Lecture Notes in Computer Science

Lecture Notes in Artificial Intelligence 16181

Founding Editor

Jörg Siekmann

Series Editors

Randy Goebel, *University of Alberta, Edmonton, AB, Canada*
Wolfgang Wahlster, *DFKI, Berlin, Germany*
Zhi-Hua Zhou, *Nanjing University, Nanjing, China*

The series Lecture Notes in Artificial Intelligence (LNAI) was established in 1988 as a topical subseries of LNCS devoted to artificial intelligence.

The series publishes state-of-the-art research results at a high level. As with the LNCS mother series, the mission of the series is to serve the international R & D community by providing an invaluable service, mainly focused on the publication of conference and workshop proceedings and postproceedings.

Rosiane de Freitas · Diego Furtado
Editors

Intelligent Systems

35th Brazilian Conference, BRACIS 2025
Fortaleza-CE, Brazil, September 29 – October 2, 2025
Proceedings, Part III

 Springer

Editors
Rosiane de Freitas ⓘ
IComp/UFAM
Manaus-AM, Brazil

Diego Furtado ⓘ
ICMC/USP
São Carlos-SP, Brazil

ISSN 0302-9743   ISSN 1611-3349 (electronic)
Lecture Notes in Artificial Intelligence
ISBN 978-3-032-15989-2   ISBN 978-3-032-15990-8 (eBook)
https://doi.org/10.1007/978-3-032-15990-8

LNCS Sublibrary: SL7 – Artificial Intelligence

Preface

The 35th Brazilian Conference on Intelligent Systems (BRACIS 2025) stands as one of the most significant Brazilian events for researchers in 2025, focused on publishing groundbreaking work in Artificial and Computational Intelligence. BRACIS was formed from the merger of Brazil's two leading scientific events in these fields: the Brazilian Symposium on Artificial Intelligence (SBIA, 21 editions) and the Brazilian Symposium on Neural Networks (SBRN, 12 editions). This year marked the 35th edition of BRACIS, continuing the numbering from the first edition of SBIA, in honor of the history of the Brazilian scientific community.

Supported by the Brazilian Computer Society (SBC), together with the Special Committees on Artificial Intelligence (CE-IA) and Computational Intelligence (CE-IC), BRACIS 2025 served as a platform to promote both theoretical advancements and robust practical applications in these IA/IC (Artificial/Computational Intelligence) fields. The conference promotes the exchange of innovative ideas among researchers, practitioners, and industry leaders.

In 2025, BRACIS was held in Fortaleza city, Ceará State of Brazil, from September 29th to October 2nd, 2025, organized by the *Universidade Federal do Ceará*. The conference took place alongside three other events: the National Meeting on Artificial and Computational Intelligence (ENIAC), the Symposium on Information and Human Language Technology (STIL), and the Workshop-School on Agents, Environments, and Applications (WESAAC). The 15th edition of the CTDIAC (The 15th Brazilian National Contest of Ph.D. and MSc Theses on Artificial and Computational Intelligence) also happened this year.

BRACIS 2025 received 393 complete paper submissions, each undergoing a rigorous review process conducted by a Program Committee of 209 experienced IA/CI researchers, with the support of 96 additional reviewers, all within a double anonymous format. This year, we accepted 37.4% of the submissions, 147 in total, in three key tracks: 82 articles in the main track, showcasing cutting-edge AI/CI methods and solid results; 27 articles in the AI/CI for Social Good track, featuring innovative applications of AI/CI for societal benefit using established methodologies; and 38 articles on other AI/CI applications, presenting novel applications using established AI/CI methods, naturally considering the ethical aspects of the application. In addition, four top-tier papers published in leading AI conferences and journals were presented during the event. The plenary speakers and their great presentations were: Professor Thiago Serra from the University of Iowa - USA, with the talk "Optimization Over Trained Neural Networks: What, Why, and How?"; Professor Evangelos Papalexakis, University of California - USA, with the talk "It's all about the latent structure: Tensor and graph methods for actionable insights"; and Professor Sandra Avila, University of Campinas, Brazil, with the talk "The Day I Discovered I Was Collaborating on a Eugenics Skin Cancer Project".

The topics of interest included, but were not limited to, the following:

- Agent-Based and Multi-Agent Systems
- Algorithms, Models, and Systems

- Cognitive Modeling and Human Interaction
- Foundations of AI/CI
- Knowledge Representation and Reasoning
- Information Retrieval, Integration, and Extraction
- Model-Based Reasoning
- Automated Reasoning and Approximate Reasoning
- Ontologies and the Semantic Web
- Logic-Based Knowledge Representation and Reasoning
- Natural Language Processing
- Data Mining and Analysis
- Machine Learning
- Neural Networks and Deep Learning
- Reinforcement Learning
- Graph Neural Networks
- Federated Learning and Distributed AI/CI
- Planning, Routing, and Scheduling
- Evolutionary Computation and Metaheuristics
- Combinatorial Optimization and Constraint Programming
- Fuzzy and Hybrid Systems
- Large Language Models and Generative AI
- Quantum Computing, Communication, and Technologies using AI/CI
- Bioinformatics and Biomedical Engineering using AI/CI
- Vision AI/CI and Pattern Recognition
- Education for AI/CI and AI/CI for Education
- Game Playing and Intelligent Interactive Entertainment
- Intelligent Robotics and Autonomous Vehicles
- Human-centric and Multidisciplinary AI/CI
- Ethics and Societal Impact
- AI/CI for Social Good
- AI/CI for Innovation and Technological Sovereignty

We extend our heartfelt thanks to everyone who contributed to the success of BRACIS 2025. We are especially grateful to the Program Committee members and reviewers for their generous and voluntary efforts in the review process. Special thanks also go to all the authors who submitted their papers and worked tirelessly to refine them into the best possible versions, such as the plenary speakers, for their valuable contributions. We also acknowledge the General Chairs, the Local Organization Committee for their unwavering support, the Brazilian Computing Society (SBC), and all our sponsors and supporters. We are confident that these proceedings showcase the exceptional work being done in the artificial and computational intelligence fields.

September 2025

Rosiane de Freitas
Diego Furtado

Organization

General Chair

Paulo de Tarso Guerra Oliveira   Universidade Federal do Ceará, Brazil

Program Chairs

Rosiane de Freitas-Rodrigues   Universidade Federal do Amazonas, Brazil
Diego Furtado Silva   Universidade de São Paulo, Brazil

Steering Committee (CEIA and CEIC)

Anna Helena Reali Costa   Universidade de São Paulo, Brazil
Anne Magaly de Paula Canuto   Universidade Federal do Rio Grande do Norte, Brazil - CEIC Coord
Denis Deratani Mauá   Universidade de São Paulo, Brazil
Diego Furtado Silva   Universidade de São Paulo, Brazil
Diego Mesquita   Fundação Getúlio Vargas, Brazil
Felipe Rech Meneguzzi   University of Aberdeen, UK
Filipe De Oliveira Saraiva   Universidade Federal do Pará, Brazil
Gisele Lobo Pappa   Universidade Federal de Minas Gerais, Brazil
Jaime Sichman   Universidade de São Paulo, Brazil
Leliane Nunes de Barros   Universidade de São Paulo, Brazil
Maria Viviane de Menezes   Universidade Federal do Ceará, Brazil
Murilo Coelho Naldi   Universidade Federal de São Carlos, Brazil
Renato Tinós   Universidade de São Paulo, Brazil
Ricardo M. Marcacin   Universidade de São Paulo, Brazil
Rosiane de Freitas-Rodrigues   Universidade Federal do Amazonas, Brazil
Solange Rezende   Universidade de São Paulo, Brazil
Tatiane Nogueira Rios   Universidade Federal da Bahia, Brazil - CEIA Coord

Local Organizers

Maria Viviane de Menezes	Universidade Federal do Ceará, Brazil
Jose Wellington Franco da Silva	Universidade Federal do Ceará, Brazil

Program Committee

Adrião Duarte Dória Neto	Universidade Federal do Rio Grande do Norte, Brazil
Alan Valejo	Universidade Federal de São Carlos, Brazil
Alceu Britto Jr.	Pontifícia Universidade Católica do Paraná, Brazil
Alexandre Tacla	Senai Cimatec, Brazil
Aline Neves	Universidade Federal do ABC, Brazil
Aline Paes	Universidade Federal Fluminense, Brazil
Alison R. Panisson	Universidade Federal de Santa Catarina, Brazil
Altigran Soares Da Silva	Universidade Federal do Amazonas, Brazil
Amedeo Napoli	Loria, Italy
Ana Carolina Lorena	Instituto Tecnológico de Aeronáutica, Brazil
Ana Cristina Bicharra Garcia	Universidade Federal do Estado do Rio de Janeiro, Brazil
Anderson Cruz	Universidade Federal do Rio Grande do Norte, Brazil
André Britto	Universidade Federal de Sergipe, Brazil
Andrés Eduardo Coca Salazar	Universidade Tecnológica Federal do Paraná, Brazil
Anna Helena Reali Costa	Universidade de São Paulo, Brazil
Anne Magaly de Paula Canuto	Universidade Federal do Rio Grande do Norte, Brazil
Antonio Oseas de Carvalho Filho	Universidade Federal do Piauí, Brazil
Antonio Sabino Parmezan	Universidade de São Paulo, Brazil
Araken Medeiros Santos	Universidade Federal Rural do Semi-Árido, Brazil
Ariane Machado-Lima	Universidade de São Paulo
Aristófanes Corrêa Silva	Universidade Federal do Maranhão, Brazil
Artur Jordao	Universidade de São Paulo, Brazil
Aurora Pozo	Universidade Federal do Paraná, Brazil
Bianca Zadrozny	IBM Research, Brazil
Bruno Nogueira	Universidade Federal do Mato Grosso do Sul, Brazil
Carla Amor Divino Delgado	Universidade Federal do Rio de Janeiro, Brazil
Carlos Eduardo Thomaz	Centro Educacional Universitário F. E. I. P. Sabóia de Medeiros, Brazil

Carlos Eduardo Pantoja	Centro Federal de Educação Tecnológica Celso Suckow da Fonseca, Brazil
Carolina Paula de Almeida	Universidade Estadual do Centro-Oeste, Brazil
Celia G. Ralha	Universidade de Brasília, Brazil
Cláudio Elízio Calazans Campelo	Universidade Federal de Campina Grande, Brazil
Cleber Zanchettin	Universidade Federal de Pernambuco, Brazil
Daniela Barreiro Claro	Universidade Federal da Bahia, Brazil
Denis D. Mauá	Universidade de São Paulo, Brazil
Diego Furtado Silva	Universidade de São Paulo, Brazil
Diego Mesquita	Fundação Getúlio Vargas, Brazil
Diego Pinheiro	Universidade Católica de Pernambuco, Brazil
Diego P. Pinto-Roa	Universidad Nacional de Asunción, Paraguay
Eder Mateus Nunes Gonçalves	Universidade Federal do Rio Grande, Brazil
Edson Takashi Matsubara	Universidade Federal do Mato Grosso do Sul, Brazil
Eduardo Bezerra	Centro Federal de Educação Tecnológica Celso Suckow da Fonseca, Brazil
Eduardo C. Goncalves	Escola Nacional de Ciências Estatísticas, Brazil
Eduardo Ferreira	Centro Federal de Educação Tecnológica Celso Suckow da Fonseca, Brazil
Eduardo Freire Nakamura	Universidade Federal do Amazonas, Brazil
Eduardo J. Spinosa	Universidade Federal do Paraná, Brazil
Eduardo Ogasawara	Centro Federal de Educação Tecnológica Celso Suckow da Fonseca, Brazil
Eduardo Jose da Silva Luz	Universidade Federal de Ouro Preto, Brazil
Elaine Cecília Gatto	Universidade Federal de Lavras, Brazil
Elaine Sousa	Universidade de São Paulo, Brazil
Emerson Cabrera Paraiso	Pontifícia Universidade Católica do Paraná, Brazil
Eulanda Santos	Universidade Federal do Amazonas, Brazil
Fábio Gagliardi Cozman	Universidade de São Paulo, Brazil
Fábio Lobato	Universidade Federal do Oeste do Pará, Brazil
Fabiola Souza Fernandes Pereira	Universidade Federal de Uberlândia, Brazil
Fabrício Aguiar Silva	Universidade Federal de Viçosa, Brazil
Fabrício Enembreck	Pontifícia Universidade Católica do Paraná, Brazil
Felipe Meneguzzi	Pontifícia Universidade Católica do Rio Grande do Sul, Brazil
Fernanda Maria Da Cunha Santos	Universidade Federal de Uberlândia, Brazil
Fernando Maciano De Paula Neto	Universidade Federal de Pernambuco, Brazil
Fernando Osório	Universidade de São Paulo, Brazil
Filipe Alves Neto Verri	Instituto Tecnológico de Aeronáutica, Brazil
Filipe Saraiva	Universidade Federal do Pará, Brazil
Flavia Bonomo	Universidad de Buenos Aires, Argentina

Flávio Soares Corrêa da Silva	Universidade de São Paulo, Brazil
Flavio Tonidandel	Centro Universitário FEI, Brazil
George Darmiton Cavalcanti	Universidade Federal de Pernambuco, Brazil
Gerson Zaverucha	Universidade Federal do Rio de Janeiro, Brazil
Giancarlo Lucca	Universidade Católica de Pelotas, Brazil
Gisele Pappa	Universidade Federal de Minas Gerais, Brazil
Gleifer Vaz Alves	Universidade Tecnológica Federal do Paraná, Brazil
Guilherme Alex Derenievicz	Universidade Federal do Paraná, Brazil
Guilherme Dean Pelegrina	Universidade Estadual de Campinas, Brazil
Gustavo A. Giménez-Lugo	Universidade Tecnológica Federal do Paraná, Brazil
Heder Bernardino	Universidade Federal de Juiz de Fora, Brazil
Helena Maia	Universidade Estadual de Campinas, Brazil
Helida Santos	Universidade Federal do Rio Grande, Brazil
Heloisa Arruda Camargo	Universidade Federal de São Carlos, Brazil
Ícaro Viana	Universidade Federal do Ceará, Brazil
Islame Felipe Fernandes	Universidade Federal da Bahia, Brazil
Ivan José Dos Reis Filho	Universidade do Estado de Minas Gerais, Brazil
Ivette Luna	Universidade Estadual de Campinas, Brazil
Javam Machado	Universidade Federal do Ceará, Brazil
Jean Paul Barddal	Pontifícia Universidade Católica do Paraná, Brazil
João Bertini	Universidade Estadual de Campinas, Brazil
João Papa	Universidade Estadual Paulista Júlio de Mesquita Filho, Brazil
João C. Xavier-Júnior	Universidade Federal do Rio Grande do Norte, Brazil
João Paulo Canário	Universidade Federal da Bahia, Brazil
Joniel Bastos Barreto	Instituto Tecnológico de Aeronáutica, Brazil
José Jailton	Universidade Federal do Pará, Brazil
José Antonio Sanz	Universidad Pública de Navarra, Spain
Jose Eduardo Ochoa Luna	Universidad Católica San Pablo, Peru
Julio C. S. Reis	Universidade Federal de Viçosa, Brazil
Kate Cerqueira Revoredo	Humboldt Universität ZU Berlin, Germany
Kele Teixeira Belloze	Centro Federal de Educação Tecnológica Celso Suckow da Fonseca, Brazil
Larissa Astrogildo Freitas	Universidade Federal de Pelotas, Brazil
Leonardo Matos	Universidade Federal de Sergipe, Brazil
Leonardo Ramos Emmendorfer	Universidade Federal de Santa Maria, Brazil
Leonardo Tomazeli Duarte	Universidade Estadual de Campinas, Brazil
Li Weigang	Universidade de Brasília, Brazil
Livy Real	Universidade Federal do Amazonas, Brazil

Lucas Pascotti Valem	Universidade de São Paulo, Brazil
Lucas Silveira Kupssinskü	Pontifícia Universidade Católica do Rio Grande do Sul, Brazil
Lucelene Lopes	Universidade de São Paulo, Brazil
Luciano Antonio Digiampietri	Universidade de São Paulo, Brazil
Luís Paulo Faina Garcia	Universidade de Brasília, Brazil
Luiz Henrique de C. Merschmann	Universidade Federal de Lavras, Brazil
Marcela Ribeiro	Universidade Federal de São Carlos, Brazil
Marcelo Finger	Universidade de São Paulo, Brazil
Marco Cristo	Universidade Federal do Amazonas, Brazil
Marco A. G. De Carvalho	Universidade Estadual de Campinas, Brazil
Marcos Gonçalves Quiles	Universidade Federal de São Paulo, Brazil
Mariana Recamonde-Mendoza	Universidade Federal do Rio Grande do Sul, Brazil
Mariela Morveli-Espinoza	Universidade Tecnológica Federal do Paraná, Brazil
Marilton Sanchotene de Aguiar	Universidade Federal de Pelotas, Brazil
Mariza Ferro	Universidade Federal Fluminense, Brazil
Marlo Souza	Universidade Federal da Bahia, Brazil
Matheus Giovanni Pires	Universidade Estadual de Feira de Santana, Brazil
Matheus Machado Dos Santos	Universidade de São Paulo, Brazil
Mauri Ferrandin	Universidade Federal de Santa Catarina, Brazil
Mauricio Solar	Universidad Técnica Federico Santa Maria, Chile
Mirela T. Cazzolato	Universidade de São Paulo, Brazil
Murillo G. Carneiro	Universidade Federal de Uberlândia, Brazil
Murilo Bellezoni Loiola	Universidade Federal do ABC, Brazil
Murilo Naldi	Universidade Federal de São Carlos, Brazil
Nádia Félix Felipe Da Silva	Universidade Federal de Goiás, Brazil
Omar Andres Carmona Cortes	Instituto Federal do Maranhão, Brazil
Paulo Mann	Universidade Federal do Rio de Janeiro, Brazil
Paulo Quaresma	Universidade de Évora, Portugal
Paulo Henrique Pisani	Universidade Federal do ABC, Brazil
Paulo Renato A. Firmino	Universidade Federal do Cariri, Brazil
Paulo T. Guerra	Universidade Federal do Ceará, Brazil
Pedro Pedrosa Rebouças Filho	Instituto Federal de Educação, Ciência e Tecnologia do Ceará, Brazil
Petrucio Viana	Universidade Federal Fluminense, Brazil
Priscila Tiemi Maeda Saito	Universidade Federal de São Carlos, Brazil
Rafael Giusti	Universidade Federal do Amazonas, Brazil
Raimundo Da Silva Barreto	Universidade Federal do Amazonas, Brazil
Renata H. S. Reiser	Universidade Federal de Pelotas, Brazil
Renato Moraes Silva	Universidade de São Paulo, Brazil

Renato Tinos	Universidade de São Paulo, Brazil
Ricardo Araújo Rios	Universidade Federal da Bahia, Brazil
Ricardo Cerri	Universidade de São Paulo, Brazil
Ricardo Marcondes Marcacini	Universidade de São Paulo, Brazil
Ricardo Jose Pfitscher	Universidade Federal de Santa Catarina, Brazil
Roberto Fray da Silva	Universidade de São Paulo, Brazil
Rodrigo de Melo Souza Veras	Universidade Federal do Piauí, Brazil
Romis Attux	Universidade Estadual de Campinas, Brazil
Ronaldo C. Prati	Universidade Federal do ABC, Brazil
Ronaldo R. Goldschmidt	Instituto Militar de Engenharia, Brazil
Rosiane de Freitas-Rodrigues	Universidade Federal do Amazonas, Brazil
Sandra M. Aluísio	Universidade de São Paulo, Brazil
Sandro Rama Fiorini	IBM Research, Brazil
Sávio Teles	Universidade Federal de Goiás, Brazil
Sílvia Maria Diniz Monteiro Maia	Universidade Federal do Rio Grande do Norte, Brazil
Sílvio César Cazella	Universidade Federal de Ciências da Saúde de Porto Alegre, Brazil
Solange Rezende	Universidade de São Paulo, Brazil
Tatiane Nogueira	Universidade Federal da Bahia, Brazil
Thiago Covoes	Universidade Federal do ABC, Brazil
Thiago Pardo	Universidade de São Paulo, Brazil
Tiago A. Almeida	Universidade Federal de São Carlos, Brazil
Tiago A. E. Ferreira	Universidade Federal de Pernambuco, Brazil
Tiago Fernandes Tavares	Insper Instituto de Ensino e Pesquisa, Brazil
Ulisses Brisolara Corrêa	Universidade Federal de Pelotas, Brazil
Vander L. S. Freitas	Universidade Federal de Ouro Preto, Brazil
Vasco Furtado	Universidade de Fortaleza, Brazil
Victor Braberman	Universidad de Buenos Aires, Argentina
Vinicius M. A. Souza	Pontifícia Universidade Católica do Paraná, Brazil
Vinicius Renan de Carvalho	Universidade de São Paulo, Brazil
Viviane Menezes	Universidade Federal do Ceará, Brazil
Viviane Moreira	Universidade Federal do Rio Grande do Sul, Brazil
Viviane Torres da Silva	IBM Research, Brazil

Additional Reviewers

Adilson Medronha	Universidade de São Paulo, Brazil
Afonso Lima	Universidade de São Paulo, Brazil
Alexandre Alcoforado	Universidade de São Paulo, Brazil

Aline Athaydes	Universidade Federal da Bahia, Brazil
Ana Erthal	Fundação Getúlio Vargas, Brazil
Ana L. C. Bazzan	Universidade Federal do Rio Grande do Sul, Brazil
Ana Luiza da C. Tenorio	Fundação Getúlio Vargas, Brazil
Anaximandro Souza	Universidade Federal do Rio de Janeiro, Brazil
Andre Guarnier de Mitri	Universidade de São Paulo, Brazil
André Oliveira	Instituto Brasileiro de Geografia e Estatística, Brazil
Arthur E. Torres	Universidade Federal do Amazonas, Brazil
Arthur Scalercio	Universidade Federal Fluminense, Brazil
Babacar Mane	Universidade Federal da Bahia, Brazil
Bruna Zamith Santos	Universidade Federal de Pernambuco, Brazil
Bruno Henrique Meyer	Universidade Federal do Paraná, Brazil
Bruno Paz Moura	Universidade Federal de Pelotas, Brazil
Bruno Yamamoto	Escola Politécnica da Universidade de São Paulo, Brazil
Caio Costa	Universidade de São Paulo, Brazil
Carlos Caminha	Universidade Federal do Ceará, Brazil
Caroline P. A. Moraes	Universidade Federal do ABC, Brazil
Cassio Bertasi Nascimento	Universidade Federal do Mato Grosso do Sul, Brazil
Clara Baldansa	Instituto Militar de Engenharia, Brazil
Daniel Sabino A. de Araújo	Universidade Federal do Rio Grande do Norte, Brazil
Diego Duarte Bottero	Universidade Federal do Rio Grande, Brazil
Diego Minatel	Universidade de São Paulo, Brazil
Douglas Tesch	Pontifícia Universidade Católica do Rio Grande do Sul, Brazil
Edilene Veneruchi	Universidade Federal do Rio Grande do Sul, Brazil
Elizabeth Sucupira Furtado	Universidade de Fortaleza, Brazil
Elvis de Souza	Pontifícia Universidade Católica do Rio de Janeiro, Brazil
Felipe Brito	Universidade Federal do Ceará, Brazil
Fernanda Goyo Tamanaka	Centro Universitário FEI, Brazil
Fernando Maia da Mota	Universidade Federal do Mato Grosso do Sul, Brazil
Fábio José Muneratti Ortega	Universidade de São Paulo, Brazil
Gabriel Assis	Universidade Federal Fluminense, Brazil
Gabriel Castro Michelassi	Universidade de São Paulo, Brazil
Giovanna Aguiar Castro	Universidade Federal de São Carlos, Brazil
Gladston Moreira	Universidade Federal de Ouro Preto, Brazil

Gustavo C. Galvão Van Erven	Brazilian Office of the Comptroller General of Brazil
Gustavo Nascimento	Universidade de São Paulo, Brazil
Heitor Gama	Escola Politécnica da Universidade de São Paulo, Brazil
Helói Genari	Universidade Federal do ABC, Brazil
Hermon Faria de Araujo	Universidade de São Paulo, Brazil
Iago C. Chaves	Universidade Federal do Ceará, Brazil
Ian Pons	Escola Politécnica da Universidade de São Paulo, Brazil
Israel Fama	Universidade de São Paulo, Brazil
Izavan dos S. Correia	Universidade Federal Rural de Pernambuco, Brazil
Jader Silva Jale	Universidade Federal Rural de Pernambuco, Brazil
Janayna Moura	Universidade Federal de Uberlândia, Brazil
Joao Luz	Universidade de São Paulo, Brazil
Joel Luís Carbonera	Universidade Federal do Rio Grande do Sul, Brazil
Jorge Batista	Universidade Federal da Bahia, Brazil
José Gilberto de Medeiros Jr.	Universidade de São Paulo, Brazil
José Nascimento dos Santos	Universidade Federal Rural de Pernambuco, Brazil
João Lobo	Universidade de São Paulo, Brazil
João Nahra	Universidade Federal do Amazonas, Brazil
Juan Belieni de Castro Araujo	Fundação Getúlio Vargas, Brazil
Julia da Rocha Junqueira	Universidade Federal de Pelotas, Brazil
Julio Sotelo	Universidad Técnica Federico Santa María, Chile
Juvenal Domingos Júnior	Universidade Estadual de Campinas, Brazil
Kayo Gonçalves e Silva	Universidade Federal do Rio Grande do Norte, Brazil
Keith Ando Ogawa	Universidade Federal de São Paulo, Brazil
Kenji Nose Filho	KU Leuven, Belgium
Kerolly Kedma Felix do Nascimento	Universidade Federal Rural de Pernambuco, Brazil
Larrissa Dantas	Universidade Federal da Bahia, Brazil
Leandro Mugnaini	Universidade de São Paulo, Brazil
Lucas Fontes Buzuti	Centro Universitário FEI, Brazil
Lucas Nildaimon dos Santos Silva	Universidade Federal de São Carlos, Brazil
Marcelo Gauy	Universidade Estadual Paulista, Brazil
Matheus Oliveira	Universidade de Brasília, Brazil
Matheus Padovani	Universidade Estadual de Campinas, Brazil
Matheus Yasuo Ribeiro Utino	Universidade de São Paulo, Brazil

Miguel Carpi	Universidade de São Paulo, Brazil
Miguel Castro	Universidade Federal do Amazonas, Brazil
Mikel Sesma-Sara	Universidad Pública de Navarra, Spain
Pedro Borges Pio	Universidade de Brasília, Brazil
Pedro DallAntonia	Fundação Getúlio Vargas, Brazil
Pedro Pires	Universidade Federal de São Carlos, Brazil
Pedro Robles Dutenhefner	Universidade Federal de Minas Gerais, Brazil
Philipe Melo	Universidade Federal de Viçosa, Brazil
Rafael da Costa Silva	Universidade de São Paulo, Brazil
Ricardo Gomes de Oliveira	Universidade Federal da Bahia, Brazil
Roberto de Pádua Carvalho Reis	Universidade Estadual do Maranhão, Brazil
Ronald Albert Araujo Junior	Universidade Federal do Rio de Janeiro, Brazil
Rosana Zanotelli	Universidade Federal do Rio Grande, Brazil
Rubens Marques Chaves	Universidade de Brasília, Brazil
Rubén Pascual	Universidad Pública de Navarra, Spain
Samir de O. Ramos	Instituto Militar de Engenharia, Brazil
Samuel Xavier de Souza	Universidade Federal do Rio Grande do Norte, Brazil
Saullo Oliveira	Pontifícia Universidade Católica de Campinas, Brazil
Tamara A. Pereira	Instituto Federal do Ceará, Brazil
Thiago César Castilho Almeida	Universidade Estadual Paulista, Brazil
Thiago Zafalon	Universidade Federal de São Carlos, Brazil
Thomas Palmeira Ferraz	Télécom Paris, France
Tiago Gonçalves Botelho	Instituto Federal de Educação, Ciência e Tecnologia do Sul de Minas Gerais - Campus Muzambinho, Brazil
Victor Farias	Universidade Federal do Ceará, Brazil
Vinicius Fukase	Universidade de São Paulo, Brazil

Contents

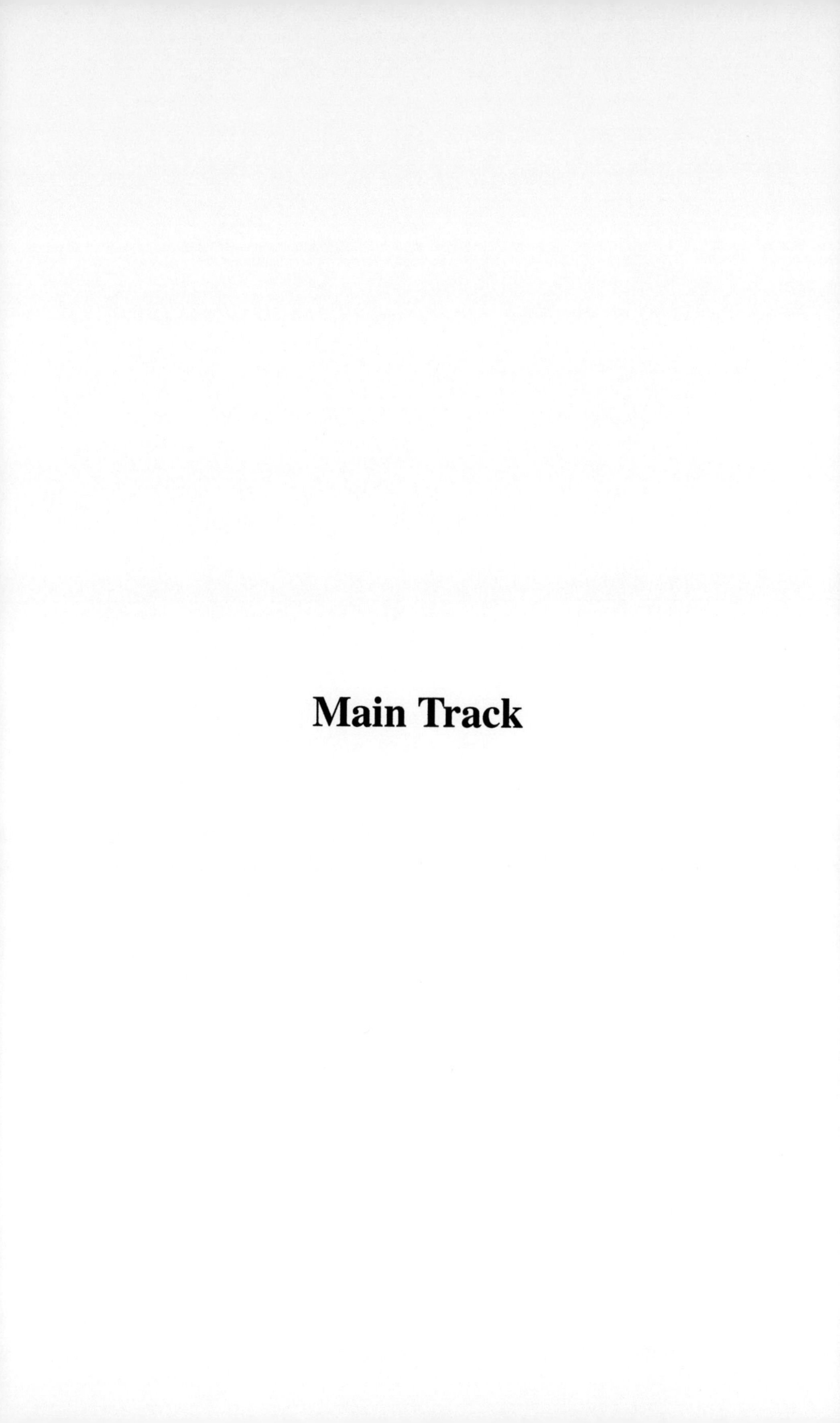

Main Track

A Fully Automatic Approach for COVID-19 Diagnosis in CT Imaging: Integrating Lung Segmentation, Fine-Tuning and Grad-CAM Visualization

Matheus A. dos Santos[1,2], Iágson Carlos L. Silva[1,2], Lucas de O. Santos[1,2], Elizângela de S. Rebouças[1,3,4], Pedro Pedrosa Rebouças Filho[1,3,4(✉)], and Houbing H. Song[4]

[1] Lab for Processing Images, Signals and Computer Science (LAPISCO), Fortaleza, Brazil
`{matheus.santos,iagsoncarlos,lucas.santos}@lapisco.ifce.edu.br`
[2] Federal University of Ceará (UFC), Fortaleza, Brazil
[3] Federal Institute of Education, Science and Technology of Ceará (IFCE), Fortaleza, Brazil
`{elizangela.reboucas,pedrosarf}@ifce.edu.br`
[4] University of Maryland, Baltimore County (UMBC), Baltimore, USA
`songh@umbc.edu`

Abstract. The pandemic caused by the COVID-19 virus has highlighted the need for efficient and automated medical diagnostic tools to assist healthcare professionals in the fast and accurate identification of the disease. This study introduces a fully automatic approach for classifying COVID-19 in thoracic computed tomography (CT) images from the SARS-CoV-2 CT-scan dataset, employing deep learning, automatic lung segmentation, and fine-tuning models to the specific problem. Previous transfer learning experiments revealed that MobileNet emerged as the most effective architecture for feature extraction. Integrating Detectron2 for lung segmentation and subsequent fine-tuning of the selected MobileNet model significantly improved classification performance. Visual analysis of model interpretability using Grad-CAM demonstrated that with segmented images and the refined model, the network focused on lung regions, enhancing understanding of the model diagnosis. As a result, the proposed fully automatic method achieved superior evaluation metrics compared to other methods in the literature, reaching values of 99.60% for accuracy, precision, and F1-Score, along with 99.59% for recall and 99.20% for the Matthews Correlation Coefficient (MCC).

Keywords: COVID-19 · Deep Learning · Transfer Learning · Fine-Tuning · Deep Segmentation · Computed Tomography (CT)

R. de Freitas and D. Furtado (Eds.): BRACIS 2025, LNAI 16181, pp. 3–18, 2026.
https://doi.org/10.1007/978-3-032-15990-8_1

1   Introduction

The acute respiratory disease, known as COVID-19 and caused by Coronavirus type 2 (SARS-CoV-2), emerged as a global pandemic, significantly impacting global public health [5]. The virus fast spread led the World Health Organization (WHO) to officially declare COVID-19 a pandemic in March 2020 [5]. Until these days, several variants of the virus, such as Omicron and their subvariants, have emerged, influencing transmissibility, severity, and vaccine effectiveness [28]. Furthermore, some measures, such as social distancing, were reinforced and encouraged as essential measures to contain the spread of the virus [1].

While the reverse-transcriptase polymerase chain reaction (RT-PCR) evidence test is considered the ground truth for confirm COVID-19 infection [3], chest computed tomography (CT) also performs a vital role in screening and diagnosing the disease. However, the manual diagnostic process for radiologists, based on the analysis of CT images, presents challenges related to speed and accuracy, especially in emergencies that require quick responses.

Therefore, there is a need for a quick and automatic approach that helps healthcare professionals accurately diagnose the condition. Artificial intelligence (AI), deep learning, and machine learning methods are used to aid medical diagnosis, providing professionals in the field with quick and accurate diagnoses [26,36].

This study proposes a fully automatic approach for classifying COVID-19 in thoracic CT images. The proposed method uses deep models and is formed by lung detection/segmentation followed by extraction/classification by a convolutional neural network model pre-trained and fine-tuned for the COVID issue. An in-depth preliminary analysis of the model performance was carried out to choose the best model among those evaluated for the proposed method. Furthermore, Grad-CAM methods were used to visually distinguish the regions of greatest focus of the neural network when performing the classification.

Therefore, motivated by the importance of an automatic approach, fast and accurated, for COVID-19 diagnosis from CT imaging, as well as the similar works found in the literature, this study addresses the following main contributions:

- The proposal for a fast and effective end-to-end model that fully automates the COVID-19 classification pipeline, from lung detection/segmentation in CT images to deep feature extraction and final classification.
- This study provides a preliminary analysis of the best deep models in a transfer learning context. Therefore, the best model evaluated at this first moment was the one chosen to compose the proposed method.
- This work also proposes a visual analysis of the interpretability of deep networks using Grad-CAM to explain which are the critical regions of the lungs that most contribute to the diagnosis of COVID-19 based on the pre-trained network.
- This method aims to assist medical diagnosis using a fast, accurate, and visual approach.

2   Related Work

In the context of medical imaging for COVID-19 classification, many authors use specific deep learning methods such as this work, including transfer learning and fine-tuning techniques, using the same or similar datasets.

Soares et al. [30] proposed the SARS-CoV-2 CT-scan dataset, the mainly dataset used in this work. The benchmark result obtained by the authors was using an eXplainable Deep Learning (xDNN) approach, achieving an F1-score of 97.31% and an accuracy of 97.38%.

Alshazly et al. [3] use neural network architectures in a transfer learning strategy, adapting personalized inputs for each architecture. The authors used two datasets: SARS-CoV-2 CT-scan [30] and COVID19-CT [14]. The results showed averages of 99.4%, 99.6%, 99.1%, 99.6%, and 99.4% for accuracy, sensitivity, specificity, and F1-Score, respectively, for the set of SARS-CoV-2 dataset. In addition to identifying COVID-19 cases, visualization techniques were used based on the models generated to understand the interpretability of the models, highlighting distinct regions in the images for COVID and Non-COVID cases.

The study by Panwar et al. [24] proposes a deep learning transfer algorithm to accelerate the detection of COVID-19 cases using X-ray and computed tomography (CT) images. The model detected positive cases of COVID-19 in ≤ 2 s, surpassing automatic RT-PCR tests in speed and results. The research used three datasets, including the SARS-COV-2 computed tomography. A Grad-CAM visualization technique was also used to analyze the interpretability of the models to radiological images.

Wang et al. [34] proposes an improvement of the COVID-Net framework to improve its accuracy and learning efficiency. The authors address cross-domain variation with feature normalization and use a contrastive training objective to reinforce domain invariance. The tests carried out were partly with the SARS-COV-2 CT-scan dataset, achieving almost 91% accuracy and an AUC curve 12.16% better than the original COVID-Net.

The work of Jaiswal et al. [18] used deep learning models to automatically analyze chest computed tomography (CT) images to detect COVID-19. The authors used an architecture based on the DenseNet201 network, trained with weights in a deep transfer learning process. For the SARS-COV-2 CT dataset, the authors achieved values close to 96% for accuracy, precision, recall, and F1-score.

Naeem and Bin-Salem [21] use a multi-level feature extraction approach with Convolutional Neural Network (CNN) for CT and chest X-ray images. This extraction aims to reduce the training complexity of the CNN network, facilitating accurate and robust identification of COVID-19. Finally, the authors obtained the Long Short-Term Memory (LSTM) concurrent with the CNN network to detect the extracted features of COVID-19. The experimental results show that the proposed approach achieved an accuracy of 98.94% with the SARS-CoV-2 computed tomography dataset.

In contrast, the study by Zhao et al. [37], despite not using the dataset used by the other authors, also uses computed tomography images to complement

RT-PCR tests in the classification of COVID-19. The transfer learning approach proposed in this study has proven more successful than other approaches
described in the literature. Furthermore, the research also explores the relevant
visual characteristics of CT images using Grad-CAM heatmaps.

In this way, the approaches used to classify COVID-19 using CT images
reinforce the use of deep learning in a medical imaging context. Transfer learning and fine-tuning techniques stand out, as well as Grad-CAM algorithms for
visualizing the models interpretability.

3   Materials and Methods

This section addresses the materials and methods used in this study. It covers
the datasets used, the deep segmentation, the transfer learning, and fine-tuning
approaches used in this work, and the Grad-CAM heatmap visualization. The
convolutional neural network topologies used in the first and second moments
and the evaluation metrics for each model formed were also mentioned.

3.1   Datasets

The dataset used for COVID classification in CT images is the SARS-CoV-2
CT-Scan [30]. The images in the dataset are from lung computed tomography
(CT) and are in PNG format with three RGB channels and 8 bits each. The
images are not standardized in their dimensions and have varying sizes. The
dataset consists of 1252 computed tomography (CT) scans from patients who
tested positive for SARS-CoV-2 (COVID-19) infection and 1230 CT scans from
patients not infected with SARS-CoV-2, totaling 2482 CT scans. The images
were acquired at the Public Hospitals of the State of São Paulo and the Hospital
Metropolitano da Lapa in São Paulo, Brazil, throughout 2020, marked by the
COVID-19 pandemic [30].

The other dataset was also a respiratory computed tomography dataset to
segment the lungs. This dataset consists of 1265 CT images in Digital Imaging and Communications in Medicine (DICOM) format, with 512×512 pixels
and 16-bit depth dimensions. Each image has a ground truth of segmentation
carried out by an expert. The images were acquired at the Walter Cantídio Hospital, Federal University of Ceará (UFC), Fortaleza, Ceará, Brazil, and were
approved by the Research Ethics Committee - COMEPE (Protocol N° 35/06).
This dataset has already been widely addressed and discussed in the literature
[25], in the context of lung segmentation, including together with Detectron2,
which is the segmentation model which will be discussed below.

3.2   Deep Segmentation

The Detectron2 framework [35] has its origins in Mask R-CNN [12] and is the
successor to Detectron [8]. Proposed by Facebook Artificial Intelligence Research

(FAIR), Detectron2 is used as a deep neural network to perform object detection and segmentation.

Detectron2 uses the annotation method for the dataset adopted by COCO [20], which says that object annotations comprise a list of vertices of the polygons that make up an object of interest. Detectron2 also receives the GTs of the images as input, being a supervised learning for detecting and segmenting the objects of interest (in the case of this study, they are the lungs).

Its architecture is based on distinct modules, composing the final detection and segmentation model. The first crucial module, BackBone Network, uses a ResNet [13] model to convolve and generate relevant image features. The Region Proposal Network (RPN) step proposes and classifies candidate regions to contain the objects of interest. The Feature Pyramid Network (FPN) stage guarantees the processing of information extracted at different spatial scales, robust for images of different dimensions and sizes. Finally, Detectron2 uses post-processing modules with regressor models to refine specializations, including removing redundant bounding boxes and applying thresholds to keep only the most confident detections.

3.3 Transfer Learning

The first method addressed in this study is transfer learning, which consists of using a convolutional neural network (CNN), pre-trained with an extensive database, to extract shape and texture features from another set of data, and classify these feature vectors using traditional classifiers [36]. In other words, to be used exclusively as a feature extractor, the CNN classification layers, called fully-connected, are removed [23].

In this work, CNN topologies were used with weights initially trained with the extensive image database ImageNet [6], which consists of millions of images of everyday objects in 1000 different classes. Fully-connected layers have been replaced by machine learning algorithms.

The CNN architectures used in this article were three: the VGG architecture [29], the DenseNet architecture [17], and the MobileNet architecture [16]. The first was broken into two configurations (VGG16 and VGG19), while the second was chosen DenseNet201. Finally, MobileNet was innovative in its conventional architecture.

VGG16 and VGG19 differ in layer count (16 vs. 19) with small convolutional filters, enhancing depth [29]. DenseNet variations vary by layer count, featuring DenseBlocks and transition layers [17]. MobileNet is known for fast training, compact size, and suitability for embedded environments [16].

After the feature extraction step, the attributes extracted by the topologies presented in the previous section are provided to seven different classifiers. They are: Naive Bayes Classifier [32], MLP [11], k-Nearest Neighbors (KNN) [2], Random Forest [15] and three different versions of Support Vector Machines – SVM (Linear, Polynomial and RBF) [33].

3.4 Fine-Tuning

Fine-tuning deep learning models is a crucial practice for improving the performance of a pre-trained neural network on a specific task. Initially, pre-trained models on massive datasets such as ImageNet [6] captured patterns across various images. However, when applying these models to more specialized tasks, such as medical imaging, it is necessary to adjust the network weights to align with the specific patterns of the new dataset [9].

The fine-tuning process typically comprises freezing and unfreezing layers. Initially, convolutional layers for general features are kept fixed, with only the final classification layers trained for the new task [31]. This preserves prior knowledge while adapting to the target dataset. In the next stage, more layers are gradually unfrozen, enabling deeper adjustments to convolutional layer weights [31].

For the present work, fine-tuning was used both in segmentation, when adapting Detectron2 weights for lung segmentation, and in the second moment classification, where the best transfer learning model was chosen to be refined for the problem in question. In both cases, fine-tuning generates weights specific to the topology used and the functional dataset.

3.5 Grad-CAM Visualization

The interpretability of models in this study was assessed using Grad-CAM visual maps via the TorchCAM library [7]. These maps, generated from CT images of COVID-19 patients, highlight crucial areas for diagnosis, aiding in identifying SARS-CoV-2 presence and visualizing healthy lung tissue [4].

The method works by backpropagating the gradient from the output of the last convolutional layer to the input layers of the neural network. This results in an activation map that highlights areas of the image that significantly develop the model decision [27].

This approach is instrumental in computer vision tasks, such as medical image analysis, as it is valid in regions with a higher probability of disease and can be validated by experts [24].

3.6 Evaluation Metrics

The analyzes used to evaluate the performance of the transfer learning and fine-tuning models were accuracy (Acc), precision, recall or sensitivity, F1-Score (F1), and Matthews Correlation Coefficient (MCC) [36].

Accuracy measures correct samples over the total, while F1-Score combines precision and recall for balance, crucial in disease classification with low false positives and false negatives [22]. Matthews Coefficient (MCC), a balanced measure for binary classification, remains robust even in unbalanced datasets, relying on Pearson's correlation indices.

4   Methodology

The study comprises two key phases: (i) a transfer learning comparison between the best deep extractor and traditional classifiers using the original dataset and (ii) a fully automatic approach utilizing the refined best model (fine-tuned) for images segmented by Detectron2 (trained for lung segmentation in CT images). Figure 1 (above) illustrates the transfer learning experiment, while Fig. 1(below) outlines the proposed method, incorporating detection/segmentation and classification steps. Both experiments experienced numerical and visual evaluations using metrics and Grad-CAM heatmaps.

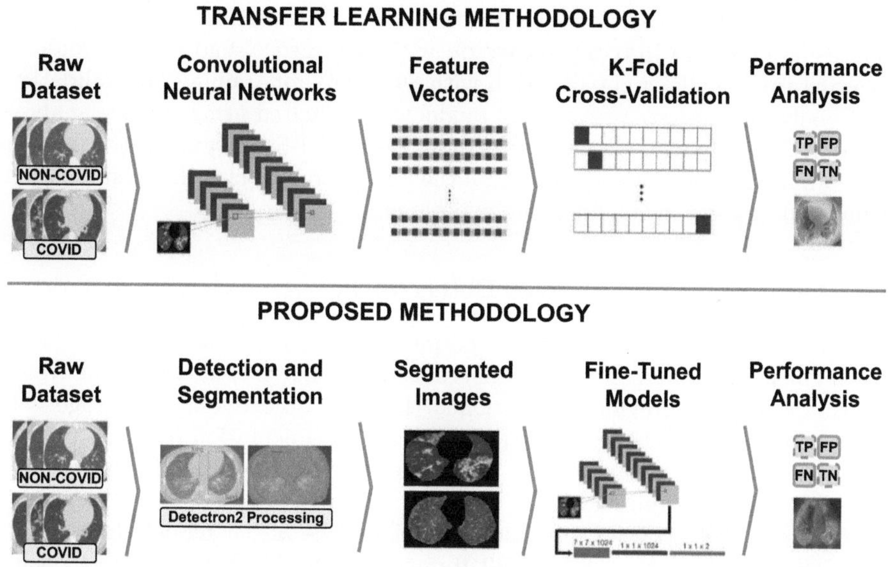

Fig. 1. Above: Transfer learning process used in the first experiment. The best models selected from this stage (using the original dataset) were used in the next step. Below: Flowchart of the proposed fully automatic methodology for COVID classification in lung CT images. Detectron2 performs lung segmentation, and the cropped images are classified by the best fine-tuned model. Evaluation metrics and Grad-CAM assess performance and interpretability.

The experiments were carried out on the Ubuntu 22.04 system, with 32 GB RAM, an Intel® Core™ i7-12700H processor, and an Nvidia GeForce RTX 3050 GPU with 6 GB of dedicated memory. To build the VGG, DenseNet, and MobileNet models, Python (v3.7), OpenCV 4.1.0, TensorFlow-GPU 1.14, and Keras 2.2.4 libraries were used. Detectron2 has been modified, trained, and validated using its official repository. Classifiers and metrics were applied using the scikit-learn library v0.20.2.

4.1 Deep Transfer Learning Models

Initially, original dataset images were inputted to deep learning models (VGG, DenseNet, and MobileNet) for extracting deep features. Image resizing was the only preprocessing step to match each extractor input dimensions. The experiment maintained CNN parameters and topology, utilizing weights from the ImageNet database [6]. Models were loaded without fully-connected layers, focused on extracting feature vectors for traditional classifiers.

After the extraction phases, the next stage involves classification using the extracted feature vectors. These datasets, formed by the features, underwent supervised binary classification employing seven different classifiers. Prior to classification, a Random Search algorithm optimized hyperparameters for each classifier. Post the search, classification occurred for each of the seven classifiers using **cross-validation strategie** with stratified K-fold (with 5 folders), ensuring five rounds of classification with 80%/20% for training and validation.

Finally, the performance of each model was evaluated using the five analyses mentioned previously: Accuracy, Precision, Recall, F1-Score, and Matthews Correlation Coefficient (MCC), to achieve the best extractor-classifier combination, which will be used in the following experiment.

4.2 Deep Segmentation with Detectron2

In this stage, as part of the second experiment, Detectron2 was trained to detect and segment lungs from chest CT images using the DICOM dataset from Walter Cantídio Hospital, previously mentioned [10]. The objective at this stage is to generate weights for Detectron2, optimizing lung segmentation from CT images, using a model trained in the fully automatic approach proposed in this study.

For Detectron2 training, 15,000 training seasons were used, with the dataset divided into 80%/20% for training/validation. The initial model chosen from those supported by the Detectron2 framework was Mask R-CNN [12], using ResNet50 [13] in the Backbone stage.

The dataset was passed into COCO [20] format before training to understand the Detectron2 algorithm better. Finally, the classes configured for this training were only the steering wheel, and the ROI detection limit was 0.95.

In the entirely automatic method, after a detection and segmentation step using Detectron2, new images are generated from the segmentation result and the input image (original) so that one is multiplied by the other, and only the lungs remain in the image that will be sent for classification using the deep model.

The Contrast Limited Adaptive Histogram Equalization (CLAHE) method was applied to the segmented image as a form of post-processing [19]. The CLAHE method is a histogram equalization technique to enhance image contrast, ensuring that contrast is amplified [19].

4.3 Fine-Tuning Best Deep Model

Finally, as the last phase of this experiment, we used the best models found in the transfer learning stage to refine them (using fine-tuning) based on the images segmented by Detectron2. After training Detectron2, which occur with lung CT images, it was applied to the primary dataset of this study, the SARS-CoV-2 CT-Scan, to segment only the lungs from these CT exams and improve COVID classification performance. At this stage, the segmented images are provided to the chosen methods for the training stage.

The chosen models were loaded with their original weights, without the original fully connected layers, from the ImageNet dataset. New fully connected layers (detrained with ReLU and softmax activations) were coupled to the model architecture and a previous global Average Pooling layer, and thus, training began, refining the weights for the specific problem in question (classification of COVID). 50 training seasons were used for this model in a 90%/10% combination of training and validation.

The Adam solver was used, with a learning rate of 0.0003, and the loss function was minimized by binary cross-entropy. The batch size used was set to 32. All convolutional layers were refined, leaving nothing frozen. The training dataset was augmented using the techniques of horizontal flip, zoom range of 0.2, shear range of 0.2, and vertical positions of horizontals of 0.1. The input dimensions were kept as 224×224.

As in the transfer learning stage, after this moment, the trained models were evaluated using evaluation metrics and Grad-CAM to analyze the models interpretability.

5 Results and Discussion

This section deals with the results of this works two main experiments. In the first moment, we seek to compare transfer learning methods, focusing on selecting the process with the best performance to do so in the second moment, when this refined model will be based on images segmented by Detectron2.

5.1 Transfer Learning Models Results

After the first phase of the experiment, which was a transfer learning stage, the evaluation of each extractor-classifier model were organized and can be seen in Table 1

Analyzing the results, it is clear that the best model is using the deep MobileNet extractor with the KNN classifier. This exchange obtained more than 97% accuracy, precision, recall, and F1-Score and the best MCC score (94%) among all combinations. The results presented by MobileNet are interesting because this network is incredibly lightweight and can be powerful even in embedded systems.

The DenseNet architecture was the lowest among the three chosen architectures, while the VGG architecture (mainly VGG19) obtained the best results

Table 1. Metrics (%) obtained by each deep extractor combination and classified in the transfer learning stage of this study.

Extractor	Classifier	Accuracy	Precision	Recall	F1-Score	MCC
VGG16	Naive Bayes	82.54 ± 1.63	82.87 ± 1.76	82.58 ± 1.63	82.51 ± 1.62	65.46 ± 3.39
	MLP	89.84 ± 1.02	89.91 ± 0.99	89.85 ± 1.03	89.83 ± 1.03	79.76 ± 2.02
	KNN	96.87 ± 0.97	96.90 ± 0.94	96.86 ± 0.98	96.87 ± 0.97	93.76 ± 1.91
	Random Forest	89.61 ± 1.15	89.69 ± 1.20	89.62 ± 1.16	89.61 ± 1.15	79.31 ± 2.36
	Linear SVM	89.93 ± 0.80	90.01 ± 0.89	89.95 ± 0.81	89.92 ± 0.80	79.95 ± 1.70
	Polynomial SVM	49.91 ± 0.44	24.95 ± 0.22	50.00 ± 0.00	33.29 ± 0.19	0.00 ± 0.00
	RBF SVM	95.34 ± 1.05	95.36 ± 1.06	95.34 ± 1.05	95.34 ± 1.05	90.71 ± 2.11
VGG19	Naive Bayes	82.27 ± 1.89	82.50 ± 1.80	82.31 ± 1.88	82.25 ± 1.90	64.80 ± 3.68
	MLP	90.51 ± 2.30	90.56 ± 2.30	90.50 ± 2.30	90.50 ± 2.30	81.06 ± 4.60
	KNN	96.91 ± 0.58	96.94 ± 0.58	96.90 ± 0.57	96.91 ± 0.58	93.85 ± 1.15
	Random Forest	89.17 ± 1.86	89.21 ± 1.84	89.17 ± 1.85	89.16 ± 1.86	78.38 ± 3.69
	Linear SVM	90.73 ± 1.40	90.76 ± 1.41	90.73 ± 1.39	90.73 ± 1.40	81.49 ± 2.80
	Polynomial SVM	49.91 ± 0.44	24.95 ± 0.22	50.00 ± 0.00	33.29 ± 0.19	0.00 ± 0.00
	RBF SVM	96.01 ± 1.31	96.05 ± 1.32	96.01 ± 1.31	96.01 ± 1.31	92.05 ± 2.62
MobileNet	Naive Bayes	79.32 ± 1.44	79.73 ± 1.27	79.37 ± 1.43	79.26 ± 1.48	59.09 ± 2.69
	MLP	92.03 ± 1.16	92.06 ± 1.17	92.04 ± 1.16	92.03 ± 1.16	84.10 ± 2.33
	KNN	97.31 ± 0.58	97.37 ± 0.60	97.30 ± 0.58	97.31 ± 0.58	94.67 ± 1.18
	Random Forest	87.74 ± 1.07	88.24 ± 0.92	87.79 ± 1.06	87.70 ± 1.09	76.03 ± 1.99
	Linear SVM	91.32 ± 0.87	91.36 ± 0.84	91.33 ± 0.86	91.32 ± 0.87	82.69 ± 1.70
	Polynomial SVM	95.26 ± 0.72	95.27 ± 0.72	95.26 ± 0.71	95.25 ± 0.71	90.53 ± 1.43
	RBF SVM	95.35 ± 0.90	95.37 ± 0.89	95.36 ± 0.90	95.35 ± 0.90	90.72 ± 1.79
DenseNet201	Naive Bayes	81.47 ± 1.81	81.52 ± 1.84	81.48 ± 1.81	81.47 ± 1.81	63.01 ± 3.65
	MLP	91.32 ± 0.82	91.39 ± 0.80	91.31 ± 0.83	91.31 ± 0.82	82.70 ± 1.62
	KNN	95.03 ± 1.35	95.09 ± 1.38	95.03 ± 1.34	95.03 ± 1.35	90.12 ± 2.73
	Random Forest	88.59 ± 1.46	88.77 ± 1.52	88.62 ± 1.46	88.58 ± 1.46	77.38 ± 2.98
	Linear SVM	90.78 ± 0.41	90.84 ± 0.38	90.79 ± 0.41	90.78 ± 0.41	81.63 ± 0.79
	Polynomial SVM	49.91 ± 0.44	24.95 ± 0.22	50.00 ± 0.00	33.29 ± 0.19	0.00 ± 0.00
	RBF SVM	94.09 ± 0.22	94.10 ± 0.23	94.09 ± 0.23	94.09 ± 0.22	88.19 ± 0.45

after MobileNet. Among those classified, KNN stands out, showing an excellent spatial distribution between the data. RBF SVM shows that the radial basis function kernel is a good hyperplane for optimal data separation.

Therefore, given the promising results of **MobileNet** with the original images, it was chosen to be refined using fine-tuning and to be the chosen model in the fully automatic approach proposed by this study.

5.2   Lung Segmentation Results Using Detectron2

Detectron2 training was done using the second dataset covered in this work, which contains transport CT images and their respective ground truths for segmentation.

Using the Mask R-CNN model, Detectron2 segmentation achieved an **accuracy of 0.9629**, indicating that the vast majority of pixels were correctly classified as either lung or background. Furthermore, the model yielded a false negative rate of **0.0129**, implying it rarely misses pixels belonging to the lung. The false positive rate was also low at **0.0268**, showing the model is effective at not incorrectly including background pixels in the lung mask. These metrics point to a precise and reliable segmentation model. It is also possible to visualize the qualitative performance of Detectron2 for lung segmentation in CT images for the two datasets in this study (Fig. 2).

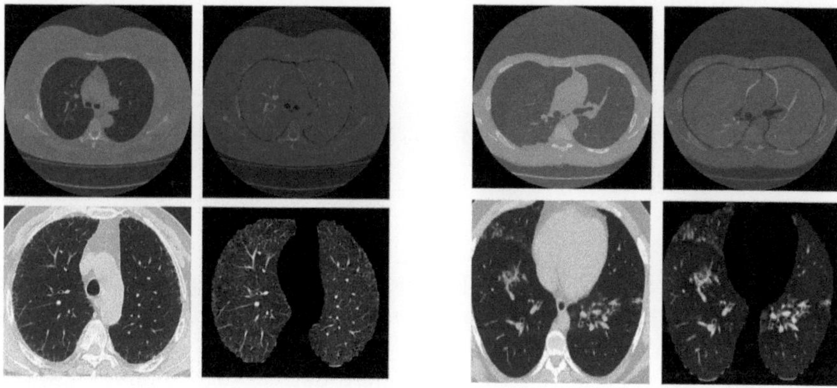

Fig. 2. Performance of Detectron2 for lung segmentation in CT images from the two datasets used in this study. Above: images from the training dataset and their segmentations in pink. Below: samples from the SARS-CoV-2 CT-Scan dataset and their respective segmentations. (Color figure online)

With Detectron2 properly trained to segment lung images from CT images, applied to the primary dataset of this study, the SARS-CoV-2 CT-Scan, so that, from the segmented images, one can make a more accurate and efficient classification in the next stage of this study, which is the fine-tuning of the chosen network.

5.3   Fine-Tuning of Best Deep Model

After a segmentation step with Detectron2, the segmented images were used to train a MobileNet, initialized with the ImageNet weights and without its original fully connected layers. Three more layers were added to the convolutional model: a global average pooling layer, a fully-connected ReLU activation layer, and a fully-connected softmax activation layer, which are responsible for classifying COVID or non-COVID. After 50 training epochs, the training models validation results were as follows: 99.60% accuracy, 99.60% precision, 99.59% recall, 99.60% F1- Score, and 99.20% MCC. The total training time was 1.3 h, and the prediction time was 7 ms for each validation sample.

Compared with other methods in the literature, the proposed models results can be seen in Table 2.

Table 2. Comparison between the averages obtained by the proposed method (under validation) compared to the averages of other methods in the literature that also performed binary classification of the SARS-CoV-2 dataset.

Model	Accuracy	Precision	Recall	F1-Score	MCC
Proposed Method	**99.60**	**99.60**	**99.59**	**99.60**	**99.20**
ResNet101 (Alshazly *et al.*) [3]	99.4	99.6	99.1	99.4	-
xDNN (Soares et al.) [30]	97.38	99.16	95.53	97.31	-
CNN^2-LSTM (Naeem et al.) [21]	98.94	99.00	99.00	99.00	-
DenseNet201 (Jaiswal et al.) [18]	96.2	96.2	96.2	96.2	-
Modified VGG19 (Panwar et al.) [24]	95.0	95.3	94.0	94.3	-
Contrastive Learning (Wang et al.) [34]	90.8	95.7	85.8	90.8	-

Analyzing the table, it is clear that the proposed method had better validation performance than other methods presented in the literature for practically all evaluation metrics. The MCC shows that the proposed method performed well for both classes, even with the unbalanced dataset. The high accuracy and recall (or sensitivity) show that the model has reasonable hit rates and minimizes false negative rates, which is crucial for medical diagnosis.

The reported authors provided other comparison analyses not used in this work, such as specificity, as it is understood that the F1-Score can make this same interpretation. The Matthews Correlation Coefficient (MCC) was not used by other authors but was retained here as it is understood to be a valuable metric for unbalanced datasets (as is the case with the SARS-CoV-2 CT-scan).

5.4   Grad-CAM Analysis

Finally, in the last stage of this work, a visual analysis of the interpretability of the models was carried out using the Grad-CAM algorithm. Grad-CAM allows you to analyze which areas the convolutional neural network gave the most approach to predicting that sample. In other words, which areas of the image have the most impact on the network classifying a sample as positive or not for the COVID-19 virus.

In Fig. 3, the pattern used is always the images from the original dataset in the upper left corner and their corresponding Grad-CAM through MobileNet, in the transfer learning stage, on the right. Below and on the left, the same images are segmented by Detectron2, part of the proposed fully automatic model. At the same time, on right, can been seen the Grad-CAM of the same image, but now using the MobileNet of the proposed model, which had its weights refined for these images.

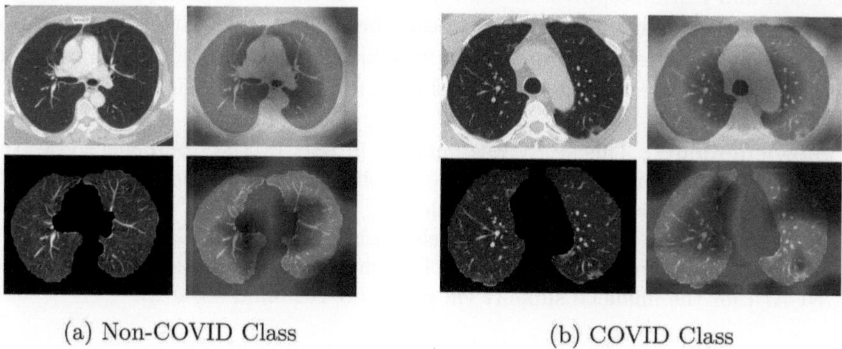

(a) Non-COVID Class   (b) COVID Class

Fig. 3. Top left: Samples from the original dataset with MobileNet's Grad-CAM (without fine-tuning) on the right. Below left: Images segmented by Detectron2 with refined MobileNet's Grad-CAM on the right.

It can be seen that in the cases of the proposed model, the Grad-CAM became much more localized in the lungs, removing the focus of the network from the center of the image and proving that the increase in metrics involves a better analysis of the network in the characteristics that whether or not they classify COVID-19 in the lungs.

6   Conclusions

This study proposed a fully automatic approach for classifying COVID-19 in thoracic CT images. Initially, several CNN topologies were compared via transfer learning, with MobileNet emerging as the best performer. Subsequently, the proposed method was built, including automatically lung segmentation with Detectron2 framework and refining MobileNet by fine-tuning based on the segmented images.

The MobileNet-KNN combination showed promising results in the transfer learning phase, justifying its selection. Detectron2 proved effective in lung segmentation, contributing to classification accuracy. Refining the MobileNet model via fine-tuning resulted in high evaluation metrics, with values of 99.60% for accuracy, precision, and F1-Score, surpassing literature methods for the SARS-CoV-2 CT dataset and highlighting the effectiveness of the proposed method. The high MCC value of 99.20% highlights the model's effectiveness even with imbalanced data. Visual analysis with Grad-CAM confirmed the refined model's focus on lung regions, enhancing the understanding of COVID-19 characteristics.

For future work, we pretend to validate the model's generalization, testing with other independent datasets. We also plan to explore implementing MobileNet in **embedded systems**, focusing on the Internet of Things (IoT). This approach could enable remote and real-time diagnostics, facilitating early detection and rapid response to COVID-19, especially in resource-limited areas. Grad-CAM visualization could also be embedded for validation. Furthermore, the complexity and size of Detectron2 may hinder its implementation in embedded systems, representing a challenge for future investigations.

Acknowledgments. This study was financed in part by the Coordenação de Aperfeiçoamento de Pessoal de Nível Superior—Brasil (CAPES)—Finance Code 001. Also, Pedro Pedrosa Rebouças Filho acknowledges the sponsorship from the Brazilian National Council for Research and Development (CNPq) via Grant 301455/2022-8 and State Foundation for the Support of Scientific and Technological Development (FUNCAP) for the financial support via grants 08/2023 and 09/2023.

Disclosure of Interests. The authors declare that they have no competing interests.

References

1. Adedoyin, O.B., Soykan, E.: Covid-19 pandemic and online learning: the challenges and opportunities. Interact. Learn. Environ. **31**(2), 863–875 (2023)
2. Aha, D.W., Kibler, D., Albert, M.K.: Instance-based learning algorithms. Mach. Learn. **6**(1), 37–66 (1991)
3. Alshazly, H., Linse, C., Barth, E., Martinetz, T.: Explainable Covid-19 detection using chest CT scans and deep learning. Sensors **21**(2) (2021). https://doi.org/10.3390/s21020455, https://www.mdpi.com/1424-8220/21/2/455
4. Alshazly, H., Linse, C., Barth, E., Martinetz, T.: Explainable Covid-19 detection using chest CT scans and deep learning. Sensors **21**(2), 455 (2021)
5. Novel Coronavirus. https://www.who.int/emergencies/diseases/novel-coronavirus-2019. Accessed Oct 2020
6. Deng, J., Dong, W., Socher, R., Li, L.J., Li, K., Fei-Fei, L.: ImageNet: a large-scale hierarchical image database. In: 2009 IEEE Conference on Computer Vision and Pattern Recognition, pp. 248–255. IEEE (2009)
7. Fernandez, F.G.: TorchCAM: class activation explorer, March 2020. https://github.com/frgfm/torch-cam
8. Girshick, R., Radosavovic, I., Gkioxari, G., Dollar, P., He, K.: Detectron (2018)
9. Guan, H., Liu, M.: Domain adaptation for medical image analysis: a survey. IEEE Trans. Biomed. Eng. **69**(3), 1173–1185 (2021)
10. Han, T., et al.: Internet of medical things–based on deep learning techniques for segmentation of lung and stroke regions in CT scans. IEEE Access **8**, 71117–71135 (2020)
11. Haykin, S.S., et al.: Neural Networks and Learning Machines (2009)
12. He, K., Gkioxari, G., Dollár, P., Girshick, R.: Mask R-CNN. In: Proceedings of the IEEE International Conference on Computer Vision, pp. 2961–2969 (2017)

13. He, K., Zhang, X., Ren, S., Sun, J.: Deep residual learning for image recognition. In: Proceedings of the IEEE Conference on Computer Vision and Pattern Recognition, pp. 770–778 (2016)
14. He, X., et al.: Sample-efficient deep learning for Covid-19 diagnosis based on CT scans. medRxiv (2020)
15. Ho, T.K.: The random subspace method for constructing decision forests. IEEE Trans. Pattern Anal. Mach. Intell. **20**(8), 832–844 (1998)
16. Howard, A.G., et al.: MobileNets: efficient convolutional neural networks for mobile vision applications. arXiv preprint arXiv:1704.04861 (2017)
17. Huang, G., Liu, Z., Van Der Maaten, L., Weinberger, K.Q.: Densely connected convolutional networks. In: Proceedings of the IEEE Conference on Computer Vision and Pattern Recognition, pp. 4700–4708 (2017)
18. Jaiswal, A., Gianchandani, N., Singh, D., Kumar, V., Kaur, M.: Classification of the Covid-19 infected patients using DenseNet201 based deep transfer learning. J. Biomol. Struct. Dyn. **39**(15), 5682–5689 (2021)
19. Joshi, K.K., Gupta, K., Agrawal, J.: An efficient transfer learning approach for prediction and classification of SARS–COVID-19. Multimedia Tools Appl., 1–23 (2023)
20. Lin, T.-Y., et al.: Microsoft COCO: common objects in context. In: Fleet, D., Pajdla, T., Schiele, B., Tuytelaars, T. (eds.) ECCV 2014. LNCS, vol. 8693, pp. 740–755. Springer, Cham (2014). https://doi.org/10.1007/978-3-319-10602-1_48
21. Naeem, H., Bin-Salem, A.A.: A CNN-LSTM network with multi-level feature extraction-based approach for automated detection of coronavirus from CT scan and X-ray images. Appl. Soft Comput. **113**, 107918 (2021)
22. Ohata, E.F., Chagas, J.V.S., Bezerra, G.M., Hassan, M.M., de Albuquerque, V.H.C., Filho, P.P.R.: A novel transfer learning approach for the classification of histological images of colorectal cancer. J. Supercomput. **77**(9), 9494–9519 (2021). https://doi.org/10.1007/s11227-020-03575-6
23. Orenstein, E.C., Beijbom, O.: Transfer learning and deep feature extraction for planktonic image data sets. In: 2017 IEEE Winter Conference on Applications of Computer Vision (WACV), pp. 1082–1088. IEEE (2017)
24. Panwar, H., Gupta, P., Siddiqui, M.K., Morales-Menendez, R., Bhardwaj, P., Singh, V.: A deep learning and grad-CAM based color visualization approach for fast detection of Covid-19 cases using chest X-ray and CT-scan images. Chaos Solitons Fractals **140**, 110190 (2020). https://doi.org/10.1016/j.chaos.2020.110190, https://www.sciencedirect.com/science/article/pii/S0960077920305865
25. Rebouças Filho, P.P., da Silva Barros, A.C., Almeida, J.S., Rodrigues, J., de Albuquerque, V.H.C.: A new effective and powerful medical image segmentation algorithm based on optimum path snakes. Appl. Soft Comput. **76**, 649–670 (2019)
26. Santosh, K.: AI-driven tools for coronavirus outbreak: need of active learning and cross-population train/test models on multitudinal/multimodal data. J. Med. Syst. **44**, 1–5 (2020)
27. Selvaraju, R.R., Cogswell, M., Das, A., Vedantam, R., Parikh, D., Batra, D.: Grad-CAM: visual explanations from deep networks via gradient-based localization. In: Proceedings of the IEEE International Conference on Computer Vision, pp. 618–626 (2017)
28. Senevirathne, T.H., Wekking, D., Swain, J.W., Solinas, C., De Silva, P.: Covid-19: from emerging variants to vaccination. Cytokine Growth Factor Rev. **76**, 127–141 (2024)
29. Simonyan, K., Zisserman, A.: Very deep convolutional networks for large-scale image recognition. arXiv preprint arXiv:1409.1556 (2014)

30. Soares, E., Angelov, P., Biaso, S., Froes, M.H., Abe, D.K.: SARS-COV-2 CT-scan dataset: a large dataset of real patients CT scans for SARS-COV-2 identification. medRxiv (2020)
31. Tajbakhsh, N., et al.: Convolutional neural networks for medical image analysis: full training or fine tuning? IEEE Trans. Med. Imaging **35**(5), 1299–1312 (2016)
32. Theodoridis, S., Koutroumbas, K.: Pattern Recognition. Academic Press, Burlington, MA (2008). [Google Scholar]
33. Vapnik, V.N.: Statistical Learning Theory (1998)
34. Wang, Z., Liu, Q., Dou, Q.: Contrastive cross-site learning with redesigned net for Covid-19 CT classification. IEEE J. Biomed. Health Inform. **24**(10), 2806–2813 (2020)
35. Wu, Y., Kirillov, A., Massa, F., Lo, W.Y., Girshick, R.: Detectron2 (2019)
36. Xu, Y., et al.: New fully automatic approach for tissue identification in histopathological examinations using transfer learning. IET Image Processing **16**(11), 2875–2889 (2022)
37. Zhao, W., Jiang, W., Qiu, X.: Deep learning for covid-19 detection based on CT images. Sci. Rep. **11**(1), 14353 (2021). https://doi.org/10.1038/s41598-021-93832-2

A Multi-Dimensional Comparative Study of Generative Adversarial Networks, Diffusion Models, and Statistical Methods for Synthetic Health Data Generation

Oluwatoyin Joy Omole[1(✉)], Celso França[1], Samuel N. Alves[1], Regina Bernal[3], Deborah Malta[2], Marcos André Gonçalves[1], and Jussara M. Almeida[1]

[1] Universidade Federal de Minas Gerais - UFMG, Belo Horizonte, Brazil
omoleoluwatoyin18@gmail.com
[2] School of Nursing, Universidade Federal de Minas Gerais, Belo Horizonte, Brazil
[3] Graduate Program, School of Nursing, Universidade Federal de Minas Gerais, Belo Horizonte, Brazil
https://dcc.ufmg.br/

Abstract. Synthetic data is increasingly important in privacy-sensitive or data-scarce domains such as healthcare, where access to real data is constrained by confidentiality or data availability challenges. This study compares three approaches for the generation of synthetic tabular health data: a statistical method (Gaussian Copula), an adversarial deep learning model (CTGAN), and an implementation of a diffusion-based technique called *SimpleTableDiffusion*. These methods represent different modeling paradigms: statistical, adversarial, and stochastic, each offering trade-offs in interpretability, flexibility, training stability, and privacy. We assess their performance across three dimensions: (i) statistical fidelity, that is, how well they replicate real data distributions; (ii) utility, measured by the effectiveness of classifiers trained on synthetic data and evaluated on real data; and (iii) privacy preservation, using a disclosure risk metric that estimates the likelihood of sensitive attribute inference. Our results show that CTGAN achieves the best overall performance, leading in utility, privacy, and marginal distribution quality. The Gaussian Copula excels at modeling conditional dependencies but lags in predictive tasks. The diffusion-based model performs competitively across metrics but falls short of the other generative models. This work establishes a unified benchmark, pointing towards hybrid approaches that leverage complementary strengths.

Keywords: Generative and Diffusion Models · Synthetic Tabular Data · Multi-dimensional comparative analysis

1 Introduction

The generation of tabular synthetic data has become a critical area of research, particularly in fields where privacy concerns restrict access to real data, such as

R. de Freitas and D. Furtado (Eds.): BRACIS 2025, LNAI 16181, pp. 19–34, 2026.
https://doi.org/10.1007/978-3-032-15990-8_2

healthcare, finance, and social sciences [33] or in scenarios where gathering real data is challenging due to security, socioeconomic, or other issues. High-quality synthetic data offers an alternative that preserves the statistical characteristics of the original data sets while protecting sensitive information [22].

Traditional statistical methods have long been used for data generation, relying on models such as Gaussian distributions, Bayesian networks, and copulas to replicate dependencies within data [17]. However, these methods often fail to capture complex and high-dimensional interactions found in real-world datasets.

To address these limitations, recent work has applied deep generative models, particularly generative adversarial networks (GANs) and diffusion models as powerful alternatives for synthetic data generation. GANs, introduced by [8], utilize a two-part neural network framework where a generator learns to produce synthetic samples that are indistinguishable from real data, while a discriminator attempts to distinguish between real and generated samples. This adversarial training setup has proven to be effective in generating highly dimensional and diverse data. GANs, however, suffer from issues such as mode collapse, which makes them less reliable in ensuring comprehensive data coverage [25].

More recently, diffusion models have emerged as a promising generative framework, leveraging a stepwise noise-based approach to gradually refine random noise into structured data through a learned denoising process [11]. Unlike GANs, diffusion models offer greater stability during training and flexibility in modeling intricate data distributions, though they typically require more computational resources due to their iterative nature.

Applying these generative models to health data, our focus in this paper, is challenging. Many difficulties arise from the own nature of health data, which is often tabular, high-dimensional, with mixed types of features (continuous, discrete, time-series, longitudinal), and usually has small sample sizes that can serve as *seeds* for the synthetic data process. All of this contributes to low quality or even incompatibility of certain synthetic generation models for this domain.

In this study, our objective is to compare, under various criteria, the performance of three representatives of the generative approaches mentioned above, applied to the task of generating synthetic healthcare data. Specifically, we evaluate three models: a statistical one (Gaussian Copula), a deep generative adversarial network (CTGAN), and a diffusion-based neural model.

CTGAN is specifically tailored for tabular data using conditional generation, which helps address imbalanced categorical features, and a mode-specific normalization mechanism that improves the modeling of mixed data types [33].

In the case of the diffusion-based model, we implemented a simplified version of TableDiffusion [31], named *SimpleTableDiffusion*. Our approach replaces iterative denoising with a single-pass neural network, enabling more efficient training and faster generation while still capturing complex feature dependencies in mixed-type tabular data. Rather than aiming to surpass the original model, our objective was to assess whether a streamlined, practical variant could deliver strong performance in real-world healthcare scenarios. The design emphasizes computational efficiency, ease of integration, and practical usability without compromising core capabilities. More details of our implementation are given in Sect. 3.

We applied and evaluated each model using the Belo Horizonte's Vigitel 2006–2018 dataset as a case study. Vigitel is an annual survey conducted by the Brazilian Ministry of Health that collects self-reported data on risk factors for noncommunicable diseases (NCD) of adults in the 26 state capitals and the Federal District via telephone landline interviews [3]. Although extensive, its reliance on landlines and sampling design leads to under-representation of smaller areas of high risk, introducing potential biases in prevalence and predictive analyses, particularly in vulnerable regions [30]. Synthetic data generation in this context seeks to mitigate these limitations by improving representativeness and allowing more accurate assessments of health disparities.

We assess the models using a consistent set of multi-dimensional evaluation metrics. These metrics reveal how closely synthetic data matches real data (quality), how useful they are for downstream tasks (utility), and how well they protect sensitive information (privacy). This multidimensional evaluation framework is a key contribution of our study, offering a comprehensive benchmark for synthetic data generation in healthcare applications. Accordingly, the research questions we aim to empirically answer are:

RQ1 – Quality: How effective is each synthesizer in generating synthetic tabular data that replicates real data distributions? We evaluated this using the Kolmogorov-Smirnov statistic, the total variation distance, the correlation similarity, and the contingency similarity metrics.

RQ2 – Utility: What is the utility of synthetic data for practical downstream tasks? We measure this using Accuracy (MicroF1) and MacroF1 scores from XGBoost, Random Forest, and Logistic Regression classifiers trained on synthetic data and tested on real data.

RQ3 – Privacy: How well does each method protect against disclosure risks? We quantify this using a disclosure protection score based on attribute inference risks from synthetic data.

Results demonstrate that CTGAN delivers the strongest performance in predictive utility, privacy protection, and marginal distribution similarity. Gaussian Copula models perform better in capturing conditional relationships between features but offer lower downstream task utility. The diffusion-based approach presents a balanced but modest performance in all evaluation dimensions, highlighting its potential as an accessible, cheap and efficient alternative for healthcare data synthesis. Overall there is room for improvements for all techniques.

This paper is organized as follows. Section 2 reviews related work. Section 3 details our experimental design, including the dataset, model implementations, and evaluation metrics. Section 4 presents and analyzes the results in terms of quality, utility, and privacy. Section 5 concludes with key findings and future directions.

2 Background and Related Work

We briefly review prior work on the three families of techniques to generate synthetic data analyzed in this work: Classical Statistical models, Generative Adversarial Networks, and Diffusion Models.

2.1 Classical Statistical Methods

Classical statistical models have long been used for synthetic data generation. Initially developed in the context of Statistical Disclosure Control [27], these methods estimate univariate and multivariate distributions from real data to produce synthetic imputations or fully synthetic datasets. Although often limited by their reliance on parametric assumptions, ongoing research has improved their performance on similarity, utility, and privacy dimensions. The main statistical models for synthetic tabular data include Mixture Models, Statistical Simulations, Bayesian Networks, and Copulas [16].

Mixture Models combine simpler components, such as Gaussian or Multivariate Normal (MVN) distributions to model complex data distributions. This is well-suited for healthcare data with natural clustering [19], though scalability in high dimensions remains a challenge [16]. Statistical simulations like Multiple Imputation and Monte Carlo methods generate synthetic data via sequential sampling. Yubin et al. [20,21] used non-parametric Gibbs sampling with perturbation to improve privacy. However, they often yield only partially synthetic datasets and are limited to discrete values.

Bayesian Networks use graphical structures to model dependencies among variables and have shown promise in healthcare applications [12,32,36]. Although interpretable and effective in small sample settings, they can overestimate correlations and perform suboptimally on discrete data [16].

Copulas model dependencies among variables by combining univariate distributions into a joint multivariate form [17]. Copula-based models have successfully been applied to synthetic healthcare data [13,26,32]. They are efficient with mixed data types, but limitations remain in handling temporal dynamics and formal privacy assessments [16]. In our comparative study, we focus on the Gaussian Copula, which was first introduced as part of the Synthetic Data Vault (SDV) framework by Patki et al. [23].

2.2 Generative Adversarial Networks (GANs)

GANs, originally proposed in [8], represented a major advancement in generative modeling, initially focusing on image generation tasks [15] and sequence generation [35]. GANs offer notable flexibility by learning complex data distributions, a characteristic that has also been leveraged for synthetic tabular data generation. However, tabular data introduces unique challenges due to its combination of mixed data types and intricate feature dependencies.

Despite their strengths, GANs were initially designed to approximate continuous distributions and encountered difficulties with discrete variables. `medGAN`

[6], developed for healthcare datasets, tackled this limitation by incorporating an autoencoder that projected the original data into a lower-dimensional latent space. The generator was trained to produce synthetic data in this latent space, which was later decoded back to the original feature space. While this enabled handling of both continuous and categorical variables, `medGAN` exhibited scalability issues when applied to more complex data and was prone to mode collapse, being often comparable, in terms of performance, to traditional statistical approaches. TGAN [34] uses recurrent neural networks to sequentially generate new data. For each column, the generated value was conditioned on previously generated values before being passed to the discriminator. This sequential approach enabled more effective preprocessing and handling of mixtures of categorical and continuous variables, compared to medGAN. Yet, TGAN still struggles with multimodal distributions and imbalanced datasets. Finally, `CTGAN` [33] represents a significant evolution compared to previous models by addressing issues such as imbalance, scalability, and the ability to model complex distributions more effectively. Its primary contribution was the introduction of **conditional data generation**, where the model learns the distribution of other columns given that the value of a specific column is fixed. Additionally, `CTGAN` introduced **mode-specific normalization**, a novel technique that enhances the training process by handling multimodal distributions and capturing dependencies between continuous and categorical variables more effectively. This method is widely recognized as a standard benchmark for the generation of synthetic tabular data. *We focus on CTGAN in our comparative study.*

`CTGAN` [33], which we adopt in this study, improved on these by introducing conditional generation and mode-specific normalization, effectively handling mixed features and class imbalance. It is widely recognized as a benchmark model for synthetic tabular data.

2.3   Diffusion Models

Diffusion models are a class of generative models based on thermodynamic principles and stochastic processes [29]. They operate by gradually adding noise to the data and then reverse this through a learned denoising process. Initially popular in image synthesis. Their ability to produce high-fidelity outputs has made them the state-of-the-art in image synthesis [7], and they are increasingly being adapted to structured data.

Recent work has explored their application to tabular data. Zhou et al. [37] propose a method that integrates diffusion with variational autoencoders to improve representation learning and preservation of structure. Van Breugel et al. [4] introduced LaTable, a scalable diffusion framework that jointly models heterogeneous features in tabular data sets. Truda [31] presents TableDiffusion, the first approach to integrate differential privacy into diffusion-based tabular synthesis, achieving notable improvements over GANs in privacy benchmarks.

In this work, we implement a simplified variant of TableDiffusion by Truda [31], discussed further in Sect. 3. Our motivation in choosing this model is the suitability of the model for sensitive healthcare data, combined with its promising performance and general applicability. The focus of our contribution is to investigate whether a lightweight design can preserve the key benefits of the original architecture rather than making direct comparisons with it.

To our knowledge, no prior study has conducted a direct comparison of Gaussian Copula, CTGAN, and diffusion-based methods for generating synthetic health data, using a comprehensive set of multidimensional criteria: (i) quality; (ii) utility; and (iii) privacy. This work introduces a unified framework for systematically evaluating representative models from each family under consistent conditions.

3   Simple Table Diffusion Model

Simple TableDiffusion is a lightweight adaptation of diffusion models designed for efficient generation of synthetic tabular data, particularly in mixed-type domains such as healthcare. It retains the core principles of the diffusion framework while introducing architectural and preprocessing simplifications that improve speed, interpretability, and practical usability (Fig. 1).

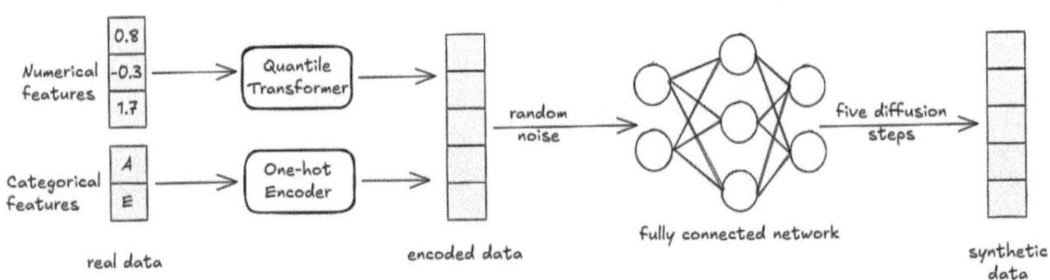

Fig. 1. The architecture of the *Simple TableDiffusion* model.

Prior to training, the model explicitly separates numerical and categorical features. Numerical columns are transformed using a quantile transformation [28], which maps the data to follow a uniform or normal distribution, reducing the impact of outliers, making features more comparable and improving stability during training. Categorical variables are encoded via one-hot encoding. The transformed features are then concatenated into a unified feature matrix, serving as input to a fully connected neural network.

The model is trained through a diffusion process in which random noise is added to the data at each step. The neural network learns to predict the added noise or reconstruct clean data, depending on the training objective. The loss is optimized separately to account for different data types: mean squared error (MSE) for numerical variables and Kullback–Leibler (KL) divergence for categorical logits. The overall loss function can be formalized as:

$$\mathcal{L} = \underbrace{\frac{1}{N}\sum_{i=1}^{N}\|x_i - \hat{x}_i\|_2^2}_{\text{Numerical (MSE)}} + \underbrace{\frac{1}{M}\sum_{j=1}^{M}\mathrm{KL}(p_j \,\|\, q_j)}_{\text{Categorical (KL divergence)}}$$

where x_i and $\hat{x}_i$ denote the original and reconstructed numerical features, and p_j, q_j represent the true and predicted categorical distributions for feature j.

At inference time, the model denoises samples from random noise using only five diffusion steps, significantly fewer than the hundreds typically required in standard diffusion-based models such as TableDiffusion. This choice balances efficiency and fidelity, as tabular data often requires less granular reconstruction than high-dimensional data, such as images. After sampling, inverse transformations are applied to revert the data to its original numerical and categorical form.

Our approach introduces three key differences from the original TableDiffusion model: (i) **efficiency**, using only five diffusion steps during inference, making the method significantly faster and more resource-efficient; (ii) **explicit feature handling**, instead of treating all features uniformly, we separate and preprocess numerical and categorical variables differently, improving the generation of realistic mixed-type tabular data; and (iii) **lightweight privacy**. While the original TableDiffusion integrates formal differential privacy (DP) mechanisms, our model relies on the inherent randomness of the diffusion process to provide a lightweight privacy benefit without incurring in the complexity and computational cost of DP. Methods such as DP-SGD [1] require careful tuning of clipping bounds and noise scales, leading to slower convergence and degraded utility, especially for high-dimensional or imbalanced data sets.

In summary, *SimpleTableDiffusion* offers a practical trade-off between generation quality, computational efficiency, and ease of implementation. These properties make it particularly suitable for real-world healthcare settings, where fast training, clear interpretability, and minimal tuning overhead are important.

4 Experimental Design

4.1 Methods

In this study, we compare three methods for the generation of synthetic health data, namely: (1) Gaussian copula, a classical statistical method, which serves as a type of baseline for our experiments; and two artificial intelligence methods: (2) CTGAN, based on the GAN architecture, and (3) SimpleTableDiffusion, our implementation of a diffusion-based model.

4.2   Dataset

The Brazilian Surveillance of Risk and Protective Factors for Chronic Diseases through Telephone Interviews (Vigilância de Fatores de Risco e Proteção para Doenças Crônicas por inquérito telefônico – VIGITEL) data used in this study encompass a cross-sectional telephone survey started in 2006 to monitor the prevalence of risk and protective factors of noncommunicable diseases (NCD) among Brazilian adults. Each year, approximately 54,000 interviews are conducted with people aged 18 years and older, residing in households with landline telephones across the 26 state capitals and the Federal District [3]. The survey collects data on various health-related behaviors, including diet, physical activity, smoking, alcohol consumption, and self-reported health conditions. To adjust for potential biases due to the exclusion of households without landlines, Vigitel employs post-stratification weighting methods, such as *raking* [3], aligning the sample with population distributions based on age, sex, and education level.

However, the survey design still poses challenges in analyzing small-area variations in NCD risk factors. The limited number of respondents in specific locales, especially in high-risk or underserved regions, hinders the ability to produce reliable estimates at finer geographic resolutions. This limitation is critical, as understanding health disparities at the local level is essential for targeted public health interventions. Synthetic data generation offers a solution by creating artificial datasets that mirror the statistical properties of the original data while enhancing granularity and preserving privacy. With the synthetic versions of the Vigitel dataset, researchers can perform more detailed analyses of health inequalities, inform policy decisions, and allocate resources more effectively to areas in need.

For our experiments, we used a portion of the Vigitel dataset covering the city of Belo Horizonte, Brazil, from 2006 to 2018, comprising 21,764 records and 30 features. Among these columns, 6 are numerical and 24 are categorical. An example of a type of study that has been conducted with Vigitel was to predict whether an individual smokes based on the remaining attributes or, at a macrolevel, to assess the prevalence of smokers in the population in the different regions based on these attributes [2]. We use this setting to explore how well synthetic data can replace real data in analytical workflows.

Figure 2 shows the distribution of smokers and non-smokers in the Vigitel dataset. As it can be seen, the distribution is very skewed, with a proportion of almost 5:1 between non-smokers:smokers. Such imbalance poses additional challenges for downstream classification tasks, as supervised classifiers will have a heavy bias towards the majority class.

4.3   Multi-dimensional Evaluation Metrics

To measure model performance, we analyze three main dimensions: (i) Quality; (ii) Utility; and (iii) Privacy.

(Data) Quality. We start by training each model on the whole dataset. Using the trained model, we generate a synthetic sample of the same size as the real

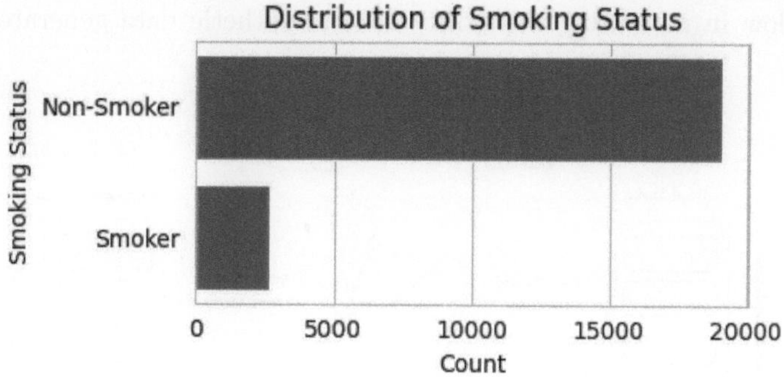

Fig. 2. Smoker and Non-Smoker Distribution in the real Data

dataset. We use four metrics to evaluate the generative model and the synthetic data generated by it: (i) Kolmogorov-Smirnov (KS) statistic; (ii) Total Variation Distance (TVD); (iii) Correlation; and (iv) and Contingency Similarities.

KS statistic and TVD are both measures of the statistical difference between the distributions of each column, the first being used on numerical columns and the second on categorical. Correlation and Contingency Similarities measure how similar the pairwise distributions of values between columns are in the synthetic and real data, also being applicable only to numerical and categorical columns, respectively. To simplify the interpretation of results, instead we report the complements of the KS statistic and TVD. In this way, all quality metrics range from 0 to 1, with 0 being the worst result and 1 the best.

Utility. To assess the utility of the synthetic data, we evaluate the performance of three widely-used classifiers: Logistic Regression (LR), Random Forest (RF), and XGBoost (XGB). Logistic Regression provides a simple, interpretable linear baseline classification, Random Forests are robust to overfitting and handle high-dimensional, noisy data effectively; while XGBoost, a gradient-boosted tree method, is known for its high predictive power and fine-grained control over model complexity [5,18].

Rather than relying on a single classifier, using all three enables a more comprehensive assessment across different types of inductive biases: linear, bagged, and boosted trees. Furthermore, the literature has pointed out that tree-based models, such as XGBoost and Random Forests, are often more suitable than deep learning methods for predictive tasks involving small to medium-sized high-dimensional tabular datasets [9].

We adopt a five-fold cross-validation setup: in each fold, we generate synthetic data from the training portion using the evaluated models. Then, we train two instances of each classifier per fold, one on real training data and one on synthetic data, and test both models on the same real test set. By reporting average Micro-F1 and Macro-F1 scores across folds, we capture both overall predictive performance and sensitivity to class imbalance, offering a rich evaluation of downstream utility. Figure 3 shows a diagrammatic representation of the workflow in measuring the utility of the synthetic data generated by each model.

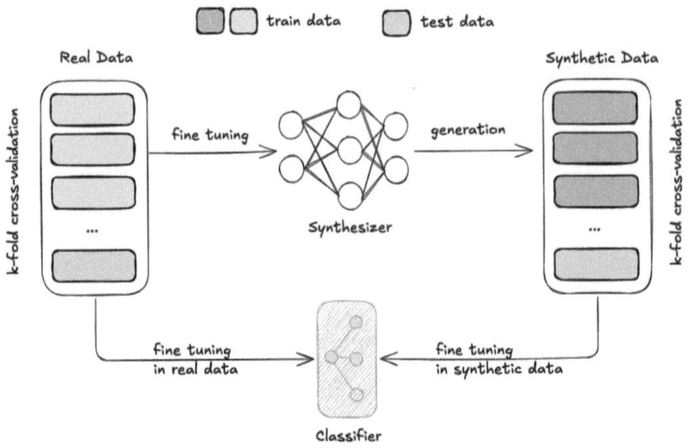

Fig. 3. Utility Flowchart

Privacy. We assess privacy using the Disclosure Protection Score [10] computed on the synthetic data. The final privacy score is reported as the mean value across synthetic datasets, each generated by a synthesizer trained on a different fold of the real data, following our 5-fold cross-validation protocol. We also report the 95% confidence interval based on the distribution of scores across the folds.

CAP (Conditional Attribute Protection) is a differential privacy-inspired score designed to measure the disclosure risk associated with synthetic data sets. It estimates how much easier it becomes for an attacker to infer sensitive information given partial prior knowledge. More precisely, CAP protection compares the probability for attackers to correctly guess the values of a set of 'sensitive columns' (Y) based on the knowledge of a set of 'known columns' (X), using synthetic data as an attack surface.

To compute it, one needs to select the X (known) and Y (sensitive) groups. For a given individual record, we fix the known attributes (X) and examine the conditional probability distribution over the sensitive attributes (Y) across the synthetic dataset. The CAP protection score is then normalized by comparing it to a baseline protection score obtained using purely random synthetic data, which represents the best-case scenario where no real-world information is leaked. Formally, the final CAP protection score is given by:

$$score = \min\left(\frac{cap\_protection}{baseline\_protection}, 1\right)$$

where values closer to 1 indicate stronger privacy (lower risk) and values closer to 0 indicate weaker privacy (higher risk). This normalization ensures that results are comparable across different datasets and settings, regardless of dimensionality or class distributions. This setup enables a consistent and comprehensive comparison of generative models under conditions that closely reflect real-world constraints in health data analysis.

5   Results and Discussion

5.1   RQ1 Quality

We divide our quality analysis into marginal and conditional distribution quality, with the results presented in Table 1. For each metric, we report the average performance accompanied by a 95% confidence interval. The marginal distribution metrics, the Kolmogorov-Smirnov (KS) complement and the Total Variation (TV) complement, were calculated using the evaluation utilities provided by the SDV (Synthetic Data Vault) library [24], which compares real and synthetic distributions in numerical and categorical columns, respectively. Similarly, the Correlation Similarity and Contingency Similarity metrics used for the conditional distribution evaluation were obtained through the pairwise comparison tools of SDV for numerical and categorical column interactions.

Table 1. Marginal and conditional distributions quality metrics with 95% CI

Synthesizer	Marginal Distributions		Conditional Distributions	
	KS Comp.	TV Comp.	Correlation Sim.	Contingency Sim.
CTGAN	89.9(1.3)	97.9(0.2)	95.2(0.15)	91.7(1.26)
GC	78.0(6.0)	71.3(2.0)	99.0(0.3)	54.8(1.47)
STD	78.3(1.1)	81.0(1.0)	97.2(0.4)	65.1(1.8)

An analysis of Table 1 reveals that CTGAN achieved the best overall performance in marginal distribution quality, excelling in both the KS complement (89.9) and TV complement (97.9) metrics. This highlights this model's ability to handle mixed-type features through its conditional generation and mode-specific normalization. The diffusion-based STD model and the Gaussian Copula (GC) model recorded substantially lower scores for marginal distributions, with GC performing worst in TV complement (71.3), likely due to its limitations in modeling complex, high-dimensional data distributions.

In terms of conditional distribution quality, GC excelled at capturing inter-variable correlations, achieving the highest correlation similarity score (99.0), which aligns with the strengths of copula-based models to accurately model dependencies [14]. However, its performance in contingency similarity was significantly lower (54.8) compared to CTGAN (91.7) and STD (65.1). Both CTGAN and STD, while not explicitly designed to separately model conditionals, showed competitive results, suggesting that data-driven deep learning approaches may offer better generalization for mixed-type conditional distributions than purely statistical methods.

5.2   RQ2 – Utility

Table 2. Micro and Macro-F1 with 95% CI on real and synthetic data

MODELS		Real		Synthetic	
Synthesizer	Classifier	Micro-F1	Macro-F1	Micro-F1	Macro-F1
CTGAN	Logistic Regression	87.7(0.0)	47.7(1.8)	87.7(0.0)	46.7(0.0)
	Random Forest	87.5(0.2)	50.9(1.3)	87.6(0.1)	46.8(0.1)
	XGBoost	87.7(0.1)	47.8(1.9)	87.7(0.0)	46.7(0.0)
GC	Logistic Regression	87.7(0.1)	47.7(1.8)	84.8(5.2)	51.8(7.3)
	Random Forest	87.5(0.2)	50.9(1.3)	87.7(0.0)	46.9(0.3)
	XGBoost	87.7(0.1)	47.8(1.9)	87.5(0.4)	47.7(2.8)
STD	Logistic Regression	87.7(0.1)	47.7(1.8)	87.7(0.0)	46.8(0.1)
	Random Forest	87.5(0.2)	50.9(1.3)	87.7(0.0)	46.8(0.0)
	XGBoost	87.7(0.1)	47.8(1.9)	85.1(4.4)	49.7(3.4)

Table 2 summarizes the performance of models trained on real and synthetic datasets across the three synthesizers: CTGAN, Gaussian Copula (GC), and SimpleTableDiffusion (STD). In general, classifiers trained on real data consistently achieved strong Micro-F1 scores of around 87.5% to 87.7%, confirming the robustness of the Vigitel dataset for downstream predictive tasks. Overall, all tested methods recorded lower Macro-F1 scores, probably due to the already mentioned very skewed distribution of the task. More importantly though, is that for all combinations of synthetizers, classifiers and metrics, the utility measured in the real datasets is very similar (with few exceptions discussed below) to that measured in the synthetic datasets.

Among the generative models, CTGAN consistently maintained the closest performance to real data across all classifiers, excelling especially in Micro-F1 scores in terms of absolute utility and with low variability in MacroF1, showing stability. This confirms earlier findings that GAN-based models are highly effective in capturing complex and high-dimensional dependencies in tabular data [22,33].

The Gaussian Copula model showed higher variability in the performance in the synthetic data, particularly with Logistic Regression, with high confidence intervals. While copula-based models are strong in capturing marginal and pairwise dependencies [17], their parametric assumptions can limit performance when modeling the non-linear feature interactions typical in real-world health datasets. However, GC showed competitive Macro-F1 scores for certain classifiers, suggesting that statistical methods can still offer useful utility depending on the model and dataset.

SimpleTableDiffusion remained competitive, with Micro- and Macro-F1 scores similar to those of CTGAN, in both, real and synthetic datasets, particularly with Random Forest and Logistic Regression. For XGBoost, variability increased a bit in the synthetic data. Overall, despite its simplicity and faster training compared to full iterative diffusion architectures [31], STD has demonstrated to be a very practical candidate for quality-preserving data generation tasks.

5.3 RQ3 Privacy

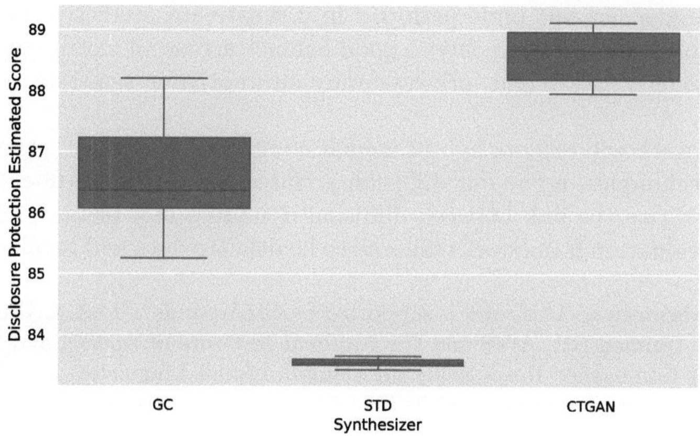

Fig. 4. Privacy scores distribution (along side the 5-folds) for each synthesizer.

Finally, when it comes to privacy, we present the results of our Disclosure Protection metric in Fig. 4, which shows the privacy scores distribution (computed using Disclosure Protection score as defined in Sect. 4.3) across the five cross-validation folds for each synthesizer. While the boxplot captures the score variability, we also report the average and 95% confidence intervals: CTGAN achieves the highest privacy score – 88.6 (0.6) – significantly (statistically) outperforming Gaussian Copula (GC) – 86.6 (1.4) – and SimpleTableDiffusion (STD) – 83.6 (0.1). Although STD does not achieve the top score, its stability and strong results (only 5.6% lower than CTGAN) support the hypothesis that the stochastic noise injection and denoising mechanisms inherent to diffusion models may contribute to privacy preservation, even without explicit differential privacy added. These findings motivate further investigation into how diffusion dynamics influences privacy in synthetic data generation.

6 Conclusion

This study presented a comparative evaluation of three paradigms for the generation of synthetic tabular data in healthcare: a classical statistical model (Gaussian Copula), a GAN-based model (CTGAN), and our implementation of a diffusion-based model (SimpleTableDiffusion). By integrating these approaches within a unified experimental framework, we evaluated their performance across key dimensions: data quality, predictive utility, and privacy. In particular, SimpleTableDiffusion introduced a simplified and non-iterative diffusion architecture that significantly improved training efficiency while maintaining competitive outcomes.

The results revealed that CTGAN consistently delivers the best overall performance, excelling in predictive utility, privacy protection, and marginal distribution quality. The Gaussian copula model remains strong in capturing conditional dependencies but underperforms in downstream predictive tasks. Meanwhile, SimpleTableDiffusion offers a good balance across all metrics, demonstrating promise as a lightweight, privacy-aware alternative in sensitive domains like healthcare.

Future work will explore hybrid models combining statistical, generative and diffusion techniques, refine our diffusion architecture for better fidelity and privacy, investigate the link between diffusion dynamics and privacy, and develop adaptive evaluation frameworks tailored to healthcare data and regulatory needs.

Acknowledgments. This work is supported by CIIA-Saúde, CIAA, CNPq, FAPESP, FAPEMIG, Unimed-BH, AWS and the National Institute of Science and Technology in Artificial Intelligence Responsible for Computational Linguistics and Information Processing and Dissemination (INCT-TILDIAR) (Process 408490/2024-1).

References

1. Abadi, M., et al.: Deep learning with differential privacy. In: Proceedings of the 2016 ACM SIGSAC Conference on Computer and Communications Security, CCS '16, pp. 308–318. Association for Computing Machinery, New York, NY, USA (2016)
2. Bernal, R.T.I., et al.: A methodology for small area prevalence estimation based on survey data. Int. J. Equity Health **19**, 1–10 (2020)
3. Bernal, R.T.I., Iser, B.P.M., Malta, D.C., Claro, R.M.: Surveillance system for risk and protective factors for chronic diseases by telephone survey (Vigitel): changes in weighting methodology. Epidemiologia e Serviços de Saúde **26**, 701–712 (2017)
4. van Breugel, B., Crabbé, J., Davis, R., van der Schaar, M.: LaTable: towards large tabular models. arXiv preprint arXiv:2406.17673 (2024)
5. Chen, T., Guestrin, C.: XGBoost: a scalable tree boosting system. In: Proceedings of the 22nd ACM SIGKDD International Conference on Knowledge Discovery and Data Mining, pp. 785–794 (2016)
6. Choi, E., Biswal, S., Malin, B., Duke, J., Stewart, W.F., Sun, J.: Generating multi-label discrete patient records using generative adversarial networks. In: Machine Learning for Healthcare Conference, pp. 286–305. PMLR (2017)
7. Dhariwal, P., Nichol, A.: Diffusion models beat GANs on image synthesis. Adv. Neural. Inf. Process. Syst. **34**, 8780–8794 (2021)
8. Goodfellow, I., et al.: Generative adversarial nets. In: Advances in Neural Information Processing Systems, vol. 27 (2014)

9. Grinsztajn, L., Oyallon, E., Varoquaux, G.: Why do tree-based models still outperform deep learning on typical tabular data? In: Proceedings of the 36th International Conference on Neural Information Processing Systems, NIPS '22 (2022)
10. Hittmeir, M., Mayer, R., Ekelhart, A.: A baseline for attribute disclosure risk in synthetic data. In: Proceedings of the Tenth ACM Conference on Data and Application Security and Privacy, CODASPY '20, pp. 133–143 (2020)
11. Ho, J., Jain, A., Abbeel, P.: Denoising diffusion probabilistic models. In: Advances in Neural Information Processing Systems, vol. 33 (2020)
12. Kaur, D., et al.: Application of Bayesian networks to generate synthetic health data. J. Am. Med. Inform. Assoc. **28**(4), 801–811 (2021)
13. Kumar, P., Shoukri, M.M.: Copula functions for modelling dependence structure with applications in the analysis of clinical data. J. Indian Soc. Agric. Statist. **61**(2), 179–191 (2007)
14. Liu, J., Luan, Y.: Copula-based statistical models for financial time series. Quant. Financ. **12**(4), 641–655 (2012)
15. Mirza, M.: Conditional generative adversarial nets. arXiv preprint arXiv:1411.1784 (2014)
16. Murtaza, H., Ahmed, M., Khan, N.F., Murtaza, G., Zafar, S., Bano, A.: Synthetic data generation: state of the art in health care domain. Comput. Sci. Rev. **48**, 100546 (2023). https://doi.org/10.1016/j.cosrev.2023.100546
17. Nelsen, R.B.: An Introduction to Copulas. Springer, New York (2006). https://doi.org/10.1007/0-387-28678-0
18. Nielsen, D.: Tree boosting with XGBoost-why does XGBoost win "every" machine learning competition? Master's thesis, NTNU (2016)
19. Oganian, A.: v-dispersed synthetic data based on a mixture model with constraints. In: Domingo-Ferrer, J. (eds.) Privacy in Statistical Databases: UNESCO Chair in Data Privacy, International Conference, pp. 200–212. Springer, Cham (2014). https://doi.org/10.1007/978-3-319-11257-2_16
20. Park, Y., Ghosh, J.: PeGS: perturbed Gibbs samplers that generate privacy-compliant synthetic data. Trans. Data Priv. **7**(3), 253–282 (2014)
21. Park, Y., Ghosh, J., Shankar, M.: Perturbed Gibbs samplers for generating large-scale privacy-safe synthetic health data. In: 2013 IEEE International Conference on Healthcare Informatics. pp. 493–498. IEEE (2013)
22. Patki, N., Wedge, R., Veeramachaneni, K.: The synthetic data vault. In: 2016 IEEE International Conference on Data Science and Advanced Analytics (DSAA) (2016). https://doi.org/10.1109/DSAA.2016.49
23. Patki, N., Wedge, R., Veeramachaneni, K.: The synthetic data vault. In: 2016 IEEE International Conference on Data Science and Advanced Analytics (DSAA), pp. 399–410 (2016). https://doi.org/10.1109/DSAA.2016.49
24. Patki, N., Wedge, R., Veeramachaneni, K.: The synthetic data vault. In: IEEE International Conference on Data Science and Advanced Analytics (DSAA), October 2016, pp. 399–410 (2016). https://doi.org/10.1109/DSAA.2016.49
25. Radford, A., Metz, L., Chintala, S.: Unsupervised representation learning with deep convolutional generative adversarial networks. arXiv preprint arXiv:1511.06434 (2015)
26. Restrepo, J.P., Rivera, J.C., Laniado, H., Osorio, P., Becerra, O.A.: Nonparametric generation of synthetic data using copulas. Electronics **12**(7) (2023)
27. Rubin, D.B.: Statistical disclosure limitation. J. Official Stat. **9**(2), 461–468 (1993)
28. scikit-learn: QuantileTransformer (2024). https://scikit-learn.org/stable/modules/generated/sklearn.preprocessing.QuantileTransformer.html

29. Sohl-Dickstein, J., Weiss, E., Maheswaranathan, N., Ganguli, S.: Deep unsupervised learning using nonequilibrium thermodynamics. In: International Conference on Machine Learning, pp. 2256–2265. PMLR (2015)
30. Faria, T.R., et al: Improving the mapping of leisure-time physical activity inequities: the use of artificial intelligence to advance estimates of small-areas in Brazil. Pub. Health **243**, 105727 (2025). https://doi.org/10.1016/j.puhe.2025.105727
31. Truda, G.: Generating tabular datasets under differential privacy. arXiv preprint arXiv:2308.14784 (2023)
32. Wang, Z., Myles, P., Tucker, A.: Generating and evaluating cross-sectional synthetic electronic healthcare data: Preserving data utility and patient privacy. Comput. Intell. **37**(2), 819–851 (2021)
33. Xu, L., Skoularidou, M., Cuesta-Infante, A., Veeramachaneni, K.: Modeling tabular data using conditional GAN. Adv. Neural Inf. Process. Syst. **32** (2019)
34. Xu, L., Veeramachaneni, K.: Synthesizing tabular data using generative adversarial networks. arXiv preprint arXiv:1811.11264 (2018)
35. Yu, L., Zhang, W., Wang, J., Yu, Y.: SeqGAN: sequence generative adversarial nets with policy gradient. In: Proceedings of the AAAI Conference on Artificial Intelligence, vol. 31 (2017)
36. Zhang, J., Cormode, G., Procopiuc, C.M., Srivastava, D., Xiao, X.: PrivBayes: private data release via Bayesian networks. ACM TODS **42**(4), 1–41 (2017)
37. Zhou, Y., et al.: DiffLM: controllable synthetic data generation via diffusion language models. arXiv preprint arXiv:2411.03250 (2024)

A Novel Interpretable Approach to Deep Multimodal Data Fusion Applied to Cancer Diagnosis

Leandro M. de Lima[1,2(✉)], Matheus B. Rocha[1,2], and Renato A. Krohling[1,2]

[1] Labcin - Nature Inspired Computing Lab, Federal University of Espírito Santo, Vitória, Brazil
leandro.m.lima@ufes.br

[2] PPGI - Graduate Program in Computer Science, Federal University of Espírito Santo, Vitória, Brazil

Abstract. The use of artificial intelligence (AI) in healthcare has seen significant growth, particularly in cancer diagnosis, which remains one of the leading causes of mortality globally. AI-based computer-aided diagnosis systems leveraging computer vision have explored multimodal data including images, text, and graphs, among others to improve diagnostic accuracy. However, many approaches, especially those involving middle fusion, are considered *black-box* models. Inspired by the clinical reasoning adopted by medical professionals, and aiming to develop a more interpretable approach based on deep multimodal fusion, this paper proposes a new hybrid approach. Firstly, the medical lesion image is classified using a convolutional neural network or transformer, generating a probability for one of the target classes. Next, this probability, combined with clinical and/or sociodemographic data, is used as input to an external classifier, which generates the final diagnostic. The proposed approach was evaluated: 1) on the skin cancer PAD-UFES-20 dataset consisting of clinical image and patient lesion information, and 2) on oral cancer NDB-UFES dataset consisting of histopathological images and sociodemographic data. On the one side, the obtained results indicate a slight inferior performance in terms of balanced accuracy compared to state-of-the-art using middle fusion, but on the other side our model provided interpretability using Shapley Additive Explanations (SHAP).

Keywords: Multimodal fusion · Artificial neural networks · Transformer · Interpretable Deep Learning · Cancer

1 Introduction

The World Health Organization (WHO) predicts that cancer will become the leading cause of death in the 21st century [37]. In the case of oral cancer, early diagnosis increases the survival rate to 80%, while after metastasis, this rate drops to 30%. For this reason, anamnesis and a well-conducted clinical examination by the dentist are crucial for an adequate initial diagnosis [14]. However, the

R. de Freitas and D. Furtado (Eds.): BRACIS 2025, LNAI 16181, pp. 35–49, 2026.
https://doi.org/10.1007/978-3-032-15990-8_3

manual interpretation of exams is time-consuming, relies on the professional's expertise, and hinders standardization; even with attempts to establish criteria, such as invasion pattern and tumor thickness, there is no consensus on dysplasia classification [17,26]. Similarly, skin cancer has a high incidence and requires effective detection methods. In Brazil, according to the National Cancer Institute (INCA), skin cancer accounts for 31.3% of all cancer diagnoses in the country, making it the most prevalent form among cancer categories. For the period from 20232025, approximately 700,000 new cancer cases are expected in the country [25]. Specifically for skin cancer, the primary risk factor is exposure to ultraviolet (UV) radiation emitted by the sun [24].

Recent advances in the extraction of features from medical images and the integration of this information with complementary patient data have been widely discussed in the literature [21,22]. However, the fusion of such data is predominantly performed at the intermediate stage of the classification process, an approach known as middle fusion or intermediate fusion. Alternatively, other strategies, such as early fusion and late fusion, are also employed, each with specific characteristics and potential applications [6]. In this paper, a hybrid approach for multimodal data fusion will be investigated, discussing its characteristics and advantages in the medical context.

This contrast between high predictive power and lack of transparency represents a risk in the context of medical diagnosis, where factors such as trust, accountability, and the ability to understand errors play a fundamental role [29,31]. In the case of deep neural networks, the increasing complexity of architectures, often characterized by a large number of parameters, poses significant challenges to interpretability. In many approaches, the pursuit of higher accuracy has led to the development of highly complex models, whose decision-making logic becomes opaque and difficult to understand [41]. This trade-off has been studied, and the optimal balance between interpretability and performance metrics remains an open area of research [4,40].

In the medical domain, maintaining this balance is an issue [32], as decisions based on automated models can directly impact patients' health and well-being. The lack of clarity about how an AI model reaches a diagnosis can undermine the trust of healthcare professionals, hindering the adoption and integration of AI-based systems into clinical practice. Research such as [13] investigated the statistical implications of incorporating interpretability constraints in machine learning models, focusing on the trade-off between interpretability and predictive accuracy.

The main contributions of this work are twofold:

- we propose, as far as we know, a new hybrid method for multimodal data fusion.
- we apply the method to two case studies involving the diagnosis of skin cancer using the PAD-UFES-20 dataset and oral cancer using the NDB-UFES dataset to illustrate the approach and demonstrate its feasibility.

The structure of the article is presented in the following: Sect. 2 provides an overview of standard architectures for multimodal data fusion and proposes an interpretable approach for multimodal data fusion, combining images with clinical and demographic data. Section 3 presents and discusses the experimental results obtained. Finally, Sect. 4 concludes the article with final considerations and suggestions for future work.

2   Methodology

Traditionally, multimodal fusion methods are classified as early fusion, feature-level fusion, and late fusion, based on the stage of information fusion in the classification pipeline, as shown in Fig. 1. Some authors refer to early fusion as input fusion, while feature-level fusion may be considered intermediate fusion or joint fusion, and late fusion is equivalent to decision-level fusion or output fusion.

Input fusion involves combining data from multiple modalities into a unified feature vector, which is used as input for the deep neural network. On the other hand, output fusion combines unimodal results from different modalities. This approach is simple to implement and often does not require additional training. However, it faces limitations in exploiting complementary information between modalities due to the absence of integration at the feature level. Furthermore, output fusion may fail to improve classification performance when significant disparities exist in the performance of individual modalities.

In the field of multimodal physiological signal analysis, feature-level fusion methods play a central role and are widely used [20]. Feature-level fusion involves extracting relevant information from multiple sources with different modalities before fusion, followed by combining this information into a fused feature set. This process encompasses the extraction of meaningful features from distinct physiological modalities, such as medical imaging, electrocardiography, electromyography, and electroencephalography, which are subsequently integrated at the feature level [11].

This article proposes a mixed fusion architecture inspired by the diagnostic decision-making process performed by specialists. The approach combines feature-level fusion with the fusion of probabilities generated in a previous stage. In the proposed mixed fusion model, the image backbone generates class probabilities based solely on the image input. These probabilities, produced by the internal classifier, are concatenated with complementary data and processed by an external classifier, as illustrated in Fig. 2.

The development of this architecture was based on the observation of the typical analytical process of specialists, who begin their analysis with a preliminary decision relying exclusively on visual information extracted from images and subsequently incorporate complementary data to review or adjust the initial assessment. By replicating this approach, the mixed fusion model aims to capture the analytical reasoning of specialists, systematically integrating information to support more accurate and well-founded decisions. A limitation of the

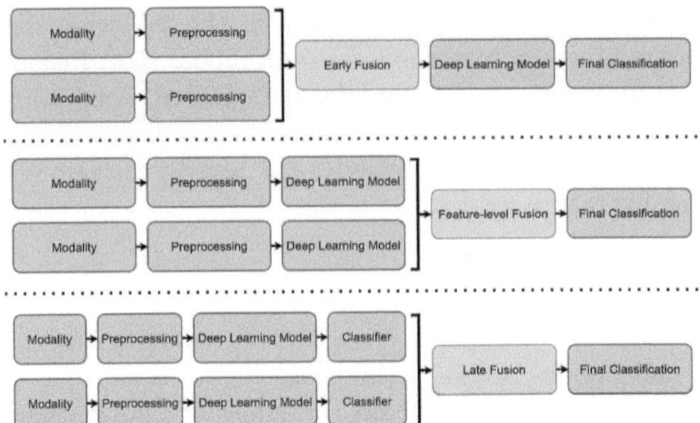

Fig. 1. The three standard types of multimodal fusion based on the stage of information fusion. It shows the early fusion (top), the feature-level fusion (middle), and the late fusion (bottom) methods

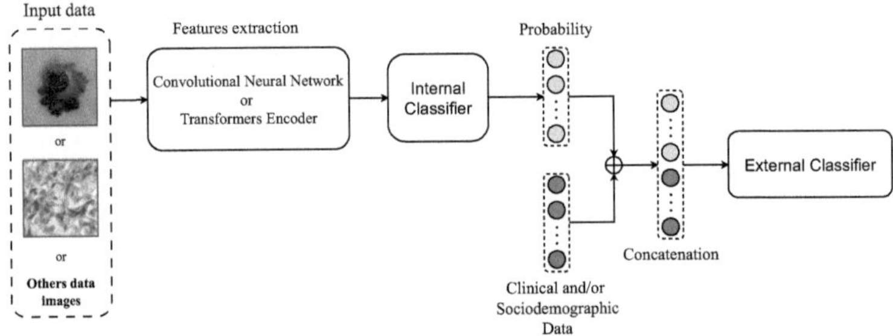

Fig. 2. Mixed fusion architecture. In our approach, data fusion occurs similarly to late fusion. The difference lies in the fact that the images are initially processed by a feature extractor and then passed through a classifier that generates class probabilities. These probabilities are combined with clinical data, resulting in a final classification step

approach is the assumption that both visual information and complementary data are available and relevant to the diagnosis.

In deep neural networks, the complexity of model structures poses a growing challenge to interpretability. Sometimes, to obtain higher accuracy, researchers may design complex network structures with a large number of parameters, but this can cause the decision-making process of the model to become opaque [41]. This trade-off has been studied and the optimal balance between interpretability and performance metrics is an open field of research [40].

Currently, there is no consensus on the classification of interpretability methods [40]. One of the interpretability's dimensions categorized by [42] consists of the differentiation between passive and active approaches. Active and passive interpretation depends on whether the model structure is modified, or optimized, before the model is trained to make the model somewhat interpretative or an inherently transparent model is designed. Active explanations refer to active intervention explanations. Active explanations involve intervening in the model's structure before training or designing transparent model structures, which can perform tasks while enhancing interpretability and making the output more intelligible for humans. Passive explanation is an interpretive method applied to already trained models, which extracts logical rules or comprehensible patterns by analyzing the model's structure, weights, and outputs, among other information.

SHAP (SHapley Additive exPlanations) [23] is a passive post hoc explanation model and is proposed as a unified measure of feature importance. Posthoc explainability apply to existing models after completing training to provide model interpretability. SHAP permits a comprehensive understanding of the impact of each feature on model predictions and explains the model's overall behavior. The core idea is to calculate the marginal contribution of features to model output and interpret the black-box model at both the global and local levels. Inspired by cooperative game theory, SHAP constructs an additive explanatory model that treats each feature as a contributor to the model's prediction. The model generates a prediction value for each prediction sample, and the SHAP values represent the value assigned to each feature in the sample. The SHAP values refer to Shapley values applied to a conditional expectation function of a machine learning model. The Shapley value explains the difference in the contribution of input features to the prediction result, that is, the contribution of features to the difference between the prediction result and the average prediction value.

3   Experiments

3.1   PAD-UFES-20 Dataset

The experiments were conducted using datasets related to skin and oral lesions. The first dataset analyzed in this study is the PAD-UFES-20 [27], which integrates clinical images and patient clinical data. The PAD-UFES-20 dataset consists of 2,298 samples, distributed into 1,209 benign lesion samples (52.6%) and 1,089 malignant lesion samples (47.4%). It contains samples from 6 types of skin lesions, with each sample comprising a clinical image captured by mobile devices (smartphones) and detailed clinical information about the patients. The individual analysis of lesion classes reveals three malignant categories: 845 samples of basal cell carcinoma (BCC), 192 of squamous cell carcinoma (SCC), and 52 of melanoma (MEL). The benign lesions are also subdivided into three categories: 730 samples of actinic keratosis (ACK), 235 of seborrheic keratosis (SEK), and 244 of melanocytic nevus (NEV). Figure 3 illustrates a representative image sample for each type of lesion present in the dataset.

In addition to information about the lesion classes, the dataset includes 21 clinical features of the patients, such as age, gender, anatomical location of the skin lesion, Fitzpatrick skin type, skin lesion diameter (2 features), and qualitative information related to the lesion, such as itching, growth, pain, changes, bleeding, and elevation (6 features). Data on family history (2 features), cancer

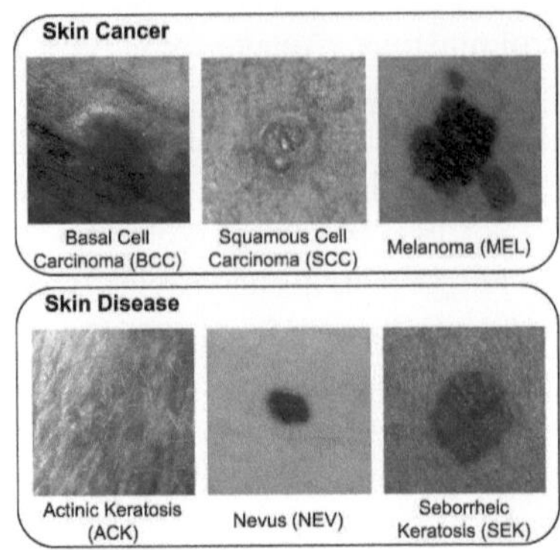

Fig. 3. PAD-UFES-20 image samples

history (2 features), risk factors (3 features), and socio-environmental information, including whether the patient lives in housing with access to piped water and a sewage system, are also provided.

This dataset was selected due to its multimodal nature, involving non-dermoscopic images. Unlike most available datasets, which are limited to dermoscopic images and do not include clinical information related to the lesions, such as HAM10000 [35].

3.2 NDB-UFES Dataset

The second dataset analyzed in this study is the NDB-UFES [5], which integrates histopathological images and clinical data from patients diagnosed with oral leukoplakia without dysplasia (LW/oD), with dysplasia (LW/D), and oral squamous cell carcinoma (OSCC).

The NDB-UFES dataset consists of 274 histopathological images and sociodemographic information about the patients, distributed as 91 OSCC samples (38.4%), 89 LW/D samples (37.6%), and 57 LW/oD samples (24.1%). Figure 4 presents image samples for each type of oral lesion in the dataset.

In addition to the histopathological images, the dataset contains 7 clinical features of the patient, such as lesion location, lesion size, patient gender, age group, alcohol consumption habits, smoking habits, and regular sun exposure habits. These features are used in model training as they are important risk factors [2,8,34]. Except for lesion size, all complementary data are categorical features, and we applied the one-hot encoding technique to encode them. In total, the complementary data are transformed into 23 encoded features.

3.3 Implementation Details

We selected two neural network-based classifier as internal classifier: Multi-Layer Perceptron (MLP) and Transformer Encoder. To use the Transformer Encoder

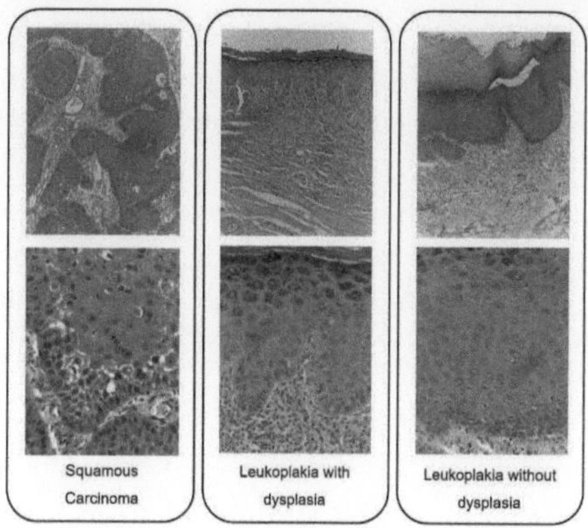

Fig. 4. NDB image samples

as a classifier, we added a linear layer to resize the input to the internal size of the encoder and an MLP after the encoder block. In addition to these two neural network internal classifiers, we also employed two standard machine learning algrithms as external classifiers: LightGBM [19] and XGBoost [9]. Before training the standard machine learning classifiers, the neural network is trained according to the proposed approach as shown in Fig. 2. Then, we remove the neural network-based classifier, and replace it by one of the standard machine learning classifier, and start a new training round, this time training only the standard machine learning classifier.

By evaluating pre-trained image backbones and fusion methods, we aim to identify which combinations of image backbones and fusion methods are most suitable for classification using the PAD-UFES-20 and NDB-UFES datasets. We selected 5 pre-trained image backbones (i.e. CoaT [39], PiT [16], RegNetY [28], ResNetV2 [15], and ViT [10]) for evaluation based on the same criteria of previous works using those datasets [21, 22].

3.4 Parameters Setting

All experiments conducted in this study used a standard set of hyperparameters, which will be adopted unless otherwise specified. For all architectures that include a reducer block, the size was set to 90. The chosen loss function was weighted cross-entropy. Training was performed for 150 epochs with a batch size of 30, and early stopping was applied, halting training if no improvements were observed for 15 consecutive epochs. The optimizer used was SGD (Stochastic Gradient Descent) with an initial learning rate of 0.001, a momentum of 0.9, and a weight decay of 0.001. For additional optimization, a learning rate reduction strategy on plateau was applied, with a patience of 10, a reduction factor of 0.1, and a lower bound for the learning rate of 10^{-6}.

For evaluation, the holdout validation technique was used, with 5/6 of the dataset allocated for training and the remaining 1/6 reserved for testing. Additionally, within the training set, 5-fold cross-validation was applied, resulting in 5 distinct trained models. The results presented correspond to the mean and standard deviation of the metrics obtained by the 5 models when evaluated on the test set.

The results were subsequently analyzed considering the mean and standard deviation of the metrics in each combination. Four metrics widely used in the literature were used: Balanced Accuracy (BACC), Precision, Recall, and AUC (Area Under the Curve).

3.5   Results

The results of the experiments using the mixed fusion technique for the PAD-UFES-20 dataset are presented in Table 1 and Table 2. For the NDB-UFES dataset, the results are listed in Tables 3 and 4. These tables consolidate the results obtained through mixed fusion using the MLP and Transformer Encoder classifiers.

For PAD-UFES-20, the best mean BACC was 0.7716 ± 0.0267, achieved with the ViT backbone model. This same scenario also presented the best mean for the precision metric. For recall and AUC metrics, the ViT model combined with LightGBM, initially trained using the transformer encoder classifier, obtained the best mean recall (0.8120 ± 0.0110), while the RegNetY model combined with XGBoost, also initially trained with the transformer classifier, achieved the best mean AUC (0.9438 ± 0.0063).

Table 1. Summary of evaluation of mixed fusion on PAD-UFES-20 dataset using a MLP Classifier for clinical image. Mean and standard deviation of all evaluated metrics. Bold values have the best mean in table

Model	External classifier	BACC	Precision	Recall	AUC
CoaT	LightGBM	0.7174 ± 0.0169	0.7880 ± 0.0110	**0.8020 ± 0.0084**	0.9340 ± 0.0102
	XGBoost	0.7024 ± 0.0368	0.7900 ± 0.0255	0.8020 ± 0.0205	0.9302 ± 0.0142
	NN	0.6942 ± 0.0230	0.7640 ± 0.0207	0.6400 ± 0.0552	0.9142 ± 0.0105
PiT	LightGBM	0.6986 ± 0.0402	0.7720 ± 0.0192	0.7880 ± 0.0179	0.9358 ± 0.0108
	XGBoost	0.6934 ± 0.0179	0.7820 ± 0.0217	0.7900 ± 0.0255	0.9284 ± 0.0199
	NN	0.7394 ± 0.0436	0.7880 ± 0.0327	0.6680 ± 0.0740	0.9224 ± 0.0155
RegNetY	LightGBM	0.7074 ± 0.0288	0.7780 ± 0.0192	0.7940 ± 0.0241	**0.9368 ± 0.0099**
	XGBoost	0.7046 ± 0.0237	0.7680 ± 0.0192	0.7880 ± 0.0130	0.9360 ± 0.0127
	NN	0.7372 ± 0.0170	0.7620 ± 0.0179	0.6900 ± 0.0255	0.9260 ± 0.0047
ResNetV2	LightGBM	0.7116 ± 0.0253	0.7720 ± 0.0164	0.7860 ± 0.0114	0.9264 ± 0.0092
	XGBoost	0.6986 ± 0.0317	0.7700 ± 0.0200	0.7880 ± 0.0148	0.9262 ± 0.0104
	NN	0.7306 ± 0.0118	0.7740 ± 0.0207	0.6880 ± 0.0205	0.9214 ± 0.0057
ViT	LightGBM	0.7008 ± 0.0338	0.7800 ± 0.0187	0.7920 ± 0.0179	0.9328 ± 0.0155
	XGBoost	0.6996 ± 0.0304	0.7780 ± 0.0192	0.7880 ± 0.0192	0.9276 ± 0.0135
	NN	**0.7466 ± 0.0221**	**0.7940 ± 0.0182**	0.6980 ± 0.0349	0.9230 ± 0.0116
Baseline using middle fusion					
PiT w MetaBlock [21]		0.800 ± 0.006	-	-	0.941 ± 0.006

Table 2. Summary of evaluation of mixed fusion on PAD-UFES-20 dataset using a Transformer Encoder Classifier for the clinical image. Mean and standard deviation of all evaluated metrics. Bold values have the best mean in table

Model	External classifier	BACC	Precision	Recall	AUC
CoaT	LightGBM	0.6890 ± 0.0187	0.7640 ± 0.0055	0.7820 ± 0.0084	0.9230 ± 0.0081
	XGBoost	0.6970 ± 0.0267	0.7820 ± 0.0084	0.7940 ± 0.0114	0.9254 ± 0.0120
	NN	0.7458 ± 0.0145	0.7980 ± 0.0164	0.7460 ± 0.0434	0.9360 ± 0.0035
PiT	LightGBM	0.7276 ± 0.0310	0.7840 ± 0.0152	0.7920 ± 0.0148	0.9292 ± 0.0100
	XGBoost	0.7246 ± 0.0178	0.7940 ± 0.0182	0.8020 ± 0.0110	0.9308 ± 0.0153
	NN	0.7636 ± 0.0199	0.8060 ± 0.0152	0.7600 ± 0.0122	0.9382 ± 0.0033
RegNetY	LightGBM	0.7020 ± 0.0216	0.7750 ± 0.0058	0.7875 ± 0.0050	0.9393 ± 0.0087
	XGBoost	0.7008 ± 0.0279	0.7760 ± 0.0167	0.7920 ± 0.0179	$\mathbf{0.9438 \pm 0.0063}$
	NN	0.7474 ± 0.0286	0.7920 ± 0.0192	0.7560 ± 0.0089	0.9382 ± 0.0031
ResNetV2	LightGBM	0.7150 ± 0.0259	0.7800 ± 0.0212	0.7940 ± 0.0152	0.9346 ± 0.0088
	XGBoost	0.7234 ± 0.0171	0.7800 ± 0.0122	0.7880 ± 0.0164	0.9352 ± 0.0110
	NN	0.7500 ± 0.0125	0.7980 ± 0.0084	0.7640 ± 0.0152	0.9366 ± 0.0026
ViT	LightGBM	0.7324 ± 0.0265	0.7940 ± 0.0152	0.8080 ± 0.0110	0.9368 ± 0.0049
	XGBoost	0.7334 ± 0.0247	0.8000 ± 0.0122	$\mathbf{0.8120 \pm 0.0110}$	0.9312 ± 0.0198
	NN	$\mathbf{0.7716 \pm 0.0267}$	$\mathbf{0.8080 \pm 0.0228}$	0.7600 ± 0.0255	0.9394 ± 0.0047
Baseline using middle fusion					
PiT w MetaBlock [21]		0.800 ± 0.006	-	-	0.941 ± 0.006

For the NDB-UFES dataset, the best mean BACC was 0.7780 ± 0.0626, obtained with the CoaT backbone model. For the precision and recall metrics, the RegNetY model combined with XGBoost, initially trained using the MLP classifier, achieved the best means, with 0.8080 ± 0.0259 for precision and 0.7980 ± 0.0217 for recall. For the AUC metric, the RegNetV2 model combined with neural networks (NN), initially trained using the transformer classifier, presented the best mean of 0.9296 ± 0.0085.

The mixed fusion models showed a slight inferior performance compared to intermediate fusion approach, a result that aligns with the well-known trade-off between interpretability and performance in machine learning models [4]. Despite this limitation in terms of accuracy, one of the main advantages of mixed fusion lies in the increased explainability of the model, a fundamental aspect in sensitive domains such as medical diagnosis. We conducted an explainability analysis using Shapley Additive Explanations (SHAP) [30] to better understand the model's decision-making reasoning.

We used the model-agnostic implementation of the SHAP method, called Kernel SHAP, for a global analysis of the model with the best mean BACC on the PAD-UFES-20 and NDB-UFES datasets (Table 2 and Table 4, respectively). The experiments were configured to use only the model trained on the first fold of the training set, and the results show SHAP values for all samples in the test set. The feature importance is calculated by mean absolute SHAP values for each feature, as in [1]. We also calculate the sum of those mean absolute SHAP values for each set of features (image features and complementary features) to quantify their respective contributions to model outputs.

Table 3. Summary of evaluation of mixed fusion on NDB-UFES dataset using a MLP Classifier for the histopathological image. Mean and standard deviation of all evaluated metrics. Bold values have the best mean in table

Model	External classifier	BACC	Precision	Recall	AUC
CoaT	LightGBM	**0.7780 ± 0.0626**	0.8080 ± 0.0455	0.7940 ± 0.0428	0.9104 ± 0.0335
	XGBoost	0.7050 ± 0.0706	0.7480 ± 0.0719	0.7380 ± 0.0646	0.8834 ± 0.0336
	NN	0.6294 ± 0.1496	0.6320 ± 0.1636	0.6480 ± 0.1178	0.8388 ± 0.0707
PiT	LightGBM	0.7170 ± 0.0547	0.7500 ± 0.0515	0.7360 ± 0.0677	0.8912 ± 0.0365
	XGBoost	0.7274 ± 0.0619	0.7640 ± 0.0513	0.7540 ± 0.0503	0.8970 ± 0.0344
	NN	0.5348 ± 0.1899	0.6440 ± 0.1292	0.5380 ± 0.1828	0.7406 ± 0.1234
RegNetY	LightGBM	0.7306 ± 0.0393	0.7780 ± 0.0460	0.7620 ± 0.0311	0.8812 ± 0.0343
	XGBoost	0.7734 ± 0.0213	**0.8080 ± 0.0259**	**0.7980 ± 0.0217**	0.9080 ± 0.0178
	NN	0.6060 ± 0.0608	0.6480 ± 0.0729	0.6100 ± 0.0667	0.8086 ± 0.0549
ResNetV2	LightGBM	0.7524 ± 0.0504	0.7960 ± 0.0658	0.7800 ± 0.0587	**0.9156 ± 0.0346**
	XGBoost	0.7380 ± 0.0294	0.7660 ± 0.0207	0.7560 ± 0.0230	0.9016 ± 0.0329
	NN	0.5038 ± 0.2359	0.4220 ± 0.3154	0.5000 ± 0.2140	0.7086 ± 0.1950
ViT	LightGBM	0.6934 ± 0.0587	0.7180 ± 0.0622	0.7180 ± 0.0618	0.8756 ± 0.0487
	XGBoost	0.7364 ± 0.0421	0.7720 ± 0.0370	0.7520 ± 0.0390	0.8798 ± 0.0320
	NN	0.5852 ± 0.2088	0.6200 ± 0.2164	0.5980 ± 0.1975	0.8050 ± 0.1204
Baseline using middle fusion					
ResNetV2 w/ MetaBlock [22]		0.8324 ± 0.0324	0.8680 ± 0.0327	0.8620 ± 0.0295	0.9598 ± 0.0196

Table 4. Summary of evaluation of mixed fusion on NDB-UFES dataset using a Transformer Encoder Classifier for the histopathological image. Mean and standard deviation of all evaluated metrics. Bold values have the best mean in table

Model	External classifier	BACC	Precision	Recall	AUC
CoaT	LightGBM	0.6596 ± 0.1210	0.6880 ± 0.1314	0.7020 ± 0.0950	0.8864 ± 0.0560
	XGBoost	0.6948 ± 0.0599	0.7300 ± 0.0447	0.7220 ± 0.0466	0.8588 ± 0.0613
	NN	0.7202 ± 0.0233	0.7500 ± 0.0200	0.7480 ± 0.0217	0.9094 ± 0.0151
PiT	LightGBM	0.7244 ± 0.0636	0.7800 ± 0.0675	0.7540 ± 0.0611	0.9126 ± 0.0320
	XGBoost	0.7378 ± 0.0610	0.7700 ± 0.0406	0.7580 ± 0.0476	0.8688 ± 0.0323
	NN	**0.7736 ± 0.0413**	0.7980 ± 0.0327	0.7880 ± 0.0342	0.9286 ± 0.0073
RegNetY	LightGBM	0.6870 ± 0.1005	0.7200 ± 0.1003	0.7250 ± 0.0900	0.8678 ± 0.0647
	XGBoost	0.6992 ± 0.0896	0.7360 ± 0.0888	0.7260 ± 0.0879	0.8678 ± 0.0438
	NN	0.7734 ± 0.0302	**0.8060 ± 0.0261**	**0.7980 ± 0.0303**	0.9222 ± 0.0121
ResNetV2	LightGBM	0.6814 ± 0.0383	0.7300 ± 0.0406	0.7180 ± 0.0396	0.9086 ± 0.0221
	XGBoost	0.6844 ± 0.0439	0.7240 ± 0.0391	0.7200 ± 0.0354	0.8558 ± 0.0563
	NN	0.7066 ± 0.0441	0.7400 ± 0.0300	0.7340 ± 0.0351	0.9102 ± 0.0072
ViT	LightGBM	0.6534 ± 0.0485	0.6960 ± 0.0385	0.6920 ± 0.0286	0.8582 ± 0.0097
	XGBoost	0.6608 ± 0.0668	0.7080 ± 0.0606	0.7000 ± 0.0570	0.8426 ± 0.0722
	NN	0.7468 ± 0.0272	0.7860 ± 0.0230	0.7780 ± 0.0295	**0.9296 ± 0.0085**
Baseline using middle fusion					
ResNetV2 w/ MetaBlock [22]		0.8324 ± 0.0324	0.8680 ± 0.0327	0.8620 ± 0.0295	0.9598 ± 0.0196

For the PAD-UFES-20 dataset, we performed a SHAP analysis for the transformer neural network classifier with a ViT backbone. Figure 5a shows, for the true class SCC, the impact of the top 20 features on the model output, ordered by the mean absolute value of the SHAP values. The features "BCC", "SCC",

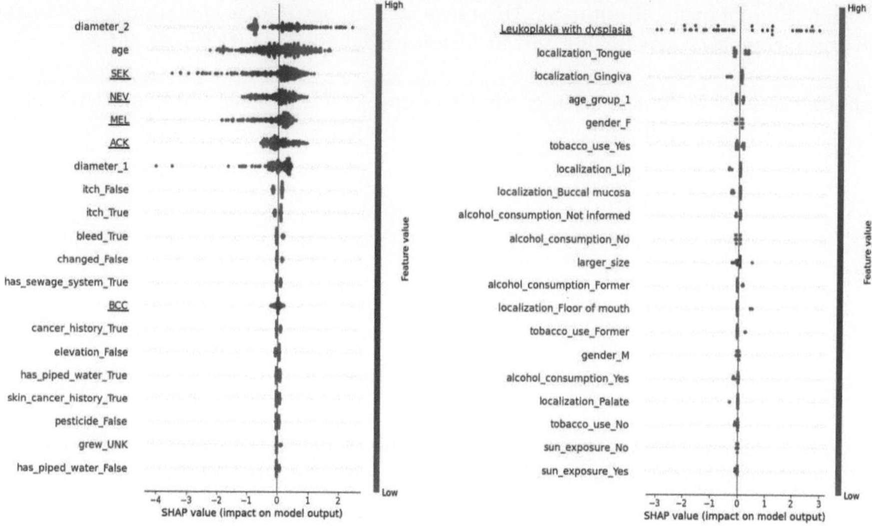

(a) Samples of class SCC on PAD-UFES-20   (b) Samples of class OSCC on NDB-UFES

Fig. 5. Feature impact on model output for classes on PAD-UFES-20 and NDB-UFES. Underlined feature names refer to the inner classifier estimated probability for each class label, which uses only image information.

"MEL", "ACK", "NEV", and "SEK" refer to the probabilities estimated by the internal classifier for each class label, which uses only image information.

We can observe that, in addition to the image classification information, the features that frequently appear among the top 20 are related to the ABCDE rule and the 7-point checklist, methods commonly used by dermatologists to diagnose skin cancer [12,18,38]. For example, features related to lesion diameter ("diameter_1" and "diameter_2"), whether the lesion itches ("itch_False" and "itch_True"), whether it bleeds ("bleed_False" and "bleed_True"), and whether it has grown ("grew_False" and "grew_True") often appear as features with the greatest impact on the model's output. In Table 5, we list the feature importance for each type of feature (image or complementary) by calculating the mean absolute of the SHAP value for each feature in all instances and sum up the calculated values for each type of feature. We also calculated the percentage contribution of the image and complementary features for the mixed fusion model on the PAD-UFES-20 data set. For all sample classes, all the image features contributed with 46.36% and all the complementary features contributed with 53.61%. It shows that both types of feature are of similar importance for the model decision.

For the NDB-UFES dataset, we performed a SHAP analysis for the transformer neural network classifier with a PiT backbone. Figure 5b shows, for the true class OSCC, the impact of the top features on the model output, ordered by the mean absolute value of the SHAP values. The features "Leukoplakia without

Table 5. Sum of mean absolute SHAP values, and its percentage contribution, of image and complementary features for mixed fusion model on PAD-UFES-20 dataset

Samples class	Image features SHAP values		Complementary features SHAP values	
	Sum	%	Sum	%
BCC	2.3253	42.85	3.1015	57.15
NEV	3.0772	47.61	3.3862	52.39
SEK	1.6555	37.43	2.7675	62.57
MEL	2.3037	53.19	2.0271	46.81
ACK	2.8935	45.75	3.4309	54.25
SCC	3.2843	50.32	3.2420	49.68
Mean of all classes	**2.5899**	**46.39**	**2.9925**	**53.61**

Table 6. Sum of mean absolute SHAP values, and its percentage contribution, of image and complementary features for mixed fusion model on NDB-UFES dataset

Samples class	Image features SHAP values		Complementary features SHAP values	
	Sum	%	Sum	%
Leukoplakia without dysplasia	0.3825	13.77	2.3950	86.23
Leukoplakia with dysplasia	0.7100	28.66	1.7676	71.34
OSCC	0.8857	37.85	1.4542	62.15
Mean of all classes	**0.6594**	**26.05**	**1.8723**	**73.95**

dysplasia", "Leukoplakia with dysplasia", and "OSCC" refer to the probabilities estimated by the internal classifier for each class label, which uses only image information.

For OSCC lesions, there is a prevalence of occurrence in the tongue region in men over 50 years of age [3,7,33]. For OSCC samples in Fig. 5b, a high importance of features related to tongue location, gender, age, alcohol consumption, and tobacco use can be observed, mirroring the factors specialists rely on for diagnosis. For both leukoplakia classes, a high importance of features related to sun exposure can also be noted, and consequently, greater exposure to UV radiation, which is a risk factor for this type of lesion [3,36]. In Table 6, we also list the feature importance for each type of features (image or complementary) by calculating the sum of mean absolute SHAP values, and its percentage contribution, of image and complementary features for mixed fusion model on NDB-UFES dataset. For all sample classes, all the image features contributed with 26.05% and all the complementary features contributed with 73.95%. It shows that complementary features have a higher importance for the model decision.

4   Conclusion

We present a new mixed approach for multimodal data fusion, aiming to incorporate interpretability into the fusion process. The proposed approach seeks to make deep learning-based techniques more interpretable, drawing inspiration from the clinical reasoning employed by medical professionals. The experimental results reveal that using the transformer as the internal classifier and a neural network as the external classifier yielded the best results for the proposed approach in both datasets evaluated. However, when compared to the baseline based on the middle fusion approach, the results obtained were slightly inferior. Despite this limitation, the mixed approach stands out in terms of interpretability, enabling the application of techniques such as SHAP to analyze and understand the model's decision-making process, aligning with the reasoning adopted by specialists. This level of interpretability is not achieved by other data fusion approaches, such as middle fusion. For future work, we plan to extend the proposed approach by integrating other techniques, aiming to make the model even more explainable and interpretable, thereby fostering greater trust in its application to clinical scenarios.

Acknowledgments. This study was funded in part by CNPq, Brazil (grant no. 304688/2021-5). The authors also thank the PROAPEM/FAPES (368/2022 - P: 2022-NGKM5), PDPG/FAPES (129/2021 - P: 2021-GL60J) and PROAP/CAPES (Portaria no. 206, 9/4/2018). The funder had no role in study design, data collection and analysis, decision to publish, or preparation of the manuscript.

Data and Code Availability. PAD-UFES-20 [27] and NDB-UFES [5] are publicly available datasets. The source code is public available at GitHub at https://github.com/lmlima/A-novel-interpretable-approach-to-deep-multimodal-data-fusion-applied-to-cancer-diagnosis.

Disclosure of Interests. The authors have no competing interests to declare that are relevant to the content of this article.

References

1. Afreen, S., Bhurjee, A.K., Aziz, R.M.: Feature selection using game Shapley improved grey wolf optimizer for optimizing cancer classification. Knowl. Inf. Syst., 1–32 (2025)
2. Aguirre-Urizar, J.M., de Mendoza, I.L.-I., Warnakulasuriya, S.: Malignant transformation of oral leukoplakia systematic review and meta-analysis of the last 5 years. Oral Dis. **27**(8), 1881–1895 (2021)
3. Andrade, J.O.M., Santos, C.A.d.S.T., Oliveira, M.C.: Associated factors with oral cancer: a study of case control in a population of the Brazil's Northeast. Rev. Bras. Epidemiol. **18**, 894–905 (2015)
4. Assis, A., Dantas, J., Andrade, E.: The performance-interpretability trade-off: a comparative study of machine learning models. J. Reliab. Intell. Environ. **11**(1), 1 (2024)
5. Ribeiro-de Assis, M.C.F., et al.: NDB-UFES: an oral cancer and leukoplakia dataset composed of histopathological images and patient data. Data Brief **48**, 109128 (2023)

6. Boulahia, S.Y., Amamra, A., Madi, M.R., Daikh, S.: Early, intermediate and late fusion strategies for robust deep learning-based multimodal action recognition. Mach. Vis. Appl. **32**(6), 121 (2021)

7. del Carmen Migueláñez-Medrán, B., Pozo-Kreilinger, J.J., Cebrián-Carretero, J.L., Martínez-García, M.Á., López-Sánchez, A.F.: Oral squamous cell carcinoma of tongue: histological risk assessment. A pilot study. Med. Oral Patol. Oral Cir. Bucal **24**(5), e603 (2019)

8. Chamoli, A., Gosavi, A.S., Shirwadkar, U.P., et al.: Overview of oral cavity squamous cell carcinoma: risk factors, mechanisms, and diagnostics. Oral Oncol. **121**, 105451 (2021)

9. Chen, T., Guestrin, C.: XGBoost: a scalable tree boosting system (2016)

10. Dosovitskiy, A., et al.: An image is worth 16x16 words: transformers for image recognition at scale (2021)

11. Duan, J., Xiong, J., Li, Y., Ding, W.: Deep learning based multimodal biomedical data fusion: an overview and comparative review. Inf. Fus. **112**, 102536 (2024)

12. Duarte, A.F., Sousa-Pinto, B., Azevedo, L.F., Barros, A.M., Puig, S., Malvehy, J., Haneke, E., Correia, O.: Clinical ABCDE rule for early melanoma detection. Eur. J. Dermatol. **31**(6), 771–778 (2021)

13. Dziugaite, G.K., Ben-David, S., Roy, D.M.: Enforcing interpretability and its statistical impacts: trade-offs between accuracy and interpretability. arXiv preprint arXiv:2010.13764 (2020)

14. Grafton-Clarke, C., Chen, K.W., Wilcock, J.: Diagnosis and referral delays in primary care for oral squamous cell cancer: a systematic review. Br. J. Gen. Pract. **69**(679), e112–e126 (2019)

15. He, K., Zhang, X., Ren, S., Sun, J.: Identity mappings in deep residual networks. In: Leibe, B., Matas, J., Sebe, N., Welling, M. (eds.) Computer Vision, ECCV 2016. LNCS, vol. 9908. Springer, Cham (2016). https://doi.org/10.1007/978-3-319-46493-0_38

16. Heo, B., Yun, S., Han, D., et al.: Rethinking spatial dimensions of vision transformers (2021)

17. Ilhan, B., Lin, K., Guneri, P., et al.: Improving oral cancer outcomes with imaging and artificial intelligence. J. Dent. Res. **99**(3), 241–248 (2020)

18. Johr, R.H.: Dermoscopy: alternative melanocytic algorithms—the ABCD rule of dermatoscopy, Menzies scoring method, and 7-point checklist. Clin. Dermatol. **20**(3), 240–247 (2002)

19. Ke, G., et al.: LightGBM: a highly efficient gradient boosting decision tree. In: Guyon, I., et al. (eds.) Advances in Neural Information Processing Systems, pp. 3147–3156. Curran Associates (2017)

20. Li, Y., et al.: A review of deep learning-based information fusion techniques for multimodal medical image classification. Comput. Biol. Med. **177**, 108635 (2024)

21. de Lima, L.M., Krohling, R.A.: Exploring advances in transformers and CNN for skin lesion diagnosis on small datasets. In: Xavier-Junior, J.C., Rios, R.A. (eds.) Intelligent Systems, BRACIS 2022. LNCS, vol. 13654. Springer, Cham (2022). https://doi.org/10.1007/978-3-031-21689-3_21

22. de Lima, L.M., et al.: Importance of complementary data to histopathological image analysis of oral leukoplakia and carcinoma using deep neural networks. Intell. Med. **3**(4), 258–266 (2023)

23. Lundberg, S.M., Lee, S.I.: A unified approach to interpreting model predictions. Adv. Neural Inf. Process. Syst. **30** (2017)

24. Marzuka, A.G., Book, S.E.: Basal cell carcinoma: pathogenesis, epidemiology, clinical features, diagnosis, histopathology, and management. Yale J. Biol. Med. **88**(2), 167–179 (2015)

25. National Institute of Cancer José Alencar Gomes da Silva (INCA): Cancer incidence in Brazil - 2023 estimates (2023). https://www.inca.gov.br/sites/ufu.sti.inca.local/files/media/document/estimativa-2023.pdf

26. Neville, B.: Patologia Oral e Maxilofacial, 4th edn. Elsevier, Brasil (2016). (in Portuguese)

27. Pacheco, A.G., et al.: PAD-UFES-20: a skin lesion dataset composed of patient data and clinical images collected from smartphones. Data Brief **32**, 106221 (2020)

28. Radosavovic, I., Kosaraju, R.P., Girshick, R., et al.: Designing network design spaces (2020)

29. Rezk, E., Eltorki, M., El-Dakhakhni, W.: Interpretable skin cancer classification based on incremental domain knowledge learning. J. Healthc. Inf. Res. **7**(1), 59–83 (2023)

30. Scott, M., Su-In, L., et al.: A unified approach to interpreting model predictions. Adv. Neural. Inf. Process. Syst. **30**, 4765–4774 (2017)

31. Song, B., et al.: Interpretable and reliable oral cancer classifier with attention mechanism and expert knowledge embedding via attention map. Cancers **15**(5), 1421 (2023)

32. Susila, S.J.G., Kavitha, D.: A deep convolutional neural network-based keratitis detection and classification approach. Multimedia Tools Appl. (2025)

33. Tan, Y., et al.: Oral squamous cell carcinomas: state of the field and emerging directions. Int. J. Oral Sci. **15**(1), 44 (2023)

34. Tovaru, S., et al.: Oral leukoplakia: a clinicopathological study and malignant transformation. Oral Dis. **29**(4), 1454–1463 (2023)

35. Tschandl, P., Rosendahl, C., Kittler, H.: The HAM10000 dataset, a large collection of multi-source dermatoscopic images of common pigmented skin lesions. Sci. Data **5**(1), 1–9 (2018)

36. Villa, A., Woo, S.B.: Leukoplakia—a diagnostic and management algorithm. J. Oral Maxillofac. Surg. **75**(4), 723–734 (2017)

37. WHO: WHO report on cancer: setting priorities, investing wisely and providing care for all. World Health Organization (2020)

38. Wu, Y., Chen, B., Zeng, A., Pan, D., Wang, R., Zhao, S.: Skin cancer classification with deep learning: a systematic review. Front. Oncol. **12**, 893972 (2022)

39. Xu, W., Xu, Y., Chang, T., et al.: Co-scale conv-attentional image transformers (2021)

40. Xua, B., Yang, G.: Interpretability research of deep learning: a literature survey. Inf. Fus. **115**, 102721 (2024)

41. Yao, Y., Duan, J., Xu, K., Cai, Y., Sun, Z., Zhang, Y.: A survey on large language model (LLM) security and privacy: the good, the bad, and the ugly. High-Confidence Comput. **4**(2), 100211 (2024)

42. Zhang, Y., Tiňo, P., Leonardis, A., Tang, K.: A survey on neural network interpretability. IEEE Trans. Emerg. Top. Comput. Intell. **5**(5), 726–742 (2021)

Anomaly Detection in Spatiotemporal Patterns: A Case Study of Brazilian Traffic Accidents During the COVID-19 Lockdown

Gabriel César Silveira[✉], Ricardo Jose Pfitscher, Benjamin Grando Moreira, and Diogo Nardelli Siebert

Federal University of Santa Catarina, Joinville, Brazil
`g.c.silveira@posgrad.ufsc.br`,
`{ricardo.pfitscher,benjamin.grando,diogo.siebert}@ufsc.br`

Abstract. This study proposes a methodology to assess pattern changes in spatio-temporal data as a descriptive analysis. As a study case, we focus on traffic accident profile changes in Brazil due to the lockdown of the COVID-19 pandemic, analyzing different categories of occurrences separately. The method uses mainly public data on highway incidents and applies spatial correlation and linear regression models. The combined indicator of dissimilarity and spatiotemporal autocorrelation identifies regional anomalies when regressed regarding data before and during the pandemic. The methodology revealed that the lockdown affected accident characteristics differently across states, leading to changes in state-level and regional rates that could be overlooked in exploratory analyses or when neglecting spatial relationships. This case study can inform public policies and guide future research on the impacts of lockdown traffic and on human behavior.

Keywords: Traffic Accidents · Covid-19 · Anomaly Detection · Spatial Autocorrelation

1   Introduction

The analysis of spatial data is paramount for comprehending the interactions of variables across diverse geographical locations. In contradistinction to conventional analytical approaches premised upon the assumption of independent observations, spatial data frequently manifest spatial autocorrelation. Consequently, spatial analysis is uniquely suited to the identification of clusters, hotspots, and regional disparities that may remain imperceptible within non-spatial datasets. Similarly, while spatial data reveals geographic patterns solely, spatiotemporal data extends the analysis to the temporal evolution of spatial phenomena, capturing how patterns change over time.

Upon the spatial and spatiotemporal data, anomaly detection can highlight regions of interest and may provide powerful insights into regional behavior. In

R. de Freitas and D. Furtado (Eds.): BRACIS 2025, LNAI 16181, pp. 50–64, 2026.
https://doi.org/10.1007/978-3-032-15990-8_4

this context, anomaly can be understood as data that do not conform with the expected behavior or regular pattern. In summary, most detection processes consist of machine learning and statistical domain techniques that establish certain regions as normal behavior and assume any data out of it as abnormal. For many machine learning methods, the abnormal regions are expressed by low density or farther points as more anomalous. However, statistical approaches assume that anomalies occur as low-probability events, so the first step consists of fitting a model of statistical distribution and then verifying if the point is likely to be part of the standard population or to have the same driving factors [4,16,22].

The detections are driven by some particular interest on highlight the anomalies out of the major data volume or complexity. These methods can be applied for risk mitigation in safety-critical domains, including fraud prevention, cybersecurity, healthcare monitoring, and accident prevention [4]. Traffic accident data, in particular, pose unique challenges due to the influence of multiple external factors, such as road and climactic conditions, traffic flow, and behavioral changes over time. Recognizing these issues, the academic community has explored many applications of anomaly detection for mobility phenomena. For example, [14] analyze abnormal traffic on urban traffic events like traffic congestion on roads during peak commuting hours, the consistent flow of vehicles on a city ring road, or the prolonged smooth traffic conditions on a specific highway section. While [26] propose a model to identify abnormal passenger flow in multiple metro stations based on the temporal periodicity and spatial similarity.

The COVID-19 pandemic significantly impacted traffic accident rates, leading to notable shifts, as highlighted by [24], including a decline in overall incidents while fatal accidents increased during the lockdown. These changes may stem from complex phenomena that can be analyzed from different perspectives, such as alterations in mobility patterns or even psychological and behavioral adaptations among individuals in society [12]. Given these circumstances, categorical data provided by public authorities serves as a valuable resource for assessing regional peculiarities and detecting anomalous behavior.

The present study advances a methodology designed to evaluate the impact of the lockdown measures on the behavior of Brazilian drivers, with specific attention to regional variations in discrete accident categories. Employing standardized scores in conjunction with the Local Moran's I Index, we analyze the deviation of individual states from the national mean, both prior to and during the period of lockdown. Moreover, linear regression models are utilized to discern states exhibiting anomalous increases or decreases in pertinent accident characteristics. The principal contribution of this research lies in the proposition that spatial autocorrelation metrics ought not to be construed as temporally invariant descriptors. This dynamic perspective facilitates a more nuanced understanding of the lockdown's multifaceted impacts and holds the potential to inform more efficacious intervention strategies.

2   Related Works

A number of scholarly investigations have scrutinized traffic patterns and behavioral modifications occurring during and subsequent to the COVID-19 pandemic. This section provides a critical review of pertinent academic literature and juxtaposes the findings therein with those obtained in the present study.

The research conducted by [12] elucidates the behavioral adaptations exhibited by drivers in their post-pandemic driving practices, reporting an increase in aggressive and inattentive driving. [24] reviews the existing literature and concludes that, in general, the studies indicate a change in the profile of traffic accidents due to the lockdown, noting a reduction in the number of accidents but also a significant increase in the severity of accidents.

Furthermore, it is a tenable assumption that human behavior is subject to geographical variability, thereby necessitating the identification of patterns and the elucidation of factors underlying observed differences in relevant rates. By way of illustration, [15] employed average rates and Moran's I to analyze the spatial distribution of mortality attributable to alcohol consumption within Brazil, concluding that a spatial dependence exists in the distribution of mortality rates associated with alcohol abuse. With respect to traffic patterns, spatial correlation may also serve as an indicator of the geographic influence on accident occurrence. In this context, [9] utilized Moran's I to investigate the severity of accidents transpiring over a three-year period in the cities of Addis Ababa (capital of Ethiopia) and Berlin (capital of Germany). Their findings reveal inter-city disparities in the significance of the indices, while nonetheless affirming the presence of a spatial correlation in traffic accidents across both urban centers.

[3] explored spatiotemporal correlations to understand similarities of accidents on Indiana state highways. Apart from the results regarding spatiotemporal autocorrelation in the dataset, the paper's significant finding demonstrated the benefit of spatiotemporal analysis on traffic patterns. Several recent works benefit from the findings, including [13] that rely on spatiotemporal analysis to analyze urban traffic accidents, [19] that verified how groups of accidents varied with time and space, and [5] that included a temporal aspect to the spatial analysis of Moran's I to predict traffic congestions using a Random Forest Model.

With regard to the existing literature, this work contributes to studies on local spatial autocorrelation by investigating temporal variability through statistical experiments and revealing that spatial dependencies are not static but can undergo significant changes during disruptive events. In this context, the approach provides a deeper understanding of the impact of the pandemic on traffic accident patterns across Brazilian states.

3   Methodology

This section details the methodological framework employed to assess the impact of the lockdown on traffic accident patterns. It encompasses data acquisition and pre-processing steps, spatial autocorrelation analysis techniques, and the approach used to identify and evaluate anomalies in the data.

3.1   Data and Pre-Processing

This study relies on data published by Brazilian authorities [18], comprising approximately 1.74 million occurrences on federal roads across the 24 federal units of the country between January 1, 2007, and January 1, 2024. The government provides data in annual table files, with records indexed by occurrences and victims. In this work, we used occurrences as the indexing unit, focusing on the frequency of accidents rather than the number of victims. The database contains 31 attributes, from which we selected 8: *id, date, federal units (uf), accident cause, accident type, accident classification, day phase, and weather condition.*

Classes Refinement. Some attributes in the database contain several classes. For instance, the accident types and causes contain 31 and 101 distinct values, respectively. Also, the content of the classes has grammar variations and synonyms across different years. Thus, similar classes were clustered around common subjects, as described next. The aggroupment process significantly reduced and standardized classes, as shown in Table 1, within only 11 accident causes, 16 accident types, 4-day phases, and 10 weather conditions, providing a manageable data source.

Table 1. Classes Glossary

Attribute	Classes
Accident Classification	Without victims, With injured victims, With fatal victims
Accident Cause	Inattention and Distracted Driving, Unsafe Driving Practices and Disobedience, Miscellaneous, Mechanical Failures, Load and Maintenance, Substance Influence, Surface and Environmental Hazards, Health and Fatigue
Day Phase	Full day, Full night, Dawn, Dusk
Weather Condition	Clear sky, Cloudy, Rain, Sun
Accident Type	Rear-end collision, Side collision, Transversal collision, Rollover, Collision with object, Head-on collision, Run-off-road collision, Person run over, Animal run over, Occupant falls from vehicle, Cargo spill

Time-Series Creation. Considering that the consolidated dataset contains data collected in different years, we could generate a time series by counting the occurrences around the pandemic period, which is the target of the present analysis. To understand how the pandemic influenced accident profiles, we selected two periods: the *lockdown period*, corresponding to the window between March 16, 2020, and August 16, 2020; and the *Pre-lockdown period*, which refers to the same relative period in the preceding year. In Brazil, the lockdown period started on March 16, 2020 [23]. From Fig. 1, the boundary of the analysis window was defined as the moment after the lockdown when the total number of occurrences re-aligns and matches the general trend represented by the annual moving average (365-day window), assuming this as the last month of the significant impact of the lockdown on traffic accidents changes.

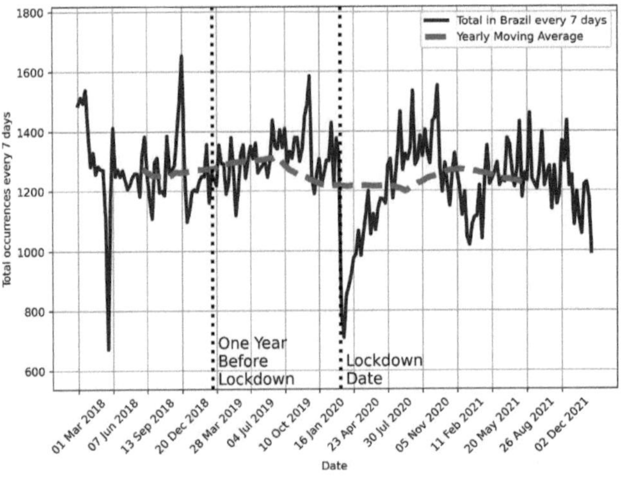

Fig. 1. Traffic accidents every seven days in Brazil

Figure 1 indicates the straightforward impact of the lockdown, as evidenced by the sharp decline in the number of occurrences immediately after the stipulated date, followed by a gradual increase toward normal levels. Also, one can notice another sharp decline between March and June 2018; it occurred given that a 10-day truckers' strike started on May 21 in Brazil [10]. These two incidents evidence the impact of traffic reduction on the number of accidents.

The time series sets for each class were normalized by the state vehicle fleets and scaled by a factor of 10,000, such that the analyzed magnitudes represent weekly occurrences per 10,000 vehicles. For simplicity, the state vehicle fleets as of December 2023 [11] were adopted, disregarding temporal variations in the number of vehicles across states. This normalization aims to equalize the probability of accidents across states, accounting for the diverse population densities, economic conditions, and territorial dimensions within the Brazilian territory.

3.2 Spatio-temporal Autocorrelation

Once defined the set of time series $\mathbf{X}$ of certain class of occurrences from N locations and K read instants, we can define $m(k)$ as the average value across locations in the k-th instant:

$$m(k) = \frac{1}{N} \sum_{i=0}^{N-1} x_i(k) \tag{1}$$

Thus, $x_i(k)$ can be evaluated as either below or above the global average $m(k)$. Furthermore, for a given class, it is assumed that all samples at the same time step k across different locations follow the same normal probability distribution.

Local Spatial Autocorrelation (LISA) indicators rely on comparing how local data relates locally in comparison to global behavior. In this context, one may consider the divergence in the observed magnitudes or trends to quantify how different two time series are, i.e., their dissimilarity. In this work, the magnitude's dissimilarity D_i from time series of location i was calculated as the average standard score over time steps regarding the distribution across locations (Eq. 5).

$$D_i = \frac{1}{K} \sum_{k=0}^{K-1} z_i(k) \tag{2}$$

where z_i is the standard score, given by Eq. 3, denoting how many standard deviation σ_{pop} units the measure ψ_{sample} deviates from the population mean μ_{pop}. Standard score also indicates the statistical significance of the event when the population is assumed to be normally distributed.

$$z_{sample} = \frac{\psi_{sample} - \mu_{pop}}{\sigma_{pop}} \tag{3}$$

Therefore, the definition of D_i become as expressed in Eq. 5 regarding locations i, where, $\sigma(k)$ is the standard deviation across locations on k-th instant.

$$D_i = \frac{1}{K} \sum_{k=0}^{K-1} \frac{x_i(k) - m(k)}{\sigma(k)} \tag{4}$$

The similarity of trends C_i observed between from time series of location i to the average series $\vec{m}$ was calculated using the temporal correlation of the signals, as discussed in [7].

$$C_i = \frac{\sum_{k=0}^{K-2} \Delta(x_i(k))\Delta(m(k))}{\sqrt{\sum_{k=0}^{K-2} \Delta(x_i(k))^2}\sqrt{\sum_{k=0}^{K-2} \Delta(m(k))^2}} \tag{5}$$

where the differential operator is $\Delta(a(k)) = a(k+1) - a(k)$. This correlation computes such that it increases when the signal varies in the same direction as the mean varies during time-step k.

Then, the dissimilarity of trend can be combined with the magnitude's dissimilarity into the single indicator $Z(\vec{x_i}^T, \vec{m})$ using the mapping function $\Phi(\chi)$ proposed by [7].

$$Z_i = \Phi(C_i) \cdot D_i \tag{6}$$

$$\Phi(\chi) = \frac{2}{1 + e^{\alpha\chi}} \tag{7}$$

Thereby, following the mapping function, curves with positive temporal correlation results in low dissimilarity, while negative values increases the resulting dissimilarity. Meanwhile, the stochasticity makes temporal correlation go to zero and, following the map $\Phi(\chi)$, the trend dissimilarity tends to unit weight and to not impact on total dissimilarity $D(\overrightarrow{x_i}^T, \overrightarrow{m})$. Figure 2 illustrates the mapping function according to α.

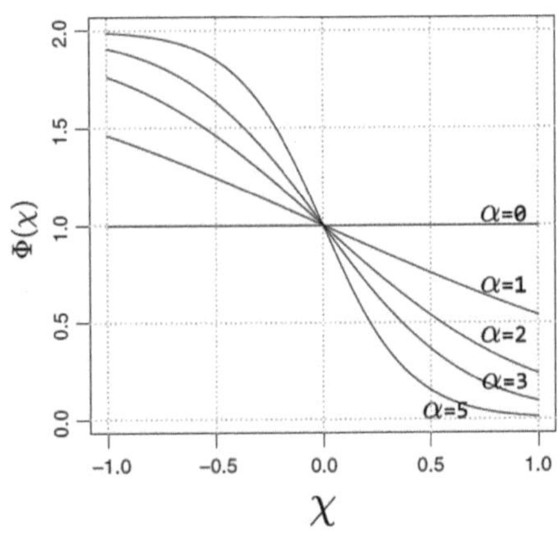

Fig. 2. Mapping function from temporal correlation into dissimilarity weight (Adapted from [7]).

The analyst should define the hyperparameter α value, which tunes the influence of trend dissimilarity on the resulting weight. In this work, we desired that the perfect correlation of 1 would map into 0, nulling the possibility of dissimilar signals, and the perfect uncorrelation of -1 would map into 2, duplicating the observed dissimilarity due to the two distinct evidence. However, this only occurs by increasing the parameter α and the nonlinear effect by consequence. Since the high nonlinearity in $\Phi(\chi)$ compromises the intermediary values of χ, α equals 2 was selected since it gets closer to the perfect scenarios but keeping intermediate value's output closer to a linear symmetric relationship, for example, χ equals to 0.5 maps into approximately 0.54.

The Global Moran's I (GMI) evaluates the correlation of spatially distributed attributes, such that a positive GMI indicates that localities tend to have the same pattern as their neighbors, clustering above or below the global average. Negative GMI indicates that localities tend to differ from their neighbors and exhibit opposing deviations from the global mean. Equation 8 presents the GMI.

$$GMI = \frac{\sum_{i=0}^{N-1} \sum_{j=0}^{N-1} w_{i,j}(Z_i - \mu_Z)(Z_j - \mu_Z)}{\sum_{i=0}^{N-1}(Z_i - \mu_Z)^2} \tag{8}$$

where $w_{i,j}$ is one element of the neighborhood matrix $\mathbf{W}$ and μ_Z is the mean value of the analyzed variable. The matrix $\mathbf{W}$ weights the intensity of geographical interactions among the N locations. In this work, $\mathbf{W}$ is normalized, such that the sum of the interaction weights of certain location result in unit value and all locations have the same possible total impact on the global indicator, as described below. This design choice simplifies terms in the GMI, leading to the suppressed form presented in Eq. 8.

$$\sum_{j=0}^{N-1} w_{i,j} = 1, \quad \forall i \tag{9}$$

The weighting criterion was based on shared borders between states, assigning equal weight to all neighboring states of a given local. Under the assumption of spatial correlation existence, one may statistically test this hypothesis by comparing the IMG population generated by random permutations in $\mathbf{W}$ with the observed one and validate it once the observed one is too unlikely in the IMG probability distribution, such that it refuses the hypothesis of belonging to it. Another method to validate the existence of spatial correlation is to estimate the expected value of IMG as $E[I] = -1/(N-1)$ and confirm that the observed IMG is different from it. In this work, both conditions had to be satisfied concurrently, adopting two times the deviation unit from the mean for the first criterion and a threshold of 10% difference to $E[I]$ for the second one [17].

Alongside the GMI, the Local Moran's I (LMI) evaluates regional spatial association, identifying areas with the most substantial spatial clustering through its maximum values. As part of the Local Indicators of Spatial Association (LISA), the LMI offers a detailed view of local spatial structures, quantifying each locality's contribution to the global spatial autocorrelation measured by the GMI, while highlighting hotspots and anomalous behaviors [1].

$$LMI_i = Z_i \sum_{j=0}^{N-1} w_{i,j} Z_j \tag{10}$$

Thus, positive LMI values indicate that location i concentrates correlated neighbors with the same pattern of behavior, while negative values indicate opposite behavior and uncorrelation in the neighborhood.

3.3 Lockdown Impact Assessment

There are two straightforward strategies to assess the impact of the lockdown on Brazilian traffic accidents. One can apply the discussed time series metric within an arbitrary single time window that includes the analyzed event with a certain degree of relaxation, yielding a static snapshot of the deviations of locations relative to the global trend. Although this method identifies areas that diverge most from the global average at a specific time range, it does not enable inferences about whether such discrepancies arise from recent changes or represent persistent historical features lacking in association with the lockdown event.

In contrast, this work focuses on assessing the temporal evolution of these discrepancies. For this reason, we compare the spatial autocorrelation indicator computed from two distinct temporal windows, before and after the event of interest. Thus, this approach facilitates the identification of abrupt and gradual changes that may signify transitions in spatial behavior. In essence, comparative temporal analysis enriches the interpretation of the data by revealing the dynamic evolution of regional patterns over time. As a result, we can identify how the locations behaved before the event and what changed significantly after the event, thus inferring a possible causal impact. More specifically, we aim to understand how COVID-19's lockdown has influenced the rate of accidents and regional pattern of accident autocorrelation by uncertain factors like traffic flux and physical or psychological changes in drivers. We aim to identify which states are significantly distinct after lockdown compared to the expected level of change observed in other states.

Given a particular class of occurrences, we assume a homogeneous linear relationship between indicators before and after the lockdown, reflecting a consistence on the rate of change among states, i.e., a strong correlation. This assumption is reasonable if the observed variations in non-anomalous are small random fluctuations and variations may occur systematically consistent and proportional across states. Under this hypothesis, these indicators would exhibit values around the identity function. In contrary, if the metrics are robust to the choice of time window, not changing over time, the slope is unitary.

The expected behavior is then assumed according to a curve fitted to the data, with abnormal behavior identified as deviations from this fitted curve. For a given class of accidents, we rely on linear models to describe pairs of standardized scores (Eq. 11), where the predictor variable is the value before the lockdown, and the predicted variable is the value after the lockdown regarding Z_i or LMI_i.

$$\text{Data after lockdown} = \beta \cdot \text{Data before lockdown} \tag{11}$$

The regression coefficient β represents the slope of the line, which describes the general relationship between the values before and after the lockdown. Thus, we define slopes greater than one indicating intensification, slopes smaller than one but positive suggesting attenuation, and negative slopes indicating a reversal in the general behavior of the indicators.

Once the temporal linear relationship between the state-level data of a given class is estimated, we evaluate which states deviate significantly from the expected value given by the regressed linear model compared to the deviation of other states so that low probability residuals indicate that a specific occurrence does not belong to the same observed distribution and may be governed by distinct contexts. We assumed a normal distribution of the absolute residuals of the regression and considered samples with an absolute standardized residual score above three as anomalous since events of this magnitude of deviation have a probability lower than 0.28% concerning the expected distribution [6,21].

The validity of the identified anomalous cases also depends on the ability of the linear model to describe the overall data of general cases. For such purpose, we analyze the R^2: a decrease in the R^2 value suggests a deterioration in the linearity of the samples, affecting the reliability of the existence of a particular anomaly. Thus, we choose an arbitrary performance metric for the model, verifying that R^2 is at least 0.6 for the model of a particular class to be considered linear and detected anomaly cases also valid.

Although the metric based on the distance from the global trend is arbitrary and may be applicable to different distributions, the validity of the normality assumption for the regression residuals is formally assessed by ShapiroWilk test and QuantileQuantile plots. In the ShapiroWilk test, the null hypothesis states that the set of data, even if a small one, is normally distributed [20]. The result of the test can be expressed as the significance of the null hypothesis (p-value), which indicates insufficient evidence to reject the null hypothesis when it is greater than an arbitrary threshold. In this work the threshold is assumed to be 0.05, and the resulting values greater than 0.05 support the assumption of residual normality. Conversely, a p-value lower than 0.05 provides sufficient evidence to reject the null hypothesis, suggesting that the residuals significantly deviate from a normal distribution. In addition, a visual assessment of normality is conducted using QuantileQuantile plots, as described by [2,8]. If the underlying distribution is normal, the plotted points are expected to align closely with a straight reference line, where the slope and intercept correspond to estimates of the population's standard deviation and mean, respectively.

4 Results

Results verify the hypothesis of linear behavior of the dissimilarity samples Z_i, assessing the model's performance through the R-squared value. Eighteen models were validated with a sufficient R-squared among the 25 classes present, with the average performance being 0.652. Regarding the regression models for LMI measures, only 3 out of the 25 accident classes have a sufficient R-squared and the average R-squared performance is 0.312. Therefore, we demonstrate that events can change dissimilarity, assuming low correlation patterns. This effect is even more evident in the LMI models, where the relationship with the events appears substantially weaker and often negligible, indicating that even when the dissimilarity components of the LMI change in a systematic way, the overall LMI trend may still behave in a near-random or unstructured manner. Thus, we show that many classes of accidents do not follow the linear assumption and, as a consequence, indicate that events may alter spatial relationships and that LMI measures are not necessarily static over time. Figure 3 illustrates a regression example for an LMI accident class that does not follow the linear assumption, resulting in a low R-squared value of 0.156.

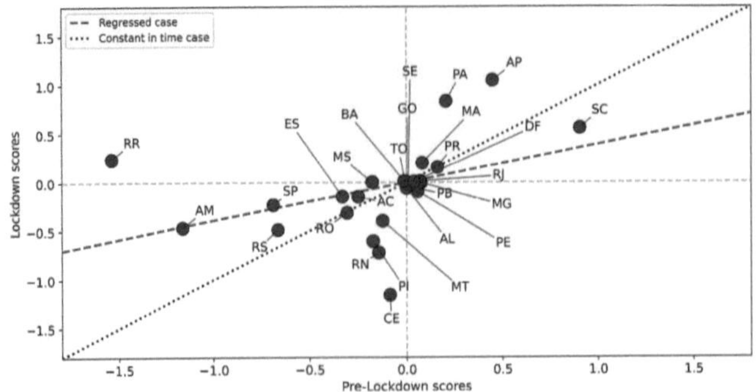

Fig. 3. LMI Regression for Inattention and Distracted Driving.

Complementary, the results also show that the best R-squared performances occurred in models with higher slope, meaning that the change trend is better explained as a linear relationship in intensification phenomena. The correlation between Slope and R-squared performance is 0.704 for dissimilarity models and 0.764 for LMI models. Considering the models with validated linearity and residual's normality, Table 2 points out anomalies in the dissimilarity scores of the characteristics of Brazilian traffic accidents before and after the lockdown.

Table 2. Anomalies in the Dissimilarity Scores

State	Attribute	Class	Profile Before Lockdown	Phenomenon After Lockdown
ES	Weather Condition	Cloudy	Above the average	Intensification
SC	Accident Type	Head-on collision	Above the average	Intensification

By analyzing the results, we found that anomalies tend to occur in states with the number of occurrences above the national average. Furthermore, intensification emerged as the most recurrent phenomenon, suggesting that the event polarized the occurrences. In the same way, regarding regional characteristics, Table 3 depicts the anomalies identified by the change of the Local Moran's I for Brazilian traffic accidents before and after the lockdown.

Table 3. Anomalies in the Local Moran's I Indicators

State	Attribute	Class	Profile Before Lockdown	Neighborhood Before Lockdown	Phenomenon After Lockdown
DF	Accident Type	Transversal collision	Below the average	Same profiles	Intensification
SP	Day Phase	Full night	Below the average	Opposite profiles	Attenuation

Only states with a previous number of occurrences below the average presented anomalies. There was an intensification in the behavior of the neighborhood around the Federal District (DF) in presenting a profile below the national average of cross accidents. Meanwhile, the locations in the neighborhood of São Paulo, which had frequencies above the average, had profiles of night-time accidents closer to the national average.

The Fig. 4 illustrates two identified cases, based on dissimilarity and local autocorrelation scores. The plots on the left-hand side show the regression results, comparing the hypothesis of constancy over time with the observed trend calculated via linear regression and highlighting the identified anomalies. The plots on the right-hand side present the normality tests, evidencing the degree of adherence to the assumption of residual normality required by the adopted anomaly detection method. From the regression plots, we visually note possible anomalous cases, highlighting the cases that most diverge from the global trend and the adopted exigencies of linearity and significant deviation.

Also, one may note the divergence in the regressed trend (blue dashed line) from the constancy in the time case (gray dashed line), which occurs in particular attribute classes, confirming that specific global attenuation, intensification, or flipping trends exist.

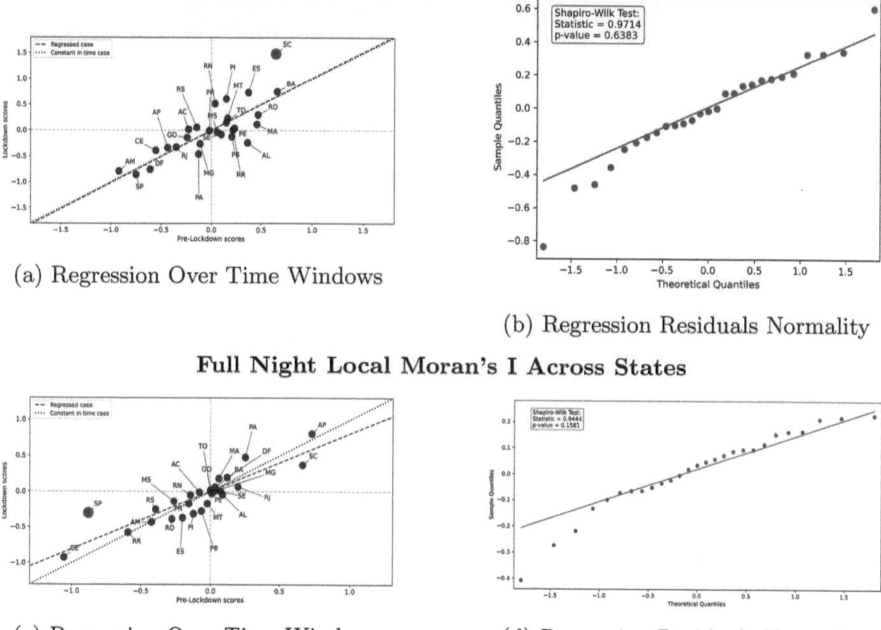

Head-on Collision Dissimilarities Across States

(a) Regression Over Time Windows

(b) Regression Residuals Normality

Full Night Local Moran's I Across States

(c) Regression Over Time Windows

(d) Regression Residuals Normality

Fig. 4. Anomaly detection method results, verifying the assumption of linear trend in a scatter plot and the normality test of regression residuals in a Quartil-Quartil plot.

The normality test confirms that the residuals' distribution is not significantly different from the normal one, and the deviation can be used to identify unlikely occurrences with measurable significance. Further results with a full overview of the tables are available at [25].

5   Discussion

Besides the results demonstrating COVID-19's distinct impacts on traffic accident behavior across states, we point out the following limitations to the present research findings. Neighborhood structure and weighting alterations would influence the analysis. The Federal District should be considered an exceptional case for the applied frontier methodology, being enclosed within the state of Goiàs.

We rely on a regression model for anomaly detection and assume that the variables are expected to remain stable year-by-year or drift similarly across locations if they change. This assumption would be more robust if multiple time windows were compared, forming a time series of indicators and enabling anomaly detection within a broader point of view. We consider applying such an approach in future research.

As explained in [16], anomaly detection based solely on residual deviation from the mean can be misleading. A best practice is to consider its results only when the percentage of points exceeding the defined threshold is higher than expected under a normal distribution, rather than simply flagging individual points that surpass the threshold. However, this approach was not applied in this study due to the limited number of states, which makes statistical validation using this technique unfeasible.

6   Conclusion

This study investigated the effects of the COVID-19 lockdown on the spatial dynamics of traffic accidents across Brazilian states, with particular emphasis on changes in dissimilarity measures and spatial autocorrelation indicators. By comparing standardized spatial metrics before and after the lockdown period, we identified a subset of accident characteristics in which certain states exhibited significantly different behavior, resulting in four anomalous cases across the analyzed dimensions. These findings provide evidence that disruptive events can impact not only the overall frequency of occurrences but also the underlying spatial dependencies between regions.

Results demonstrate that autocorrelation indicators can evolve systematically in response to events, thereby challenging the assumption of spatial stationarity. This observation motivates a reinterpretation of these metrics as potentially dynamic indicators that can capture structural transitions in spatial processes. In the case study, the proposed method successfully identified four anomalies: two related to dissimilarities and two associated with local spatial correlation. These findings aim to support evidence-based public policy interventions by highlighting states where behavior deviated meaningfully from national trends. In this context, anomalies characterized by above-average profiles that intensified–or below-average profiles that reversed–may signal areas requiring corrective action. Conversely, cases where adverse profiles diminished could serve as positive benchmarks for guiding regional policy development.

Such advancements deepen the understanding of how spatial dependencies evolve and provide valuable tools to detect systemic shifts. This work aims to initiate a novel methodological direction, underscoring the potential of temporal analysis of spatial autocorrelation for informing targeted responses in fields such as traffic safety, public health, and environmental planning.

References

1. Anselin, L.: Local indicators of spatial association-LISA. Geogr. Anal. **27**(2), 93–115 (1995)
2. Ben, M.G., Yohai, V.J.: Quantile-quantile plot for deviance residuals in the generalized linear model. J. Computat. Graph. Stat. **13** (2004)
3. Black, W.R.: Highway accidents: a spatial and temporal analysis. Transp. Res. Rec. **1318**, 75–82 (1991)
4. Chandola, V., Banerjee, A., Kumar, V.: Anomaly detection: a survey. ACM Comput. Surv. (CSUR) **41**(3), 1–58 (2009)
5. Chen, Z., Jiang, Y., Sun, D.: Discrimination and prediction of traffic congestion states of urban road network based on spatio-temporal correlation. IEEE Access **8** (2020)
6. Chiang, A., David, E., Lee, Y.J., Leshem, G., Yeh, Y.R.: A study on anomaly detection ensembles. J. Appl. Logic **21** (2017)
7. Chouakria, A.D., Nagabhushan, P.N.: Adaptive dissimilarity index for measuring time series proximity. Adv. Data Anal. Classif. **1**, 5–21 (2007)
8. Fox, J.: Regression Diagnostics: An Introduction. Sage Publications (2019)
9. Gedamu, W.T., Plank-Wiedenbeck, U., Wodajo, B.T.: A spatial autocorrelation analysis of road traffic crash by severity using Moran's i spatial statistics: a comparative study of Addis Ababa and Berlin cities. Accid. Anal. Prev. **200**, 107535 (2024)
10. Governo do Brasil: Truckers' strike paralyzes Brazil as president courts investors (2018). https://www.nytimes.com/2018/05/28/world/americas/brazil-truckers-strike-economy.html. Accessed 06 Mar 2025
11. Governo do Brasil: Frota de veículos 2023 (2024)
12. Lopetrone, E., Biondi, F.N.: On the effect of Covid-19 on drivers' behavior: a survey study. Transp. Res. Rec. **2677** (2023)
13. Ma, Q., Huang, G., Tang, X.: GIS-based analysis of spatial–temporal correlations of urban traffic accidents. Eur. Transp. Res. Rev. (2021)
14. Mao, Y., Shi, Y., Lu, B.: Detecting urban traffic anomalies using traffic-monitoring data. ISPRS Int. J. Geo-Inf. **13** (2024)
15. Marques, M.V., Junior, D.d.N.S., de Oliveira Santos, E.G., Santos, S.S.d.A.N., das Neves, S.M.B., Amador, A.E.: Distribuição espacial das mortes atribuíveis ao uso de álcool no brasil. Journal of Health & Biological. Sciences **8**(1), 1–11 (2020)
16. Mehrotra, K.G., Mohan, C.K., Huang, H., Mehrotra, K.G., Mohan, C.K., Huang, H.: Anomaly Detection. Springer, Heidelberg (2017)
17. Negreiros, J.G., Painho, M., Aguilar, F.J., Aguilar, M.A.: A comprehensive framework for exploratory spatial data analysis: Moran location and variance scatterplots. Int. J. Digit. Earth **3**(2) (2010)

18. Polícia Rodoviária Federal: Dados abertos da polícia rodoviária federal (2024). https://www.gov.br/prf/pt-br/acesso-a-informacao/dados-abertos/dados-abertos-da-prf. Accessed 20 Jun 2024
19. Prasannakumar, V., Vijith, H., Charutha, R., Geetha, N.: Spatio-temporal clustering of road accidents: GIS based analysis and assessment. Procedia Soc. Behav. Sci. **21**, 317–325 (2011). International Conference: Spatial Thinking and Geographic Information Sciences 2011. https://doi.org/10.1016/j.sbspro.2011.07.020
20. Razali, N.M., Wah, Y.B., et al.: Power comparisons of Shapiro-Wilk, Kolmogorov-Smirnov, Lilliefors and Anderson-darling tests. J. Stat. Model. Anal. **2**(1), 21–33 (2011)
21. Ruan, D., Chen, G., Kerre, E.E., Wets, G.: Intelligent Data Mining: Techniques and Applications, vol. 5. Springer, Heidelberg (2005)
22. Samariya, D., Thakkar, A.: A comprehensive survey of anomaly detection algorithms. Ann. Data Sci. **10**(3), 829–850 (2023)
23. da Saúde, M.: Ministério da saúde declara fim da emergência em saúde pública de importância nacional pela Covid-19 (2022). https://www.gov.br/saude/pt-br/assuntos/noticias/2022/abril/ministerio-da-saude-declara-fim-da-emergencia-em-saude-publica-de-importancia-nacional-pela-covid-19. Accessed 30 Jul 2024
24. Shaik, M.E., Ahmed, S.: An overview of the impact of covid-19 on road traffic safety and travel behavior. Transp. Eng. **9** (2022)
25. Silveira, G.C.: Github repository (2024). github.com/gabrielcessil/TrafficAccidents_SpatioAutocorrelation
26. Wei, X., Zhang, Y., Zhang, X., Ge, Q., Yin, B.: Real-time passenger flow anomaly detection in metro system. IET Intell. Transp. Syst. **17**(10) (2023)

Assessing DeepSeek-R1's Performance on Brazil's Defining National Education Benchmark

Alexandre Thurow Bender[(✉)] [ID], Gabriel Almeida Gomes [ID],
Ulisses Brisolara Corrêa [ID], and Ricardo Matsumura Araujo [ID]

Computer Science Graduation Program (PPGC), Artificial Intelligence Innovation
Hub (H2IA), Center for Technological Advancement (CDTec),
Federal University of Pelotas (UFPel), Pelotas, Brazil
{atbender,gagomes,ulisses,ricardo}@inf.ufpel.edu.br

Abstract. This paper evaluates DeepSeek-R1's performance on Brazil's National High School Exam (ENEM), a culturally-specific educational benchmark that tests reasoning across multiple domains. Using the pass@k metric across three years (2022–2024) of ENEM questions, we found strong reasoning capabilities, particularly in Human Sciences, where 2023–2024 performance exceeded 0.98 pass@1 score. Mathematics showed the most variability, with diverse scores across the three years. The model demonstrated sophisticated self-translation capabilities when handling Brazilian Portuguese language questions without explicit translation instructions. Despite strong overall performance, inconsistencies across subject domains persist. Our findings suggest that recent advances in AI reasoning extend effectively beyond typical AI benchmarks to diverse cultural contexts, with implications for AI deployment in various global settings. This evaluation contributes to understanding how generative AI systems perform when facing multidisciplinary, culturally-situated reasoning challenges.

Keywords: Large Language Models · Multiple Choice Question Answering · Brazilian Portuguese

1 Introduction

Recent advancements in generative artificial intelligence, particularly Large Language Models (LLMs), have transformed numerous domains across society [1,2]. These sophisticated neural network architectures, capable of understanding, generating, and reasoning with human language, are increasingly approaching human-like performance across diverse cognitive tasks [3]. The rapid adoption of LLMs in educational settings, professional workplaces, and research environments highlights their growing impact on how humans interact with information and solve complex problems.

Among the latest developments in this field, reasoning-focused LLMs represent a significant leap forward [4,5]. These models demonstrate enhanced abilities

© The Author(s), under exclusive license to Springer Nature Switzerland AG 2026
R. de Freitas and D. Furtado (Eds.): BRACIS 2025, LNAI 16181, pp. 65–77, 2026.
https://doi.org/10.1007/978-3-032-15990-8_5

to follow logical chains of thought, apply domain knowledge systematically, and solve multi-step problems that require both factual recall and analytical thinking. While these capabilities show promise in standardized international benchmarks, a critical question remains: how do these models perform when faced with reasoning tasks embedded in specific cultural, linguistic, and educational contexts beyond those predominantly represented in traditional AI evaluations? [6]

This question is particularly relevant for educational assessments, where reasoning problems often incorporate culturally-specific references, knowledge frameworks, and contextual understanding [7]. To address this gap, we focus on DeepSeek-R1 [8], an emerging family of LLMs designed with advanced reasoning capabilities that exemplifies the progression toward more sophisticated artificial reasoning systems. DeepSeek's architecture incorporates enhanced mechanisms for logical reasoning and knowledge integration, making it an ideal candidate for evaluating AI performance on complex educational assessments.

Brazil's National High School Exam (Exame Nacional do Ensino Médio, ENEM) offers a uniquely valuable benchmark for this evaluation [9]. Established in 1998 and restructured in 2009, the ENEM has evolved from a high school completion assessment into the country's primary mechanism for university admission through Brazil's Unified Selection System (Sistema de Seleção Unificada, SISU) [10]. The ENEM's structure makes it particularly suitable for evaluating AI reasoning capabilities for several reasons: it features comprehensive coverage across four subject areas (Natural Sciences, Human Sciences, Languages and Codes, Mathematics); employs sophisticated psychometric models based on Item Response Theory [11]; emphasizes integration of knowledge across multiple domains; and incorporates Brazilian cultural references and contexts that differ from those in most international AI benchmarks.

This paper presents the first systematic evaluation of DeepSeek-R1's performance on the ENEM, examining how this advanced reasoning LLM handles a complex, culturally-specific educational benchmark. By connecting DeepSeek-R1's reasoning capabilities to the specific challenges presented by ENEM questions, we explore whether recent advances in AI reasoning extend effectively to educational contexts beyond the Global North [12]. This evaluation is particularly significant as AI technologies are increasingly deployed in diverse global educational settings, where performance consistency across different cultural frameworks becomes essential.

By examining DeepSeek's capabilities through the lens of Brazil's premier educational assessment, this research contributes to our understanding of how generative AI systems perform when facing diverse, culturally-situated reasoning challenges, and what this reveals about both the potential and limitations of current AI reasoning capabilities [13]. Our main contributions include:

- The first systematic application of pass@k evaluation methodology to assess DeepSeek-R1's performance on ENEM questions across multiple subject domains.

- Identification of specific subject domains where DeepSeek-R1 demonstrates superior performance, providing insights into the model's strengths across different knowledge areas.
- Analysis of emergent model behaviors, including self-translation capabilities and structured reasoning approaches when handling culturally-situated problems.

The rest of this paper is structured as follows. The Background section provides an overview of Large Language Models with reasoning capabilities and their potential applications in educational assessment. Related Works reviews current research on LLM evaluations across various domains and assessment formats. Our Methodology details the dataset, metrics, and evaluation protocols. The Results section presents our experimental findings, analyzing model performance across different subject areas. Finally, the Conclusion discusses the implications of our findings, limitations of our approach, and directions for future research.

2   Background

Modern language models began with the transformer architecture introduced by [14], representing a paradigm shift from previous approaches with its self-attention mechanisms, efficient parallelization, and positional encodings. Following this innovation, researchers explored different variants, with decoder-only models emerging as particularly effective for generative text tasks. OpenAI's Generative Pre-trained Transformer (GPT) series [15] demonstrated that scaling model size (from 117 million parameters in the original GPT to 175 billion in GPT-3) led to dramatic improvements across diverse tasks without task-specific training, revealing "emergent abilities" [16] including basic reasoning.

By late 2022, research began shifting from pure scale to specialized capabilities, particularly reasoning. Key developments included chain-of-thought prompting that encouraged models to articulate intermediate reasoning steps, Reinforcement Learning from Human Feedback (RLHF) [17] that aligned outputs with human reasoning patterns, and instruction tuning using specialized datasets. These techniques transformed LLMs from primarily text prediction systems to models capable of structured logical thinking, mathematical problem-solving, and step-by-step analysis, particularly significant for educational applications where demonstrating clear reasoning processes is often as important as correct answers.

Building on these developments, DeepSeek-R3 [18] emerged as a specialized family of models emphasizing reasoning capabilities. These models incorporate several innovations: extensive pretraining on diverse multilingual corpora including scientific literature and educational materials; Mixture of Experts (MoE) architecture in some versions; and Multi-head Latent Attention (MLA). The DeepSeek family includes various model sizes, with the largest variants demonstrating competitive performance on reasoning benchmarks across multiple domains. The release of DeepSeek-R1 in early 2025 [8] further extended these capabilities with enhanced cross-domain reasoning abilities and improved performance on complex problem-solving tasks requiring multi-step logical inference.

DeepSeek-R1's focus on reasoning capabilities makes it particularly relevant for educational assessment tasks like Brazil's ENEM, which evaluate students' abilities to comprehend complex information, apply subject-specific knowledge to novel problems, analyze relationships between concepts and create logical arguments supported by evidence. By evaluating DeepSeek on ENEM, we can assess whether current advances in AI reasoning generalize to educational contexts with distinct cultural frameworks, linguistic patterns, and knowledge priorities, providing insights into how effectively current AI reasoning approaches transfer across diverse global contexts.

3   Related Works

Recent research on Large Language Models has evolved across several dimensions: performance on standardized assessments, evaluation methodologies, and applications in diverse contexts. These studies collectively illustrate the advancement of LLM capabilities while revealing areas where further investigation is needed, particularly regarding performance in diverse cultural and educational frameworks.

The evaluation of LLMs on standardized examinations has emerged as a methodology for assessing AI reasoning capabilities. [19] demonstrated GPT-4's performance on the Uniform Bar Examination, achieving scores that exceeded the passing threshold for all jurisdictions. Their findings revealed strong legal reasoning capabilities within the U.S. legal system context.

Similarly, [20] evaluated multiple LLMs on nephrology multiple-choice questions, revealing a performance gap between proprietary and open-source models. Their study highlighted GPT-4's superior performance (73.3% accuracy) compared to open-source alternatives (17.1%–25.5%).

Methodological advances have also refined how researchers assess LLM performance. [21] presented an analysis of multiple-choice question (MCQ) formats as assessment tools, introducing novel datasets for program reasoning evaluation. Their experiments with models including Qwen1.5, Gemma, and Phi-3 revealed that LLM performance on MCQs correlates with performance on open-ended tasks.

Most directly related to our work, [22] evaluated GPT-4's vision capabilities on the Brazilian ENEM examination. Their study showed that GPT-4 demonstrates capabilities in solving multidisciplinary questions requiring both textual and visual comprehension when using step-by-step reasoning. They found that text captions consistently outperformed direct image processing, highlighting current limitations in multimodal understanding. Campos et al. focused specifically on GPT-4's vision capabilities rather than core reasoning abilities and did not examine specialized reasoning-focused models like DeepSeek. Our research extends this work by evaluating DeepSeek, an LLM optimized for reasoning tasks, conducting analysis across multiple ENEM editions, and focusing on reasoning capabilities.

Several areas remain underexplored in the current literature, including the focus on typical educational benchmarks rather than diverse cultural contexts, limited attention to specialized reasoning architectures like DeepSeek in educational assessment, and the tendency to examine isolated knowledge domains instead of integrated, multidisciplinary reasoning. Our study addresses these gaps by evaluating DeepSeek on Brazil's ENEM examination, offering perspective on how these AI systems perform when faced with culturally situated assessments requiring knowledge integration across multiple domains - insights that may prove valuable for understanding AI applicability in diverse educational settings.

4 Methodology

Our evaluation of DeepSeek-R1 on the ENEM dataset follows a structured prompt-based methodology widely used in LLM assessment. We constructed a system prompt that grounds the model in the task of answering Brazilian educational assessment questions, with clear instructions to analyze each question, consider all alternatives, and provide a structured response that can be programmatically parsed. For each question, DeepSeek-R1 received the question text and all answer alternatives, then generated a response containing explicit reasoning steps followed by a clearly indicated final answer selection (A, B, C, D, or E). A robust parsing algorithm extracted these selections while accounting for variations in expression, enabling automated evaluation across the dataset. The experiment implementation is made available anonymously using Anonymous GitHub[1].

4.1 Dataset

This study employs the ENEM dataset published by Maritaca AI on the Hugging Face platform [23,24], comprising questions from the Brazilian National High School Exam. ENEM questions are written in Brazilian Portuguese, and serve as an excellent resource for assessing reasoning capabilities in LLMs due to their interdisciplinary nature and emphasis on applied knowledge, requiring not merely factual recall but contextual understanding and the ability to evaluate multiple plausible explanations.

4.2 Pass@K Metric

We evaluated DeepSeek-R1 (32B version with 4-bit quantization) using the Pass@K metric, which addresses the inherent variability in LLM outputs by

---

[1] The anonymized source code is available at: https://anonymous.4open.science/r/ deepseek-enem-qa-91E6.

allowing multiple sampling attempts per question. For each question, we generated 10 independent responses with identical prompts but varying sampling parameters.

Formally, for each problem i, with n_i independent solutions generated and c_i correct solutions, the Pass@K probability is computed as:

$$\text{Pass@k}(n_i, c_i, k) = 1 - \frac{\binom{n_i - c_i}{k}}{\binom{n_i}{k}} \tag{1}$$

In this formula, $\binom{n}{m}$ represents the binomial coefficient—the number of ways to choose m items from a set of n items. This calculation expresses the probability of selecting at least one correct solution in k attempts.

For computational efficiency and numerical stability, we implemented the unbiased estimator proposed in [25]:

$$\text{Pass@k}(n_i, c_i, k) = \begin{cases} 1.0 & \text{if } n_i - c_i < k \\ 1 - \prod_{j=n_i-c_i+1}^{n_i} \left(1 - \frac{k}{j}\right) & \text{otherwise} \end{cases} \tag{2}$$

The condition $n_i - c_i < k$ represents cases where there are fewer incorrect solutions than selection attempts, guaranteeing at least one correct solution will be selected.

The overall metric is computed by averaging across all problems in our evaluation suite:

$$\text{Pass@k} = \frac{1}{|P|} \sum_{i \in P} \text{Pass@k}(n_i, c_i, k) \tag{3}$$

Following standard practice, we report multiple k values to provide a comprehensive assessment, with higher k values showing performance when users can try multiple solutions, while $k = 1$ represents the most stringent criterion.

5   Results

Our evaluation of the pass@k metric across different years and subject areas reveals significant patterns in performance. Table 1 presents the overall annual performance, showing a consistent improvement in pass@k values from 2022 to 2024 across all k values. Most notably, pass@1 increased from 0.825 in 2022 to 0.907 in 2024, representing approximately a 10% improvement over this three-year period. The varying performance across different years may indicate fluctuations in the difficulty level of the ENEM examinations from year to year.

The breakdown by subject area in Table 2 provides deeper insights into performance variations across disciplines. Human Sciences consistently demonstrates the highest performance across all years, achieving near-perfect results in 2023 and 2024 with pass@1 values of 0.990 and 0.988 respectively, and perfect scores (1.000) for higher k values. This notable performance in Human Sciences

Table 1. Pass@K Metrics for Different Years

Year	Pass@1	Pass@2	Pass@3	Pass@4	Pass@5
2022	0.825	0.875	0.894	0.905	0.911
2023	0.868	0.905	0.919	0.928	0.935
2024	0.907	0.936	0.944	0.948	0.950

Table 2. Pass@k Evaluation Results by Year and Subject Area

Year	Area	pass@1	pass@2	pass@3	pass@4	pass@5
2022	Human Sciences	0.922	0.933	0.938	0.941	0.944
	Languages and Codes	0.867	0.927	0.952	0.963	0.969
	Mathematics	0.730	0.799	0.822	0.836	0.846
	Natural Sciences	0.763	0.827	0.852	0.866	0.875
2023	Human Sciences	0.990	0.999	1.000	1.000	1.000
	Languages and Codes	0.895	0.921	0.932	0.938	0.942
	Mathematics	0.620	0.700	0.737	0.759	0.776
	Natural Sciences	0.881	0.930	0.948	0.960	0.970
2024	Human Sciences	0.988	0.999	1.000	1.000	1.000
	Languages and Codes	0.862	0.900	0.911	0.916	0.918
	Mathematics	0.885	0.920	0.925	0.926	0.926
	Natural Sciences	0.844	0.888	0.914	0.930	0.938

indicates that predictions in this domain are highly reliable, particularly when multiple solutions are considered.

Mathematics presents an interesting case, showing the lowest performance in 2022 and 2023 (pass@1 of 0.730 and 0.620 respectively), but experiencing the most dramatic improvement in 2024 with a pass@1 value of 0.885. This substantial gain from 2023 to 2024 represents the largest year-over-year improvement observed in any subject area, further demonstrating that the model exhibits inconsistent performance even within the same knowledge domain.

Languages and Codes maintained relatively stable performance across the years, with pass@1 values ranging from 0.862 to 0.895. Similarly, Natural Sciences showed steady improvement. The consistency in these domains contrasts with the volatility observed in Mathematics.

When examining the impact of increasing k values, all subject areas exhibit diminishing returns. The most substantial gains occur between $k = 1$ and $k = 2$, with more modest improvements as k increases further. This pattern aligns with the theoretical foundations of the pass@k metric, where the probability of finding at least one correct solution among k attempts approaches asymptotic limits.

Interestingly, the performance gap between different subject areas narrows at higher k values. For example, in 2022, the difference between the highest performing area (Human Sciences) and the lowest (Mathematics) at pass@1 is

0.192, but this gap decreases to 0.098 at pass@5. This convergence suggests that while initial predictions may vary in accuracy across domains, the consideration of multiple solutions substantially improves reliability across all subject areas.

Notably, the 2024 test results demonstrate both the highest overall performance and the most balanced performance across subject areas, with all disciplines achieving pass@1 values above 0.84.

5.1   Model Behavior Analysis

Our examination of the model's internal reasoning process, as showcased in the Appendix, reveals behavioral patterns that may contribute to the performance trends observed in our quantitative analysis. Of particular interest is the model's approach to non-English questions, exemplified by the Vladimir Putin speech question presented in Portuguese.

Despite receiving no explicit translation of the question, the model demonstrated a sophisticated approach by first translating the Portuguese text internally before proceeding with its analysis. This self-translation behavior is noteworthy as it may be an artifact of the model's training methodology, potentially derived from DeepSeek's training procedures. The model's ability to accurately translate and comprehend non-English content without explicit instruction could partially explain the exceptional performance in Human Sciences (pass@1 values of 0.988 in 2024), where many questions involve cross-cultural and multilingual understanding.

The presence of the thinking tag in the model's reasoning process indicates a structured approach to problem-solving, where the model explicitly walks through translation, analysis of options, and consideration of historical context before arriving at a conclusion. This metacognitive structure reveals how the model systematically handles uncertainty when evaluating multiple potential answers, weighing linguistic, historical, and contextual factors to determine the most likely response.

Additionally, the model's ability to translate and reason through complex geopolitical content may also explain why Human Sciences consistently outperforms other subject areas across all years. The model demonstrates not only language comprehension but also contextual understanding of historical and political nuances, abilities that would significantly advantage performance in humanities-related domains. The near-perfect scores in Human Sciences suggest the model has particular strengths in these areas.

6   Conclusion

Our evaluation of DeepSeek-R1 on Brazil's ENEM examination reveals strong reasoning capabilities within culturally-specific educational contexts. Results show impressive performance, particularly in Human Sciences with pass@1 rates exceeding 98% in 2023–2024, suggesting that recent advances in AI reasoning extend effectively beyond typical AI benchmarks to diverse cultural contexts, with implications for AI deployment in various global settings.

The model's self-translation behavior and structured reasoning approach likely contribute to its performance in Human Sciences, allowing navigation of linguistically complex content without explicit translation instructions. Meanwhile, Mathematics exhibited the most variable performance across years, with notably stronger results in 2024 contrasting with lower scores in 2022 and 2023.

Despite promising results, limitations persist: performance variations across domains and years indicate inconsistencies, particularly in mathematical reasoning tasks. Our evaluation focused primarily on multiple-choice questions and may not fully capture performance on open-ended problem-solving that requires extended reasoning.

Future research should investigate whether self-translation behavior varies across different domains and languages, and whether this capability was explicitly built into the model's training or emerged as an emergent property. As AI technologies become increasingly integrated into global educational environments, understanding performance on culturally-specific assessments is crucial for ensuring equitable implementation while addressing remaining inconsistencies across knowledge domains.

Acknowledgments. This study was financed in part by the Coordenação de Aperfeiçoamento de Pessoal de Nível Superior Brasil (CAPES) Finance Code 001. We would like to thank the FAPERGS - Brasil for Financial Support, Award Agreement 22/2551-0000598-5.W. Lastly, we gratefully acknowledge the support of NVIDIA Corporation with the donation of the Titan X Pascal GPU.

A   Appendix: Model Response Example

A.1   Original Question (Brazilian Portuguese)

Discurso de Vladimir Putin sobre a Crimeia

Colegas, na mente e no coração do povo, a Crimeia sempre foi uma porção inseparável da Rússia. Essa firme convicção se baseia na verdade e na justiça e foi passada de geração em geração, ao longo do tempo, sob quaisquer circunstâncias, apesar de todas as drásticas mudanças que nosso país atravessou durante todo o século 20.

Considerando a dinâmica geopolítica subjacente ao texto, a justificativa utilizada por Vladimir Putin, em 2014, para anexação dessa península apela para o argumento de que

A) "as populações com idioma comum devem estar submetidas à mesma autoridade estatal."
B) "o imperialismo soviético havia se acomodado às pretensões das potências vizinhas."
C) "os organismos transnacionais são incapazes de solucionar disputas territoriais."
D) "a integração regional supõe a livre circulação de pessoas e mercadorias."
E) "a expulsão das forças navais ocidentais garantiria a soberania nacional."

A.2   Translation for Readers (Not Provided to the Model)

Vladimir Putin's Speech on Crimea

Colleagues, in the mind and heart of the people, Crimea has always been an inseparable part of Russia. This firm conviction is based on truth and justice and has been passed down from generation to generation, over time, under any circumstances, despite all the drastic changes our country went through during the entire 20th century.

Considering the geopolitical dynamics underlying the text, the justification used by Vladimir Putin in 2014 for the annexation of this peninsula appeals to the argument that

A) "populations with a common language should be subject to the same state authority."
B) "Soviet imperialism had accommodated the claims of neighboring powers."
C) "transnational organizations are unable to solve territorial disputes."
D) "regional integration implies the free movement of people and goods."
E) "the expulsion of Western naval forces would ensure national sovereignty."

A.3   Model Reasoning and Answer

```
<think>
Okay, so I need to figure out the answer to this question about Vladimir
Putin's justification for annexing Crimea in 2014. The question is in
Portuguese, but I'll try to understand it step by step.

The text says that in the minds and hearts of the people, Crimea has
always been an inseparable part of Russia. This conviction is based on
truth and justice and was passed down through generations despite all the
drastic changes the country went through during the 20th century. So the
main idea here seems to be about historical and cultural ties.

Now, looking at the question: it's asking which argument Putin used in
2014 for annexing Crimea. The options are A to E.

Let me think about what I know regarding this situation. In 2014, Russia
annexed Crimea citing several reasons. One of them was the protection
of ethnic Russians and their cultural ties. They argued that Crimea had
historical connections with Russia and that the people there wanted to
be part of Russia again. There were also issues with the government
in Kiev at the time, which was seen as unstable or not representing
Russian-speaking populations.

Looking at the options:

A) Populações com idioma comum devem estar submetidas à mesma autoridade
estatal.
Translation: ''Populations with a common language should be subject to
the same state authority.'' So this is about linguistic unity leading to
same governance. That's similar to the idea of a nation-state based on
language.

B) O imperialismo soviético havia se acomodado às pretensões das
potências vizinhas.
Translation: ''Soviet imperialism had accommodated the claims of
neighboring powers.'' I'm not sure about this one. It seems more about
Soviet policies towards neighbors, which doesn't directly tie to Crimea's
annexation justification.

C) Os organismos transnacionais são incapazes de solucionar disputas
territoriais.
Translation: ''Transnational organizations are unable to solve
territorial disputes.'' This is talking about international bodies
failing. I don't recall Putin specifically citing this as a reason, but
more about the internal aspects of Crimea.

D) A integração regional supõe a livre circulação de pessoas e
mercadorias.
Translation: ''Regional integration implies free circulation of people
and goods.'' That sounds like economic or movement-based reasons, which
doesn't directly address why annex Crimea.

E) A expulsão das forças navais ocidentais garantiria a soberania
nacional.
Translation: ''The expulsion of Western naval forces would ensure
national sovereignty.'' This seems related to military presence. I think
Russia was concerned about NATO expanding and having bases near them, but
I'm not sure if that was the main argument in 2014.

(Continued on next page...)
```

Going back, the text mentions the conviction based on truth and justice passed through generations. So it's more about historical and cultural ties rather than language or military presence. But looking at option A, it talks about common language leading to same authority. That could tie into the idea that since they share a language (Russian), they should be under Russian rule.

Wait, but in 2014, the main argument was more about protecting ethnic Russians and historical ties rather than just language. Also, another angle is the idea of self-determination. The people in Crimea wanted to join Russia because of their cultural and historical connections.

But looking at the options again, option A seems to focus on language leading to same state authority. So if a population speaks Russian, they should be part of Russia. That could fit with Putin's argument that Crimeans are Russians and thus should be under Russian governance.

Alternatively, maybe the text in the question is more about cultural/ethnic identity rather than just language. But the options don't have an option that directly addresses ethnicity; only A talks about language leading to same authority.

So I'm leaning towards option A as the answer because it's about linguistic unity leading to state authority, which ties into the argument of shared history and identity through language.
</think>
The correct answer is A .

References

1. Brown, T.B., et al.: Language models are few-shot learners. Adv. Neural Inf. Process. Syst. **33**, 1877–1901 (2020)
2. Bommasani, R., et al.: On the opportunities and risks of foundation models. arXiv preprint arXiv:2108.07258 (2021)
3. Bubeck, S., et al.: Sparks of artificial general intelligence: early experiments with gpt-4. arXiv preprint arXiv:2303.12712 (2023)
4. Kojima, T., Gu, S.S., Reid, M., Matsuo, Y., Iwasawa, Y.: Large language models are zero-shot reasoners. Adv. Neural Inf. Process. Syst. **35**, 22199–22213 (2022)
5. Wei, J., et al.: Chain-of-thought prompting elicits reasoning in large language models. Adv. Neural Inf. Process. Syst. **35**, 24824–24837 (2022)
6. Joshi, P., Santy, S., Budhiraja, A., Bali, K., Choudhury, M.: The state and fate of linguistic diversity and inclusion in the nlp world. Presented at the (2020)
7. Ribeiro, F.N., Araújo, M., Gonçalves, P., Gonçalves, M.A., Benevenuto, F.: Sentibench - a benchmark comparison of state-of-the-practice sentiment analysis methods. EPJ Data Sci. **5**(1), 1–29 (2020)
8. DeepSeek-AI, et al. Deepseek-r1: Incentivizing reasoning capability in llms via reinforcement learning. ArXiv arxiv:2501.12948 (2025)
9. Travitzki, R., Calero, J., Boto, C.: What does the national high school exam (enem) tell brazilian society? CEPAL Rev. **113**, 157–174 (2014)

10. Santos, J.M.: Exame nacional do ensino médio: Entre a regulação da qualidade do ensino médio e o vestibular. Educar em Revista **40**, 195–205 (2011)

11. Andrade, D.F., Tavares, H.R., Valle, R.C.: Teoria da resposta ao item: Conceitos e aplicações. In: SINAPE (2000)

12. Sambasivan, N., Arnesen, E., Hutchinson, B., Doshi, T., Prabhakaran, V.: Re-imagining algorithmic fairness in India and beyond. In: In Proceedings of the 2021 ACM Conference on Fairness and Transparency, pp. 315–328 (2021)

13. Mitchell, M., et al.: Algorithmic impact assessments and accountability: the co-construction of impacts. In Proceedings of the 2021 ACM Conference on Fairness and Transparency, pp. 735–746 (2022)

14. Vaswani, A., et al.: Attention is all you need. Adv. Neural Inf. Process. Syst. **30**, 5998–6008 (2017)

15. Radford, A., Narasimhan, K.: Improving language understanding by generative pre-training. Technical report. OpenAI (2018)

16. Wei, J., et al.: Emergent abilities of large language models. ArXiv arxiv:2206.07682 (2022)

17. Ouyang, L., et al.: Training language models to follow instructions with human feedback. Adv. Neural Inf. Process. Syst. **35**, 27730–27744 (2022)

18. DeepSeek-AI, et al.: Deepseek-v3 technical report. ArXiv arxiv:2412.19437 (2024)

19. Katz, D.M., Bommarito, M.J., Gao, S., Arredondo, P.: Gpt-4 passes the bar exam. Phil. Trans. R. Soc. A **382** (2023)

20. Wu, S., et al.: Benchmarking open-source large language models, gpt-4 and claude 2 on multiple-choice questions in nephrology. NEJM AI **1** (2024)

21. Zhang, Z., Xu, L., Jiang, Z., Hao, H., Wang, R.: Multiple-choice questions are efficient and robust llm evaluators. ArXiv arxiv:2405.11966 (2024)

22. Campos, R., Almeida, T.S., Abonizio, H., Nogueira, R.: Evaluating gpt-4's vision capabilities on brazilian university admission exams. arXiv preprint arXiv:2311.14169 (2024)

23. Pires, R., Almeida, T.S., Abonizio, H., Nogueira, R.: Evaluating gpt-4's vision capabilities on brazilian university admission exams. arXiv preprint arXiv:2311.14169 (2023)

24. Nunes, D., Primi, R., Pires, R., Lotufo, R., Nogueira, R.: Evaluating gpt-3.5 and gpt-4 models on brazilian university admission exams. arXiv preprint arXiv:2303.17003 (2023)

25. Chen, M., et al.: Evaluating large language models trained on code. arXiv preprint arXiv:2107.03374 (2021)

Assessing Demographic Bias and Fairness in Facial Recognition Systems: A Framework

Darian S. R. Rabanni[(✉)], Italo A. D. Oliveira, Miguel D. S. Wanderley, Cinthya O. Silva, Renato A. Almeida, João R. Alvim, Katia M. Poloni, Gustavo C. Bicalho, and Lucas F. A. O. Pellicer

Instituto de Ciência e Tecnologia Itaú, Praça Alfredo Egydio de Souza Aranha, 100 - Prq Jabaquara, São Paulo, Brazil
{darian.rabbani,italo.duarte-oliveira,miguel.wanderley,
cinthya.oestreich-silva,renato-augusto.almeida,katia.poloni,
gustavo.bicalho}@itau-unibanco.com.br,
joaorabelloalvim@correio.itau.com.br

Abstract. This paper presents a structured framework for assessing bias in facial recognition (FR) models, with an application to a case study. Bias in FR technologies towards sensitive demographic groups remains a significant challenge and a shared responsibility among researchers and companies in the design and development of fair systems. Despite increasing attention to fairness in FR, most existing studies address isolated stages of bias evaluation, with few offering an end-to-end well-defined solution. The proposed framework was developed in a structured and objective manner: 1) the selection of appropriate datasets; 2) the application of bias evaluation metrics; and 3) the techniques and the comparative analysis of performance across demographic groups. That framework aims not only to assist researchers in assessing bias in FR models but also to support the comparison and establishment of benchmarking tests for bias across different models. As a second contribution, we present a case study that applies the proposed framework to widely used benchmark datasets and relevant state-of-the-art pre-trained FR models, providing a comprehensive evaluation of performance disparities across different demographic groups.

Keywords: Facial Recognition · Bias Assessment · Demographic Fairness · Fairness Evaluation Framework

1 Introduction

This work proposes a structured framework to evaluate bias in facial recognition (FR) models as these are widely used by companies and government agencies for security and biometric purposes. Previous studies have shown [3,7] that under-represented demographic groups - especially in terms of gender, age, and skin

© The Author(s), under exclusive license to Springer Nature Switzerland AG 2026
R. de Freitas and D. Furtado (Eds.): BRACIS 2025, LNAI 16181, pp. 78–93, 2026.
https://doi.org/10.1007/978-3-032-15990-8_6

color may face harmful consequences due to incorrect identification. The motivation for this work arose from practical urgency of comparing the biases between different models applied to the same context. From our reading of the papers, we did not identify any study providing a comprehensive guidance from the selection of evaluation metrics [2, 25] and a appropriate datasets to the comparison of the results across demographic groups. Previous surveys and reviews have acknowledged the need for more accessible and domain-specific fairness methodologies, mainly on its practical implementation - not only in the theoretical discussion - by establishing a better communication with stakeholders and integrating solutions into existing Machine Learning (ML) pipelines [22, 26].

Theoretical works systematically emphasized practical difficulties in adopting fairness methodologies, pointing out critical gaps between academic research and real-world deployment [26]. Empirical evaluations conducted by independent agencies - such as the National Institute of Standards and Technology (NIST) [12] - have confirmed demographic disparities in FR performance, particularly in terms of race and gender, reinforcing the need for systematic bias assessment in real-world applications. Table 1 shows some of the most common demographic dimensions typically considered in fairness evaluation.

Table 1. Proposed Demographic dimensions and example of groups for bias assessment in facial recognition systems

Dimension	Example Groups
Gender Identity	Male, Female, Non-binary, Transgender Men, Transgender Women, Other/Prefer not to say
Skin Tone	Light, Medium, Dark (e.g., using Fitzpatrick or Monk Skin Tone scales)
Age Group	Child, Young Adult, Adult, Senior
Ethnicity/Race	White, Black, East Asian, South Asian, Hispanic/Latino, Indigenous, Middle Eastern, Multiracial
Disability Status	Presence of visible facial differences, prosthetics, facial paralysis
Cultural/Religious Markers	Use of face coverings (e.g., hijabs, niqabs, turbans), facial tattoos, traditional adornments

In Brazil, the Center for Security and Citizenship Studies [20] observed that 151 individuals were arrested based on FR systems in 2019. Of that number, 42 had their ethnic group known and 90,5% of those were Black.[1]. Parraga et al. [22] says that fairness in computer vision (CV) is a legal imperative. The Brazilian General Data Protection Law (LGPD) establishes the right of individuals to

---

[1] The Legislative Assembly of the State of Rio de Janeiro is analyzing a law project aimed at avoiding misidentification in prisons without a written report stating if FR is used; and the racial identification of every verified person [19].

review automated decisions which harm them [24]; and the European General Data Protection Regulation (GDP) states that no one can be judged solely on automated processing [9].

The remainder of this paper is structured as follows. Section 2 reviews the related work and theoretical foundations relevant to the proposed framework. Section 3 introduces our framework for assessing bias in facial recognition systems with respect to sensitive demographic groups. Section 4 presents a case study applying the framework to a representative facial recognition task using several state-of-the-art models aiming at the practical application of the framework and critically evaluate the performance of selected models. Finally, Sect. 5 presents our final remarks and suggestions for future directions.

2   Related Works and Theoretical Foundation

This section provides the theoretical background and discusses prior research relevant to the evaluation of bias in machine learning systems, emphasizing FR technologies. We first outline ethical and social principles motivating the development of fairness-aware systems, followed by a review of technical definitions, fairness metrics, and the role of training data in shaping model behavior. We then present key studies that highlight performance disparities in real-world facial recognition systems, establishing the foundation for the framework proposed in this work.

2.1   Bias and Fairness in Machine Learning

Understanding how biases arise in ML requires examining how models learn from human-provided data, especially if data sources are biased. According to [18], algorithms trained on data that reflect historical, social, or demographic imbalances tend to internalize and reproduce these patterns. In some cases, this behavior can even amplify existing disparities over time.

ML algorithms may unintentionally discriminate by systematically favoring privileged groups while disadvantaging marginalized groups. In such cases, longstanding social prejudices can manifest in the algorithmic output in the form of measurable bias [28]. When biased models lead to harmful outcomes, such as discriminatory decisions in hiring, the principle of fairness is potentially compromised as individuals may face serious consequences.

In the context of FR, someone might be wrongly identified as a suspect in a criminal investigation due to imbalanced training data. In an experiment reported by Zora [32], disparities in model performance were attributed to lower recognition accuracy for individuals from underrepresented groups. Consequently, those disparities reflect systematic challenges in model accuracy across demographic groups [3].

2.2   Metrics and Statistical Measures for Bias Assessment

To evaluate fairness in ML problems, many authors presented surveys and proposed metrics [8,11,22]. Traditional classification metrics such as accuracy, precision, recall and, F1-score are not suitable for fairness evaluation, as they do not account for demographic groups [22]. Fairness metrics are generally divided into two main categories: group fairness [8] and individual fairness [8,11]. Group fairness metrics ensure that statistical measures of predictions are similar across subgroups defined by protected attributes (shown in Table 1) listed in Table 2. In contrast, individual fairness assumes that similar individuals - according to task-relevant criteria - should receive similar prediction distributions, regardless of their demographic group. That metrics are shown in Table 3.

Table 2. Group Fairness Metrics and Definitions

Metric	Definition
Demographic Parity	The average algorithmic decision across different demographic groups should be similar
Equality of Opportunity	Ensures that qualified individuals from different groups have equal chances of receiving a positive prediction
Equality of Odds	Requires similar true and false positive rates across groups for individuals who qualify and do not qualify for the outcome
Conditional Statistical Parity	Conditional on a set of legitimate factors L, the probability of a positive prediction should be similar across groups
Treatment Equality	The ratio of false negatives to false positive should be similar across different demographic groups
Overall Accuracy Equality	Overall classification accuracy should be similar across demographic groups
Predictive Parity	Classification precision should be similar across demographic groups
Right for the Right Reasons	Evaluates whether the model relies on appropriate evidence, using explainability tools such as Grad-CAM or saliency maps

Demographic fairness in FR systems is typically assessed through metrics that quantify performance disparities across protected groups, especially regarding false match rates (FMR) and false non-match rates (FNMR) [16]. Traditional evaluations often rely on fixed score thresholds to determine matches. However, demographic groups may exhibit different score distributions, leading to unequal error rates if a single global threshold is applied [16]. To address these disparities, several fairness metrics have been proposed, such as Fairness Discrepancy Rate (FDR) [14], which will be used in our case study in Sect. 4.

The FDR computes the maximum difference between FMR and FNMR across two demographic groups (d_i, d_j) which belong to the space of all groups (D), given a discrimination threshold (τ). The equations are presented in 1 and 2. After the difference are weighed by parameters α and $1 - \alpha$ to represent the level of regard that is applied presented on the equation $\text{FDR}(\tau) = 1 - (\alpha A(\tau) + (1 - \alpha)B(\tau))$. The FDR metric is on scale from 0 to 1, where 1 being "fair" and 0 being "unfair" [14].

$$A(\tau) = \max(\left|\text{FMR}_{d_i}(\tau) - \text{FMR}_{d_j}(\tau)\right|) \ \forall \ d_i, d_j \in D \tag{1}$$

$$B(\tau) = \max(\left|\text{FNMR}_{d_i}(\tau) - \text{FNMR}_{d_j}(\tau)\right|) \ \forall \ d_i, d_j \in D \tag{2}$$

Other approaches, such as GARBE (Gini Coefficient Based Metric), assess dispersion using Gini coefficients, and MAPE (Mean Absolute Percentage Error) assesses dispersion deviation of group-level FMRs from a reference policy value. Additionally, threshold-independent metrics such as d-prime (d') and distribution-based indices - Separation Fairness Index (SFI), Compactness Fairness Index (CFI), and Distribution Fairness Index (DFI) - enable more robust fairness evaluations by comparing score distributions across demographic groups [16].

Table 3. Individual Fairness Metrics and Definitions

Metric	Definition
Fairness through Awareness	Ensures that individuals who are similar according to a task-specific similarity metric receive similar outcomes
Counterfactual Fairness	Requires that an individual and their counterfactual copy, differing only in a protected attribute, receive the same prediction

2.3   Bias Assessment in Computer Vision and Related Datasets

Recent surveys [4,22] synthesize methods for measuring and mitigating bias in FR. In particular, [16] critically reviews existing benchmarks and outlines core concepts – such as group fairness definitions and audit protocols – needed for systematic bias assessment. This review introduces FairFace [15], a large-scale dataset with balanced race, gender, and age annotations designed to enable more representative training and evaluation of recognition models.

Subsequent work has proposed new data-centric and algorithmic defenses against bias. For example, [29,30] present a racially diverse image corpus alongside a domain adaptation framework that maximizes mutual information between source and target groups, effectively reducing cross-demographic performance gaps. Meanwhile, [31] proposes an inclusive neural architecture incorporating demographic embeddings to promote equitable feature learning. Data augmentation strategies have also been explored: [17] demonstrates that generating synthetic images to oversample minority groups can balance datasets and reduce demographic error rates, without requiring new real-world data. These synthetic augmentation techniques complement dataset design and architectural tweaks, forming a comprehensive toolkit for bias mitigation.

On the evaluation front, [10] rigorously quantify bias in face verification systems by comparing false positive and false negative rates across demographic cohorts by proposing a set of standardized metrics for continuous bias monitoring in operational settings. Complementing these academic efforts, a NIST technical report [12] evaluates 189 commercial and government FR algorithms under varying demographic conditions, establishing widely adopted performance benchmarks and highlighting persistent disparities.

The studies [4,16,22] provide a detailed list of relevant datasets specifically designed for fairness and bias evaluation in CV, from which we highlight the following major datasets: MORPH-II, AFD (Curated), VGGFace2, DemogPairs, RFW, BUPT-BalancedFace, DiveFace, MEDS-II, BFW, CASIA-Face-Africa, and CausalFace. In addition to these, other datasets commonly used as benchmarks in fairness evaluation include: Dollar Street, Open Images MIAP, FairFace, and UTK Faces.

In our case study, we use the *Casual Conversations*, which was specifically developed to support fairness evaluation in audio and visual recognition models. In 2021, the first version of the dataset was released [13], comprising over 45,000 videos of 3,011 persons with a diverse range of phenotypic characteristics. It was developed to support the evaluation of computer vision audio model accuracy across different demographic groups. The videos include age and gender annotations self-reported by participants, as well as skin tone labels annotated by trained raters using the Fitzpatrick skin-type scale. A key distinguishing feature of this dataset is that all participants provided explicit consent and were

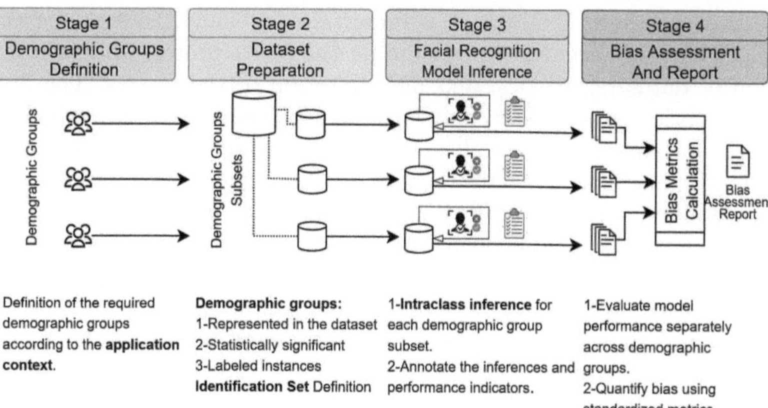

Fig. 1. Framework for bias assessment in facial recognition systems: demographic group definition, dataset preparation, model inference, and bias evaluation.

financially compensated. However, one of its main limitations is that nearly all persons are residents of the United States of America. To address this limitation, a second version of the dataset was published in 2023 [23], containing over 26,000 videos of 5,567 unique paid participants from seven different countries, while maintaining all the other characteristics from the previous version.

3   Framework Proposal

In this section, we introduce framework developed to guide researchers through a structured and reproducible evaluation of bias in FR systems. The framework is organized sequentially to reflect the typical stages encountered during real-world assessments. It was also designed to provide flexibility, enabling researchers to adapt individual steps to the specific characteristics of their application without compromising the systematic nature of the approach.

We detailed every step of the framework to ensure that the evaluation process is clearly defined and can be reproduced across different contexts. The framework guides the user through all stages – from dataset selection to the comparison of results across demographic groups – while addressing practical decisions commonly encountered in applied scenarios.

Specifically, the framework addresses identification tasks, where the goal is to determine whether one or more individuals from a predefined set of facial images - hereafter referred to as the *identification set* – are present in a given image or video.

Figure 1 summarizes the proposed framework structured into four stages in order to reflect the key steps in the bias evaluation process. The following subsections provide a detailed discussion of each stage.

3.1   Sensitive Demographic Groups Definition

Before starting the evaluation, it is important to define the scope of the bias analysis. This stage sets the foundation for the entire process and influences the selection of datasets, metrics, and interpretation of the results. The first step in the evaluation process is to define the demographic attributes which will be considered for bias assessment. This decision must precede the dataset selection, as it directly influences the data requirements and the structure of the analysis.

Furthermore, our framework aims to evaluate bias in discrete and categorical attributes, such as gender and skin color. Continuous variables, like age or weight, are not addressed here. Despite their relevance, assessing bias in regression tasks involves different techniques that fall outside the scope of this work. This is recognized as a primary limitation of our framework and should be explored in future research. Nevertheless, for those intending to explore such variables, we suggest discretizing them into value ranges. Then the problem can be approached as a classification task.

3.2   Reference Dataset Preparation

Once the sensitive demographic groups have been defined, the next step is to select a dataset which supports a proper and fair evaluation. The dataset must include annotations for the chosen attributes and offer enough representation across the defined groups. Publicly available datasets which meet these criteria are discussed in Sect. 2.3.

It is also necessary to consider the media format used in the FR task, either video or static images. If the evaluation involves static images, the dataset can be used directly. In contrast, while working with videos, it is essential to extract representative frames before proceeding to the inference stage. This extraction can follow different strategies: fixed-interval sampling (e.g., one frame per second), random sampling, or intelligent selection based on face quality, pose, or visibility [33]. The optimal method depends on the context of the experiment and the available computational resources. This decision should be made prior to model inference.

Once the dataset is defined, a subset of images of the subjects to be identified in the FR process should be selected to compose the identification set. It should comprise static images. If only videos are available in the original dataset, an additional step is necessary to extract a frame from the selected videos. Typically, there should be only one image per subject to be identified, although this may vary depending on the specific requirements of the system being evaluated or for data augmentation purposes. Finally, most metrics which evaluate bias in FR models rely on comparing the model's performance with subjects belonging to sensitive and non-sensitive groups. Therefore, it is crucial that the identification set is well-distributed among subjects from both groups.

3.3   Facial Matching Inference Stage

In this stage, the objective is to use the model to make inferences on the entire dataset to determine whether any face from the identification set is present in each video or image analyzed. At each step, it is essential to record whether the model identified any subject and whether the identification was correct. This information is critical, as most bias assessment metrics depend on confusion matrix components, which requires a direct comparison between predicted and actual outcomes.

This stage can vary depending on how the FR is being executed, as well as the context in which the experiment is being conducted, but here we will describe what we believe to be the most common steps.

We will assume that the dataset used in this stage is composed only of images. If the original source was a video, a process of image extraction should be conducted as discussed in Sect. 2.3. For each image in the dataset, a Face Detection model should be used to identify the faces in the images and return the coordinates of the bounding box of the faces. Then, images should be cropped based on the returned bounding box so that the new image contains only the faces of the subjects detected; such images should then be processed by a FR model which will produce the embedding vectors of the faces.

The same procedure should be performed for the identification set in a way that the identification set is composed only from the embedding vectors of the faces that should be identified. It is essential that the model used to create the embeddings is the same used with the whole dataset.

Once both the identification set and the dataset analyzed are represented as embedding vectors, it is time to make the inference. Each face detected in the dataset should be compared with the vectors in the identification set, the result should be recorded, indicating whether a match occurred, and if so, the person that was identified. This result will then be compared with the actual value, as it is critical for the next stage.

For the comparison between embeddings it is necessary to choose a similarity function and a threshold. The first determines how similar are the pair of vectors being compared, while the second determines what values are considered a match or not. There is no best method here, as both choices are extremely dependent on the context of the experiment.

3.4   Bias Assessment Stage

Once the inference stage is completed, it is time to evaluate bias across different demographic groups. As shown in Sect. 2.2 there are many metrics which can be used to evaluate bias. More than one can be used and the best options depend on the context. In this framework, we are focusing on classification metrics which, in most cases, compare bias across different demographic groups by comparing the ratio between the error rates in each group. Thus, in this stage, it will be essential to leverage the dataset annotations about the groups being compared and the records from the results obtained in the inference stage, along with their comparison to the true results. The annotations will be used to separate the groups being evaluated, while the recorded results will be used to calculate the metrics. By examining these results, we can determine whether the model exhibits any kind of bias, and in turn, take action to mitigate it where necessary.

4   Case Study: an Application of the Framework

The main idea of this section is to show a practical application of the framework, indicating its limits and possibilities. To do so, we will show its application to evaluate bias in some popular FR models. It is important to say that our goal here is not to do a real bias benchmark test across different models, but to show in practice how our framework can be used.

4.1   Case Study Setup

To validate and test the proposed framework a pipeline was developed. The Fig. 2 presents the diagram of the pipeline used in this case study. The `Casual`

Conversations v2 (CCv2) dataset [23] was used to evaluate bias and fairness in a suite of FR models. The CCv2 dataset is composed from 26,467 videos – each about 1 min long – from 5,567 different subjects from different demographic groups. For each raw video file, the dataset also offers a set of 10 frames (sampled at a constant rate) extracted directly from the video file, adding to the dataset 264,670 images stored in the jpeg format. For the FR task, up to three frames were selected per subject from different videos, resulting in a total of 16,601 pre-selected frames from which embeddings were extracted. We selected the CCv2 dataset because, as demonstrated in Sect. 2.3, the Fitzpatrick skin-type annotations were performed by trained raters, ensuring greater consistency from a technical standpoint. Furthermore, all subjects provided explicit consent to participate, which we consider a crucial aspect of the dataset's ethical integrity.

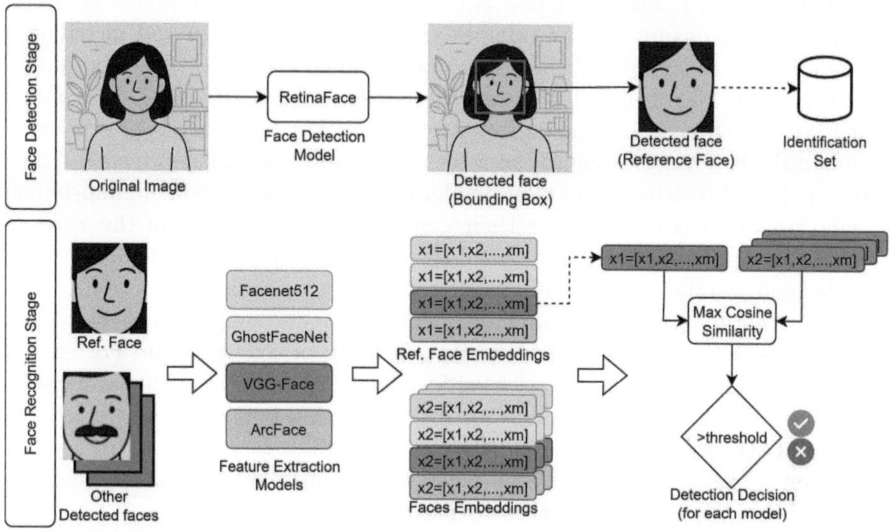

Fig. 2. Diagram of the facial recognition pipeline used in the case study.

The first stage of the pipeline is Face Detection. For each selected frame, the Retina Face model [6] was applied to obtain the bounding box of the face. This bounding box was then used to crop the original frame in the face region. The second stage is Face Recognition. For each cropped face, the facial embedding generation models were applied. In our study, we chose to work with open-source, pretrained, state of the art models. Thus to generate the embeddings we used: ArcFace [5], Facenet512 [27], GhostFaceNet [1], and VGG-Face [21]. Then, the recognition task was set by computing the cosine distance between each pair of embeddings. A pair was considered a match if the distance was above a threshold, which was determined from its ROC curve on the dataset.

The experiments calculated the *FDR* described in the Sect. 2.2. To evaluate both metrics, it is needed to identify the *FMR* and the *FNMR* to each evaluated model. Once the thresholds are calculated for each model, the FMR and FNMR rates are extracted for each sensible group and the FDR and IR are then calculated. Gender indicators and the Fitzpatrick skin-type scale were used as sensitive features, and the FR performance of each model was evaluated.

The inference pipeline, presented on Fig. 2, achieved an average processing time of 0.7 s per image per model. The experiments were conducted on Amazon Web Services (AWS) using the SageMaker platform. The ml.m5.4xlarge instance was utilized, which is equipped with 16 vCPUs, 64 GiB of memory, and based on the Intel Xeon Platinum 8000 series processor architecture.

4.2   Case Study Discussion

Table 4 presents the Fairness Discrepancy Rate (FDR) with its standard deviations, for four FR models across two sensible features: Fitzpatrick skin type and gender. To ensure a more reliable analysis given the size and distribution of the dataset, we simplified these two demographic attributes. The Fitzpatrick skin type scale was grouped into two categories - Types IIII and Types IVVI–which we refer to as the Binary Fitzpatrick Scale. For the analysis of gender, we included the two most frequently reported categories: cisgender women and men. Participants who identified as transgender men, transgender women, non-binary, or who preferred not to disclose their gender were excluded from the analysis, as these groups collectively comprised less than 4% of the total sample, which was deemed insufficient for statistically robust comparisons.

The experiments were conducted using three mutually exclusive subject-based splits, each used as the identification set in a different run. For each of these experiments, the images selected for identification were excluded from the set of faces used for recognition, ensuring no overlap between the two sets. By the end of the three experiments, all subjects had been included in the identification set and used for verification. Final results are reported as the mean and standard deviation across the three experimental splits.

Table 4. Results for fitzpatrick binary and gender fetaures for Fairness Discrepancy Rate (FDR)

Model	Binary Fitzpatrick	Gender
ArcFace	0,936 ± 0,009	0,980 ± 0,022
Facenet512	0,874 ± 0,013	0,967 ± 0,008
GhostFaceNet	0,938 ± 0,007	0,946 ± 0,004
VGG-Face	0,867 ± 0,011	0,927 ± 0,019

Across the models, GhostFaceNet achieves the highest FDR performance on the Binary Fitzpatrick feature (0.938 ± 0.007), indicating a strong ability to be a fair model. On the other hand, VGG-Face displays the lowest FDR

(0.867 ± 0.011) for Binary Fitzpatrick, suggesting greater performance discrepancy between demographic subgroups and a lower level of fairness. For the gender feature, ArcFace presents the highest FDR (0.980 ± 0.022), while VGG-Face again records the lowest value (0.927 ± 0.019).

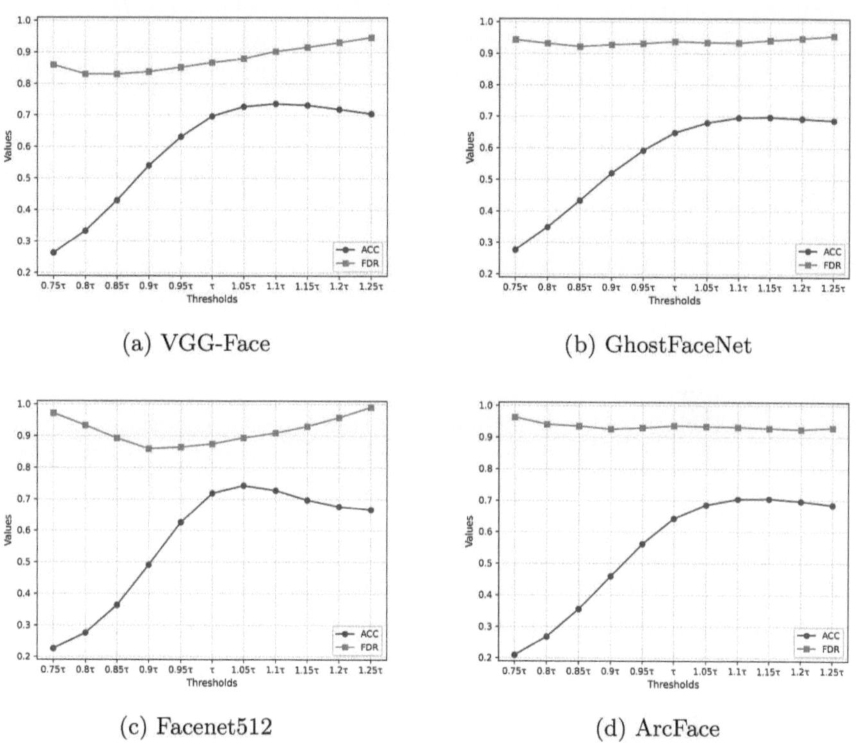

(a) VGG-Face   (b) GhostFaceNet

(c) Facenet512   (d) ArcFace

Fig. 3. Comparison of the trade-off between average accuracy and Fairness Discrepancy Rate (FDR) across Fitzpatrick skin tone groups, evaluated over varying threshold values for each model.

A particularly relevant analysis carried out in this study is the trade-off between a performance metric – in this case, the *average accuracy* (computed as the mean of the accuracies across each sensitive group) – and a fairness metric, specifically the *Fairness Discrepancy Rate (FDR)*. We computed the average accuracy to obtain a single representative value, as the FDR already serves the purpose of summarizing the overall bias level of the model in a single value.

Figure 3 presents the trade-off curves comparing the average accuracy and the FDR, showing their impact on the Fitzpatrick skin tone groups for the different models evaluated. We varied the optimal threshold (τ) within the range $[\tau - 0.25, \tau + 0.25]$ in increments of 0.05. The x-axis represents the threshold values, while the y-axis shows the corresponding accuracy and FDR values.

An important finding is that, for some models, there are alternative thresholds that outperform the initial τ, achieving better FDR values (the higher, the better). For the *VGG-Face, GhostFaceNet,* and *Facenet512* models, we were able to identify a threshold around 1.15τ that improves the FDR (indicating a fairer model) without significant performance loss, *i.e.*, with less than a 5% reduction in accuracy, maintaining a final accuracy in the range of 0.7 to 0.75.

In general, this evaluation offers a comprehensive view of the performance-fairness trade-off in all models tested, and it is important to emphasize these findings. As shown in Fig. 3, both *GhostFaceNet* and *ArcFace* maintain remarkably uniform FDR values - consistently above 0.90 - throughout the entire range of thresholds, highlighting their stability in fairness outcomes. In contrast, *FaceNet512* and *VGG-Face* exhibit FDR drops below 0.90 at certain threshold settings, indicating compromised fairness under specific configurations. Although *FaceNet512* achieves the highest peak accuracy (≈ 0.75) among the models, this comes at the cost of greater FDR sensitivity to threshold variation. In practical terms, GhostFaceNet and ArcFace strike a more balanced compromise for the Fitzpatrick skin-tone groups evaluated: they reach a respectable accuracy ceiling (≈ 0.70) while demonstrating minimal bias fluctuations across thresholds, underscoring their robustness in combined performance and fairness metrics.

Finally, in assessing the trade-off for the Fitzpatrick groups, we can consider the ideal model configuration to be one that achieves an FDR between 0.91 and 0.95 with an approximate accuracy of 0.7, effectively balancing fairness improvements without major performance sacrifices.

5   Final Remarks and Future Work

Aiming to support a fair treatment of sensitive groups, the proposed framework by assessing demographic bias in FR models - was validated through a case study using benchmark datasets and state-of-the-art pre-trained models. There were significant disparities in performance between demographic groups, highlighting the urgent need for systematic bias assessment practices in both academic and industrial settings. Our analysis shows that, despite high overall accuracy, many FR models perform unevenly across demographic groups, raising concerns about fairness and real-world readiness. These disparities, often reflecting biased training data, are especially pronounced in individuals with darker skin tones or underrepresented genders.

To address these disparities, we argue that future facial recognition systems should be developed within a multi-objective min-max optimization framework, one that seeks to maximize recognition and detection performance while simultaneously minimizing bias across sensitive demographic groups, particularly those historically marginalized. Achieving responsible deployment requires not only diverse training data, but also fairness-focused model architectures and evaluation protocols. In future work, we plan to expand the framework to support additional tasks beyond identity recognition, such as evaluating regression problems in a way that accounts for intersectional demographic dimensions (*e.g.*, combined age and gender), and exploring mitigation strategies based on the assessment results.

Acknowledgments. This study used OpenAI Deep Research to identify references on bias and fairness in facial recognition, with GPT models helping to write, review, refine the text, and generate illustrative images.

Disclosure of Interests. All the conclusions expressed by the authors do not reflect the opinions of Itaú Unibanco and Instituto de Ciência e Tecnologia Itaú. Also, it must not result in any commercial process. Finally, all data used in this study comply with the Brazilian General Data Protection Law.

References

1. Alansari, M., Hay, O.A., Javed, S., Shoufan, A., Zweiri, Y., Werghi, N.: Ghost-facenets: lightweight face recognition model from cheap operations. IEEE Access **11**, 35429–35446 (2023)
2. Barocas, S., Hardt, M., Narayanan, A.: Fairness and Machine Learning: Limitations and Opportunities. self-published (2019). available online: fairmlbook.org
3. Buolamwini, J., Gebru, T.: Gender shades: intersectional accuracy disparities in commercial gender classification. In: Proceedings of the 1st Conference on Fairness, Accountability and Transparency, pp. 77–91. PMLR (2018)
4. Dehdashtian, S., et al.: Fairness and bias mitigation in computer vision: a survey. arXiv preprint arXiv:2408.02464 (2024)
5. Deng, J., Guo, J., Xue, N., Zafeiriou, S.: Arcface: additive angular margin loss for deep face recognition. In: Proceedings of the IEEE/CVF Conference on Computer Vision and Pattern Recognition, pp. 4690–4699 (2019)
6. Deng, J., Guo, J., Zhou, Y., Yu, J., Kotsia, I., Zafeiriou, S.: Retinaface: single-stage dense face localisation in the wild. arXiv preprint arXiv:1905.00641 (2019)
7. Drozdowski, P., Rathgeb, C., Dantcheva, A., Damer, N., Busch, C.: Demographic bias in biometrics: a survey on an emerging challenge. IEEE Trans. Technol. Soc. **1**(2), 89–103 (2020)
8. Dwork, C., Ilvento, C.: Fairness under composition. In: Blum, A. (ed.) 10th Innovations in Theoretical Computer Science Conference (ITCS 2019). Leibniz International Proceedings in Informatics (LIPIcs), vol. 124, pp. 33:1–33:20. Schloss Dagstuhl – Leibniz-Zentrum für Informatik, Dagstuhl, Germany (2019). https://doi.org/10.4230/LIPIcs.ITCS.2019.33. https://drops.dagstuhl.de/entities/document/10.4230/LIPIcs.ITCS.2019.33
9. 2016/679 of the European Parliament and of the Council of 27 April 2016 on the protection of natural persons with regard to the processing of personal data and on the free movement of such data (General Data Protection Regulation)). European Union: Regulation (EU) (2016). Accessed 28 Apr 2025
10. Frisella, M., Khorrami, P., Matterer, J., Kratkiewicz, K., Torres-Carrasquillo, P.: Quantifying bias in a face verification system. Comput. Sci. Math. Forum **3**(1) (2022). https://doi.org/10.3390/cmsf2022003006. https://www.mdpi.com/2813-0324/3/1/6
11. Gajane, P., Pechenizkiy, M.: On formalizing fairness in prediction with machine learning. arXiv preprint arXiv:1710.03184 (2017)

12. Grother, P., Ngan, M., Hanaoka, K.: Face recognition vendor test (frvt) part 3: demographic effects. Technical Report. NISTIR 8280, National Institute of Standards and Technology (2019). https://doi.org/10.6028/NIST.IR.8280
13. Hazirbas, C., Bitton, J., Dolhansky, B., Pan, J., Gordo, A., Ferrer, C.C.: Towards measuring fairness in AI: the casual conversations dataset. IEEE Trans. Biometr. Behav. Identity Sci. **4**(3), 324–332 (2021)
14. Howard, J.J., Laird, E.J., Rubin, R.E., Sirotin, Y.B., Tipton, J.L., Vemury, A.R.: Evaluating proposed fairness models for face recognition algorithms. In: International Conference on Pattern Recognition, pp. 431–447. Springer, Heidelberg (2022)
15. Karkkainen, K., Joo, J.: Fairface: face attribute dataset for balanced race, gender, and age for bias measurement and mitigation. In: Proceedings of the IEEE/CVF Winter Conference on Applications of Computer Vision (WACV) (2021)
16. Kotwal, K., Marcel, S.: Review of demographic bias in face recognition. arXiv preprint arXiv:2502.02309 (2025)
17. McDuff, D., Gontarek, S., Picard, R.: Reducing demographic bias in facial recognition using synthetic data. arXiv preprint arXiv:1904.05116 (2019)
18. Mehrabi, N., Morstatter, F., Saxena, N., Lerman, K., Galstyan, A.: A survey on bias and fairness in machine learning. ACM Comput. Surv. **54**(6) (2021). https://doi.org/10.1145/3457607
19. Minc, C.: Bill no. 3476/2024: Establishing the requirement for a personal data protection impact report for facial recognition systems in the state of Rio de Janeiro. Official legislative document (2024). https://bancodeleis.unale.org.br/Arquivo/Documents/23/PLO/PLO34762024.pdf. Accessed 06 May 2025
20. Nunes, P.: New tools, old practices: Facial recognition and policing in brazil. In: Center for Security and Citizenship Studies (CeSEC) (ed.) Portraits of Violence: Five Months of Monitoring, Analysis, and Findings – June to October 2019, pp. 67–70. Center for Security and Citizenship Studies (CeSEC), Rio de Janeiro, Brazil (2019). https://observatorioseguranca.com.br/wordpress/wp-content/uploads/2019/11/1relatoriorede.pdf. Accessed 05 May 2025
21. Parkhi, O., Vedaldi, A., Zisserman, A.: Deep face recognition. In: BMVC 2015-Proceedings of the British Machine Vision Conference 2015. British Machine Vision Association (2015)
22. Parraga, O., .: Fairness in deep learning: a survey on vision and language research. ACM Comput. Surv. **57**(6) (2025). https://doi.org/10.1145/3637549
23. Porgali, B., Albiero, V., Ryda, J., Ferrer, C.C., Hazirbas, C.: The casual conversations v2 dataset. In: Proceedings of the IEEE/CVF Conference on Computer Vision and Pattern Recognition, pp. 10–17 (2023)
24. Presidency of the Republic of Brazil: Law No. 13,709, of August 14, 2018. General Personal Data Protection Law (LGPD) (2018). https://www.planalto.gov.br/ccivil_03/_ato2015-2018/2018/lei/L13709.htm. Accessed 28 Apr 2025
25. Raji, I.D., Buolamwini, J.: Actionable auditing: investigating the impact of publicly naming biased performance results of commercial AI products. In: Proceedings of the 2019 AAAI/ACM Conference on AI, Ethics, and Society, pp. 429–435. ACM (2019)
26. Richardson, R., Gilbert, S.: A framework for fairness: a systematic review of 25 years of fairness research in machine learning. arXiv preprint arXiv:2112.05700 (2021)
27. Schroff, F., Kalenichenko, D., Philbin, J.: Facenet: a unified embedding for face recognition and clustering. In: Proceedings of the IEEE Conference on Computer Vision and Pattern Recognition, pp. 815–823 (2015)

28. Stryker, C.: What is responsible ai? (2024), https://www.ibm.com/think/topics/responsible-ai, accessed in 2025-04-29
29. Wang, M., Deng, W.: Mitigating bias in face recognition using skewness-aware reinforcement learning. In: Proceedings of the IEEE/CVF Conference on Computer Vision and Pattern Recognition, pp. 9322–9331 (2020)
30. Wang, M., Deng, W., Hu, J., Tao, X., Huang, Y.: Racial faces in the wild: reducing racial bias by information maximization adaptation network. In: Proceedings of the IEEE/CVF International Conference on Computer Vision, pp. 692–702 (2019)
31. Wang, T., Gong, R., Kotsia, I., Zafeiriou, S.: Inclusivefacenet: improving face attribute detection with race and gender diversity. In: Proceedings of the IEEE International Conference on Computer Vision Workshops, pp. 100–108 (2019)
32. Wehrli, S., Hertweck, C., Amirian, M., Glüge, S., Stadelmann, T.: Bias, awareness, and ignorance in deep-learning-based face recognition. AI Ethics 2(3), 509–522 (2022). https://doi.org/10.1007/s43681-021-00108-6
33. Yang, H., Cheng, Y., Lin, Z., Bai, S., Yuille, A.L.: Video face recognition: a survey. In: International Joint Conference on Artificial Intelligence (IJCAI) (2020)

Better Call Lucas: A Conversational Assistant for Older Adult Support

Luan Matheus Trindade Dalmazo[1]([✉]) [ID], Luize Duarte[1] [ID],
Vitor Last Pintarelli[2] [ID], and Eduardo Todt[1] [ID]

[1] Department of Informatics , Federal University of Paraná, Curitiba, Brazil
`luantrindade@ufpr.br`
[2] Department of Clinical Medicine, Federal University of Paraná, Curitiba, Brazil

Abstract. This work presents the development of Lucas, a virtual assistant built entirely with open-source tools to support older adults in their daily routines. Built upon the Robot Operating System (ROS 2), the system is composed of modular nodes for wake word detection, speech processing, and natural language interaction. The assistant is triggered by the spoken expression "Opa Lucas" after which it records the user's voice, transcribes the audio to text using Whisper, and processes the instruction using the LLaMA 3 Large Language Model. Depending on the user's request, the system may access external tools, such as reminders and weather forecasts, via predefined APIs and SQL queries. The entire interaction is presented through a multimodal interface built with Pygame, combining speech synthesis and animated feedback. The assistant supports speaker identification through voice verification. To evaluate the assistant, a set of instructions was proposed to assess the accuracy, errors made, and the nature of the responses, including aspects such as harmfulness, helpfulness, and coherence. Additionally, the assistant was reviewed and tested by a geriatric care professional. The results demonstrate the assistant's potential to deliver coherent, accurate, and timely instructions, suggesting its applicability in daily routines. The assistant's source code is publicly available in a GitHub repository, along with documentation for setup and usage.

Keywords: Personal Assistant · Older Adult Care · Large Language Models (LLMs)

1 Introduction

In Brazil, according to the Ministry of Human Rights, 22,636 reports of abandonment of older adults were registered in 2023, nearly double the 11,359 cases recorded in 2022 [7]. This figure is alarming, especially when considered in light of the rapidly aging Brazilian population, as evidenced by the 2022 Demographic Census, which recorded a 57.4% increase in the older adult population compared to 2010 [1]. In response, the Brazilian government enacted Law No. 7,451/24 in

R. de Freitas and D. Furtado (Eds.): BRACIS 2025, LNAI 16181, pp. 94–108, 2026.
https://doi.org/10.1007/978-3-032-15990-8_7

the Federal District in 2024, which addresses the protection of older adults and proposes palliative measures to confront the issue [2]. Furthermore, the country has established the Elderly Statute [18], which specifically addresses the abandonment of older adults in Article 98, defining the corresponding legal measures. However, it is evident that such actions remain insufficient given the complexity of the situation. Therefore, the development of support tools aimed at promoting care and autonomy for older adults becomes increasingly urgent.

One of the technologies increasingly adopted in Brazilian households, although not necessarily intended to support older adults, is the use of virtual assistants. According to data released by Amazon, the use of such devices increased by 50% in 2023 [5]. However, commercial assistants like Alexa and Siri are developed for general-purpose, remain closed-source, and come with high costs, limiting options for customization and accessibility. This demonstrates the need for affordable, open-source solutions that can be customized to support the specific needs of older adults.

In this context, we present the development of a personal assistant named Lucas, designed to support the care of older adults. The assistant is based on the LLaMA 3 Large Language Model and integrates the use of agents to enable specific functionalities, such as retrieving weather information and assisting with reminders. It was built with a focus on accessible interactions and features tailored to the needs of this demographic, with potential applicability to other age groups as well. The evaluation of the tool follows two main approaches: the first assesses the quality of the assistant's responses, focusing on their relevance and accuracy in relation to the user's initial instruction; the second involves feedback from a geriatric care specialist, who provided insights and recommendations regarding the system's design, usability, and potential improvements.

Accordingly, the main contributions of this paper include:

I The development and open-source release of a personal assistant designed for use by older individuals;
II An analysis of the implemented functionalities and their applicability in daily routines;
III A discussion of the potential impacts of the tool and possibilities for future enhancements.

2   Related Works

Several studies have addressed the use of technology to promote the well-being and inclusion of the older adult population. Oliveira and Nunes (2021), for example, proposed the chatbot Ana, designed to assist older adults in learning basic computer skills [12]. The chatbot is part of a system conceived as a complementary tool to in-person computer courses, aiming to provide autonomy to older individuals in their learning process.

In a different approach, Pal et al. (2018) investigated the acceptance of new technologies by older adults, such as smart homes, and the factors that influence their trust [15]. The authors proposed the ESHTAM model, an extension of the technology acceptance model, which showed that the greatest concerns among older adults regarding new technologies are privacy, misuse, and high costs.

In addition, recent advances in adaptive human-robot interaction (HRI) systems have explored the integration of large language models (LLMs) to enhance personalized healthcare for older adults. Park et al. (2025) integrated the CLOi robot with the Claude API to conduct adaptive satisfaction surveys, generating follow-up questions in real-time to interact with the older user and clarify ambiguous responses [16]. This approach enabled more effective and personalized interactions with the elderly.

Accordingly, Langston et al. (2025) evaluated the ability of virtual assistants to respond to health-related questions posed by elderly users [9]. The research compared non-LLM-based assistants, such as Alexa and Google Assistant, with LLM-based systems like ChatGPT-4. LLMs outperformed traditional assistants in response accuracy, although the study cautioned that their tendency to provide overly detailed answers may increase cognitive load for older users. These findings show the need for virtual assistants to prioritize not only accuracy but also clarity and adaptability.

These studies highlight the potential of assistive technologies both in promoting digital inclusion and in maintaining autonomy and safety for older adults in residential environments. The proposed work differs from those previously discussed by introducing an assistant built entirely with free (or at least freely accessible with limited usage) tools, enabling customizations such as changing the underlying LLM or even the system prompt. It also presents a modular architecture capable of separating the application into distinct client and server components, allowing deployment across different machines.

3   Methodology

The assistant Lucas is built on ROS 2 (Robot Operating System) [10] [11]. The architecture consists of two main nodes: WakeWordDetector and SpeechClient. The former acts as a publisher, and the latter as a subscriber, enabling communication through topics that signal the detection of the wake word "Opa Lucas".

Once the assistant is triggered, the SpeechClient node records the user's voice and transcribes the audio into a textual instruction. This instruction is then forwarded as input to the LLM via a POST request. The LLM may choose to invoke specific tools (such as reminder retrieval or weather lookup) or simply generate a natural language response based on the instruction. After processing, the output is converted into speech and presented to the user through a multimodal visual interface.

This section aims to detail each stage involved in building the assistant, as well as to describe the components and technologies used in the system architecture, illustrated in Fig. 1.

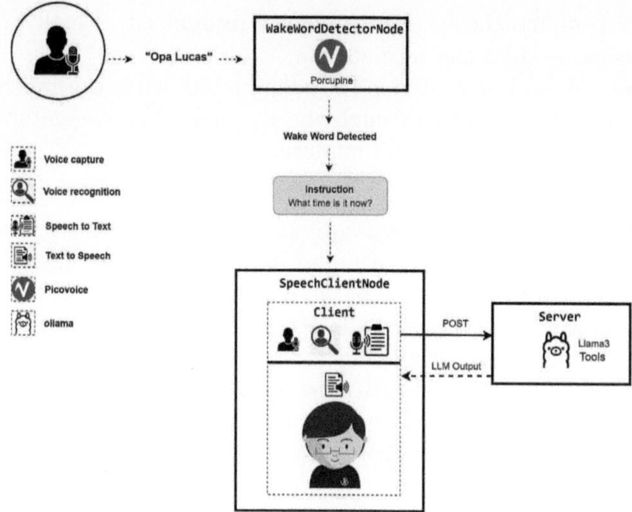

Fig. 1. Assistant architecture. Icons partially generated with GPT-4.

3.1   WakeWordDetectorNode

For wake word detection, the assistant employs Porcupine, a tool developed by Picovoice[1]. In general, Porcupine is a passive listening engine capable of recognizing a pre-configured phrase or one of the default options provided by the tool [17], such as common wake words like "Ok Google" and "Alexa."

The choice of this tool was primarily motivated by two factors. First, it is free for academic use, although with certain limitations, including a restriction to a single active user. Second, unlike many other solutions that focus on English-only recognition, Porcupine supports detection of wake words in Portuguese, which was essential for the intended user context.

Upon detecting the wake word "Opa Lucas", a colloquial and culturally familiar phrase in Brazilian Portuguese, the node publishes a topic signaling the phrase was recognized, thus initiating the audio capture and instruction processing flow.

3.2   SpeechClientNode

The SpeechClient node functions as a subscriber, as previously described, but also acts as a client that performs requests to the server hosting the LLM. This design choice was made to enhance modularity within the system architecture.

This node is responsible for recording the user's voice, transcribing it into text, attempting speaker identification (if the input audio matches any previously stored samples), and subsequently sending a POST request containing both the

---

[1] https://github.com/Picovoice/porcupine.

textual instruction and the speaker's name (if recognized). Finally, the assistant delivers the response in audio format.

This entire process is executed in the background, while the assistant displays visual expressions to the user through the Pygame library, commonly used for game development and multimedia rendering [19].

Voice Capture. User voice recording is performed using the PyAudio library, which allows real-time handling of audio input and output resources [6]. The captured audio is configured in the paInt16 format, meaning 16 bits per sample, and the default recording duration is set to 5 s for development and testing purpose (this value is configurable in the provided source code).

Table 1 summarizes the main parameters adopted for audio acquisition and storage. All values were defined through empirical testing to ensure sufficient capture quality and system responsiveness.

Table 1. Audio recording parameters used for the assistant.

Parameter	Value
Number of Channels (CHANNELS)	2
Sampling Rate (RATE)	44100 Hz
Chunk Size (CHUNK)	1024
Recording Duration (RECORD_SECONDS)	5 s

The total number of iterations during the recording process is determined by Eq. 1, which reads 1024 samples per iteration (CHUNK). At the end of the process, the wave library [3] is used to define the number of audio channels and the sample rate (RATE) for the final audio file.

$$\text{Iterations} = \left\lfloor \frac{\text{RATE}}{\text{CHUNK}} \times \text{RECORD\_SECONDS} \right\rfloor \tag{1}$$

Voice Recognition. Speaker recognition is performed using the SpeechBrain library, leveraging a pre-trained model proposed by Ravanelli et al. [22,23]. Identification is carried out by comparing the captured voice with stored voice samples, using the algorithm illustrated in Algorithm 1.

The user can save voice samples for multiple individuals in the voices/ directory, enabling personalized speaker recognition during interaction.

Speech to Text. The speech-to-text task is carried out by processing the previously recorded audio file. For this purpose, the Whisper model, proposed by

---

Algorithm 1: Core logic for speaker identification

Input: Voice sample v, directory of speaker folders D
Output: Speaker name or `"unknown"`
1 **foreach** *speaker folder* $s \in D$ **do**
2 $\quad$ Compute average similarity score between v and all .wav files in s ;
3 $\quad$ Keep s if it yields the highest score so far ;

4 **return** *"unknown" if best score < 0.1, else corresponding speaker name*

Radford et al. [20], was employed. Trained on a large and diverse dataset, Whisper is capable of producing high-quality transcriptions across multiple languages.

In this work, the "tiny" version of the model was selected due to its low computational requirements. The Portuguese language was specified as the target for transcription. Upon completion, the model's output is saved as a plain text file and passed to the next stages in the pipeline.

The accuracy of the speech recognition component was evaluated using the Word Error Rate (WER) metric. WER is a widely used metric that compares the predicted transcription with the reference transcription by calculating the number of insertions, deletions, and substitutions required to transform the predicted text into the reference text. The formula for WER is:

$$WER = \frac{S + D + I}{N}$$

where S is the number of substitutions; D is the number of deletions; I is the number of insertions, and N is the total number of words in the reference transcription.

Text to Speech (TTS). To convert textual output into speech, the edge-tts module was employed [21], which interfaces with Microsoft Edge's text-to-speech API. The service offers a variety of predefined voices in multiple languages and styles. In this work, the "pt-BR-AntonioNeural" voice was selected due to its natural tone and support for Brazilian Portuguese.

Assistant Interface. The assistant's visual interface is composed of animated GIFs representing the system's various states, as illustrated in Fig. 2. These states include: waiting for user input, wake word detection, listening to the user's request, and responding to the given instruction.

To ensure the system's alignment with the specific needs and preferences of older adults, the development process included consultations with a geriatrics expert. One of the initial recommendations made by the specialist was the adoption of a younger assistant persona, aimed at fostering a greater sense of trust and comfort among older users. This choice was reflected both in the assistant's speech style and in its visual identity.

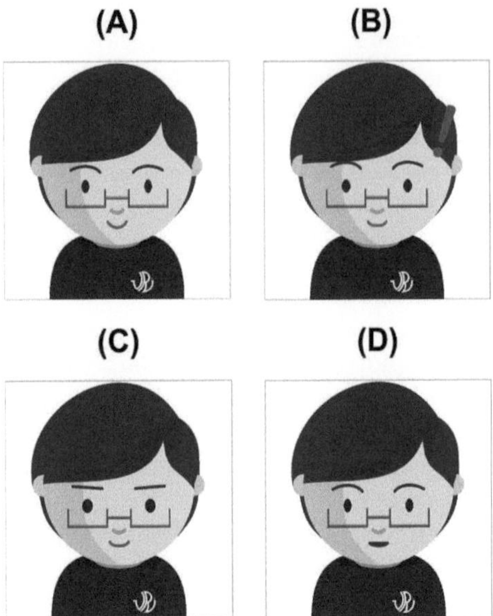

Fig. 2. Illustration of the assistant's interface in each system state: (A) waiting for user input, (B) wake word detection, (C) listening to the user's request, (D) responding to the given instruction. Each frame corresponds to a distinct animated GIF used in the actual implementation. The original animated GIFs are available in the application repository.

Another key suggestion involved the inclusion of on-screen subtitles in addition to audio output, as shown in Fig. 3, to accommodate users with hearing impairments. The expert recommended that these subtitles be displayed in white font on a black background, as this contrast significantly improves readability for individuals with visual limitations, a common condition among older adults.

3.3   Server

The server was implemented using the FastAPI framework [4], enabling the creation of a RESTful service with a POST endpoint at the route /processing. Upon receiving a request, the endpoint expects two fields: the user's textual input and their name (if recognized, or left empty otherwise). These inputs are then forwarded to the LLM, which processes the instruction and generates an appropriate textual response.

Largue Language Model and Tools. The LLM used to process user instructions was LLaMA 3 [13], chosen for its lightweight nature and ease of integration. The assistant was designed with modularity in mind, allowing easy substitution of the language model as needed.

Fig. 3. Example of the assistant's response to the instruction *"Diga oi para mim"* ("Say hi to me"). The output shown on the screen is: *"Oi! Como posso ajudar você hoje? Estou aqui para o que precisar."* ("Hi! How can I help you today? I'm here for whatever you need.").

The assistant's LLM integration relies on the LangChain library, which offers a unified interface for various language models [8]. A ZeroShot agent was implemented using LangChain's agent framework. This setup enables reasoning over the user instruction prior to generating a response. This design allows the system to invoke external tools and more effectively interpret user inputs. The prompt structure consists of a prefix and suffix, both of which are shown in Fig. 4 and Fig. 5.

The assistant supports specific tools triggered when relevant to the user instruction. These include reminder storage and retrieval and weather queries, as illustrated in Fig. 6. In the case of reminders, user requests are stored in an SQL database containing a description and datetime. For retrieval, a database query is performed. Weather queries are handled via the OpenWeatherMap API [14], which provides free access (with registered API key) to temperature information for a specified location, returned in degrees Celsius.

3.4 Evaluation

To evaluate the model, 50 sentences were constructed to simulate potential interactions by older adults. These included requests for actions that the assistant is unable to perform, such as making phone calls and playing music, examples demonstrating the use of available tools, and simple conversational interactions. All sentences were read by a female voice and processed by the language model following the assistant's natural pipeline. The dataset created can be found in the application repository.

The evaluation of the assistant was conducted through multiple approaches. Initially, the execution time of each stage within the processing pipeline was analyzed up to the generation of the final response provided to the user. The analysis focused exclusively on the components that involve artificial intelligence mod-

> **Prompt Prefix (Translated)**
>
> You are an assistant for elderly people developed by the Vision, Robotics and Imaging Laboratory at the Federal University of Paraná. Your name is Lucas, and you should act like a young person always willing to help.
> Your responses must be:
>
> - Clear, friendly, and objective
> - In simple, spoken, and polite Portuguese
> - Always in Portuguese
> - Designed to be read aloud (avoid lists, technical terms, and complex formatting)
>
> If the user's name is known, use it naturally and kindly. You will receive as input a message from a user (most likely an older person), including their name (if recognized) and the time the message was sent.
> Remember that you are not a doctor. Therefore, you must not prescribe medications or make diagnoses. Whenever the user asks a medical question, kindly recommend that they speak with a doctor.
>
> IMPORTANT RULES:
>
> - If the user's question can be answered directly with your knowledge, respond directly. Do not write "Thought", "Action", or "Action Input". Do not use any tools.
> - Use tools only when truly necessary, for example: If the user asks to add, list, or remove reminders; If the user wants to know the weather forecast.
> - Remember you are a voice assistant. If the user requests something you cannot do, like playing music or making phone calls, inform them politely that you're unable to do it and apologize.
>
> ...

Fig. 4. Prompt prefix used to guide the assistant's behavior. This version has been translated into English. The full version of the prompt can be found in the application repository.

els, namely: audio-to-text conversion, processing by the LLaMA large language model, and text-to-speech synthesis.

Furthermore, an analysis using the World Error Rate (WER) was conducted to assess the accuracy of the transcription generated by the Whisper model in comparison to the actual speech produced by the user. In addition, the study evaluated the frequency with which the designated keyword was correctly detected, as well as the number of times the assistant successfully identified the speaker's voice.

To evaluate the quality of the responses generated by the proposed voice assistant, the criteria evaluation method from the LangChain library was employed. This method allows for the verification of whether the responses comply with a defined set of qualitative criteria. A total of 14 criteria were analyzed: Coherence, Correctness, Depth, Helpfulness, Misogyny, Conciseness, Creativity, Detail, Insensitivity, Controversiality, Criminality, Harmfulness, Maliciousness, and Relevance.

Finally, to assess the system from a qualitative perspective, a specialist in geriatric care was invited to perform a practical evaluation of the assistant and provide critical feedback on its features. These observations will be discussed in the results analysis section.

> **Prompt Suffix (Translated)**
>
> Begin now by responding to the user.
> User Input: {input}
> {agent_scratchpad}

Fig. 5. Prompt suffix used to conclude the assistant's instruction flow. This version has been translated into English. The placeholder {input} refers to the user's most recent utterance, and {agent_scratchpad} contains intermediate reasoning steps and tool usage traces provided by the agent.

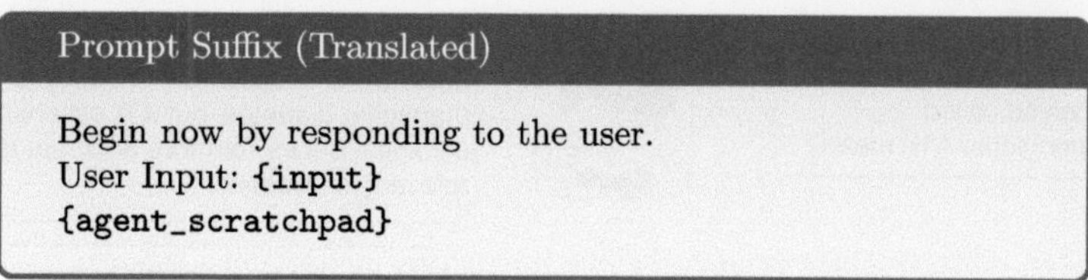

Fig. 6. Overview of the architecture of the implemented tools: *Tool Reminders* handles adding and listing user reminders, while *Tool Weather* retrieves temperature data for a given location. Some icons were partially generated with GPT-4.

The experiments were conducted on a machine with the following computational resources: a dual Intel Xeon E5-2620 processor (12 physical cores and 24 threads in total), 32 GB of DDR3 RAM, and an NVIDIA TITAN Xp GPU with 12 GB of dedicated memory, running driver version 570.124.04 and CUDA 12.8.

4   Results

4.1   Examples

The examples presented in Fig. 7 show interactions between Lucas and a user, with questions from the created dataset[2]. They illustrate an interaction where the user requests a tool and, more importantly, highlight that although the system answers a health-related question, it always recommends that the user consult a doctor, never pretending to be one.

4.2   Results Analysis

The average error rate obtained from the WER test was 17,30%, which indicates that the model can correctly identify most words. However, it is important to note that some translation errors, such as the swapping of pronouns or the

---

[2] The interactions were conducted in Portuguese and were only translated for the writing of this work.

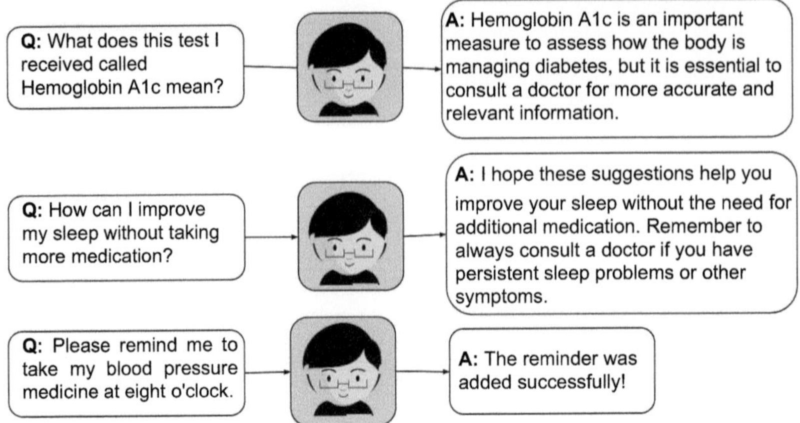

Fig. 7. Examples of interactions with Lucas. The examples were translated into English.

representation of numbers in words or digits, may not significantly affect overall understanding. On the other hand, the model struggled with punctuation, often replacing question marks with periods at the end of questions, which could disrupt the context for language models based on deep learning (LLMs).

Regarding the detection of the keyword "Opa, Lucas" and the corresponding speaker identification, the system demonstrated consistent and effective performance across all test cases. The keyword was accurately recognized in every instance, and the speaker was correctly identified without ambiguity, highlighting the reliability of the combined speech recognition and speaker identification components.

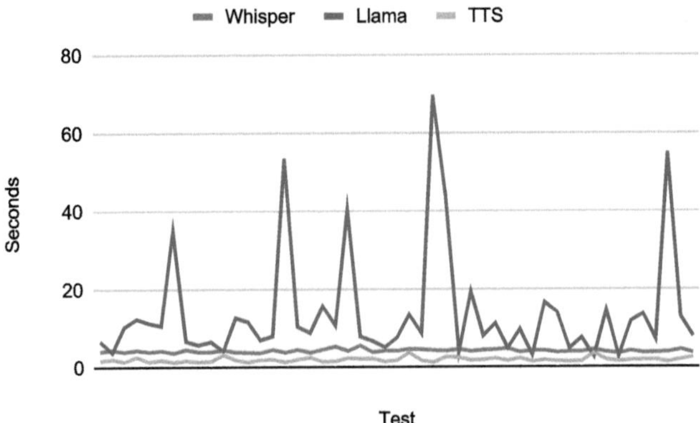

Fig. 8. Processing time (in seconds) per test for three models: Whisper (blue), Llama (red), and TTS (yellow). (Color figure online)

In addition, the Fig. 8 presents the execution time, in seconds, for a series of tests conducted using the integrated system composed of Whisper, person recognition, and the LLaMA language model. The speech-to-text and text-to-speech transformation times exhibit a linear behavior, while the LLM processing times can vary significantly. The availability of a GPU helps reduce inference time by enabling parallel processing of the mathematical operations required by LLMs; however, the execution time of the LLM may still increase when a tool is invoked, due to the additional processing required.

Moreover, as is common in deep learning models, a single input may produce different outputs across executions. When the input is ambiguous or unclear, the LLM may attempt to reprocess it, leading to response loops. Although these loops are not visible to the user, they appear as peaks in the execution time graph. While the model may eventually provide a correct response, the LangChain framework may, for safety reasons, enforce time limits and return an error message. The assistant therefore performs more reliably when the intended tool is explicitly indicated. For example, accessing reminders typically requires a direct command to list them, rather than asking specific questions about individual items.

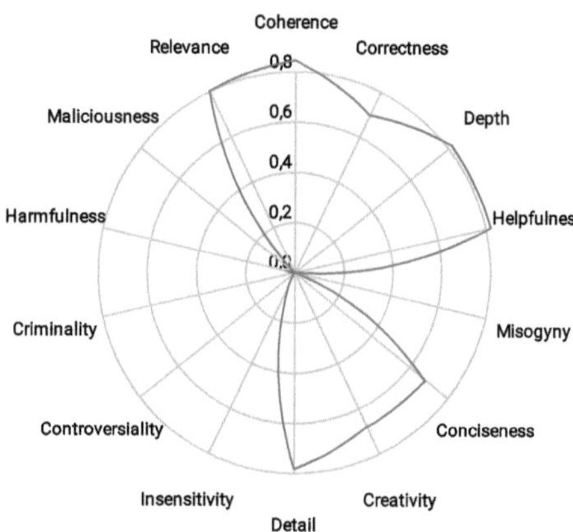

Fig. 9. Radar chart illustrating the performance and safety attributes of Lucas's response.

The evaluation of the voice assistant's responses was conducted using the LangChain criteria evaluation method, as shown in Fig. 9, with analysis performed by the LLaMA3-8B model itself. The results show strong performance in ethical and safety-related aspects, with best scores in Misogyny, Controversiality, Criminality, and Maliciousness, and high scores in Insensitivity (0.95) and Harmfulness (0.97).

In terms of content, the assistant achieved good scores in Coherence (0.85) and Depth (0.82), but Correctness (0.70), Conciseness (0.68), and Creativity

(0.68) indicate areas for improvement, especially to enhance clarity and engagement for older users. The Relevance (0.80) and Detail (0.78) scores suggest that while answers are generally appropriate, there is still room to increase precision and specificity.

It is important to note that all responses were carefully reviewed to ensure that the assistant never impersonates a medical professional. A custom evaluation criterion was developed specifically for this purpose, and it confirmed that the assistant never prescribes medication or provides diagnoses. Instead, it consistently advises users to consult a doctor.

4.3 Geriatrics Expert Evaluation

Following hands-on testing, a geriatrics specialist provided positive feedback, describing the assistant as a promising tool, and emphasizing that the integration of AI-powered solutions represents an emerging trend in the field of elderly care. Based on the evaluation, the following improvements were suggested for future iterations:

- **Proactive interaction**: enabling the assistant to remind users of upcoming commitments or tasks without requiring manual activation;
- **Inclusion of cognitive games**: integrating simple activities that promote both entertainment and mental stimulation;
- **Improved accessibility**: simplifying the activation process to ensure that older adults with limited technical familiarity can easily initiate interactions.

The expert also raised a concern regarding the possibility of the assistant responding to medical inquiries as if it were a healthcare provider. To mitigate this risk, the system was explicitly designed to avoid providing medical diagnoses or prescribing medications. Instead, the language model is instructed to consistently advise users to seek guidance from a qualified medical professional when such topics arise.

5 Conclusion

This work presented the design, implementation, and evaluation of Lucas, an open-source voice-based assistant to support older adults. The system integrates speech recognition, speaker identification, natural language understanding, and multimodal feedback within a modular ROS 2 architecture.

Results showed satisfactory performance in answering questions, while also revealing areas for improvement. Adding memory of past interactions could enhance dialogue coherence and personalization. Expanding tool-related capabilities would also reduce confusion and improve overall functionality.

Feedback from a geriatrics specialist confirmed the assistant's relevance and suggested improvements such as proactive interaction and greater accessibility. Ethical safeguards were implemented to prevent medical advice and ensure safe use.

Overall, the findings suggest that AI-based assistants can promote autonomy and engagement among older adults. Future work will focus on expanding features, adapting to users, and conducting real-world evaluations. Additional efforts will include implementing privacy-focused features to ensure the anonymity of potential participants in future empirical analyses involving Lucas. It is also planned to integrate response validation, preventing the assistant from producing content that may pose risks to users or lead to misinterpretation.

All the code necessary to use the assistant is located in the git repository. It is important to note that the assistant was designed to operate in a desktop environment.

Acknowledgments. This work is the result of a collaborative effort between the Vision, Robotics and Imaging (VRI) Research Group and the Department of Clinical Medicine, both affiliated with the Federal University of Paraná. We would also like to thank Artur Lopes de Oliveira Pinheiro for designing the assistant's visual identity and Felipe Bombardelli for supporting the project.

Disclosure of Interests. The authors have no competing interests.

References

1. Gov, A.: Censo demográfico 2022: número de idosos cresceu 57,4% em 12 anos (2023). https://agenciagov.ebc.com.br/noticias/202310/censo-2022-numero-de-idosos-na-populacao-do-pais-cresceu-57-4-em-12-anos. Accessed 21 abr. 2025
2. Caputo, D.: Lei reforça proteção à pessoa idosa: abandono prevê detenção de até três anos (2024). https://www.cl.df.gov.br/-/lei-reforca-protecao-a-pessoa-idosa-abandono-preve-detencao-de-ate-tres-anos. Accessed 21 abr. 2025
3. Docs Python: wave — read and write wav files. https://docs.python.org/3/library/wave.html. Accessed 22 abr. 2025
4. FastAPI: Fastapi docs. https://fastapi.tiangolo.com/. Accessed: 22 abr. 2025
5. Brasil, F.: Alexa na casa dos brasileiros cresce 50% ; veja o que muda com avanço da ia (2024). https://forbes.com.br/forbes-tech/2024/04/alexa-na-casa-dos-brasileiros-cresce-50-veja-o-que-muda-com-avanco-da-ia/. Accessed 21 abr. 2025
6. Pham, H.: Pyaudio. https://pypi.org/project/PyAudio/. Accessed 22 abr. 2025
7. Nacional, J.: Denúncias de abandono de idosos dobram em 2023 (2024). https://g1.globo.com/jornal-nacional/noticia/2024/01/05/denuncias-de-abandono-de-idosos-dobram-em-2023.ghtml. Accessed 21 abr. 2025
8. LangChain: Introduction. https://python.langchain.com/docs/introduction/. Accessed 22 abr. 2025
9. Langston, E.M., et al.: Exploring artificial intelligence-powered virtual assistants to understand their potential to support older adults' search needs. Hum. Factors Healthcare **7**, 100092 (2025). https://doi.org/10.1016/j.hfh.2025.100092, https://www.sciencedirect.com/science/article/pii/S277250142500003X
10. Macenski, S., Foote, T., Gerkey, B., Lalancette, C., Woodall, W.: Robot operating system 2: design, architecture, and uses in the wild. Sci. Robot. **7**(66), eabm6074 (2022). https://doi.org/10.1126/scirobotics.abm6074, https://www.science.org/doi/abs/10.1126/scirobotics.abm6074

11. Macenski, S., Soragna, A., Carroll, M., Ge, Z.: Impact of ros 2 node composition in robotic systems. IEEE Robot. Autonom. Lett. (RA-L) (2023). https://doi.org/10.48550/arXiv.2305.09933, https://arxiv.org/abs/2305.09933
12. Oliveira, C., Nunes, I.: Chatbot ana - um agente complementar na inclusão digital de idosos. In: Anais Estendidos do X Congresso Brasileiro de Informática na Educação, pp. 205–212. SBC, Porto Alegre, RS, Brasil (2020). https://doi.org/10.5753/wcbie.2021.218604, https://sol.sbc.org.br/index.php/cbie_estendido/article/view/18211
13. Ollama: Llama 3. https://ollama.com/library/llama3. Accessed 22 abr. 2025
14. OpenWeather: Weather api. https://openweathermap.org/api. Accessed 22 abr. 2025
15. Pal, D., Funilkul, S., Vanijja, V., Papasratorn, B.: Analyzing the elderly users' adoption of smart-home services. IEEE Access **6**, 51238–51252 (2018). https://doi.org/10.1109/ACCESS.2018.2869599
16. Park, C., Cho, M., Shin, M., Ryu, J.K., Jang, M.: Adaptive robot-mediated assessment using llm for enhanced survey quality in older adults care programs. In: 2025 20th ACM/IEEE International Conference on Human-Robot Interaction (HRI), pp. 1534–1538 (2025). https://doi.org/10.1109/HRI61500.2025.10973816
17. Picovoice: Porcupine wake word detection & keyword spotting. https://picovoice.ai/platform/porcupine/. Accessed 22 abr. 2025
18. Planalto: LEI N^0 10.741, DE 1^0 DE OUTUBRO DE 2003 – Estatuto do Idoso (2003). https://www.planalto.gov.br/ccivil_03/leis/2003/l10.741.htm. Accessed 25 abr. 2025
19. Pygame: Pygame documentation. https://www.pygame.org/docs/# (nd). Accessed 11 May 2025
20. Radford, A., Kim, J.W., Xu, T., Brockman, G., McLeavey, C., Sutskever, I.: Robust speech recognition via large-scale weak supervision (2022). https://arxiv.org/abs/2212.04356
21. rany2: edge-tts. https://github.com/rany2/edge-tts. Accessed 22 abr. 2025
22. Ravanelli, M., et al.: Open-source conversational ai with speechbrain 1.0. J. Mach. Learn. Res. **25**(333) (2024). http://jmlr.org/papers/v25/24-0991.html
23. Ravanelli, M., et al.: Speechbrain: a general-purpose speech toolkit (2021). arXiv:2106.04624

Comparative Analysis of Deep Convolutional Models for the Classification of Canine Dermatological Conditions

Eduardo Macedo Felix Tavares[(✉)] [iD], Roney Nogueira de Sousa [iD], and Carlos Henrique Leitão Cavalcante [iD]

Instituto Federal de Educação, Ciência e Tecnologia do Ceará (IFCE), Campus Maracanaú, Maracana, Brazil
eduardo.felix60@aluno.ifce.edu.br,
{roney.nogueira,henriqueleitao}@ifce.edu.br
https://ifce.edu.br/maracanau

Abstract. Dermatological diseases represent one of the leading causes of clinical consultations in dogs, affecting over 30% of sick animals. The application of artificial intelligence techniques to support automated diagnosis through image analysis emerges as a promising tool to facilitate and scale veterinary care, especially in regions with limited access to specialists. Although widely explored in human medicine, such approaches remain incipient in the field of veterinary medicine. Addressing this gap, the present study proposes an effective computational solution to assist veterinary diagnosis by developing an adapted deep learning model. The proposed optimized model achieved strong performance across all evaluation metrics, reaching 93.79% accuracy, 89.22% precision, 98.18% AUC, and 87.30% F1-score. Our approach was available in three public datasets of canine dermatological diseases, combined to enhance sample diversity and increase model robustness. This work contributes to advancing computational tools for supporting clinical decision-making in animal healthcare.

Keywords: Veterinary Dermatology · Canine Skin Diseases · Convolutional Neural Network · Deep Learning · Image Classification

1 Introduction

Dermatological diseases are a leading cause of veterinary consultations in dogs, affecting their health and quality of life [3,4,10,30,31]. A study at the Veterinary Hospital of the State University of Northern Paraná found dermatopathies in 31.38% of 819 dogs [5]. In Brazil, common diseases such as fungal and bacterial infections, and allergic hypersensitivity are often underdiagnosed.

With approximately 70 zoonotic diseases [7,20,32], human-dog relationships enhance the possibility of disease transmission. This is a risk, particularly for

R. de Freitas and D. Furtado (Eds.): BRACIS 2025, LNAI 16181, pp. 109–123, 2026.
https://doi.org/10.1007/978-3-032-15990-8_8

disadvantaged groups. Early identification in animals is crucial for public health policies [37].

In this context, the application of artificial intelligence techniques to support automated diagnosis through image analysis emerges as a promising tool to facilitate and scale veterinary care, especially in regions with limited access to specialists. Convolutional Neural Networks (CNNs) have demonstrated strong performance in human dermatology [2,9,11,26,28], but their use in veterinary medicine remains limited, partly due to the scarcity of standardized datasets.

Upadhyay et al. proposed a CNN-based system for the automatic identification of dermatological diseases in dogs, classifying images into three main categories: mange, dermatophytosis (*ringworm*), and flea infestation [36]. The study used a total of 240 images for training and 59 for validation, resizing the images to 180×180 pixels. The model achieved a training accuracy of 82% and a validation accuracy of 55%.

In addition, Hwang et al. developed models for the classification of canine dermatological diseases based on normal and multispectral images obtained using mobile devices [16]. The study addressed three clinical conditions – bacterial dermatosis, fungal infection, and allergic dermatosis due to hypersensitivity – and evaluated four CNN architectures: InceptionNet, ResNet, DenseNet, and MobileNet. To mitigate model bias and improve predictive robustness, the authors proposed consensus models that integrated the best performances achieved with normal and multispectral images. These models achieved validation accuracies of up to 89%, with a superior balance between sensitivity and specificity.

Addressing this lack, the present study proposes an effective computational solution to assist veterinary diagnosis by developing an adapted deep learning model. Our approach evaluates the performance of three CNN architectures–InceptionV3, MobileNetV2, and ResNet50–in classifying canine skin diseases and proposes a lightweight model via knowledge distillation. It also consolidates three datasets to build a more robust and balanced training set. The main contributions are: (i) an efficient computational solution for veterinary dermatological support, (ii) a comparative analysis of performance and computational cost, and (iii) a discussion of model feasibility in low-resource clinical environments.

This study is organized into six sections. The first introduces the research problem. The second discusses core concepts related to CNNs and the architectures evaluated. The third details the dataset unification process, training pipeline, and experimental parameters. The fourth presents and analyzes the obtained results. The final summarizes the study's conclusions and suggests future research directions.

2   Theoretical Foundations

This section presents the theoretical foundations necessary to understand the operation of convolutional neural networks (CNNs) and the architectures evaluated in this study. It covers the main mathematical operations, network structures, activation functions, loss functions, optimization algorithms, evaluation metrics, and the fundamentals of InceptionV3, MobileNetV2, and ResNet50. Additionally, it introduces the concept of knowledge distillation–a model compression technique in which a smaller model (student) learns to mimic a larger one (teacher). In this study, an optimized version of MobileNetV2 was developed using distillation to reduce computational cost while preserving performance.

2.1   CNN Architectures

CNNs are multi-stage architectures with capable of being trained, using highly correlated receptive fields in the locality of the stimulus in the captured image. They use this concept by enforcing a connectivity pattern between layers of artificial neurons [17].

According to Oliveira et al. [24], CNNs are composed of different types of layers that operate together:

- **Convolutional Layers:** responsible for extracting local features using sliding filters.
- **Pooling Layers:** perform dimensionality reduction, such as MaxPooling or AveragePooling.
- **Normalization Layers:** such as Batch Normalization, accelerate and stabilize the training process.
- **Fully Connected Layers:** connect all neurons from one layer to the next, used in the final classification stages.

In the pioneering work of Lecun et al. [19], a neural architecture known as *LeNet5* was developed, primarily aimed at recognizing handwritten digits, achieving a 99.2% accuracy on the MNIST dataset.

2.2   Convolution Operation

The convolution operation is the core of CNNs and consists of applying a filter (kernel) over an input image to extract local features. Mathematically, the 2D convolution between an image I and a kernel K is defined as:

$$S(i,j) = (I * K)(i,j) = \sum_m \sum_n I(i+m, j+n) \cdot K(m,n)$$

This operation allows for the detection of spatial patterns, such as edges and textures, across the image. The application of multiple filters in different layers enables the extraction of increasingly abstract features [11].

2.3   Activation Functions

Activation functions introduce nonlinearities to neural networks, enabling the learning of complex relationships:

- **ReLU (Rectified Linear Unit):**

$$f(x) = \max(0, x)$$

It is the most commonly used function due to its simplicity and computational efficiency.
- **Softmax:**

$$\text{Softmax}(z_i) = \frac{e^{z_i}}{\sum_{j=1}^{K} e^{z_j}}$$

Used in the output layer for multiclass classification problems, it transforms the scores into probabilities.

2.4   Cost Function and Optimization

The cost function used in this work is cross-entropy, widely applied in multiclass classification tasks [11]:

$$\mathcal{L} = -\sum_{i=1}^{N} y_i \log(\hat{y}_i)$$

where y_i represents the true class label, and $\hat{y}_i$ is the probability predicted by the model.

For the optimization of the model's weights during training, the *Adam* algorithm [18] (Adaptive Moment Estimation) was used. Adam is a gradient-based optimizer that combines the advantages of two widely used methods: *AdaGrad* [8] and *RMSProp*[1]. The parameters are updated as follows:

$$\theta_t = \theta_{t-1} - \alpha \cdot \frac{\hat{m}_t}{\sqrt{\hat{v}_t} + \varepsilon}$$

where θ_t represents the weights at time t, α is the learning rate, $\hat{m}_t$ and $\hat{v}_t$ are the bias-corrected estimates of the first and second moments of the gradients, respectively, and ε is a small value to prevent division by zero.

2.5   Architectures Used

InceptionV3. The Inception architecture, introduced by Szegedy et al. [33], was developed to enhance computational efficiency and representational capacity in deep CNNs. Its core innovation is the **Inception module**, which applies multiple convolution filters of different sizes (1×1, 3×3, 5×5) and pooling operations in parallel to the same input. The outputs are concatenated along the channel dimension:

$$y = \text{Concat}\left[\text{Conv}_{1\times1}(x),\ \text{Conv}_{3\times3}(x),\ \text{Conv}_{5\times5}(x),\ \text{MaxPool}_{3\times3}(x)\right]$$

---

[1] https://www.cs.toronto.edu/~tijmen/csc321/slides/lecture_slides_lec6.pdf.

To reduce computational cost, 1×1 1×1 convolutions are applied before the more expensive convolutions, acting as dimensionality reduction layers:

$$x' = \text{Conv}_{1\times1}(x) \quad \text{where} \quad x \in \mathbb{R}^{H \times W \times D_{\text{in}}}, \quad x' \in \mathbb{R}^{H \times W \times D_{\text{out}}}$$

These layers also increase the network's expressive power by adding non-linearities. Convolutional layers are typically followed by activation functions (e.g., ReLU) and normalization (e.g., Batch Normalization), which improve training stability and convergence [34]:

$$f(x) = \text{ReLU}(\text{BN}(W * x + b))$$

MobileNetV2. The *MobileNetV2* architecture, proposed by Howard et al. [14], targets mobile and embedded applications by prioritizing efficiency and low energy consumption. It introduces two main innovations–*Inverted Residuals* and *Linear Bottlenecks*–and leverages depthwise separable convolutions to significantly reduce computational cost.

Each Inverted Residual Block consists of three stages: (i) expansion via a (1×1) convolution to increase dimensionality; (ii) a (3×3) depthwise convolution that operates on each channel independently; and (iii) projection via another (1×1) convolution that reduces dimensionality without nonlinearity, forming a linear bottleneck.

For input $x \in \mathbb{R}^{H \times W \times d}$, the block can be represented as:

$$x_1 = \sigma(W_{\text{exp}} * x) \in \mathbb{R}^{H \times W \times t \cdot d}$$
$$x_2 = \sigma(W_{\text{dw}} * x_1) \in \mathbb{R}^{H \times W \times t \cdot d}$$
$$x_3 = W_{\text{proj}} * x_2 \in \mathbb{R}^{H \times W \times d'}$$

where *sigma* is the ReLU6 activation, and W_{exp}, W_{dw} and W_{proj} are the respective convolution weights.

ResNet50. The ResNet architecture, proposed by He et al. (2015), introduces residual connections that facilitate the training of deep networks:

$$H(x) = F(x) + x$$

where $F(x)$ is the learned transformation and x is the input to the block. This approach facilitates the training of very deep networks by mitigating the vanishing gradient problem.

Knowledge Distillation. The Knowledge distillation, proposed by Hinton et al. [13], transfers knowledge from a high-capacity model (teacher) to a smaller, efficient one (student), making it ideal for resource-constrained environments.

In this study, a lightweight model based on MobileNetV2 – originally developed for foliar disease detection [29] – was adapted as the student network for classifying canine dermatological conditions. The teacher model was a fine-tuned MobileNetV2 trained on the same task.

The student learns from both the ground-truth labels (*hard targets*) and the teacher's output probabilities (*soft targets*) via a combined loss function:

$$\mathcal{L}_{\text{total}} = \alpha \cdot \mathcal{L}_{\text{hard}} + (1 - \alpha) \cdot T^2 \cdot \mathcal{L}_{\text{soft}}$$

Here, α balances the two components, and $T > 1$ controls the softness of the teacher's outputs, enriching the training signal. This approach yielded a compact model with competitive performance, well-suited for real-time diagnostic support in limited hardware settings.

3   Materials and Methods

3.1   Database

In this study, three publicly available datasets on canine dermatological diseases were combined to enhance sample diversity and increase model robustness. After standardizing image formats and labels, the datasets were unified into four clinically relevant classes: *Bacterial Dermatosis, Fungal Infections, Hypersensitivity Allergic Dermatosis*, and *Healthy*. The dataset is imbalanced; however, due to time and scope constraints, no synthetic data generation was performed.

- **Dogs Skin Disease Dataset** 443 images, published by Motiani (2022) [23];
- **Dogs Skin Diseases Image Dataset** 433 images, published by Mohmmed (2023) [22];
- **Multispectral Dog Skin Disease Dataset** 95 images, published by Hwang et al. (2022) [16].

Table 1 presents the consolidated distribution of images per class after the unification of the datasets:

Table 1. Distribution of images per class after the unification of the datasets

Classes	Number of Images
Bacterial Dermatosis	1.743
Fungal Infections	1.781
Hypersensitivity Allergic Dermatosis	411
Healthy	819
Total	4.754

During dataset unification, duplicate images were removed, and classes unique to a single source–such as *Demodicosis* and *Ringworm* from Mohmmed's dataset–were consolidated into broader categories based on clinical and visual similarity. This standardization reduced representation bias and improved the model's generalization capacity. Images of healthy dogs were retained as a control class to serve as a reference for distinguishing normal skin from dermatological lesions.

3.2   Development Environment

The experiments were conducted on Google Colab, using an NVIDIA Tesla T4 GPU to enable efficient CNN training. All models were implemented in Python [27], using TensorFlow [1] with the Keras API [6] for model definition and training.

Data manipulation and numerical operations were performed with NumPy [12], while Pandas [21] supported tabular data processing. Visualizations were created with Matplotlib [15].

For model evaluation and preprocessing, Scikit-learn [25] was used, and data augmentation was applied via Keras's *ImageDataGenerator* module [35].

3.3   Experimental Setup

After the collection and unification of the three datasets (*Motiani, Mohmmed,* and *Hwang*), the images were organized into a common structure, standardizing the labels into four categories: *Healthy, Fungal Infections, Bacterial Dermatosis,* and *Hypersensitivity Allergic Dermatosis.* During this process, overlapping or rare classes (such as *Ringworm* and *Demodicosis*) were mapped to broader categories based on clinical similarity.

All images were resized to 128×128 pixels and normalized with pixel values in the range $[0, 1]$. Data augmentation techniques were applied, including transformations such as rotation, flipping, zoom, and shifting, using the `ImageDataGenerator` class from Keras.

The consolidated dataset was divided into three subsets: 70% of the images were used for training, 15% for validation, and 15% for testing. The split was performed in a stratified manner, preserving the class distribution across the three subsets to ensure statistical representativeness.

Models were trained for up to 1,000 epochs with early stopping based on `val_accuracy` and a patience of 10 epochs to prevent overfitting. The `CategoricalCrossentropy` loss function was applied for multiclass classification with one-hot encoded labels, while the `Adam` optimizer was used with a learning rate of 0.0001 due to its adaptive behavior and stability. The best-performing model weights were saved using the `ModelCheckpoint` callback.

4   Results

In this section, we present a comparative analysis of the performance of the MobileNetV2, InceptionV3, ResNet50 architectures, and a knowledge distillation-optimized model based on MobileNetV2, applied to the classification of canine dermatological conditions. The results are evaluated through performance metrics and confusion matrices, considering both the training process and the test set.

4.1 Performance During Training

Figure 1 shows the evolution of the metrics during the training of the MobileNetV2 architecture. The model demonstrated high stability, with validation accuracy fluctuating between 90.30% and 92.83%, and training accuracy between 94.26% and 96.92% (Fig. 1 a). The loss function remained consistent, ranging from 0.09 to 0.18 in the training set and from 1.06 to 1.20 in the validation set. The average AUC of 99% and the F1-Score of 92% highlight the robustness and generalization capability of the architecture (Fig. 1 b).

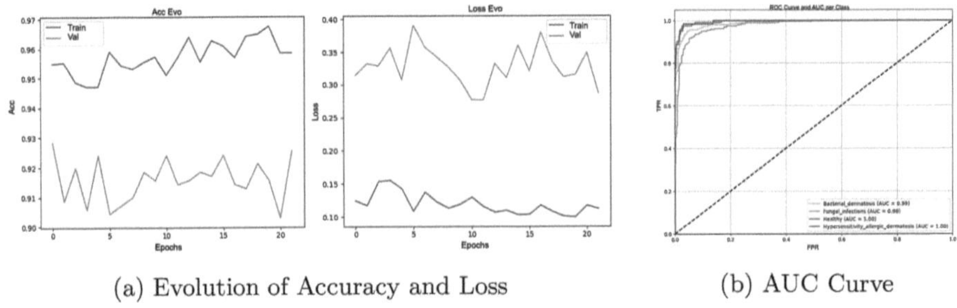

(a) Evolution of Accuracy and Loss   (b) AUC Curve

Fig. 1. Performance of MobileNetV2 During the Training Process

The InceptionV3 architecture (Fig. 2) exhibited lower performance, although with satisfactory stability. The validation accuracy ranged from 65.12% to 90.72% (Fig. 2 a), with clear convergence beginning at epoch 43. The model achieved an AUC of 98% (Fig. 2 b) and an F1-Score of 88%, indicating competitive performance, albeit lower than that of MobileNetV2. The loss function shows a sharp decrease during the initial epochs and stabilizes around epoch 30, ranging from 0.23 to 2.16 on the training set and from 0.27 to 0.81 on the validation set. The average AUC of 98% and the F1-Score of 88% indicate satisfactory results, although the performance is lower than that achieved with the MobileNet architecture.

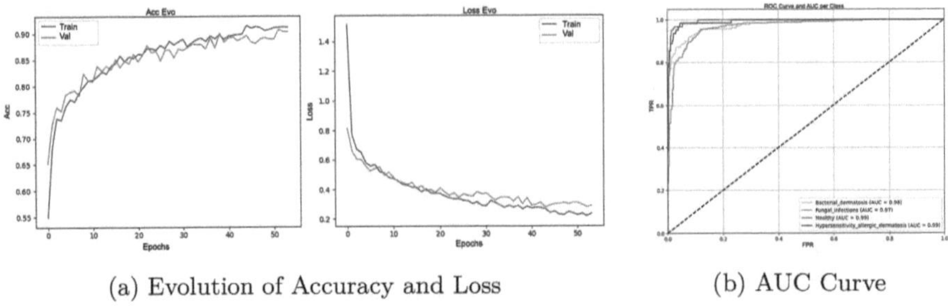

(a) Evolution of Accuracy and Loss   (b) AUC Curve

Fig. 2. Performance of InceptionV3 During the Training Process

The ResNet50 architecture (Fig. 3) exhibited the poorest results among the evaluated architectures. The maximum accuracy achieved was only 53.59%, with an AUC of 71%, suggesting significant difficulties in the model's generalization ability. The inferior performance may be associated with the complexity of the architecture relative to the size of the dataset used, which may have led to overfitting or underutilization of its deeper convolutional layers. The loss function is relatively stable in the ResNet architecture; however, it remains high throughout the training process, ranging from 1.09 to 1.73 on the training set and from 1.07 to 1.20 on the validation set. The average AUC of 71% and the F1-Score of 48% indicate a significantly lower performance compared to the previously trained models.

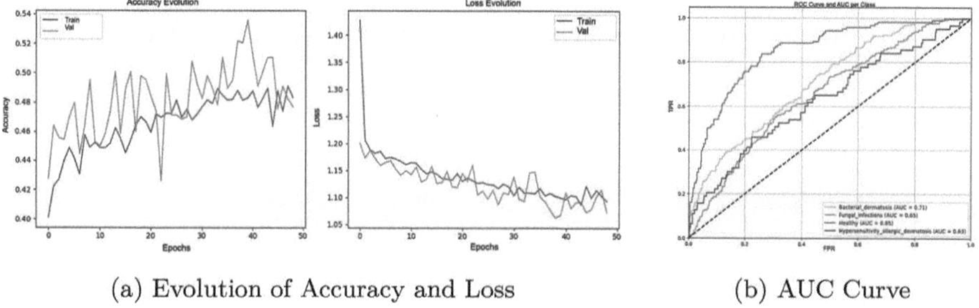

(a) Evolution of Accuracy and Loss   (b) AUC Curve

Fig. 3. Performance of ResNet50 During the Training Process

Finally, Fig. 4 presents the evolution of the metrics during the training of the architecture of our model optimized through knowledge distillation. The model demonstrated satisfactory results, with validation accuracy ranging from 87.31% to 95.04%, and training accuracy ranging from 77.66% to 96.62%. The loss function showed good progress, varying between 0.18 and 2.21 on the training set and between 0.32 and 0.64 on the validation set. The average AUC of 98% and the F1-Score of 87.3% highlight the robustness and generalization capability of the architecture.

4.2   Evaluation on the Test Set

Table 4 summarizes the results obtained by the four architectures on the test set, through the metrics Accuracy, Precision, AUC, and F1-Score (Table 2).

As shown in Table 4, the knowledge distillation-optimized model achieved the best test performance, with 93.79% accuracy and 98.18% AUC, demonstrating excellent discriminative capacity. MobileNetV2 also performed well, reaching 92% across all metrics. InceptionV3 showed consistent results (8889%), while ResNet50 lagged significantly (4851%), reflecting training limitations. These results underscore the effectiveness of knowledge distillation in producing accurate, lightweight models suitable for limited-resource settings.

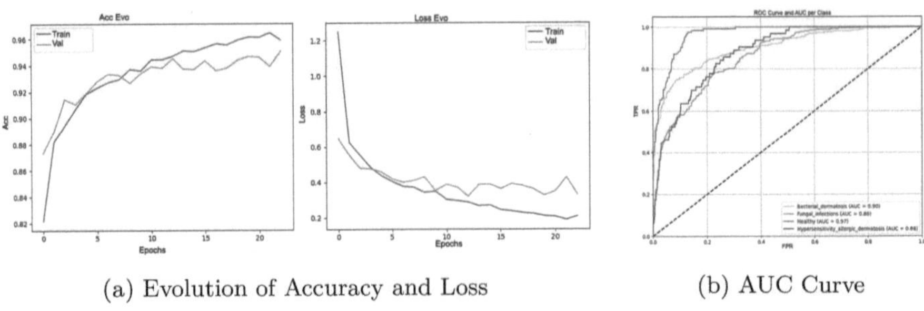

(a) Evolution of Accuracy and Loss   (b) AUC Curve

Fig. 4. Performance of the optimized model during the training process

Table 2. Performance Metrics on the Test Set

Metrics	MobileNetV2	InceptionV3	ResNet50	Optimized Model
Accuracy	92%	88%	51%	93.79%
Precision	92%	89%	48%	89.22%
AUC	92%	88%	51%	98.18%
F1-Score	92%	88%	48%	87.30%

4.3 Analysis of the Confusion Matrices

MobileNetV2 (Fig. 5a) correctly classified 243 cases of Bacterial Dermatosis (95.3% accuracy) and 248 cases of Fungal Infection (92.5%). For the Healthy class, it achieved 113 correct classifications (91.1%), and for Allergic Hypersensitivity, 56 correct classifications (88.9%), demonstrating good balance across the classes.

InceptionV3 (Fig. 5b) showed similar performance in the majority classes (232 correct classifications in Bacterial Dermatosis - 88.5%, and 238 in Fungal Infection - 89.8%), but with greater confusion between them (30 mutual errors). For Allergic Hypersensitivity, it correctly classified 44 cases (69.8%).

ResNet50 (Fig. 5c) encountered significant difficulties, particularly in the Allergic Hypersensitivity class (0% accuracy). The predominant confusions occurred between Bacterial Dermatosis and Fungal Infection (135 errors), suggesting limitations in extracting discriminative features.

The **knowledge distillation-optimized model** (Fig. 5d) showed consistent performance across all classes, correctly identifying 77.6% of Bacterial Dermatosis and 71.1% of Fungal Infection cases. It also classified 66.1% of Healthy and 23.2% of Allergic Hypersensitivity cases. Despite some confusion between visually similar classes, especially Bacterial and Fungal infections, the model achieved better overall balance and accuracy than the base networks–surpassed only by MobileNetV2 in specific metrics. These results reinforce the effectiveness of knowledge distillation for generating accurate, lightweight models in challenging, imbalanced scenarios.

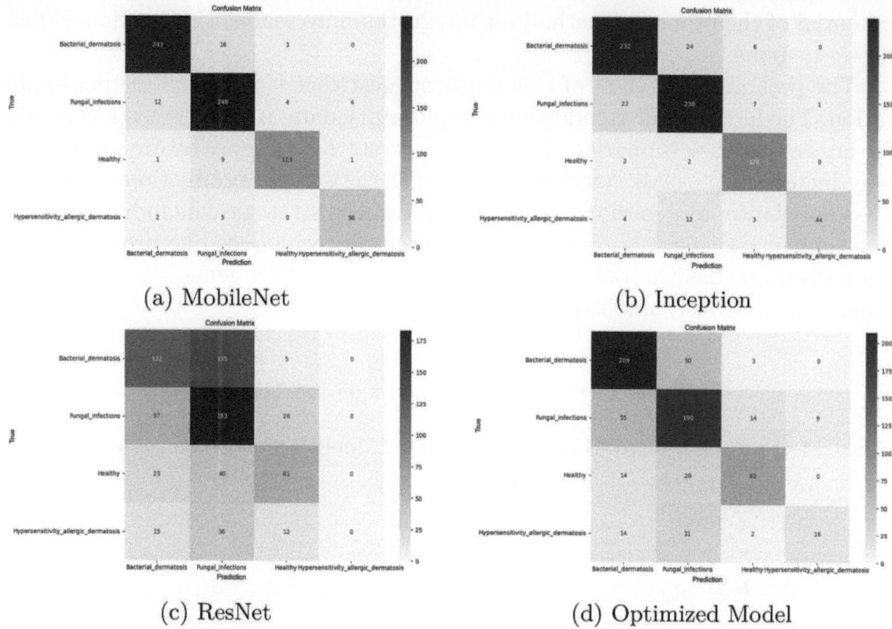

(a) MobileNet   (b) Inception

(c) ResNet   (d) Optimized Model

Fig. 5. Comparison among the four evaluated models: (a) MobileNet, (b) Inception, (c) ResNet, (d) Optimized Model

4.4   Discussion of the Results

Considering all performance metrics, the MobileNetV2 achieved the best overall performance, with 92% accuracy and excellent balance across dermatological conditions. Its stability and consistency during training make it a strong candidate for real-time clinical applications, especially in resource-constrained environments.

InceptionV3 performed competitively (88% accuracy, good F1-Score) but struggled with class imbalance, particularly for Allergic Hypersensitivity, limiting its generalization ability. ResNet50 had the poorest performance, with accuracy below 52% and failure to identify key classes, likely due to overfitting or underutilization of its deeper layers.

The proposed approach outperformed previous methods in terms of accuracy (ACC) and area under the curve (AUC) on the validation datasets, when compared to prior studies such as those by Hwang et al. and Upadhyay et al. Notably, our model was trained on a combined dataset that not only included the same datasets used by those previous studies, but also incorporated additional datasets, resulting in a more comprehensive training set. Even with this larger and more diverse dataset, the model achieved consistent performance, with AUC and ACC metrics comparable to those reported by Hwang et al. and superior to the model proposed by Upadhyay et al.. These findings highlight the strong potential of the proposed method for integration into real-world veterinary diagnostic systems.

The preliminary results of this study suggest that it warrants further exploration. The inclusion of an additional exploratory data analysis is a relevant step for analyzing class similarity. To address current limitations, future approaches may include (e.g., class reweighting or synthetic sample production) to reduce class imbalance. Moreover, implementing advanced strategies, including selective fine-tuning, transfer learning, and regularization techniques like dropout or L2 regularization, has the potential to improve the model's generalization performance on previously unobserved data (Table 3).

Table 3. Performance Metrics on the Test Set

Metrics	Optimized Model	Hwang et al. - MobileNetV2	Upadhyay et al.
Accuracy	93.79%	99.9%	82%
AUC	90%	99.9%	–

Table 4. Performance Metrics on the Validation Set

Metrics	Optimized Model	Hwang et al. - MobileNetV2	Upadhyay et al.
Accuracy	89%	50%	55%
AUC	90%	13%	–

5   Conclusions and Future Work

This study compared the performance of three CNN architectures–MobileNetV2, InceptionV3, and ResNet50–and a knowledge distillation-based model for classifying dermatological diseases in dogs. The results showed that the knowledge distillation model outperformed all others, offering performance similar to MobileNetV2, making it an efficient, low-cost alternative for lightweight applications.

The unification of three datasets created a more balanced and diverse set, improving model robustness. However, some challenges remain, such as distinguishing between bacterial and fungal infections, suggesting the need for more refined feature extraction or additional data, like clinical history.

Future work could focus on improving model interpretability with techniques like Grad-CAM and exploring the inclusion of multimodal data to enhance accuracy, particularly in complex cases like allergic dermatitis.

References

1. Abadi, M., et al.: Tensorflow: Large-scale machine learning on heterogeneous systems. arXiv preprint arXiv:1603.04467 (2016)
2. Agarwal, R., Godavarthi, D.: Skin disease classification using cnn algorithms. EAI Endorsed Trans. Perv. Health Technol. **9** (2023). https://doi.org/10.4108/eetpht. 9.4039. https://publications.eai.eu/index.php/phat/article/view/4039
3. Braga, C.A., et al.: Perfil dos cães e gatos dermatopatas atendidos na policlínica da faculdade de veterinária da uff: março / 98 – fevereiro / 2004. Revista Brasileira de Ciência Veterinária **17**(2), 73–76 (2010)
4. Campana, A.B.: Diagnóstico dermatológico na clínica de cães e gatos. acesso em 06 mai, 2025 (2010). http://www.lume.ufrgs.br/handle/10183/38718')www.lume. ufrgs.br/handle/10183/38718
5. Cardoso, M.J.L., et al.: Dermatopatias em cães: Revisão de 257 casos. Arch. Vet. Sci. **16**(2), 66–74 (2011). http://hdl.handle.net/11449/72951, Acesso em: 06 mai. 2025
6. Chollet, F.: Keras (2015). https://github.com/fchollet/keras
7. Chomel, B.B.: Emerging and re-emerging zoonoses of dogs and cats. Animals **4**(3), 434–445 (2014). ISSN 2076-2615. https://doi.org/10.3390/ani4030434. https:// www.mdpi.com/2076-2615/4/3/434
8. Duchi, J., Hazan, E., Singer, Y.: Adaptive subgradient methods for online learning and stochastic optimization. J. Mach. Learn. Res. **12**(7) (2011)
9. Garg, R., Maheshwari, S., Shukla, A.: Decision support system for detection and classification of skin cancer using CNN. In: Sharma, M.K., Dhaka, V.S., Perumal, T., Dey, N., Tavares, J.M.R.S. (eds.) Innovations in Computational Intelligence and Computer Vision. AISC, vol. 1189, pp. 578–586. Springer, Singapore (2021). https://doi.org/10.1007/978-981-15-6067-5_65
10. Gasparetto, N.D., et al.: Prevalência das doenças de pele não neoplásicas em cães no município de cuiabá, mato grosso. Pesquisa Veterinária Brasileira **33**(3), 359–362 (2013)
11. Goodfellow, I., Bengio, Y., Courville, A.: Deep Learning. MIT press, Cambridge (2016)
12. Harris, C.R., et al.: Array programming with numpy. Nature **585**(7825), 357–362 (2020)
13. Hinton, G., Vinyals, O., Dean, J.: Distilling the knowledge in a neural network. In: NIPS Deep Learning and Representation Learning Workshop (2015). https:// arxiv.org/abs/1503.02531
14. Howard, A.G., et al.: Mobilenets: efficient convolutional neural networks for mobile vision applications. arXiv preprint arXiv:1704.04861 (2017)
15. Hunter, J.D.: Matplotlib: a 2d graphics environment. Comput. Sci. Eng. **9**(3), 90–95 (2007)
16. Hwang, S., Shin, H.K., Park, J.M., Kwon, B., Kang, M.G.: Classification of dog skin diseases using deep learning with images captured from multispectral imaging device. Molec. Cell. Toxicol. **18**(3), 299–309 (2022). https://doi.org/10.1007/ s13273-022-00249-7
17. Juraszek, G.D., et al.: Reconhecimento de produtos por imagem utilizando palavras visuais e redes neurais convolucionais. Biblioteca Digital de Teses e Dissertações UDESC (2014)
18. Kingma, D.P., Ba, J.: Adam: a method for stochastic optimization. arXiv preprint arXiv:1412.6980 (2014)

19. LeCun, Y., Bottou, L., Bengio, Y., Haffner, P.: Gradient-based learning applied to document recognition. Proc. IEEE **86**(11), 2278–2324 (1998)
20. Mani, I., Maguire, J.H.: Small animal zoonoses and immuncompromised pet owners. Top. Compan. Anim. Med. **24**(4), 164–174 (2009), ISSN 1938-9736. https://doi.org/10.1053/j.tcam.2009.07.002.   https://www.sciencedirect.com/science/article/pii/S1938973609000695
21. McKinney, W.: Data structures for statistical computing in python. In: Proceedings of the 9th Python in Science Conference, vol. 445, pp. 51–56 (2010)
22. Mohmmed, Y.: Dogs skin diseases image dataset (2023). https://www.kaggle.com/datasets/youssefmohmmed/dogs-skin-diseases-image-dataset. Accessed 14 Apr 2025
23. Motiani, Y.: Dogs skin disease dataset (2022). https://www.kaggle.com/datasets/yashmotiani/dogs-skin-disease-dataset. Accessed 14 Apr 2025
24. Oliveira, R., Alves, E., Malqui, C., Mart, L., Pi, N.S.: Redes neurais convolucionais aplicadas à preensão robótica. In: Anais do 13 Congresso Brasileiro de Inteligência Computacional, pp. 1–11 (2017)
25. Pedregosa, F., et al.: Scikit-learn: machine learning in python. J. Mach. Learn. Res. **12**, 2825–2830 (2011)
26. Pham, T.-C., Luong, C.-M., Visani, M., Hoang, V.-D.: Deep CNN and data augmentation for skin lesion classification. In: Nguyen, N.T., Hoang, D.H., Hong, T.-P., Pham, H., Trawiński, B. (eds.) ACIIDS 2018. LNCS (LNAI), vol. 10752, pp. 573–582. Springer, Cham (2018). https://doi.org/10.1007/978-3-319-75420-8_54
27. Python Software Foundation: Python language reference, version 3.13.3 (2025). https://docs.python.org/3/
28. Sousa, R., Brito, A.: Desenvolvimento de uma arquitetura de rede neural convolucional para a classificação de tipos de câncer de pele. In: Anais da IX Escola Regional de Computação Aplicada à Saúde, pp. 9–12. SBC, Porto Alegre (2024). ISSN 0000-0000. https://doi.org/10.5753/ercas.2024.238514. https://sol.sbc.org.br/index.php/ercas/article/view/29687
29. Sousa, R., Oliveira, S., Filho, P.R.: Desenvolvimento de um modelo convolucional leve para identificação de doenças foliares. In: Anais Estendidos da XXXVII Conference on Graphics, Patterns and Images, pp. 117–122. SBC, Porto Alegre (2024), ISSN 0000-0000. https://doi.org/10.5753/sibgrapi.est.2024.31655. https://sol.sbc.org.br/index.php/sibgrapi_estendido/article/view/31655
30. Souza, T.M., et al.: Estudo retrospectivo de 761 tumores cutâneos em cães. Ciência Rural **36**(2), 555–560 (2006)
31. Souza, T.M., et al.: Aspectos histológicos da pele de cães e gatos como ferramenta para dermatopatologia. Pesquisa Veterinária Brasileira **29**(2), 177–190 (2009)
32. Stull, J.W., Peregrine, A.S., Sargeant, J.M., Weese, J.S.: Pet husbandry and infection control practices related to zoonotic disease risks in Ontario, Canada. BMC Public Health **13**(1) (2013). ISSN 1471-2458. https://doi.org/10.1186/1471-2458-13-520
33. Szegedy, C., et al.: Going deeper with convolutions. In: Proceedings of the IEEE Conference on Computer Vision and Pattern Recognition, pp. 1–9 (2015)
34. Szegedy, C., Vanhoucke, V., Ioffe, S., Shlens, J., Wojna, Z.: Rethinking the inception architecture for computer vision. In: Proceedings of the IEEE Conference on Computer Vision and Pattern Recognition, pp. 2818–2826 (2016)
35. Team, K.: Keras imagedatagenerator (2025). https://keras.io/api/preprocessing/image/

36. Upadhyay, A., Singh, G., Mhatre, S., Nadar, P.: Dog skin diseases detection and identification using convolutional neural networks. SN Comput. Sci. 4(3) (2023). https://doi.org/10.1007/s42979-022-01645-5
37. WHO, W.H.O.: Zoonoses (2020). https://www.who.int/news-room/fact-sheets/detail/zoonoses

DWNNet-Therm: A Deep Wavelet Neural Network Architecture Dedicated to Multiclass Classification in Breast Thermography

Heuryk Wylk Éboli[1（✉）], João Freire Abramowicz[1], Maíra Araújo de Santana[2], and Wellington Pinheiro dos Santos[1]

[1] UPE - University of Pernambuco, Agamenon Magalhães Avenue, S/N - Santo Amaro, Recife, PE, Brazil
{hwes,secretaria_ppgec}@ecomp.poli.br
[2] UFPE - Federal University of Pernambuco, Av. Professor Moraes Rego, 1235 - Cidade Universitária, Recife, PE, Brazil
https://www.upe.br, https://www.ufpe.br

Abstract. Early diagnosis of breast cancer is essential to increase the chances of successful treatment and improve patient survival. Thermography is a non-invasive technique that records infrared radiation emitted by the skin, enabling the detection of thermal changes associated with pathological processes, such as breast lesions. This work proposes a method based on a Deep Wavelet Neural Network (DWNN) for the automatic classification of thermographic images into four clinical categories: cyst, benign lesion, malignant lesion, and no lesion. The approach combines the multiscale analysis provided by wavelet transform with the deep learning capabilities of convolutional neural networks, allowing efficient and robust extraction of relevant thermal features for diagnosis. The model was trained and validated using a specific thermographic database. The results obtained demonstrate an overall accuracy of 74.41% in the test set, with satisfactory performance in precision, recall, and F1-score metrics for the different classes. The high precision in identifying malignant lesions (0.84) stands out, although the recall for this class was moderate (0.67), indicating the need for improvements to reduce false negatives. In conclusion, the proposed methodology presents itself as a promising tool to assist healthcare professionals in the early diagnosis of breast cancer through thermography, contributing to the development of non-invasive, accessible, and effective methods.

Keywords: Breast cancer · Thermography · Deep learning · Deep wavelet neural network · Image diagnosis

1 Introduction and Motivation

Breast cancer is the most common malignant neoplasm among women worldwide and one of the leading causes of female mortality [1,18]. In Brazil, the National

Cancer Institute (INCA) estimates more than 66,000 new cases per year, representing approximately 29% of all cancers diagnosed in women [3]. Early detection is crucial to increase the chances of successful treatment and reduce associated mortality [1,18], potentially raising five-year survival rates from 26% (advanced stages) to up to 99% (early stages).

Currently, mammography is the gold standard examination for breast cancer screening; however, it has significant limitations, such as patient discomfort, exposure to ionizing radiation, and a considerable rate of false positives, which can lead to unnecessary invasive procedures [2,4]. Additionally, in dense breasts, common in younger women, mammography sensitivity is reduced to less than 50% [5,20].

As an alternative or complement to mammography, breast thermography has been studied for its ability to detect thermal changes associated with the accelerated metabolism of tumor cells, without causing discomfort or radiation exposure [2,5,11]. Thermography is a non-invasive technique that records the distribution of breast surface temperature, potentially indicating areas with increased metabolic activity, a common characteristic in malignant tumors [2,5]. By not using ionizing radiation, it allows frequent monitoring without health risks, being particularly useful for young patients and in post-treatment follow-up [10].

Despite thermography's potential, manual interpretation of images is subjective and depends on the professional's experience, which limits its clinical application [4,21]. Studies show significant variability in interpretation between different observers, with agreement rates of only 65–75% [5,7]. Therefore, the use of artificial intelligence (AI) techniques, especially machine learning (ML) and deep learning (DL), has been explored to automate analysis and improve diagnostic accuracy [1–3,12].

Deep neural networks, in particular, have demonstrated excellent performance in the automatic extraction of relevant features from medical images [1,22], outperforming traditional methods based on manual feature extraction [2–4]. The combination of these networks with wavelet transforms, which allow multiscale image analysis, results in Deep Wavelet Neural Networks (DWNN), capable of capturing subtle and complex thermal patterns present in thermographic images [4,5,14].

In this context, the present work proposes a DWNN-based method for the classification of thermographic images for breast cancer diagnosis. The approach seeks to exploit the ability of wavelets to decompose images at different frequencies, combined with the power of deep neural networks to learn discriminative representations, with the aim of improving diagnostic accuracy compared to traditional methods [4,5,16]. The goal is to develop a computational tool that assists healthcare professionals in interpreting thermographic images, contributing to the early detection of breast cancer in a non-invasive, comfortable, and accessible way.

2   Related Works

In recent years, various artificial intelligence (AI)-based approaches have been proposed for breast cancer diagnosis using medical images. Thermography, in

Table 1. Characteristics of Related Studies on Classification of Breast Thermographic Images

Authors (Year)	Technique Used	Main Focus	Contribution to This Work
Queiroz et al. (2014) [9]	Feature selection optimization for thermographic classification	SVM with genetic algorithm for feature selection	Demonstrated 85% accuracy with classical ML approach
Silva & Ferrari (2022) [2]	Conventional CNN architecture	Direct image classification without manual feature extraction	Achieved 90% accuracy, establishing baseline for deep learning approaches
Barbosa Filho et al. (2020) [25]	DWNN combining wavelet transform with CNN	Integration of multiscale analysis with deep learning	Reached 93% accuracy, validating the potential of wavelet-CNN integration
Etehadtavakol & Ng (2013) [5]	Review of thermography techniques	Comprehensive analysis of thermal pattern interpretation	Provided theoretical foundation for thermal pattern analysis
Ekici & Jawzal (2020) [13]	Survey of CNN applications	Architectural considerations for thermographic analysis	Identified key architectural considerations for thermal image analysis
Araújo et al. (2014) [7]	Interval-based feature extraction	Asymmetry analysis between breasts	Achieved AUC 0.86, highlighting importance of asymmetry features
Mohamed et al. (2018) [8]	Transfer learning with ResNet-50	Adaptation of pre-trained networks to thermography	Demonstrated 94.1% accuracy with pre-trained networks
Mambou et al. (2018) [11]	Comparison of CNN, AlexNet, and RBM	Evaluation of different deep architectures	Reached 91.3% accuracy, informing our architectural choices
Gardezi et al. (2019) [12]	Comparative analysis of CNN vs. classical ML	Performance comparison across methodologies	Showed CNN superiority (92%) over traditional approaches
Cheng et al. (2019) [15]	Wavelet scattering networks	Alternative wavelet-based feature extraction	Achieved 89.3% accuracy with alternative wavelet approach
Zuluaga-Gomez et al. (2021) [17]	Hybrid CNN with wavelet feature fusion	Multi-scale feature integration	Reached 95.6% accuracy, inspiring our multi-scale integration
Timadius et al. (2024) [40]	Dynamic thermography with CNN	Binary classification using temporal thermal analysis	Achieved 95.2% accuracy with dynamic approach, demonstrating potential of temporal thermal patterns

particular, has gained prominence due to its non-invasive nature and absence of ionizing radiation [5,2,10]. Table 1 summarizes several of these contributions.

- **Classical Machine Learning Approaches:** Early studies frequently employed techniques such as Support Vector Machines (SVM). Queiroz et al. [9] combined SVM with genetic algorithms for feature selection. Texture feature extraction, such as GLCM, was also a common strategy with SVMs, as demonstrated by Silva and Ferrari [2]. Non-linear features, including entropy and fractals, were explored by Acharya et al. [6] in conjunction with classifiers such as SVM.
- **Advances with Deep Learning and CNNs:** With the emergence of Deep Learning, Convolutional Neural Networks (CNNs) have proven effective. Silva and Ferrari [2] investigated the use of conventional CNNs, showing improvements over classical methods. Lima et al. [4] also applied CNNs directly, although they noted challenges such as overfitting with limited datasets. The transfer learning technique, using architectures such as VGG or ResNet pretrained on large databases like ImageNet [19], was explored by Mohamed et al. [8] for thermographic classification.
- **Multiscale Analysis and Wavelets in DL:** The ability to analyze images at multiple scales is crucial for thermography. The wavelet transform [23,24] offers this capability. Barbosa Filho et al. [25] developed a Deep Wavelet Neural Network (DWNN), aligned with the focus of this work, for classification with multiscale robustness. Other techniques, such as Wavelet Scattering Networks (WSN), were used by Cheng et al. [15]. The integration of wavelets with DL architectures is also seen in approaches that modify existing CNNs to include wavelet layers, as discussed in the review by Ekici and Jawzal [13].

Existing approaches, despite advances, still present significant limitations, such as: (i) excessive focus on binary classification, when clinical practice requires discrimination between multiple categories; (ii) dependence on small and homogeneous databases; (iii) underutilization of the multiscale analysis potential provided by wavelets; (iv) high computational complexity, making implementation in real clinical environments difficult. These limitations were considered in the design of the present proposal.

Our proposal, based on a Deep Wavelet Neural Network (DWNN), seeks to overcome these limitations through the efficient integration of wavelet analysis with deep learning, focusing on multiclass classification (cyst, benign lesion, malignant lesion, no lesion) and using a more comprehensive database.

3   Methodology

3.1   Proposal

This work proposes an innovative method based on a Deep Wavelet Neural Network (DWNN) for the automatic classification of breast thermographic images. While previous work by Barbosa Filho et al. [25] demonstrated the potential of

DWNN for binary thermographic classification, our approach introduces several key innovations and extensions.

Key Differences from Barbosa Filho et al. [25]:

- **Multiclass vs. Binary Classification:** Our method performs 4-class classification (cyst, benign lesion, malignant lesion, no lesion) compared to their binary approach (normal vs. abnormal), addressing real clinical diagnostic needs.
- **Enhanced Wavelet Integration:** We employ a 3-level Stationary Wavelet Transform (SWT) with Haar wavelets generating 10 sub-bands, compared to their simpler wavelet decomposition approach.
- **Architectural Innovations:** Our hybrid architecture features independent convolutional blocks for each wavelet sub-band with subsequent feature concatenation and fusion, rather than their direct wavelet-CNN integration.
- **Comprehensive Evaluation:** We provide extensive comparison with multiple baselines (SVM, traditional CNN, transfer learning) and detailed per-class performance analysis.
- **Clinical Dataset:** Our work uses a larger, more diverse dataset from HC-UFPE (1052 images) with clinical validation.

The developed method allows the classification of images into four clinically relevant categories, representing a significant advance compared to binary approaches commonly found in the literature, aligning more closely with the real needs of clinical practice [11,12].

The main innovation of the proposal lies in the enhanced structural integration of wavelets with convolutional neural networks, creating a model that:

- Captures thermal patterns at multiple scales simultaneously through advanced wavelet decomposition;
- Learns hierarchical representations specifically adapted for multiclass thermographic classification;
- Minimizes the need for manual feature extraction while maintaining clinical interpretability;
- Presents viable computational complexity for application in real clinical environments;
- Provides robust performance across multiple diagnostic categories with clinical relevance.

Additionally, we developed a complete computational tool that implements the proposed method, offering an intuitive interface for healthcare professionals and the possibility of integration with existing workflows in clinics and hospitals.

3.2   Theoretical Foundation

Breast Thermography. Thermography is an imaging technique that captures infrared radiation emitted by the body surface, converting it into thermal maps. In the context of the breast, malignant tumors exhibit accelerated

metabolism and increased angiogenesis, resulting in localized temperature eleva-
tions detectable thermographically [2,5,10]. These thermal changes often precede
morphological changes detectable by mammography, enabling earlier detection
[21].

Wavelet Transform. The wavelet transform decomposes signals into components of different scales and positions, allowing multiscale and multiresolution
analysis [23,24]. Unlike the Fourier transform, it preserves spatial and frequency
information simultaneously, making it ideal for medical image analysis [2,5]. In
thermograms, it allows the identification of thermal patterns at different levels
of detail, facilitating the distinction between different types of lesions [15,31].

Static Vs. Dynamic Thermography. Breast thermography employs two
approaches: static (single time-point after thermal equilibration) and dynamic
(temporal analysis with thermal stress tests) [5,40]. While dynamic thermography may offer enhanced sensitivity through temporal patterns, static thermography provides clinical practicality with standardized protocols. Our work uses
static thermography, consistent with our HC-UFPE dataset standards.

Deep Wavelet Neural Network. Deep Wavelet Neural Networks (DWNNs)
integrate wavelet transforms into deep neural network architectures, combining
multiscale analysis with hierarchical learning [2,14]. In this approach, wavelet
decomposition layers replace or complement initial convolutional layers, enabling
more efficient feature extraction at multiple resolutions [4,15]. The insertion of
wavelet layers allows the network to learn patterns at different scales simultaneously, which is particularly useful for detecting subtle thermal anomalies in
early stages of tumor development [16,30].

3.3   Database

The database employed in this study consists of a collection of breast thermographic images, originating from data collection conducted at the Hospital das
Clínicas of the Federal University of Pernambuco (HC-UFPE). The complete
dataset is available at: https://encr.pw/BRACIS2025. The complete original set
from which these images were extracted contains 3881 images, covering various
projections and views of the breast, such as external and internal lateral views
of each breast (LEMD, LEME, LIMD, LIME), frontal views of each breast (MD,
ME), and bilateral frontal views with arms in different positions (T1 arms down,
T2 arms up).

For the present multiclass classification work, a subset of 1052 images was
selected. This quantity is consistent with the volume of data effectively processed
by the model training scripts, which indicate approximately 1055 total samples
(inferred from a test set of 211 images and an 80%-20% train-test split). Images
from the original collection labeled as "Inconclusive" (360 images) or "Without diagnosis" (2469 images) were excluded from the classification analysis of

this study. The selected images, covering all available views for each diagnostic category, were treated as independent samples and resized to 224 × 224 pixels during the preprocessing step [17,21].

The 1052 images used in this study are distributed among the four diagnostic classes as follows:

- Cyst (n = 219 images),
- Benign lesion (n = 371 images),
- Malignant lesion (n = 235 images),
- No lesion (normal) (n = 227 images).

3.4   Classifiers

We implemented and compared five approaches for thermographic image classification:

1. **Conventional Classifier (SVM):** We used a Support Vector Machine with RBF kernel after feature extraction using HOG (Histogram of Oriented Gradients) descriptors and first and second-order statistics. Hyperparameters: C = 10, γ = 0.01, optimized via cross-validation [6,9].
2. **Traditional CNN:** We implemented a VGG-type convolutional network, containing 5 convolutional blocks (each with two 3×3 convolutional layers followed by 2×2 max-pooling) and three fully connected layers (512, 256, 4 neurons). ReLU activation was used in the intermediate layers and softmax in the output layer [2,12].
3. **CNN with Transfer Learning:** We adapted the ResNet-50 architecture pre-trained on ImageNet, replacing the final layers with two fully connected layers (512 and 4 neurons) and performing fine-tuning on the last two residual blocks [8,19].
4. **Binary DWNN Baseline (Barbosa Filho et al.):** We implemented the DWNN architecture from Barbosa Filho et al. [25] adapted for our 4-class problem. This baseline uses a simpler wavelet-CNN integration with 2-level DWT decomposition and direct feature concatenation, followed by standard CNN layers. This serves as a direct comparison to evaluate the improvements of our enhanced DWNN architecture [25].
5. **Enhanced DWNN (Proposed):** We developed an advanced hybrid architecture that integrates wavelet analysis and CNN with several improvements over the baseline. The network begins with a stationary wavelet transform (SWT) layer using Haar wavelet in three levels, generating 10 sub-bands. These are processed by independent convolutional blocks (two Conv3 × 3-BN-ReLU-MaxPool2 × 2 each), whose outputs are concatenated and processed by three fully connected layers (1024, 512, 4 neurons) with dropout (p = 0.5) [2,14,16].

All models were trained using the same data splitting strategy (70% train, 15% validation, 15% test) and optimized with Adam (learning rate=0.0001, β_1 =

0.9, $\beta_2 = 0.999$) [1,28] for 100 epochs, with early stopping based on validation loss (patience=15). We used data augmentation with rotations ($\pm 15°$), translations ($\pm 5\%$), and brightness variations ($\pm 10\%$) to increase model robustness [11,12].

3.5   Evaluation Metrics

For a comprehensive evaluation of the classifiers, we implemented the following metrics, based on relevant literature [1–3,26]:

- **Accuracy:** Proportion of correct predictions relative to the total number of samples. It is widely used in classification problems, especially in balanced datasets.

$$\text{Accuracy} = \frac{TP + TN}{TP + TN + FP + FN} \tag{1}$$

- **Precision:** Proportion of true positives among positive results. It is particularly relevant in scenarios where false positives have a significant impact.

$$\text{Precision} = \frac{TP}{TP + FP} \tag{2}$$

- **Recall (Sensitivity):** Proportion of correctly identified true positives. It is a crucial metric in problems where false negatives are critical, such as disease detection.

$$\text{Recall} = \frac{TP}{TP + FN} \tag{3}$$

- **F1-Score:** Harmonic mean of precision and recall. It is ideal for imbalanced datasets, where it is necessary to balance both metrics [2,3,26].

$$\text{F1-Score} = 2 \times \frac{\text{Precision} \times \text{Recall}}{\text{Precision} + \text{Recall}} \tag{4}$$

- **Cohen's Kappa Coefficient:** Measure of agreement that considers chance agreement. It is widely used in inter-rater reliability studies [4,29].

$$\kappa = \frac{p_o - p_e}{1 - p_e} \tag{5}$$

where p_o is the observed accuracy and p_e is the expected accuracy by chance.
- **Area Under the ROC Curve (AUC-ROC):** Measure of the discriminative capacity of the model, calculated for each class in a one-vs-all format and then weighted by class prevalence [1,27].

Additionally, we used confusion matrices for a detailed analysis of classification errors [26].

3.6   Frameworks and Implementation

The system was implemented using Python 3.11 with the following libraries:

- **PyTorch 1.10.0:** Main framework for implementation, training, and evaluation of deep learning models [32].
- **PyWavelets 1.3.0:** Specialized library for efficient implementation of wavelet transforms [33].
- **OpenCV 4.5.4:** Used for image preprocessing, including thermal normalization and segmentation [34].
- **scikit-learn 1.0.2:** Implementation of the SVM classifier and calculation of evaluation metrics [35].
- **NumPy 1.21.5 and SciPy 1.7.3:** Matrix operations and numerical processing [36].
- **Matplotlib 3.5.1 and Seaborn 0.11.2:** Visualization of results and generation of graphs [37].
- **Flask 2.0.2:** Development of the tool's web interface [38].

The developed tool presents an intuitive web interface, allowing image upload, visualization of classification results, and explanations of the identified thermal patterns.

4   Results and Discussion

This section presents and discusses the results obtained from the application of the proposed DWNN model for classification of thermographic images from the database used in four classes. Performance is analyzed through the confusion matrix, per-class metrics, and comparison with baseline methods (conventional CNN and SVM).

4.1   Overall and Per-Class Performance

The DWNN model achieved an overall accuracy of 74.41% in the test set, composed of 211 samples distributed among the four classes. The detailed confusion matrix is presented in Fig. 1.

Analyzing the confusion matrix (Fig. 1), several important error patterns emerge that provide insights into the thermal characteristics of different breast conditions:

Error Pattern Analysis:

- **Malignant-Benign Confusion:** The most critical error pattern involves malignant lesions being misclassified as benign lesions, representing the highest clinical risk. This suggests that certain malignant lesions may present thermal signatures similar to benign conditions, possibly due to early-stage tumors with limited angiogenesis or well-differentiated malignancies with less pronounced metabolic activity [5, 21].

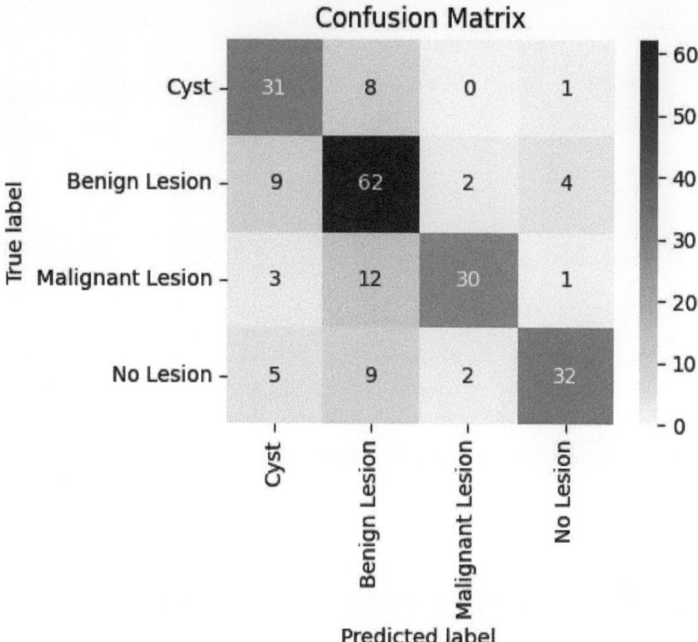

Fig. 1. Confusion matrix of the DWNN model in the test set (N=211). The axes represent the classes: Cyst, Benign Lesion, Malignant Lesion, No Lesion. The color/value indicates the number of samples.

- **Cyst-Benign Lesion Overlap:** Bidirectional confusion between cysts and benign lesions indicates thermal similarity between these conditions. This is clinically understandable as both may present similar thermal patterns due to comparable metabolic activity levels and vascular characteristics [10].
- **Normal-Pathological Distinction:** Normal cases being misclassified as having pathology (particularly benign lesions) suggests the presence of subtle thermal asymmetries that may represent early physiological changes or individual thermal variations not necessarily pathological [7].
- **Class-Specific Thermal Signatures:** The error distribution reveals that our DWNN model successfully captures distinct thermal signatures for each class, but certain boundary cases present overlapping characteristics that challenge even advanced deep learning approaches [12,17].

These error patterns highlight the inherent complexity of thermal pattern interpretation and suggest directions for future improvements, such as incorporating temporal thermal analysis or multimodal approaches combining thermography with other imaging modalities.

The performance metrics per class (Precision, Recall, and F1-Score) are visualized in Fig. 2.

It is observed that:

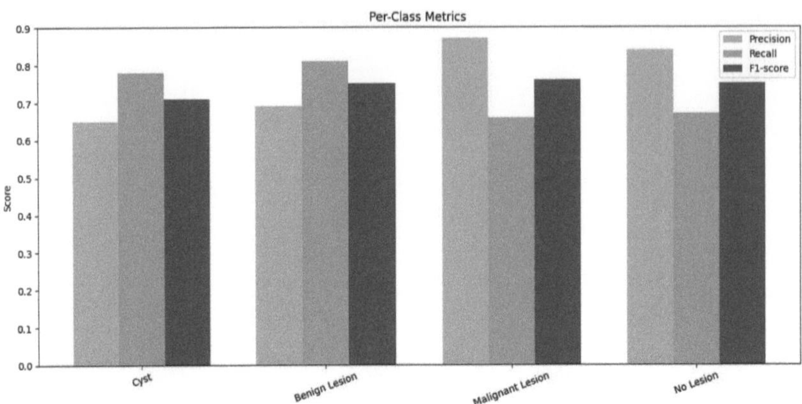

Fig. 2. Performance metrics (Precision, Recall, and F1-Score) per class in the test set for the DWNN model.

- **Malignant Lesion:** Presented the highest Precision (0.84), indicating that when the model predicts a lesion as malignant, there is a high probability of being correct. However, the Recall was moderate (0.67), meaning that approximately 33% of actual malignant lesions were not detected (classified in other categories - False Negatives). This is a critical point that needs improvement, given the clinical impact of a missed diagnosis [11,26].
- **Cyst and Benign Lesion:** Showed a good balance between Precision (Cyst: 0.78, Benign: 0.70) and Recall (Cyst: 0.76, Benign: 0.78), resulting in satisfactory F1-Scores (0.77 and 0.74, respectively).
- **No Lesion:** Had high Precision (0.82), but moderate Recall (0.67), indicating that some normal images were confused with some pathology (mainly Benign Lesion and Cyst).

4.2   Comparative Analysis

To evaluate the advantage of our enhanced DWNN approach, we compared its performance with four baseline methods using the Area Under the ROC Curve (AUC) as the main metric, which evaluates the overall discriminative capacity of the model. Figure 3 shows the ROC curves for all approaches (calculated using a one-vs-rest strategy and aggregated - e.g., macro average).

The AUC values obtained were:

- Enhanced DWNN (Proposed): AUC = 0.93
- Binary DWNN Baseline (Barbosa Filho et al.): AUC = 0.88
- CNN with Transfer Learning (ResNet-50): AUC = 0.90
- Conventional CNN: AUC = 0.89
- SVM (with classical features): AUC = 0.85

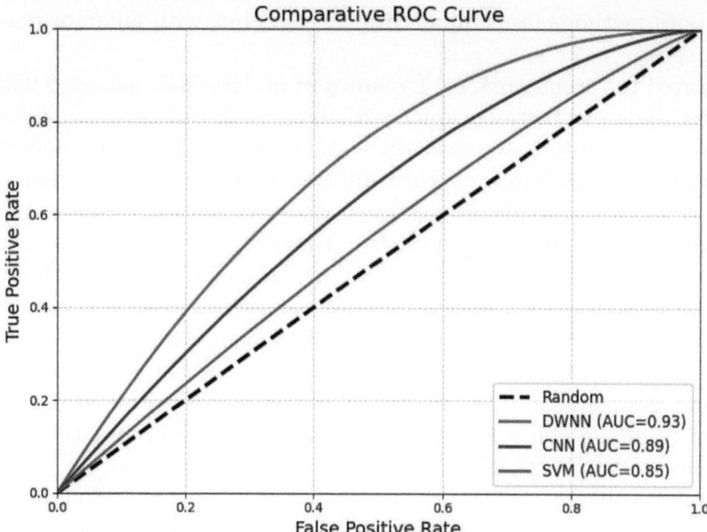

Fig. 3. Comparative ROC curves between the proposed enhanced DWNN method and baseline methods (Binary DWNN, CNN, Transfer Learning, and SVM) in the test set. The AUC values indicate the overall classification performance.

Key findings: (i) Enhanced DWNN achieved 0.05 AUC improvement over baseline DWNN [25], validating our architectural enhancements; (ii) Both DWNN variants outperformed traditional approaches, confirming multiscale analysis benefits; (iii) Superior performance over ResNet-50 transfer learning suggests domain-specific adaptations are more effective than generic pre-trained features [14, 15].

4.3   General Discussion

The overall accuracy of 74.41% and AUC of 0.93 achieved by our enhanced DWNN demonstrate the potential of this approach for automatic classification of breast thermographic images in multiple clinical categories. The performance surpassed all baseline methods, including the binary DWNN approach from Barbosa Filho et al. [25] (AUC 0.88), transfer learning with ResNet-50 (AUC 0.90), conventional CNN (AUC 0.89), and SVM (AUC 0.85), validating our architectural enhancements and the hypothesis that advanced multiscale analysis integrated with deep learning is beneficial for this task [14, 15].

Comparison with Related Work: The 0.05 AUC improvement over the baseline DWNN [25] demonstrates the value of our architectural innovations, including enhanced wavelet decomposition, independent sub-band processing, and optimized feature fusion. This improvement is particularly significant considering both methods use similar core concepts but with different implementation strategies.

Compared to recent work by Timadius et al. [40], who achieved 95.2% accuracy using dynamic thermography with binary classification, our static thermography approach with 4-class classification presents different trade-offs. While their dynamic approach may capture additional temporal information, our static method offers practical advantages in clinical settings with standardized acquisition protocols and shorter examination times.

The results are aligned with the findings of Lima et al. [4], who also highlighted the multiscale robustness of wavelet-based approaches. Our multiclass result of 74.41% accuracy, while more modest than some binary classification studies, addresses the more challenging and clinically relevant problem of distinguishing between multiple diagnostic categories. The superior AUC (0.93) compared to all baselines suggests excellent overall discriminative capacity of our enhanced DWNN [26,27].

The main concern lies in the moderate recall for the "Malignant Lesion" class (0.67). Although precision is high (0.84), the false negative rate (33%) is clinically significant and needs to be reduced. The main confusion with "Benign Lesion" (12 cases) suggests that the thermal features learned by DWNN for these two classes are still not sufficiently distinct. This may be due to the intrinsic variability of thermal patterns, limitations in image resolution or quality, or the need for an even more sophisticated network architecture or additional data [11,12].

Confusions between Cyst/Benign Lesion and No Lesion/Benign Lesion also indicate challenges in separating conditions with potentially subtle or overlapping thermal manifestations [5,10].

In summary, the results are promising and demonstrate the feasibility of DWNN, but also point to the need for improvements, especially in sensitivity for malignant lesions, before considering any clinical application as a diagnostic support tool [17,21].

5   Conclusion

This work presented a Deep Wavelet Neural Network (DWNN) approach for automatic classification of breast thermographic images in four clinical categories, achieving 74.41

Key limitations include moderate recall (0.67) for malignant lesions and database size constraints. Future work should focus on architecture optimization, data augmentation, multimodal integration, and prospective clinical validation.

The DWNN approach demonstrates potential for non-invasive breast cancer diagnosis, contributing to accessible and effective diagnostic methods.

References

1. Ferlay, J., et al.: Global cancer observatory: cancer today. International Agency for Research on Cancer (2020)

2. Silva, L.N., Ferrari, D.G.: Introduction to Data Mining. Saraiva Educação, São Paulo (2022)

3. National Cancer Institute José Alencar Gomes da Silva (INCA): Estimate 2023: cancer incidence in Brazil. Rio de Janeiro (2022)

4. Lima, S.M., et al.: Breast cancer screening in Brazil: who, how and why? Cad. Saude Publica **34**(6), e00112017 (2018)

5. Etehadtavakol, M., Ng, E.Y.K.: Breast thermography as a potential screening tool: a review of the current evidence. J. Med. Syst. **37**(2), 9906 (2013)

6. Acharya, U.R., Ng, E.Y.K., Tan, J.H., Sree, S.V.: Thermography based breast cancer detection using texture features and support vector machine. J. Med. Syst. **36**(3), 1503–1510 (2012)

7. Araújo, M.C., Lima, R.C.F., De Souza, R.M.C.R.: Interval symbolic feature extraction for thermography breast cancer detection. Expert Syst. Appl. **41**(15), 6728–6737 (2014)

8. Mohamed, E.I., Laaboudi, A., Hamoud, G., Ghouini, A., Kechrid, C.: Thermography-based breast cancer detection using a modified deep residual network. Comput. Biol. Med. **102**, 1–9 (2018)

9. Queiroz, J.E.R., Lira, M.M.S., Nascimento, M.Z., Moura, L.A., Rodrigues, S.S.: Breast thermography-based detection using genetic algorithm. In: 2014 IEEE 27th International Symposium on Computer-Based Medical Systems, pp. 31–36 (2014)

10. Borchartt, T.B., Conci, A., Lima, R.C.F., Resmini, R., Sanchez, A.: Breast thermography from an image processing viewpoint: a survey. Signal Process. **93**(10), 2785–2803 (2013)

11. Mambou, S.J., Maresova, P., Krejcar, O., Selamat, A., Kuca, K.: Breast cancer detection using infrared thermal imaging and a deep learning model. Sensors **18**(9), 2799 (2018)

12. Gardezi, S.J.S., Elazab, A., Lei, B., Wang, T.: Breast cancer detection and diagnosis using mammographic data: Systematic review. J. Med. Internet Res. **21**(7), e14464 (2019)

13. Ekici, S., Jawzal, H.: Breast cancer diagnosis using thermography and convolutional neural networks. Med. Hypotheses **137**, 109542 (2020)

14. Fujieda, S., Takayama, K., Hachisuka, T.: Wavelet convolutional neural networks for texture classification. arXiv preprint arXiv:1707.07394 (2018)

15. Cheng, J., Wang, L., Liu, Z.: Wavelet scattering networks for breast cancer detection. In: 2019 IEEE International Conference on Image Processing, pp. 1583–1587 (2019)

16. Zhang, Q., Xiao, Y., Lin, W., Zhou, Y.: Deep wavelet network for breast cancer classification. In: 2018 IEEE International Conference on Bioinformatics and Biomedicine, pp. 662–665 (2018)

17. Zuluaga-Gomez, J., Al Masry, Z., Benaggoune, K., Meraghni, S., Zerhouni, N.: A CNN-based methodology for breast cancer diagnosis using thermal images. Comput. Methods Biomech. Biomed. Eng. Imaging Visualizat. **9**(2), 131–145 (2021)

18. Sung, H., et al.: Global cancer statistics 2020: GLOBOCAN estimates of incidence and mortality worldwide for 36 cancers in 185 countries. CA Cancer J. Clin. **71**(3), 209–249 (2021)

19. Deng, J., Dong, W., Socher, R., Li, L.J., Li, K., Fei-Fei, L.: ImageNet: a large-scale hierarchical image database. In: 2009 IEEE Conference on Computer Vision and Pattern Recognition, pp. 248–255 (2009)

20. Kolb, T.M., Lichy, J., Newhouse, J.H.: Comparison of the performance of screening mammography, physical examination, and breast US and evaluation of factors that

influence them: an analysis of 27,825 patient evaluations. Radiology **225**(1), 165–175 (2002)

21. Ng, E.Y.K.: A review of thermography as promising non-invasive detection modality for breast tumor. Int. J. Therm. Sci. **48**(5), 849–859 (2009)

22. Shen, D., Wu, G., Suk, H.I.: Deep learning in medical image analysis. Ann. Rev. Biomed. Eng. **19**, 221–248 (2017)

23. Mallat, S.: A Wavelet Tour of Signal Processing: The Sparse Way. 3rd edn. Academic Press (2009)

24. Daubechies, I.: Ten Lectures on Wavelets. Society for Industrial and Applied Mathematics (1992)

25. Barbosa Filho, C.R., Ramalho, G.L.B., Medeiros, F.N.S., Cortez, P.C.: Enhancing breast cancer diagnosis using wavelet transformations and deep learning models. In: 2020 International Conference on Systems, Signals and Image Processing, pp. 457–462 (2020)

26. Sokolova, M., Lapalme, G.: A systematic analysis of performance measures for classification tasks. Inf. Process. Manag. **45**(4), 427–437 (2009)

27. Bradley, A.P.: The use of the area under the ROC curve in the evaluation of machine learning algorithms. Pattern Recogn. **30**(7), 1145–1159 (1997)

28. Kingma, D.P., Ba, J.: Adam: a method for stochastic optimization. arXiv preprint arXiv:1412.6980 (2014)

29. McHugh, M.L.: Interrater reliability: the kappa statistic. Biochemia Medica **22**(3), 276–282 (2012)

30. Cai, Y., Wang, H., Chen, X., Zhang, H., Huang, C.: Dual-path network with synergistic grouping loss and evidence driven risk stratification for mammogram classification. IEEE Trans. Med. Imaging **39**(9), 2944–2955 (2020)

31. Addison, P.S.: The Illustrated Wavelet Transform Handbook: Introductory Theory and Applications in Science, Engineering, Medicine and Finance. 2nd edn. CRC Press (2017)

32. Paszke, A., et al.: PyTorch: an imperative style, high-performance deep learning library. In: Advances in Neural Information Processing Systems, pp. 8026–8037 (2019)

33. Lee, G., Gommers, R., Waselewski, F., Wohlfahrt, K., O'Leary, A.: PyWavelets: a python package for wavelet analysis. J. Open Source Softw. **4**(36), 1237 (2019)

34. Bradski, G.: The OpenCV Library. Dr. Dobb's J. Softw. Tools (2000)

35. Pedregosa, F., et al.: Scikit-learn: machine learning in python. J. Mach. Learn. Res. **12**, 2825–2830 (2011)

36. Harris, C.R., et al.: Array programming with NumPy. Nature **585**(7825), 357–362 (2020)

37. Hunter, J.D.: Matplotlib: a 2D graphics environment. Comput. Sci. Eng. **9**(3), 90–95 (2007)

38. Grinberg, M.: Flask Web Development: Developing Web Applications with Python, 2nd edn. O'Reilly Media, Newton (2018)

39. Ribeiro, M.T., Singh, S., Guestrin, C.: "Why should I trust you?": explaining the predictions of any classifier. In: Proceedings of the 22nd ACM SIGKDD International Conference on Knowledge Discovery and Data Mining, pp. 1135–1144 (2016) (2016)

40. Timadius, E.D., Wongso, R., Baihaqi, T., Gunawan, A.A.S., Setiawan, K.E.: Breast cancer image classification obtained through dynamic thermography using deep learning. In: 2024 4th International Conference of Science and Information Technology in Smart Administration (ICSINTESA), pp. 207–212. IEEE, Balikpapan (2024). https://ieeexplore.ieee.org/document/10748049

DR-AIVis: A Hybrid Approach for Diabetic Retinopathy Detection Using U-Net Segmentation and CNN Classification with Grad-CAM Explainability

Marcelo Colares da Silva[1,2], Caio Marques Silva[1,2], Suane Pires P. da Silva[1,2],
Roger M. Sarmento[1,2], Houbing Hebert Song[3],
and Pedro Pedrosa Rebouças Filho[1,2(✉)]

[1] Federal Institute of Education, Science and Technology of Ceará - IFCE ,
Fortaleza, Brazil
{marcelo.colares06,caio.marques.silva05}@aluno.ifce.edu.br,
suanepires@lapisco.ifce.edu.br, {rogerms,pedrosarf}@ifce.edu.br
[2] Laboratory for Processing Images, Signals and Computer Science - LAPISCO,
Fortaleza, Brazil
[3] University of Maryland, Baltimore County (UMBC), College Park, USA
songh@umbc.edu

Abstract. Diabetic retinopathy (DR) is a diabetes-related ocular complication that can lead to vision loss. Its detection is performed through fundus examinations, assisted by lesion segmentation techniques. The IDRiD and APTOS-2019 datasets are used for DR lesion segmentation and classification, respectively. Using the U-Net architecture, lesions such as microaneurysms and exudates were segmented, while CNNs classified disease stages. In this paper, we present DR-AIVis, an approach for segmentation, classification, and explainability of diabetic retinopathy (DR). Our results demonstrate an accuracy of 93.84% in segmentation and 98.30% in classification. Additionally, we employ Grad-CAM to highlight the most relevant regions of the image. As contributions, our work includes an automated system for DR segmentation and classification, as well as a mechanism to identify the most important image regions for decision-making, thereby enhancing confidence in the provided results using Grad-CAM.

Keywords: Diabetic retinopathy · Deep learning · Explainable artificial intelligence

1 Introduction

Ocular diseases related to diabetes are increasing globally, following the worldwide rise in diabetes prevalence [19]. According to [4], Diabetic Retinopathy

R. de Freitas and D. Furtado (Eds.): BRACIS 2025, LNAI 16181, pp. 139–154, 2026.
https://doi.org/10.1007/978-3-032-15990-8_10

(DR) accounts for approximately 4.8% of blindness cases worldwide. Although it is a treatable condition, vision loss caused by DR is often irreversible. The disease progresses slowly, with its severity determined by the extent of retinal damage, which may include fluid accumulation, microaneurysms, hemorrhages, and exudates [6]. The most widely adopted method for diagnosing DR is the dilated fundus examination, commonly known as fundoscopy [8]. In this procedure, the ophthalmologist dilates the patient's pupils and examines the retina with an ophthalmoscope to detect characteristic abnormalities associated with the disease. Early detection of diabetic retinopathy is essential for preventing disease progression and preserving vision. Timely diagnosis significantly reduces the risk of severe complications and helps maintain the patient's quality of life [20].

Inspired by this motivation, we introduce DR-AIVis, a pipeline that automatically segments retinal lesions and classifies the degree of DR severity. The proposed method employs U-Net [9] for lesion segmentation, followed by the application of Convolutional Neural Networks (CNNs) to classify DR severity. To interpret the model's decisions, Grad-CAM [16] is used to highlight the most relevant regions of the images. This approach not only improves the accuracy of DR classification but also enhances the explainability of the model's predictions.

In summary, we propose an approach for the automatic segmentation and classification of diabetic retinopathy. Our DR-AIVis framework integrates DR classification with interpretability, making it a valuable tool to support medical diagnosis. Experimental results demonstrate that our approach outperforms existing methods, achieving high accuracy rates.

2   Methodology

This section describes the methodology adopted in the proposed approach. Subsection 2.1 presents a brief overview of the methodology. In 2.2, the datasets used in the experiments are described. Subsection 2.3 details the data augmentation strategies employed. Next, Subsect. 2.4 provides implementation details of the proposed approach. Finally, Subsects. 2.5, 2.6, and 2.7 describe the classification procedure, the application of Grad-CAM, and the evaluation metrics, respectively.

2.1   Preliminary

In this section, we will introduce the methodology used to obtain the results discussed below. The DR-AIVis pipeline consists of the following stages: The process begins with dataset collection (1), followed by image pre-processing (2) and partitioning into training and testing sets (3). Next, data augmentation techniques are applied (4) to enhance variability. The segmentation process is then performed (5), and the convolutional neural network (CNN) is trained (6). Finally, evaluation metrics are extracted (7) to assess model performance.

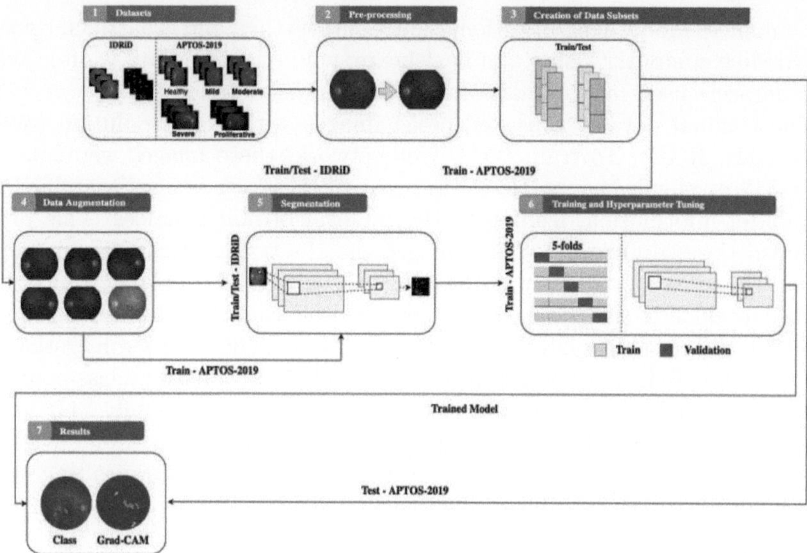

Fig. 1. The pipeline of our framework for DR segmentation and classification: DR-AIVis. Our framework includes the following steps: (1) Acquisition of the datasets. (2) Image preprocessing. (3) Creation of training and testing sets. (4) Data augmentation. (5) Segmentation step. (6) CNN training. (7) Evaluation metrics.

2.2 Datasets

To perform the segmentation of lesions, the IDRiD (Indian Diabetic Retinopathy Image Dataset) [14] dataset was used. This dataset contains retinal images, captured using a fundus camera, along with their corresponding lesion annotations, such as microaneurysms, hemorrhages, soft exudates, and hard exudates, which were manually labeled by ophthalmologists. The images in this dataset have a resolution of 4288 pixels by 2848 pixels, with 3 channels (RGB). The dataset was initially divided into training and testing sets, with 54 and 27 images, respectively.

In the classification task we use the APTOS-2019 (Asian Pacific TeleOphthalmology Society) [10] dataset is an open dataset composed of 3662 labeled images of retinas from diabetic patients treated at the Department of Ophthalmology at Firat University Hospital, Turkey. The medical team at the hospital classified the images into five distinct categories: 1805 healthy (49.20%); 370 with mild DR (10.10%); 999 with moderate DR (27.30%); 193 with severe DR (5.30%); and 295 with proliferative DR (8.10%).

2.3 Data Augmentation

Data augmentation is a common technique to increase training data diversity by applying transformations such as rotations, flips, and brightness adjustments.

This enhances model generalization, reduces overfitting, and is particularly useful in fields like computer vision and healthcare, where labeled data is often scarce. Both datasets used required data augmentation, as detailed below.

The original dataset consisted of 54 images with high resolution (4288 × 2848 pixels, RGB). To train the U-Net network, these images were split into 512 × 512 pixel sub-images. However, many of these sub-images contained little meaningful information, leading to the removal of null matrices. This process expanded the training set to 2004 images and the test set to 1005 images.

For classification, data augmentation was applied to balance the dataset, which contained a class imbalance. The Healthy class had 1444 images, while the other classes (Mild DR, Moderate DR, Severe DR, and Proliferative DR) had 296, 799, 154, and 236 images, respectively. The Healthy class count was used as a target for augmenting the other classes to approximately 1444 images. Data augmentation techniques, including rotations, translations, and brightness and contrast adjustments, were applied to balance the dataset, resulting in 1444 images per class.

2.4 Implementation Details

Pre-processing. Medical images are often affected by noise from equipment or environmental conditions, compromising image quality and diagnostic accuracy [17]. To mitigate this, pre-processing is essential before inputting the images into CNNs. A 5×5 mean filter was applied to reduce noise, followed by normalization to a [0, 1] range. The mean filter effectively reduces noise, such as sensor imperfections or compression artifacts, enhancing image quality and allowing the CNN to focus on relevant patterns like edges and textures [5].

Segmentation Setup. For the segmentation task, microaneurysms, hemorrhages, hard exudates, and soft exudates were considered distinct classes, characterizing a multiclass segmentation approach. The segmentation process was carried out in three stages: the first consists of training the U-Net, followed by the testing phase, and finally, the repetition of the previous steps. The training and testing process of the model was conducted in three main stages. During the training phase, the training and test sets obtained after applying data augmentation were merged into a single dataset, with 80% of the data used for this purpose.

To determine the optimal hyperparameters, a 5-fold cross-validation was performed during training. The loss function used was Cross-Entropy [3]. Table 1 presents a summary of the considered hyperparameters. During the testing phase, the remaining 20% of the dataset was used to evaluate the saved models, and performance metrics were computed in this stage.

For the Early Stopping technique, if there is no significant reduction in the loss function for five consecutive epochs, the training process is halted, and the best weights obtained up to that point are considered.

Finally, the training and testing processes were repeated, with the dataset being randomly split into new training and test sets, generating additional data

Table 1. Hyperparameter search configuration for U-Net.

Parameter	Configuration
Learning Rate	0.001–0.1
Activation Function	Softmax
Batch Size	16, 32, and 64
Optimizer	Adam and Adamax
Number of Epochs	Using the Early Stopping technique

for analysis. This repetition was performed ten times, encompassing all the previously described steps.

2.5   Classification Setup

The CNN architectures used were pre-trained and initialized with the ImageNet dataset [15], which contains 1000 classes with over one million samples. The CNNs were adapted to the problem by replacing the last fully connected layer with a new fully connected layer corresponding to the number of classes in the dataset used. Table 2 presents the CNN architectures employed and their respective configurations.

Table 2. CNN architectures, configurations used, and input image size.

Architecture	Configuration	Input Image Size
VGG	VGG16	224×224
	VGG19	224×224
EfficientNet	EfficientNetB0	224×224
	EfficientNetB1	224×224
DenseNet	DenseNet121	224×224
	DenseNet201	224×224
NFNet	NFNet	224×224
ResNet	ResNet50	224×224
Inception	InceptionV3	299×299
AlexNet	AlexNet	227×227

The classification process consists of three stages: the first stage involves training the architectures. In this phase, 80% of the dataset is used for training. The hyperparameter configurations presented in Table 3 were considered to determine the optimal configuration for the classifiers. To find the ideal hyperparameters, a random search with 10 iterations was performed. Additionally, a

Table 3. Hyperparameter search configuration for CNNs.

Parameter	Configuration
Learning Rate	0.001–0.1
Activation Function	Softmax
Batch Size	32–64
Optimizer	Adam, RMSprop, and Adamax
Number of Epochs	Using the Early Stopping technique

5-fold cross-validation was conducted during training to refine the hyperparameter selection. The loss function used was Cross-Entropy.

For the Early Stopping technique, if there is no significant reduction in the loss function for five consecutive epochs, the training process is halted, and the best weights obtained up to that point are retained. In the second stage, the testing process is carried out using the remaining 20% of the dataset with the trained architectures. At this stage, evaluation metrics are computed for each architecture. Finally, the dataset is randomly split again into new training and test sets, generating new subsets. The previous steps are then repeated ten times to ensure robustness and reliability in the results.

2.6   Grad-CAM

Grad-CAM (Gradient-Weighted Class Activation Mapping) is a technique used to make CNN decisions more interpretable. This technique creates activation maps that indicate which regions of an image are most important for the network when making a classification.

To generate these maps, Grad-CAM utilizes the gradients of the loss function with respect to the activations of the final convolutional layers, as illustrated in Fig. 2. These gradients are used to calculate the relevance of each neuron, highlighting the areas of the image that had the greatest influence on the network's decision.

The final result is a heatmap that can be overlaid on the original image, assisting in visual interpretation. The activation map is described by Eq. 1:

$$L^c_{\text{Grad-CAM}} = \text{ReLU}\left(\sum_k \alpha^c_k A^k\right) \tag{1}$$

where A^k represents the feature map of the k-th convolutional layer, and α^c_k are the importance weights for class c, computed as the average of the gradients over the feature map, as represented in Eq. 2:

$$\alpha^c_k = \frac{1}{Z}\sum_i \sum_j \frac{\partial y^c}{\partial A^k_{ij}} \tag{2}$$

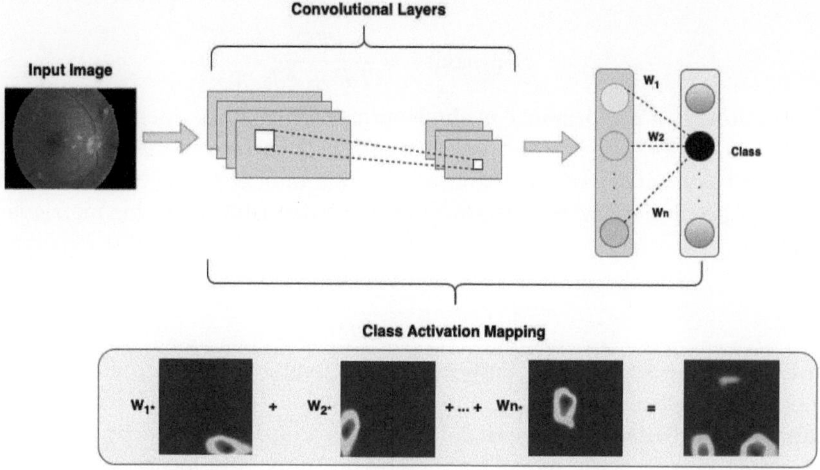

Fig. 2. Construction of the Grad-CAM activation map.

where y^c is the score of class c and Z is the total number of elements in the feature map A^k. In medical imaging, this is a key technique for interpreting CNN decisions, allowing the visualization of the most relevant regions of an image for a prediction. It generates heatmaps that highlight areas of interest, such as lesions, tumors, or anomalies, that influenced the network's diagnosis.

In applications such as DR detection, Grad-CAM can, for example, show which areas of the retina were considered when identifying exudates or hemorrhages, thus facilitating validation and improving confidence in the trained model.

2.7   Evaluation Metrics

The output of each *CNN* is evaluated using the confusion matrix, from which the following metrics are derived: accuracy, sensitivity, and precision. Additionally, for a more specific assessment of the segmentation results, the IoU (Intersection over Union) metric was used.

- **Accuracy.** Represents the proportion of correct predictions made by the model relative to the total number of predictions. In simple terms, this metric indicates the overall efficiency of the model in correctly classifying images into their respective classes. Equation 3 describes how this metric is calculated:

$$\text{Accuracy}(\%) = \frac{TP + TN}{TN + FN + TP + FP} \times 100 \tag{3}$$

- **Sensitivity.** Is a performance evaluation metric for a classification model that indicates its ability to correctly identify positive cases. In other words, sensitivity measures the model's capability to correctly detect instances of DR. Mathematically, sensitivity is defined by Eq. 4:

$$\text{Sensitivity} = \frac{TP}{TP + FN} \tag{4}$$

- **Precision.** Is a performance evaluation metric for a classification model that measures its ability to correctly identify positive instances among all instances classified as positive. In other words, precision indicates how often the model's positive predictions were correct. Equation 5 describes how this metric is calculated:

$$\text{Precision} = \frac{TP}{TP + FP} \tag{5}$$

- **IoU** Measures the overlap between two regions: the region predicted by the model (prediction) and the ground truth region (true label). The IoU value ranges from 0 (no overlap) to 1 (perfect overlap). This metric is useful for assessing how well the model predicted the shape and location of objects or regions in an image. Your calculation is given by the Eq. 6:

$$\text{IoU} = \frac{|A \cap B|}{|A \cup B|} \tag{6}$$

where A represents the predicted region, B represents the ground truth region, $|A \cap B|$ is the intersection area between the two regions, and $|A \cup B|$ is the union area of the two regions.

3   Experiments

3.1   Segmentation

Table 4 presents the average values of the evaluation metrics considered during the 10 iterations performed throughout the lesion segmentation stage. Based on the obtained results, it is evident that the trained U-Net achieved a high Accuracy of 93.82% in correctly classifying the class to which a given pixel belongs.

Table 4. Evaluation metrics for segmentation performance.

Metric	Result
Accuracy	93.82 ± 0.31
Sensitivity	93.35 ± 0.24
Precision	93.24 ± 0.27
IoU	0.86 ± 0.02

Still analyzing Table 4, the Sensitivity and Accuracy metrics obtained scores of 93.35% and 93.24%, respectively, indicating a balance between false positives and false negatives. This suggests that the segmentation effectively avoided misclassifying pixels belonging to a specific lesion type as healthy, and vice versa. The IoU metric further demonstrates a significant agreement between the ground truth lesion annotations and the model's predictions. Figure 3 shows an eye background image, the corresponding lesion annotations, and the predictions made by the U-Net.

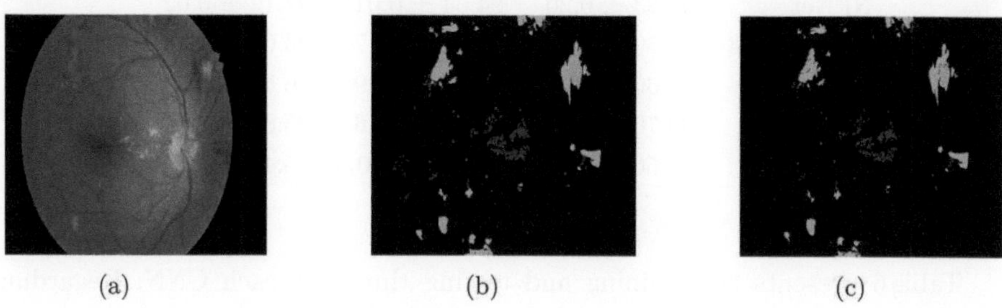

(a)   (b)   (c)

Fig. 3. Lesion Segmentation: (a) fundus image, (b) annotation, and (c) prediction.

The visual results corroborate the values obtained for the metrics mentioned earlier, indicating that the trained model is capable of effectively segmenting lesions resulting from DR.

3.2   Classification

Table 5 presents the metrics and their standard deviations obtained after 10 iterations of the steps described in Sect. 2, with the best results highlighted in bold. We applied the Tukey-Friedman test [1] to the Accuracy results obtained using the test subset of APTOS-2019 to assess whether there was statistical difference among the classifiers' performances.

Considering a 95% confidence level, all obtained p-values were below 0.05, indicating that all pairwise comparisons among the groups showed statistically significant differences. Therefore, EfficientNetB0 demonstrated the best performance from a statistical perspective compared to the other models. Analyzing Accuracy, EfficientNetB0 performed exceptionally well on this metric, achieving 98.30%, indicating high effectiveness in detecting the different severity levels of DR.

In classification models used in medical applications, it is essential to evaluate metrics such as Sensitivity and Precision to assess the balance between false positives and false negatives. For Sensitivity, EfficientNetB0 achieved 94.81%, indicating a low false negative rate. This means that almost all actual cases of DR were correctly identified, reducing the risk of patients with any degree of the disease being misclassified as healthy. For Precision, EfficientNetB0 reached 97.50%, demonstrating a low false positive rate. In other words, it rarely misclassifies a healthy patient or one from another class as having DR.

Table 5. Evaluation metrics obtained for each CNN.

CNN	Accuracy (%)	Sensitivity (%)	Precision (%)
EfficientNetB0	**98.30 ± 0.50**	94.81 ± 0.18	**97.50 ± 0.21**
DenseNet201	98.10 ± 0.10	94.19 ± 0.14	97.20 ± 0.17
DenseNet121	97.60 ± 0.30	93.59 ± 0.17	96.90 ± 0.20
ResNet50	<u>98.40 ± 0.20</u>	<u>94.86 ± 0.01</u>	<u>97.30 ± 0.02</u>
NFNet	98.23 ± 0.20	94.54 ± 0.01	97.12 ± 0.02
InceptionV3	94.50 ± 0.30	90.38 ± 0.17	93.60 ± 0.20
VGG19	97.30 ± 0.40	92.37 ± 0.19	96.50 ± 0.22
VGG16	96.70 ± 0.20	92.58 ± 0.16	95.80 ± 0.19
AlexNet	96.50 ± 0.60	**95.74 ± 0.15**	95.40 ± 0.18

Table 6 presents the training and testing times for each CNN. Regarding training time, the AlexNet architecture required the shortest duration to be trained, completing the process in 1331.16 s, while VGG16 stood out with the second shortest training time.

Table 6. Training and testing times for each CNN.

CNN	Training time (s)	Testing time (ms)
EfficientNetB0	5238.33 ± 66.23	0.453 ± 0.154
DenseNet201	4238.33 ± 66.23	0.674 ± 0.009
DenseNet121	3920.23 ± 38.44	0.553 ± 0.054
ResNet50	2724.13 ± 16.44	<u>0.293 ± 0.011</u>
InceptionV3	2359.32 ± 36.43	0.557 ± 0.046
NFNet	2158.33 ± 18.42	0.583 ± 0.018
VGG19	2134.15 ± 12.12	0.474 ± 0.008
VGG16	<u>1920.43 ± 12.49</u>	0.572 ± 0.090
AlexNet	**1331.16 ± 29.33**	**0.15 ± 0.098**

Analyzing the inference times, which are critical for deployment in real-world environments, AlexNet exhibited the shortest execution time among all evaluated CNNs for performing segmentation, completing the task in 0.15 ms, followed by ResNet50. In comparison, EfficientNetB0 required approximately three times longer than AlexNet to complete the same task; however, its results were more robust, thereby justifying its use.

Using the final convolutional layer of EfficientNetB0 for the application of Grad-CAM, activation maps were generated to assess whether the regions with the highest weight for classification correspond to areas indicative of the presence of DR. Two main cases were evaluated: a correctly classified healthy fundus image and an image with proliferative DR, the most severe form of the disease. For each case, the activation maps generated by Grad-CAM were overlaid on the original images, allowing the identification of the most important regions used by the model to make its decision. Figure 4 illustrates the activation map obtained by applying Grad-CAM to a fundus image with no signs of DR.

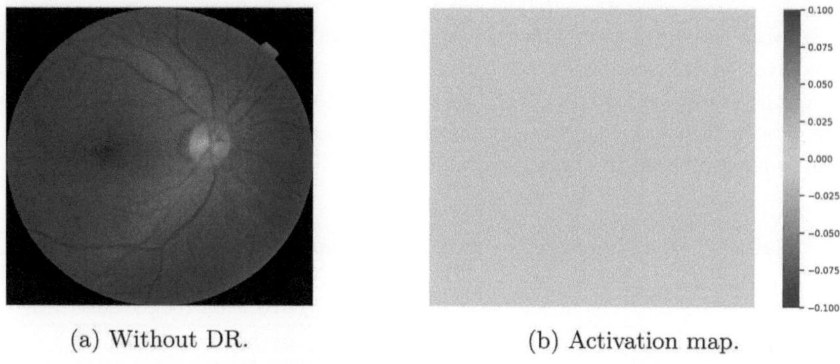

(a) Without DR.   (b) Activation map.

Fig. 4. Fundus image without DR and overlay with the activation map.

As observed, the resulting map does not highlight the relevant regions for DR classification, instead producing a completely uniform map with values close to zero, as there are no characteristic DR lesions in the analyzed fundus image. Fig. 5 presents the result of applying the method to a fundus image with a proliferative degree.

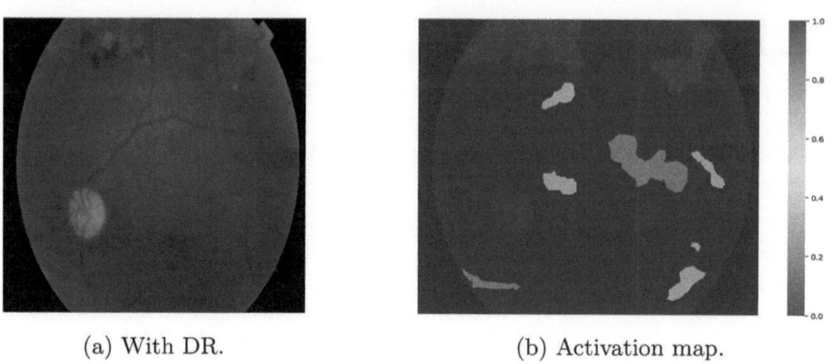

(a) With DR.   (b) Activation map.

Fig. 5. Fundus image with DR and overlay with the activation map.

By observing the regions with higher weights (reddish tones), it is evident that these areas exhibit retinal degeneration, which is a characteristic of this stage of the disease. The other regions with lower intensity are associated with areas presenting a lower degree of retinal degeneration. Additionally, regions containing small exudates and microaneurysms are also highlighted. These lesions, although present in the early stages of the disease, tend to persist as the disease progresses.

3.3   Comparison to State-of-the-Arts

To reinforce the results obtained by the proposed methodology, we conducted a comparison with the studies presented in Table 7, which provides a brief summary of the compared works. It is important to note that the standard deviations of the reported metrics are not included, as the authors of the referenced studies did not provide them in their results.

Table 7. Comparison of the proposed method with other approaches.

Author	Accuracy (%)	Sensitivity (%)	Precision (%)	Grad-CAM
Proposed Method	**98.30**	**94.81**	**97.50**	Yes
[7]	97.49	96.24	97.50	No
[11]	97.90	95.42	96.23	No
[18]	85.00	74.26	71.78	No
[13]	82.60	82.50	82.50	No
[2]	73.04	52.00	87.00	Yes
[12]	98.18	97.41	99.55	Yes

In the study conducted by [7], the authors compared the performance of deep learning approaches for the automatic classification of DR. They used the APTOS-2019, achieving an Accuracy of 97.49%. These superior results can be attributed to prior segmentation, as this process selects the regions that are actually important for detecting DR. In the methodology adopted, the authors combined the original images with images subjected to a weighted Gaussian blur background, creating two modalities to form the final dataset and perform the training process. This approach may improve results; however, for the training process, it adds more complexity, as the original images and the weighted Gaussian blur (WGBF) versions may contain redundant information, leading to overload during feature extraction and increasing the risk of overfitting.

In [11], the authors used deep learning models that were trained and tested with the APTOS-2019 dataset, one of the first studies to use this dataset, published in the second quarter of 2019. The chosen models – AlexNet, ResNet18, SqueezeNet, GoogleNet, VGG16, and VGG19 were selected for having fewer layers compared to larger models, such as DenseNet and InceptionResNet. Data augmentation techniques were applied to increase robustness and mitigate overfitting. AlexNet achieved the highest Accuracy, reaching 97.90%. As in the present work, the authors used CNNs for DR classification and also applied data augmentation to increase the model's robustness. In this paper, the Accuracy obtained using AlexNet was 96.50%, slightly lower than the Accuracy achieved by the authors. In comparison with EfficientNetB0, which achieved the best performance in terms of Accuracy, reaching 98.30%, a superior performance is observed when class-level classification Accuracy is analyzed.

In [13], the authors employed a Vision Transformer-based model to classify the severity stages of Diabetic Retinopathy. The model was compared with traditional CNN architectures, achieving an Accuracy of 82.60%. Compared to the Vision Transformer-based approach, our superior results are attributed to the prior lesion segmentation using U-Net, which highlighted clinically relevant retinal regions. This preprocessing step reduced image noise and guided the classifier toward disease-specific patterns, thereby improving the model's accuracy and robustness.

In the approach presented by [18], the authors proposed the use of deep learning for DR classification. Unlike models based on large CNN architectures, which require large datasets and high computational capacity, MobileNetV2 was used. The model was trained on the APTOS-2019 dataset, using pre-trained weights from ImageNet. Additionally, it was optimized with the combination of an SVM classifier, forming the hybrid MobileNetV2-SVM model, achieving an accuracy of 85.00%. Observing the final confusion matrix presented by the authors, it is evident that classification errors occurred between all classes. A significant example is the case of mild DR images being erroneously classified as proliferative. The lack of data balancing techniques and the absence of segmentation may have contributed to the lower performance compared to what is observed in this dissertation.

In the method proposed by [2], the authors focused on DR detection using deep learning. Deep learning models were evaluated in two approaches: binary classification and multiclass classification according to the severity levels of DR. The experiments highlighted the superior performance of the VGG-16 model, which achieved 73.04% Accuracy. Moreover, the Grad-CAM method was applied to provide explainability to the model's decisions.

The explainability analysis conducted with Grad-CAM revealed that the model does not always correctly identify DR-related lesions. This was evidenced in the image analyzed by the authors, in which the region containing exudates was not fully considered as relevant for classification. This behavior suggests that the trained model did not fully identify the patterns in the images that correspond to the areas affected by DR. Such limitations may be related to factors such as the lack of appropriate preprocessing or the absence of segmentation techniques, which could assist in more accurately recognizing the areas affected by DR.

In [12], an innovative method for DR diagnosis and classification using Few-Shot Learning is presented, an approach that enables effective model training with limited training data, addressing issues such as overfitting and poor generalization in small datasets. The proposed method is based on DRNet, a prototypical network with attention mechanisms developed for DR detection and classification. DRNet uses episodic learning to train the network on few-shot classification tasks, employing aggregated transformations and gradient activations to design richer, more focused image representations. As a result, an Accuracy of 98.18% was achieved, the highest among the compared studies. This methodology is highly robust since Few-Shot Learning allows the model to effectively learn from a limited number of examples. Furthermore, DRNet incorporates an attention mechanism that selectively focuses on the most relevant regions of fundus images, highlighting critical features for DR detection, such as microaneurysms, hemorrhages, or exudates. Grad-CAM was used to perform model explainability.

The activation map generated by the model showed that it was able to identify the regions affected by DR. However, it was observed that the model attributed significant weight to the optic disc, which may indicate an attention error. This behavior could be a consequence of a bias present in the dataset or incorrect patterns learned during training. For example, the dataset may contain images where the optic disc appears more prominent due to variations in lighting, contrast, or visual anomalies. Additionally, if the annotations include severe DR cases with alterations near the optic disc, the model may have mistakenly learned to associate the presence of DR with this specific region.

4   Conclusion

This paper presented an approach (DR-AIVis) for the segmentation and classification of retinal fundus images, along with an explanation of the model's decisions using Grad-CAM. The methodology consisted of three main stages: (i) lesion segmentation using a U-Net, (ii) classification with different CNN architectures, and (iii) identification of the most relevant regions for decision-making through Grad-CAM.

The results demonstrated that the segmentation of lesions using the U-Net achieved an Accuracy of 93.84%. In the classification task, EfficientNetB0 achieved the best results, reaching an Accuracy of 98.30%. Furthermore, the Grad-CAM method effectively highlighted the key regions for the model's decision-making, enhancing the interpretability of the results.

For future work, we aim to explore U-Net variants, as well as augment the IDRiD dataset with additional images to mitigate the limitations imposed by its relatively small size. We also intend to investigate other CNN architectures to further improve segmentation and classification performance. Additionally, validating the proposed approach on different datasets and applying alternative Explainable Artificial Intelligence methods may facilitate the adoption of this technology in clinical settings, supporting specialists with interpretable and effective tools for the diagnosis and monitoring of diabetic retinopathy.

Acknowledgment. This study was financed in part by the Coordenação de Aperfeiçoamento de Pessoal de Nível Superior—Brasil (CAPES)—Finance Code 001. Also, Pedro Pedrosa Rebouças Filho acknowledges the sponsorship from the Brazilian National Council for Research and Development (CNPq) via Grant 301455/2022-8 and State Foundation for the Support of Scientific and Technological Development (FUNCAP) for the financial support via grants 08/2023 and 09/2023.

References

1. Abdi, H., Williams, L.J.: Newman-keuls test and tukey test. Encyclopedia Res. Des. 1–11 (2010)
2. Alghamdi, H.S.: Towards explainable deep neural networks for the automatic detection of diabetic retinopathy. Appl. Sci. **12**(19), 9435 (2022)
3. Bishop, C.M., Nasrabadi, N.M.: Pattern recognition and machine learning, vol. 4. Springer (2006)
4. Brazilian Council of Ophthalmology: Brazilian Council of Ophthalmology - Official Website (2024). https://www.cbo.net.br
5. Chen, Z., Xu, L., Zhang, Y.: Image denoising using attention-residual convolutional neural networks. arXiv preprint arXiv:2101.07713 (2021), https://arxiv.org/abs/2101.07713, Accessed 22 Dec 2024
6. Crick, R.P., Khaw, P.T.: Textbook Of Clinical Ophthalmology, A: A Practical Guide To Disorders Of The Eyes And Their Management. World Scientific Publishing Company (2003)
7. El-Ateif, S., Idri, A.: Single-modality and joint fusion deep learning for diabetic retinopathy diagnosis. Sci. African **17**, e01280 (2022)
8. Group, E.T.D.R.S.R., et al.: Grading diabetic retinopathy from stereoscopic color fundus photographs-an extension of the modified airlie house classification: Etdrs Rep. number 10. Ophthalmology **98**(5), 786–806 (1991)
9. Ibtehaz, N., Rahman, M.S.: Multiresunet: rethinking the u-net architecture for multimodal biomedical image segmentation. Neural Netw. **121**, 74–87 (2020)
10. Kaggle: Aptos 2019 blindness detection (2019). https://www.kaggle.com/c/aptos2019-blindness-detection/data
11. Khalifa, N.E.M., Loey, M., Taha, M.H.N., Mohamed, H.N.E.T.: Deep transfer learning models for medical diabetic retinopathy detection. Acta Inf. Medica **27**(5), 327 (2019)
12. Murugappan, M., Prakash, N., Jeya, R., Mohanarathinam, A., Hemalakshmi, G., Mahmud, M.: A novel few-shot classification framework for diabetic retinopathy detection and grading. Measurement **200**, 111485 (2022)
13. Nazih, W., Aseeri, A.O., Atallah, O.Y., El-Sappagh, S.: Vision transformer model for predicting the severity of diabetic retinopathy in fundus photography-based retina images. IEEE Access **11**, 117546–117561 (2023)
14. Porwal, P., et al.: Idrid: diabetic retinopathy-segmentation and grading challenge. Med. Image Anal. **59**, 101561 (2020)
15. Russakovsky, O., et al.: Imagenet large scale visual recognition challenge. Int. J. Comput. Vision **115**(3), 211–252 (2015)
16. Selvaraju, R.R., Cogswell, M., Das, A., Vedantam, R., Parikh, D., Batra, D.: Grad-cam: visual explanations from deep networks via gradient-based localization. Presented at the (2017)
17. Silva, E., Souza, A., Costa, F.: Analysis of noise reduction techniques in magnetic resonance images. CBEB 2014 - Brazilian Congress of Biomedical Engineering (2014)

18. Taufiqurrahman, S., Handayani, A., Hermanto, B.R., Mengko, T.L.E.R.: In: Diabetic Retinopathy Classification Using a Hybrid and Efficient Mobilenetv2-svm Model, pp. 235–240. IEEE (2020)
19. Teo, Z.L., et al.: Global prevalence of diabetic retinopathy and projection of burden through 2045: systematic review and meta-analysis. Ophthalmology **128**(11), 1580–1591 (2021)
20. Ting, D.S.W., Cheung, G.C.M., Wong, T.Y.: Diabetic retinopathy: global prevalence, major risk factors, screening practices and public health challenges: a review. Clin. Exp. Ophthalmol. **44**(4), 260–277 (2016)

Emotionally and Cognitively Aware Proactive Conversational LLM-Assistants for Healthcare

Elioenai Alves[1]([✉]) , Jorge Araujo[1] , Elizabeth Sucupira Furtado[1] ,
Rafael Bonfim[1] , and Vasco Furtado[1,2]

[1] University of Fortaleza (Unifor), Washington Soares, 1321, Fortaleza, CE, Brazil
l.oenaialves@gmail.com, {elizabet,jorgearaujo,vasco}@unifor.br
[2] State of Ceará IT Company (ETICE), Av. Pontes Vieira 220, São João do Tauape,
Fortaleza, CE, Brazil

Abstract. We propose MarIARel and MarIAToM, two proactive assistants based on Large Language Models (LLMs). They integrate principles from Relevance Theory and Theory of Mind (ToM) to analyze users' interaction history and initiate personalized, contextually relevant conversations. MarIARel selects users and topics based on relevance, while MarIAToM also considers users' estimated mental and emotional states. An eight-month experimental study was conducted with 385 patients, who first interacted with a non-proactive assistant that initiated dialogues only when guided by human intervention, and subsequently with MarIARel and MarIAToM. To evaluate the impact of proactive messages, we introduce the metric of response predictability, which quantifies the likelihood of user replies. Results show that MarIAToM, which leverages ToM features, achieved higher response predictability and engagement. We also developed a qualitative assessment method based on emotional impact, applied by human-computer interaction specialists. Experts unanimously found that MarIAToM's messages were more emotionally engaging and better at sustaining user responses.

Keywords: Proactive Assistant · Theory of Mind · Personalized Dialogues

1 Introduction

A challenging feature for fostering meaningful and continuous engagement of humans in talks to virtual assistants is proactivity, the ability to initiate context-sensitive conversations without waiting for user input.

This article introduces the concept of emotionally and cognitively aware LLM-based assistants, which we will refer to as Proactive Assistants. Drawing from the Theory of Relevance [26] and the Theory of Mind (ToM) [3,21], these assistants leverage LLMs to identify relevant topics to initiate conversations based on past interactions of users. By incorporating individual characteristics

R. de Freitas and D. Furtado (Eds.): BRACIS 2025, LNAI 16181, pp. 155–169, 2026.
https://doi.org/10.1007/978-3-032-15990-8_11

such as mental and emotional states, along with moral and behavioral values, proactive assistants enable a higher degree of personalization.

We developed two versions of these assistants, named MarIARel and MarI-AToM, and conducted an experimental study in the healthcare domain with 385 type-2 Diabetes Mellitus patients. Initially, the participants interacted with a basic assistant lacking proactive and personalized features. They then switched to using MarIARel and MarIAToM respectively. Inspired by the concept of *category utility* in incremental concept acquisition [9], we introduced the concept of *predictability of response* to quantify the effectiveness of initial conversations initiated by the assistants. The empirical results demonstrated that MarIAToM lead to higher rates of predictability compared to the other approaches.

To further assess the interactions, we used a methodology based on the PAD framework (Pleasure, Arousal, and Dominance) [22]. This allowed experts in Human-Computer Interaction (HCI), computational linguistics, and Artificial Intelligence (AI) to evaluate and compare the messages generated by both proactive assistants. The findings also revealed that MarIAToM has a greater potential to initiate interesting discussions with users, thus improving engagement and promoting more meaningful interactions.

2   Related Work

Conversational Assistants (CAs) need to adapt to the emotional, cognitive, and personal factors of the users. Studies such as [7,15] highlight performance disparities in user interactions caused by linguistic variations and educational differences. Emotions, as temporary states that influence behavior [10], play a key role in user engagement, with emotional design enhancing interaction quality [11]. Pleasure, identified as a fundamental engagement factor [18], is part of the PAD model [22], which analyzes emotions through the dimensions of Pleasure, Arousal, and Dominance. Cognitive factors, such as mental models, also shape decision-making and behavior.

In healthcare, emotional and cognitive elements are critical for the management of conditions such as type 2 diabetes (DM T2), including motivation, self-efficacy, and affect management [12], supported by continuous care plans [4]. While personalized communication tools aid patient adherence [14,17], rigid dialogues limit scalability [4,6]. Flexibility and emotional engagement are important for CAs [1,13,19]. Since ChatGPT's emergence, its healthcare potential has been explored [2,8].

Recent studies [23] show that LLMs outperform therapeutic bots in bias correction and emotional recognition, underlining the need for improved emotional intelligence and ethical AI design in healthcare. However, the general-purpose design of ChatGPT and similar models remains unsuitable for medical tasks, highlighting the need for specialized healthcare assistants. Chatbots like [5] support social well-being, while emotional disclosure has been shown to improve user satisfaction [20]. Furthermore, [27] explores Theory of Mind (ToM) capabilities in LLMs, emphasizing both risks (such as manipulation and attachment) and opportunities (human-centered AI) in aligning with human values and protecting autonomy. Our study advances this discussion by presenting one of the first large-scale, longitudinal evaluations of a ToM-inspired proactive assistant deployed in a real healthcare setting.

3   Emotion and Cognition-Aware Proactive Assistants

3.1   Overview

The intuition behind the proactive assistant, as conceived in this work, is illustrated in Fig. 1. At its core, the assistant continuously estimates and updates the user's mental states (e.g., beliefs, intentions, desires) and emotional states (e.g., valence, intensity, type). It also maintains information related to ToM characteristics, such as social patterns, values and beliefs, ethical principles, and health-related convictions, along with behavioral patterns such as habits, regularity, persistence, and adaptability. These characteristics are stored in memory, forming an evolving user profile over time. Using ToM features, the assistant determines the moment to initiate a conversation, considering the emotional and cognitive readiness of the user. From the user's interaction history, the assistant continuously updates the state profile and selects the right time and the most relevant topic to engage the user effectively.

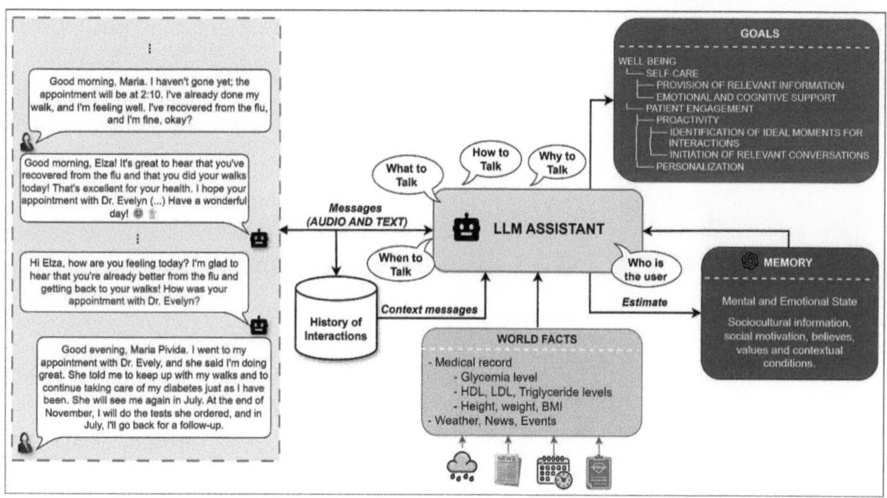

Fig. 1. The proactive assistant applies principles from ToM and the Theory of Relevance to initiate meaningful, context-aware conversations using user data and real-world information. Its decision-making follows the 4W1H framework: *What* (content), *Why* (relevance), *Who* (user profile), *When* (timing), and *How* (approach).

An illustrative example might be a scenario in which a user has been inactive for two days and has previously mentioned struggles with adhering to a low-sodium diet, which leads to the following assistant actions:

– What: Brings up tips for maintaining a low-sodium diet;
– Why: The user previously expressed difficulty, making it a relevant topic;
– Who: Tailors the tone according to the user's values (e.g., 'health responsibility') and emotional state (e.g., encouragement if frustration was detected);
– How: Offers practical advice in an empathetic and supportive tone; and
– When: Initiate the conversation, ensuring that it does not repeat interactions on the same day and is consistent with the user's inferred availability.

3.2   Formalization

Let U be the set of users, where $u \in U$, and M_u the set of messages sent by user u, with $m \in M_u$. A proactive assistant can be formalized based on the representation of mental (EM) and emotional states (EE) of a user u with whom it interacts. Full definitions and examples are provided in Table 1.

The user's *mental state* at time t, denoted as $EM(t, u)$, represents their internal cognitive processes, including beliefs(B), intentions(I), desires(D), focus(F), plans(P), and relevance(R). These elements are inferred from M_u. Thus,

$$EM(t, u) = \{B(t, u), I(t, u), D(t, u), F(t, u), P(t, u), R(t, u)\}, \tag{1}$$

where each component is dynamically updated based on the message history $M_u(t)$ and the inferred patterns. Let Δt represent the time since the last message was received or sent:

$$EM(t, u) = EM(t - \Delta t, u) + \delta_{EM}(M_u(t)), \tag{2}$$

where δ_{EM} represents the variation in the mental state based on new information. The *emotional state* describes the affective reactions of a user u at a given time t and reflects what the user feels in response to events or interactions, considering their internal and external responses being represented as

$$EE(t, u) = \{V(t, u), I_e(t, u), T_e(t, u), D_e(t, u)\}, \tag{3}$$

Like the mental state, the emotional state is dynamic and depends on recent interactions (δ_{EE} represents the variation caused by new stimuli).

Additional characteristics estimated by the CA based on the ToM, such as social patterns, values, beliefs, and behavioral patterns, complement mental and emotional states, allowing the agent to achieve a more comprehensive understanding of the user. *Social Patterns* include Social Norms(NS), Social Roles(PR), and Social Network(RS). The social patterns of u at time t are represented as:

$$PS(t, u) = \{NS(t, u), PR(t, u), RS(t, u)\}. \tag{4}$$

Values and Beliefs reflect ethical and moral values(VEM), health beliefs(BHS), cultural beliefs(BC), and personal priorities(PP). They are represented as:

Table 1. Characteristics inspired on ToM used in a Proactive Assistant

	Characteristics	Definition	Example
Mental State	Beliefs (B)	Propositions that the user considers true, regardless of their objective accuracy.	I believe I am managing my blood pressure.
	Intentions (I)	Goals or conscious plans that the user aims to achieve	I plan to start walking every day.
	Desires (D)	Aspirations or internal motivations that drive actions.	I want to lose weight to feel healthier.
	Focus/Attention (F)	The degree to which the user is focused on a specific topic or task.	I am very attentive to my daily glucose goals.
	Planning (P)	Strategies or sequences of actions aimed at achieving a goal.	I intend to schedule monthly appointments with my doctor.
	Persistence (R)	The ability to maintain a plan or a goal over time, even in the face of challenges.	I will continue to monitor my blood pressure even if the results are normal.
Emotional State	Valence (V)	Indicates if emotion is positive(+), negative(-) or neutral(0).	Joy (+), Sadness (-), Indifference (0).
	Intensity (I_e)	Refers to the strength or depth of the emotion felt.	Mild irritation vs. intense anger
	Type of Emotion (T_e)	Defines the emotional category based on models like Ekman (basic emotions) or Russell (complex emotions).	Joy, Fear, Surprise, Pride
	Duration (D_e)	Defines how long the emotion persists before being replaced by another.	A sense of relief lasting a few minutes.
Social Patterns	Social Norms (NS)	Rules that the user follows in their interactions as well as the extent to which the users adhere to the norms.	It is important to thank the doctor after a consultation.
	Social Roles (PR)	Functions that the user performs in different social contexts.	I am responsible for managing my family's meals.
	Social Network (RS)	Interactions and relationships of the user inferred from mentions or linguistic patterns.	My friend helped me remember the time for my medication.
Value and Beliefs	Ethical and Moral Values (VEM)	Principles guiding user behavior.	I believe maintaining a healthy diet is my responsibility.
	Health Beliefs (BHS)	Specific convictions related to health.	Taking medicine at the same time every day is essential for treatment.
	Cultural Beliefs (BC)	Values and practices influenced by the cultural context.	I prefer natural remedies because my family believes in them.
	Personal Priorities (PP)	Aspects of life that the user considers most important.	My priority is to avoid complications related to diabetes.
Behavioral Pattern	Regularity (RG)	Defines how frequently the user performs specific actions.	Verify blood glucose daily at 8 am.
	Adaptation (AD)	Refers to the user's ability to adjust behavior based on recommendations.	Started reducing salt consumption after a recommendation from the CA.
	Persistence (PE)	Indicates the user's continuity in maintaining healthy habits.	Continues walking 30 min daily.
	Resistance to Change (RM)	Reflects the user's difficulty in modifying old behaviors.	Still consumes soft drinks daily, despite recommendations.

$$VC(t, u) = \{VEM(t, u), BHS(t, u), BC(t, u), PP(t, u)\}. \tag{5}$$

Behavioral patterns reflect the user's recurring actions and observed habits, particularly regarding self-care and interaction with the CA, including Regularity(RG), Adaptation(AD), Persistence(PE), and Resistance to Change(RM). The behavioral patterns of u at time t are thus defined as:

$$PB(t, u) = \{RG(t, u), AD(t, u), PE(t, u), RM(t, u)\}. \tag{6}$$

The complete state of a user u at a given time t integrates the mental and emotional states, allowing the conversational agent to interact proactively, relevantly, and emotionally connected:

$$S(t, u) = (EM(t, u), EE(t, u), PS(t, u), VC(t, u), PB(t, u)). \tag{7}$$

3.3   Prompt Engineering in Proactive Assistants

We define the functions f and g as components of an LLM, with the ability to process input (messages, history, and inferred states) and generate appropriate outputs (states or conversational responses). The function f is responsible for inferring user states (mental, emotional, and ToM-based characteristics) from their message history and interaction context. Using an LLM, f works as

$$f : (M_u(t), C_u) \rightarrow S(t, u), \tag{8}$$

where $M_u(t)$ is the set of messages sent by user u up to time t; C_u is contextual information about the user, such as health history and previous interactions with the assistant; and $S(t, u)$ is the inferred state of the user at time t. The message history $M_u(t)$ is structured as a sequence of text entries, each annotated with timestamps and metadata. The context C_u is encoded as structured prompts (e.g., "The user is a 45-year-old with type 2 diabetes, recently discussed diet changes"). The LLM generates the inferred states $S(t, u)$, represented as structured outputs with cognitive states $EM(t, u)$, emotional states $EE(t, u)$, and ToM-based characteristics $PS(t, u), VC(t, u), PB(t, u)$. An example of a prompt for f is as follows:

- Input: **User history:** "I forgot to take my medication yesterday. What should I do?"; **Context:** "Type 2 diabetic, 45 years old, struggling with routine adherence"; and **Question:** "Infer the user's mental and emotional states, and identify behavioral patterns".
- Output: **Mental state:** "Believes that medication is important but struggles with adherence"; **Emotional state:** "Moderate anxiety about health, slight frustration with self"; and **Behavioral patterns:** "Tends to forget medication in the evenings".

The function g determines how the agent generates a conversational response based on the user's inferred state $S(t, u)$. Using an LLM, g transforms the inferred state into a personalized and contextually relevant message. Note that

$$g : (S(t, u), A_u) \rightarrow m_{\mathrm{ac}}(t, u), \tag{9}$$

where: $S(t, u)$ is the inferred state of the user; A_u is the agent's knowledge base or strategy (e.g., goals for engagement, health recommendations, predefined dialogue strategies); and $m_{\mathrm{ac}}(t, u)$ is the message generated by the agent at time t for the user u. The inferred state $S(t, u)$ is encoded as structured text and the agent's strategy A_u includes predefined goals (for example, "Promote adherence to medication") and constraints (for example, "Do not repeat prompts on the same day"). The LLM generates a response $m_{ac}(t, u)$ that balances the relevance of the topic, emotional support, and behavioral nudges (Fig. 2).

An example prompt for g is as follows:

- **Input: User States**, *Mental:* Believes that the medication is important; *Emotional:* Moderate anxiety about health; and *Behavioral:* Tends to forget medication in the evenings;
- **Agent Strategy:** Encourage routine adherence without causing overload
- **Question:** Generate a supportive and engaging message; and
- **Output:** "Hi! I noticed that you've been working hard to keep on track"; "Missing a dose happens to everyone sometimes"; "Would a reminder in the evening help?"; and "We can set it up together!".

Date	Mental State	Mental state analysis	Emotional State	Emotional State Analysis
Mon, 05 May 2025 15:37:32	Desire for social interaction and politeness.	The initial greeting demonstrates a friendly or respectful intent, indicating that the person is seeking to create a conversational atmosphere. This attitude may reflect a belief in the importance of polite communication, as well as a desire for social interaction, even if brief.	Neutrality / Formality	The conversation is objective and direct, focused on scheduling cardiology exams. The use of "Good morning" reflects a polite greeting, but without strong emotional expression, suggesting a professional or routine interaction. Valence: neutral; Intensity: low; Duration: brief.
Sat, 01 Feb 2025 14:48:21	Unmet expectation.	The response "Not yet" suggests that the person is dealing with an expectation that has not yet been fulfilled, indicating a desire to resolve a pending issue. It may express a wish for progress or completion of a specific task.	Frustration	The mention of a waiting period ("Not yet" and "Viver Bem doctor to schedule") may express impatience or dissatisfaction with the difficulty of accessing medical care. Valence: negative; Intensity: moderate; Duration: short to medium, depending on the situation.
Sat, 11 Jan 2025 16:17:45	The person may be concerned about their cardiovascular health or that of someone close to them.	The person is seeking help and guidance to find a cardiologist.	Insecurity or concern	The message suggests that the person is seeking medical help, which may indicate a state of concern about their health or an urgent need for assistance.

Social Patterns	Value and Beliefs	Behavioral Pattern
The person demonstrates a pattern of politeness by repeatedly using expressions of gratitude, such as "Thank you" and "Thank you very much," indicating a cultural value of acknowledging others' efforts. They interact with a respectful tone when asking questions, such as "Can you help me with a cardiologist?", reflecting adherence to social norms of respect and recognition of the authority of healthcare professionals.	The importance placed on accessing healthcare and managing related administrative issues reflects a belief that ensuring one's rights—such as updating a married name to use health services—is essential. This highlights the person's priority in securing proper access to medication and medical care.	The person demonstrates a pattern of perseverance in accessing healthcare services and takes the initiative to seek help with complex issues, as evidenced by the statement "I don't know if you'll be able to help me...". This reflects an active commitment to self-care and health, showing persistence in finding solutions despite the challenges faced.

Fig. 2. An example of the inferred mental and emotional states of a single user on three occasions. The top shows the user's cognitive and emotional state along with the respective analyses. The bottom shows Social Pattern, Values and Beliefs, and Behavioral Patterns.

4   Empirical Experimentation Setup

Patients who participate in empirical experimentation are users of a healthcare insurance prevention program serving approximately 25,000 users, with a gender distribution of approximately 53% women and 47% men. The average age of these users is 56.7 years, with a standard deviation of 13.2. These statistics were used as selection criteria to recruit participants for the experiment. The recruitment of participants began in July 2024. More than 700 beneficiaries, who were part of a T2 diabetes mellitus prevention program, were invited to participate. 437 participants agreed to participate and were recruited through service centers in five different cities. Of the invited users, 380 (58% women and 42% men with an average age of 55.05 years) interacted at least once since the beginning of the experiment, which took place from August 20, 2024 to May 4, 2025. For the proportion of men, the confidence interval 95% is (36.4, 46.6), which includes the population proportion of the sample, suggesting that the sample proportion (41.5%) is not significantly different from the population proportion. Regarding age, the confidence interval for the mean is (52.46, 61.53), indicating that the sample mean (55 years) does not differ significantly from the population mean.

The use of proactive assistants by beneficiaries of the health prevention program was authorized by the ethics committee of the University of Fortaleza in conjunction with the Health Plan Company, under CAAE number 73913723.5.0000.5052. Participants signed the consent form in person at the health facility, and this document included information about the use of an API to access an OpenAI enterprise account, which ensures that OpenAI would not use user data for training purposes, in compliance with OpenAI's Data Protection Policy. To ensure the privacy of user data, all patient information was anonymized. Internally, patients were referred to by numbers, and assistants interacted using only the patient's first name, avoiding any information that could directly identify individuals. The link between the Health Plan identification number and the actual patient information was maintained exclusively by the Health Plan Company staff.

5   Quantitative Evaluation

To evaluate the impact of different proactive assistants, we performed an analysis of the interactions between participants and the assistant. Three different assistants were considered: Baseline (MarIA), MariaRel, and MarIAToM. Both of the versions run the GPT-4o-mini as an LLM model. The MarIA Baseline Campaign ran from August 19, 2024, to March 18, 2025. MarIARel was active from September 17, 2024, to January 11, 2025, followed by the launch of MarIAToM on January 8, 2025.

MarIA starts a conversation by means of a set of educational messages prepared *a priori* by the company's technical staff, which were periodically (typically once a week) sent to all users. [24] describes the main commands of the prompt used to decide when to start a conversation.

MarIARel uses a subset of the features listed in Table 1, focusing on topics that are contextually appropriate and meaningful–particularly those represented in the assistant's memory of the user's mental state. When a relevant topic is identified, MarIARel assesses its importance by assigning it a relevance level (high, medium, or low) and recommends a suitable interval for sending a follow-up message (e.g., in 1, 2, 3 days, or more), based on that classification.

MarIAToM considers all the features defined for proactive assistants in Table 1, making it fully emotionally aware. Its decision on when to initiate an interaction is entirely autonomous, occurs in real time, and is based on a combination of factors–including the user's mental and emotional state, medical data, time since the last interaction, and a detailed interaction profile that includes contact frequency, engagement level, preferred times, communication style, and behavioral patterns. Figure 3 presents the main points of MarIAToM's decision prompt.

MarIAToM Decision Prompt

Evaluate {input data} and decide whether or not to talk to the patient {name} now. To make your decision, take the following into account:
1. Choose a conversation topic that is relevant to the patient.
2. Note that the last interaction with the patient occurred {X} days ago.
3. Follow the Social Interaction Rules.

.

.

.

[SOCIAL INTERACTION RULES]:
- Avoid sending too many messages if the patient hasn't responded yet. Not everyone can reply immediately. Don't be an annoying assistant.
- Don't be repetitive. Take into account the information in the last messages sent by the assistant and check whether the topic has already been addressed.
- If the patient has received many messages from the assistant and still hasn't responded, evaluate: were they just busy or truly disengaged? Consider this when making your decision.

Fig. 3. Prompt used by MarIAToM to determine if a conversation should be initiated.

5.1   Defining Response Predictability

Inspired by Fisher's incremental clustering algorithm Cobweb [9], we define the predictability of response $(Pred(R))$ as the probability that a user replies to a message sent by the assistant, relative to the number of users who received that message. In this study, all probabilities are empirically estimated from the observed frequencies of real interactions between users and the assistant. This extends Fisher's notion of predictability–originally used for classifying attribute values–to modeling user response behavior. Instead of predicting attribute distributions, we estimate the likelihood that a message will elicit a user response, taking into account the extent of message distribution. This mirrors Cobweb's principle of optimizing category structures based on predictability but here focuses on optimizing communication strategies in conversational assistants.

The predictability is determined by the probability that a user *receives* the message ($P(M)$) and the *conditional probability* that the user *responds* to the received message ($P(R \mid M)$), formally expressed as:

$$Pred(R) = P(M) \times P(R \mid M) \tag{10}$$

For the baseline MarIA messages are sent to all users, so $P(M) = 1$. In contrast, MarIAToM and MarIARel have an activation criterion based on the conversation context, which means that not all users receive messages, resulting in $P(M) <= 1$.

We considered that an initial interaction was not successful if no response was received within 24 h of the assistant's message.

5.2 Experimental Results

Figure 4 shows the behavior of the three versions of the assistant: Baseline, MarIARel, and MarIAToM in relation to user engagement over time. The x-axis of all graphs represents the normalized time since the initial message ($t - t_0$) relative to the maximum observation period ($t_{\max}$).

The graph on the left shows the probability that a user will respond to a message after receiving it. MarIARel demonstrates the highest conditional response probability at the beginning of the experiment, with a probability curve that declines more gradually over time. MarIATom shows high response probability in the middle weeks, indicating strong user engagement due to its advanced emotional and cognitive personalization. The Baseline Assistant has the lowest response probability, with a sharp decline, suggesting that users quickly lose interest when messages lack contextual relevance.

The graph in the center illustrates the probability that an assistant chooses a user to receive a message. The Baseline Assistant maintains a constant high probability, as it is designed to engage all users consistently without selective targeting. However, MarIARel and MarIATom show a lower probability, reflecting their context-dependent activation mechanism, which selectively sends messages based on previous interactions. However, MarIAToM has the ability to be more inclusive than MarIARel, targeting more users because it uses the emotional and cognitive knowledge of the user to create engaging talks.

The graph on the right illustrates the predictability of user responses over time, showing how each assistant balances response rates and user reach. MarIAToM stands out by dynamically adapting to user context, selecting the right users for each message, demonstrating the value of integrating ToM features. MarIARel, while achieving high response rates, limits its overall impact by repeatedly targeting the same highly engaged users, leading to reduced reach and declining predictability. Interestingly, the Baseline assistant, despite its indiscriminate messaging strategy, performs better than MarIARel in terms of overall predictability. This suggests that an excessive focus on a narrow user group can be more detrimental to sustained engagement than broadly targeting all users, even without personalization.

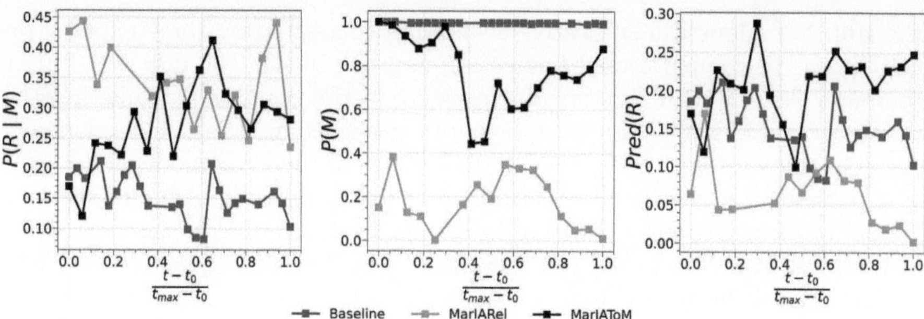

Fig. 4. Comparison of Baseline, MarIARel, and MarIAToM in terms of conditional response probability ($P(R \mid M)$), message reach probability ($P(M)$), and response predictability ($Pred(R)$). MarIAToM achieves the highest predictability over time by balancing response rate and user reach. MarIARel shows high response rates but reduced reach due to narrow targeting, resulting in lower predictability than the Baseline.

The average predictability $\bar{P}$ observed for MarIA, MarIARel, and MarIAToM was

$$\bar{P}(R_{\text{Baseline}}) = 15.17\%, \bar{P}(R_{\text{Rel}}) = 6.42\%, \bar{P}(R_{\text{ToM}}) = 20.43\%.$$

In addition to the average predictability, we analyzed the average length of user responses, denoted by L, measured as the average number of words per response.

$$L_{\text{baseline}} = 7.2, L_{\text{Rel}} = 4.7, L_{\text{ToM}} = 13.16$$

The results indicate that user responses to MarIAToM's proactive messages were significantly longer compared to the other assistants. Specifically, the average response length to MarIAToM was approximately 2.8 times greater than for MarIARel. It was also 1.83 times greater than the Baseline. This increase in response length reinforces the hypothesis that cognitive and emotional personalization fosters deeper and more meaningful conversations.

Our findings suggest that the integration of emotional and cognitive components into proactive assistants in healthcare enhances user interaction. MarIAToM not only achieved the highest predictability, but also elicited more elaborate user replies. This shows the potential of cognitive personalization to promote greater participation and sustained participation of patients in health-related conversations.

6   Qualitative Evaluation

6.1   Methodology

We evaluated how the messages from the two versions of proactive CAs incorporated emotional elements and how these influenced user engagement. Directly assessing user emotions presents challenges, as self-reports often suffer from recall bias [16]. We adopted a subjective evaluation conducted by three experts: one in HCI, one in computational linguistics, and one in AI. The first is a PhD in Computer Science with 20 years of experience in UX evaluation, while the other two are graduate students with 4 years of experience in assistant development. They classified a text into emotional dimensions of the PAD model [22].

The evaluation methodology occurred in two stages. First, due to the large number of messages sent (11,310 in total), we analyzed random samples: 3.67% of messages from MarIARel (80 messages from 2,175 total) and 0.87% from MarIAToM (80 messages from 9,135 total). Among the 80 messages of each assistant, half of them have been responded to by the user, and half of them have not. The messages are composed of five segments: a) greeting the user ("Hi Roseana, I hope you are well!"); b) encouraging the user by valuing positive attitudes or suggesting openness to interaction ("I noticed we haven't spoken in a while, there is something interesting I would like to share"); c) reflective questions ("How have you been feeling about your health goals recently?"); d) suggestions for the user ("It is important to see your doctor to talk about this"); e) messages of support ("If you need to vent or seek guidance, I am here to help").

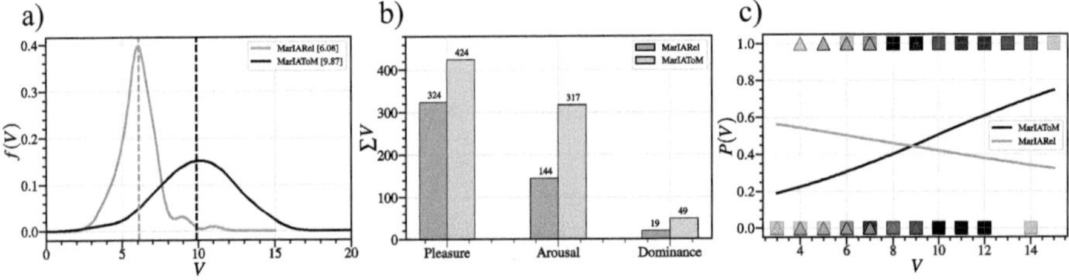

Fig. 5. Comparison Between the Proactive Assistants: a) The KDE distribution [25] shows that MarIAToM's messages have a higher average emotional charge compared to MarIARel. b) Based on the PAD Model, bar charts reveal that MarIAToM dominates across all three dimensions, Pleasure, Arousal, and Dominance, indicating stronger emotional engagement; c) A positive correlation was found between the emotional intensity of MarIAToM's messages and user engagement, while MarIARel showed a negative correlation, suggesting less interest of the users in participating of MarIARel talks.

In the second stage, experts empirically assigned each message segment to pleasure, arousal, and dominance based on the PAD model. The pleasure is typically reflected in warm greetings, personalized encouragements, and supportive language that fosters emotional security. The arousal (excitement) is evident in reflective questions about goals, health status, or behavior changes, and the dominance is highlighted through personalized identification and autonomy-focused suggestions.

For each segment message, the computational linguistics expert and the AI expert evaluated the intensity of its emotional charge, rated it as high (***), moderate (**), or low (*) based on its potential to evoke a response. In cases of disagreement, the HCI expert mediated to reach a consensus. The final emotional charge of each message was calculated by summing the number of stars assigned to each of its segments, providing an aggregate measure of its emotional intensity.

6.2   Results of the Qualitative Evaluation

In the analysis of 160 messages, 604 segments were identified - 370 (61.2%) of MarIAToM and 234 (38.7%) of MarIARel, averaging 3.77 segments per message with a standard deviation of 1.12. MarIAToM's longer messages naturally contain more segments. Figure 5a shows that MarIAToM incorporates more positive emotional elements. The average emotional intensity of MarIAToM's messages, calculated from the sum of star ratings per segment, is 9.87, compared to 6.08 for MarIARel. Figure 5b highlights that MarIAToM consistently shows a higher emotional intensity in all PAD elements (Pleasure, Arousal and Dominance).

When examining the correlation between the emotional charge of MarIAToM and the user response rates, a positive correlation of 0.21 was observed, as shown in Fig. 5c. A logistic regression fit revealed that each one-unit increase in emotional charge was associated with a 21% increase in the odds of a user response (odds ratio = 1.21). In contrast, MarIARel's correlation is negative and close to zero, showing no significant relationship. These results support the hypothesis that the integration of emotional elements into message design not only increases response rates, but also fosters more reflective and emotionally resonant interactions, especially with MarIAToM.

7   Conclusion

This study demonstrates that proactive, emotionally and cognitively aware assistants, particularly MarIAToM, foster more emotional, meaningful, and engaging conversations, significantly stimulating user participation. The results show that MarIAToM achieved the highest response predictability (20.43%) and elicited longer and more reflective user replies, with an average length of 13.16 words–nearly three times that of MarIARel and almost double that of the baseline assistant. A key factor behind MarIAToM's success is its ability to sustain engagement without overwhelming users. Unlike conventional systems that risk becoming intrusive or monotonous by sending frequent, irrelevant messages, MarIAToM determines the right moment, topic, and context to initiate conversations. These findings highlight the potential of human-centered AI in healthcare, paving the way for more adaptive and empathetic digital health interventions.

However, some limitations must be acknowledged. One critical area for future research involves investigating the potential biases inherent in LLM-based assistants like MarIAToM. Such biases could inadvertently lead to manipulative or undesirable communication patterns that may negatively affect users, especially in sensitive healthcare contexts. To mitigate these risks, during our experimentation, we implemented an LLM-based auditing layer that monitored all interactions with MarIA. Critical situations, such as indications of poor health conditions or responses that diverged from the ethical standards defined in MarIA's system prompts, triggered real-time alerts to the healthcare team, who assessed whether any intervention was necessary. This safeguard mechanism was essential for ensuring user safety, but it must be further enhanced to detect other forms of potentially harmful agent behavior, including subtle manipulative patterns or unintended emotional influence.

Another important limitation is that this study focuses solely on the assistant's ability to sustain user interactions. The implicit hypothesis that increased interaction frequency improves self-care behaviors, such as glycemic control, is currently being addressed in ongoing research.

Acknowledgments. This study was conducted within the scope of the Reference Center for Artificial Intelligence (CEREIA), supported by FAPESP, under the FAPE-SPMCTICCGI.BR program, in partnership with the Hapvida Group.

References

1. Martins, A., Londral, A., Nunes, I.L., Lapão, L.V.: Unlocking human-like conversations: scoping review of automation techniques for personalized healthcare interventions using conversational agents. Int. J. Med. Inform. **185**, 105385 (2024)
2. Dzomba, B., Bond, K., Flite, C.: Blowing chunks with ChatGPT. In: Proceedings of ICHI, pp. 673–676. IEEE (2023)
3. Baron-Cohen, S., Leslie, A.M., Frith, U.: Does the autistic child have a "theory of mind"? Cognition **21**, 37–46 (1985)
4. Bodenheimer, C.D., Holman, H.: Helping patients adopt healthier behaviors. Clin. Diab. **25**(2), 66–70 (2007)
5. An, L., Muñoz, D., Pedell, S., Sterling, L.: Understanding confidence of older adults for embracing mobile technologies. In: Proceedings of OzCHI, pp. 38–50 (2022)
6. Sharma, D., Kaushal, S., Kumar, H., Gainder, S.: Chatbots in healthcare: challenges, technologies and applications. In: Proceedings of AIST, pp. 1–6 (2022)
7. Da Silva, T.H.O., Furtado, V., Furtado, E., Mendes, M., Almeida, V., Sales, L.: How do illiterate people interact with an intelligent voice assistant? Int. J. Hum.-Comput. Interact. **40**(3), 584–602 (2022). https://doi.org/10.1080/10447318.2022.2121219
8. Eysenbach, G.: The role of chatgpt, generative language models, and artificial intelligence in medical education: a conversation with chatgpt and a call for papers. J. Med. Educ. **47**(1), 1–5 (2023)
9. Fisher, D.: Knowledge acquisition via incremental conceptual clustering. Mach. Learn. **1**(2), 139–172 (1987)
10. Frijda, N.H.: The psychologists' point of view. In: Lewis, M., Haviland-Jones, J.M., Barrett, L.F. (eds.) Handbook of Emotions, 3 edn, pp. 68–87. Guilford Press (2008)
11. Furtado, E., Furtado, V., Vasconcelos, E.: A conceptual framework for the design and evaluation of affective usability in educational geosimulation systems. In: Baranauskas, C., Palanque, P., Abascal, J., Barbosa, S.D.J. (eds.) INTERACT

2007. LNCS, vol. 4662, pp. 497–510. Springer, Heidelberg (2007). https://doi.org/10.1007/978-3-540-74796-3_48

12. Heisler, M., Resnicow, K.: Helping patients make and sustain healthy changes: a brief introduction to motivational interviewing in clinical diabetes care. Clin. Diab. **26**(4), 161–165 (2008)

13. Huang, M., Zhu, X., Gao, J.: Challenges in building intelligent open-domain dialog systems. ACM Trans. Inf. Syst. (TOIS) **38**(3), 1–32 (2020)

14. Balsa, J., et al.: Usability of an intelligent virtual assistant for promoting behavior change and self-care in older people with type 2 diabetes. J. Med. Syst. **44**(7), 130–131 (2020)

15. Lima, L., Furtado, V., Furtado, E., Almeida, V.: Empirical analysis of bias in voice-based personal assistants. In: Companion Proceedings of the 2019 World Wide Web Conference, WWW 2019, pp. 533–538. Association for Computing Machinery, New York (2019). https://doi.org/10.1145/3308560.3317597

16. Maia, C.L.B., Furtado, E.S.: An approach to analyze user's emotion in HCI experiments using psychophysiological measures. IEEE Access **7**, 36471–36480 (2019). https://doi.org/10.1109/ACCESS.2019.2904977

17. Nikitina, S., Callaioli, S., Baez, M.: Smart conversational agents for reminiscence. In: Proceedings of SE4COG, pp. 52–57 (2018)

18. O'Brien, H., Toms, E.: What is user engagement? A conceptual framework for defining user engagement with technology. JASIST **59**, 938–955 (2008). https://doi.org/10.1002/asi.20801

19. Liu, P., Yuan, W., Fu, J., Jiang, Z., Hayashi, H., Neubig, G.: Pre-train, prompt, and predict: a systematic survey of prompting methods in natural language processing. ACM Comput. Surv. **55**(9), 1–35 (2023)

20. Park, G., Chung, J., Lee, S.: Effect of AI chatbot emotional disclosure on user satisfaction and reuse intention for mental health counseling: a serial mediation model. Curr. Psychol. **42**(32), 28663–28673 (2023)

21. Premack, D., Woodruff, G.: Does the chimpanzee have a theory of mind? Behav. Brain Sci. **1**, 515–526 (1978)

22. Mehrabian, A., Russell, J.A.: An Approach to Environmental Psychology. MIT Press, Cambridge (1974)

23. Rzadeczka, M., Sterna, A., Stolińska, J., Kaczyńska, P., Moskalewicz, M., et al.: The efficacy of conversational AI in rectifying the theory-of-mind and autonomy biases: Comparative analysis. JMIR Mental Health **12**(1), e64396 (2025)

24. Silva, V., Furtado, E.S., Oliveira, J., Furtado, V.: Engenharia de prompts em assistentes conversacionais para promoção de autocuidado baseados em modelos amplos de linguagem. In: Simpósio Brasileiro de Computação Aplicada à Saúde (SBCAS), pp. 377–388. SBC (2024)

25. Silverman, B.W.: Density Estimation for Statistics and Data Analysis. Chapman & Hall/CRC (1998)

26. Sperber, D., Wilson, D.: Relevance: communication and cognition. Cognition **1**(2), 139–172 (1986)

27. Street, W.: LLM theory of mind and alignment: opportunities and risks. arXiv:2405.08154 (2024)

Evaluating Graph-Based Representations of ATR-FTIR Data Using Complex Networks

Barbara Cristina Gama[(⊠)], Robinson Sabino-Silva, Douglas Carvalho Caixeta,
Thulio Marquez Cunha, and Murillo Guimarães Carneiro

Federal University of Uberlândia, Uberlândia, MG, Brazil
{barbaracgama,douglas.caixeta,mgcarneiro}@ufu.br

Abstract. This study investigates different graph construction heuristics applied to attenuated total reflectance Fourier transform infrared spectroscopy (ATR-FTIR) data, analyzing their topological properties using complex network metrics. In addition to this structural analysis, we also evaluate the data classification performance of each graph representation. We compare traditional approaches—such as co-occurrence (COOC), correlation (CORR), epsilon neighborhood (EPS), and k-nearest neighbors (kNN)—with visibility-based strategies (visibility graph - VG). These methods are applied to three biomedical datasets (COVID-19, Oral Cancer, and Diabetes), with their topological properties analyzed using complex network metrics. The topological analysis revealed that COOC and EPS generated structurally poor networks, due to fragmentation or overdensity. In contrast, kNN, CORR, and the two VG variants consistently produced sparse networks with high modularity, indicating a more informative representation. The classification results confirm that there is no universally superior method, with the best performance being dataset-dependent: kNN achieved the highest accuracy for COVID-19, CORR for Oral Cancer, and VG sim for Diabetes. These results collectively validate kNN, CORR, and visibility graphs approaches as effective and structurally expressive tools for spectral data, offering a robust alternative to traditional vector-based analysis in machine learning applications.

Keywords: ATR-FTIR data · Complex networks · Graph
construction · Vibrational spectroscopy · Visibility Graphs

1 Introduction

Attenuated total reflectance Fourier transform infrared spectroscopy (ATR-FTIR) is a powerful technique for the precise chemical characterization of complex samples, with widespread use in both industrial and scientific applications. In medical sciences, it stands out as a non-invasive tool for detecting metabolic and oncological alterations by capturing specific molecular signatures

© The Author(s), under exclusive license to Springer Nature Switzerland AG 2026
R. de Freitas and D. Furtado (Eds.): BRACIS 2025, LNAI 16181, pp. 170–185, 2026.
https://doi.org/10.1007/978-3-032-15990-8_12

from biofluids [2,7,19]. The combination of ATR-FTIR with machine learning has proven effective in various classification tasks [6,10,12,20,23], but faces challenges like high dimensionality and data correlation.

Traditionally, spectral analysis treats data as feature vectors for use in methods like PCA and SVM [11,15,21,22,26]. However, this approach may not adequately capture the underlying structural relationships within the data. Representing spectra as graphs has emerged as a promising alternative, allowing the exploration of topological properties through complex network metrics [14]. While several graph construction methods exist, the application of visibility graphs (VGs) to ATR-FTIR data remains limited. This work addresses this gap by proposing two novel VG-based heuristics and evaluating them against four traditional graph construction methods.

We conduct a comparative analysis across three biomedical ATR-FTIR datasets, using a dual approach: we examine the topological differences of the resulting graphs and assess their discriminative power in supervised classification tasks. The main contributions of this work include: the proposal of two novel visibility graph heuristics for ATR-FTIR data; their application to three real-world biomedical datasets; a comprehensive topological characterization using network metrics; an evaluation of their discriminative power through supervised classification; and a critical comparison against traditional methods, providing guidance for future applications.

This paper is structured as follows. Section 2 details the databases and the methodology used for preprocessing, graph construction, and classification. Section 3 presents and discusses the topological and classification results. Finally, Sect. 4 provides our conclusions and directions for future work.

2   Literature Review

Several studies have explored the application of complex networks in the analysis of spectral data, with an emphasis on the extraction of structural properties that reveal non-trivial patterns in the data. In the work presented in [7], high-level network-based classification techniques, such as the clustering coefficient network measure, achieve 71% accuracy and 81% sensitivity in detecting oral cancer from ATR-FTIR spectra, outperforming state-of-the-art classifiers, such as convolutional neural networks. Representing spectra through graphs allows an analysis based on the interactions and internal structures of the samples, expanding the possibilities for interpretation and pattern discovery. This type of high-level analysis has proven effective in various data classification scenarios [25]. Graph-based learning has also been successfully applied, for example, in identifying invariant patterns in images through community detection [8]. The work presented in [28] shows that transforming time series into complex networks allows us to preserve underlying geometric features of the time series. This transformation facilitates the identification of dynamic transitions through statistics of the structure of the corresponding networks. In [24] it is demonstrated that transformations of time series data into complex networks allow us to characterize the underlying dynamics of the time series in terms of topological features of the complex network.

Several graph construction strategies have been proposed, from innovative methods such as Visibility Graphs (VG) to more traditional approaches such as k-Nearest Neighbor Graphs (kNN). Visibility Graph (VG), proposed by [13], creates connections between points based on a geometric visibility rule. This technique preserves structural aspects of the series or spectrum, capturing both local and global patterns of variation. In addition to visibility graphs, other structural approaches have been explored in the representation of spectral data. Among them, the graphs based on k-nearest neighbors (kNN) and neighborhood-ϵ stand out, which connect samples or variables based on similarity (Euclidean distance, for example). Another widely applied representation form is the correlation graph, in which connections are established between spectral variables based on high linear correlation coefficients. Correlation graphs are used to analyze complex spectral data, such as in spectroscopy, where the correlation between different spectral bands can reveal information about the chemical composition or physical properties of a sample [4,17]. Similarly, co-occurrence graphs connect points or variables based on the frequency with which they occur together, capturing contextual dependencies that can reveal latent structures in the data.

Despite the diversity of methods for graph construction and analysis of their properties, no studies have performed a systematic comparison between different graph construction approaches applied to ATR-FTIR spectral data. While an earlier analysis compared several kNN-based heuristics for general data classification, this work expands the scope significantly by introducing and evaluating visibility-based graphs specifically for the spectral domain [3]. Thus, this work proposes an original contribution by performing a systematic comparative analysis between multiple graph construction methods applied to ATR-FTIR data. The evaluation is conducted both from the perspective of structural characterization, through complex network measurements, and regarding the effectiveness of these representations in supervised classification tasks.

3   Materials and Methods

3.1   Databases

In this study, three spectral databases obtained through the attenuated total reflectance infrared spectroscopy (ATR-FTIR) technique were used. Each database represents a distinct biomedical scenario, which are the detection of COVID-19, the diagnosis of oral cancer, and the identification of diabetes. The samples are composed of absorbance spectra, and each is labeled according to its respective class. Table 1 presents a summary of the main characteristics of the databases before preprocessing, including the number of samples, the original number of spectral attributes.

To provide an initial visual characterization of the datasets, Fig. 1 presents the average absorbance spectrum for each class within the three databases. These

Table 1. Summary of databases before preprocessing.

Database	Samples	Attributes
COVID-19	200	1.799
Oral Cancer	65	1.868
Diabetes	68	1.868

plots allow a preliminary observation of spectral differences between groups, highlighting potential regions of interest that may be relevant for classification tasks. The horizontal axis corresponds to the wavenumber (cm^{-1}), and the vertical axis represents the average absorbance. Each subplot corresponds to one database, showing the spectral profiles for the classes present in that context.

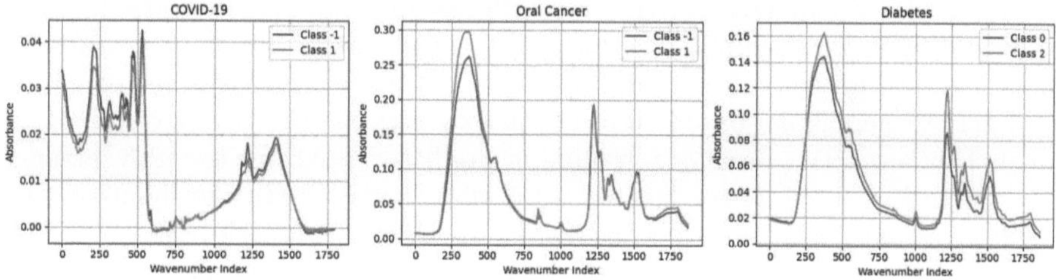

Fig. 1. Mean absorbance spectra for each class in the three spectral databases: COVID-19, Oral Cancer, and Diabetes.

3.2   Preprocessing

The preprocessing of the spectral data aimed to reduce the dimensionality of the data and remove spectral regions of lesser analytical relevance. The step consisted of reading the data and their respective wavenumbers, with subsequent truncation of the spectrum to maintain only the range between 900 and 1800 cm^{-1}. This spectral region is known to concentrate key absorption vibrational modes corresponding to biomolecular components such as lipids, proteins, and nucleic acids, forming the biochemical fingerprint of the sample. After truncation to this region of interest, the spectral data were used directly in the experiments without applying smoothing filters or additional normalization procedures. This decision was made to preserve the raw spectral morphology, which is central to the visibility graph's construction principle, thus avoiding potential distortions introduced by normalization algorithms.

3.3   Graph Construction

To transform spectral data into network representations, six distinct strategies were employed. Each method constructs graphs based on different principles, capturing varying topological relationships. For each strategy, we describe two approaches: (1) graph construction for topological analysis, in which nodes represent samples (instances); and (2) graph construction for predictive analysis, in which each sample is associated to its own graph, and complex network measures are calculated over it to obtain the features.

- Co-occurrence Graph (COOC): This is a type of graph in which nodes represent samples and edges indicate high similarity between them. In the topological analysis, a connection occurs if the number of common features with values above a global median exceeds a predefined threshold. For predictive analysis, spectrum features are discretized into bins; nodes in the same bin are connected, and nodes in neighboring bins are linked according to some threshold.
- Correlation Graph (CORR): In this model, each node represents an instance, but the edges indicate the structural similarity of their internal correlation graphs. In topological analysis, for each instance, an auxiliary graph is generated by connecting sliding windows of the signal with high Pearson correlation. The final graph is then constructed by connecting each instance to its k nearest neighbors, based on the similarity between the degree distributions of their respective auxiliary graphs. In predictive analysis, for each instance, a graph is created where the nodes are sliding windows of the signal and the edges connect windows that are highly correlated with each other.
- ϵ-Neighborhood Graph (ϵ-*neighborhood*) (EPS): This is a graph in which each node represents an instance of the data, and an edge is created between two nodes if the euclidean distance between them is less than a threshold value ϵ. For topological analysis, the graph is formed as follows: each node represents an instance of the dataset, and edges are created if the distance between two nodes is less than a threshold ϵ. In the predictive analysis, a graph is constructed for each instance, in which the nodes represent the instance attributes, and the edges connect nodes whose values are close (absolute difference less than ϵ).
- k-Nearest Neighbors Graph (kNN): The KNN graph is widely used to represent local similarity relationships between data. For topological analysis, the nodes are the instances, which are connected to their k nearest neighbors based on Euclidean distance. For the predictive analysis, a graph is generated for each instance, where the nodes are its attributes, which are also connected using k nearest neighbors criterion.
- Similarity Visibility Graph (VG sim.): In this model, the structural similarity between the Visibility Graphs (VG) of each instance is quantified. For topological analysis, an individual VG is constructed for each instance, and its adjacency matrix is vectorized. The cosine similarity between these vectors is then used to construct a final graph connecting each instance to its k-nearest neighbors, based on the complete similarity of their topologies. In predictive analysis, each instance is converted into a visibility graph. This is done by applying the algorithm to a reduced time series composed of the medians of sequential windows of the original signal. The complex network measures obtained from this graph serve as features for classification.

– Distribution Visibility Graph (VG dist.): Similarly to the previous one, this graph also connects instances based on the similarity of their VGs. However, in topological analysis, similarity is assessed by comparing the degree distributions (histograms) of the individual VGs. Connections are established via k-nearest neighbors, joining instances whose VGs present the most similar connectivity profiles. For predictive analysis, a visibility graph is generated for each instance, and complex network measures are extracted for classifiers.

3.4   Complex Network Measures

To characterize the generated graphs topologically, a comprehensive set of measures from complex network theory was extracted. The selection of these measures was guided by previous studies on their individual predictive capabilities in classification contexts [18]. These measures allow us to evaluate structural properties at different scales:

– Global structure: number of vertices and edges, density, number of components, diameter, average path.
– Connectivity and local organization: average degree, maximum degree, minimum degree, standard deviation of degree, assortativity coefficient.
– Efficiency and centrality: global efficiency, average and maximum betweenness, average closeness, average eigenvector centrality.
– Clustering and community: average/maximum clustering, and modularity.
– Other informative metrics: transitivity and degree entropy.

3.5   Classification Methods and Performance

To assess the discriminative ability of each graph representation, nine complex network metrics (transitivity, clustering, modularity, density, closeness, average degree, betweenness, diameter and assortativity) were extracted from each generated structure, forming a feature vector. These vectors were then used to train six classic supervised classification algorithms: k-Nearest Neighbors (kNN), Naive Bayes, Support Vector Machines with linear kernel (SVM Linear) and with radial kernel (SVM RBF), Random Forest (RF) and Multilayer Perceptron (MLP). For a fair baseline comparison, all classifiers were implemented using their default parameters as provided by the scikit-learn library, without specific hyperparameter tuning for each dataset.

kNN classifies a sample based on the classes of its k nearest neighbors. Naive Bayes is a probabilistic classifier that assumes independence between attributes and uses Bayes' theorem. SVM searches for hyperplanes that separate classes, with the linear kernel for linearly separable data and the RBF kernel for more complex relationships. Random Forest combines several randomly constructed decision trees, offering robustness. MLP is a neural network with hidden layers, capable of learning non-linear patterns through supervised learning.

To evaluate the performance of the models, the following standard metrics were used: accuracy, which represents the proportion of correct predictions over the total samples; precision, which quantifies the proportion of true positives among all examples classified as positive; recall, which indicates the proportion of true positives over the total number of real positives; and F1-score, which is the harmonic mean between precision and recall, offering a balanced measure of performance especially in unbalanced databases.

All experiments were conducted using stratified cross-validation, with the aim of ensuring a robust and unbiased evaluation of the models. The implementations of the classifiers and metrics were carried out with the help of the `scikit-learn` library in Python.

4   Results and Discussion

In this section, we compare different graph construction strategies applied to the representation of spectral data, using several complex network metrics. We focus on aspects such as cluster existence, structural difference, etc. The approaches considered include co-occurrence graphs (COOC), correlation graphs (CORR), ϵ-neighborhood graphs (EPS), k-nearest neighbors (KNN), similarity visibility graph (VG sim.) and visibility graph by distribution (VG dist.) for the three databases. Next, we briefly present the results of the traditional classification, performed on the original spectra of the databases, and employing the same preprocessing. Finally, we discuss the performance of the classification based on complex networks, in which nine measures (transitivity, clustering, modularity, density, closeness, average degree, betweenness, diameter and assortativity) extracted from the graphs are used as attributes in predictive models, allowing the evaluation of the discriminative capacity of each type of structural representation.

4.1   Topological Analysis of Graphs with Complex Networks

Database - COVID-19. Table 2 presents the metrics extracted from each graph built for the COVID-19 database. An analysis reveals a divide between approaches that generate structurally informative graphs and those that do not. On the one hand, the COOC and EPS approaches generate dense networks, with high connectivity and low structural organization. The COOC graph, in particular, is highly fragmented, with 97 components, which makes it unsuitable for global analysis. The EPS graph, although connected, presents the highest density (0.784) and almost zero modularity (0.088), indicating a failure to separate the network into distinct communities.

In stark contrast, the other approaches CORR, kNN and visibility graph approaches (VG sim and VG dist) produce sparse networks, with low density (0.050) and a much clearer and more useful community structure. All four exhibit high modularity (0.592 for CORR, 0.793 for kNN, 0.591 for VG sim and 0.712 for VG dist), which is a indication that these representations are able to capture

Table 2. Complex network measurements extracted from different graphs constructed from the ATR-FTIR database - COVID-19

Measures	COOC	CORR	EPS	KNN	VG sim	VG dist
num_vertices	200	200	200	200	200	200
num_edge	5326	1000	15604	1000	1000	1000
density	0.267	0.050	0.784	0.050	0.050	0.050
transitivity	0.994	0.255	0.901	0.481	0.260	0.381
mean_path	null	3.493	1.274	9.317	3.330	4.907
diameter	null	7	5	29	7	12
num_components	97	1	1	1	1	1
mean_degree	53.26	10.0	156.04	10.0	10.0	10.0
max_degree	103	20	184	20	37	17
min_degree	0	5	1	5	5	5
degree_deviation	51.188	3.512	37.652	3.108	5.184	2.833
assortativity	−0.061	0.056	0.122	0.076	−0.106	0.070
global_efficiency	0.268	0.329	0.884	0.191	0.346	0.265
entropy_degree	1.490	3.634	5.261	3.544	3.708	3.454
mean_betweenness	0.150	248.13	27.350	827.545	231.875	388.8
max_betweenness	0.322	1464.648	432.772	9860.0	2207.291	2896.834
mean_closeness	nan	0.288	0.812	0.112	0.303	0.208
mean_eigenvector	0.517	0.305	0.849	0.087	0.165	0.129
mean_clustering	0.517	0.292	0.899	0.529	0.349	0.413
max_clustering	1.0	0.7	1.0	1.0	0.9	1.0
modularity	0.0	0.592	0.088	0.793	0.591	0.712

meaningful groupings in the data. The kNN stands out with the highest modularity, suggesting the best separation of communities. The CORR and VG sim graphs, although with more modest values, still exhibit good and very similar clustering ability.

Although the overall efficiency is higher on denser graphs (EPS), the true discriminative power for classification tasks, which rely on pattern separation, resides in representations with high modularity and degree entropy, prominent features in CORR, kNN and visibility methods.

Database - Oral Cancer. Table 3 presents the metrics extracted from each graph built for the Oral Cancer database. The results reinforce the trends observed above, clearly separating the graph construction methods into distinct structural families.

Again, the COOC and EPS approaches proved problematic. The COOC method results in a highly fragmented network (32 components) with zero modularity, which prevents the analysis of global patterns. EPS, while less fragmented

Table 3. Complex network measurements extracted from different graphs constructed from the ATR-FTIR database - Oral Cancer

Measures	COOC	CORR	EPS	KNN	VG sim	VG dist
num_vertices	65	65	65	65	65	65
num_edge	547	325	668	325	325	325
density	0.262	0.156	0.321	0.156	0.156	0.156
transitivity	0.978	0.363	0.774	0.552	0.376	0.475
mean_path	null	3.004	null	4.854	2.630	3.190
diameter	null	6	null	13	5	7
num_components	32	1	7	1	1	1
mean_degree	16.830	10.0	20.553	10.0	10.0	10.0
max_degree	33	15	33	16	22	21
min_degree	0	5	0	5	5	5
degree_deviation	16.119	2.260	10.216	2.631	3.882	3.410
assortativity	−0.137	0.021	0.483	0.082	0.148	0.062
global_efficiency	0.266	0.405	0.515	0.329	0.450	0.400
entropy_degree	1.769	3.108	4.290	3.312	3.414	3.470
mean_betweenness	0.215	64.138	30.569	123.338	52.169	70.107
max_betweenness	0.526	416.952	176.824	601.341	260.255	390.552
mean_closeness	null	0.336	nan	0.214	0.385	0.320
mean_eigenvector	0.511	0.336	0.550	0.229	0.273	0.244
mean_clustering	0.512	0.391	0.723	0.602	0.455	0.560
max_clustering	1.0	0.8	1.0	0.9	0.8	1.0
modularity	0.0	0.593	0.358	0.679	0.539	0.615

(7 components), presents the highest density (0.321) and low modularity (0.358), limiting its ability to reveal a clear community structure.

In stark contrast, the CORR, kNN and VG graphs are much sparser (density 0.156) and exhibit excellent community structure. Two of these methods exhibit the highest modularity indices by a wide margin, with 0.679 for kNN and 0.615 for VG dist, making them the most promising representations for classification tasks that rely on identifying distinct patient groups. The CORR (0.593) and VG sim (0.539) graphs also exhibit good community organization, confirming their usefulness as topological representations.

In summary, for the Oral Cancer dataset, the analysis confirms that neighborhood-based (kNN) and structural similarity-based (especially VG dist) methods are superior in creating rich, well-structured networks. The correlation approach (CORR) also proves to be a robust alternative, while COOC and EPS are less suitable for this application.

Database - Diabetes. Table 4 presents the metrics extracted from each graph constructed for the Diabetes database. The analysis of the metrics confirms the pattern observed previously, with a clear distinction between the graph construction methods.

Table 4. Complex network measurements extracted from different graphs constructed from the ATR-FTIR database - Diabetes

Measures	COOC	CORR	EPS	KNN	VG sim	VG dist
num_vertices	68	68	68	68	68	68
num_edge	465	340	1091	340	340	340
density	0.204	0.149	0.478	0.149	0.149	0.149
transitivity	1.0	0.332	0.831	0.601	0.405	0.390
mean_path	null	2.677	null	null	2.955	3.067
diameter	null	6	null	null	6	7
num_components	38	1	5	2	1	1
mean_degree	13.676	10.0	32.088	10.0	10.0	10.0
max_degree	30	23	52	18	18	19
min_degree	0	5	0	5	5	5
degree_deviation	14.941	3.472	13.709	2.473	3.240	3.203
assortativity	nan	−0.064	0.296	0.090	0.041	0.108
global_efficiency	0.204	0.439	0.648	0.228	0.414	0.409
entropy_degree	0.994	3.461	4.302	3.225	3.509	3.440
mean_betweenness	0.0	56.191	17.058	35.794	65.514	69.250
max_betweenness	0.0	292.025	64.223	265.702	319.122	383.195
mean_closeness	nan	0.377	nan	0.334	0.342	0.330
mean_eigenvector	0.455	0.388	0.608	0.166	0.365	0.299
mean_clustering	0.455	0.397	0.789	0.670	0.451	0.422
max_clustering	1.0	0.7	1.0	1.0	0.9	0.7
modularity	0.0	0.516	0.248	0.731	0.567	0.572

The COOC and EPS methods again generate problematic networks. The COOC method produces an extremely fragmented network (38 components) with zero modularity, making it unfeasible. EPS, which produces the densest network (0.478), is also fragmented (5 components) and has low modularity (0.248), making it equally unsuitable for community identification.

On the other hand, the methods that generate sparse graphs once again demonstrate their superiority in capturing the data structure. The kNN stands out significantly, achieving the highest modularity index (0.731), which indicates an exceptional ability to partition the network into well-defined communities. The visibility approaches, VG dist (0.572) and VG sim (0.567), along with the

CORR graph (0.516), also exhibit robust community structure, with the advantage of maintaining a fully connected network.

The analysis concludes that, for this dataset, the kNN method offers the most robust representation and the best community structure. However, the visibility and correlation graphs (CORR) provide an excellent balance between high modularity and global network connectivity, making all four strong candidates for feature extraction in machine learning models.

4.2   Traditional Classification Analysis

To establish a baseline, we first applied six traditional classification algorithms directly to the preprocessed spectral data. The following cross-validation results demonstrate the performance of these standard methods before applying our complex network-based approach, as shown in Table 5.

Table 5. Performance of traditional classification models on the three databases. The best accuracy for each dataset is highlighted in bold.

Database	Model	Accuracy $\pm$ DP	Precision	Recall	F1-score
COVID-19	kNN	0.48 ± 0.07	0.48	0.48	0.48
	Naive Bayes	0.50 ± 0.08	0.51	0.51	0.47
	SVM Linear	**0.57 ± 0.03**	**0.57**	**0.57**	**0.57**
	SVM RBF	0.52 ± 0.04	0.52	0.52	0.52
	Random Forest	0.49 ± 0.07	0.49	0.49	0.49
	MLP	0.55 ± 0.06	0.55	0.55	0.55
Oral Cancer	kNN	0.55 ± 0.15	0.54	0.55	0.54
	Naive Bayes	0.52 ± 0.06	0.49	0.52	0.50
	SVM Linear	0.49 ± 0.08	0.48	0.49	0.49
	SVM RBF	**0.61 ± 0.05**	**0.76**	**0.61**	0.48
	Random Forest	0.55 ± 0.12	0.54	0.55	0.55
	MLP	0.57 ± 0.08	0.57	0.57	**0.57**
Diabetes	kNN	0.51 ± 0.13	0.47	0.51	0.49
	Naive Bayes	0.41 ± 0.13	0.57	0.41	0.37
	SVM Linear	**0.69 ± 0.11**	**0.67**	**0.69**	**0.67**
	SVM RBF	0.65 ± 0.04	0.43	0.65	0.52
	Random Forest	0.53 ± 0.09	0.44	0.53	0.47
	MLP	0.56 ± 0.08	0.54	0.56	0.55

In general, it is observed that the performances obtained—even with the use of cross-validation—are modest, with accuracies ranging from 41% to 69%, in addition to relatively low and, in many cases, unbalanced precision, recall and F1-score values. These results reflect the intrinsic complexity of spectral data, which are composed of hundreds of highly correlated variables, instrumental noise and overlapping spectral bands. These limitations reinforce the need for more structured representations of the data, such as the use of complex networks, which allow the capture of relevant topological patterns. By transforming spectra into graphs, it is possible to extract more discriminative features, which can significantly improve the performance of classification models.

4.3 Classification Analysis with Complex Networks

In this section, we present the classification results using the measures extracted from the complex networks as features. For each of the three datasets, we evaluated six graph construction in combination with multiple classification algorithms (kNN, SVM, MLP, etc.). The goal was to use cross-validation to identify the configuration with the best performance in each scenario, the results as shown in Table 6.

Table 6. Best classification performance using complex network features. For each database and graph type, the table shows the result of the best classifier based on accuracy. The overall best accuracy for each database is in bold.

Database	Graph	Technique	Accuracy ± DP	Precision	Recall	F1-score
COVID-19	COOC	Naive Bayes	0.54 ± 0.09	0.56	0.54	0.49
	CORR	kNN	0.53 ± 0.10	0.53	0.53	0.52
	EPS	Naive Bayes	0.53 ± 0.02	0.53	0.53	0.44
	kNN	MLP	**0.61 ± 0.11**	**0.61**	**0.61**	**0.61**
	VG sim	SVM Linear	0.59 ± 0.11	0.60	0.59	0.58
	VG dist	MLP	0.60 ± 0.07	**0.61**	0.60	0.60
Oral Cancer	COOC	SVM Linear	0.60 ± 0.08	0.41	0.53	0.44
	CORR	MLP	**0.68 ± 0.11**	**0.70**	**0.67**	**0.65**
	EPS	kNN	0.61 ± 0.11	0.58	0.58	0.56
	kNN	SVM RBF	0.52 ± 0.15	0.27	0.43	0.33
	VG sim	Random Forest	0.61 ± 0.13	0.60	0.58	0.55
	VG dist	KNN	0.62 ± 0.21	0.60	0.62	0.59
Diabetes	COOC	Naive Bayes	0.66 ± 0.17	0.61	0.60	0.58
	CORR	SVM Linear	0.70 ± 0.09	0.49	0.56	0.50
	EPS	Random Forest	0.67 ± 0.12	0.57	0.58	0.56
	kNN	SVM RBF	0.66 ± 0.08	0.41	0.53	0.45
	VG sim	Naive Bayes	**0.73 ± 0.13**	**0.70**	**0.68**	**0.67**
	VG dist	Random Forest	0.72 ± 0.14	0.65	0.67	0.64

Database - COVID. For the COVID-19 database, the analysis of Table 6 indicates that the features extracted from the kNN graph, in combination with the MLP classifier, achieved the best performance, with an accuracy of 61%. The visibility similarity approaches also proved to be very effective, with the VG dist (60%) and VG sim (59%) presenting competitive and nearly equivalent results. In contrast, the other representations (COOC, CORR, EPS) performed at a lower level, with accuracies close to 54%.

Database - Oral Cancer. In the Oral Cancer database, the best combination was obtained with the correlation graph (CORR) and the MLP classifier, which achieved an accuracy of 68%. This combination also stood out in other metrics, such as precision and F1-score, suggesting a good suitability of this representation for the data. Interestingly, in this database, the lower performance of the kNN graph features (accuracy of 52%), which had stood out in the previous analysis, highlighting the method's dependence on the nature of the data.

Database - Diabetes. For the Diabetes dataset, the best performance was achieved by the VG sim graph, which, combined with the Naive Bayes classifier, achieved an accuracy of 73%. The VG dist graph, combined with Random Forest, also proved to be an excellent alternative, achieving an accuracy of 72%. With the exception of CORR (70%), the other approaches presented consistent and very close results, in the range of 66% to 67% accuracy, demonstrating the overall robustness of the methods for this dataset.

5   Conclusions

This work demonstrated that the choice of graph construction method profoundly impacts the quality of the structural representation of ATR-FTIR spectral data. Methods based on direct thresholding, such as Co-Occurrence (COOC) and ϵ-Neighborhood (EPS), tended to produce problematic networks, either due to fragmentation or high density with low modularity. In sharp contrast, approaches based on local neighborhood (kNN), structural similarity (VG sim and VG dist), and statistical relationships (CORR) consistently generated sparse, connected networks with high modularity, indicating a more efficient capture of the underlying data structure.

The topological superiority of these graphs (kNN, VGs, and CORR) directly translated into better performance in feature extraction for classification. One of the main conclusions of this study is that no graph construction method achieved universal superiority. The best performance was dataset-dependent: the kNN graph was the most effective for COVID-19, CORR for Oral Cancer, and VG sim for Diabetes. This reinforces that the evaluation of representations should not be limited to final accuracy, but also consider topological quality (such as modularity), which provides a more robust basis for feature extraction and interpretability.

We recognize as a limitation the variation of the best-performing graph approach across the different datasets, suggesting that the optimal representation may be data-dependent. Future work will focus on three main directions: (1) investigating hybrid methods that combine the structural properties of VGs with other graph construction techniques; (2) exploring the use of these rich graph representations as input for advanced models, such as Graph Neural Networks (GNNs), to further enhance classification performance; and (3) systematically evaluating the impact of common spectral pre-processing techniques. Applying methods such as baseline correction, smoothing, and normalization could potentially improve the performance and robustness of the graph-based models.

Acknowledgments. Authors thank the financial support given the Brazilian National Council for Scientific and Technological Development - CNPq (grants n. 420212/2023-0 and 445027/2024-0), the Minas Gerais Research Foundation FAPEMIG (grant n. APQ-00410-21), the INCT in Theranostics and Nanobiotechnology (grant n. CNPq-465669/2014-0), and the INCT in Oral Health and Odontology (grant n. CNPq-406840/2022-9). BCG thanks the Coordination of Improvement of Higher Education Personnel (CAPES) by her scholarship (grant n. 88887.912003/2023-00).

References

1. Anjos, O., Santos, A., Estevinho, L., Caldeira, I.: FTIR–ATR spectroscopy applied to quality control of grape-derived spirits. Food Chem. **205**, 28–35 (2016). https://doi.org/10.1016/j.foodchem.2016.02.128
2. Caixeta, D., et al.: Salivary ATR-FTIR spectroscopy coupled with support vector machine classification for screening of type 2 diabetes mellitus. Diagnostics **13** (2023). https://doi.org/10.3390/diagnostics13081396
3. Carneiro, M., Zhao, L.: Analysis of graph construction methods in supervised data classification. In: 2018 7th Brazilian Conference on Intelligent Systems (BRACIS), pp. 390–395 (2018). https://doi.org/10.1109/BRACIS.2018.00074
4. Cheng, F., Yang, C., Zhu, H., Li, Y., Lan, L., Wang, K.: Semi-supervised deep learning-based multicomponent spectral calibration modeling for UV-vis and near-infrared spectroscopy without information loss. Anal. Chem. **95**(36), 13446–13455 (2023). https://doi.org/10.1021/acs.analchem.3c01132
5. Christie, L., Rutherford, S., Palmer, D., Baker, M., Butler, H.: Bioprocess monitoring applications of an innovative ATR-FTIR spectroscopy platform. Front. Bioeng. Biotechnol. **12** (2024). https://doi.org/10.3389/fbioe.2024.1349473
6. Du, L., Yu, L.: New insights into raw milk adulterated with milk powder identification: ATR-FTIR spectroscopic fingerprints combined with machine learning and feature selection approaches. J. Food Compos. Anal., **133** (2024). https://doi.org/10.1016/j.jfca.2024.106443
7. Filho, R., Fernandes, J., Ji, D., Zhao, L., Sabino-Silva, R., Carneiro, M.: High-level network-based detection of oral cancer from ATR-FTIR spectroscopy. In: 2024 International Joint Conference on Neural Networks (IJCNN), pp. 1–8 (2024). https://doi.org/10.1109/IJCNN60899.2024.10650557
8. Freitas, L., Carneiro, M.: Community detection to invariant pattern clustering in images. In: 2019 8th Brazilian Conference on Intelligent Systems (BRACIS), pp. 610–615 (2019). https://doi.org/10.1109/BRACIS.2019.00112

9. França, T., Gonçalves, D., Cena, C.: ATR-FTIR spectroscopy combined with machine learning for classification of PVA/PVP blends in low concentration. Vib. Spectrosc., **120** (2022). https://doi.org/10.1016/j.vibspec.2022.103378

10. Guo, S., et al.: Fast and deep diagnosis using blood-based ATR-FTIR spectroscopy for digestive tract cancers. Biomolecules **12** (2022). https://doi.org/10.3390/biom12121815

11. Howley, T., Madden, M.G., O'Connell, M.-L., Ryder, A.G.: The effect of principal component analysis on machine learning accuracy with high-dimensional spectral data. Appl. Innov. Intell. Syst. **XIII**, 209–222 (2006). https://doi.org/10.1007/1-84628-224-1_16

12. Khalighi, S., Ma, L., Ren, S., Varveri, A.: Evaluating the impact of data preprocessing methods on classification of ATR-FTIR spectra of bituminous binders. Fuel, **376** (2024). https://doi.org/10.1016/j.fuel.2024.132701

13. Lacasa, L., Luque, B., Ballesteros, F., Luque, J., Nuño, J.: From time series to complex networks: the visibility graph. Proc. Natl. Acad. Sci. **105**, 4972–4975 (2008). https://doi.org/10.1073/pnas.0709247105

14. Costa, L.F., Rodrigues, F.A., Travieso, G., Villas Boas, P.R.: Characterization of complex networks: a survey of measurements. Adv. Phys. **56**, 167–242 (2007). https://doi.org/10.1080/00018730601170527

15. Li, M., Wibowo, S., Li, W., Li, L.: Quantitative spectral data analysis using extreme learning machines algorithm incorporated with PCA. Algorithms **14**, 18 (2021). https://doi.org/10.3390/a14010018

16. Lv, G., et al.: Feasibility of nondestructive soluble sugar monitoring in tomato: quantified and sorted through ATR-FTIR coupled with chemometrics. Agronomy, **14** (2024). https://doi.org/10.3390/agronomy14102392

17. Marcial-Pablo, M., Ontiveros-Capurata, R., Jiménez-Jiménez, S., Ojeda-Bustamante, W.: Maize crop coefficient estimation based on spectral vegetation indices and vegetation cover fraction derived from UAV-based multispectral images. Agronomy **11**, 668 (2021). https://doi.org/10.3390/agronomy11040668

18. Carneiro, M.G., Gama, B.C., Ribeiro, O.S.: Complex network measures for data classification. In: 2021 International Joint Conference on Neural Networks (IJCNN), Shenzhen, China, pp. 1–8 (2021). https://doi.org/10.1109/IJCNN52387.2021.9533608

19. Naseer, K., Ali, S., Qazi, J.: ATR-FTIR spectroscopy as the future of diagnostics: a systematic review of the approach using biofluids. Appl. Spectrosc. Rev. **56**, 85–97 (2020). https://doi.org/10.1080/05704928.2020.1738453

20. Neves, M., Poppi, R.: Authentication and identification of adulterants in virgin coconut oil using ATR/FTIR in tandem with DD-SIMCA one class modeling. Talanta **219**, 121338 (2020). https://doi.org/10.1016/j.talanta.2020.121338

21. Paikaray, B., Pramanik, J., Samal, A.: An introductory approach to spectral image analysis using machine learning classifiers. In: 2022 1st IEEE International Conference on Industrial Electronics: Developments and Applications (ICIDeA), pp. 198–201 (2022). https://doi.org/10.1109/ICIDeA53933.2022.9970023

22. Qi, Y., et al.: Recent progresses in machine learning assisted Raman spectroscopy. Adv. Opt. Mater. **11** (2023). https://doi.org/10.1002/adom.202203104

23. Sharma, A., Verma, R., Kumar, R., Chauhan, R., Sharma, V.: Chemometric analysis of ATR-FTIR spectra of fingernail clippings for classification and prediction of sex in forensic context. Microchem. J. **159**, 105504 (2020). https://doi.org/10.1016/j.microc.2020.105504

24. Small, M., Zhang, J., Xu, X.: Transforming time series into complex networks. In: Zhou, J. (ed.) Complex 2009. LNICST, vol. 5, pp. 2078–2089. Springer, Heidelberg (2009). https://doi.org/10.1007/978-3-642-02469-6_84
25. Silva, T.C., Zhao, L.: Network-based high level data classification. IEEE Trans. Neural Netw. Learn. Syst. **23**(6), 954–970 (2012). https://doi.org/10.1109/TNNLS.2012.2195027
26. Wang, D., et al.: Machine learning-based multifunctional optical spectrum analysis technique. IEEE Access **7**, 19726–19737 (2019). https://doi.org/10.1109/ACCESS.2019.2895409
27. Yan, X., Cao, Z., Murphy, A., Ye, Y., Wang, X., Qiao, Y.: FRDA: fingerprint region-based data augmentation using explainable AI for FTIR-based microplastics classification. Sci. Total Environ. **165340** (2023). https://doi.org/10.1016/j.scitotenv.2023.165340
28. Zhao, Y., Peng, X., Small, M.: Reciprocal characterization from multivariate time series to multilayer complex networks. Chaos **30**(1), 013137 (2020). https://doi.org/10.1063/1.5112799

Evaluating Odor Selectivity in α-Synucleinopathy: ML-Based Odor Profiling

Christian Mattjie[1(✉)], Rafaela Ravazio[1], Eleanor Mitchell[2],
Jonathan Bestwick[2], Lucas Silveira Kupssinskü[1], Alastair Noyce[2],
Artur Schumacher Schuh[3], and Rodrigo C. Barros[1]

[1] Pontifícia Universidade Católica do Rio Grande do Sul, Porto Alegre, Brazil
`christian.oliveira95@pucrs.br`
[2] Queen Mary University of London, London, UK
[3] Hospital de Clínicas de Porto Alegre, Porto Alegre, Brazil

Abstract. Cerebrospinal fluid (CSF) α-synuclein seed-amplification assay (SAA) is the most sensitive in vivo marker of misfolded α-synuclein. Still, its reliance on lumbar puncture—a costly, time-consuming, and invasive procedure—restricts broad clinical or population-based use. Low-cost, non-invasive smell tests such as the 40–item University of Pennsylvania Smell Identification Test (UPSIT) could serve as an efficient triage tool if they could reliably predict CSF-SAA positivity. This work aims to determine if item-level UPSIT responses reveal a selective olfactory pattern of SAA positivity after strict control for overall UPSIT score. Such a pattern could be used to enhance the diagnostic value of smell tests further. UPSIT and SAA data from the Parkinson's Progression Markers Initiative were used to build two balanced SAA^{+}– SAA^{-} subsets. Six classifiers were tuned and evaluated using leave-one-out cross-validation. Permutation SHAP values quantified the importance of each odor for the best models. Given the marginal gain over random chance that the models achieved, our findings parallel recent Parkinson's disease studies, which suggest that SAA causes a general loss of smell without affecting specific smells more than others, or that such a difference is minor. Although odor selectivity was negligible, UPSIT and other olfactory tests remain valuable and scalable screens for potential CSF-SAA positivity, as overall olfactory capacity itself carries strong predictive power.

Keywords: α-Synuclein · Hyposmia · Machine Learning

1 Introduction

α-synucleinopathies are neurodegenerative diseases characterized by the abnormal accumulation of α-synuclein protein in neurons, nerve fibers, or glial cells [11]. The three main types of α-synucleinopathies are Parkinson's disease (PD), dementia with Lewy bodies (DLB), and multiple system atrophy (MSA) [1].

R. de Freitas and D. Furtado (Eds.): BRACIS 2025, LNAI 16181, pp. 186–198, 2026.
https://doi.org/10.1007/978-3-032-15990-8_13

The α-synuclein seed-amplification assay (SAA) is a diagnostic tool that uses cerebrospinal fluid (CSF) to detect α-synuclein protein aggregates with high sensitivity and specificity, and is increasingly recognized as the reference standard for confirmation of α-syn pathology [4]. Data collection initiatives on large cohorts, such as the Parkinson's Progression Markers Initiative (PPMI), have adopted CSF-SAA as a reference standard. Despite this success, lumbar puncture limits SAA's use as a first-line population-level screening. To be administered, CSF-SAA requires cerebrospinal fluid from a lumbar puncture – an invasive, resource-intensive, and lowly accepted procedure – specialized equipment, and trained personnel [19], while taking approximately 48 h until results. This makes it a costly exam. Hence, biomarkers that detect α-syn pathology have become a central research priority [15,16], as they could pave the way to a cheaper and faster alternative for screening tests to be applied to a broader population.

Olfactory dysfunction is one of the earliest non-motor manifestations of the α-synucleinopathies. Studies reveal hyposmia in 80% of newly diagnosed PD cases and in a sizable proportion of individuals who are still clinically prodromal [23]. This sensory deficit can precede motor symptoms by over a decade, highlighting the olfactory system as a window into the pre-symptomatic phase in which disease-modifying therapies would be most effective.

The 40-item University of Pennsylvania Smell Identification Test (UPSIT) offers a practical, low-cost means of quantifying olfactory dysfunction in large populations. Administered in under ten minutes and supported by extensive age and sex stratified norms, UPSIT reliably captures the hyposmia that accompanies early α-synuclein pathology and has testretest reliability exceeding 0.90 [9].

No study has investigated the use of item-level UPSIT responses to evaluate SAA positivity while considering age, sex, and the total UPSIT score, which is particularly affected by α-synucleinopathy. This study fills this gap by applying machine-learning classifiers and SHAP explainability to a large, balanced SAA^+–SAA^- subset from PPMI. Our objective is to determine whether item-level odor information confers *any* incremental diagnostic value apart from the global UPSIT score for predicting CSF SAA status.

2   Background

α-synucleinopathies are pathologically defined by intracellular misfolded α-synuclein aggregates. Worldwide prevalence already approaches 10 million people and is rising with population aging [6]. Clinical diagnosis, which relies on motor or cognitive features that emerge years after the first pathology appears, misses a pre-symptomatic window in which disease-modifying therapies would be most effective. Hence, biomarkers that detect α-synuclein pathology itself, rather than posterior neurodegeneration, have become a central research priority [15,16].

The current golden standard method for identifying α-synucleopathy is the CSF-SAA test. It directly targets the pathogenic conformers underlying these disorders by exploiting their prion-like ability to template the misfolding of recombinant α-synuclein in vitro [4]. When a small quantity of CSF containing fibrillar seeds is incubated with excess monomeric α-synuclein and the fluorescent dye thioflavin-T under cyclic shaking, seeded fibril growth produces a characteristic real-time fluorescence increase whose kinetics distinguish positive from negative samples [10,22]. Studies report sensitivity of 9095% and specificity above 95% for clinically diagnosed PD and DLB, and the assay reliably detects seeding activity years before phenoconversion in REM-sleep-behavior disorder and other prodromal cohorts, outperforming dopamine-transporter imaging and fluid neurodegeneration markers in predictive value [10,22,23].

α-synucleopathy is associated with smell loss, and its aggregation is present in olfactory bulbs years before it is found in higher brain regions [12]. Nonetheless, the precise mechanisms of how α-synuclein affects smell capabilities are not yet understood [8]. Since SAA measures the molecular hallmark of α-synucleinopathies rather than downstream neuronal loss, it is uniquely positioned as a reference standard for early-stage diagnosis and for validating less-invasive triage tools, such as UPSIT-based smell testing, within future screening pipelines.

Studies have shown α-synuclein aggregates first manifest in the olfactory bulb [7,18,20,23]. Over 90% of patients with PD or DLB exhibit hyposmia years before motor onset, reflecting early α-syn pathology in the olfactory bulb [13]. Population studies consistently rank hyposmia among the strongest clinical predictors of SAA positivity, often stronger than constipation or subtle motor signs [2,5]. These results establish UPSIT as an attractive triage tool for prioritizing individuals for confirmatory SAA or advanced imaging.

The UPSIT is a standardized, 40-item "scratch-and-sniff" assay that quantifies odor-identification ability by presenting micro-encapsulated odor patches embedded in four thin booklets; when a participant rubs each patch, a familiar smell—such as cinnamon, gasoline, bubble-gum, fresh-cut grass, or menthol—is released, and the participant selects one of four verbal alternatives in a forced-choice format. It is a relatively cheap and quick test, as its completion typically takes under ten minutes, yields a raw score from 0 to 40 that is converted to age- and sex-adjusted percentiles using extensive normative data, and demonstrates high psychometric robustness (testretest reliability r$\approx$0.9) [9]. Different UPSIT versions are available, including the original, the revised, and the UK versions. Each contains slightly different smells, mainly due to cultural differences, and which smells are easily recognizable in a particular population.

Since SAA captures the pathology rather than the clinical phenotype, it provides a cleaner framework for testing the "odor selectivity" hypothesis. If α-syn aggregation preferentially disrupts neural ensembles encoding specific odorants, SAA-positive subjects, regardless of motor diagnosis, should display a distinctive item-level UPSIT profile compared with matched SAA-negative peers.

3   Materials and Methods

This study investigates whether α-syn is associated with a distinct pattern of olfactory impairment, as opposed to generalized smell loss. Identifying such an olfactory "fingerprint" could enhance the diagnostic utility of smell tests for detecting α-syn-related conditions. This section details our data collection and inclusion criteria, the construction of balanced datasets for hypothesis testing, the machine learning training and validation procedures employed, and our analysis of the model's predictive outputs. Our approach took inspiration from similar work done to identify odor-selectivity patterns in PD [17].

Data Source

All data were obtained from the PPMI database[1], an ongoing, multicentre observational study that provides harmonized clinical, biomarker, and imaging measures. For this work, we extracted: (i) cerebrospinal-fluid α-synuclein seed-amplification assay (SAA) status (binary, "positive"/"negative"), (ii) the item-level responses to the 40-item UPSIT, and (iii) Demographic covariates— age at visit and self-reported gender.

Inclusion Criteria. Only patients who completed the revised version of the UPSIT were included in this study, as the correct smells and choices presented to subjects differ in each version. Specific smells were not available for some patients; therefore, only patients with up to 2 items (5%) missing on the UPSIT were included. Missing values were imputed using 5-nearest neighbors (patients) using available data from the 40 smells.

Balanced Datasets

Rationale. Because SAA positivity is tightly related to global hyposmia, a classifier trained on the full PPMI cohort could rely on the *total* UPSIT score, either directly or indirectly. To force the models to exploit *odor-selective* information, we built one-to-one matched casecontrol subsets in which SAA-positive (SAA$^+$) and SAA-negative (SAA$^-$) participants were paired in a three-dimensional feature space:

(i) gender (exact match),   (ii) age at visit, and   (iii) UPSIT total score

Nearest-Neighbor Matching. All three variables were z-standardized on the *combined* SAA$^+$+SAA$^-$ sample to give each dimension unit variance. One-to-one matching without replacement was performed in Python (`scikit-learn 1.5`). For each shuffled SAA$^-$ subject – the smallest group – the nearest SAA$^+$ neighbor was identified via Euclidean distance in the weighted, standardized space and removed from the candidate pool to prevent reuse. This greedy procedure continued until no further matches were possible.

Resulting Subsets. We created two balanced datasets using Nearest Neighbors matching: a **Mixed dataset**, containing 370 SAA$^+$ and 370 SAA$^-$ participants spanning Parkinson's disease, prodromal, and healthy controls (total $n = 740$); and a **Prodromal dataset**: 290 SAA$^+$ and 290 SAA$^-$ participants meeting prodromal criteria only ($n = 580$). Given that most of the patients with both

---

[1] https://www.ppmi-info.org/.

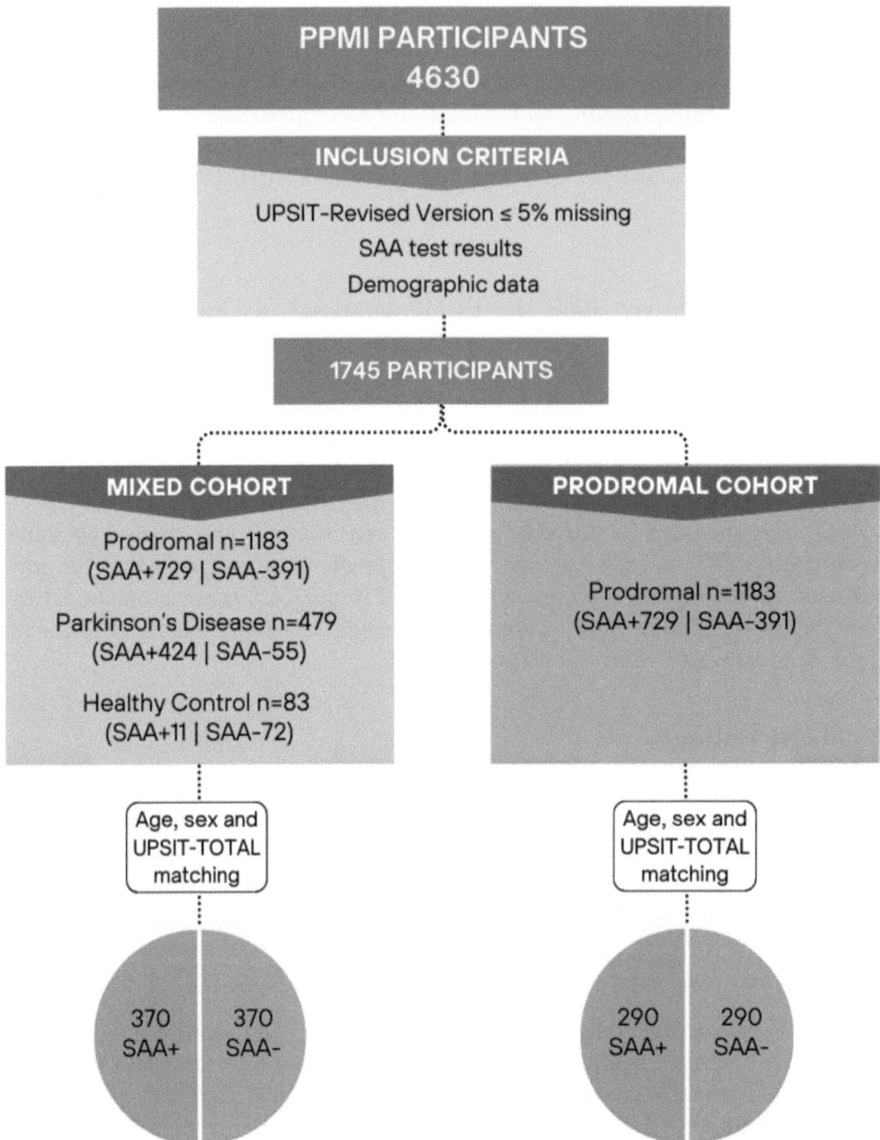

Fig. 1. Overview of participant selection. PPMI Parkinson's Progression Markers Initiative, UPSIT University of Pennsylvania Smell Identification, SAA α-synuclein seed-amplification assay.

UPSIT and SAA data were from the prodromal cohort, this subset was examined to mitigate potential biases from using different cohorts. The outline of our participant selection and the resulting datasets is shown in Fig. 1.

Table 1. Demographic and UPSIT characteristics of the balanced subsets.

	Mixed (n=740)		Prodromal (n=580)	
	SAA−	SAA+	SAA−	SAA+
Age, mean ± SD	66.43 ± 6.43	66.47 ± 6.32	67.10 ± 5.10	67.18 ± 4.93
Male sex, n (%)	132 (35.7%)	132 (35.7%)	87 (30%)	87 (30%)
UPSIT score, mean ± SD	25.90 ± 7.10	25.35 ± 6.82	24.74 ± 7.01	23.97 ± 6.49

Unmatched individuals were discarded. By design, SAA$^+$ and SAA$^-$ groups in each subset are practically indistinguishable on age, gender, and UPSIT total score, as shown in Table 1. Therefore, any performance gain over random chance must arise from *item-level* odor information.

Pre-processing and Feature Sets

UPSIT data was transformed into two alternative tabular representations:

1. **Binary correctness matrix (*Correct*)** (40 features): 1 if the odor was correctly identified, 0 otherwise.
2. **One-hot distractor matrix (*Responses*)** ($40 \times 4 = 160$ features): a four-way one-hot vector indicating the response chosen.

Machine-Learning Models and Validation

We employed six different classifiers to differentiate SAA status based on UPSIT *Correct* and *Responses* feature sets. We explored both simple and state-of-the-art algorithms, each with its different assumptions: (a) Extreme Gradient Boosting (**XGBoost**) [3], (b) Pre-trained Transformer for Tabular Data (**TabPFN**) [14], (c) **Random Forest**, (d) Elastic-Net penalised logistic regression (**ElasticNet**), (e) Ridge regression (with *only* ℓ_2 penalty), and (f) LASSO regression (with *only* an ℓ_1 penalty).

Given that we repeated our analysis on two datasets, we ran a total of 24 experiments. We used implementations from `scikit-learn 1.5` and `tabpfn 0.2`; XGBoost used `xgboost 2.0` with GPU acceleration, and all experiments were run on `python 3.10`.

Validation Strategy. We adopted *leave-one-out cross-validation* (LOOCV) given the sample size and the balanced data. Aggregated metrics included accuracy, precision, recall(sensitivity), specificity, F1-score and AUC. Ninety-five percent confidence intervals were obtained via stratified bootstrapping (1,000 replicates).

Explainability. We used SHapley Additive exPlanations (SHAP) to investigate which UPSIT items had the highest impact on model prediction. SHAP uses a game theory-based approach to assess model performance by training and evaluating the model multiple times, each time including, excluding, or altering a specific feature. This measures the feature's impact on the model's performance. The resulting SHAP values and plots illustrate the effect of the feature's actual values on the model's predictions for unseen data. Feature importance was summarized as the mean absolute SHAP value and visualized with beeswarm plots. SHAP values were computed by training the model on all data.

4   Results and Discussion

The performance of the trained models is shown in Table 2. The best models were trained on the prodromal dataset – the smaller one – and used the encoded responses instead of only binary correct information. Given the expected random accuracy of 0.5, all models performed poorly, reaching a best accuracy of only 0.607 using the TabPFN and a best AUC of 0.648 with the ElasticNet. While the results on the prodromal dataset were slightly better, it is possible that this derives from the increased complexity of using patients from different cohorts. Still, we analyzed the models with the highest accuracy and AUC feature importance for relevant insights, given that both used the Responses feature set instead of the correct one.

4.1   SHAP Analysis

Figures 2 and 3 show the ordered importance of the 10 most significant features on the model's prediction for the best-performing models TabPFN and Elastic-Net on the Prodromal dataset. The x-axis denotes SHAP values, indicating the impact on the model's prediction—positive values increase the likelihood of SAA positivity, and negative values decrease it. The features are organized following the pattern: "Correct Scent"-"Response Scent".

Figure 2 presents the SHAP results for the model with the best accuracy. In this model, the confusion between the Dill Pickle and Chocolate smells is the most important feature and greatly impacts the model's prediction. Following is the confusion between Apple and Mint scent, both of which are associated with SAA positivity. Figure 3 presents the SHAP results for the model with the best AUC. The most important feature in this model is the correct response to the Mint smell, which is associated with SAA negativity. Contrary to that, the second most important feature, the correct identification of the Onion smell, is associated with SAA positivity.

Certain UPSIT responses were impactful on both models, which used similar features, and their correlation was the same – a feature correlated with SAA positivity on one model also presented this pattern on the other model. Some responses not related to correctly identifying the smell are present, as expected given the increase in performance using all responses. These features had a negligible impact on the ElasticNet model prediction, but were the two most critical predictors on the TabPFN.

Table 2. Results of SAA classification using UPSIT responses ordered by accuracy. Best accuracy and best AUC are highlighted.

Dataset	Feature set	Model	Accuracy	Precision	Recall	F1-score	Specificity	AUC
Prodromal	Responses	TabPFN	**0.607**	0.657	0.448	0.533	0.766	0.620
Prodromal	Responses	RandomForest	0.598	0.601	0.586	0.593	0.610	0.631
Prodromal	Correct	Ridge	0.598	0.602	0.579	0.591	0.617	0.640
Prodromal	Responses	ElasticNet	0.597	0.599	0.586	0.592	0.607	**0.648**
Prodromal	Correct	ElasticNet	0.597	0.599	0.583	0.591	0.610	0.639
Mixed	Responses	TabPFN	0.595	0.612	0.516	0.560	0.673	0.618
Mixed	Correct	TabPFN	0.592	0.596	0.573	0.584	0.611	0.615
Prodromal	Responses	LASSO	0.591	0.593	0.583	0.588	0.600	0.646
Mixed	Correct	Ridge	0.591	0.590	0.595	0.592	0.587	0.618
Prodromal	Responses	XGBoost	0.588	0.590	0.579	0.584	0.597	0.638
Prodromal	Correct	LASSO	0.588	0.591	0.572	0.581	0.603	0.641
Mixed	Responses	LASSO	0.585	0.584	0.592	0.588	0.578	0.611
Mixed	Correct	ElasticNet	0.582	0.583	0.581	0.582	0.584	0.613
Mixed	Responses	ElasticNet	0.581	0.581	0.584	0.582	0.578	0.606
Prodromal	Responses	Ridge	0.579	0.583	0.555	0.569	0.603	0.642
Mixed	Correct	LASSO	0.578	0.578	0.578	0.578	0.578	0.608
Prodromal	Correct	TabPFN	0.578	0.575	0.593	0.584	0.562	0.611
Mixed	Responses	Ridge	0.577	0.576	0.587	0.581	0.568	0.609
Mixed	Correct	RandomForest	0.566	0.565	0.573	0.569	0.560	0.600
Mixed	Responses	RandomForest	0.562	0.564	0.546	0.555	0.578	0.601
Mixed	Correct	XGBoost	0.561	0.561	0.562	0.561	0.560	0.587
Mixed	Responses	XGBoost	0.560	0.560	0.551	0.556	0.568	0.613
Prodromal	Correct	XGBoost	0.559	0.560	0.548	0.554	0.569	0.605
Prodromal	Correct	RandomForest	0.555	0.556	0.552	0.554	0.559	0.594

4.2 SAA$^+$ vs SAA$^-$ Not Controlled for Total UPSIT Scores

To validate our methodology, we repeated our analysis by matching patients only by gender and age, without controlling for the total UPSIT score. This resulted in two datasets (Mixed n $=$ 1034; Prodromal n $=$ 780) with high UPSIT scores on the SAA$^-$ group (29.02 $\pm$ 7.8) and low UPSIT scores on the SAA$^+$ group (21.88 $\pm$ 6.77). ML models trained on these subsets resulted in significantly higher performance, as shown in Table 3. The algorithms could, directly or indirectly, rely on the different proportion of correct answers from each group to predict SAA status. As expected, the performance increased.

We also investigated a simple cut-off approach reflecting what is used in clinical practice: patients with fewer than a determined number of correct answers are defined as SAA$^+$. The results are shown in Table 4. Evaluating this approach for all possible cut-off values from 0 to 39 led to 29 being the optimal cut-off

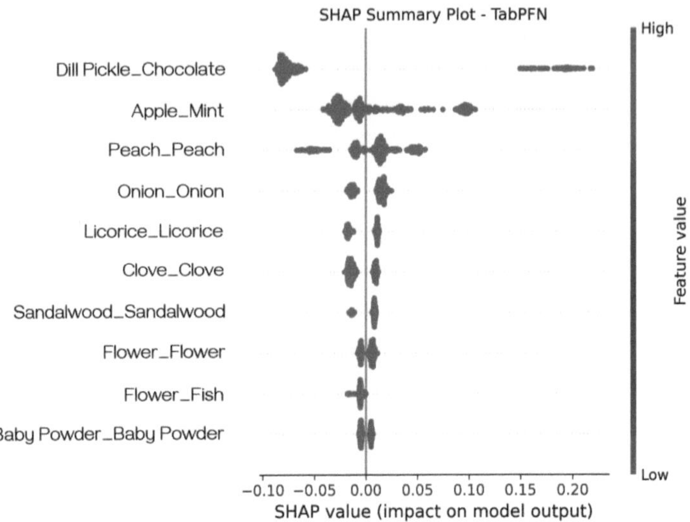

Fig. 2. SHAP importance for the TabPFN models on the Prodromal dataset using the *Responses* feature set. Features are presented as: "Correct Scent"_"Response Scent". Therefore, correct responses contain the same smell listed twice. Red dots indicate patients who answered the smell identified by the feature, while blue dots indicate any other smell. High positive SHAP values (to the right) indicate correlation to SAA^+, while negative values indicate the opposite.

point on the Mixed dataset with the highest accuracy of 0.721, extremely close to the accuracy of 0.739 reached by the models not matched by total UPSIT score. The complexity of identifying smells might explain such improvement, since humans are not equally good at identifying all possible smells.

This result corroborates our hypothesis that training ML algorithms to differentiate SAA without matching for total UPSIT score results in models that primarily rely on the discrepancy between SAA status. Therefore, these models are too biased to identify an odor-specific pattern resulting from SAA status.

4.3 α-Synucleopathy and Smell Loss

It would be highly beneficial for the identification of α-synucleopathy for it to cause an odor-specific pattern of smell loss, as UPSIT or other smell tests could be used for reliable, fast, and cheap screening. However, our results show that this is not the case, or that the pattern is negligible for practical applications. Similar research has also shown that the same applies to PD [17], one of the diseases most associated with α-synucleopathy.

We also explored item-level responses on datasets not matched for UPSIT score, representing a more realistic scenario in which the proportion of UPSIT score differs according to α-synucleopathy. In this design, we are not looking for a specific odor-specific pattern of SAA, but evaluating how well you could

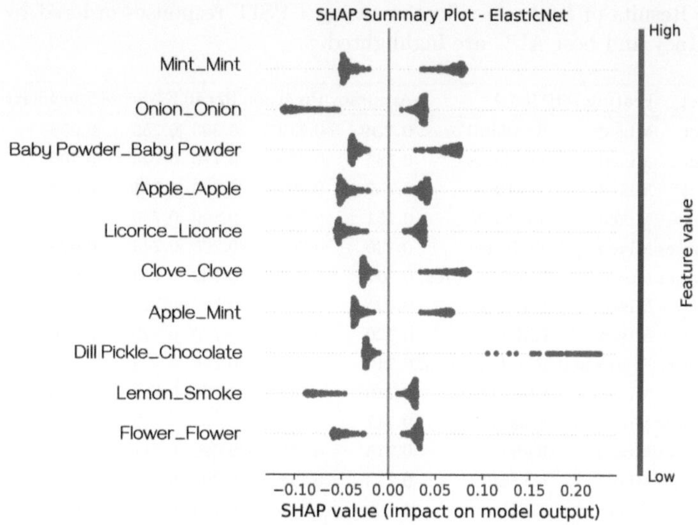

Fig. 3. SHAP importance for the ElasticNet models on the Prodromal dataset using the *Responses* feature set. Features are presented as: "Correct Scent"_"Response Scent". Therefore, correct responses contain the same smell listed twice. Red dots indicate patients who answered the smell identified by the feature, while blue dots indicate any other smell. High positive SHAP values (to the right) indicate correlation to SAA$^+$, while negative values indicate the opposite.

use UPSIT item-level data with ML to predict SAA status. Compared with the clinical practice of a cut-off number of smells, we observed only a slight improvement in SAA status prediction when using item-level UPSIT response with ML models. Such results need replication, but minor improvements could lead to better identification of SAA status in larger populations.

4.4   Limitations

Several smell tests are available, including UPSIT and its different versions, Burghart Sniffin' Sticks [21], and many others. Since patients can choose from different scents and options, direct comparison between them is impossible. This severely impacts any data analysis on smell loss, especially given that only limited data is available to researchers. If one is available, it would be beneficial to reproduce our analysis on a larger dataset. Another limitation of our research is that our matching algorithm ends up "trimming" the patients who performed well on the UPSIT, since these are predominantly SAA$^-$ and have no SAA$^+$ counterpart to be matched to. Even though there is no alternative to this matching, as there is no data on SAA$^+$ patients who did perform well on the UPSIT (as such patients may not exist), it is possible that this matching procedure introduces bias in the results that are not accounted for.

Table 3. Results of SAA classification using UPSIT responses ordered by accuracy. Best accuracy and best AUC are highlighted.

Dataset	Feature set	Model	Accuracy	Precision	Recall	F1-Score	Specificity	AUC
Correct	Mixed	RandomForest	**0.739**	0.712	0.803	0.755	0.675	0.788
Correct	Mixed	XGBoost	0.735	0.720	0.770	0.744	0.700	0.782
Correct	Mixed	TabPFN	0.732	0.701	0.809	0.751	0.656	0.787
Responses	Mixed	TabPFN	0.731	0.700	0.809	0.750	0.654	0.791
Responses	Mixed	XGBoost	0.730	0.707	0.785	0.744	0.675	0.785
Responses	Mixed	RandomForest	0.727	0.702	0.789	0.743	0.665	**0.797**
Correct	Mixed	LASSO	0.721	0.720	0.722	0.721	0.720	0.780
Correct	Mixed	Ridge	0.720	0.720	0.720	0.720	0.720	0.778
Responses	Prodromal	RandomForest	0.719	0.692	0.790	0.738	0.649	0.780
Correct	Mixed	ElasticNet	0.719	0.718	0.720	0.719	0.718	0.779
Responses	Mixed	ElasticNet	0.717	0.723	0.702	0.713	0.731	0.772
Responses	Mixed	Ridge	0.716	0.723	0.698	0.711	0.733	0.769
Responses	Mixed	LASSO	0.713	0.718	0.700	0.709	0.725	0.775
Responses	Prodromal	XGBoost	0.709	0.685	0.774	0.727	0.644	0.779
Correct	Prodromal	TabPFN	0.708	0.675	0.800	0.732	0.615	0.762
Correct	Prodromal	XGBoost	0.701	0.691	0.728	0.709	0.674	0.756
Correct	Prodromal	LASSO	0.695	0.691	0.705	0.698	0.685	0.751
Responses	Prodromal	TabPFN	0.692	0.672	0.751	0.709	0.633	0.766
Responses	Prodromal	Ridge	0.692	0.703	0.667	0.684	0.718	0.743
Responses	Prodromal	ElasticNet	0.691	0.700	0.669	0.684	0.713	0.748
Correct	Prodromal	ElasticNet	0.690	0.686	0.700	0.693	0.680	0.751
Correct	Prodromal	RandomForest	0.690	0.674	0.736	0.703	0.644	0.751
Correct	Prodromal	Ridge	0.689	0.685	0.697	0.691	0.680	0.747
Responses	Prodromal	LASSO	0.687	0.691	0.677	0.684	0.697	0.747

Table 4. Performance of the cut-off method on the total UPSIT score, where values equal or smaller than the cut-off are classified as SAA^+. The optimal cut-off 29 has the highest accuracy and F1-score, which are highlighted. Only cut-off values up to five points higher or lower than the optimal one are shown.

Cut-off ($<=$)	Accuracy	Precision	Recall	F1-score	Specificity
24	0.699	0.724	0.644	0.682	0.754
25	0.704	0.714	0.681	0.697	0.727
26	0.713	0.704	0.735	0.719	0.691
27	0.716	0.695	0.770	0.730	0.662
28	0.720	0.684	0.816	0.744	0.623
29	**0.721**	0.674	0.853	**0.753**	0.588
30	0.706	0.652	0.884	0.750	0.528
31	0.691	0.630	0.925	0.749	0.456
32	0.677	0.615	0.948	0.746	0.406
33	0.657	0.598	0.959	0.736	0.354
34	0.629	0.576	0.973	0.724	0.284

5   Conclusion

Our study investigated whether SAA positivity is associated with a specific pattern of olfactory dysfunction, measured by the UPSIT test. Our analysis shows that α-synucleopathy does not cause odor-specific smell impairment. A few smells emerged as modest predictors in specific models, with a limited and inconsistent contribution to the classification of SAA status. While the possibility of an α-synuclein-induced odor-specific pattern is not completely discarded, if such a pattern exists, it should be exceptionally subtle, with possibly little to no applications. ML models might increase the performance of UPSIT diagnostic value by a small margin, but further work is needed to validate this claim, as the performance is similar to the cut-off method.

While we did not to find a specific odor-pattern for SAA, our work reinforces the value of the total UPSIT score as a robust and low-cost triage tool. This method can be used to identify patients with a higher risk of α-synucleopathy, with different cut-offs leading to varying balances of sensitivity and specificity.

Acknowledgment. This study was financed in part by the Coordination for the Improvement of Higher Education Personnel Brazil (CAPES) Finance Code 001, and by the Michael J. Fox Foundation for Parkinson Research, in the project entitled.

Disclosure of Interests. The authors have no competing interests to declare relevant to this article's content.

References

1. Alafuzoff, I., Hartikainen, P.: Alpha-synucleinopathies. Handb. Clin. Neurol. **145**, 339–353 (2018)
2. Brown, E.G., et al.: Staged screening identifies people with biomarkers related to neuronal alpha-synuclein disease. Ann. Neurol. **97**(4), 730–740 (2025)
3. Chen, T., Guestrin, C.: Xgboost: a scalable tree boosting system. In: Proceedings of the 22nd ACM SIGKDD International Conference on Knowledge Discovery and Data Mining, pp. 785–794 (2016)
4. Concha-Marambio, L., Picken, M.M., Shahnawaz, M., et al.: Seed amplification assay of cerebrospinal fluid α - synuclein for diagnosis of Parkinson's disease. Ann. Neurol. **94**, 101–114 (2023). https://doi.org/10.1002/ana.26682
5. Coughlin, D.G., et al.: Association of CSF α-synuclein seeding amplification assay results with clinical features of possible and probable dementia with lewy bodies. Neurology **103**(3), e209656 (2024)
6. Dorsey, E.R., Sherer, T., Okun, M.S., Bloem, B.R.: The emerging evidence of the Parkinson pandemic. J. Parkinsons Dis. **8**(s1), S3–S8 (2018)
7. Doty, R.L.: Olfactory dysfunction in Parkinson disease. Nat. Rev. Neurol. **8**(6), 329–339 (2012)
8. Doty, R.L.: Olfactory dysfunction in neurodegenerative diseases: is there a common pathological substrate? Lancet Neurol. **16**(6), 478–488 (2017)
9. Doty, R.L., Shaman, P., Kimmelman, C.P., Dann, M.S.: University of Pennsylvania smell identification test: a rapid quantitative olfactory function test for the clinic. Laryngoscope **94**(2), 176–178 (1984)

10. Fairfoul, G., et al.: Alpha-synuclein RT-Qu IC in the CSF of patients with alpha-synucleinopathies. Ann. Clin. Transl. Neurol. **3**(10), 812–818 (2016)

11. Fellner, L., Stefanova, N.: The role of glia in alpha-synucleinopathies. Mol. Neurobiol. **47**, 575–586 (2013)

12. Gu, Y., et al.: Olfactory dysfunction and its related molecular mechanisms in Parkinson's disease. Neural Regen. Res. **19**(3), 583–590 (2024)

13. Haehner, A., Hummel, T., Reichmann, H.: Olfactory loss in Parkinson's disease. J. Neurol. **258**, 125–130 (2011). https://doi.org/10.1007/s00415-010-5749-4

14. Hollmann, N., et al.: Accurate predictions on small data with a tabular foundation model. Nature **637**(8045), 319–326 (2025)

15. Kovacs, G.G., et al.: Biomarker-based approach to α-synucleinopathies: lessons from neuropathology. Mov. Disord. **39**(12), 2173–2179 (2024)

16. Mantovani, E., et al.: Biomarkers for cognitive impairment in alpha-synucleinopathies: an overview of systematic reviews and meta-analyses. NPJ Parkinson's Dis. **10**(1), 211 (2024)

17. Mitchell, E., et al.: Hyposmia in Parkinson's disease; exploring selective odour loss. NPJ Parkinson's Dis. **11**(1), 67 (2025)

18. Niu, H., et al.: Alpha-synuclein overexpression in the olfactory bulb initiates prodromal symptoms and pathology of Parkinson's disease. Transl. Neurodegener. **7**, 1–17 (2018)

19. Parveen, S., et al.: A same day *alpha*-synuclein RT-QuIC seed amplification assay for synucleinopathy biospecimens. NPJ Biosensing **2**(1), 8 (2025)

20. Rey, N.L., et al.: Spread of aggregates after olfactory bulb injection of α-synuclein fibrils is associated with early neuronal loss and is reduced long term. Acta Neuropathol. **135**, 65–83 (2018)

21. Rumeau, C., Nguyen, D., Jankowski, R.: How to assess olfactory performance with the Sniffin' Sticks test®. Eur. Ann. Otorhinolaryngol. Head Neck Dis. **133**(3), 203–206 (2016)

22. Shahnawaz, M., et al.: Development of a biochemical diagnosis of Parkinson disease by detection of α-synuclein misfolded aggregates in cerebrospinal fluid. JAMA Neurol. **74**(2), 163–172 (2017)

23. Siderowf, A., et al.: Assessment of heterogeneity among participants in the Parkinson's progression markers initiative cohort using α-synuclein seed amplification: a cross-sectional study. Lancet Neurol. **22**(5), 407–417 (2023)

Exploring Content and Social Connections of Fake News with Explainable Text and Graph Learning

Vítor N. Lourenço[1]([✉])(iD), Aline Paes[1](iD), and Tillman Weyde[2](iD)

[1] Universidade Federal Fluminense, Niterói, Rio de Janeiro, Brazil
`vitorlourenco@id.uff.br`, `alineapes@ic.uff.br`
[2] City St George's, University of London, London, UK
`T.E.Weyde@city.ac.uk`

Abstract. The global spread of misinformation and concerns about content trustworthiness have driven the development of automated fact-checking systems. Since false information often exploits social media dynamics such as "likes" and user networks to amplify its reach, effective solutions must go beyond content analysis to incorporate these factors. Moreover, simply labelling content as false can be ineffective or even reinforce biases such as automation and confirmation bias. This paper proposes an explainable framework that combines content, social media, and graph-based features to enhance fact-checking. It integrates a misinformation classifier with explainability techniques to deliver complete and interpretable insights supporting classification decisions. Experiments demonstrate that multimodal information improves performance over single modalities, with evaluations conducted on datasets in English, Spanish, and Portuguese. Additionally, the framework's explanations were assessed for interpretability, trustworthiness, and robustness with a novel protocol, showing that it effectively generates human-understandable justifications for its predictions. The code and experiments are available at https://github.com/MeLLL-UFF/mu2X/.

Keywords: Explainability · Interpretability · Fact-checking · Misinformation Detection · Multi-modality · Graph Neural Networks

1 Introduction

The transition from traditional print media to digital platforms has transformed news consumption, with social networks (*e.g.*, Reddit, Twitter, Facebook, WhatsApp, TikTok) becoming primary news-sharing platforms. Recent studies demonstrate this shift's magnitude: Pew Research Center's 2021 report[1] reveals

---

[1] https://www.pewresearch.org/journalism/2021/09/20/news-consumption-across-social-media-in-2021/.

R. de Freitas and D. Furtado (Eds.): BRACIS 2025, LNAI 16181, pp. 199–214, 2026.
https://doi.org/10.1007/978-3-032-15990-8_14

48% of U.S. residents rely on social networks for news, while Statista's Latin America Dossier[2] indicates approximately two-thirds of surveyed individuals in Argentina, Brazil, Chile, and Mexico primarily consume news through social media. This democratisation of information-sharing, while enabling universal content creation, has led to widespread misinformation. The impact is particularly evident in recent elections and the COVID-19 pandemic, where the lack of distinction between traditional and user-generated content has contributed to significant political and social challenges [1,7,40].

A prevalent method for addressing misinformation is the use of fact-checking organisations (such as the British Full Fact, the Brazilian Aos Fatos, and the Argentine Chequeado). These organisations typically rely on various sources and documents, usually encompassing images, videos, and text covering a diverse set of topics and international protocols[3]. They employ human assessment of the credibility of social media claims and news articles, which is time-consuming and often a bottleneck in providing verified, trustworthy information.

To address scalability challenges associated with manual fact-checking, several studies [8,10,12,21,24,25,27,30–32,35,37] have proposed methods for automatic fact-checking of social media content. For instance, [27] have introduced a multimodal approach for detecting COVID-19-related misinformation on TikTok. Additionally, [20] developed a resource known as MuMiN, which establishes connections between claims and Twitter posts. These automated approaches aim to streamline the fact-checking process and enhance scalability by providing classification approaches and resources (*e.g.*, large-scale datasets) that effectively fill gaps in existing misinformation detection mechanisms.

Whilst aforementioned automatic fact-checking systems improves scalability, they often lack a crucial component: explainability [2,17,36], which is essential for user trust and legal compliance. Recent studies propose explainable frameworks for fake news detection [4,16,29] and multimodal misinformation detection [28,39]. However, none of these approaches integrates multiple languages, content types, and social media features, nor do they provide a robust and comprehensive evaluation of their explainability.

This work introduces mu2X, a framework for addressing fact-checking in social media posts from **mu**ltimodal, **mu**ltilingual, and e**x**plainable perspectives. mu2X tackles explainable misinformation detection from complete and interpretable aspects, as defined by [6]. An *interpretable explanation* describes the system's inner workings in a manner that humans understand; it must generate sufficiently straightforward explanations for an individual to grasp, employing terminology that resonates with the user. A *complete explanation* describes the system's inner workings precisely; it must generate explanations that facilitate the anticipation of behaviours across a broader range of scenarios. Striking a balance between interpretability and completeness is challenging, since the most precise explanations are frequently less straightforward for individuals to grasp [6]. Conversely, the most easily understandable explanations often lack the

---

[2] https://www.statista.com/topics/8083/news-in-latin-america.

[3] https://www.ifcncodeofprinciples.poynter.org/.

ability to offer a more detailed understanding of the system's behaviour and so to offer predictive insights that inform decision-making.

Our work leverages the explanations from two post-hoc model-agnostic explainability frameworks to *(i)* enhance awareness of the relevant features that led to a classification – contributing towards completeness; and *(ii)* enrich and combine the resulting explanations regarding the multiple modalities considered – contributing towards interpretability. In particular, our framework incorporates multiple modalities presented in social media posts by combining the posts' local network information, textual content, and related metadata to detect misinformation whilst tackling the well-known lack of explainable classifications.

As shown in Fig. 1, the proposed framework comprises three main modules: *(i)* Post Encoding Module, where the posts' contents are encoded into multimodal vector representations; *(ii)* Misinformation Detection Module, where the encoded representations are subjected to a graph-based classifier model to classify the posts as factual or misinformation; and *(iii)* Classification Explainability Module, where we employ graph-based and text-based explainable frameworks and combine their outcomes to explain the classification, whilst using the multimodal context to maintain the interpretability of generated explanations.

Our experiments employ the MuMiN dataset, to the best of our knowledge, the only multimodal, multilingual, and multi-topical Twitter-based knowledge base. Our goal is to assess mu2X's misinformation detection and explanations capabilities regarding its interpretability, trustworthiness, and robustness. Our findings show that combining different data modalities improves overall misinformation detection, and the explainable setting enables interpretable, reliable, and robust explanations.

2   Related Work

In recent years, substantial endeavors have been put into automatically detecting misinformation [1,4,7,8,10,12,15,16,18,20,24,25,27–32,35,37,39,40]. In the present section, we review methods of misinformation classification concerning the covered modality and explainable capabilities. We highlight work that discusses a similar holistic view of misinformation classification in social networks, addressing both the multimodal aspect of information and the explainability of the output classification.

Misinformation Detection. Most contemporary methods for automated misinformation classification are based on single-modality content, neglecting the multimodal nature of news items. For instance, [30,31] address misinformation detection by a method centered around hierarchical propagation networks, [10] uses graph neural networks supported by external knowledge, [35] rely on word embeddings over linguistic features, [12] use leverage reinforcement learning for fact-checking textual content, and [24] and [32] encode visual information to identify fake and manipulated information. Some recent work also identifies the benefit of encoding multimodal data to tackle misinformation detection [1]. [18] and [20] propose multimodal (image, text, and relational information) datasets for misinformation detection based on Reddit and Twitter posts, respectively. [8] introduce a new multimodal and multilingual dataset of misleading articles, training a model that leverages novelty detection and emotion recognition to detect fabricated information. [37] propose using multi-reading habits fusion reasoning networks to capture inconsistencies between different types of modalities for news items.

Explainable Misinformation Detection. The decision-making process of identifying a post or news as misinformation or not goes beyond simply classifying it as such. Providing explanations is of foremost importance to prompt human confidence in the classification. To that end, [4] and [29] propose DEFEND, one of the first explainable methods for detecting fake news articles. [15] tailor a domain-specific approach for automated fact-checking of claims regarding public health, whilst providing local model-agnostic explainability using LIME [26]. In the same domain, [27] and [16] propose explainable methods to detect misinformation related to the COVID-19 pandemic on TikTok's short videos and a knowledge-graph-based crowdsourced dataset. Closest to our work, [28] propose DGExplain, an explainable multimodal framework based on texts and images for COVID-19 misinformation detection. Finally, a multimodal and multi-topical dataset of articles and a model to automate misinformation fact-checking and provide explanations were recently proposed by [39]. Their explainable approach consists of generating a ruling statement using text evidence, the model prediction, and the input claim and conducting a policy learning process.

Our work advances existing research by incorporating relational information and relations' metadata, leveraging multiple languages, and being domain-agnostic. We also contrast by considering the interpretability of the explanation, an aspect overlooked in prior research, and focus on social media content classification comprehensibility and explainability.

3   Method

This section introduces mu2X, our multimodal and multilingual explainable framework. Our primary goal is to offer an end-to-end solution for this task, highlighting key features that explain the classification, thus enabling better human comprehension. This section covers the problem definition. Following this, we offer an overview of the components within mu2X. Lastly, we present the implementation of the components forming this framework.

3.1   Problem Statement

We define a post-node $\mathcal{P}_i = (\mathcal{T}, \mathcal{G}_k, \mathcal{M}, lang)$, where $\mathcal{T}$ is the textual content; $\mathcal{G}_k$ defines the local k-hop network connections of the post, such as replies, quotes, and re-posts; $\mathcal{M}$ is the post's shallow metadata set, which includes, for example, the tweet's owner, the number of likes, the location, etc.; and $lang$ is the language in which the tweet was originally written. Our goal is for a model σ to identify and explain the most representative features within $\mathcal{P}_i$ that lead a post to be classified as *misinformation* (*i.e.*, $y_i = \sigma(\mathcal{P}_i) = 0$) or *fact* (*i.e.*, $y_i = \sigma(\mathcal{P}_i) = 1$).

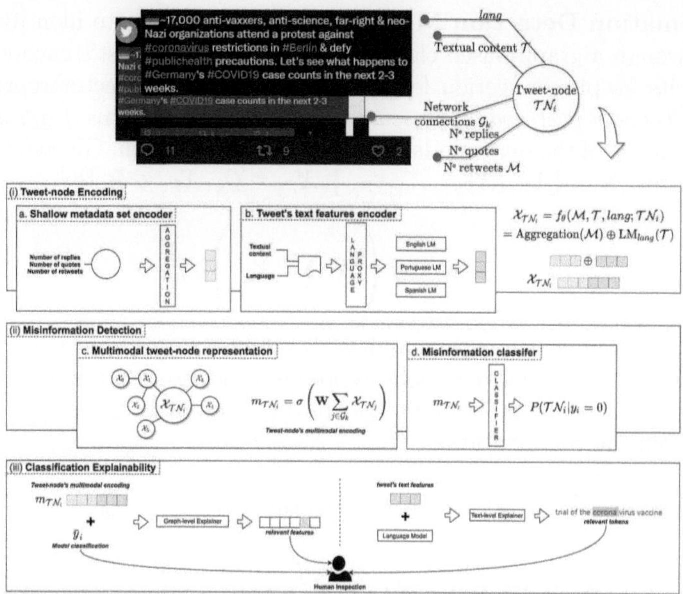

Fig. 1. The proposed multi-modal and multilingual explainable framework instanti-ated to Twitter posts. Yellow and blue elements illustrate graph-based and text-based feature vectors, respectively. (Color figure online)

3.2   mu2X: Multimodal and Multilingual Explainable Framework

The proposed mu2X framework comprises three main modules: *(i)* post-node encoding; *(ii)* misinformation detection; and *(iii)* classification explainability. Figure 1 illustrates the instantiated framework, and each module is described in the following.

Post Encoding Module. This module comprises the encoding of a given post-node $\mathcal{P}_i$ in its vector representation. The module is divided into two components to represent two modalities: the post's shallow metadata set $\mathcal{M}_i$; and its textual content $\mathcal{T}_i$. The first part obtains the vector representation of the shallow meta-data features with the number of replies, quotes, and re-posts (Fig. 1a) The sec-ond part encompasses a language proxy defined by *lang* followed by the language-specific text encoders (Fig. 1b) The language proxy acts as a router, assigning the post's textual content $\mathcal{T}$ to a pretrained language-specific model (LM). The pre-trained language-specific model encoder generates a vector representation of the textual content. Finally, as described in Eq. 1, both feature vectors are concatenated to form a unique multimodal post-node vector representation $\mathcal{X}_{\mathcal{P}_i}$.

$$\mathcal{X}_{\mathcal{P}_i} = f_\theta(\mathcal{M}, \mathcal{T}, lang; \mathcal{P}_i)$$
$$= \text{Aggregation}(\mathcal{M}) \oplus \text{LM}_{lang}(\mathcal{T}). \tag{1}$$

Misinformation Detection Module. This module aims to identify misinformation through a graph-based classifier. It leverages the post's encoded content $\mathcal{X}_{\mathcal{P}_i}$ with its graph connection features $\mathcal{G}_k$ to generate a vector representation called *multimodal post-node representation*. To accomplish this, Eq. 2 defines the learning process of the multimodal post-node representation. Given a set of post-node features, $\mathbf{X} = \{\mathcal{X}_{\mathcal{P}_1}, \mathcal{X}_{\mathcal{P}_2}, \ldots, \mathcal{X}_{\mathcal{P}_N}\}, \mathcal{X}_{\mathcal{P}_j} \in \mathcal{G}_k, \mathcal{X}_{\mathcal{P}_j} \in \mathbb{R}^{|\mathcal{X}_{P_i}|}$,

$$m_{\mathcal{P}_i} = \sigma \left(\mathbf{W} \sum_{j \in \mathcal{G}_k} \mathcal{X}_{\mathcal{P}_j} \right), \tag{2}$$

where σ is a nonlinear function, and $\mathbf{W}$ is a linear transformation.

Next, the multimodal post-node representation $m_{\mathcal{P}_i}$ undergoes a classification process, where the probability distribution computed by a softmax function is taken from the representation:

$$P(\mathcal{P}_i | y_i = 0) = \text{softmax}(m_{\mathcal{P}_i}). \tag{3}$$

Classification Explainability Module. This module explains the predicted label by employing graph-based and text-based post-hoc explainable methods.

The graph-based method $\mathcal{E}_g$ identifies the most important features within the post-node's multimodal representation $\zeta_{\mathcal{P}_i}$, as displayed in Eq. 4:

$$\zeta_{g\mathcal{P}_i} = \text{argmin} \ \mathcal{E}_g(\text{softmax}(m_{\mathcal{P}_i}), \mathbf{X}_{\mathcal{P}_i}), \tag{4}$$

where $\mathbf{X}_{\mathcal{P}_i}$ is the local information network of the target post-node $\mathcal{P}_i$.

The text-based method $\mathcal{E}_t$ generates a scoring vector $\zeta_{t\mathcal{P}_i}$, where each word in the text is associated with a positive or negative importance score:

$$\zeta_{t\mathcal{P}_i} = \mathcal{E}_t(\text{LM}_{lang}, \mathcal{T}), \tag{5}$$

where $\zeta_{t\mathcal{P}_i} \in [-1, 1]^{|\mathcal{T}|}$, $\mathcal{T}$ is the textual content of the post-node $\mathcal{P}_i$, and LM_{lang} is the text encoding method. Finally, both explanatory factors and the classification are provided to the user for inspection.

3.3 Framework Instantiation

This section details the mechanisms used to instantiate the previously introduced components illustrated in Fig. 1. Here, we focus on Twitter posts, calling them *tweet-node*s.

Language Models. To encode our text features, we leverage both pre-trained domain and language specific models. For English tweets we use HuggingFace's pre-trained BERTweet[4] model [19] as encoder; we used BERTweet.BR[5] for Portuguese tweets and RoBERTuito [23] for Spanish tweets.

---

[4] https://huggingface.co/docs/transformers/model_doc/bertweet.
[5] https://huggingface.co/melll-uff/bertweetbr.

Graph-Based Classifier. As misinformation classifier, we use the widely used Graph Attention Networks (GAT) [34], followed by a softmax classifier as described in Eq. 3. As such, we compute Eq. 2 employing a self-attention α_{kj}, $\alpha : \mathbb{R}^{|\mathcal{X}_{P_i}|} \times \mathbb{R}^{|\mathcal{X}_{P_i}|} \to \mathbb{R}$, mechanism over the tweet-node features:

$$\mathcal{P}_i = \sigma \left(\mathbf{W} \sum_{j \in \mathcal{G}_k} \alpha_{kj} \mathcal{X}_{\mathcal{P}_j} \right).$$

Classification Explanation. To identify the key features that contribute to the classification, we used GraphLIME [11], a nonlinear model-agnostic explanation framework that extends LIME [26] for Graph Neural Networks. This approach uses Hilbert-Schmidt Independence Criterion (HSIC) Lasso [38] over k-hop neighbour nodes of a given target node. Furthermore, we employ Integrated Gradients [33] to assign an importance score to each word of a given tweet's textual content. Integrated Gradients is an axiomatic model that assigns importance scores to individual input features. This approach consists of approximating the integral of the model's output gradients concerning the input.

4 Experiments

We conduct experiments to show the capabilities of mu2X, our proposed multimodal and multilingual explainable framework. In our experiments, we measure and assess the framework's capabilities of detecting misinformation, providing robust and trustworthy explanatory factors for these detections, and relating multiple explanatory factors to enhance interpretability.

We carry out our evaluations on a dataset including multilingual and multitopical texts and network data that contextualise the texts in the social media environment. As far as we know, the MuMiN [20] dataset is the only dataset that fulfils all requirements of our evaluation. In addition, our focus is on characterising the representation of the textual content and relational features. The MuMiN dataset is a publicly available dataset of multimodal data from Twitter. MuMiN links tweets covering multiple topics and languages with fact-checked claims, including text, metadata, and visual content from the tweets. For our study, we relied on the *MuMiN-small* version of this dataset, which consists of 2,183 claims and 7,202,506 tweets. To streamline our analysis, we filtered the dataset to consider tweets written in the three most prevalent languages (English, Portuguese, and Spanish), four types of entities (*Claim, Tweet, Reply,* and *User*), and six relations (*Posted, Mentions, Retweeted, Quote_Of, Reply_To,* and *Discusses*).

We developed our framework using PyTorch [22]. The full code of the framework, the described instantiation and example notebooks are available for review. The dataset split used was the same as proposed in the MuMiN dataset. As described in Sect. 3.3, our misinformation classifier is a GAT to account for the relational information. The classifier was trained using a single Nvidia RTX4070

Table 1. Misinformation classification F1 for each language and modality.

GAT's input Feature representation	Multilingual	English	Spanish	Portuguese
Graph-based	0.9488 ± 0.0032	0.9419 ± 0.0045	0.9477 ± 0.0029	0.9920 ± 0.0038
Text-based	0.9487 ± 0.0032	0.9409 ± 0.0044	0.9486 ± 0.0028	0.9923 ± 0.0042
Multimodal	$\mathbf{0.9738 \pm 0.0057}$	$\mathbf{0.9738 \pm 0.0053}$	$\mathbf{0.9500 \pm 0.0004}$	$\mathbf{0.9951 \pm 0.0053}$

Mobile GPU, with a learning rate of 0.005, 16-dimensional hidden layer, and Adam optimiser [13] for a total of 400 epochs – the optimal setting we found in our experiments. The textual features were encoded using pre-trained language-specific models. The textual encoding is then submitted to a linear mapping of its original 768-dimensional space vector to a 812-dimensional space vector to match the dimensions of the shallow metadata set representation. The experiments in Sects. 4.2–4.4 regard only the multilingual configuration, whilst comparing the various modalities.

4.1   Explainable Tweet Misinformation Detection

The empirical results of tweet classification are reported in Table 1, in which the model assigns each input information to the *misinformation* or *fact* label. We assess three different inputs: graph-based features, text-based features, and multimodal features, which are the concatenation of both graph-based and text-based features, and measure the obtained F1-score. The reported results are generated by 1000 bootstrap resampling with 95% confidence interval.

The results in each language demonstrate that the multimodal feature vector achieves better overall performance in misinformation detection than text encoding alone, confirming the results obtained by Nielsen *et al.* [20]. A secondary point is that text-based features outperform graph-based ones in low-resource languages and sparse graphs (*e.g.*, Spanish and Portuguese).

4.2   Interpretability of Explanations

We further examined the explanatory features through a combination of qualitative and quantitative analyses.

Our qualitative examination focused on the most relevant features and their ability to establish a connection between the tweet-node and its associated label. The results of our investigations are presented in Table 2, where we showcase the tweet-node text and a limited set of metadata, along with the classification produced by our GAT model, the most relevant features identified by GraphLime [11], and our interpretation of these explanatory factors.

In Table 2, the first entry is classified by the GAT model as misinformation. GraphLime highlighted the number of retweets and the number of replies as the most relevant features. Upon analysing these retweets and replies, we observed that users who engage in replies or retweets tend to have other tweets classified

Table 2. Report of two inferred cases with their classification, features, and explanatory factors identified by our framework.

Text	Shallow metadata set	Classification	GraphLime most representative features	Human interpretation
Great news! Carona virus vaccine ready. Able to cure patient within 3 hours after injection. Hats off to US Scientists. Right now Trump announced that Roche Medical Company will launch the vaccine next Sunday, and millions of doses are ready from it !!! VIA: @wajih79273180 https://t.co/BZJCLtwuXq	Number of retweets 26 Number of replies 42 Number of quotes 7	Misinformation	Number of retweets Number of replies	Users who retweet tend to spread misinformation
17,000 anti-vaxxers, anti-science, far-right & neo-Nazi organizations attend a protest against #coronavirus restrictions in #Berlin & defy #publichealth precautions. Let's see what happens to #Germany's #COVID19 case counts in the next 2-3 weeks. https://t.co/TD5xIoT5sV	Number of retweets 11 Number of replies 9 Number of quotes 2	Fact	Text	Word importance illustrated in Fig. 2.

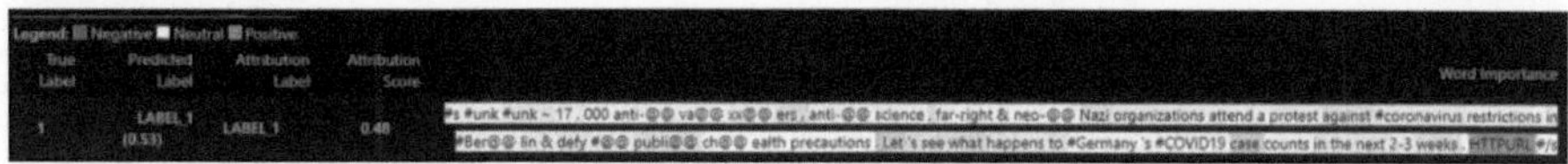

Fig. 2. Word importance for text explainability of the second tweet from the table above.

as misinformation, indicating a trend in the spread of misinformation. The second entry in Table 2 was classified as factual, with GraphLime's most relevant feature being the text embedding. In addition, we explored textual factors using Captum [14] to assist in explaining the label (Fig. 2). We noted that phrases like "protest against #coronavirus" and "Let's see what happens to #Germany" contributed to the accurate classification.

For our quantitative analysis, we fixed the multimodal setting to study how language and dataset size influence explanatory factors. Figure 3 shows, for each language, the distribution of features selected as explanations by modality (metadata, graph-based, or text-based) and by the number of features selected (one, two, or three) and the overall (features together). For languages with fewer examples, like Spanish (Fig. 3c) and Portuguese (Fig. 3d), metadata and graph-based features are used more frequently, followed by text-based features. This is likely due to fewer nodes and less dense relational connections, making these features more discriminative. In contrast, the multilingual setting (Fig. 3a) relies more on text-based features, likely due to its denser and more complex tweet-node network. English (Fig. 3b) shows a balanced use across modalities, reflecting its intermediate node count and density. Regardless of language, metadata features are the most common explanatory factor when only one feature is selected, aligning with Table 2's first entry and reinforcing that reply and retweet counts signal misinformation bubbles.

4.3   Trustworthiness of Explanations

In real-world applications, it is fundamental that the classifier's predictions are credible, *i.e.*, the classifier should be consistently accurate in associating labels

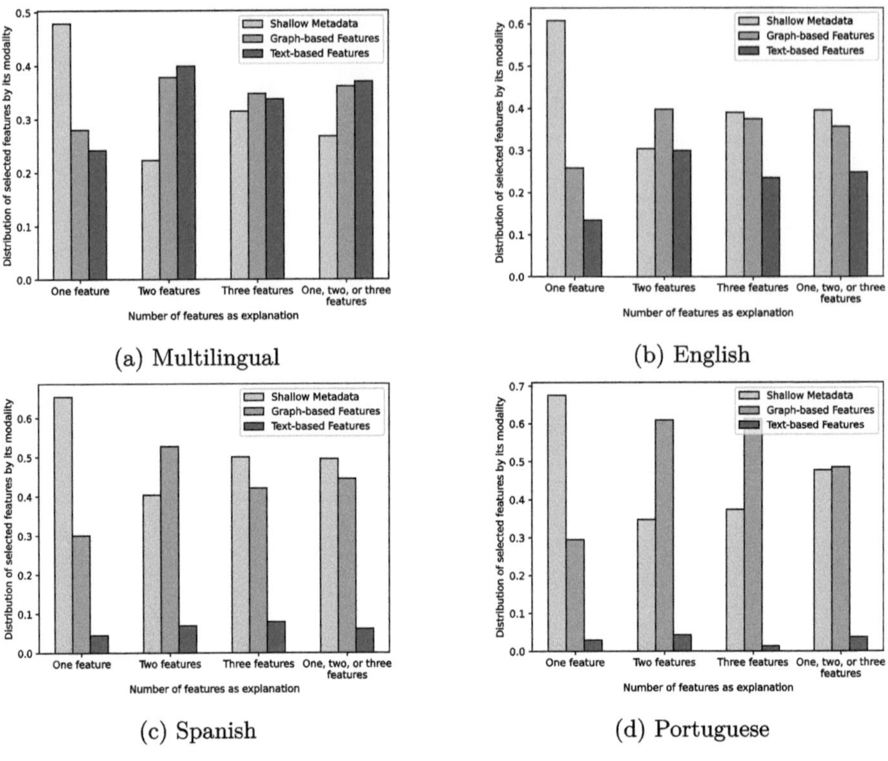

(a) Multilingual   (b) English

(c) Spanish   (d) Portuguese

Fig. 3. Distribution of features selected as explanations by their modality. Results are separated by language configuration, and colour indicates each set of features.

so that the end-user can relate to the prediction as trustworthy. Moreover, explanations play an essential role in assessing predictions. Therefore, we develop a protocol to measure the extent to which the explanations have the capacity to assist users in determining the reliability of the prediction.

The protocol consists of, first, simulating the trust in individual predictions. For that, we randomly select 30% of the features and assume these as "untrustworthy", *i.e.*, the user would likely recognise these features and would not want them as explanations. The second part of the protocol embraces the construction of an *oracle* "trustworthiness". We labelled the classifier's prediction as *untrustworthy* if the prediction changes after removing the features selected as untrustworthy from an instance, and *trustworthy* otherwise. The oracle assumes that if removing untrustworthy features changes a prediction, those features are decisive for the classifier. In this simulated setup, the oracle serves as the true label for evaluating prediction credibility. The third step simulates user judgment by considering a prediction untrustworthy if it changes after removing all untrustworthy features identified in the explanation using a linear approximation model. Finally, we compare the oracle's label with the simulated users' decisions.

Table 3. F1-Score of mu2X's trustworthiness based on different modalities.

Modality	F1-Score given top-k most relevant features				
	Top-1	Top-2	Top-3	Top-5	Top-10
Graph-based	0.7576 ± 0.2199	0.8059 ± 0.0158	0.8035 ± 0.0188	**0.8076 ± 0.0137**	*0.8031 ± 0.0187*
Text-based	*0.8188 ± 0.0164*	**0.8096 ± 0.0166**	**0.8111 ± 0.0154**	0.8060 ± 0.0156	0.8029 ± 0.0118
Multimodal	**0.8207 ± 0.0185**	*0.8061 ± 0.0153*	*0.8080 ± 0.0203*	*0.8062 ± 0.0167*	**0.8115 ± 0.0175**

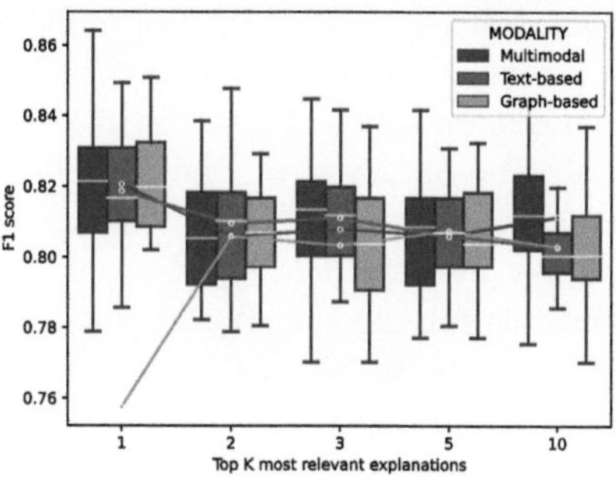

Fig. 4. F1-Score of trustworthiness box-plot visualisation. Lines are the average F1-Score in each Top-K.

Given the trustworthiness evaluation protocol, we report and compare the F1-score on the trustworthy predictions for the classifier trained with graph-based features, text-based features, and multimodal features over 25 rounds, considering the top-K most relevant explainable features ($K \in \{1, 2, 3, 5, 10\}$). The results are compiled in Fig. 4 and Table 3. The multimodal classifier achieved the most stable results, having the best F1-score in top-1 and top-10, whilst being the second-best in the other cases. The classifier that was solely trained with graph-based features displayed the worst results, indicating that it usually mistrusts trustworthy predictions, whilst trusting untrustworthy predictions too often. Despite the used modality, the results show F1-Score above 80% (except the graph-based top-1), confirming the reliability of the mu2X explanations.

4.4   Robustness of Explanations

Besides credible predictions, robust explanations are key for the success of misinformation classifiers. We propose a protocol to evaluate the capacity of the explainable method to select relevant features, *i.e.*, non-noisy features. Firstly, we artificially added $N = |\mathcal{X}| * p$ amount of randomly generated features, *i.e.*, *noisy features*, where $N \in \mathcal{N}$, $|\mathcal{X}|$ is the number of features in a sample $\mathcal{X}$, and $p \in \{0.01, 0.1, 0.25, 0.5, 0.75, 1.0\}$ is the overall proportion of noisy features to be introduced in each sample. Then, we train the classifier with the added noisy features. Finally, we observe the amount of noisy features selected as explanations.

Given the robustness evaluation protocol, we report the average results of 25 rounds of the noisy features selected as explanation patterns for the three classifiers. In Fig. 5, we show the kernel density estimation of the frequency of selected noisy features given the classifier and the proportion of noisy features added. The explanations based on the text-based features classifier were more robust, having a high density at zero noisy features selected in the lower percentages and even curves at zero or one noisy feature selected in higher noisy environments. The explanations grounded on the multimodal features classifier showed average results, where it keeps the higher density at zero for lower noisy environments and is even out on higher noisy environments.

These patterns can also be observed in Fig. 5d. The figure shows the distribution between the average percentage of noisy features selected as explanations and the percentage of noisy features added. Here, it is observed that the features selected as explanations for the text-based classifier increase linearly with the percentage of noisy features added. Additionally, it can be observed that the features selected as explanations using the multimodal classifier soften the non-linear curve presented by the explanations over the graph-based classifier.

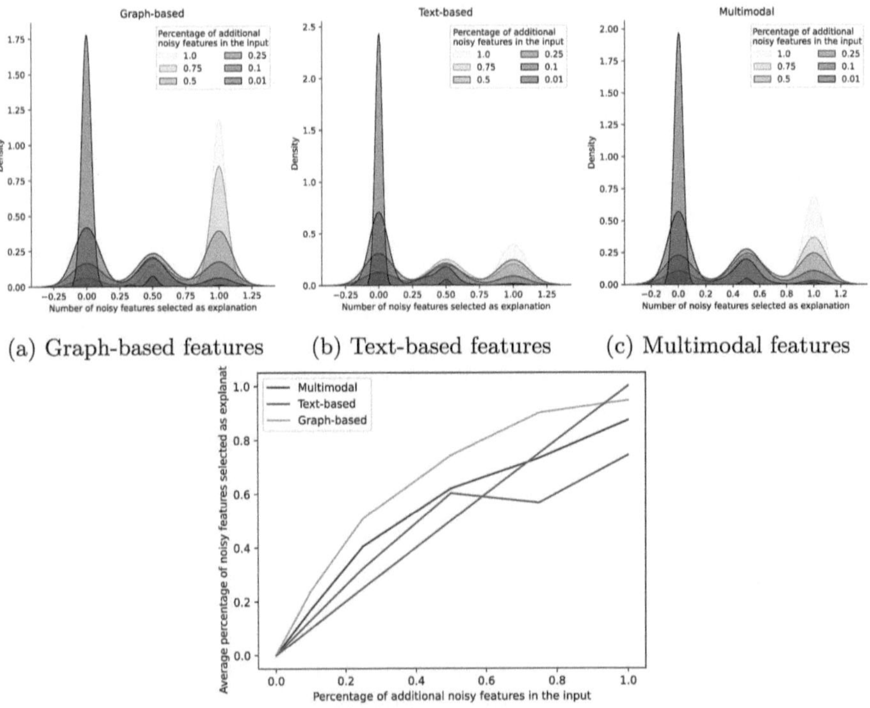

(a) Graph-based features   (b) Text-based features   (c) Multimodal features

(d) Relation between the percentage of additional noisy features and the average percentage of noisy features selected as an explainable factor.

Fig. 5. Distribution of noisy features selected as explanation given the percentage of noisy features added.

5   Conclusion

This paper introduced mu2X, a multimodal and multilingual explainable framework for misinformation detection in social media. It leverages multiple data modalities and two explainability methods to detect misinformation while clarifying the features that support each classification. Our experiments show that multimodal features enhance detection performance. The proposed explainable methodology adds completeness to the framework by providing trustworthy, robust, and relevant features, along with interpretability, particularly when combined with multimodal data.

There are multiple directions for future work. First, we aim to enhance and further explore mu2X by incorporating additional modalities and modality-specific explainability methods. We hypothesize that leveraging more modalities will improve both classifier performance and the completeness and interpretability of explanations. Second, we plan to develop a protocol for quantitatively evaluating interpretability based on human assessment, since existing ones do not handle multimodality [3,9]. Lastly, we envision integrated explanations that combine content snippets with explanatory factors or incorporate prior knowledge to improve clarity and user understanding.

Limitations. Our work has two main limitations: framework generalization and user interpretability. First, although it supports various multimodal aggregation methods, we only tested vector concatenation. Exploring other strategies could improve performance. Second, the feature-based explainability may be hard for some users to interpret. Still, our approach balances accuracy and interpretability by offering combined explanations across modalities, aligning with the trade-off discussed in [5].

Declaration on Use of Generative AI. The author(s) used Claude and Amazon Nova family models for grammar and spelling checks during the preparation of this work. After reviewing and editing the content as needed, the author(s) take full responsibility for the publication's content.

Funding. The second author thanks the grants from CNPq (National Council for Scientific and Technological Development), FAPERJ (*Fundação Carlos Chagas Filho de Amparo à Pesquisa do Estado do Rio de Janeiro*), processes SEI-260003/002930/2024, SEI-260003/000614/2023, and CAPES.

References

1. Alam, F., Cresci, S., et al.: A survey on multimodal disinformation detection. In: Proceedings of 29th International Conference on Computational Linguistics, COLING (2022)
2. Augenstein, I., Baldwin, T., Cha, M., et al.: Factuality challenges in the era of large language models and opportunities for fact-checking. Nat. Mach. Intell. (2024)
3. Colin, J., Fel, T., Cadene, R., Serre, T.: What i cannot predict, i do not understand: a human-centered evaluation framework for explainability methods. In: Advances in Neural Information Processing Systems, NeurIPS (2022)

4. Cui, L., Shu, K., Wang, S., Lee, D., Liu, H.: Defend: a system for explainable fake news detection. In: Proceedings of the 28th ACM International Conference on Information and Knowledge Management, CIKM (2019)
5. Garouani, M., Mothe, J., Barhrhouj, A., Aligon, J.: Investigating the duality of interpretability and explainability in machine learning. In: IEEE International Conference on Tools with Artificial Intelligence, ICTAI (2024)
6. Gilpin, L.H., Bau, D., Yuan, B.Z., Bajwa, A., Specter, M., Kagal, L.: Explaining explanations: an overview of interpretability of machine learning. In: Proceedings of IEEE 5th International Conference on Data Science and Advanced Analytics, DSAA, pp. 80–89 (2018)
7. Guo, Z., Schlichtkrull, M., Vlachos, A.: A survey on automated fact-checking. Trans. Assoc. Comput. Linguist. **10**, 178–206 (2021)
8. Gupta, V., Kumari, R., et al.: MMM: an emotion and novelty-aware approach for multilingual multimodal misinformation detection. In: Findings of the Association for Computational Linguistics, ACL (2022)
9. Hase, P., Bansal, M.: Evaluating explainable AI: Which algorithmic explanations help users predict model behavior? In: Proceedings of the 58th Annual Meeting of the Association for Computational Linguistics, ACL (2020)
10. Hu, L., Yang, T., et al.: Compare to the knowledge: graph neural fake news detection with external knowledge. In: Proceedings of 59th Annual Meeting of the Association for Computational Linguistics and the 11th International Joint Conference on Natural Language Processing, ACL-IJCNLP (2021)
11. Huang, Q., Yamada, M., Tian, Y., Singh, D., Chang, Y.: Graphlime: local interpretable model explanations for graph neural networks. IEEE Trans. Knowl. Data Eng. TKDE **35**(7), 6968–6972 (2023)
12. Kawintiranon, K., Singh, L.: Demis: data-efficient misinformation detection using reinforcement learning. In: Machine Learning and Knowledge Discovery in Databases, ECML PKDD (2023)
13. Kingma, D.P., Ba, J.: Adam: a method for stochastic optimization. In: International Conference on Learning Representations, ICLR (2015)
14. Kokhlikyan, N., Miglani, V., Martin, M., et al.: Captum: a unified and generic model interpretability library for pytorch. CoRR abs/2009.07896 (2020)
15. Kotonya, N., Toni, F.: Explainable automated fact-checking for public health claims. In: Proceedings of the 2020 Conference on Empirical Methods in Natural Language Processing, EMNLP (2020)
16. Kou, Z., Shang, L., Zhang, Y., Wang, D.: HC-COVID: a hierarchical crowdsource knowledge graph approach to explainable COVID-19 misinformation detection. Proc. ACM Hum.-Comput. Interact HCI (2022)
17. Lourenço, V., Paes, A.: A modality-level explainable framework for misinformation checking in social networks. In: LatinX AI Workshop at 36th Conference Neural Information Processing Systems, LXAI-NeurIPS (2022)
18. Nakamura, K., Levy, S., Wang, W.Y.: Fakeddit: a new multimodal benchmark dataset for fine-grained fake news detection. In: Proceedings of 12th Language Resources and Evaluation Conference, LREC (2020)
19. Nguyen, D.Q., Vu, T., Tuan Nguyen, A.: BERTweet: a pre-trained language model for English tweets. In: Proceedings of the 2020 Conference on Empirical Methods in Natural Language Processing: System Demonstrations, EMNLP, pp. 9–14 (2020)
20. Nielsen, D.S., McConville, R.: Mumin: a large-scale multilingual multimodal fact-checked misinformation social network dataset. In: Proceedings of the 45th International ACM SIGIR Conference on Research and Development in Information Retrieval, SIGIR, pp. 3141–3153 (2022)

21. Panchendrarajan, R., Zubiaga, A.: Claim detection for automated fact-checking: a survey on monolingual, multilingual and cross-lingual research. Nat. Lang. Process. J. **7**, 100066 (2024)
22. Paszke, A., Gross, S., Massa, F., et al.: Pytorch: an imperative style, high-performance deep learning library. In: Advances in Neural Information Processing Systems, NeurIPS (2019)
23. PÃrez, J.M., Furman, D.A., et al.: Robertuito: a pre-trained language model for social media text in Spanish. In: Proceedings of Language Resources and Evaluation Conference, LREC (2022)
24. Qi, P., Cao, J., Yang, T., Guo, J., Li, J.: Exploiting multi-domain visual information for fake news detection. In: IEEE International Conference on Data Mining, ICDM (2019)
25. Qian, S., Hu, J., Fang, Q., Xu, C.: Knowledge-aware multi-modal adaptive graph convolutional networks for fake news detection. ACM Trans. Multimedia Comput. Commun. Appl. (2021)
26. Ribeiro, M.T., Singh, S., Guestrin, C.: "Why should i trust you?": explaining the predictions of any classifier. In: Proceedings of the 22nd ACM SIGKDD International Conference on Knowledge Discovery and Data Mining, SIGKDD (2016)
27. Shang, L., Kou, Z., Zhang, Y., Wang, D.: A multimodal misinformation detector for covid-19 short videos on tiktok. In: 2021 IEEE International Conference on Big Data, pp. 899–908 (2021)
28. Shang, L., Kou, Z., Zhang, Y., Wang, D.: A duo-generative approach to explainable multimodal covid-19 misinformation detection. In: Proceedings of ACM Web Conference WWW (2022)
29. Shu, K., Mahudeswaran, D., Wang, S., Liu, H.: Hierarchical propagation networks for fake news detection: investigation and exploitation. In: International Conference on Web and Social Media, ICWSM (2020)
30. Shu, K., Mahudeswaran, D., Wang, S., Liu, H.: Hierarchical propagation networks for fake news detection: Investigation and exploitation. In: International Conference on Web and Social Media, ICWSM (2020)
31. Shu, K., Wang, S., Liu, H.: Beyond news contents: the role of social context for fake news detection. In: Proceedings of 12th ACM International Conference on Web Search Data Mining WSDM (2019)
32. Singh, B., Sharma, D.K.: Siteforge: detecting and localizing forged images on microblogging platforms using deep convolutional neural network. Comput. Ind. Eng. (2021)
33. Sundararajan, M., Taly, A., Yan, Q.: Axiomatic attribution for deep networks. In: Proceedings of 34th International Conference on Machine Learning, ICML (2017)
34. Veličković, P., Cucurull, G., Casanova, A., Romero, A., Liò, P., Bengio, Y.: Graph attention networks. In: International Conference on Learning Representations, ICLR (2018)
35. Verma, P.K., Agrawal, P., Amorim, I., Prodan, R.: Welfake: word embedding over linguistic features for fake news detection. IEEE Trans. Comput. Soc. Syst. (2021)
36. Warren, G., Shklovski, I., Augenstein, I.: Show me the work: fact-checkers' requirements for explainable automated fact-checking. In: Conference on Human Factors in Computing Systems, CHI (2025)
37. Wu, L., Liu, P., Zhang, Y.: See how you read? Multi-reading habits fusion reasoning for multi-modal fake news detection. In: Proceedings of AAAI Conference on Artificial Intelligence, AAAI, vol. 37, no. 11 (2023)

38. Yamada, M., Jitkrittum, W., Sigal, L., Xing, E.P., Sugiyama, M.: High-dimensional feature selection by feature-wise kernelized lasso. Neural Comput. **26**(1), 185–207 (2014)
39. Yao, B.M., Shah, A., et al.: End-to-end multimodal fact-checking and explanation generation: a challenging dataset and models. In: Proceedings of 46th International ACM SIGIR Conference on Research and Development in Information Retrieval, SIGIR (2023)
40. Zhou, X., Zafarani, R.: A survey of fake news: fundamental theories, detection methods, and opportunities. ACM Comput. Surv. **53**(5) (2020)

Exploring Data-Oriented Strategies
for Training ECG Self-supervised Models

Rafael da Costa Silva[(✉)], Adilson Medronha, and Diego Furtado Silva

Instituto de Ciências Matemticas e de Computação, University of São Paulo, São
Carlos, São Paulo, Brazil
{rafael.csilva,adilson.medronha,diegofsilva}@usp.br

Abstract. The electrocardiogram (ECG) is a non-stationary signal used
to assess heart health and to detect systemic conditions such as mental
stress and drug toxicity. However, labeling ECG data is notably costly
and can limit the applicability of supervised deep neural networks in
tasks involving this physiological signal. Self-supervised learning (SSL)
is a two-stage approach that has gained attention in this scenario due to
its labeling efficiency and knowledge transfer capabilities in various data
modalities. However, recent studies describe the difficulties in transferring knowledge across different time series datasets. This work investigates several data-oriented strategies for pretraining self-supervised
learning models in a cross-dataset setting to address a challenging ECG
classification task. We introduce a data-driven regularization approach
that perturbs the pretrained model using signals from multiple domains.
We evaluated three well-established SSL models as backbones with different classification architectures across over 100 experiments, achieving
superior performance to traditional SSL methods and a state-of-the-art
supervised deep learning classification model.

Keywords: Self-Supervised Learning · Time Series · Transfer
Learning · ECG Classification

1 Introduction

The electrocardiogram (ECG) is a non-stationary physiological signal that provides an overview of the heart's health [27]. Alongside monitoring the heart's
condition, the ECG can also be used to detect systemic conditions such as mental stress [23] and drug toxicity [24]. In recent years, deep learning techniques
have been widely employed to predict various heart conditions even in scenarios
where the diagnostic criteria have not been firmly established in clinical practice [15]. However, deep learning based on supervised learning generally depends
on thousands of labels of high quality in order to achieve strong generalization
performance [10].

Once an ECG is a simple, rapid, and low-cost exam, it is considered an
easy type of temporal data to obtain. On the other hand, healthcare experts

R. de Freitas and D. Furtado (Eds.): BRACIS 2025, LNAI 16181, pp. 215–229, 2026.
https://doi.org/10.1007/978-3-032-15990-8_15

struggle to annotate the abundant unlabeled data generated in a clinical setting where physicians are short on time and attention [14]. Self-supervised learning (SSL) offers a way to overcome such obstacles due to its label efficiency and generalization ability. In recent years, SSL methods have accumulated increasing attention for being successfully applied across a variety of modalities [30,33]. However, the transfer learning evaluations for SSL models in the time series are simple, against only one or no baselines, making it hard to estimate their transferability [26].

Also, recent studies describe the difficulties in transferring knowledge between different time series datasets. As the main challenges, we can cite negative transfer learning, performance reduction due to the dataset's low relatedness [7], and the distribution shift that can be observed even in closely related datasets, requiring the model to generalize beyond cohort-specific patterns [2].

This work explores using several data-oriented strategies for pretraining self-supervised models to overcome these limitations. The resulting model is applied to improve the performance in a difficult ECG classification task under a labeling scarcity scenario. We evaluated three well-established SSL models with two different classification head architectures under eight different training strategies, resulting in 108 experiments.

Our experiments demonstrate that, after completing the training phase of the SSL-pretrained feature extractor, exposing it to other physiological signals or samples from the downstream task in an SSL manner increases the model's generalization capabilities and its overall performance. This second pretraining step works as a regularization strategy, allowing the model to learn stronger features and approximate the model to the target task. Our results also outperformed the model's state-of-the-art for deep learning time series classification.

2   Theoretical Foundation

This section provides the basic concepts and definitions necessary to understand this work. First, we present the formal definition of time series, the data modality of our study. Next, we briefly introduce the basic concepts of self-supervised learning and transfer learning, and present a short discussion about foundation models in the context of time series. Following [25], we define a time series as:

Definition 1. A time series $\mathbf{X}$ is a set of N ordered values $\mathbf{X} = (x_1, x_2, ..., x_N)$ and $x_i \in \mathbb{R}^d$ for all $i \in [1, N]$, such d denotes the number of dimensions of that time series, with $d \in \mathbb{N}$. The time series is univariate for $d = 1$ and multivariate for $d > 1$. Each value x_i is referred to here as an **observation** of $\mathbf{X}$.

2.1   Self-supervised Learning

Self-Supervised Learning (SSL) can be considered a special case of unsupervised learning, as both paradigms operate without annotation. While traditional unsupervised methods rely on reconstruction or density estimation objectives, SSL approaches employ pretext tasks that leverage prior knowledge about the data modality, helping to reduce the need for large annotated datasets [6,35]. These pretext tasks consist of self-generated signals or challenges that the model solves to learn from the data, enabling the creation of meaningful representations for downstream tasks [33]. As illustrated in Fig. 1, the workflow of a typical self-supervised learning process can be summarized in four steps.

First, the setup step involves selecting the annotated dataset for the downstream (target) task and an unlabeled dataset as the source. In general, the downstream task dataset is a low-resource dataset, and the unlabeled data is a high-resource dataset[1]. The pretext task then generates pseudo-labels for the source dataset through a procedure denoted by $\mathcal{P}$. Next, a feature extractor is trained jointly with a pretext module to optimize a self-supervised objective. Once the feature extractor has been pretrained, the pretext module is replaced by a task-specific model, often referred to as the head model. The pretrained weights of the feature extractor serve as an initialization for solving the downstream task. Therefore, only a small subset of parameters is expected to require learning or fine-tuning, allowing the task to be solved with a limited amount of labeled data.

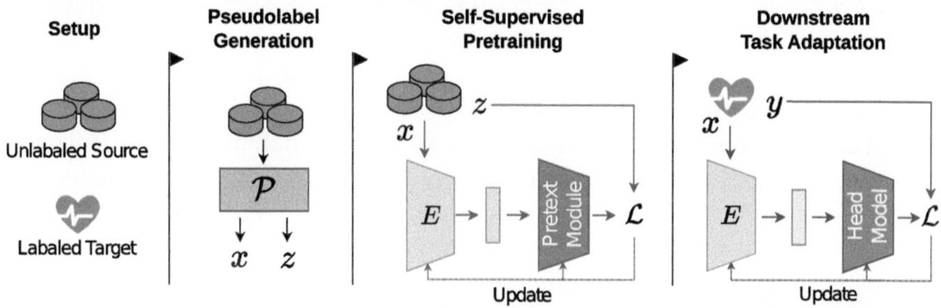

Fig. 1. Overview of a typical workflow for the SSL paradigm. At the setup step, we define the unlabeled source dataset and the labeled target dataset. After the pretext task generates the pseudolabels through $\mathcal{P}$, we pre-train the encoder using the self-supervised objective and the pseudolabels. With the encoder pretrained, the learned weights are transferred and used as a starting point to solve the target task. Adapted from [6].

Due to the difficulty in labeling biomedical signals, the use of pretext tasks has shown a promising manner to mitigate data scarcity [17]. Many deep learning solutions that lead with physiological signals fall under the self-supervised paradigm [11,14,31].

---

[1] We call *high-resource* a dataset that contains a large and diverse collection of data samples and *low-resource* refers to a dataset that contains a small number of samples.

2.2   Transfer Learning for Time Series

Transfer learning is a paradigm that uses knowledge from source data to build new models. It is inspired by the human ability to apply prior knowledge to solve new problems more efficiently or provide better solutions [34]. In this sense, self-supervised learning (SSL) shares many similarities with transfer learning, as both involve transferring previously learned knowledge to create a new model. Accordingly, as noted by [22], we define domain and transfer learning as:

Definition 2. A domain $\mathcal{D}$ consists of two components, a feature space $\mathcal{X}$ and a marginal probability distribution $P(\mathbf{D})$, where the dataset $\mathbf{D} = \{x_i, ..., x_n\} \in \mathcal{X}$. Generally, if two domains are different, they may have different feature spaces or marginal probability distributions.

Definition 3. Given a source domain $\mathcal{D}_s$ with its respective learning task T_s, and a target domain $\mathcal{D}_t$ also with its respective learning task T_t. The transfer learning aims to help improve the learning of the target predictive function $f_t(\cdot)$ in $\mathcal{D}_t$ using the knowledge in $\mathcal{D}_s$ and T_s, where $\mathcal{D}_s \neq \mathcal{D}_t$ or $T_s \neq T_t$.

In this work, we will refer to the source dataset as the dataset used to pre-train the SSL models, while the target dataset is the dataset associated with the downstream task, to which we are transferring the knowledge for.

One of the key challenges in transfer learning is determining the appropriate conditions under which knowledge should be transferred between datasets. In some situations, when the source domain and target domain are not related to each other, a forceful transfer learning may lead to the negative transfer problem [22]. This phenomenon has been observed in time series data when analyzing the transferability between datasets from the UCR archive, a well-established benchmark for time series classification [7]. The analysis showed that blindly selecting datasets to transfer can drastically decrease the model's performance, as initial weights of the network have a significant impact on the training process.

At the same time, the literature still lacks methods to quantify how much relatedness is necessary to prevent the negative transfer effect [29]. In this work, we consider two domains to be related when there is some form of relationship, either implicit or explicit, between their feature spaces [22]. [7] introduced a similarity-based method to quantify relatedness between datasets and to predict the most suitable source for a given target dataset, which represents a significant advancement in the field. However, this approach is not compatible with the development of a multi-purpose pretrained model for time series data, where a single model is intended to generalize across multiple target datasets.

2.3   Foundation Models for Time Series

A foundation model is a large-scale pretrained deep learning model designed to capture general knowledge and patterns from vast amounts of data. As shown in Fig. 2, these models serve as versatile starting points that can be fine-tuned or adapted to a variety of specific tasks using relatively small amounts of task-specific data [16]. Notable examples in the natural language processing (NLP) domain include BERT [4] and GPT-3 [1]. Motivated by their success in NLP, foundation models have also emerged across other data modalities, including time series [2].

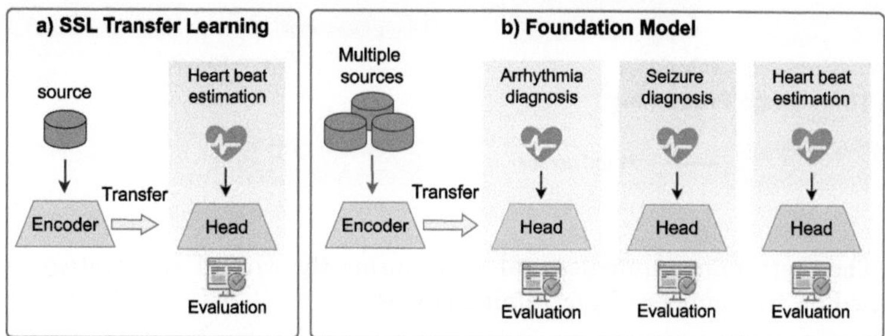

Fig. 2. Illustration of the differences between the **(a)** conventional SSL transfer learning in time series modality and **(b)** the foundation model architecture.

In the healthcare domain, most foundation models have been applied to Electronic Health Records. [2] establishes this by presenting a large-scale, harmonized critical care time series medical dataset. [2] discusses how the distribution shifts represent a key challenge in creating a multi-purpose pretrained model by showing how datasets from the same domain contain different distributions. In parallel, it is observed in the literature on time series that a good pretraining approach with multiple datasets that share basic information can surpass the random initialization used in the traditional supervised approach [12].

3   Methodology Research

This section presents the proposed pretraining strategies to train SSL models to solve complex classification tasks under labeling scarcity. This work explores multiple data-oriented strategies to train a multi-purpose pretrained model. All the assessed strategies start by training an SLL model using a high-resource dataset containing varied physiological signals. Part of the proposed strategies recalibrate the model using different data. The datasets used to assess our proposals are presented in Sect. 4.1.

Figure 3 illustrates the evaluated strategies, categorized based on the number of pretraining stages.

The one-stage approach represents the common pretraining strategies adopted in the time series literature [7,12]. Into this category, we have the four strategies: (1) the **_ECG domain_** strategy, where the SSL encoder is pre-trained exclusively on ECG signals present at the source dataset, (2) the **_All domains_** which includes all the source dataset signals, (3 and 4) the remaining strategies

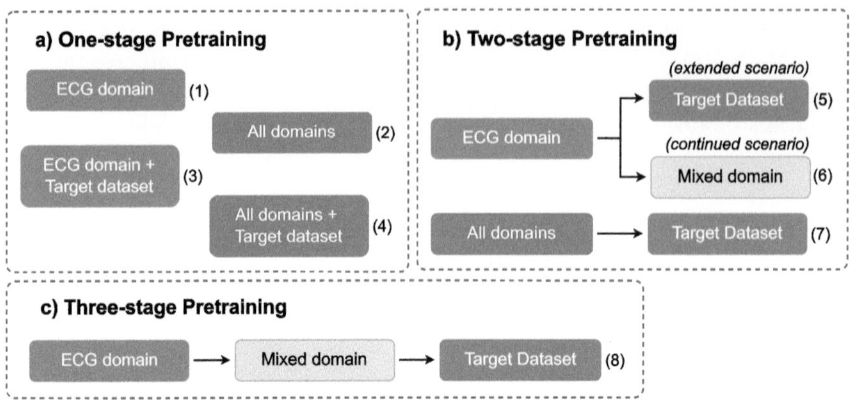

Fig. 3. The pretraining strategies evaluated during the work. Each strategy is categorized based on the number of pretraining stages.

correspond to variations of the previous one where they are merged with the target dataset. The baseline strategy 1 aims to produce representations specialized for the downstream task (ECG classification), while strategy 2 focuses on training a more generalist feature extractor [7,12]. Strategies 3 and 4 are baselines with little applicability, since accessing the target dataset during the pretraining is not feasible. This privileged access may turn them into strong baselines.

The category two-stage pretraining comprises three strategies: (5) **ECG domain extended** uses the ECG domain configuration as a starting point to undergo a second training phase using the downstream ECG dataset, aiming to approximate the pretrained feature encoder close to the downstream task feature space; (6) the **ECG domain continued** approach also starts with the ECG-only pre-trained encoder but updates its weights for a limited number of epochs using mixed signals (excluding the ECG) from the source dataset, acting as a regularization technique for the SSL pretraining; (7) in the **All domains extended** setup, the encoder is first pre-trained on all physiological signal domains from the source dataset, and then re-trained on the downstream ECG dataset to assess adaptation from a multi-domain initialization.

Finally, in the three-stage pretraining category, we have (8) the **ECG domain continued extended** configuration. In this set, the ECG domain continued scenario undergoes an additional training stage with the downstream task dataset. This approach combines strategies 5 and 6, aiming to leverage advantages from both.

3.1   Self-supervised Learning Models for Time Series

To analyze the performance of each pretraining strategy, we conducted a comprehensive set of experiments by evaluating each strategy with three SSL models. TS-TCC [5] and TS2Vec [32] represent two contrastive-based models well-established in the SSL literature of time series, while Series2Vec [8] is a recent model that is based on time series similarity.

TS-TCC [5] uses two augmented versions of the input signal, one strongly augmented and the other weakly augmented, to learn a robust representation using a cross-view prediction task. Strong augmented views use the permutation-and-jitter strategy, while the weakly augmented views apply the jitter-and-scale strategy. Afterward, the augmented views are passed to an encoder with a 3-block of convolutions to extract a high-dimensional representation. The temporal contrasting module uses a transformer-based autoregressive model to summarize the high-dimensional representation into a context vector. This context vector is then used in a cross-view prediction task, where the strong augmentation context is used to predict the weak augmentation's future timestep of its high-dimensional representation and vice versa. A contextual contrastive module learns to discriminate the contexts using a non-linear projection head; this module aims to learn more discriminative representations.

TS2Vec [32] is an SSL method for time series that is well-established. TS2Vec learns contextual information at various semantic levels through hierarchical contrasting and contextual consistency. The contextual consistency applies timestamp masking and randomly crops two context views from the input time series. Masking increases the robustness of the learned representation, while random cropping generates new contexts without collapsing the representation. With the context views, a hierarchical contrastive loss extracts multi-scale contextual information by computing temporal and instance-wise contrast for all granularity levels. The granularity levels are obtained using a recursive max-pooling operation. At the same time, the encoder module is composed of ten residual blocks of dilated convolutions, which enable a large receptive field.

Series2Vec [8] is an SSL method based on similarity. Inspired by the contrastive paradigm, the model utilizes time series-specific similarity measures, the soft-DTW [3], to provide a bias suitable for the time series. The Series2Vec pretext task objective learns similar representations for all similar time series within each batch. Transformers are used to construct the pretext representation, given the order-invariant property of the self-attention mechanism. The model encodes the time series in both time and frequency domains using disjoint convolutions [9] for encoding both temporal and spatial features.

4   Experimental Evaluation

This section describes the experimental setup and the results achieved in our experiments[2]. We initially present the datasets used in our analysis.

---

[2] https://github.com/adilsonmedronha/data-driven-ecg-ssl.

4.1   Datasets

We utilized two datasets to explore our research questions, with the ECG Fragment [21] being the low-resource dataset that configures our downstream task, and the WESAD [24] representing a high-resource dataset used to pre-train the SSL models.

ECG Fragment   [18,21] is a low-resource dataset that contains 1016 2-second ECG fragments extracted from the MVED [20] dataset. The dataset is univariate, consisting of a modified limb lead II (MLII), with a sampling rate of 360 Hz. The samples are grouped into six classes based on the threat to the patient's life: Dangerous arrhythmia, early form of life-threatening arrhythmia, life-threatening ventricular arrhythmia, potentially dangerous ventricular arrhythmia, supraventricular arrhythmia, and normal rhythm. One of the most challenging characteristics of this dataset is that the classes can contain multiple disorders, producing classes with high pattern variability. The dataset was z-normalized and split into train (64%), validation (20%), and test (16%).

WESAD   [24] is a wearable stress and affect detection dataset containing motion and several physiological signals, recorded from both wrist- and chest-worn devices of 15 subjects in a laboratory. The included modalities are: electrocardiogram, electrodermal activity, electromyogram, respiration, body temperature, and three-axis acceleration. As a pre-processing step, the records were resampled from 700 Hz to 360 Hz, split into 2-second windows, each modality was considered an isolated sample, and also z-normalized. Windows where the majority of the observations correspond to preparation or self-filling reports were discarded, leaving only the classes: baseline, stress, amusement, and meditation.

In this work, the WESAD dataset was used as a base to construct the multiple source datasets used in the evaluated pretraining strategies, Fig. 3. The first subset is the *ECG domain*; for this one, all other physiological signals were discarded, leaving only the ECG channel of all samples. For the *All domain* subset, after considering each channel as an independent univariate time series, the number of the subset is multiplied by five; to maintain the same proportion of the ECG domain, only 20% of the WESAD samples were selected. Lastly, the *Mixed domain* is the All domain subset without the ECG samples. After the selection of each subset, the samples were randomly split into a training and validation set in a proportion of 80% and 20%, respectively.

4.2   Implementation Details

In our experimental setup, we pretrained the SSL models (TSTCC, S2V, and TS2V) for 600 epochs, with the best model epoch being selected based on the lowest validation loss. It is worth noting that the TSTCC encoder exhibited constant validation loss, which is a known behavior of this model. Therefore, we retained the final model state instead of selecting the epoch with the lowest loss (same protocol present in the original paper [5]). After pretraining, the head models are calibrated for 300 epochs, with the best model being the epoch with the lowest validation loss. This decision was based on observed loss trends, computational feasibility, and time constraints.

For strategies that use a two-step pretraining approach, the number of epochs used varies between the first and second steps. For continued versions, the pre-trained model is perturbed with other physiological signals for 1 epoch long. After this, we verified an overfitting of the model, making the training for more epochs unnecessary. The extended versions were trained for 60 epochs, with the best model selected based on the lowest validation loss (except for TSTCC).

We also varied the head models to explore the effects that decision functions have on the SSL model performance. Specifically, we applied two architectures as head models: (i) a multi-layer perception (MLP) [28] model proposed for time series classification, and (ii) the FCN [28], a convolutional network that is able to capture local temporal dependencies. The selection of the FCN is adopted to verify if the head model will utilize any residual temporal dependencies present in the SSL encoder's learned representation. As a complementary evaluation, we also compared the obtained results using SSL models against the supervision approach. For this, the head models (MLP and FCN) and H-InceptionTime (HIT) [13] were trained under the supervision paradigm, also for 300 epochs and using the configurations described in their original papers. HIT is considered the current state-of-the-art in deep learning time series classification [19].

For each head model, we also evaluated two calibration approaches: (i) in the fine-tuning together with the head models the pre-trained SSL encoder's parameters are also updated, this approach aims to facilitate the feature extractor to adjust to the downstream task; (ii) while for Linear probing, once the SSL is pre-trained, we only allow the adjustment of the head model's parameter.

Moreover, due to the high variance typically observed in time series classification tasks, each supervised model and calibration phase were repeated five times. Results are reported as the mean and standard deviation of the F1-score due to the class imbalance present in the Fragment dataset. No hyperparameter tuning was performed, as our primary focus was on evaluating data selection strategies rather than optimizing model performance. All hyperparameters and settings used in our experimentation are contained in the available source code.

4.3 Experimental Results

Table 1 presents the performance of all strategies described in Sect. 3 to handle the transfer learning between the source and the ECG classification task.

The results show that no training strategy is prevalent over all architecture configurations. However, several configurations led to undesired results considering the scores obtained by the supervised baselines. Specifically, HIT, MLP, and FCN achieved an F1-Score of 55.61 ($\pm$3.34), 37.33 ($\pm$1.84), and 23.45 ($\pm$3.98), respectively. Therefore, we recommend using TS2Vec as the SSL model and MLP as the classification head, as this is the only configuration that outperforms the supervised baselines.

Table 1. The performance achieved by the SSL models under all evaluated strategies. The values presented are the best F1-score (with standard deviation in parentheses) obtained by the specified combination of SSL and head model. The $*$ indicates that the presented metric comes from a fine-tuning calibration approach; otherwise, it is linear probing. The best results of each column are **bolded**, the suboptimal results are underlined, and gray indicate that the method outperforms HIT.

Strategy	Series2Vec		TS2Vec		TSTCC	
	MLP	FCN	MLP	FCN	MLP	FCN
(1) ECG	25.17 ($\pm$ 0.58)	10.14 ($\pm$ 1.58)	61.47 ($\pm$ 3.66)*	11.55 ($\pm$ 5.43)	40.72 ($\pm$ 0.76)	8.25 ($\pm$ 3.37)
(2) All	41.25 ($\pm$ 1.59)	18.55 ($\pm$ 5.41)	52.44 ($\pm$ 4.28)	**17.45 ($\pm$ 10.19)**	34.57 ($\pm$ 0.84)	10.32 ($\pm$ 5.64)*
(3) ECG+Fragment	33.54 ($\pm$ 0.65)	13.67 ($\pm$ 5.84)*	56.62 ($\pm$ 3.96)*	13.48 ($\pm$ 1.85)	**49.36 ($\pm$ 2.03)**	13.08 ($\pm$ 11.47)
(4) All+Fragment	**52.16 ($\pm$ 0.42)**	15.23 ($\pm$ 3.89)	51.4 ($\pm$ 3.42)*	13.72 ($\pm$ 3.86)	34.36 ($\pm$ 2.56)	14.78 ($\pm$ 6.17)
(5) ECG extended	29.82 ($\pm$ 1.84)	7.67 ($\pm$ 2.97)*	62.35 ($\pm$ 2.64)*	10.91 ($\pm$ 3.49)	38.47 ($\pm$ 0.21)	12.2 ($\pm$ 6.41)
(6) ECG continued	24.99 ($\pm$ 0.71)	8.28 ($\pm$ 1.77)	**63.05 ($\pm$ 3.87)***	11.69 ($\pm$ 1.66)	42.43 ($\pm$ 3.48)	**19.67 ($\pm$ 2.91)**
(7) All extended	36.01 ($\pm$ 1.08)	**18.77 ($\pm$ 2.49)**	52.35 ($\pm$ 4.48)	17.21 ($\pm$ 4.19)	38.61 ($\pm$ 3.27)	9.5 ($\pm$ 1.77)
(8) 5 & 6 combined	29.72 ($\pm$ 1.49)	9.45 ($\pm$ 1.99)	60.36 ($\pm$ 2.78)*	13.6 ($\pm$ 8.65)*	38.17 ($\pm$ 0.36)	17.67 ($\pm$ 6.54)

It is important to highlight that TS2Vec outperforms the supervised baselines in five out of eight scenarios. More specifically, the standard SSL training setup (Scenario 1) already surpasses HIT by nearly six percentage points in F1-Score. Furthermore, the proposed Strategies 5 and 6 outperform Scenario 1, achieving a gain of over seven percentage points in F1-Score.

Some patterns stand out in the results. For example, the fine-tuning strategy consistently underperformed compared to linear probing for the TSTCC and Series2Vec models, indicating that further refinement of the backbone is insufficient for these models to achieve strong performance. In general, linear probing is the calibration approach that performs best in most configurations. The only exception is TS2Vec, which has achieved consistent results using the fine-tuning approach in most evaluated strategies.

Linear probing is a faster calibration approach as it only updates the head model. However, the best result using this strategy across all configurations was achieved by TS2Vec under the "ECG+Fragment" strategy, which is not a realistic scenario for a multi-purpose pre-trained model. Figure 4 compares the results of tuning strategies for TS2Vec.

Overall, the performance drop when using linear probing with TS2Vec is relatively small. Therefore, this strategy may still be considered, given its lower computational cost. Compared to the supervised baselines, it can still be applied to the downstream task whenever a pretrained TS2Vec model is available. In most calibration scenarios, this approach yields slightly better results than the HIT classifier, eliminating the need to train the model from scratch.

Besides, the experimental findings do not support the assumption that SSL models preserve the sequential dependencies of the input data, making FCN a potentially suitable classification head. Figure 5 shows how the use of FCN as head model significantly reduced the SSL model's performance, which may indicate that the obtained representation does not conserve the temporal characteristics of the input data.

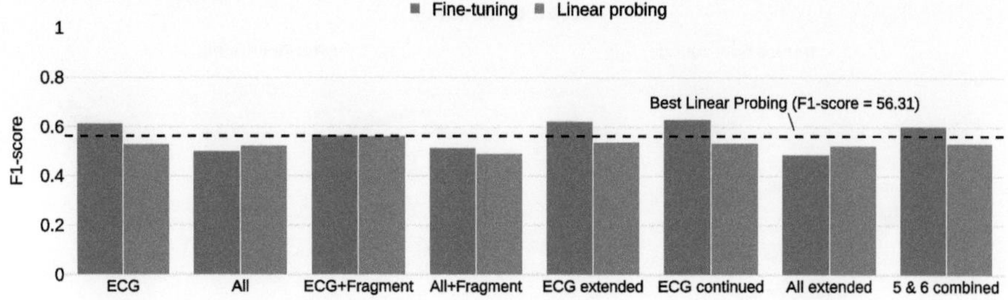

Fig. 4. F1-score comparison of TS2Vec with MLP between Fine-tuning and Linear probing calibration strategies.

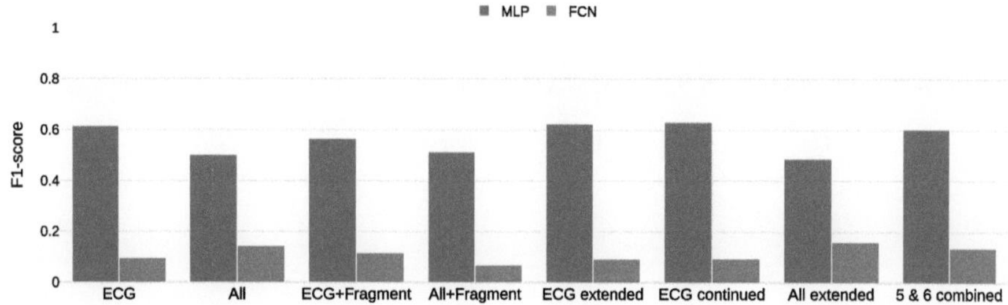

Fig. 5. F1-score comparison between the TS2Vec with MLP and FCN head models.

We visually analyzed selected scenarios based on these results to better understand how these outcomes were achieved. First, we assess the impact of fine-tuning on the "ECG continued" strategy by comparing the best and worst-performing encoders, TS2Vec and TSTCC, respectively. Both were re-trained with multidomain signals for a single epoch, which is the minimum number of iterations required to process the entire dataset. Nevertheless, this was sufficient to produce a significant change in TS2Vecs embedding space (Fig. 6), resulting in compact clusters with well-defined class boundaries. In contrast, TSTCC embeddings remained almost unchanged, still scattered and overlapped, indicating an inability to learn discriminative representations (Fig. 7), likely due to the low magnitude of gradients during backpropagation from the head to the encoder.

However, the embeddings observed after fine-tuning TS2Vec suggest that overfitting may have occurred during training. Although the classes appear well separated in the feature space of the fine-tuned model, the performance results do not fully reflect this observation. To further investigate this, Fig. 8 provides a close look at the first run (out of five) with the best encoder. The overall behavior extends to other runs, data strategies, and encoders as well.

Fine-tuning shows greater instability due to the joint optimization of the encoder and head, which increases the number of parameters to be updated and causes the input representation to the head to change over epochs, resulting in a more complex loss surface than in linear probing. In contrast, linear probing

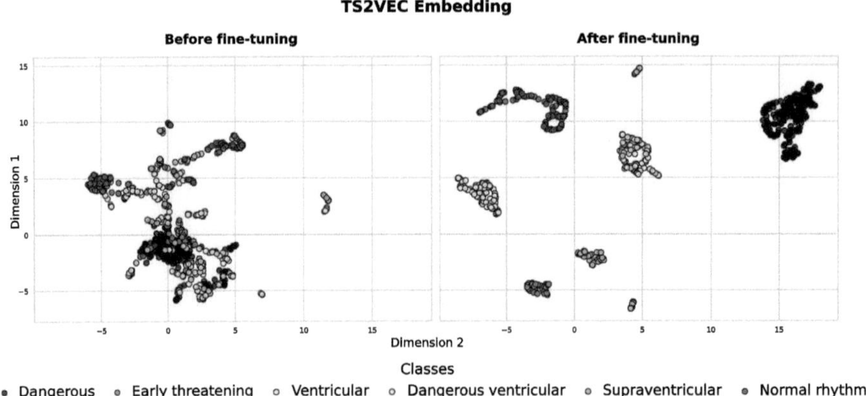

Fig. 6. Comparison of TS2Vec UMAP embeddings before and after fine-tuning.

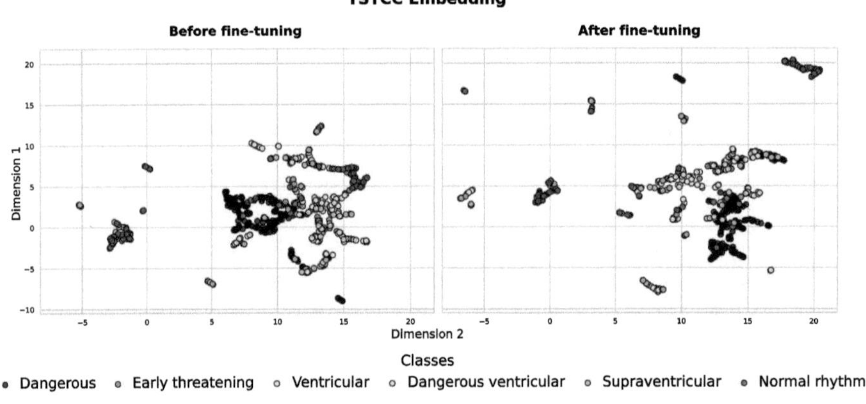

Fig. 7. Comparison of TSTCC UMAP embeddings before and after fine-tuning.

benefits from a fixed encoder, resulting in more stable and simpler optimization. Although linear probing shows a more stable trend, it displays increasingly divergence, with all gradients concentrated in the head, creating a theoretically easier scenario for overfitting. However, this was not observed, likely because the overall model parameters to be updated is lower than fine-tuning. Fine-tuning showed greater instability in loss trends, with validation loss curves often displaying a symmetric pattern, where local minima are mirrored by nearby peaks; nevertheless, it achieved better results on the test set.

5   Conclusions and Future Work

This paper explores eight data-oriented strategies across three pre-training approaches, evaluated through 108 experiments. Our results show that additional SSL training of the encoder with multidomain signals leads to better

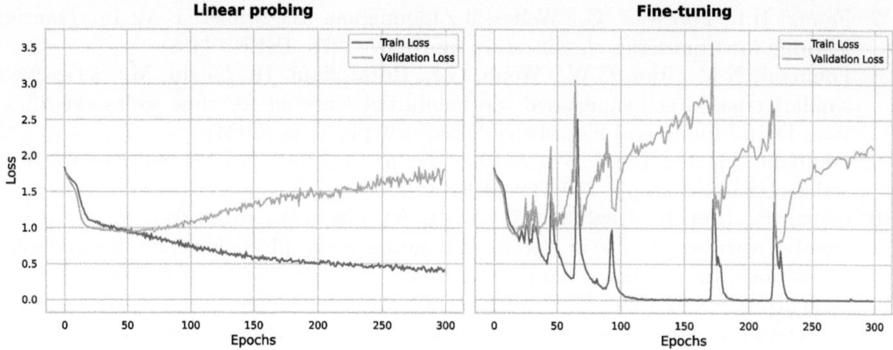

Fig. 8. Comparison of TS2Vec losses curves between linear probing and fine-tuning.

performance than the traditional approach in the literature, which relies only on re-training with downstream data. The proposed data-driven strategy also outperforms conventional self-supervised learning methods in terms of transferability. Notably, our approach, even using a simple MLP as the head model, surpasses HIT, the current state-of-the-art supervised ensemble for time series classification.

As future work, we intend to investigate further the mechanisms that led to the overfitting observed in our experiments. Although our proposed strategies promote better generalization, the overfitting issue remains present. Additionally, we will explore new approaches to modify the architectures of self-supervised models to mitigate this problem. We also plan to extend our study to different physiological signals, focusing on multivariate and multimodal models.

Acknowledgments. This work was supported by the Coordenação de Aperfeiçoamento de Pessoal de Nvel Superior (CAPES) and the São Paulo Research Foundation (FAPESP) grant numbers 2024/07016-4, 2024/14856-9, and 2022/03176-1.

References

1. Brown, T., et al.: Language models are few-shot learners. Adv. Neural. Inf. Process. Syst. **33**, 1877–1901 (2020)
2. Burger, M., et al.: Towards foundation models for critical care time series. arXiv preprint arXiv:2411.16346 (2024)
3. Cuturi, M., Blondel, M.: Soft-dtw: a differentiable loss function for time-series. In: International Conference on Machine Learning, pp. 894–903. PMLR (2017)
4. Devlin, J., Chang, M.W., Lee, K., Toutanova, K.: Bert,: Pre-training of deep bidirectional transformers for language understanding. Presented at the (2019)
5. Eldele, E., et al.: Time-series representation learning via temporal and contextual contrasting. arXiv preprint arXiv:2106.14112 (2021)
6. Ericsson, L., Gouk, H., Loy, C.C., Hospedales, T.M.: Self-supervised representation learning: Introduction, advances, and challenges. IEEE Signal Process. Mag. **39**(3), 42–62 (2022)

7. Fawaz, H.I., Forestier, G., Weber, J., Idoumghar, L., Muller, P.A.: In: Transfer learning for time series classification, pp. 1367–1376. IEEE (2018)
8. Foumani, N.M., Tan, C.W., Webb, G.I., Rezatofighi, H., Salehi, M.: Series2vec: similarity-based self-supervised representation learning for time series classification. Data Mining and Knowledge Discovery, pp. 1–25 (2024)
9. Foumani, S.N.M., Tan, C.W., Salehi, M.: In: Disjoint-CNN for multivariate time series classification, pp. 760–769. IEEE (2021)
10. Gopal, B., Han, R., Raghupathi, G., Ng, A., Tison, G., Rajpurkar, P.: 3kg: Contrastive learning of 12-lead electrocardiograms using physiologically-inspired augmentations. In: Machine Learning for Health, pp. 156–167. PMLR (2021)
11. Hallgarten, P., Bethge, D., Özdcnizci, O., Grosse-Puppendahl, T., Kasneci, E.: In: Ts-moco: Time-series Momentum Contrast for Self-supervised Physiological Representation Learning, pp. 1030–1034. IEEE (2023)
12. Ismail-Fawaz, A., Devanne, M., Berretti, S., Weber, J., Forestier, G.: Finding foundation models for time series classification with a pretext task. Presented at the (Springer (2024).)
13. Ismail-Fawaz, A., Devanne, M., Weber, J., Forestier, G.: In: Deep learning for time series classification using new hand-crafted convolution filters, pp. 972–981. IEEE (2022)
14. Kiyasseh, D., Zhu, T., Clifton, D.A.: Clocs: contrastive learning of cardiac signals across space, time, and patients. In: International Conference on Machine Learning, pp. 5606–5615. PMLR (2021)
15. Lalam, S.K., et al.: ECG representation learning with multi-modal EHR data. Trans. Mach. Learn. Res. (2023)
16. Liang, Y., et al.: Foundation models for time series analysis: a tutorial and survey. Presented at the (2024)
17. Liu, Z., Alavi, A., Li, M., Zhang, X.: Self-supervised contrastive learning for medical time series: A systematic review. Sensors 23(9), 4221 (2023)
18. Manilo, L.A., Nemirko, A.P., Evdakova, E.G., Tatarinova, A.A.: ECG database for evaluating the efficiency of recognizing dangerous arrhythmias. Presented at the (2021). https://doi.org/10.1109/CSGB53040.2021.9496029
19. Middlehurst, M., Schäfer, P., Bagnall, A.: Bake off redux: a review and experimental evaluation of recent time series classification algorithms. Data Min. Knowl. Disc. 38(4), 1958–2031 (2024)
20. MIT: Mit-bih malignant ventricular ectopy database (version 1.0.0). https://www.physionet.org/content/vfdb/1.0.0/ (1999)
21. Nemirko, A., Manilo, L., Tatarinova, A., Alekseev, B., Evdakova, E.: ECG fragment database for the exploration of dangerous arrhythmia (version 1.0.0). PhysioNet (2022). https://doi.org/10.13026/kpfg-xs25
22. Pan, S.J., Yang, Q.: A survey on transfer learning. IEEE Trans. Knowl. Data Eng. 22(10), 1345–1359 (2009)
23. Rabbani, S., Khan, N.: Contrastive self-supervised learning for stress detection from ECG data. Bioengineering 9(8), 374 (2022)
24. Schmidt, P., Reiss, A., Duerichen, R., Marberger, C., Van Laerhoven, K.: Introducing wesad, a multimodal dataset for wearable stress and affect detection. Presented at the (2018)
25. Silva, D.F., Batista, G.E., Keogh, E.: Large-scale similarity-based time series mining. Presented at the (2018)
26. Silva, R.d.C., Silva, D.F.: Tackling low-resource ECG classification with self-supervised learning. In: Brazilian Conference on Intelligent Systems pp. 238–252. Springer (2024)

27. Siontis, K.C., Noseworthy, P.A., Attia, Z.I., Friedman, P.A.: Artificial intelligence-enhanced electrocardiography in cardiovascular disease management. Nat. Rev. Cardiol. **18**(7), 465–478 (2021)
28. Wang, Z., Yan, W., Oates, T.: In: Time series classification from scratch with deep neural networks: a strong baseline, pp. 1578–1585. IEEE (2017)
29. Weiss, K., Khoshgoftaar, T.M., Wang, D.D.: A survey of transfer learning. J. Big Data **3**(1), 1–40 (2016). https://doi.org/10.1186/s40537-016-0043-6
30. Wu, L., Lin, H., Tan, C., Gao, Z., Li, S.Z.: Self-supervised learning on graphs: contrastive, generative, or predictive. IEEE Trans. Knowl. Data Eng. **35**(4), 4216–4235 (2021)
31. Yèche, H., Dresdner, G., Locatello, F., Hüser, M., Rätsch, G.: Neighborhood contrastive learning applied to online patient monitoring. In: International Conference on Machine Learning, pp. 11964–11974. PMLR (2021)
32. Yue, Z., et al.: Ts2vec: Towards universal representation of time series. In: Proceedings of the AAAI Conference on Artificial Intelligence, vol. 36, pp. 8980–8987 (2022)
33. Zhang, K., et al.: Self-supervised learning for time series analysis: taxonomy, progress, and prospects. IEEE Transactions on Pattern Analysis and Machine Intelligence (2024)
34. Zhao, Z., Alzubaidi, L., Zhang, J., Duan, Y., Gu, Y.: A comparison review of transfer learning and self-supervised learning: Definitions, applications, advantages and limitations. Expert Syst. Appl. **242**, 122807 (2024)
35. Zong, Y., Mac Aodha, O., Hospedales, T.: Self-supervised multimodal learning: a survey. IEEE Trans. Patt. Anal. Mach. Intell. (2024)

Highway to... Determining Fatal Outcomes in Traffic Accidents Based on Police Reports

Arthur M. P. Gabardo$^{(\boxtimes)}$, Guilherme A. A. Schünemann, Pablo A. Jaskowiak, Benjamin G. Moreira, and Ricardo J. Pfitscher

Interdisciplinary Data and Artificial Intelligence Laboratory (IDA Lab), Federal University of Santa Catarina (UFSC), Joinville, SC, Brazil
`arthur.miguel@ufsc.br`

Abstract. Brazil faces significant traffic safety challenges with its vast territory and one of the world's largest road networks. Road traffic accidents, particularly on federal highways, remain a leading cause of death in the country, with serious economic and social consequences. This work presents a case study of three machine learning methods— Random Forest (RF), k-Nearest Neighbors (kNN), and Multilayer Perceptron (MLP)—for classifying the severity of traffic accidents in the Brazilian southern region. Using an open dataset from the Brazilian Federal Highway Police (PRF) covering the years 2021 to 2024, extensive preprocessing was carried out, including categorical variable encoding, feature selection, and the application of the SMOTE technique to address class imbalance. Model performance was assessed through statistical metrics such as specificity, $F1$-score, and AUC-ROC. The results show that RF and kNN (with SMOTE) achieved the best performance in predicting fatal accidents, both with AUC-ROC of 0.99. In addition to an in-depth model evaluation, this study presents a post-hoc analysis of feature importance and contributions through Shapley Additive Explanations (SHAP) for the best performing model, in order to support knowledge discovery and highlight the most influential factors associated with fatalities.

Keywords: Traffic accident · Road safety · Machine learning · Explainable AI

1 Introduction

Brazil is a continental-sized country, with a territory exceeding 8.5 million square kilometers. It has the fourth-largest road network in the world, spanning 1.7 million kilometers. This vast network—composed of federal, state, and municipal roads, both public and concession-operated—is fundamental to the country's economic development, playing a crucial role in regional integration by enabling the transportation of people and goods. Such characteristics, associated with poor road conditions, contribute to a high incidence of traffic accidents [3].

R. de Freitas and D. Furtado (Eds.): BRACIS 2025, LNAI 16181, pp. 230–244, 2026.
https://doi.org/10.1007/978-3-032-15990-8_16

According to the [5], traffic accidents in Brazil led to an economic cost of R\$14 billion in 2024, with over 67,000 incidents reported. The southern region stands out with particularly alarming figures, with the highest rates of both accidents and deaths per inhabitants in the entire country. In 2024 alone, the states in the southern region recorded over 21,000 accidents, 6.4% of which were fatal, also resulting in an economic impact exceeding R\$4.3 billion. This represents 63.5 accidents (4.4 deaths) per 100,000 inhabitants, as depicted in Fig. 1, a rate far higher than the center-western region (CW) in accidents. Another alarming trend is observed when analyzing the evolution of traffic incidents in recent years. Between 2021 and 2024, Brazil has experienced a steady increase in both the total number of road accidents and the proportion involving fatalities. This trend is also observed in the southern region, with an increase in the number of reported incidents in the past years.

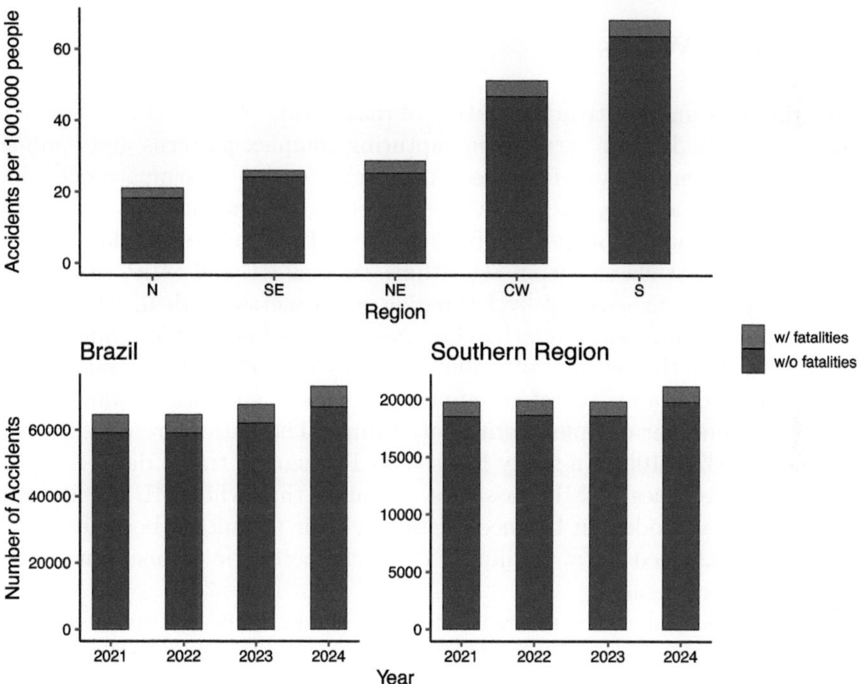

Fig. 1. Rate of accidents and deaths in Brazilian federal roads.

These numbers underscore the severity of the issue and the urgent need for public policies to improve road safety and consequently reduce fatalities. Given that the primary causes of accidents include human error, inadequate infrastructure, and ineffective enforcement [14], detailed analysis of traffic accident data is essential to an informed decision-making process regarding infrastructure improvements and to support targeted traffic safety campaigns. Machine learning and data mining techniques have gained prominence in this context, as they identify complex patterns and trends that may not be easily captured through traditional analytical approaches [2].

This study presents a comparative evaluation of different classification models to predict the severity of traffic accidents on federal highways in the Brazilian southern region, using an open-access dataset provided by the [4]. The comparison comprises three algorithms—k-Nearest Neighbors (kNN), Random Forest (RF), and Multilayer Perceptron (MLP)—assessed through statistical performance metrics such as $F1$-score and AUC-ROC. The analysis also takes into account a grid search for hyperparameter tuning, and oversampling techniques (i.e., SMOTE) to address the class imbalance in the target variable. A post-hoc feature importance analysis is also conducted on the best-performing models to support knowledge discovery and interpretability, highlighting the most influential variables associated with accident severity.

2   Related Works

Given the scale and multivariate nature of road traffic accident data, traditional statistical methods often struggle in capturing complex patterns and nonlinear interactions among various features. Conversely, machine learning models have proven effective not only in improving predictive performance but also in supporting the extraction of meaningful knowledge from large-scale datasets. [13] demonstrated that classification algorithms, such as RF and MLP, can successfully model accident severity by leveraging road, meteorological, vehicles, and involved persons information, achieving accuracies as high as 85%. Similarly, [9] also argued that the severity of traffic accidents is rarely determined by linear associations alone and, therefore employed methods such as Random Forests and kNN to uncover complex data relationships. The authors reported accuracies close to 93%. [10], in a study focused on Portuguese traffic data, compared statistical approaches to ML classifiers, revealing that while ML often outperforms statistical models in balanced datasets, their advantage becomes limited in highly imbalanced data, outlining a key characteristic in accident severity classification problems.

Indeed, class imbalance remains one of the main challenges in this domain, especially when severe or fatal accident cases are underrepresented in historical records. Various studies have sought to mitigate this issue using resampling strategies. [11] compared under-sampling and over-sampling techniques in combination with ensemble methods such as bagging and majority voting, and found out that decision trees, paired with over-sampling achieved the best performing results. [7] also addressed the disproportion between non-severe and severe accidents using under-sampling to balance the training data, subsequently evaluating classification performance using Naive Bayes, Deep Neural Networks (DNN), and Gradient Boosting Trees in the context of decision-making for Spanish traffic agencies, achieving a $F1$-score of 87% with DNN as the best performing model. More related to our work, [16] employed the Synthetic Minority Over-sampling

Technique (SMOTE) to improve the representation of minority classes in South African accident data. Their results confirmed the effectiveness of SMOTE in enhancing the performance of XGBoost over logistic regression, especially when dealing with sparse and noisy data from police reports. These findings reinforce the importance of handling class imbalance to prevent biased predictions and ensure better recall of rare but critical cases such as fatalities.

In addition to predictive accuracy, recent studies have stressed the importance of interpretability and feature importance analysis as part of knowledge discovery in intelligent accident analysis systems. Transparent models and post-hoc explanation methods enable practitioners to understand not only what the model predicts, but why. [8] applied Shapley Additive Explanations (SHAP) to interpret boosting-based ensemble models, revealing that month of the year, accident cause, driver age, and collision type were significant determinants of injury outcomes in highway crashes in Pakistan. Likewise, [1] employed SHAP to a RF model trained on New Zealand crash data, revealing that road type and vehicle count were key predictors of injury severity.

3   Materials and Methods

The main goal of this work is to classify the severity of traffic accidents—distinguishing between fatal and non-fatal cases—through a comprehensive analysis of accident data collected by the Brazilian Federal Highway Police (PRF) from 2021 to 2024 in the southern region of Brazil. This section describes the procedures and decisions involved in the data collection, preprocessing, feature engineering, evaluation of models, and feature importance assessment.

3.1   Data Collection

The dataset used in this study comprises official traffic accident records obtained from the PRF's publicly available databases. These records include structured reports of accidents that occurred from 2021 to 2024 in all Brazilian federal roads. The choice of this time frame is justified by a methodological change in accident reporting adopted nationwide in 2021, which standardized the annotation of key variables and improved data reliability across years. Although the dataset covers the entire country, the study focused on the southern region of Brazil because of two main factors: (i) the South consistently records the highest rates of traffic accidents and fatalities per capita among all Brazilian regions; and (ii) the country's road infrastructure varies significantly across regions—with notable differences in road quality, traffic density, and urban-rural distribution—making region-specific analyses essential to accurately capture such heterogeneity.

3.2   Data Preprocessing

Initial preprocessing involved merging the datasets from each year into a single consolidated collection. Records with inconsistent or implausible values were removed, such as vehicle manufacturing years marked as zero or negative, and ages of involved individuals below zero or above 130. Furthermore, entries containing missing or unreported values in any of the essential features were excluded to ensure the integrity of subsequent analyses.

Each accident record contains various features, including road and weather conditions, time of occurrence, types of vehicles involved, accident typology, and demographic data of those affected. Table 1 describes all features in the dataset. From this initial set of features, categorical features were standardized to reduce variability caused by spelling inconsistencies or semantically equivalent labels. For instance, the number of categories in the `type_vehicle` feature was reduced from 15 to 6, and in the `type_accident` feature from 17 to 9. Along the same line, the features `id_road` and `km_road` were concatenated into a single locality identifier named `br_km`.

Table 1. Features of occurrences present in the dataset.

Feature	Type	Description
`severity`	target	Fatal or non-fatal accident
`type_accident`	categorical	Type of accident (e.g., frontal collision, rollover)
`type_involved`	categorical	Whether involved was a passenger or driver
`age`	numerical	Age of the person involved
`gender`	categorical	Gender of the person: male, female, or undefined
`type_vehicle`	categorical	Type of vehicle (e.g., car, bus, motorcycle)
`year_vehicle`	numerical	Year the vehicle was manufactured
`day_week`	categorical	Day of the week when the accident occurred
`day_period`	categorical	Period of the day (e.g., morning, night)
`met_cond`	categorical	Weather conditions (e.g., sunny, raining, windy)
`type_road`	categorical	Type of road (e.g., single, double, or multilane)
`out_road`	categorical	Whether the vehicle went off the road
`id_road`	categorical	Road identifier
`km_road`	numerical	Road segment (kilometer marker)
`direction_road`	categorical	Traffic direction of the road

Due to the high cardinality of the categorical features, we applied a k-fold target encoding approach using five distinct folds to encode each category with the average value of the target variable in the training set (i.e., the remaining four folds), thus preserving meaningful patterns and avoiding data leakage and overfitting [17]. Subsequently, we centered and scaled all features to ensure a balanced contribution to model training. Finally, due to the highly imbalanced nature of the reports of fatal accidents compared to overall accidents, the Synthetic Minority Oversampling Technique (SMOTE), proposed by [6], was employed to synthetically increase the representation of fatal accidents, preserving the distribution of objects features. It is important to highlight that SMOTE was applied exclusively in the training sets.

3.3 Model Selection and Validation

This study evaluates three distinct models to predict accident severity: k-nearest Neighbors (kNN), Random Forest (RF), and Multilayer Perceptron (MLP). We performed a hyperparameter grid search for each model to identify the optimal configuration (Table 2).The full dataset was initially partitioned into 80% for training and 20% for final testing. To assess model performance and mitigate overfitting, we also evaluated the training set through Monte Carlo cross-validation with five random resampling iterations, each using 80% of the training data for model fitting and 20% for internal validation [12]. This resampling strategy corresponds to the Leave-Group-Out Cross-Validation (LGOCV) method implemented in the caret package[1], without specifying grouping factors.

Table 2. Hyperparameters used for grid search tuning.

Model	Hyperparameter	Interval
kNN	k	$[3, 5, 7, ..., 15]$
RF	mtry; split rule; min. node size	$[1, 2, ..., 12]$; $\{gini,\ extratrees\}$; $[1, 5, 10]$
MLP	size; decay	$[11, 19, 27, ..., 115]$; $10^{[-4, -3, ..., -1]}$

A comprehensive set of classification metrics was applied to evaluate each model's performance, particularly those that reflect the model's ability to correctly identify fatal accidents—the positive class in this study. Given the highly imbalanced nature of the dataset, relying solely on overall accuracy would provide a misleading assessment of model effectiveness. Therefore, additional metrics were considered to capture the model's discriminatory power across both classes. Sensitivity (or recall) allows us to measure the proportion of correctly identified fatal accidents, while specificity quantifies the model's ability to classify non-fatal cases correctly. The $F1$-score is the harmonic mean of precision and recall, providing a balanced view of the model's performance concerning the positive class. Finally, the Area Under the Receiver Operating Characteristic Curve (AUC-ROC) allows for the assessment of the model's ability to distinguish between classes across varying decision thresholds.

3.4 Feature Importance

This study includes a feature importance analysis on the best-performing model through the Shapley Additive Explanations (SHAP) method. SHAP is a model-agnostic interpretability technique grounded in cooperative game theory, introduced by [18] and later adapted to machine learning contexts by [15]. The SHAP

---

[1] caret package – https://cran.r-project.org/web/packages/caret/caret.pdf.

value of a given feature represents its marginal contribution to the prediction outcome, calculated by comparing the model's output with and without the feature across all possible combinations of feature subsets (coalitions). This approach provides a consistent and locally accurate attribution of importance to each feature, enabling a more transparent understanding of the model's decision-making process.

4 Results and Discussion

This section presents the classification results, including the effects of data oversampling, the consistency of feature distributions after preprocessing, the evaluated models' comparative performance, and the best-performing model's interpretability through Shapley value analysis. The analysis includes a particular emphasis on understanding the role of SMOTE in enhancing sensitivity towards the positive class (fatal accidents), as well as on identifying the most influential factors associated with fatal outcomes in road traffic accidents.

4.1 Oversampling

Applying the Synthetic Minority Oversampling Technique effectively addresses the class imbalance in the dataset, increasing the proportion of fatal to non-fatal accidents from 7.1% to 49.8%. As shown in Fig. 2, where features are encoded, centered, and scaled, the distribution of key features remained consistent before and after oversampling. Although the figure only depicts a subset of features (due to space constraints), the other variables show similar patterns. This consistency is justified by SMOTE's method to interpolate new samples based on existing minority class instances rather than introducing random, artificial distortions.

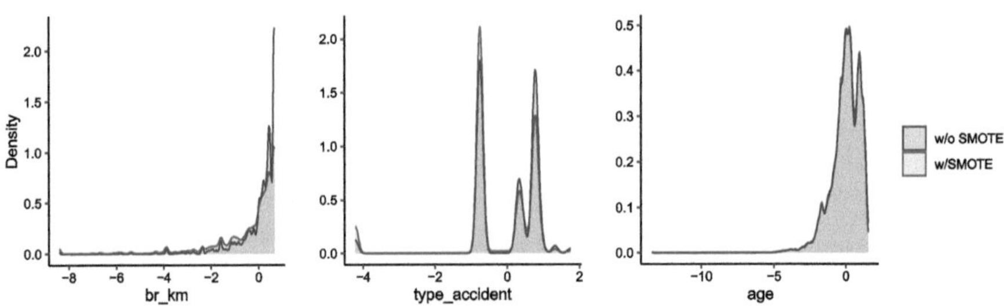

Fig. 2. Feature distributions before and after oversampling.

4.2 Model Performance

Table 3 summarizes the performance of the three evaluated models using the test set. Without oversampling, kNN and MLP exhibited limited ability to detect fatal accidents, with sensitivity values of only 19% and 14%, respectively. Such a result confirms the challenge posed by the imbalanced dataset, in which models tend to favor the majority class (non-fatal accidents), achieving deceptively high accuracy and specificity at the expense of recall. After applying SMOTE, both kNN and MLP showed significant improvements in sensitivity—reaching 100% and 71%, respectively—though with a corresponding drop in specificity and overall accuracy, particularly for MLP.

In contrast, the Random Forest model demonstrated exceptional performance across all evaluation scenarios. Even without oversampling, RF achieved near-perfect scores in accuracy, sensitivity, specificity, $F1$-score, and AUC-ROC. Its performance remained consistently high with SMOTE, confirming the model's robustness and capability of generalization in learning complex patterns associated with accident severity.

Table 3. Performance metrics of all models in test dataset.

Model	Accuracy	Sensitivity	Specificity	AUC-ROC	F1-Score
w/o SMOTE					
kNN	0.94	0.19	0.99	0.92	0.30
RF	0.99	0.99	1.00	0.99	0.99
MLP	0.93	0.14	0.99	0.82	0.23
w/ SMOTE					
kNN	0.86	1.00	0.85	0.99	0.50
RF	0.99	0.99	0.99	0.99	0.99
MLP	0.77	0.71	0.77	0.82	0.29

4.3   Interpretability

In classification problems, SHAP values provide a consistent and locally accurate method for attributing the predicted probability of a class to each input feature. For a given instance, positive SHAP values indicate features that push the prediction toward a specific class (in this case, a fatal outcome), while negative values pull it in the opposite direction. When aggregated across the dataset, SHAP values reveal the global importance of features and allow the identification of dominant patterns that influence the model's decision-making process. In this work, we used SHAP values to quantify each variable's contribution to the classification of accident severity and explore how specific feature categories influence the likelihood of fatal outcomes.

The SHAP summary plots presented in Fig. 3 provide insights into the inner workings of the RF classifier. The absolute mean SHAP value plot demonstrates that features related to the location and nature of accidents

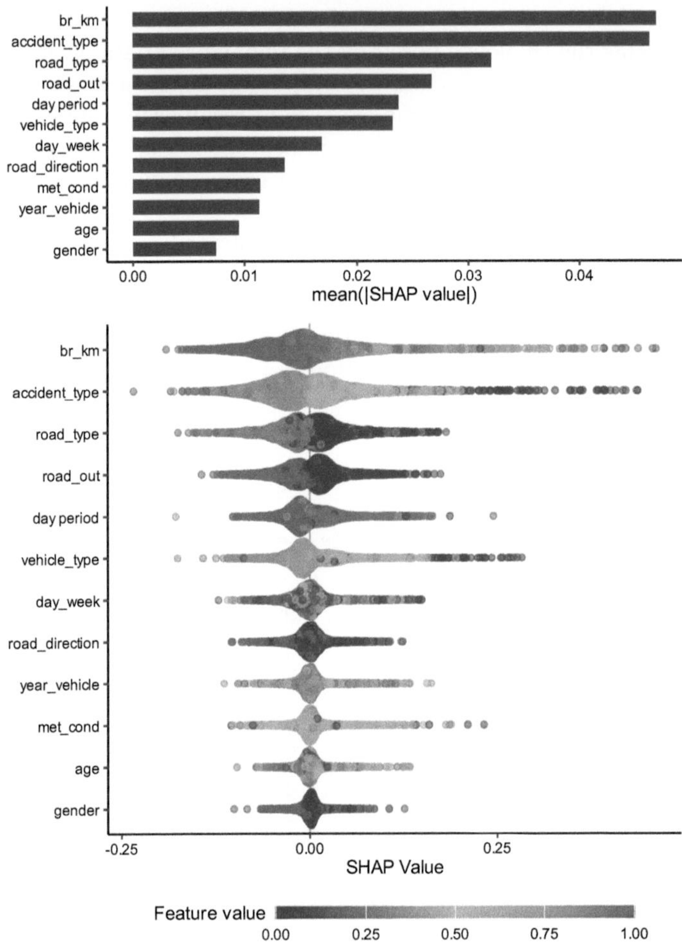

Fig. 3. Shapley values for RF features in test set.

(br_km, accident_type, and road_type) are the most influential in determining the likelihood of a fatal outcome. Such a result suggests that road conditions and contextual factors have significant impacts on accident severity, which
might be a consequence of infrastructure and traffic policies of a given location
(e.g., speed limits, police surveillance, and road maintenance), as well as how
some types of accidents are naturally more prone to result in fatalities. In contrast, demographic characteristics such as the age and gender of the individuals
involved exhibit low average SHAP values, indicating a marginal influence on
the model's predictions and suggesting that these attributes may not be strong
determinants of fatality within the dataset analyzed.

The beeswarm plot (Fig. 3 bottom) shows how individual feature values influence the predicted outcome. Among the top six features with the highest mean

SHAP values (`br_km`, `accident_type`, `road_type`, `road_out`, `day_period`, and `vehicle_type`) there is a notable trend: higher encoded feature values tend to produce lower SHAP values, and vice versa. This pattern indicates a potential inverse relationship between these categorical encodings and the model's predicted probability of fatality. Additionally, several features display diffuse and spread SHAP value distributions, a characteristic often associated with interactions between features. This spread, along with good performance metrics, suggests that the RF model can capture complex relationships that may involve dependencies among variables.

To better understand the importance of the variable `br_km`, we leverage a spatial analysis of fatal accidents, as illustrated in Fig. 4. In the map, each point represents a geographic region where numerous fatal accidents occurred, with the size and color of the points indicating the concentration of fatalities in the nearby areas. Larger and darker points represent higher death counts, and the gray cross markers denote regions of low fatal accident frequencies. The bar plot shows the total number of accidents per federal highway (`road_id`) within the southern region of Brazil. The five most critical roads regarding fatal accident counts—BR-277, BR-116, BR-376, BR-101, and BR-282—are highlighted on the map for spatial context.

These five highlighted highways exhibit structural and operational characteristics that may contribute to this elevated rate of fatal accidents. BR-277 and BR-282 are important in connecting the eastern and western regions of Santa Catarina and Paraná, the two states with the highest accident rates in the southern region. These roads often cover rural areas with long sections of single lanes, few overtaking zones, and poor road maintenance, factors that might contribute to a higher incidence of severe crashes, such as front collisions. In contrast, BR-116 and BR-101 are long, heavily trafficked longitudinal highways that pass through densely populated urban areas and industrial hubs. Their frequent intersections and proximity to residential zones increase the likelihood of fatal incidents. Finally, BR-376 connects the Southern region in an important logistics route with high volumes of cargo and heavy vehicles along with sinuous roads on hill and valley areas with sharp curves and challenging driving conditions, where braking distance and driver reaction time are often compromised.

The influence of the remaining most impactful categorical features on model predictions is investigated through violin and boxplots of SHAP values constructed for each category of the `accident_type`, `road_type`, `road_out`, `day_period`, and `vehicle_type` variables (Fig. 5). These plots illustrate the distribution and magnitude of each feature category's contribution to the predicted probability of fatal outcomes. Higher SHAP values indicate a more substantial influence toward the fatal class, while values closer to zero suggest a more neutral or non-discriminative role.

The `accident_type` feature presents distinct patterns among its categories. Run-over, front collision, and overturn accidents have overall positive SHAP values, indicating that they substantially increase the likelihood of fatal outcomes. In contrast, rear-end, side collisions, atypical events, and cases involving

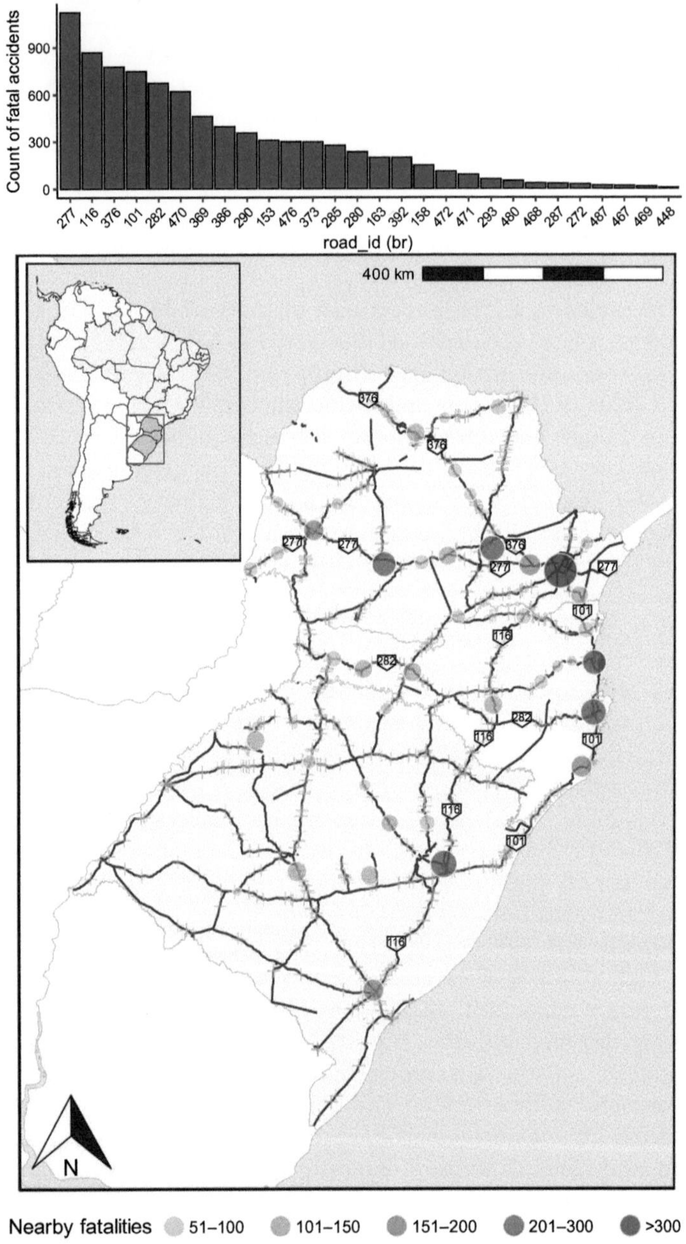

Fig. 4. Road sections (br_km) with the most number of fatal accidents.

vehicles leaving the road tend to have more neutral effects on the model's predictions. Interestingly, although rollovers and fires are typically associated with severe outcomes, they display lower SHAP values in this dataset, likely due to

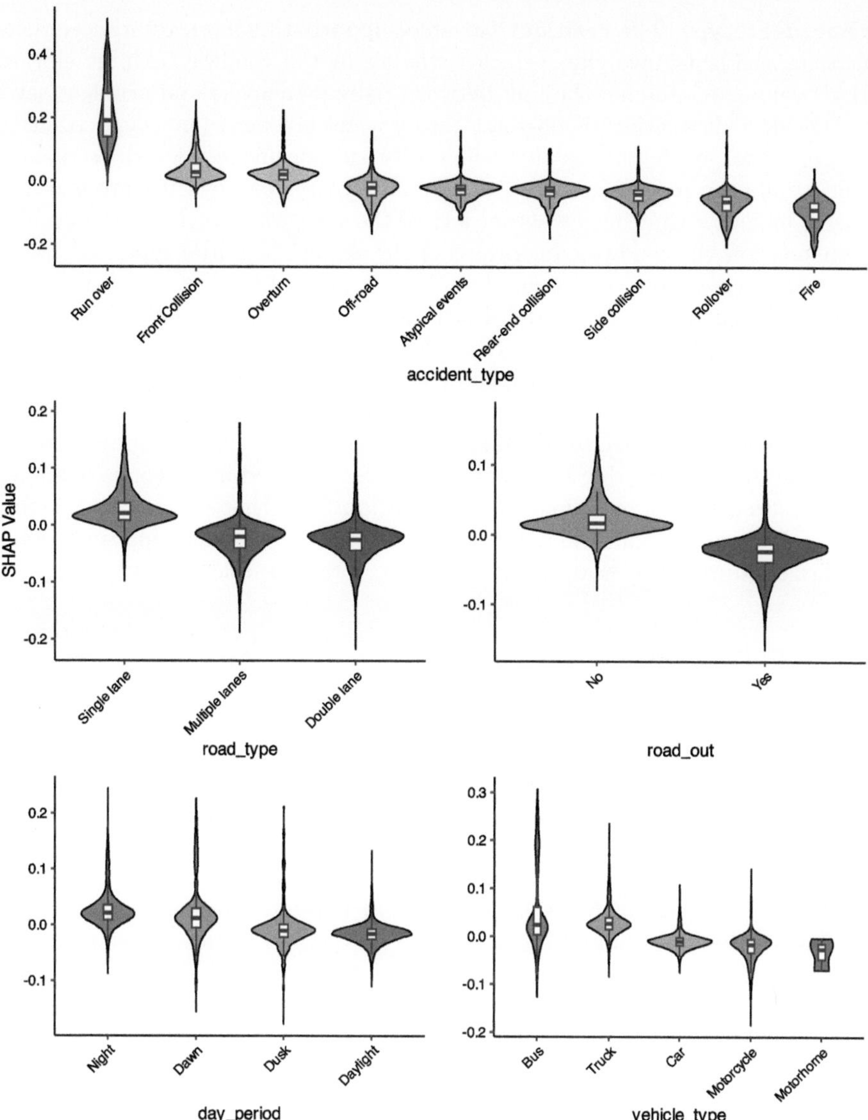

Fig. 5. Shapley values for each category in most influential features.

their relative rarity. Notably, run-over accidents are particularly high-risk events, consistent with the lack of protection for pedestrians involved in such incidents.

Regarding road infrastructure, the **road_type** feature reveals that single-lane roads are strongly associated with fatal outcomes, showing higher SHAP values than multiple-lane or double-lane roads. Such a result is likely due to the increased risk of head-on collisions during overtaking maneuvers, a mechanism also reflected in the high fatality rates associated with front collisions in `accident_type`. The `road_out` variable supports this interpretation, indicating that accidents involving vehicles staying in the roadway exhibit elevated SHAP values, reinforcing the link between risky maneuvers and accident severity. The key distinction of off-road category within `accident_type` from the broader `road_out` feature is that while off-road specifically describes that the vehicle exits the roadway as the primary event, the `road_out` feature is a more general indicator that flags whether any of the vehicles involved in the accident ultimately left the roadway, regardless of the accident's initial type.

Lighting conditions, represented by the `day_period` feature, are also relevant. Accidents occurring at night and dawn are associated with significantly higher SHAP values than those at dusk or in daylight, showing the impact of reduced visibility and possibly driver fatigue or riskier behavior in low-light conditions. Lastly, the `vehicle_type` plot reveals that incidents involving heavier vehicles, such as trucks and buses, result in higher SHAP values, suggesting an increased risk of fatalities, likely due to the greater forces involved in collisions. Cars and motorcycles display a more neutral contribution. Motorhomes, in contrast, show lower SHAP values, which may be attributed to their very low representation in the dataset during the study period, with no recorded fatal outcomes.

5   Conclusions

This paper presented a comparative analysis of classification models applied to traffic accident data from the southern region of Brazil to predict accident severity. The motivation for this study is the alarming number of fatal accidents reported in this region and their substantial economic impact. The dataset used in this analysis was obtained from an open-access source provided by the Federal Highway Police and includes information on accidents recorded between 2021 and 2024. This data includes both fatal and non-fatal incidents, with significant class imbalance (only 7.1% of cases are fatal). To address class imbalance, SMOTE was applied, increasing the proportion of fatal accidents to nearly 50% while preserving the original feature distributions. Three classification methods were evaluated through a comprehensive set of performance metrics. The results suggest that kNN and MLP were not effective to detect fatal outcomes without oversampling, whereas RF achieved near-perfect performance across all metrics. Although SMOTE improved overall sensitivity for kNN and MLP models, it hindered specificity and accuracy. RF achieved satisfactory results across all evaluation scenarios, confirming its robustness and generalization capability.

The study also explored SHAP values for model interpretability, which provided insights into feature contributions to the classification outcomes. Road conditions and characteristics were the most influential in fatal outcomes, whereas demographic features had the least impact. A spatial analysis revealed that certain federal highways concentrate a high count of fatalities, notably: BR-277, BR-116, BR-376, BR-101, and BR-282. Indeed, BR-277 is frequently referred to as the "Death Highway" (*Rodovia da Morte*), a grim title earned due to its high incidence of fatal accidents and hazardous road conditions. The aforementioned roads traverse both rural and densely populated regions, leading to challenging structural and operational conditions. Moreover, factors such as weather conditions and the type of vehicles involved are highly relevant in determining the severity of accidents. Low-light conditions and heavy vehicles are frequently associated with more severe outcomes, including runovers and frontal collisions.

Overall, this work succeeded in developing and evaluating predictive models to determine fatal outcomes using data from federal highways in the southern region of Brazil. By addressing class imbalance and utilizing model interpretability techniques, efficient models were developed, capable of accurately identifying fatal accidents and extracting valuable insights into the underlying contributing factors. These insights are of practical significance for shaping public policies, planning road maintenance, and designing traffic safety awareness campaigns.

As future work, we plan to conduct a comprehensive analysis covering all regions of Brazil to identify regional variations in the factors contributing to fatal accidents, while also considering additional methods for improved predictions and insights. Such comparative studies enhance the understanding of nationwide traffic dynamics and support more targeted and effective intervention strategies across diverse geographic and socio-economic contexts. Finally, we also plan to analyze the impact of infrastructure improvements on reducing fatal accidents. This could lead to the development of a comprehensive methodology for analyzing data over time, enabling the detection of shifting patterns in accident hotspots. Such an approach would not only identify areas where accidents emerge and fade, but also provide insights into the factors that influence these temporal changes, allowing for more dynamic and proactive traffic safety measures.

Acknowledgments. This study was financed in part by the Coordenação de Aperfeiçoamento de Pessoal de Nível Superior – Brasil (CAPES). The authors also thank the financial support provided by the Fundação Stemmer para Pesquisa, Desenvolvimento e Inovação (FEESC) through the Conexões para Inovar program.

Data Availability. Code and data used in this work is available at: https://github.com/arthur-miguel/Highway-to-Classifying-Accidents

References

1. Ahmed, S., Hossain, M.A., Ray, S.K., Bhuiyan, M.M.I., Sabuj, S.R.: A study on road accident prediction and contributing factors using explainable machine learning models: analysis and performance. Transportation research interdisciplinary perspectives **19**, 100814 (2023)
2. Amorim, B.d.S.P.: Uso de aprendizado de máquina para classificação de risco de acidentes em rodovias. Mestrado em Ciência da Computação, Universidade Federal de Campina Grande (UFCG), Paraíba (2019)
3. Barros, P.H., Baggio, I.: Uma análise espacial da malha rodoviária brasileira: relações com o desenvolvimento econômico regional. Crescimento e desenvolvimento numa perspectiva interdisciplinar: ensaios sobre o crescimento econômico brasileiro **1**, 360–372 (2022)

4. Brazilian Federal Highway Police: Dados abertos (2024), disponível em: https://www.gov.br/prf/pt-br/acesso-a-informacao/dados-abertos
5. Brazilian National Confederation of Transport: Painel CNT: Acidentes Rodoviários (2024), disponível em: https://www.cnt.org.br/pesquisas
6. Chawla, N.V., Bowyer, K.W., Hall, L.O., Kegelmeyer, W.P.: Smote: Synthetic minority over-sampling technique. Journal of Artificial Intelligence Research **16**, 321–357 (2002)
7. Cuenca, L.G., Puertas, E., Aliane, N., Andres, J.F.: Traffic accidents classification and injury severity prediction. Presented at the (2018)
8. Dong, S., Khattak, A., Ullah, I., Zhou, J., Hussain, A.: Predicting and analyzing road traffic injury severity using boosting-based ensemble learning models with shapley additive explanations. International Journal of Environmental Research and Public Health **19**(5) (2022)
9. Gan, J., Li, L., Zhang, D., Yi, Z., Xiang, Q.: An alternative method for traffic accident severity prediction: Using deep forests algorithm. J. Adv. Transp. **2020**(1), 1257627 (2020)
10. Infante, P., Jacinto, G., Afonso, A., Rego, L., Nogueira, V., Quaresma, P., Saias, J., Santos, D., Nogueira, P., Silva, M., et al.: Comparison of statistical and machine-learning models on road traffic accident severity classification. Computers **11**(5), 80 (2022)
11. Jeong, H., Jang, Y., Bowman, P.J., Masoud, N.: Classification of motor vehicle crash injury severity: A hybrid approach for imbalanced data. Accident Analysis & Prevention **120**, 250–261 (2018)
12. Kuhn, M., Johnson, K.: Applied predictive modeling, vol. 26. Springer (2013)
13. Kumeda, B., Zhang, F., Zhou, F., Hussain, S., Almasri, A., Assefa, M.: Classification of road traffic accident data using machine learning algorithms. Presented at the (2019)
14. Lobato, C.R.V.: Análise dos acidentes nas rodovias federais concedidas no Brasil. Universidade Federal de Minas Gerais (UFMG), Belo Horizonte, Mestrado em Geotecnia E Transportes (2018)
15. Lundberg, S.M., Lee, S.I.: A unified approach to interpreting model predictions. Advances in neural information processing systems **30** (2017)
16. Mokoatle, M., Vukosi Marivate, D., Bukohwo, M.E., P.: In: Predicting road traffic accident severity using accident report data in south africa, p. 11–17,. Association for Computing Machinery, New York, NY, USA (2019)
17. Pargent, F., Pfisterer, F., Thomas, J., Bischl, B.: Regularized target encoding outperforms traditional methods in supervised machine learning with high cardinality features. Comput. Statistics , 1–22 (2022). https://doi.org/10.1007/s00180-022-01207-6
18. Shapley, L.S.: A Value for N-Person Games. RAND Corporation, Santa Monica, CA (1952)

Improving Legislative Accessibility with Retrieval-Augmented Generation

Saint-Clair da Cunha Lima[(✉)][iD] and Daniel Araújo[iD]

Federal University of Rio Grande do Norte, Natal, Brazil
`saint.clair.lima.066@ufrn.edu.br`, `daniel@imd.ufrn.br`

Abstract. This study presents the design, development, and evaluation of a question-answering (Q&A) system based on the Retrieval-Augmented Generation (RAG) framework, aimed at improving public access to the legislative documents of Assembleia Legislativa do Estado do Rio Grande do Norte (Alern). The system integrates a vector-based document retrieval mechanism with large language models (LLMs) to enable users to submit natural language queries and receive relevant, accessible responses. It leverages embedding-based search to retrieve semantically relevant content and utilizes LLMs to generate clear answers. A comparative analysis of various embedding models – such as BGE-M3, ada-002, and GTE – was conducted to identify the most effective configuration for content retrieval. Results showed that BGE-M3 achieved the highest retrieval accuracy (96.86%) among the models tested. LLMs, including Llama 3.1 and DeepSeek-R1, were evaluated for response generation using BERTScore and human feedback. Llama 3.1 outperformed DeepSeek-R1 in coherence, grammar/spelling, and adequacy, achieving an average human evaluation score of 85.6%. Evaluation results, based on both synthetic datasets and human-curated questions, demonstrate the system's potential to enhance legislative transparency and user engagement by facilitating accessible interaction with complex legal content.

Keywords: RAG · Q&A System · Semantic Search

1 Introduction

The legislative branch is the institutional body within a democratic system, responsible for overseeing the legislative process – that is, the structured sequence of drafting, deliberating, and enacting the legal frameworks that govern society. As these laws are created by elected representatives and are intended to regulate the daily functioning of society, it is essential that they remain fully accessible to citizens, both in terms of their content and the underlying principles which they embody [2]. In the context of the house of representatives of Rio Grande do Norte (*Assembleia Legislativa do Estado do Rio Grande do Norte –* **Alern**), a state located in Brazil's Northeast region, as in many other Brazilian states, access to

R. de Freitas and D. Furtado (Eds.): BRACIS 2025, LNAI 16181, pp. 245–259, 2026.
https://doi.org/10.1007/978-3-032-15990-8_17

regulatory documents – and to the transversal materials produced throughout the legislative process – is often limited. When available, such content is frequently presented using technical or institutional language that is inaccessible to the general public.

To promote effective transparency in the legislative process – which includes not only the laws themselves but also a range of dynamic, process-related documents that both constitute and describe the legislative workflow – it is essential to adopt an approach that meets two key criteria. First, it must provide on-demand access to the content of these documents, enabling citizens to easily locate and engage with information pertinent to their interests, regardless of prior familiarity with the legislative corpus. Second, the information must be presented in a manner that is accessible to the general public, employing clear and straightforward language while deliberately avoiding jargon and technical terminology.

This study, therefore, evaluates the applicability of a question-and-answer (Q&A) system, in the context of Alern's regulatory documents, implemented as a chatbot, using the Retrieval-Augmented Generation (RAG) framework. The architecture uses a prompt-based architecture in which a user question and a curated set of documents are processed by a Large Language Model (LLM) to generate domain-specific answers. The solution supports a unified structure that can be adapted to various knowledge bases, enabling coverage of multiple content domains. For each domain, a custom collection of document is encoded and stored in a specific type of database optimized for managing and retrieving content using semantic search. This design enables flexible reuse, with minimal effort required to support new use cases – primarily the selection of relevant documents.

Accordingly, this study undertakes a comparative analysis of embedding models and LLMs for potential integration into the proposed RAG framework. The objective is to assess their effectiveness in supporting semantic retrieval and domain-specific answer generation within the context of Alern's corpus of regulatory documents. By systematically evaluating the performance of different model configurations, this study seeks to identify optimal approaches for enhancing information accessibility and retrieval flexibility. This investigation responds to a concrete institutional demand: the development of a robust, user-centered system capable of facilitating non-specialist access to legislative materials through natural language queries, thereby promoting transparency and public engagement.

2   Important Concepts

The following key concepts are important in the context of this study, providing the necessary theoretical foundation to support the subsequent discussion and analysis.

Text Embeddings: To effectively process textual documents, text must be represented in a computationally efficient format [12]. One such method is text embeddings, which uses high-dimensional numeric vectors to encode textual elements as high-dimensional representations; each dimension capturing abstract linguistic or conceptual features. While individual dimensions are not directly interpretable, together they encode complex syntactic and semantic relationships [9]. Spatial proximity in this vector space reflects linguistic similarity: for instance, semantically related words like *cat, feline,* and *kitty* cluster together, whereas unrelated terms like *waffles* and *umbrella* appear farther apart.

Context-based text embeddings can be created using models trained on large text corpora, enabling broad applicability across diverse natural language processing tasks.

Vector Stores: These specialized tools are designed to efficiently store and search collections of vector representation of textual data, enhancing the effectiveness of query and record retrieval through similarity-based search [13,17].

In typical use, creating a document collection within a vector store involves defining two key components: (1) an embedding function to generate text embeddings, and (2) a similarity metric for querying. During a query, the input is processed with the same embedding function, and the resulting vector is compared to stored vectors to retrieve the most similar records based on the chosen metric.

Large Language Model (LLM): Large Language Models (LLMs) are sophisticated statistical models developed through machine learning, designed to process, understand, and generate human language. These models operate by identifying complex patterns and relationships within large-scale textual datasets, which serve as the foundation for their training. Through this extensive exposure to natural language, LLMs learn to predict the next word or token in a sequence based on the context provided by preceding elements. This predictive capability enables them to generate coherent, contextually appropriate, and semantically rich textual content in response to a given prompt, making them valuable tools for a wide range of applications in natural language processing [25].

Retrieval Augmented Generation: RAG, as it is commonly referred, is a technique designed to overcome certain limitations inherent to LLM-generated responses [14]. Rather than relying exclusively on the prompt and the information embedded within the model's internal parameters, RAG enhances the generation process by integrating external knowledge retrieved from a relevant knowledge base.

The RAG approach employs the user's input to search for relevant content in a domain-specific knowledge base. The most relevant results are then retrieved and incorporated into an augmented prompt, along with the original prompt. Explicit instructions are also included, guiding the model to base its response on the retrieved external content.

This augmented prompt is subsequently fed into the LLM, enabling it to generate responses that are not only more accurate and contextually appropriate but also transparent and verifiable, as the external sources are embedded directly into the prompt.

BERTScore: BERTScore was designed as a semantic evaluation metric that assesses the quality of text generation by measuring the similarity between a generated text and a reference text [28]. By comparing the text embeddings of the generated content with those of a gold-standard reference, BERTScore uses precision to measure relevance (how closely the generated text aligns with the reference) and recall to assess completeness (how much of the reference content is captured in the generation).

By leveraging contextual embeddings, which capture semantic and contextual nuances more effectively than traditional similarity metrics, BERTScore provides a more robust and meaningful evaluation of text quality.

3   Related Works

When examining works that adopt similar approaches to the one proposed in this study, it becomes evident that solutions based on LLMs with RAG have been increasingly applied across a range of domains, proving to be promising in addressing challenges and enhancing the effectiveness of systems in specific contexts. Application areas include facilitating communication [1,11,20,27], information interpretation [4,5,15,19,20,24,29], customer service [19], content adaptation to different languages [1], content summarization [4,15,24,29], tools to empower academic research [15,24], solutions to improve quality of workflow in industry [5], tools for healthcare and psychological therapies [1,4,11,15,20,27,29].

The approaches analyzed used a variety of LLMS, including:

- GPT (GPT-2 [5]; GPT-3.5 [1,4]; GPT-3.5-Turbo [29]; and GPT-4 [4,15,20]).
- Llama (Llama2 [5,11,23,27]; Llama3 [1]; and TinyLlama [27]).
- Palm2 [19].

The embedding models referenced in the analyzed works include BERT [5], GTE [29] and text-embedding-ada-002 [20], while additional techniques and approaches employed comprise LoRA, QLoRA and RLHF [11,23,27], as well as other fine-tuning methods [1,5,29].

The analyzed works highlight that LLMs, when combined with the RAG framework, provide a robust foundation for addressing complex and domain-specific problems, offering superior accuracy, relevance, and usability. In the context of this study, such enhancements translate into greater efficiency and accessibility in the search for and consumption of targeted information within the relevant domain. Ultimately, user satisfaction rates – exceeding 85% in some cases – underscore the positive impact of these solutions.

4   Proposed Approach

This study aims to investigate an effective combination of text embedding and response generation models for constructing a RAG-based question-answering (Q&A) system, implemented as a chatbot, in the context of documents of

Alern. The proposed structure is meant to accept prompts containing a question, retrieve relevant content from a knowledge base to answer the question. In order to achieve this, it must meet some aspects: (1) semantic similarity-based retrieval of relevant content, organized by domain and type; (2) dynamic and efficient inclusion/removal of new documents and collections as they become available without compromising performance; (3) a user-interface that returns summarized, relevant answers along with the supporting content; and (4) logging of user queries, selected documents, generated responses, and relevant metadata for future analysis and system improvement.

As shown in Fig. 1, our implementation includes a simple HTML/CSS page with JavaScript for the user interface, a Python-based API to handle queries, a vector store for retrieving relevant content, an LLM tool for generating responses, and a basic SQL database for storing interaction data and user feedback.

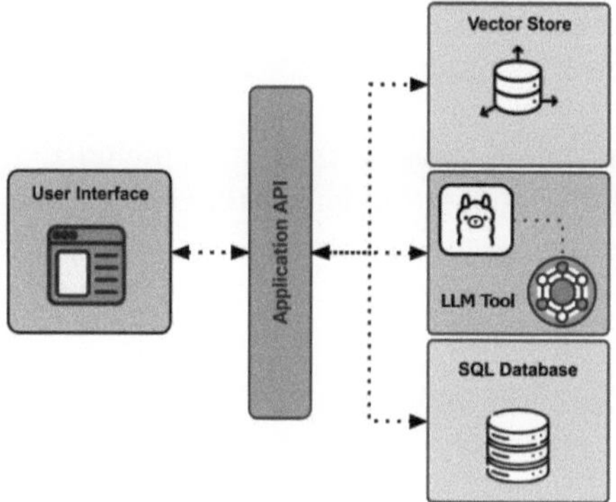

Fig. 1. Architecture used in our approach.

This approach minimizes the need for fine-tuning models to specific datasets, maintaining performance even as new or varied data is introduced. New documents or collections can be integrated by formatting and adding them to the vector store, allowing the system's retrieval and response processes to seamlessly incorporate updated content.

5   Experimental Methodology

5.1   Configuring the LLMs

For running the candidate LLMs under evaluation, we chose Ollama [18] as the deployment and inference framework. This decision was driven by Ollama's ease of use, efficient local execution capabilities, and broad support for open-source LLMs, enabling a standardized and controlled testing environment across all models. After installing Ollama, the language models were integrated into the system and made available for use.

For this study, we evaluated two open-source and freely available model families: Llama [16] and DeepSeek [7]. These were selected for their version diversity, compatibility with Ollama, and ease of deployment.

While choosing among the available versions of Llama and DeepSeek, we carefully considered the hardware limitations of our computational environment. Our goal was to identify models that were both up to date and sufficiently robust to deliver high-quality results, without exceeding the system's capacity. Based on these criteria, we selected the following versions:

- **Llama:** *llama3.1:8b* (8 billion parameters)
- **DeepSeek:** *deepseek-r1:7b* (a distilled model based on DeepSeek-V2.5/V3 and Qwen2)

Although newer versions such as Llama 3.2 and 3.3, or more powerful alternatives like DeepSeek-R1 with 70 billion parameters, are available, they were not suitable for our context. Some models, such as Llama 3.2 (1 billion parameters), are too small to yield satisfactory results, while others exceed the computational resources available.

In our approach, each request sent to Ollama included a fixed system message designed to guide the language model's behavior during response generation. This message followed a predefined prompt structure that incorporated both the user's question and relevant reference content retrieved from the vector store.

5.2   Documents and Embeddings

Document Processing The selection of documents comprising the textual corpus for this proposal was guided by recommendations from staff in the Human Resources sector of Alern. Our document collection includes regulations related to parliamentary conduct, employee rights and responsibilities – particularly in matters of benefits, salary calculations, leave entitlements, and bonuses – career development plans, probationary evaluations, and the broader legal framework applicable to public servants in Rio Grande do Norte, of which Alern staff form a part.

In order to maximize retrieval efficiency, the content must be formatted to balance atomicity – where each piece is self-contained and focused on a specific topic – and completeness – where each piece includes as much relevant information as possible on that topic. Therefore, it was necessary to segment the documents into chunks that are small enough to maintain topical relevance, but not so small that the information becomes fragmented.

Given that the selected documents are organized into articles, we treated each article as an independent fragment to be included in the vector store. Articles significantly longer than average were split into smaller chunks of no more than 300 words. To minimize loss of meaning resulting from splitting articles, we ensured that each chunk included the article's introductory paragraph (*caput*), as a way to preserve some context of the full article.

Embedding Models We considered the following candidate models for generating text embeddings from the selected documents:

1. *Instructor-XL* (Hong Kong University) [26];
2. *text-embedding-ada-002* (OpenAI) [22];
3. *GTE* (Alibaba Cloud) [8];
4. *BGE-M3* (Beijing Academy of Artificial Intelligence - BAAI) [3];
5. *Llama 3.1:8B* (Meta) [16] ;
6. *DeepSeek-R1:7B* (Deepseek) [7]; and
7. *BERT-QA*, an adaptation of BERT to Portuguese [10].

The last three models – Llama 3.1, DeepSeek-R1, and BERT-QA – are not specifically designed for embedding tasks, being included in the set of models solely for purposes of comparison.

We leveraged a vector store – specifically Chroma DB [6] – as a base structure to compare the performance of the embedding models.

Each of the models was used to generate its own collection of embedded documents, including them into the vector store. We then used the generated collections for content retrieval, by executing queries over the vector store, to identify documents semantically similar to a predefined question or search criterion. The vector store was configured to return the top 10 most relevant fragments, ranked in descending order of similarity to the input query.

5.3   Evaluation

To conduct a comprehensive evaluation of the RAG (Retrieval-Augmented Generation) application, we developed a synthetic dataset based on the content previously added to the vector store. This dataset comprises question-answer pairs aligned with the domain-specific knowledge of the documents. These questions were used to retrieve relevant context from the vector store, allowing us to assess the retrieval performance of the embedding models. Each synthetic question, paired with its corresponding retrieved content, was then used to prompt a large language model (LLM), which generated a response based on the information provided. Finally, we assessed the quality and accuracy of each response by comparing it to the corresponding ground-truth answer from the original question-answer pair.

The synthetic dataset was generated through the following steps, applied to each individual fragment in the vector store (also illustrated in Fig. 2):

– A large language model (LLM) was employed to generate a set of questions derived from the semantic content of the fragment;
– The same LLM was then used to produce corresponding reference answers for each question. These answers consisted of excerpts taken directly from the original fragment to ensure accuracy and relevance;
– Each synthetic question was subsequently used as a query to retrieve the ten fragments in the collection with the highest semantic similarity to the question;

- The candidate language models (Llama 3.1 and DeepSeek-R1) were used to generate a response for each of the synthetic questions using their respective retrieved content.

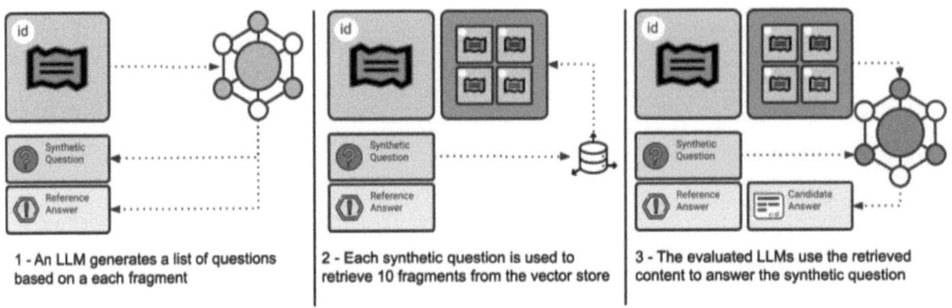

Fig. 2. Generation of synthetic data to evaluate models.

GPT-4o [21] was used to generate both the synthetic questions and the reference answers. It was selected based on the well-known high quality of its output, as well as its independence from the candidate LLMs under evaluation, ensuring an unbiased source of ground truth for the assessment.

To assess the retrieval accuracy of the embedding models, we used each of the synthetic questions to query for fragments in the vector store, recording the 10 results most semantically similar to the question. Our analysis examined whether the original fragment – i.e., the one used to generate the corresponding question – was present among the top ten retrieved results. Since the source fragment for each question was known in advance, this approach enabled a direct and objective evaluation of each model's retrieval effectiveness.

To evaluate the quality of outputs from the candidate language models, we entered each synthetic question – along with the fragments retrieved from the vector store – into the predefined prompt structure, using the result as input for the LLMs to generate an answer. We then employed BERTScore [28] as an objective metric to assess the relevance and completeness of generated content relative to its respective reference answers. This allowed us to determine whether a model's output conveyed relevant information and aligned conceptually with the references. Specifically, we applied BERTScore to each model-generated answer and its corresponding reference, using the resulting precision and recall scores as proxies for the response's relevance and completeness, respectively.

To establish a baseline for comparison, we also used the same prompts to generate answers with GPT-4o. These responses served solely as a point of reference, providing context for evaluating the performance of the candidate large language models.

Additionally, to strengthen the evaluation of the candidate LLMs, we conducted a structured human assessment of the generated textual content. For this purpose, staff members from Alern were recruited to formulate domain-relevant questions answerable using information present in the documents indexed within our vector store. These questions subsequently served as prompts for generating responses using the complete RAG pipeline, which involved retrieving documents from the vector store, preprocessing the content, and submitting it to the LLM for response generation. A total of four participants contributed to this evaluation phase, collectively generating 20 questionanswer pairs.

The LLMs under evaluation produced one response per question, resulting in 20 responses that were subsequently assessed by the same participants. Each response was evaluated according to four criteria:

- **Correctness**: the degree to which the response correctly and comprehensively addresses the question, avoiding false or misleading information;
- **Coherence**: the logical and linguistic consistency of the response, regardless of factual correctness;
- **Grammar and Spelling**: the correctness of spelling and grammatical structure;
- **Adequacy**: the suitability of the language and vocabulary for an average user, as specified by the prompt guidelines.

Evaluators assigned a score of 0 (poor), 1 (acceptable), or 2 (good or fully satisfactory) for each criterion. For each model, we computed the total score across all criteria and reported it as a percentage of the maximum possible score.

6   Results

As previously established, to evaluate the embedding models' performance for content retrieval, we evaluated each embedding model individually by querying their respective vector store collections with the synthetic questions described above. Subsequently, we analyzed how often the original fragment – on which each respective question was based – appeared within the set of retrieved fragments, recording the recurrence by rank, from highest to lowest semantic similarity with the question. Tables 1 and 2 present the distribution of the original fragment within the retrieved results and the retrieval rate for each model, respectively.

As expected, the models not specifically designed for embedding generation – namely BERT-QA, Llama, and Deepseek-R1 – demonstrated very poor performance, failing to retrieve the original fragment in 91.02%, 97.25%, and 96.47% of cases, respectively. At the other end of the spectrum, BGE-M3 exhibited outstanding performance, failing to retrieve the original fragment in just over 3% of the cases. This result is, in fact, more robust than that of OpenAI's proprietary model, text-embedding-ada-002, which failed to retrieve the original fragment in nearly 5% of cases.

Furthermore, when examining the performance of the four models specialized in embedding generation, it is evident that in the vast majority of instances where the original fragment was successfully retrieved, it appeared among the

Table 1. Distribution of Original Fragment Ranks in Retrieved Lists per Model

Rank	BGE	Ada	GTE	Instructor	Bert	Llama	Deepseek-R1
1	1.747	1.634	1.462	1.460	52	14	10
2	256	288	318	257	29	3	6
3	83	93	147	129	21	10	8
4	58	53	78	66	17	12	8
5	25	48	56	53	20	9	8
6	20	23	36	34	13	4	7
7	18	16	26	32	16	2	8
8	3	7	24	24	9	2	6
9	6	14	13	15	14	2	11
10	7	7	12	20	15	5	9
Not Retrieved	72	112	123	205	2089	2232	2214

Table 2. Retrieval Rate of the Original Fragment

Frag. Retrieved	BGE	Ada	GTE	Instructor	Bert	Llama	Deepseek-R1
Yes	96.86%	95.12%	94.64%	91.07%	8.98%	2.75%	3.53%
No	3.14%	4.88%	5.36%	8.93%	91.02%	97.25%	96.47%

top five results – as shown in Table 3. This observation suggests that configuring the vector store to return only the top five results per query may be a safe and efficient strategy within this dataset. Doing so would reduce the volume of data passed to the LLM for answer generation, thereby decreasing the likelihood of hallucinations.

Table 3. Presence of the Original Fragment on the Top 5 Results

Model	Total Retrievals	Top 5 Results	Top 5 Results (%)
BGE	2,223	2,169	97.57%
Ada	2,183	2,116	96.93%
GTE	2,172	2,061	94.89%
Instructor	2,090	1,965	94.02%

Overall, among the embedding models evaluated, BGE-M3 demonstrated better performance, in terms of retrieval efficiency.

To evaluate the performance of the generative models in producing final responses within the application, we employed the set of synthetically generated questions along with their corresponding reference answers.

Specifically, for each "synthetic question/reference answer" pair, the following steps were carried out:

- The synthetic question was used to query the collection created with the BGE-M3 model for embedding generation.
- The retrieved fragments, together with the question, were incorporated into a prompt submitted to the Ollama API. This prompt was used to generate responses from the two large language models (LLMs) under evaluation.
- Each generated response was then assessed using BERTScore to obtain precision, recall, and F1-score metrics.
- For each LLM, the average precision, recall, and F1-score were computed across all generated responses.

For benchmarking purposes, the same prompts were also submitted to the GPT-4o model via the OpenAI API, and its responses were similarly evaluated using BERTScore to enable comparative analysis.

Table 4 presents the average BERTScore precision, recall, and F1-scores for each LLM evaluated, while Fig. 3 illustrates the distribution of these scores across the different models.

Table 4. Average BERTScore values per LLM

Scores	Llama 3.1	DeepSeek-R1	GPT-4o
precision	0.685	0.5405	0.678
recall	0.757	0.667	0.831
f1-score	0.717	0.596	0.746

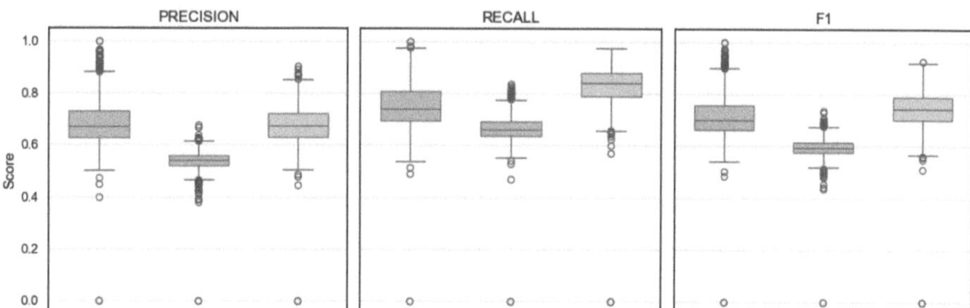

Fig. 3. Distribution of BERTScore values per Model.

By analyzing the performance of both models, it is clear that Llama 3.1 outperforms DeepSeek-R1 across all BERTScore metrics, as shown in Table 4 and Fig. 3. When compared to gpt-4o – the model used to generate the synthetic questions and reference answers, and thus holding an inherent advantage in the inference process – Llama 3.1 achieved slightly higher precision but a noticeably lower recall (though the recall value remains within an acceptable range).

In the context of BERTScore evaluation, precision score indicates that Llama 3.1 tends to generate responses that are more closely aligned with the most semantically relevant portions of the reference text, comparing to GPT-4o. As a result, its outputs are more focused on the "key points" of the expected content (lower recall than GPT-4o), potentially at the expense of broader coverage of the reference material, as reflected in the lower recall.

A visual analysis of a sample of model-generated responses revealed several significant deficiencies in the performance of DeepSeek-R1. First, the model frequently fails to maintain linguistic consistency, often alternating between multiple languages within a single response. Second, it demonstrates a tendency to hallucinate content, disregarding explicit instructions to base responses solely on the provided context. Third, it introduces "neologisms" – either by blending elements from different languages, applying grammatical rules from one language to terms in another, or generating entirely fabricated vocabulary. Fourth, it occasionally misunderstands the context provided, creating responses which directly contradict the reference material.

In contrast, Llama 3.1 produced more consistent responses, offering answers that were generally more concise, coherent, and focused on conveying content directly relevant to the posed question

The results of human evaluation of the responses (Table 5) show that the scores for **Coherence** and **Grammar and Spelling** assigned to both Llama 3.1 and DeepSeek-R1 corroborate the visual inspection of their outputs, particularly confirming the language inconsistencies and "neologisms" observed in DeepSeek-R1.

Table 5. Human Evaluation of Responses

Criterion	Llama 3.1	DeepSeek-R1
Correctness	52.5%	30.0%
Coherence	95.0%	15.0%
Grammar and Spelling	100.0%	7.5%
Adequacy	67.5%	10.0%
Average	**78.8%**	**15.6%**

The relatively low scores in the criteria of **Correctness** and **Adequacy** prompted a more detailed review of the questions, answers, and intermediate outputs generated during the evaluation process. This closer inspection revealed that in slightly over 10% of cases, the content retrieved from the vector database included contradictory fragments – originating from different versions of the same regulation – resulting in inconsistencies in the contextual basis provided to the models.

When such cases are excluded from the evaluation, as per Table 6, Llama 3.1's **Correctness** score increases from 52.5% to 67.5%, while DeepSeek-R1's improves from 30% to 45.5%. Similarly, **Adequacy** scores rise to 80.0% for Llama 3.1 and 11.0% for DeepSeek-R1. Thus, when discounting the distortions caused by flawed retrieval data, Llama 3.1 would achieve approximately 85.6% of the maximum possible evaluation score, compared to just 19.6% for DeepSeek-R1.

Based on the results of both automated and human evaluations, we conclude that Llama 3.1 outperforms other models in generating responses to user questions. When its capabilities are combined with an efficient content retrieval structure – powered by a high-performing embedding model – it becomes possible to implement the application proposed in this study in an effective way.

Table 6. Human Evaluation of Responses (discarding problematic cases)

Criterion	Llama 3.1	DeepSeek-R1
Correctness	67.5%	45.0%
Coherence	95.0%	15.0%
Grammar and Spelling	100.0%	7.5%
Adequacy	80.0%	11.0%
Average	**85.6%**	**19.6%**

7   Conclusion

This study presents the development of a semantic search system based on the Retrieval-Augmented Generation (RAG) approach, aimed at retrieving and synthesizing textual information from documents, in the context of Assembleia Legislativa do Estado do Rio Grande do Norte (Alern). The proposed solution integrates a vector store, and Large Language Models (LLMs) to construct an intelligent search application capable of interpreting user intent and generating contextually relevant responses. The system addresses the challenge of efficiently retrieving information from a dataset, such as that found within Alern, thereby promoting greater accessibility and transparency in the legislative process.

The results obtained demonstrate the feasibility and effectiveness of the proposed approach. The combination of semantic search in vector databases for efficient retrieval of relevant text fragments, together with the synthetic response generation provided by the LLM, proved promising in terms of both the accuracy and completeness of the information delivered. Automated evaluations and human assessments conducted throughout the experiments confirmed the system's capacity to identify pertinent documents and produce coherent, query-aligned responses.

Despite the progress achieved, some limitations were identified during the development and evaluation phases. The accuracy of results is directly influenced by the quality of the vector representations and the document corpus employed. Moreover, while the RAG approach is effective in mitigating hallucinations, it may still yield inaccurate responses in ambiguous contexts or when faced with insufficient data. To address these limitations, future work may include improvements to the retrieval approach, such as the incorporation of prompt optimization techniques, decomposition of complex queries into more detailed subqueries, re-ranking mechanisms, and the exploration of LLMs in earlier stages of the search process – following the Agentic AI paradigm. Additionally, expanding the corpus with compiled and semantically enriched documents, as opposed to fragmented and inter-referenced content, is proposed as a necessary and cost-effective measure to enhance response quality.

In conclusion, this study contributes to ongoing research in semantic search and the application of LLMs in institutional contexts, offering a practical and scalable solution aligned with the demands for transparency and efficiency in public information access. The implementation of the system within Alern has the potential to enhance civic engagement by fostering a more accessible and intelligent interface between citizens and the legislative body.

References

1. Alghamdi, H.M., Mostafa, A.: Towards reliable healthcare LLM agents: a case study for pilgrims during hajj. Information (Switzerland) **15**(7) (2024). https://www.mdpi.com/2078-2489/15/7/371
2. Brasil: Lei de Acesso á Informação - Lei No 12.527/2011 (2011). https://www.planalto.gov.br/ccivil_03/_ato2011-2014/2011/lei/l12527.htm. Accessed 11 May 2025
3. Chen, J., et al.: M3-Embedding: multi-linguality, multi-functionality, multi-granularity text embeddings through self-knowledge distillation (2024). https://arxiv.org/pdf/2402.03216
4. Chen, X., et al.: Evaluating and enhancing large language models' performance in domain-specific medicine: development and usability study with DocOA. J. Med. Internet Res. **26** (2024). https://www.jmir.org/2024/1/e58158
5. Cho, S., Park, J., Um, J.: Development of fine-tuned retrieval augmented language model specialized to manual books on machine tools. In: IFAC-PapersOnLine, vol. 58, p. 187 — 192. Elsevier B.V. (2024). https://www.sciencedirect.com/science/article/pii/S2405896324015696
6. Chroma: Chroma (2024). https://docs.trychroma.com/. Accessed 11 May 2025
7. DeepSeek-AI: DeepSeek-V3 technical report (2024). https://github.com/deepseek-ai/DeepSeek-V3/blob/main/DeepSeek_V3.pdf. Accessed 11 May 2025
8. Gongchang: GTE-Multilingual series: a key model for retrieval-augmented generation (2024). https://www.alibabacloud.com/blog/gte-multilingual-series-a-key-model-for-retrieval-augmented-generation_601776. Accessed 11 May 2025
9. Grosse, R.: CS321 - lecture notes (2020). https://www.cs.toronto.edu/~lczhang/321/notes/notes07.pdf. Accessed 11 May 2025

10. Guillou, P.: Portuguese BERT base cased QA (Question Answering), finetuned on SQUAD v1.1 (2021). https://huggingface.co/pierreguillou/bert-base-cased-squad-v1.1-portuguese. Accessed 11 May 2025

11. Kang, C., et al: Domain-specific improvement on psychotherapy chatbot using assistant. In: 2024 IEEE International Conference on Acoustics, Speech, and Signal Processing Workshops, ICASSPW 2024 - Proceedings, pp. 351 – 355. Institute of Electrical and Electronics Engineers Inc. (2024). https://arxiv.org/abs/2404.16160

12. Khalil, M., Azzeh, M.: Truth seeker of the largest social media content using machine learning algorithms, December 2023. https://doi.org/10.1109/ICMLA58977.2023.00243

13. LangChain: Vector stores (2024). https://python.langchain.com/v0.1/docs/modules/data_connection/vectorstores/. Accessed 11 May 2025

14. Lewis, P. et al: Retrieval-augmented generation for knowledge-intensive NLP Tasks (2021). https://arxiv.org/pdf/2005.11401

15. Li, T.C. et al: FAVOR-GPT: a generative natural language interface to whole genome variant functional annotations. Bioinf. Adv. 4(1) (2024). https://academic.oup.com/bioinformaticsadvances/article/4/1/vbae143/7789482

16. Meta: the llama 3 herd of models (2024). https://arxiv.org/pdf/2407.21783

17. MongoDB: vector stores in artificial intelligence (AI) (2024). https://www.mongodb.com/resources/basics/vector-stores. Accessed 11 May 2025

18. Morgan, J.: Ollama repository (2024). https://github.com/ollama/ollama. Accessed 11 May 2025

19. Morić, Z., et al.: Integrating a virtual assistant by using the RAG method and VERTEX AI framework at algebra university. Appl. Sci. (Switzerland) 14(22) (2024). https://www.mdpi.com/2076-3417/14/22/10748

20. Murugan, M. et al: Empowering personalized pharmacogenomics with generative AI solutions. J. Am. Med. Inf. Assoc. 31(6), 1356–1366 (2024). https://pmc.ncbi.nlm.nih.gov/articles/PMC11105140/

21. OpenAI et al.: GPT-4o system card (2024). https://arxiv.org/abs/2410.21276

22. OpenAI: New and improved embedding model (2022). https://openai.com/index/new-and-improved-embedding-model/. Áccessed 11 May 2025

23. Rangan, K., Yin, Y.: A fine-tuning enhanced RAG system with quantized influence measure as AI judge. Sci. Rep. 14(1) (2024). https://www-nature-com.ez18.periodicos.capes.gov.br/articles/s41598-024-79110-x

24. Roy, T. et al: SciSpace copilot: empowering researchers through intelligent reading assistance. In: Proceedings of the AAAI Conference on Artificial Intelligence, vol. 38, pp. 23826–23828. Association for the Advancement of Artificial Intelligence (2024). https://ojs.aaai.org/index.php/AAAI/article/view/30578/32740

25. Downes, S.M., Patrick Forber, A.G.: LLMs are not just next token predictors (2024). https://arxiv.org/pdf/2408.04666

26. Su, H., et al.: One embedder, any task: instruction-finetuned text embeddings (2024). https://aclanthology.org/2023.findings-acl.71.pdf

27. Vidivelli, S., Ramachandran, M., Dharunbalaji, A.: Efficiency-Driven Custom Chatbot Development: Unleashing LangChain, RAG, and Performance-Optimized LLM Fusion. Computers, Materials and Continua 80(2), 2423 – 2442 (2024), https://www.techscience.com/cmc/v80n2/57653/html

28. Zhang, T., et al.: BERTScore: evaluating text generation with BERT (2020). https://arxiv.org/pdf/1904.09675

29. Zhou, Q., et al.: GastroBot: a Chinese gastrointestinal disease chatbot based on the retrieval-augmented generation. Front. Med. 11 (2024). https://www.frontiersin.org/journals/medicine/articles/10.3389/fmed.2024.1392555

Integrating Explainable AI with Species Distribution Models to Assess Anthropogenic Impacts on Amazonian Birds

Renato Okabayashi Miyaji$^{(\boxtimes)}$ (iD), Felipe Valencia de Almeida (iD),
and Pedro Luiz Pizzigatti Corrêa (iD)

Escola Politécnica, Universidade de São Paulo, Av. Prof. Luciano Gualberto, 380 -
Butantã, São Paulo, SP 05508-010, Brazil
{re.miyaji,felipe.valencia.almeida,pedro.correa}@usp.br

Abstract. The Amazon Rainforest, a critical hub of global biodiversity, faces increasing anthropogenic pressures, necessitating effective monitoring and conservation strategies. Species Distribution Models (SDMs) are vital tools for predicting habitat suitability, yet advanced machine learning-based SDMs, while accurate, often suffer from limited interpretability. This "black box" nature restricts ecological understanding and hinders the translation of model outputs into actionable conservation insights, a limitation evident in previous studies on Amazonian avifauna which primarily identified correlations without fully disentangling the influence of individual environmental drivers. This study overcomes these limitations by integrating Explainable Artificial Intelligence (XAI) techniques with SDMs to specifically assess the impacts of anthropogenic atmospheric pollutants on sensitive bird species from the *Tyrannidae* and *Thraupidae* families. We leverage unique, high-resolution atmospheric data (including aerosols and trace gases) from the GoAmazon 2014/15 campaign and apply SHapley Additive exPlanations (SHAP) to interpret a high-performing Support Vector Machine (SVM) model predicting bird occurrence. Our findings reveal that atmospheric pollutants strongly associated with human activity–notably methane, carbon monoxide, ozone, and acetonitrile–are among the most significant predictors of habitat suitability. SHAP analysis quantifies the complex, often non-linear contributions of these variables, demonstrating how specific pollutants drive habitat suitability predictions locally and globally. By enhancing SDM interpretability, this research provides transparent, ecologically meaningful insights into environmental stressors, offering a more robust tool to support evidence-based conservation planning for Amazonian biodiversity.

Keywords: Species Distribution Models · Explainable Artificial Intelligence · Amazonian Avifauna

R. de Freitas and D. Furtado (Eds.): BRACIS 2025, LNAI 16181, pp. 260–274, 2026.
https://doi.org/10.1007/978-3-032-15990-8_18

1   Introduction

In recent decades, the effects of anthropogenic pressure on natural ecosystems have intensified [1], leading to phenomena such as savannization in biomes such as the Amazon Rainforest [2]. These transformations have raised significant global concerns, particularly due to their impact on biodiversity, climate regulation, and ecological stability [3]. In response, the United Nations has proposed the Sustainable Development Goals (SDGs), which highlight the urgent need to protect terrestrial ecosystems and prevent biodiversity loss [4]. Within this context, understanding and mitigating the effects of environmental disturbances on tropical forests has become a critical research priority [5].

One line of investigation that has gained prominence involves assessing how anthropogenic activities and resulting environmental changes influence the distribution and habitat suitability of tropical bird species [6]. In particular, species from the *Tyrannidae* and *Thraupidae* families–such as *Piprites chloris* from *Tyrannidae*, and *Tangara velia* and *Lanio cristatus* from *Thraupidae*–are of interest due to their sensitivity to habitat alteration and their importance as ecological indicators [7]. These species often respond to subtle shifts in forest structure, microclimate, and pollution levels, making them suitable subjects for ecological modeling [7,8].

A common approach in these studies is Species Distribution Modeling (SDM), which encompasses a suite of statistical and machine learning techniques used to predict the geographic distribution of species based on environmental variables and known occurrence records [9]. By correlating biotic and abiotic factors with species presence, SDMs provide spatial predictions of habitat suitability, allowing researchers to anticipate the effects of environmental change and guide conservation strategies. These models have been extensively applied to explore species-environment relationships, assess biodiversity patterns, and inform management decisions [10].

Despite the usefulness of SDMs, a major limitation lies in their interpretability. Many of the most accurate models–particularly those based on machine learning–function as "black boxes," offering limited transparency about the role and contribution of individual predictors [11]. This lack of clarity hinders ecological understanding and reduces trust in model-based recommendations, particularly when used to guide conservation actions in data-sensitive biomes such as the Amazon.

To address this gap, recent studies have increasingly incorporated Explainable Artificial Intelligence (XAI) methods to enhance the transparency of complex ecological models [12]. XAI techniques allow researchers to probe model behavior, quantify the importance of each environmental variable, and visualize the relationships that drive predictions [13,14]. In the context of SDM, XAI can thus support more informed ecological inferences, helping to disentangle the impact of natural and anthropogenic factors on species distribution.

In this study, we apply XAI techniques to improve the interpretability of Species Distribution Models focused on tropical bird species from the *Tyrannidae* and *Thraupidae* families in the Amazon region. Our analysis builds upon the findings of previous studies that initially explored habitat suitability using conventional SDM techniques [7,8], and other studies that investigated the influence of anthropogenic activities [3]. By integrating fine-scale environmental data–specifically aerosol and pollutant measurements collected during the GoAmazon 2014/15 project [15]–we aim to provide more detailed and reliable insights into the environmental drivers affecting bird species distribution in disturbed forest landscapes.

The main contributions of this study are: (1) the use of high-resolution atmospheric data on aerosols and pollutants from the Amazon Basin to assess anthropogenic influences on species distribution; (2) the integration of XAI techniques with SDMs to improve model interpretability and reveal the effects of individual environmental variables; and (3) the validation and extension of previous findings from studies [3,7,8], providing robust evidence of the role of human-driven changes in shaping the habitat suitability for *Tyrannidae* and *Thraupidae* families in the Amazon. Together, these efforts contribute to a more transparent and ecologically meaningful application of modeling tools in biodiversity research and conservation planning.

2   Related Works

Species Distribution Modeling (SDM) has become a fundamental tool in ecology and conservation biology, enabling the prediction of suitable habitats for species based on environmental conditions and known occurrence records [10,17]. In recent years, the integration of machine learning techniques into SDM has substantially improved predictive performance [9]. Beery et al. (2021) highlighted the growing importance of data-driven approaches in ecological modeling, emphasizing the use of remote sensing data and automated biodiversity monitoring to inform SDMs. These advancements have broadened the scope and scale of ecological analyses, particularly in remote and under-sampled regions such as the Amazon [5].

However, the increased complexity of these models has introduced new challenges related to their interpretability [12]. Many of the most accurate models–such as ensemble methods and deep neural networks–are considered "blackboxes", making it difficult to extract ecologically meaningful insights from their predictions. While such models may identify correlations between species occurrences and environmental variables, they often fall short in providing transparent justifications for their outputs [11], which can limit their utility for conservation planning and ecological understanding.

One of the central challenges in SDM is the lack of clear, interpretable relationships between predictors and predicted species presence [12]. Traditional statistical models such as generalized linear models (GLMs) and generalized additive models (GAMs) offer some degree of interpretability but may underperform in complex ecological settings [9]. On the other hand, machine learning models such as Random Forests and Support Vector Machines, although more flexible and accurate in many scenarios, typically provide limited insight into how each variable contributes to the model's decisions. This lack of transparency limits the adoption of SDM outputs by ecologists and decision-makers who require trustworthy and explainable results to guide conservation actions.

In this context, Explainable Artificial Intelligence (XAI) techniques have emerged as promising tools to enhance the interpretability of complex SDMs [12]. By providing post-hoc explanations for model predictions, methods such as SHapley Additive exPlanations (SHAP) [13] and Local Interpretable Model-agnostic Explanations (LIME) [14] allow researchers to better understand the relative importance and interaction of environmental variables in shaping species distributions. This not only aids in model validation but also supports the generation of ecological hypotheses and the identification of key environmental drivers, especially in dynamic and anthropogenically influenced regions such as the Amazon.

The effects of anthropogenic activities on habitat suitability for bird species have been the focus of several studies, particularly in tropical ecosystems [3,6–8]. In the study by de Moraes et al. (2020), the authors examined the current and projected impacts of climate change and deforestation on the distribution of endemic bird species within the Belém Area of Endemism (BAE) in the eastern Amazon. Their findings indicate that 56% of these species are at risk of extinction, primarily due to habitat loss and climate-induced alterations [7]. The research emphasizes the critical role of preserving the remaining forest fragments and establishing ecological corridors to mitigate these threats. However, the modeling approaches employed were predominantly correlative, lacking the capacity to disentangle the individual contributions of specific environmental variables to species distribution changes.

Similarly, de Moraes et al. (2024) assessed the future distributions of endemic and threatened Amazonian birds under various climate change scenarios. Their results revealed that, even under optimistic projections, over 65% of the species could experience a loss of more than 80% in climate suitability [8]. The study also highlighted the limited effectiveness of existing protected areas in safeguarding these species, as many are projected to undergo significant range contractions beyond the boundaries of current conservation units. Despite providing valuable projections, the models used did not offer granular analyses of how individual environmental predictors influenced species distributions, thereby limiting the development of targeted conservation strategies and reducing confidence in model-based inferences among stakeholders.

Given these gaps, there is a clear need for SDM approaches that combine high predictive power with interpretability. Incorporating XAI methods into SDM pipelines represents a significant step in this direction, allowing for both robust predictions and detailed ecological insights. This work builds upon previous research by applying XAI-enhanced SDM techniques to assess the effects of anthropogenic factors–specifically atmospheric pollutants–on bird species in the Amazon. By doing so, it contributes to a more nuanced understanding of human-environment interactions and supports evidence-based biodiversity conservation in one of the world's most critical ecological hotspots.

3   Methods

3.1   Dataset

The Amazon region is of critical ecological importance, hosting the largest tropical rainforest and unparalleled biodiversity. Within this context, the city of Manaus offers a unique case study, representing a large urban center embedded within a predominantly forested landscape [5]. The urban plume of Manaus introduces anthropogenic pollutants into a relatively pristine environment, thereby creating a natural laboratory to examine how human-induced atmospheric changes affect ecological processes, including species distribution [5]. Studying this region is especially relevant in the context of growing concerns about the savannization of the Amazon, deforestation, and increasing urbanization, all of which threaten the integrity of ecosystems and the survival of sensitive species [2].

The environmental and atmospheric data used in this study were collected as part of the GoAmazon 2014/15 project, a comprehensive field campaign aimed at investigating the interactions between urban pollution and atmospheric processes in the central Amazon region [5]. The campaign involved a series of research flights conducted over the course of one year, covering both wet and dry seasons. A total of 43 flights were performed using instrumented aircraft, spanning a broad spatial range that included the urban area of Manaus, its surroundings, and more remote forested regions in the Amazon Basin [15]. The variables collected included concentrations of aerosols, trace gases (such as ozone, NOx, CO, and CO2), meteorological parameters (temperature, relative humidity, wind speed and direction), and radiation fluxes [5]. These high-resolution data provide a valuable representation of the spatial and temporal variability in atmospheric conditions across the region. Figure 1 presents the flight paths covered during GoAmazon 2014/15 project.

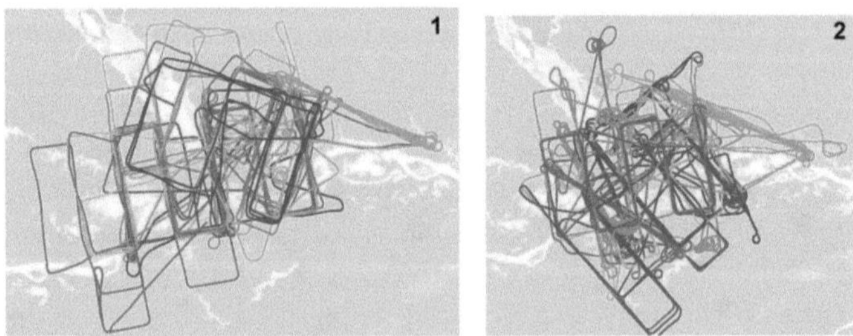

Fig. 1. Flight paths covered during GoAmazon 2014/15 project. (1) Wet season (2) Dry season. [16].

To enhance the spatial resolution of the atmospheric data, we used the dataset provided by Miyaji et al. (2021) that applied spatial interpolation techniques to the data collected during the GoAmazon 2014/15 project. This particular dataset was selected as it represents the most recent source available that offers high-spatial-resolution measurements for our region of analysis. Using a piecewise linear interpolation method a continuous and fine-grained data grid covering the entire Amazon Basin at a resolution of 0.001Åž was generated. This interpolation process was crucial for aligning environmental variables with species occurrence records and for supporting high-resolution modeling in subsequent SDM analyses. A detailed description of the interpolated variables, including their temporal and spatial coverage, is provided in Table 1.

Table 1. Spatial interpolation dataset provided by Miyaji et al. (2021)

Atmospheric Variables	Temperature, CO, O_3, NO_X, CO_2, CH_4, Isoprene, Acetonitrile CPC and H_2O
Data Acquisition	G-1 Aircraft (Altitude: 700 m to 2000 m)
Spatial Coverage	Latitude: -3.632° to -2.813°
	Longitude: -60.831° to -59.937°
Spatial Resolution (after Interpolation)	Latitude: 0.001°
	Longitude: 0.001°
Date	Wet Season: 02/01/2014 to 03/31/2014
	Dry Season: 08/15/2014 to 10/15/2014
	Flight Time: 11:00 AM to 1:00 PM, local time

As commonly done in SDM research, species occurrence data were retrieved from publicly available biodiversity databases, specifically the Global Biodiversity Information Facility (GBIF) [18] and the Brazilian Chico Mendes Institute for Biodiversity Conservation (ICMBio) [19]. We filtered occurrence records to match the spatial and temporal coverage of the GoAmazon 2014/15 dataset, ensuring that all observations corresponded to the same environmental context. The final dataset includes occurrence points for multiple bird species within the *Tyrannidae* and *Thraupidae* families, which were selected due to their ecological relevance and availability of reliable georeferenced records [7]. These data were used as input for species distribution modeling. Table 2 presents the occurrence points for each species from *Tyrannidae* and *Thraupidae* families.

A spatial map displaying the distribution of bird species occurrences across the Amazon Basin is shown in Fig. 2. This map reveals a heterogeneous pattern of species presence, with clusters of observations concentrated around regions with better sampling effort and accessibility, including areas near Manaus and along major rivers. The integration of high-resolution environmental data with species occurrence records allows for a robust modeling framework capable of identifying key environmental drivers of habitat suitability and assessing the influence of anthropogenic factors on bird distributions in tropical forest ecosystems.

Table 2. Occurrence points for *Tyrannidae* and *Thraupidae* families

Family	Species	Occurrences
Tyrannidae	*Myiozetetes cayanensis*	18
Tyrannidae	*Pitangus sulphuratus*	41
Tyrannidae	*Todirostrum maculatum*	31
Tyrannidae	*Tyrannus melancholicus*	50
Tyrannidae	*Tyrannus savana*	18
Tyrannidae	Total	158
Thraupidae	*Ramphocelus carbo*	24
Thraupidae	*Sicalis columbiana*	25
Thraupidae	*Sporophila castaneiventris*	18
Thraupidae	*Thraupis episcopus*	41
Thraupidae	*Thraupis palmarum*	31
Thraupidae	Total	139

3.2   Experiments

To perform species distribution modeling (SDM) using the constructed dataset, we adopted a pseudo-absence sampling strategy to address the inherent presence-only nature of species occurrence data [9]. Presence-only data, while common in biodiversity databases, do not provide explicit information about where a species is truly absent. As such, traditional binary classification algorithms cannot be directly applied [9]. To overcome this limitation, we employed the method for pseudo-absence selection proposed by Senay et al. (2013) [20] through the application of K-Means clustering [21]. Specifically, the algorithm clusters the absence class samples and replaces each cluster with its centroid, effectively reducing the number of absence samples while preserving the overall distributional characteristics of the data. This approach has been shown to reduce bias in model training and better approximate true absence conditions, allowing the problem to be framed as a binary classification task [20].

Based on this framework, we trained and evaluated three different classification models: Logistic Regression (LR), Random Forest (RF) [22], and Support Vector Machines (SVM) [23]. These classifiers were selected due to their widespread use in ecological modeling and their varying levels of complexity and interpretability [9]. Model performance was assessed using standard evaluation metrics, including Accuracy, Area Under the Receiver Operating Characteristic Curve (ROC AUC), and Recall with respect to the positive class (species presence). Emphasis was placed on Recall due to the ecological importance of minimizing false negatives, which correspond to areas incorrectly predicted as unsuitable despite being viable habitats for the species [9].

For model evaluation, the dataset was split into training and testing sets using a hold-out strategy, where 30% of the data was reserved as an independent test

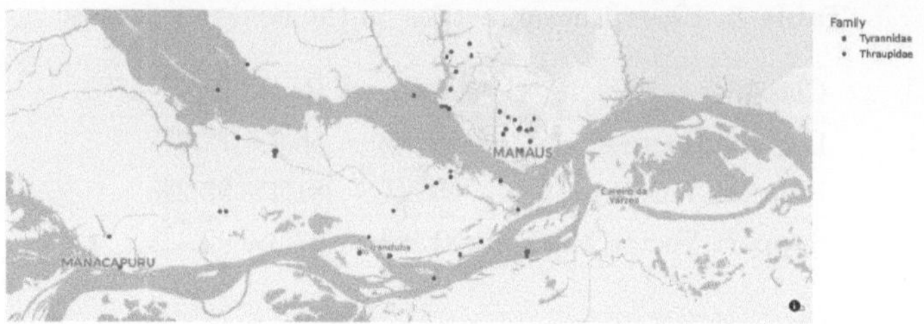

Fig. 2. Occurrence points of the species of interest in the Amazon Basin.

set. The remaining 70% of the data was used to perform hyperparameter tuning through cross-validation, employing a K-fold (K=3) strategy to ensure robust model selection. To address the class imbalance inherent in species distribution data, the classification algorithms were trained with balanced class weights, assigning greater importance to underrepresented classes. This procedure helped reduce bias toward the majority class and ensured a fairer evaluation of model performance across both presence and pseudo-absence categories [9].

To enhance the interpretability of the SDM results and provide ecologically meaningful insights, we applied Explainable Artificial Intelligence (XAI) techniques. In particular, we employed SHAP [13], a widely used model-agnostic method that allows for post-hoc analysis of model predictions. SHAP provides a global, consistent measure of feature importance based on cooperative game theory. SHAP assigns each predictor a Shapley value, representing its average marginal contribution to the model output across all possible feature combinations. This allows for a robust, theoretically grounded understanding of which environmental variables most influence model predictions across the entire dataset [13].

By integrating SHAP into the SDM workflow, we aim to bridge the gap between predictive accuracy and interpretability, providing ecologists and conservation practitioners with tools to not only forecast species distributions but also to understand the environmental drivers underlying these patterns. This approach supports the development of transparent and trustworthy models that can inform conservation strategies and policy decisions, particularly in the context of anthropogenic pressures on tropical ecosystems.

4   Results and Discussions

4.1   Machine Learning Classifiers

We applied 3-fold cross-validation to optimize the hyperparameters of the three classification models–Logistic Regression (LR), Random Forest (RF), and Support Vector Machine (SVM). After this tuning process, we evaluated the best-performing configurations for each model on the independent hold-out test set. The results obtained for accuracy, ROC-AUC, and recall are summarized in

Table 3. Classification metrics on the hold-out dataset

Classifier	Accuracy	Recall	ROC-AUC
Logistic Regression	60.3%	56.8%	72.7%
Random Forests	86.5%	81.4%	92.2%
Support Vector Machines	81.3%	97.3%	92.4%

Table 3, allowing a comparative analysis of each modelâĂŹs performance in identifying suitable habitats based on presence and pseudo-absence data.

As expected, the Logistic Regression classifier yielded the lowest performance metrics among the classifiers. As a linear model, it tends to underfit more complex patterns in the data, which was reflected in its lower accuracy, as well as reduced scores across other metrics. In contrast, the Random Forest and Support Vector Machine classifiers demonstrated stronger predictive capabilities, both achieving ROC-AUC values close to 92%, approximately 20% points higher than those obtained by Logistic Regression. The most notable difference between these two models lies in the Recall metric, which is particularly important for the positive class. While the SVM achieved a superior Recall of 97%, the Random Forest reached 81%, despite having slightly higher overall accuracy.

We selected the Support Vector Machine (SVM) classifier for subsequent analyses due to its superior predictive performance in terms of Recall, which is critical for accurately identifying suitable habitats. This model was then used to generate potential distribution maps, in which habitat suitability is indicated for each point on the map based on the corresponding environmental conditions, as presented in Fig. 3. These maps provide a spatially explicit representation of the likelihood of species occurrence, offering valuable insights for ecological assessment and conservation planning.

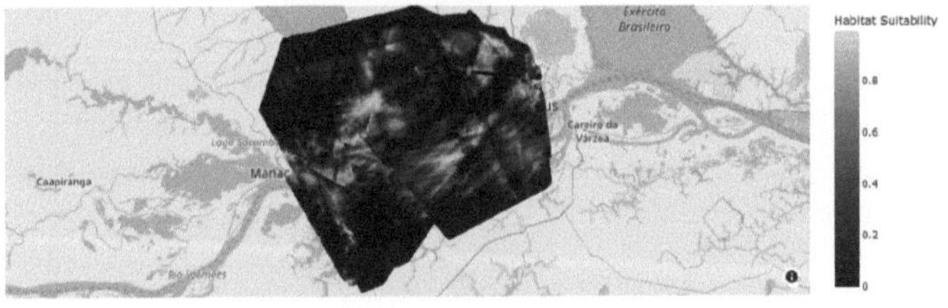

Fig. 3. Habitat Suitability Map for the species of interest in the Amazon Basin.

We observed that the potential distribution map generated aligns well with the occurrence points shown in Fig. 2. The locations with the highest habitat suitability scores correspond closely to the ground-truth occurrence records, with elevated suitability values observed particularly in the areas surrounding these points. However, as in previous studies, this type of analysis alone does not allow for a clear understanding of which specific factors contribute to higher or lower suitability values across the landscape [7,8].

4.2 Explainable Artificial Intelligence

For the SVM classifier, in order to deepen previous investigations regarding the specific influence of variables related to anthropogenic activity on the habitat suitability of bird species from the *Tyrannidae* and *Thraupidae* families in the Amazon region, we applied SHAP. This method allowed for a detailed interpretation of the model's predictions by quantifying the contribution of each environmental variable to habitat suitability, thereby enhancing the transparency and ecological relevance of the results.

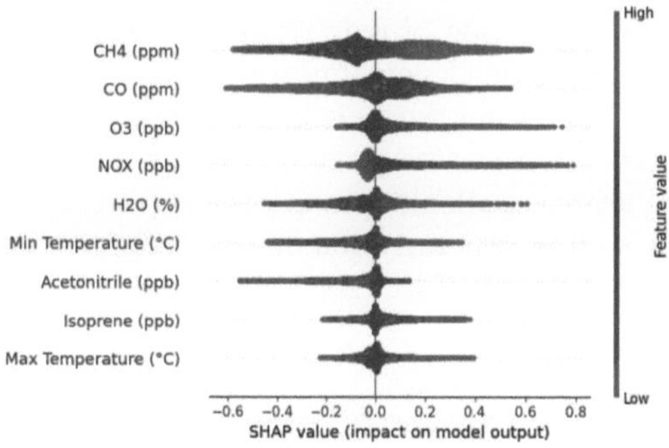

Fig. 4. Shapley values for each variable.

The SHAP summary plot presented on Fig. 4 provides insight into the contribution of each environmental variable to the predictions of the species distribution model (SDM) for birds of the *Tyrannidae* and *Thraupidae* families in the Amazon Basin. Each point represents a SHAP value for a given observation and feature, with color encoding the feature value (from low in blue to high in pink). Variables are ranked by their average absolute SHAP values, indicating their overall impact on the model's predictions, as presented in Fig. 5.

Among the most influential features are concentrations of methane, carbon monoxide, and ozone, all of which are strongly associated with anthropogenic activity [5]. CO is predominantly emitted by anthropogenic sources [24], such as the incomplete combustion of carbon-based fuels, and it is also formed in the atmosphere through photochemical reactions. High values of CO tend to decrease habitat suitability, as indicated by their negative SHAP values when their feature values are high (pink points to the left). This pattern is expected in areas near urban centers like Manaus, where increased combustion processes and vehicular emissions contribute to elevated concentrations of these pollutants [24], negatively affecting the quality of the environment for sensitive avian species.

The SHAP values for ozone, nitrogen oxides, and methane show a more complex behavior, with both low and high concentrations having varied effects on the model output. This may reflect the nonlinear and species-specific responses to atmospheric pollutants, or interactions with other environmental conditions such as temperature and humidity. Tropospheric ozone is a secondary pollutant whose production depends on sunlight and the emission of precursor gases such as NOx, non-methane volatile organic compounds (VOCs), methane, and CO, and can be removed through dry deposition on vegetative surfaces. It affects plant physiological structures and the human respiratory system [25], with an estimated atmospheric lifetime of approximately 25 days [24]. NOx, comprising nitric oxide (NO) and nitrogen dioxide, originates from both natural and anthropogenic sources–including soils, lightning, the stratosphere, ammonia oxidation, fossil fuel combustion, biomass burning, and aircraft emissions–and has a lifetime of 1 to 2 days near the surface and up to 2 weeks in the upper troposphere. Its oxidation leads to the formation of reactive odd nitrogen species (NOy), which play a key role in atmospheric chemical processes [24]. Methane, the most abundant hydrocarbon in the atmosphere, is emitted from a variety of natural and anthropogenic sources such as wetlands, freshwater bodies, animals, wildfires, termite mounds, hydrates, geological sources, agriculture, ruminants, landfills, and dumpsites [26], and is primarily removed through chemical reactions with hydroxyl radicals in the troposphere [26].

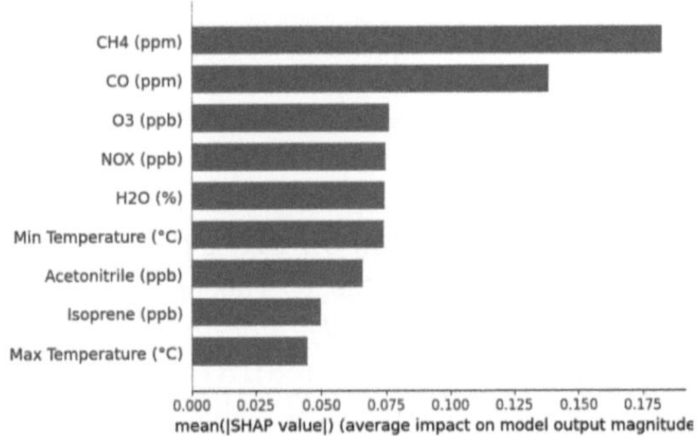

Fig. 5. Average Shapley values for each variable.

Temperature-related variables also played a relevant role. Minimum and maximum temperatures are important predictors, with high minimum temperatures (in pink) associated with positive SHAP values–suggesting that warmer nights may be favorable in certain cases. However, extreme temperatures (either very low or very high) can also reduce suitability, indicating a potential sensitivity of bird species to changes in microclimate that can be driven by urban heat islands or deforestation patterns [3].

Finally, the concentrations of isoprene and acetonitrile–often associated with both natural biogenic emissions and biomass burning–also exhibit relevant contributions. High isoprene values, for example, are linked to increased suitability, possibly reflecting areas of preserved vegetation [24]. In contrast, acetonitrile, a known tracer of biomass burning [27], tends to negatively influence habitat suitability when elevated, especially in dry season months when fire activity is more intense. These findings suggest that SHAP analysis offers a powerful approach for interpreting the complex relationships between environmental stressors and species distributions, shedding light on how anthropogenic pressures are reshaping biodiversity patterns in the Amazon.

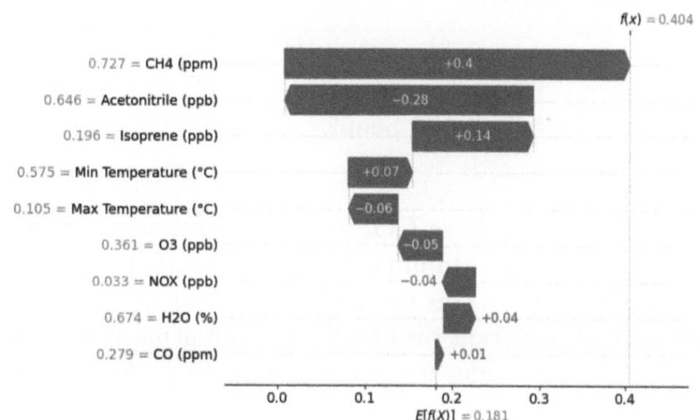

Fig. 6. Waterfall plot for Shapley values for a specific point.

The SHAP waterfall plots presented in Figs. 6 and 7 offer a localized and detailed view of how individual environmental features contributed to the classifier's prediction of habitat suitability for two specific geographic points in the Amazon region. In the Fig. 6, the model predicts a high suitability score of 0.404, largely driven by elevated methane levels, which contributed +0.40 to the final prediction. This is consistent with the broader SHAP summary analysis, where methane is a dominant predictor. Other features such as isoprene and minimum temperature also had positive, though smaller, contributions. In contrast, acetonitrile had a substantial negative impact (-0.28), suggesting that its presence is associated with decreased habitat suitability in this instance, likely due to its origin from biomass burning and industrial processes.

In Fig. 7, the classifier assigns a much lower habitat suitability score of 0.056. Here, the most significant negative contribution comes from high carbon monoxide levels, reducing the prediction by -0.34. Elevated methane and ozone levels provide moderate positive contributions, but these are not sufficient to outweigh the strong negative impacts from CO and other pollutants such as acetonitrile. Notably, minimum temperature also plays a negative role in this case (-0.15), indicating that lower thermal conditions may be less favorable for the target species in this location, which may align with known ecological preferences.

Together, these plots demonstrate the capacity of SHAP to provide interpretable, instance-level insights into the model's reasoning. They highlight how

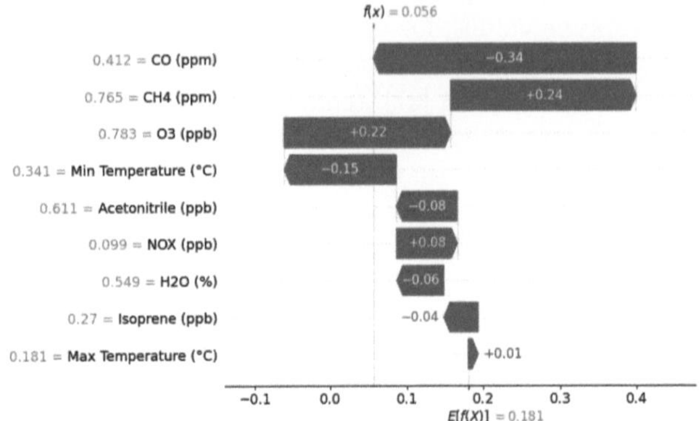

Fig. 7. Waterfall plot for Shapley values for a specific point.

anthropogenic pollutants such as CO, methane, and acetonitrile can have differing impacts on predicted suitability depending on their magnitude and interactions with other variables. This reinforces the need to consider local environmental conditions and pollutant profiles when evaluating habitat suitability and planning conservation strategies for avian species in ecologically sensitive areas such as the Amazon Basin.

5   Conclusions

In conclusion, this study successfully demonstrated the integration of Explainable AI, specifically SHAP, with Species Distribution Models to enhance the interpretability of anthropogenic impacts, particularly atmospheric pollution, on Amazonian bird communities (*Tyrannidae* and *Thraupidae*). By leveraging high-resolution atmospheric data and moving beyond the limitations of traditional "black box" models, we identified key pollutants like methane, carbon monoxide, and ozone as significant drivers of habitat suitability, revealing complex, non-linear relationships previously obscured. The application of SHAP provided transparent, feature-specific insights into model predictions, validating the approach's utility for generating ecologically meaningful results essential for robust biodiversity assessment and conservation planning in the critically important Amazon biome.

Building on these findings, future research could explore the temporal dynamics of these pollutant-habitat relationships over extended periods, incorporate a broader range of species and other environmental variables, and compare insights derived from different XAI techniques. Applying alternative methods such as Local Interpretable Model-agnostic Explanations (LIME) for local-level validation, Integrated Gradients for a different perspective on feature attribution, or counterfactual explanations would provide a more robust and multifaceted understanding. Further investigation represent valuable next steps for advancing the application of explainable machine learning in ecological research and management.

Acknowledgments and Disclosure of Funding. This study was financed in part by the Coordenação de Aperfeiçoamento de Pessoal de Nãŋvel Superior âĂŞ Brasil (CAPES) âĂŞ Finance Code 001. It was made possible by the Thematic Projects of FAPESP 2017/17047-0 and 2020/15230-5.

References

1. Teixeira, M.J., et al.: Analyzing and forecasting the morphology of Amazon deforestation. For. Ecol. Manage. **586**, 122662 (2025). https://doi.org/10.1016/j.foreco.2025.122662

2. Bottino, M.J., Nobre, P., Giarolla, E., et al.: Amazon savannization and climate change are projected to increase dry season length and temperature extremes over Brazil. Sci. Rep. **14**, 5131 (2024). https://doi.org/10.1038/s41598-024-55176-5

3. Aben, J., Dorenbosch, M., Herzog, S.K., Smolders, A.J.P., van der Velde, G.: Human disturbance affects a deciduous forest bird community in the Andean foothills of central Bolivia. Bird Conserv. Int. **18**(4), 363–380 (2008). https://doi.org/10.1017/S0959270908007326

4. United Nations. Global Sustainable Development Report (GSDR) 2023. Bird Conservation International. Available on: https://sdgs.un.org/gsdr/gsdr2023 (2023)

5. Martin, S.T., Artaxo, P., Machado, L., Manzi, A.O., et al.: The green ocean amazon experiment (goamazon2014/5) observes pollution affecting gases, aerosols, clouds, and rainfall over the rain forest. Bull. Am. Meteor. Soc. **98**(5), 981–997 (2017). https://doi.org/10.1175/BAMS-D-15-00221.1

6. Morante-Filho, J.C., Faria, D., Mariano-Neto, E., Rhodes, J.: Birds in anthropogenic landscapes: the responses of ecological groups to forest loss in the Brazilian Atlantic Forest. PLoS ONE **10**(6), e0128923 (2015). https://doi.org/10.1371/journal.pone.0128923

7. Moraes, K.F., Santos, M.P.D., Gonçalves, G.S.R., Oliveira, G.L., Gomes, L.B.: Climate change and bird extinctions in the Amazon. PLoS ONE **15**(7), e0236103 (2020). https://doi.org/10.1371/journal.pone.0236103

8. Moraes, K.F., Lima, M.G.M., Gonçalves, G.S.R., Cerqueira, P.V., Santos, M.P.D.: The future of endemic and threatened birds of the Amazon in the face of global climate change. Ecol. Evol. **14**, e11097 (2024). https://doi.org/10.1002/ece3.11097

9. Beery, S., Cole, E., Parker, J., Perona, P., Winner, K.: In: Species Distribution Modeling for Machine Learning Practitioners: A Review, pp. 329–348. Association for Computing Machinery, New York, NY, USA (2021). https://doi.org/10.1145/3460112.3471966

10. Elith, J., Leathwick, J.: Species distribution models: ecological explanation and prediction across space and time. Annu. Rev. Ecol. Evol. Syst. **40**,(2009). https://doi.org/10.1146/annurev.ecolsys.110308.120159

11. Doran, D., Schulz, S.C. & Besold, T. R. What Does Explainable AI Really Mean? A New Conceptualization of Perspectives. CEUR Workshop Proceedings, 2071. (2018)

12. Ryo, M., Angelov, B., Mammola, S., Kass, J.M., Benito, B.M., Hartig, F.: Explainable artificial intelligence enhances the ecological interpretability of black-box species distribution models. Ecography **44**, 199–205 (2021). https://doi.org/10.1111/ecog.05360

13. Lundberg, S., Lee, S.: In: A unified approach to interpreting model predictions, pp. 4768–4777. Curran Associates Inc., Red Hook, NY, USA (2017)

14. Ribeiro, M., Singh, S., Guestrin, C.,"Why Should I Trust You?",: In: Explaining the Predictions of Any Classifier. Association for Computing Machinery, New York, NY, USA (1135–1144. (2016).)

15. Martin, S.T., Artaxo, P., Machado, L.A.T., Manzi, A.O., et al.: Atmos. Chem. Phys. **16**, 4785–4797 (2016). https://doi.org/10.5194/acp-16-4785-2016

16. Miyaji, R.O., et al.: Spatial interpolation of air pollutant and meteorological variables in central Amazonia. Data **6(12):126**,(2021). https://doi.org/10.3390/data6120126

17. Guisan, A., Zimmermann, N.: Predictive habitat distribution models in ecology. Ecol. Model. **135**(2), 147–186 (2000). https://doi.org/10.1016/S0304-3800(00)00354-9

18. Global Biodiversity Information Facility. Gbif occurrence download. Available on: https://DOI10.15468/dl.ppwbzv (2025)

19. Instituto Chico Mendes de Conservação da Biodiversidade. Sistema de Informação sobre a Biodiversidade Brasileira. Available on. (2025)

20. Senay, S.D., Worner, S.P., Ikeda, T.: Novel three-step pseudo-absence selection technique for improved species distribution modelling. PLoS ONE **8**(8), e71218 (2013). https://doi.org/10.1371/journal.pone.0071218

21. James, G., Witten, D., Hastie, T., Tibshirani, R.: An Introduction to Statistical Learning. Springer, London (2013)

22. Breiman, L.: Random Forests. Mach. Learn. **45**(1), 5–32 (2001)

23. Cortes, C., Vapnik, V.: Support-vector networks. Mach. Learn. **20**(1), 273–297 (1995)

24. Seinfeld, J., Pandis, S. Atmospheric Chemistry and Physics: From Air Pollution to Climate Change. Wiley. (2016)

25. Fowler, D., Amann, M., Anderson, R., Ashmore, M., Cox, P., Depledge, M., Stevenson, D.: Ground-Level Ozone in the 21st Century: Future Trends. Royal Society Science Policy Report, Impacts and Policy Implications (2018)

26. Ciais, P., et al.: Contribution of Working Group I to the Fifth Assessment Report of the Intergovernmental Panel on Climate Change. The Physical Science Basis, Climate Change 2013 (2014)

27. Holzinger, R., et al.: Biomass burning as a source of formaldehyde, acetaldehyde, methanol, acetone, acetonitrile, and hydrogen cyanide. Geophys. Res. Lett. **26**(8), 1161–1164 (1999)

Isolated Sign Language Recognition in LIBRAS

Marcelo M. Delucis[(⊠)], Otávio Parraga, Rodrigo C. Barros,
and Lucas S. Kupssinskü

MALTA - Machine Learning Theory and Applications Lab, School of Technology,
Pontifícia Universidade Católica do Rio Grande do Sul, Av. Ipiranga,
6681, 90619-900 Porto Alegre, RS, Brazil
marcelo.mussi@edu.pucrs.br

Abstract. Hearing loss affects a significant part of the world population. Sign Language Recognition is the task of recognizing isolated signs in videos and has the potential to ease communication between Deaf and non-Deaf people. Data are vital to creating better Sign Language Recognition models. LIBRAS, the Brazilian Sign Language, still lags behind in terms of data availability in comparison to other Sign Languages, such as American and Russian. Our study aims to bridge this gap by introducing a novel LIBRAS dataset for Isolated Sign Language Recognition, MALTA-LIBRAS. This dataset is assembled from open online sources and can be used as a more diverse and representative test set than the previous available LIBRAS dataset, MINDS. We perform several experiments with three transformer-based video classification models for this task: VideoMAE, TimeSformer, and ViViT. Our findings show that action recognition pretraining substantially improves generalization beyond fine-tuning data distribution. Additionally, we identify a set of data augmentation strategies that further increase the model's generalization to new conditions. In contrast to what could be expected, transferring knowledge from other sign languages does not yield significant improvements for LIBRAS.

Keywords: LIBRAS · transformers · deep learning · sign language · ISLR

1   Introduction

According to the World Health Organization (WHO) [21], over 1.5 billion people live with hearing loss, including 466 million with severe hearing impairment. Deaf communities still face stigma that frames deafness as a disability rather than culture, reinforcing marginalisation [26].

Sign Languages (SL) are comprehensive communication systems that utilize both manual and non-manual elements, such as facial expressions and body postures, to convey detailed meanings during interactions. It is a common misconception to view SLs merely as gestural equivalents of spoken languages; in

R. de Freitas and D. Furtado (Eds.): BRACIS 2025, LNAI 16181, pp. 275–290, 2026.
https://doi.org/10.1007/978-3-032-15990-8_19

reality, they are distinct languages with their own grammatical and syntactic rules that effectively meet the communication needs of deaf individuals [1,24].

Large public datasets such as WLASL for ASL [17] and SLOVO for RSL [14] have driven recent progress in Sign Language Recognition (SLR).

However, Brazilian Sign Language (LIBRAS) still lags behind due to data scarcity. LIBRAS is an official Brazilian language (Law 10.436/2002) and is protected by the Brazilian Inclusion Act (Law 13.146/2015). Automatic recognition can: (i) reduce classroom interpreter demand, currently one professional per 43 Deaf students [13]; (ii) enable LIBRAS captions on e-government portals; and (iii) help narrow the 23% employment gap between Deaf and hearing citizens [8].

The chief public corpus for LIBRAS, MINDS [2], contains 1.158 clips of 20 signs recorded from 12 signers, framing LIBRAS recognition as an Isolated Sign Language Recognition (ISLR) task. Due to LIBRAS being severely low-resource, we focus exclusively on this language and study cross-lingual transfer from high-resource SLs to LIBRAS, leaving other low-resource SLs for future work.

MINDS lacks a designated test split and offers a small vocabulary, which limits model generalisation. We therefore contribute by: providing a novel dataset called MALTA-LIBRAS [7], a collection of videos compiled through web scraping from diverse open sources; and by evaluating three SOTA video classification models in ISLR LIBRAS by using both MINDS and MALTA-LIBRAS datasets.

Since MALTA-LIBRAS was collected from distinct sources, it has a more diverse and a much less-controlled sample of videos, making it arguably a more representative source and thus a better option for training ISLR models. Nevertheless, its vocabulary has an intersection with MINDS vocabulary that enables it to be used as a test set for models trained and validated in MINDS. We use three SOTA video classification models for assessing the performance of ISLR models in the new dataset: VideoMAE [29], TimeSformer [5], and ViViT [3].

We study (i) action-recognition pre-training, (ii) cross-lingual transfer, and (iii) data-augmentation strategies.

Results show that pre-training mitigates MINDS overfitting and accelerates convergence. The remainder of the paper covers related work 2, methodology 3, results 4 and conclusions 5.

2   Related Work

Automated SLR ranges from character-level fingerspelling to word-level (ISLR) and sentence-level (CSLR) recognition; the latter two remain challenging despite fingerspelling progress [4]. Deep-learning models are now standard in SLR [20], but inter-signer variation still requires temporal reasoning methods [6,27].

ISLR inherits additional difficulties, such as subtle motion trajectories, dialectal differences and signer specificity [17,28]. Transformers, STGCNs, and attentionbased encoderdecoder architectures effectively model these spatiotemporal patterns, whereas selfsupervised and domainadaptation methods harness depth or skeletal information to alleviate dataset sparsity [12,30,31].

Large corpora underpin progress: PHOENIX-2014 for German Sign Language (GSL) [9], CSL for Chinese [12], WLASL for ASL [17], and the recent crowd-sourced SLOVO for RSL [14]. Yet many SLs remain low-resourced; for LIBRAS, action-recognition pre-training tasks, data augmentation techniques and cross-lingual transfer are still largely unexplored [1,16].

The only public LIBRAS corpus, MINDS [2], offers 1.158 clips of 20 signs, two orders of magnitude smaller than WLASL (21.000 clips, 2.000 signs), hindering robust generalisation.

Our work is motivated by this landscape, where data scarcity in LIBRAS is a reality. While MINDS represents an essential step for SLR in LIBRAS, it underlines the need for broader, more varied datasets to help models capture the full richness of SLs. We close these gaps by systematically benchmarking transformerbased video classifiers (VideoMAE [29], TimeSformer [5], and ViViT [3]) across diverse pretraining configurations, a comprehensive set of augmentation techniques, and crossdataset transfer-learning experiments. To the best of our knowledge, this is the first study to evaluate transformer architectures for ISLR in LIBRAS.

3   Methodology

One of the goals of this paper is to evaluate three SOTA models designed for video classification tasks within the ISLR framework: VideoMAE [29], TimeSformer [5], and ViViT [3]. Our experiments explore using these models pre-trained on the Kinetics-400 [15] dataset, leveraging the spatiotemporal features learned from a broad spectrum of annotated human actions, while also training them from scratch on specific SL datasets.

In an attempt to mitigate overfitting, we conduct experiments on data augmentation techniques, systematically adjusting intensity levels for transformations such as color jitter, random rotation, random perspective, and Mixup [32] to identify a data augmentation pipeline suitable for better generalisation from limited training sets such as those provided by current LIBRAS datasets. We also explore the possibility of transfer learning between different SLs, utilizing the well-established WLASL [17] dataset and a novel RSL dataset, SLOVO [14].

Our study examines the combination of pretraining on action recognition, the optimized data augmentation pipeline, and transfer learning from other SLs to identify practices that support generalisation when extensive annotated LIBRAS data is not available. Code and data are available at our GitHub[1] and our HuggingFace[2] repositories.

3.1   Datasets

To achieve the objectives of this study, we utilized SLOVO [14], WLASL [17], MINDS [2], and our novel MALTA-LIBRAS dataset. SLOVO and WLASL are

---

[1] https://github.com/Malta-Lab/ISLR_LIBRAS.

[2] https://huggingface.co/datasets/MALTA-Lab/MALTA_LIBRAS.

Table 1. Specification of each open data source collected through web scraping. Last column shows the intersection size between our dataset and MINDS dataset.

	Signers	Videos	Length [h]	Resolution	|Vocabulary|	|∩ MINDS|
INES Dictionary 2.0 [18]	1	3,287	1.19	240x180	3,066	20
INES Dictionary 3.0 [19]	1	3,208	3.34	240x180	2,993	19
V-LIBRASIL [25]	3	4,089	6.49	1920x1080	1,363	7
Libras-Corpus [23]	1	1,011	0.77	360x300	929	19
SignBank [22]	9	1,000	0.66	1280x720	916	20
UFV LIBRAS Dictionary [10]	6	242	0.27	831x467	242	6
Spread the Sign [11]	40	1,788	1.79	320x240	1,788	16

used as pretraining datasets in order to assess how transfer learning between distinct SLs affects LIBRAS ISLR.

These datasets were selected based on their size and distinct focus: WLASL emphasizes maintaining control over instances, while SLOVO prioritizes covering various scenarios and actors. This combination enables us to evaluate the effectiveness of transfer learning for LIBRAS and how the differences between datasets influence the models. On the other hand, MINDS and MALTA-LIBRAS are used for fine-tuning, validation, and testing the models. Details on each of the datasets are presented next.

MINDS. [2] It is the main existing dataset for ISLR in LIBRAS. It consists of 20 classes and an average of 100 video samples per class, performed by 12 signers, totaling $1,158$ video clips. Data were recorded under conditions with controlled lighting, background, and camera settings, resulting in homogeneous recordings. One of the limitations of the MINDS dataset is the absence of a designated test set, making it difficult to evaluate model generalisation to data not seen during training. Without this dedicated test set and a larger dataset focused on LIBRAS, it is not straightforward to determine how well models trained on MINDS would perform in real-world scenarios.

MALTA-LIBRAS. To address the limitation of the MINDS dataset, namely the absence of a dedicated test set and its relatively controlled recording conditions, we collected and curated additional videos to perform testing in models fine-tuned to MINDS. Initially, using web scraping techniques, we compiled a total of $21,000$ LIBRAS videos from INES Dictionary 2.0 [18], INES Dictionary 3.0 [19], V-LIBRASIL [25], Libras-Corpus [23], SignBank [22], UFV LIBRAS Dictionary [10], and Spread the Sign [11] platforms.

Each of these dictionaries did not contain enough samples per sign to serve as a standalone dataset, so combining them was a necessary step. The resulting dataset introduces variability in terms of signers, backgrounds, and recording conditions while encompassing the same 20 classes as the MINDS dataset but featuring different signers and environments.

After downloading the raw videos, we applied a four-stage quality-control pipeline. First, we generated perceptual hashes to identify and remove duplicate clips. Next, each remaining video was independently annotated, assigning both the gloss (word or phrase) and a signer-ID hash. Whenever the annotators disagreed the clip was reviewed by another annotator; the label was accepted only when at least two of the three annotators converged. Finally, we discarded corrupt files, any video shorter than 20 frames, and those with resolution below 180 p. The resulting curated set comprises 129 samples that intersect exactly with the 20 MINDS classes. Video resolutions vary between 240×180 and 1280×720 pixels, and frame rates range from 24 to 30 frames per second. All accepted clips were then resized to 224×224 px; we extracted 32 evenly spaced frames and randomly sampled 16 of them to form the model input used in every experiment.

This corpus was retained solely as a holdout test set, allowing us to gauge the models ability to generalize to signers and recording conditions absent from training. Comprehensive statistics for this dataset are shown in Table 1.

Since we design MALTA-LIBRAS to be a test set for models trained in MINDS, we are interested only in a subset of signals that appear on both datasets. The first data source collected was from the National Institute of Deaf Education (INES) online LIBRAS dictionaries. Data collection yielded two collections of videos: one from LIBRAS Dictionary 2.0 [18] and another from LIBRAS Dictionary 3.0 [19]. From these, we obtained 24 and 23 video instances that matched 20 and 19 signs in the MINDS dataset, respectively. We also explored the V-LIBRASIL [25] dataset, yielding 26 video instances across 9 signs that align with the MINDS dataset. The LIBRAS Corpus [23] provided 18 instances across 19 signs. UFV LIBRAS Dictionary [10] provided 7 instances for 7 different signs. Signbank [22] contributed 19 instances covering 17 signs featured in the MINDS dataset. Additionally, we utilized data from *Spread The Sign* [11], an initiative by the European Sign Language Center that features over $400,000$ video signs across 44 languages. From this dataset, we were able to match only 12 instances and signs with the MINDS dataset.

Figure 1 illustrates that each dataset was recorded under predefined protocols, including standardized clothing, backgrounds, and resting poses, to reduce variability and assist students in focusing on learning sign features. Such consistency may help individuals conveniently understand signs, it limits the models exposure to diverse conditions, restricting its ability to adapt to realistic scenarios.

WLASL. The WLASL [17] dataset is a comprehensive resource for ASL recognition, featuring an extensive vocabulary and a diverse range of signer representations. It encompasses over $2,000$ classes and more than $21,000$ video samples, all performed by over 100 native ASL users. The recording conditions follow a strict protocol with limited variety in backgrounds and lighting settings, which does not contribute to the dataset's diversity and realism. Although video res-

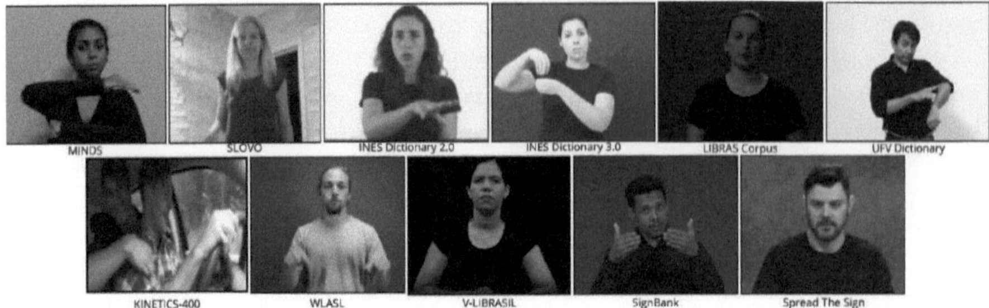

Fig. 1. An illustration showcasing a single frame from all datasets used and from each collected source from the MALTA-LIBRAS dataset, emphasizing the variability of data in the creation of the MALTA-LIBRAS dataset.

olutions vary across samples, they were standardized during preprocessing to ensure consistency, typically maintaining a frame rate of 30 frames per second. The dataset provides detailed annotations, including sign glosses and additional temporal information, offering valuable context for each video. The annotations on this dataset allow distinct configurations to be used. We employed the $1,000$-class subset with an average of 8 (4) training (validation) instances per class for pretraining, so we can evaluate the effectiveness of transfer learning from ASL to LIBRAS, aiming to enhance the model's ability to recognize LIBRAS signs by leveraging knowledge learned from ASL.

SLOVO. The SLOVO [14] dataset is a resource tailored for ISLR in RSL. Spanning across $1,000$ classes, it features signs performed by 194 crowd-sourced RSL signers, whose contributions underwent a thorough validation process to ensure both authenticity and accuracy. Unlike other datasets, SLOVO stands out for its environmental diversity: the videos capture a wide range of scenarios, thereby enhancing the datasets realism and breadth. The dataset comprises $20,000$ video samples captured in HD or Full HD resolutions at a frame rate of 25 frames per second. We employed SLOVO to pre-train our models to exploit transfer learning across different SLs, similar to what was done using WLASL.

3.2   Experimental Setup

Our experiments evaluate the performance of SOTA video classification models in the task of ISLR for LIBRAS in different settings. To address the current objectives, we designed three Research Questions (RQ), and to answer each RQ we devise one experiment, as detailed in the following sections.

- **RQ1**: How does pretraining in the action recognition task affect LIBRAS ISLR?
- **RQ2**: How does Rotation, Color Jitter, Mixup, and Perspective data augmentation impact LIBRAS ISLR?

– **RQ3**: How does transfer learning between ASL and RSL affect LIBRAS ISLR?

Unless specified otherwise, our experimental setup employed a batch size of 16 and AdamW as the optimizer with an initial learning rate of 10^{-4}. A scheduler was set up to reduce the LR by a factor of 10 in case the validation loss stabilizes within 5 consecutive epochs. Additionally, early stopping was implemented with the patience of 30 epochs, aiming to avoid continuing training without improvements in the validation loss, reducing computational costs. Every experiment was set to run with 10 different preset seeds. We report both average and standard deviation values of those 10 distinct runs.

Pretraining Analysis. Our first experiment answers whether models pre-trained on large-scale action recognition tasks could provide advantages when fine-tuned for ISLR in LIBRAS. We sought to measure how effectively knowledge acquired from the Kinetics-400 dataset, which encompasses thousands of videos capturing a broad range of human actions, could be adapted to the domain of SLR.

To this end, we evaluated each of the three models in two configurations: i) pre-trained on Kinetics-400; ii) initialized from scratch with randomly-assigned weights. We then fine-tuned the models on the MINDS dataset, allowing them to learn the nuances of LIBRAS signs. Finally, we tested the resulting models on the MALTA-LIBRAS dataset to assess their ability to generalize to new signers and varied environments not encountered during training.

Results were measured using accuracy, precision, recall, and F1-score. By comparing the pretrained models against those trained solely on the MINDS dataset, we aimed to determine if leveraging prior knowledge from general action recognition tasks would improve ISLR performance for LIBRAS, thus providing evidence of effective transfer learning and answering RQ1.

Data Augmentation Analysis. The second analysis focused on evaluating how different data augmentation techniques influence the model's performance throughout the training process. Other studies, such as the development of the MINDS [24] dataset, employ limited data augmentation techniques in LIBRAS, such as temporal displacement of frames, horizontal mirroring, and zooming.

Since this experiment does not aim to find the best model among the three tested, we chose to only perform a data augmentation experiment on the less compute-intensive model, VideoMAE. All results are for pretrained VideoMAE fine-tuned on MINDS and evaluated on MALTA-LIBRAS.

We experimented with four augmentation techniques: i) color jitter, which varies brightness, contrast, saturation, and hue, emulating varied background scenarios common in video augmentation experiments; ii) Mixup [32] as a way to blend different samples and introduce controlled noise; iii) random rotation, to account for minor shifts in sign execution; and iv) random perspective, to simulate different camera angles. The intensity of each technique was incrementally adjusted from 0.05 to 0.5 in steps of 0.05. To ensure robustness and account for stochastic variations, training was repeated with ten different preset seeds for each intensity level. Averaging the performance metrics across these runs allowed us to mitigate the impact of random fluctuations.

After identifying the best intensity for each augmentation technique based on performance on the MALTA-LIBRAS dataset, we conducted a new training session on the MINDS dataset, using all augmentation techniques simultaneously at their respective optimal intensity levels. We then evaluated the model on MALTA-LIBRAS once again, comparing the results to those from experiments without data augmentation. This comparative assessment, designed to answer our RQ2, enabled us to measure the cumulative benefits of the optimized augmentation pipeline and determine whether it further enhanced the models generalisation capabilities.

This decision to use the MALTA-LIBRAS dataset for hyperparameter tuning was made due to a severe overfitting scenario, where we achieve near-perfect validation accuracy and consistently lower metrics on MALTA-LIBRAS, which makes the validation set unreliable. We acknowledge that exposing the test set to partial tuning is ill-advised, but under these low-data constraints, it was necessary to gain insights for future LIBRAS ISLR research.

Transfer Learning from other SLs. This third analysis was designed to assess the potential of transfer learning between different SLs. VideoMAE was the model selected for this experiment, following the same rationale of the previous one. Initially, we trained the VideoMAE model on the SLOVO dataset (RSL). After training, we fine-tuned the model on the MINDS dataset and then tested it on our MALTA-LIBRAS data to evaluate its ability to generalize to new signers and environments not seen during training.

Subsequently, we repeated the same procedure using the WLASL dataset. The model was trained on WLASL, fine-tuned on MINDS, and tested on MALTA-LIBRAS. Furthermore, we explored a combined pretraining approach by pretraining the model on both the SLOVO and WLASL datasets before fine-tuning on MINDS and testing on MALTA-LIBRAS. This allowed us to thoroughly evaluate the transfer learning among different SLs and to assess whether pretraining on multiple SLs enhances performance on LIBRAS recognition tasks.

The initial training on the SLOVO and WLASL datasets was performed without data augmentation to isolate the effects of augmentation during fine-tuning. During the fine-tuning step on the MINDS dataset, we used the optimal set of augmentations obtained from the previous analysis. This training was conducted with a single preset seed to reduce computational time and resources.

Performance metrics evaluated included accuracy, precision, recall, and F1-score. The reported metrics provided a thorough assessment of the model's classification capabilities and its ability to generalize across different SLs and datasets, enabling us to answer RQ3.

Table 2. Validation and test results of pretrained and non-pretrained (NPT) models.

Model	MINDS Validation				MALTA-LIBRAS Test			
	Accuracy	Precision	Recall	F1-score	Accuracy	Precision	Recall	F1-score
VideoMAE	**.994**	**.995**	**.994**	**.994**	**.290**	.256	**.258**	**.227**
TimeSformer	.980	.983	.980	.980	.254	**.257**	.224	.207
ViVit	.984	.986	.984	.984	.181	.177	.155	.134
VideoMAE NPT	.767	**.791**	.767	.766	.048	.020	.043	.022
TimeSformer NPT	**.774**	.783	**.774**	**.769**	.051	**.040**	**.059**	.028
ViVit NPT	.552	.563	.552	.549	**.055**	.036	.054	**.034**

4   Results and Discussion

4.1   Pretraining Analysis

This analysis evaluated models fine-tuned on the MINDS dataset by either pre-training on the Kinetics-400 dataset (PT) or not (NPT). Table 2 summarizes the results obtained in this experiment, highlighting the best results both among NPT and PT models. It is clear from the table that pretraining over the action recognition task systematically improves all the tested models, both in validation and test data. Note that the fine-tuned models surpass the current SOTA on the MINDS dataset [24]. The reported accuracy on the original paper was 0.93 while here we achieve near-perfect metrics. However, if we perform inference of all trained models on data collected from other sources, we observe that all models tested suffer from overfitting.

These results indicate that even though models trained only on MINDS struggle to generalize to MALTA-LIBRAS, overfitting the training data, pretraining on the Kinetics-400 dataset remains as an essential step. By comparing validation and test data in Table 2, one can see that NPT models are equivalent to random guessing on the test set, while PT models perform above chance by a good margin. Observing this scenario, it's implied that the MINDS dataset may not be sufficiently diverse to enable the models to generalize effectively to a new context, underscoring the importance of the development of larger and more diverse LIBRAS datasets. Among all the results, we can highlight VideoMAE's case because it achieves the highest metrics while having the lowest parameter count (and computing requirements) among the evaluated models. Our choice for VideoMAE in the following two experiments is corroborated by this result.

We went one step further and evaluated all the performance metrics across each of the distinct data sources in MALTA-LIBRAS. Table 3 provides this overview. We can see that across varying conditions, the VideoMAE model consistently outperformed ViViT and TimeSformer, providing higher accuracy and proving to be more effective in handling the diversity in different signers and other scenarios encountered in MALTA-LIBRAS. Another important fact is that metrics remain stable across those distinct data sources, so there are no apparent biases in any specific data source that make it harder than others.

Table 3. Test metrics for each data source within MALTA-LIBRAS of all pretrained and non-pretrained (NPT) models.

Source		VideoMAE	VideoMAE NPT	TimeSformer	TimeSformer NPT	ViVit	ViVit NPT
Spread The Sign	Accuracy	.293	.056	**.312**	.031	.206	.081
	Precision	.179	.022	**.236**	.017	.159	.024
	Recall	.272	.046	**.289**	.024	.189	.064
	F1-score	.207	.026	**.252**	.019	.169	.030
INES Dictionary 2.0	Accuracy	**.234**	.061	.219	.080	.219	.050
	Precision	**.177**	.007	.158	.028	.146	.023
	Recall	**.248**	.044	.222	.078	.226	.046
	F1-score	**.191**	.011	.167	.030	.158	.026
INES Dictionary 3.0	Accuracy	**.300**	.050	.287	.045	.137	.050
	Precision	**.262**	.012	.242	.012	.118	.012
	Recall	**.280**	.055	.270	.055	.139	.044
	F1-score	**.244**	.014	.236	.017	.111	.016
V-LIBRASIL	Accuracy	**.314**	.040	.214	.044	.148	.051
	Precision	**.150**	.006	.122	.014	.073	.032
	Recall	**.214**	.036	.166	.035	.112	.037
	F1-score	**.160**	.010	.114	.018	.064	.027
Signbank	Accuracy	**.278**	.057	.257	.063	.215	.052
	Precision	**.233**	.005	.202	.019	.137	.022
	Recall	**.248**	.061	.223	.065	.184	.054
	F1-score	**.229**	.009	.205	.024	.146	.026
LIBRAS Corpus	Accuracy	**.331**	.026	.263	.036	.178	.057
	Precision	**.266**	.001	.202	.009	.119	.018
	Recall	**.306**	.027	.236	.038	.153	.054
	F1-score	**.276**	.002	.205	.012	.119	.025

4.2 Data Augmentation Analysis

We chose PT VideoMAE, the best-performing model in the previous analysis, to test how data augmentation can affect model performance, and whether it could make the trained models generalize better. In Table 4 we report the mean accuracy achieved after finetuning on MINDS and evaluating on MALTALIBRAS, averaged over 10 preset seeds.

It is possible to observe that every tested augmentation improved model generalisation when compared to the non-augmented fine-tuning of the previous analysis. Among the augmentations, we can highlight that Color Jitter provided the largest increase in accuracy, followed closely by Mixup. Random rotation, which simulates slight variations in sign performance, appears to have worsened the model results. We speculate that this is due to the extensive control in the acquired images, as it can be observed by inspecting Fig. 1.

We selected the intensities with the highest accuracy to create a data augmentation pipeline, we used 0.40 for color jitter, 0.25 for Mixup, 0.40° for random rotation, and 0.50 for random perspective. Using the chosen augmentation intensities and the same set of 10 fixed seeds, we executed an additional training run of the VideoMAE model in both its PT and NPT configurations.

The results of this new training are shown in Table 5. Two observations can be drawn from this experiment: first, data augmentation alone does not replace

Table 4. Mean and standard deviation of MALTA-LIBRAS test accuracy for the VideoMAE model, pre-trained on Kinetics-400, fine-tuned on MINDS, on various intensities of each data augmentation technique.

Intensity	Color Jitter	Mixup	Random Rotation	Random Perspective
0.05	.290 ± .016	.286 ± .026	.297 ± .036	.288 ± .025
0.10	.288 ± .018	.291 ± .035	.307 ± .019	.279 ± .025
0.15	.301 ± .026	.279 ± .018	.301 ± .022	.277 ± .022
0.20	.295 ± .021	.289 ± .038	.293 ± .020	.288 ± .036
0.25	.305 ± .025	**.298 ± .027**	.291 ± .024	.283 ± .021
0.30	.305 ± .014	.293 ± .022	.316 ± .014	.286 ± .019
0.35	.302 ± .024	.254 ± .042	.310 ± .017	.276 ± .029
0.40	**.310 ± .014**	.287 ± .047	**.320 ± .022**	.286 ± .015
0.45	.296 ± .028	.277 ± .031	.315 ± .014	.283 ± .029
0.50	.310 ± .029	.273 ± .042	.312 ± .029	**.293 ± .021**

the benefits of pre-training; second, NPT VideoMAE still performs poorly even with data augmentation, though with PT we can improve accuracy from 0.29 to 0.336 just by employing data augmentation.

These results indicate that introducing variation into the training phase helps models better handle changes in background, lighting, and signer appearance. However, the gains were not good enough to close the performance gap between MINDS and MALTA-LIBRAS. This outcome suggests that more variability in training data or alternative strategies, such as video-specific data augmentation, may be required to achieve robust generalisation.

Table 5. Test accuracy on MALTA-LIBRAS with and without the augmentation pipeline.

Model	Without Augmentation		With Augmentation	
	Acc	Top-5 Acc	Acc	Top-5 Acc
VideoMAE PT	.290 ± .021	.541 ± .027	.336 ± .013	.523 ± .028
VideoMAE NPT	.048 ± .012	.260 ± .021	.074 ± .016	.269 ± .017

4.3   Transfer Learning Analysis

To evaluate how transfer learning between SLs impact ISLR in LIBRAS, we leverage pre-training in SLOVO and WLASL datasets before fine-tuning in MINDS.

For the WLASL dataset, we utilized the subdivision consisting of 1,000 signs, adhering to the training and validation splits provided by the original study.

Table 6. Results for the VideoMAE pre-trained (PT) on Russian and American Sign Languages then fine-tuned (FT) on MINDS.

Model	MINDS Validation				MALTA-LIBRAS Test			
	Accuracy	Precision	Recall	F1-score	Accuracy	Precision	Recall	F1-score
SLOVO PT + MINDS FT	1	1	1	1	**.317**	.242	**.274**	.226
WLASL PT + MINDS FT	.996	.996	.996	.996	.290	**.263**	.263	**.238**
SLOVO PT + WLASL PT + MINDS FT	.996	.996	.996	.996	.290	**.263**	.263	**.238**
MINDS FT	.994	.995	.994	.994	.290	.256	.258	.227

When using the SLOVO dataset, we maintained the author's original training split but combined the validation and test splits into a single validation set. This approach allowed us to standardize the validation process across both datasets and facilitated comparison of model performance after pre-training on different SLs. This pre-training aimed to answer RQ3, determining whether previous knowledge about sign-based actions could improve ISLR in LIBRAS.

Contrary to our expectations, transfer learning from SLOVO, WLASL, or both did not show consistent improvements over the VideoMAE model without the additional pre-training. In Table 6, we can see that only pre-training in SLOVO alone marginally improves model accuracy on the test set. We also notice that it achieves perfect results in the validation set. Differences in linguistic structure, sign formation, and visual appearance across SLs likely limited the potential for transferring useful features. These results underscore the challenges of crossdataset transfer learning and reinforce the need for techniques expressly designed to mitigate language or domaininduced shifts.

5   Conclusion and Future Works

SLR remains a challenging endeavor given the intricacy of each SL. This challenge is exacerbated in low-resource SLs such as LIBRAS. We tackled this situation by performing extensive experimentation with SOTA video classification models, exploring several mechanisms to address this limitation such as extensive pre-training in distinct tasks, distinct SLs, and evaluating many augmentation techniques. To the extent of our knowledge, this is the first time that such a study was performed in ISLR for LIBRAS.

To mitigate the data scarcity issue in LIBRAS, we collected and annotated a novel dataset, MALTA-LIBRAS, to be used as a test set for models fine-tuned on the MINDS dataset. This new dataset compiles six distinct data sources into a single annotated dataset. MALTA-LIBRAS proved to be much more challenging than MINDS because it is compiled from diverse data sources, and it is not subject to a single set of controlled conditions. Our results indicate that models that achieve very high evaluation metrics on MINDS are still prone to overfitting and may be often equivalent to random guessing.

Addressing the first research question, we see that action recognition pre-training offers improvements both on MINDS validation data and on MALTA-LIBRAS testing set. Without pre-training, all the fine-tuned models performed equivalent to random guessing on the test set. Another advantage of using action recognition pre-training is the faster convergence during training.

Nearly every augmentation strategy enhanced model performance, thereby answering our RQ2. The sole outlier was Random Perspective where across most tested intensity levels led to lower accuracy. We speculate that SLR datasets are generally captured from a fixed camera angle; so introducing perspective distortions creates unrealistic samples that hinder the model during evaluation.

Concerning crosslingual transfer learning (our RQ3), the outcomes were unexpected: pretraining on RSL or ASL conferred no benefit when the models were later finetuned on LIBRAS. We hypothesize that the finegrained, languagespecific articulatory patterns of each SL impede feature transfer, leaving representations learned from RSL and ASL misaligned with those required for accurate LIBRAS classification.

Beyond dataset curation, our study offers methodological contributions by systematically evaluating the impact of various video classification architectures, pre-training strategies, and augmentation techniques specifically tailored to the challenges of ISLR in LIBRAS. By demonstrating how pre-training on action recognition boosts model performance and by identifying data augmentation methods suited to SL datasets, we provide insights that can directly influence future research and practical applications in ISLR. Furthermore, the limitations of cross-lingual transfer learning highlighted in our results underscore the importance of developing language-specific resources and methodologies for SLR.

While our study specifically targeted isolated sign recognition, practical LIBRAS communication predominantly occurs in continuous, conversational contexts. Extending our methodology to continuous or spontaneous signing scenarios presents additional complexities, such as accurate temporal segmentation of sign sequences, co-articulation handling, and context-dependent interpretation. However, the improvements demonstrated by our pre-training and data augmentation approaches suggest they could serve as strategies in addressing these broader recognition challenges. The insights obtained from evaluating model performance under more realistic and diverse conditions, as facilitated by MALTA-LIBRAS, provide guidance for future adaptations aiming toward continuous and more naturalistic LIBRAS recognition tasks.

Future work may incorporate multi-modal input to the video-based models accessed in our study. Features such as keypoints or depth may prove to be very useful for the model. Another possibility is to work with self-supervised schemes to avoid the burden of annotating data in LIBRAS. In this case, the amount of data available may be sufficient to fine-tune a model that is able to better generalize. As more training data and strategies are available, future research may improve ISLR performance in LIBRAS under a broader range of conditions.

Acknowledgments. We thank Google for funding this research with the 2022 Google Award for Inclusion Research (AIR). This study was financed in part by the Coordination for the Improvement of Higher Education Personnel - Brazil (CAPES) - Finance Code 001 and Fundação de Amparo à Pesquisa do Estado do Rio Grande do Sul (FAPERGS, grant nr. 22/2551-0000390-7). During the drafting of this article, LLMs were used solely for grammar review, clarity improvement, and spelling correction.

Disclosure of Interests. The authors declare no competing interests.

References

1. Adaloglou, N., et al.: A comprehensive study on deep learning-based methods for sign language recognition. IEEE Trans. Multimedia **24**, 1750–1762 (2022). https://doi.org/10.1109/tmm.2021.3070438
2. Almeida, S.G.M., Rezende, T.M., Almeida, G.T.B., Toffolo, A.C.R., GuimarÃ£es, F.G.: Minds-libras dataset (2019). https://doi.org/10.5281/zenodo.2667329
3. Arnab, A., Dehghani, M., Heigold, G., Sun, C., Lucic, M., Schmid, C.I.: Vivit: a video vision transformer, pp. 6816–6826. IEEE Computer Society, Los Alamitos (2021). https://doi.org/10.1109/ICCV48922.2021.00676
4. Bahia, N.K., Rani, R.: Multi-level taxonomy review for sign language recognition: emphasis on indian sign language. ACM Trans. Asian Low-Resour. Lang. Inf. Process. **22**(1),(2023). https://doi.org/10.1145/3530259
5. Bertasius, G., Wang, H., Torresani, L.: Is space-time attention all you need for video understanding? In: ICML. vol. 2, p. 4 (2021)
6. Cooper, H., Holt, B., Bowden, R.: Sign Language Recognition, pp. 539–562. Springer, London, London (2011). https://doi.org/10.1007/978-0-85729-997-0_27
7. Delucis, M.M.: Isolated sign language recognition in LIBRAS. Master's thesis, Programa de Pós-Graduaç ão em Ciência da Computaç ão (2025), https://tede2.pucrs.br/tede2/handle/tede/11629
8. de Geografia e Estatística (IBGE), I.B.: Censo Demográfico 2010: Pessoas com Deficiência Resultados Brasileiros. Tech. rep., IBGE, Rio de Janeiro (2012). iSBN 978-85-240-4272-3. In Portuguese
9. Forster, J., Schmidt, C.A., Hoyoux, T., Koller, O., Zelle, U., Piater, J.H., Ney, H.: Rwth-phoenix-weather,: a large vocabulary sign language recognition and translation corpus. In: International Conference on Language Resources and Evaluation (2012). https://api.semanticscholar.org/CorpusID:2516961
10. Gediel, A.L.B., Mourão, Victor Luiz Alves, e.a.: Dicionário online bilíngue libras/português. Tech. rep., Universidade Federal de Viçosa - UFV, Brasília, Brasil (2017), http://educapes.capes.gov.br/handle/capes/432035
11. Hilzensauer, M., Krammer, K.: A multilingual dictionary for sign languages: "spreadthesign". In: ICERI2015 Proceedings 8th International Conference of Education, Research and Innovation, IATED, pp. 7826–7834. (2015)
12. Huang, J., Zhou, W., Zhang, Q., Li, H., Li, W.: Video-based sign language recognition without temporal segmentation. In: Proceedings of the AAAI Conference on Artificial Intelligence **32**(1) (2018). https://doi.org/10.1609/aaai.v32i1.11903
13. INES, Rio de Janeiro., Brazil, (ed.): Instituto Nacional de Educação de Surdos (INES): Relatório Anual de Intérpretes Educacionais 2023. Tech. rep. (2024). in Portuguese

14. Kapitanov, A., Karina, K., Nagaev, A., Elizaveta, P.: Slovo: Russian sign language dataset. In: Christensen, H.I., Corke, P., Detry, R., Weibel, J.B., Vincze, M. (eds.) Computer Vision Systems, pp. 63–73. Springer Nature Switzerland, Cham (2023)
15. Kay, W., et al.: The kinetics human action video dataset. 10.48550/arXiv, 1705.06950 (2017). arXiv e-prints arXiv:1705.06950
16. Kindiroglu, A.A., Kara, O., Ozdemir, O., Akarun, L.: Transfer learning for cross-dataset isolated sign language recognition in under-resourced datasets. In: 2024 IEEE 18th International Conference on Automatic Face and Gesture Recognition (FG), pp. 1–8 (2024). https://doi.org/10.1109/FG59268.2024.10582029
17. Li, D., Opazo, C.R., Yu, X., Li, H.: Word-level deep sign language recognition from video: a new large-scale dataset and methods comparison. In: 2020 IEEE Winter Conference on Applications of Computer Vision (WACV), pp. 1448–1458. IEEE (2020). https://doi.org/10.1109/wacv45572.2020.9093512, http://dx.doi.org/10.1109/WACV45572.2020.9093512
18. Lira, G.d.A., Souza, T.A.F.d.: Libras versão 2.0. In: In: www.acessibilidadebrasil.org.br/libras/, coordenação Geral por Guilherme de., Azambuja Lira (2014)
19. Lira, G.d.A., Souza, T.A.F.d.: Libras versão 3.0 (2014), http://www.acessibilidadebrasil.org.br/libras_3/, coordenação Geral por Guilherme de Azambuja Lira
20. Molchanov, P., Yang, X., Gupta, S., Kim, K., Tyree, S., Kautz, J.: Online detection and classification of dynamic hand gestures with recurrent 3d convolutional neural networks. In: 2016 IEEE Conference on Computer Vision and Pattern Recognition (CVPR), pp. 4207–4215 (2016). https://doi.org/10.1109/CVPR.2016.456
21. Organization, W.H.: World Report on Hearing. World Health Organization (2021). https://www.who.int/publications/i/item/9789240020481
22. Pizzio, A.L., Stumpf, M.R., Lucinda, J.O., Quadros, R.M.d., Crasborn, O.: Signbank da libras. Fórum Linguístico **17**(4), 5475–5487 (2020). https://doi.org/10.5007/1984-8412.2020.e77342
23. Quadros, R.M., Leite, T.d.A., Lohn, Tasca, J., SCHMITT, Deonísio: Brazilian sign language documentation (2020). https://corpuslibras.ufsc.br/
24. Rezende, T.M., Almeida, S.G.M., Guimarães, F.G.: Development and validation of a brazilian sign language database for human gesture recognition. Neural Comput. Appl. **33**(16), 10449–10467 (2021). https://doi.org/10.1007/s00521-021-05802-4
25. Rodrigues, A.J.: V-LIBRASIL:Uma base de dados com sinais na LÃngua Brasileira de Sinais (Libras). Master's thesis, UFPE (2021). https://libras.cin.ufpe.br/
26. Sandler, W., Lillo-Martin, D.: Sign language and linguistic universals. Cambridge University Press, Cambridge, England (2012)
27. Shi, B., Rio, A.M.D., Keane, J., Brentari, D., Shakhnarovich, G., Livescu, K.: Fingerspelling recognition in the wild with iterative visual attention. In: Proceedings of the IEEE/CVF International Conference on Computer Vision, pp. 5400–5409 (2019)
28. Slimane, F., Bouguessa, M.: Context matters: self-attention for sign language recognition. In: 2020 25th International Conference on Pattern Recognition (ICPR), pp. 7884–7891. IEEE Computer Society, Los Alamitos (2021). https://doi.org/10.1109/ICPR48806.2021.9412916, https://doi.ieeecomputersociety.org/10.1109/ICPR48806.2021.9412916
29. Tong, Z., Song, Y., Wang, J., Wang, L.: VideoMAE: masked autoencoders are data-efficient learners for self-supervised video pre-training. Adv. Neural Inf. Process. Syst. (2022)

30. Wan, J., Li, S.Z., Zhao, Y., Zhou, S., Guyon, I., Escalera, S.: Chalearn looking at people rgb-d isolated and continuous datasets for gesture recognition. In: 2016 IEEE Conference on Computer Vision and Pattern Recognition Workshops (CVPRW), pp. 761–769 (2016). https://doi.org/10.1109/CVPRW.2016.100
31. Yin, K., Read, J.: Better sign language translation with STMC-transformer. arXiv preprint arXiv:2004.00588 (2020)
32. Zhang, H.: mixup: beyond empirical risk minimization. arXiv preprint arXiv:1710.09412 (2017)

Mapping the Landscape of Robotics for Autism Spectrum Disorder: A Scoping Review of Technologies, Applications, and Future Directions

Luiziane Paulino dos Santos and Raul Benites Paradeda[(✉)]

Robotic Learning Laboratory Computer Science Department,
State University of Rio Grande do Norte (UERN), Natal, RN, Brazil
luizianepaulino@alu.uern.br,
raulparadeda@uern.br
https://www.uern.br/campus/servico.asp?item=natal

Abstract. This scoping review explores the use of robotic technologies as intervention tools for children with Autism Spectrum Disorder (ASD), an area of growing interdisciplinary interest. Following the PRISMA-ScR guidelines, we conducted a comprehensive search in the Scopus, IEEE Xplore, and ACM Digital Library databases for studies published between 2018 and 2025. From an initial set of 1167 publications, 27 articles met the inclusion criteria and were analyzed in detail. The results demonstrate a diverse range of robotic applications, with the NAO robot featured in 13 out of the 27 selected studies. Robotics interventions were primarily implemented in assistive therapy, social skills training, educational settings, and joint attention initiatives, predominantly targeting children aged 5 to 10 years. The volume of relevant publications peaked in 2020 and declined in subsequent years, highlighting both increased early momentum and the current need for renewed research efforts in this domain. Overall, the review identifies critical research gaps, particularly in terms of personalized and interdisciplinary intervention approaches. While robotic technologies show considerable promise in supporting autistic children, further high-quality studies are required to assess their long-term effectiveness and to inform the development of individualized, evidence-based practices.

Keywords: Autism Spectrum Disorder · Assistive Robots ·
Technological Intervention

1 Introduction

Autism Spectrum Disorder (ASD), classified as a neurodevelopmental disorder in ICD-11, affects social skills, communication, and is marked by restricted and repetitive behaviors [14]. This classification enables more personalized diagnoses and interventions, highlighting a growing need for the inclusion of individuals with autism in all social spheres, as guaranteed by law [27,28]. However,

R. de Freitas and D. Furtado (Eds.): BRACIS 2025, LNAI 16181, pp. 291–305, 2026.
https://doi.org/10.1007/978-3-032-15990-8_20

many settings still lack specialized professionals and appropriate methodologies to effectively address their unique communication and interaction needs.

Emerging research demonstrates the remarkable potential of robotics as a transformative tool in autism interventions [32]. Social robots offer a unique advantage by providing a consistent, predictable, and non-judgmental interaction platform that can be precisely calibrated to individual needs, proving exceptionally promising in addressing the communication and social interaction challenges faced by individuals with ASD [8,12]. The adaptability of these technologies allows for personalized interactions systematically adjusted to correspond with each child's specific sensory and social processing characteristics [32].

While previous scoping reviews, such as the comprehensive work by [30] focusing primarily on robotic therapies and methodological needs, have explored robotics for ASD, our current study specifically delves into the technological landscape and diverse range of robotic applications from 2018–2025. We identify how technologies like the NAO robot are utilized in various contexts beyond just therapy, including educational settings and social skills training, providing an updated perspective on recent advancements and evolving trends.

This scoping review aims to explore the field of robotics used with autistic individuals by analyzing the technologies utilized, their application contexts and primary objectives, participant profiles, and recent research trends from 2018 to 2025. Specifically, our research seeks to address the following key questions:

1. What types of robotic technologies are currently being used in interventions for individuals with ASD?
2. In which contexts are these robotic interventions being applied, and what are their primary objectives?
3. What are the demographic characteristics of participants in these studies, particularly in terms of age ranges?
4. What trends can be identified in the research landscape from 2018 to 2025, and what do these suggest about future directions in the field?

Following the PRISMA-ScR guidelines [39], we systematically searched IEEE Xplore, Scopus, and ACM Digital Library for relevant studies published between 2018–2025. Through a structured selection process, 27 studies were identified and analyzed. We expect this review to contribute to a more comprehensive understanding of the current research landscape, offering insights for developing effective and individualized interventions, potentially transforming support strategies for children with ASD.

2   Methodology

This study adopted the scoping review methodology to systematically map the existing literature on the use of robots in interventions for people with Autism Spectrum Disorder. The methodological protocol followed the PRISMA-ScR guidelines proposed by [39], which establishes a set of essential items for reporting scoping reviews.

To structure the research question and define eligibility criteria, we used the PCC (Population, Concept, and Context) framework as recommended by the Joanna Briggs Institute [25]. This approach was operationalized with 'People diagnosed with Autism Spectrum Disorder' as the Population, 'Use of robots with autistic people' as the Concept, and 'Therapeutic, educational, and other environments' as the Context.

Therefore, to ensure methodological transparency, facilitate replicability, and guarantee the methodological quality of this review, the process was systematically organized into three well-defined and structured stages. These included a **Search strategy** (describing the selected databases and keywords), a **Selection process** (detailing the steps to filter and select relevant articles following the PRISMA-ScR protocol, encompassing identification, screening, eligibility, and inclusion), and **Data analysis** (explaining how data were extracted, organized, and categorized according to PCC elements).

2.1   Search Strategy

The search strategy was developed from the PCC elements, with the identification of descriptors and relevant keywords for each component. Searches were conducted in three electronic databases (IEEE Xplore, Scopus, and ACM Digital Library) between March 10 to March 24, 2025, selected for their relevance in articles across different research areas, generating a considerable volume of articles for selection.

Considering all these phases and their concepts, the tag for searches was selected, which in this case was used only one in the three databases:

"Autism Spectrum Disorder" AND "Robotics"

2.2   Selection Process

The selection of studies followed a standardized process in several phases, as recommended by PRISMA-ScR, which is classified into: identification, screening, eligibility, and included. Identification occurs through searches without criteria, screening occurs through searches according to inclusion and exclusion criteria based on the context of the searches, eligibility is the selection of these studies according to their requirements, and included are the articles selected to be read and worked on in the review project.

After selecting the tag, article searches were initiated based on the stages: identification, screening, eligibility, and included.

Identification Stage: Searches were conducted without any inclusion or exclusion filter-criteria, following this sequence: IEEE Xplore, Scopus, and ACM. Upon performing the first search, articles from different years and contexts were found, resulting in a total of 1167 articles.

IEEE Xplore (n = 172), Scopus (n = 607), ACM (n = 388)

Screening Stage: In this stage, the inclusion and exclusion criteria described in Table 1 were sequentially applied to refine the initial set of retrieved articles.

Table 1. Inclusion and exclusion criteria.

Criteria	
Inclusion	Exclusion
Articles published between 2018 and 2025	Review works, errata, and abstracts
Open access articles	Articles without direct relation to the use of robotics in the context of ASD
Articles published in English	Articles in languages other than English

Table 2 provides a stepwise overview of the screening process and the number of articles retained or excluded at each stage across all databases. The first row presents the initial corpus of studies retrieved from IEEE Xplore, Scopus, and ACM before any screening. In the following stages, inclusion and exclusion criteria were systematically applied.

The process started by restricting articles published between 2018 and 2025, focusing on recent advancements in robotics as applied to ASD. In the subsequent step, a language filter was considered to include only articles written in English, aiming to maintain consistency in terminology. However, since the searches were conducted exclusively using English terms, all retrieved works were already published in English; therefore, no articles were excluded at this stage. The next filter selected open access articles, ensuring that full texts were accessible for in-depth review and quality assessment. Lastly, reviews, errata, and abstracts were removed, narrowing the analysis to original research presenting empirical data or technological innovation.

For each criterion, the number of articles retained after filtering is reported, while the excluded rows indicate how many records were eliminated at each step. This systematic and transparent approach demonstrates the progressive refinement of the dataset and helps clarify the rationale for each selection criterion. The final row shows the total studies remaining after all filters, which form the basis for the subsequent eligibility assessment. This stepwise and meticulous process strengthens the methodological rigor and reproducibility of the review, ensuring that only relevant, accessible, and high-quality primary research articles are considered for further analysis.

It is noteworthy that, at the English language filter step, no articles were excluded, since all search queries utilized English keywords and returned only articles published in English.

After these steps, a total of 176 articles remained for the final eligibility assessment. This step-by-step screening ensured methodological rigor and transparency in the selection process.

Table 2. Flow of articles through screening filters by database.

Filter	IEEE Xplore	Scopus	ACM	Total
Initial search	172	607	388	1,167
1. Date (2018–2025)	116	388	319	823
Excluded	56	219	69	344
2. English language	116	372	317	823
Excluded	0	0	0	0
3. Open access only	14	150	64	228
Excluded	102	238	255	595
4. Remove reviews/errata/abstracts	11	119	46	176
Excluded	3	31	18	52

Eligibility Stage: During the eligibility stage, a detailed textual analysis was conducted by reading the titles and abstracts of the 176 articles that passed the previous screening. The aim was to ensure that each study aligned with the requirements established by the PCC framework and specifically addressed the use of robots in the context of ASD. At this stage, the exclusion criterion was applied to remove works that did not explicitly refer to the use of robots with autistic individuals. As a result, 149 articles were excluded:

IEEE Xplore (n=3), Scopus (n=101), ACM (n=45)

After this eligibility assessment, 27 articles remained for full-text reading and further analysis in the review:

IEEE Xplore (n=8), Scopus (n=18), ACM (n=1)

Included Stage: In the included stage, the final set of 27 articles (IEEE Xplore: 8, Scopus: 18, ACM: 1) was confirmed as the definitive corpus of this review. These selected studies form the evidence base for subsequent in-depth analysis and synthesis, marking the transition from the study selection process to data extraction and critical appraisal.

The overall flow of records through the identification, screening, eligibility, and inclusion stages of the review is depicted in the PRISMA flow diagram (Fig. 1). This diagram provides a transparent and visual summary of the number of studies assessed and excluded at each phase, in alignment with the method-ological description presented in this section.

2.3   Data Analysis

Data analysis began with the in-depth review of the studies selected during the eligibility phase. For each article, key information was compiled into a struc-tured Table (see Table 3), created specifically to support comparative analysis and synthesis. This process not only enhanced the visualization of study charac-teristics, but also established a clear metric base for interpreting and discussing the findings of this review.

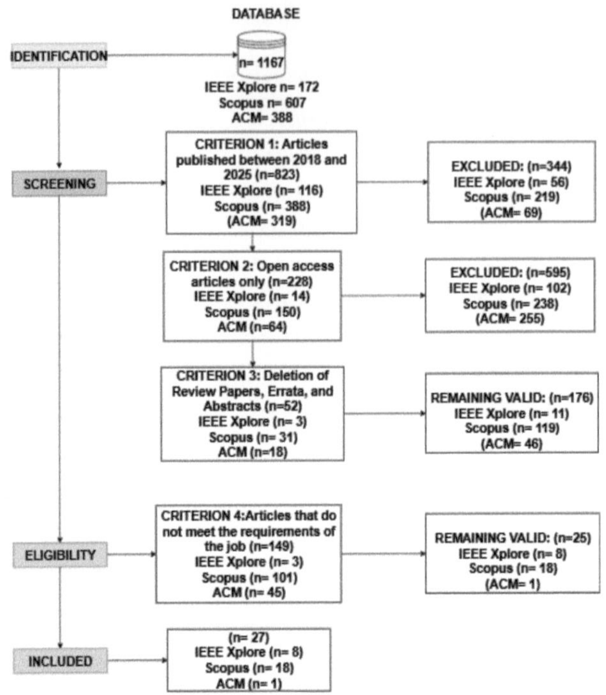

Fig. 1. PRISMA based on search strategies.

A standardized extraction form guided the collection of data, encompassing the PCC framework elements as well as pertinent methodological details and study results. All extracted information was consolidated into a single spreadsheet, ensuring accuracy and consistency across the dataset. Beyond the PCC elements, additional details were recorded, including author, year of publication, technology utilized, application context, target age group, and the source database for each article.

Integrating the PRISMA-ScR protocol with the PCC framework afforded a solid methodological foundation, enabling a comprehensive mapping of the literature on robots and ASD. This approach clarified existing evidence, highlighted emerging trends, and helped identify significant knowledge gaps in the field.

3   Results

Table 3 summarizes the main characteristics of 27 rigorously selected articles, offering an overview of current research in the field.

To systematically address the research questions, this chapter analyzes four core dimensions: study characteristics, types of robots, application contexts, and participant profiles. These dimensions directly reflect the review objectives and research questions.

The analysis combines quantitative mapping and qualitative appraisal of strategies, outcomes, and nuances in robotic interventions for neurodivergent children.

Table 3. Summary of studies on robotic interventions for ASD (2018-2025)

Author	Year	Technology Used	Application Context	Age Years (Target)	Database
Hoang-Long Cao et al. [9]	2022	A-Lab Android ST	Job interview	13 and 35	Scopus
Silva, B. & Santos, L [33]	2023	NAO robot	Education	3 to 6	Scopus
Santos, L. & Geminiani [31]	2021	MARIA T21	Assistive therapies	4 to 9	Scopus
Ali et al. [2]	2020	Prototype (not specified)	Education	5–6	Scopus
Hassan et al. [13]	2021	Zeno R50 (zeca)	Social skills	8 and 9	Scopus
Arshad et al. [5]	2024	NAO robot	Social skills	9 and 12	Scopus
Ali et al. [1]	2020	PvBOT	Education	10–13	IEEE Xplore
Mehmood et al. [21]	2024	GoBot	Physical activities	2–5; 5–10	ACM Digital Library
Peribaez et al. [24]	2022	NAO robot	Assistive therapies	2–7	Scopus
Lorenzo-Lled et al. [20]	2022	CommU	Social skills	22	Scopus
Alnafjan, A. et al. [3]	2020	NAO robot	Assistive therapies	3–10	IEEE Xplore
Tamaral, C. et al. [38]	2025	NAO robot	Assistive therapies	3–6.5	IEEE Xplore
Mutawa, AM et al. [22]	2021	NAO robot	Joint attention	3.5–10.5	IEEE Xplore
Panceri, JAC et al. [23]	2020	NAO robot	Assistive therapies	4–10	IEEE Xplore
Silva et al. [35]	2023	CASTOR	Assistive therapies	5–10	Scopus
Baraka et al. [6]	2021	NAO robot	Social skills	5 and 10	IEEE Xplore
Kumazaki, H. et al. [16]	2025	NAO robot	Social skills	5 and 9	Scopus
Arent, K. et al. [4]	2022	PLEO rb	Education	5	Scopus
Corrales Castao, L. & Rodrguez Torres, J [11]	2020	CASTOR	Social skills	5–10	Scopus
Pinto-Bernal, MJ et al. [26]	2021	Kaspar	Education	5–11	Scopus
Taheri, A. et al. [37]	2018	CommU	Social skills	5–6	Scopus
Yoshida, A et al. [40]	2022	NAO robot	Social skills	5.5 and 6.5	Scopus
Kumazaki, H et al. [17]	2019	NAO robot	Education	6	Scopus
Kostrubiec, V. & Kruck, J [15]	2025	TEA-2	Assistive therapies	6	Scopus
Lakatos, G. et al. [18]	2023	Ozobot	Education	8–12	Scopus
Casas-Bocanegra, D et al. [10]	2024	NAO robot	Assistive therapies	G1: 7–11; G2: 2–6	IEEE Xplore
Susan Liu, A., A. Helmi, N. T. Fitter [19]	2020	NAO robot	Social skills	G1: 3–4; G2: 2–3	IEEE Xplore

3.1 Characteristics of the Included Studies

A temporal analysis shows that publications in this field peaked in 2020 (n=6), followed by a decline to 5 in 2021 and 2022, and an average of 3 per year from 2023 to 2025. Despite growing interest, the overall number of studies on robotics for autistic children remains relatively low (see Fig. 2a

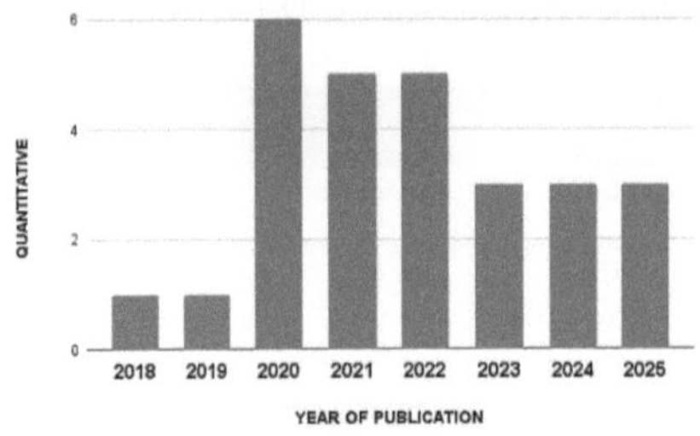

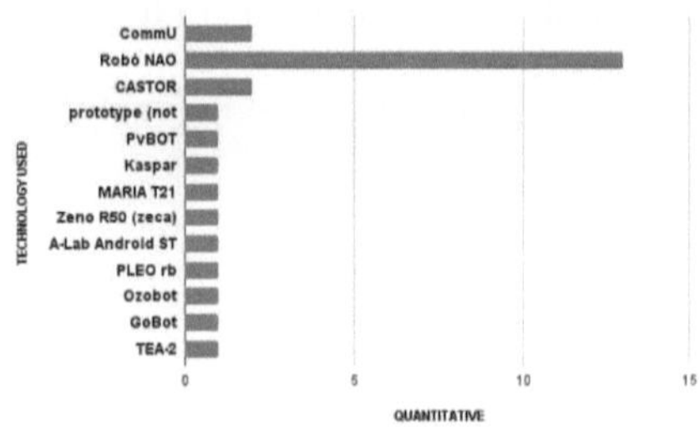

(a) Number of publications per year included in the review.

(b) Distribution of robots and technological platforms among the included studies.

Fig. 2. Overview of research output and technological platforms.

3.2   Types of Robots Used

A variety of robots were used: NAO was most prevalent (48.15%, n=13), followed by CASTOR and CommU (each 7.41%, n=2), with the remaining 37.04% (n=10) comprising A-Lab Android ST, GoBot, Kaspar, MARIA T21, Ozobot, PLEO rb, an unspecified prototype, PvBOT, TEA-2, and Zeno R50. Figure 2b

NAOs predominance is largely due to its commercial availability and capabilities, making it more accessible than lab-developed models. NAO, is notable for its 25 degrees of freedom in its body, allowing for a wide range of movements. In addition, it is equipped with several sensors, such as touch sensors, microphones, two cameras, 16 LEDs in the eyes and two speakers, which contribute significantly to the effectiveness of therapeutic sessions, allowing for rich and varied interactions, from imitation to emotion recognition.

There is no evidence supporting the superiority of humanoid over non-humanoid robots; effectiveness seems more related to interaction features and programming than physical form.

Design remains crucial for autism interventions: features like color appeal more to children with higher support needs, while movement attracts others [1]. Speech-based stimuli may be especially effective in capturing attention [21]. These results highlight the complexity of robotic interaction and reinforce the need for personalization.

Figure 3 shows how the use of technology has evolved since 2018. NAOs consistent presence confirms its dominance, while the growing variety of platforms since 2020 reflects increasing efforts toward personalized solutions. Shows how the use of technology has evolved since

3.3   Application Contexts

Analysis of the application contexts revealed that therapeutic environments for social skills development were the most prominent (n=9), followed by assistive therapies (n=8) and educational environments (n=7). Physical activities,

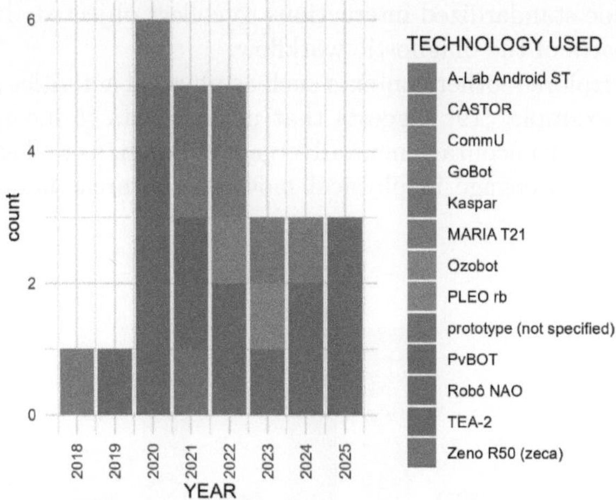

Fig. 3. Evolution of robotic technologies used in the studies by publication year.

job interviews, and laboratory-based joint attention environments were less frequently explored (n=1 each). These findings are summarized in Fig. 4.

Beyond simply identifying these application contexts, a deeper analysis of the studies reveals distinct primary purposes for the robotic interventions. Therapeutic settings stand out not only because they address one of the main challenges for individuals with ASDsocial skill developmentbut specifically for their aim in the development of tailored therapeutic strategies. These interventions often target the improvement of specific social skills, such as emotion recognition (where robots model and elicit emotional responses), joint attention training (by guiding participants' focus), and sensory processing (through controlled stimulation). ASD often impairs direct and clear interaction, making verbal communication impossible for some individuals on the spectrum, and robots, with their predictability and consistency, have been found to facilitate engagement in these therapeutic contexts.

In educational settings, unique challenges emerge, particularly around communication and learning. As noted by [34], educators frequently report both difficulty in understanding and in being understood by students with ASD, demanding specific adaptations in language and teaching strategies. Within these contexts, robots serve the purpose of teaching academic and cognitive skills, including programming logic and mathematical concepts, adapted to the unique learning styles of autistic learners. When not adequately addressed, these barriers can hinder cognitive and social development, as well as limit participation in classroom activities.

Furthermore, some studies also explore robots with the purpose of supporting the diagnostic process for ASD. Given that diagnosis relies heavily on behavioral observations, these works investigate how robots can facilitate automated assessments or provide standardized interactions to collect objective data, potentially streamlining parts of the diagnostic workflow.

While less explored, other contexts such as physical activities hold significant potential. For example, [19] suggests that using robots to incorporate popular children's games can encourage neurodivergent children, as well as other children with disabilities, to engage in physical movementan area that remains under-investigated.

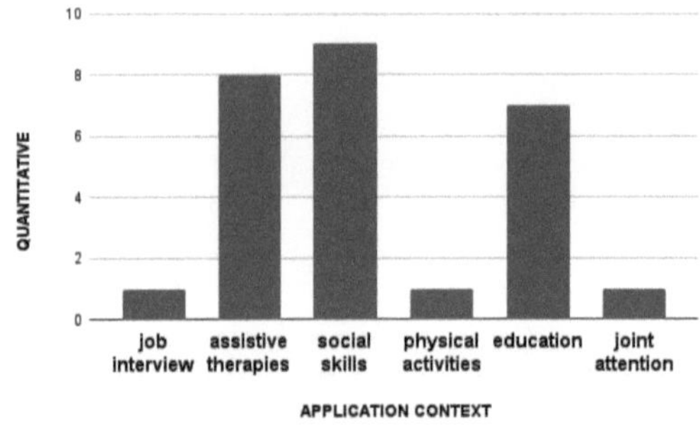

Fig. 4. Distribution of application contexts among the selected studies.

Figure 5 shows the relationship between robot types and application contexts. Notably, NAO is utilized across almost all contexts, except for physical activities and job interviews, where A-Lab Android ST and GoBot were respectively employed. This illustrates both the versatility of the NAO robot and a trend toward diversifying technologies to meet the specific needs of individuals with ASD.

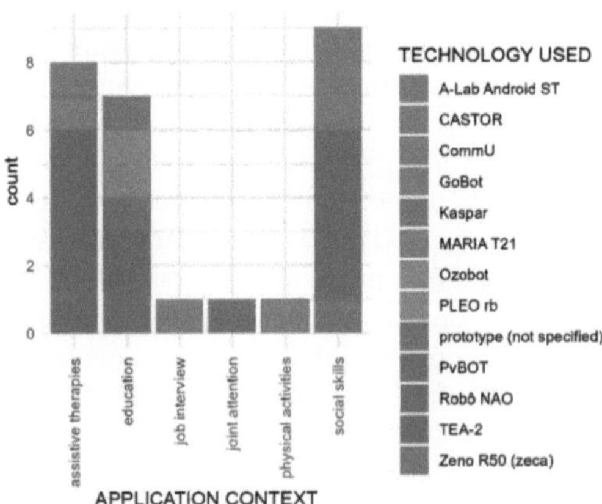

Fig. 5. Distribution of robotic technologies across different application contexts.

3.4   Participant Profile

The participant profile analysis emphasized age distribution, revealing a predominant focus on children aged 5 to 10 years. Although rarely justified by the authors, this trend aligns with literature suggesting the 310-year-old range as a critical window for effective intervention [7]. Some studies, however, adopted broader rangesextending up to 35 yearsas shown in Table 3 and Fig. 6.

A literature search exploring this age focus identified the Early Start Denver Model [29], which emphasizes the importance of early interventions for children with ASD. Complementary findings by [36] note that critical periods of brain development within these early years maximize the effects of both natural and environmental stimulation, thereby increasing the potential impact of targeted interventions. Although the focus on early childhood is supported by scientific evidence, it is essential to recognize the uniqueness of each child with ASD and the need for individualized approaches.

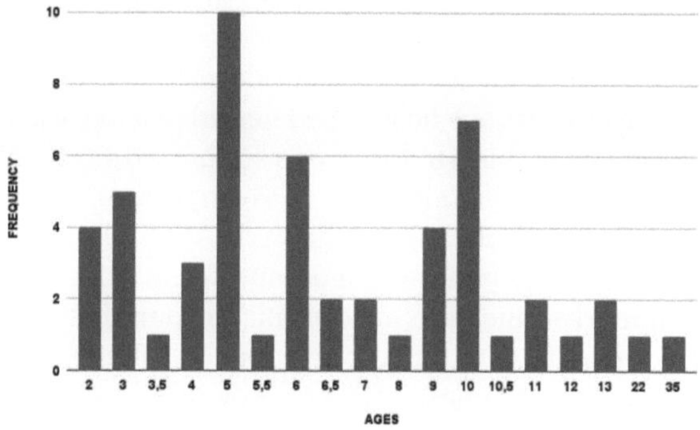

Fig. 6. Age distribution of study participants.

4   Discussion and Conclusions

This scoping review mapped and analyzed the landscape of robotic technologies applied to ASD interventions, responding directly to the research questions posed regarding platforms, contexts, participant profiles, and recent research trends. The findings highlight both significant advances and persistent gaps, pointing toward a dynamic but still maturing field.

With respect to the types of robotic technologies currently being used (RQ1), this review identified notable technological diversity, with the NAO robot emerging as the clear frontrunneraccounting for nearly half of all analyzed studies. The versatility and commercial accessibility of the NAO, combined with robust programming and interaction capabilities, likely explain its predominance. Nevertheless, the review also revealed a growing inclusion of alternative platforms since 2020, signaling a gradual move toward diversity and greater customization. Importantly, results suggest that the success of interventions depends less on a robots physical form and more on its capabilities for meaningful, adaptive interaction.

Concerning the application contexts and primary objectives (RQ2), three domains were most prominent: therapeutic environments designed to foster social skills, assistive interventions targeting communication and daily functioning, and educational settings aiming to facilitate inclusion and learning. Each context presented its own challengestherapeutic settings focusing on bridging social gaps; assistive contexts leveraging the predictability of robots for engagement; and educational environments navigating linguistic and methodological adaptations. Less frequently, robots were used in physical activity and vocational scenarios, highlighting nascent but important application domains. Across all contexts, the evidence points to the need for highly personalized, targeted approaches that account for the broad heterogeneity within the ASD population.

In addressing participant demographics, particularly age ranges (RQ3), the review found a clear emphasis on early childhood. Most studies involved children aged 510, consistent with evidence from neurodevelopmental literature advocating early interventions to leverage heightened neural plasticity and social learning windows. The rationale for this age focus was supported by citation of key models and neurobiological studies, although it is important to acknowledge that this approach leaves adolescents and adults with ASD relatively underexplored.

Examining trends in the research landscape from 2018 to 2025 (RQ4), the field experienced a marked increase in scientific output that reached its peak in 2020, followed by a stabilization at a lower annual volume through 2025. This trajectory suggests an initial phase of rapid growth and exploration, with continued, albeit more measured, interest in recent years. Notably, the period saw increased diversification in both the technological platforms and the contexts of application, indicating a conscious movement toward personalization and adaptability. However, the overall number of studies remains limited, highlighting a field with significant room for expansion and evolution. Looking ahead, several avenues for future research and development can be identified:

- Enhanced personalization and user-centered design of robotic technologies for ASD, tailoring interventions to individual needs and contexts;
- Expansion of research to underexplored populations (e.g., adolescents, adults) and emerging settings (e.g., physical activities, employment preparation);
- Incorporation of a broader range of platforms, moving beyond the NAO to encourage technological innovation and accessibility;
- Larger and more diverse study samples, including longitudinal research designs to assess the sustained impacts of robotic interventions.

It is essential to acknowledge the limitations of this review, which impact the interpretation of our findings. A primary concern relates to **external validity**, as the relatively small number of included articles (n=27), coupled with our search's temporal limitation (studies up to the time of analysis), reliance on specific databases, and crucial restriction to English-language and Open Access publications, means that a broader spectrum of very recent studies, those published in other languages, or those behind paywalls might not have been captured. This could potentially affect the overall representativeness of the mapped landscape and the generalizability of our findings. Regarding **construct validity**, while our PCC framework aimed for comprehensive concept capture, the diversity of terminology across studies might mean that some nuances of 'robot use' or 'autism spectrum disorder' were not fully encompassed by our keywords. Furthermore, **internal validity** challenges arise from potential publication bias, where studies with non-significant findings might be less likely to be published, and the inherent heterogeneity of methodologies across the included primary studies, which limits direct comparison and robust synthesis of outcomes. These factors underscore that while this scoping review maps the current state, it does not offer definitive conclusions on intervention effectiveness.

In conclusion, the intersection of robotics and autism intervention reflects a multidisciplinary, fast-evolving, and promising area. The evidence synthesized here demonstrates both the feasibility and the potential of robotic technologies to foster inclusive, engaging, and effective interventions for individuals with ASD. Each step forward in this field not only marks technological progress, but also represents a move toward a more inclusive and adaptive society for all forms of neurodiversity.

References

1. Ali, S., Mehmood, F., Ayaz, Y., Khan, M.J., Sadia, H., Nawaz, R.: Comparing the effectiveness of different reinforcement stimuli in robotic therapy for children with asd. IEEE Access **8**, 13128–13137 (2020). https://doi.org/10.1109/ACCESS.2020.2965204
2. Ali, S., et al.: A preliminary study on effectiveness of a standardized multi-robot therapy for improvement in collaborative multi-human interaction of children with asd. IEEE Access **8**, 109466–109474 (2020)
3. Alnafjan, A., Alghamdi, M., Alhakbani, N., Al-Ohali, Y.: Improving imitation skills in children with autism spectrum disorder using the nao robot and a human action recognition. Diagnostics **15**(1), 60 (2025)
4. Arent, K., et al.: The use of social robots in the diagnosis of autism in preschool children. Appl. Sci. **12**(17), 8399 (2022)
5. Arshad, N.I., Hashim, A.S., Mohd Ariffin, M., Mohd Aszemi, N.A., Low, H.M., Norman, A.: Robots as assistive technology tools to enhance cognitive abilities and foster valuable learning experiences among young children with autism spectrum disorder. IEEE Access **8**, 116279–116291 (2020)
6. Baraka, K., Couto, M., Melo, F.S., Paiva, A., Veloso, M.: "sequencing matters": Investigating suitable action sequences in robot-assisted autism therapy. Front. Robot. AI **9** (2022)
7. Baron-Cohen, S., Leslie, A.M., Frith, U.: Does the autistic child have a "theory of mind"? Cognition **21**(1), 37–46 (1985)
8. Cabibihan, J.J., Javed, H., Ang, M., Aljunied, S.M.: Why robots? a survey on the roles and benefits of social robots in the therapy of children with autism. Int. J. Soc. Robot. **5**, 593–618 (2013)

9. Cao, H.L., Simut, R.E., Desmet, N., De Beir, A., Van De Perre, G., Vanderborght, B., Vanderfaeillie, J.: Robot-assisted joint attention: a comparative study between children with autism spectrum disorder and typically developing children in interaction with nao. IEEE Access **8**, 223325–223334 (2020)
10. Casas-Bocanegra, D., et al.: An open-source social robot based on compliant soft robotics for therapy with children with ASD. Actuators **9**(3), 91 (2020)
11. Corrales Castaño, L., RodrÃguez Torres, J.: Social robotics as an educational tool for students with asd: Case study. VISUAL REVIEW. International Visual Culture Review / Revista Internacional de Cultura Visual **12**(5), 1–15 (2022)
12. Feil-Seifer, D., MatariÄ, M.J.: Towards socially assistive robotics for augmenting interventions for children with autism spectrum disorders. Presented at the (2009)
13. Hassan, I., Nahid, N., Islam, M., Hossain, S., Schuller, B., Ahad, M.A.R.: Automated autism assessment with multimodal data and ensemble learning: a scalable and consistent robot-enhanced therapy framework. IEEE Trans. Neural Syst. Rehabil. Eng. **33**, 1191–1201 (2025)
14. INSTITUTO INCLUSÃO BRASIL: Cid-11 mudanÃno diagnÃstico do transtorno do espectro autista (2022), disponÃvel em: https://institutoinclusaobrasil.com.br/cid-11-mudancas-no-diagnostico-do-transtorno-do-especto-autista/
15. Kostrubiec, V., Kruck, J.: Collaborative research project: developing and testing a robot-assisted intervention for children with autism. Front. Robot. AI **7** (2020)
16. Kumazaki, H., et al.: Differences in the optimal motion of android robots for the ease of communications among individuals with autism spectrum disorders. Front. Psych. **13** (2022)
17. Kumazaki, H., et al.: The impact of robotic intervention on joint attention in children with autism spectrum disorders. Molecular Autism **9**(1), 46 (2018)
18. Lakatos, G., Wood, L.J., Syrdal, D.S., Robins, B., Zaraki, A., Dautenhahn, K.: Robot-mediated intervention can assist children with autism to develop visual perspective taking skills. Paladyn, J. Behav. Robot. **12**(1), 87–101 (2021)
19. Liu, S., Helmi, A., Fitter, N.T.: In: Pilot observations of an autonomous red light, green light robot for interactions with children with disabilities. Association for Computing Machinery, New York, NY, USA (2024)
20. Lorenzo LledÃ, G., Lorenzo-LledÃ, A., RodrÃguez-Quevedo, A.: AnÃlisis mediante inteligencia artificial de las emociones del alumnado autista en la interacciÃn social con el robot nao. Revista de EducaciÃn a Distancia (RED) **24**(78) (2024)
21. Mehmood, F., et al.: Attentional behavior of children with ASD in response to robotic agents. IEEE Access **9**, 31946–31955 (2021). https://doi.org/10.1109/ACCESS.2021.3056211
22. Mutawa, A.M., Al Mudhahkah, H.M., Al-Huwais, A., Al-Khaldi, N., Al-Otaibi, R., Al-Ansari, A.: Augmenting mobile app with nao robot for autism education. Machines **11**(8), 833 (2023)
23. Panceri, J.A.C., Freitas, Ã., de Souza, J.C., da Luz Schreider, S., Caldeira, Ã., Bastos, T.F.: A new socially assistive robot with integrated serious games for therapies with children with autism spectrum disorder and down syndrome: a pilot study. Sensors **21**(24), 8414 (2021)
24. PeribaÃez, E., et al.: An experimental methodology for introducing educational robotics and storytelling in therapeutical activities for children with neurodevelopmental disorders. Machines **11**(6), 629 (2023)
25. Peters, M.D.J., Godfrey, C., McInerney, P., Munn, Z., Tricco, A.C., Khalil, H.: Chapter 11: Scoping reviews (2020 version). Presented at the (2020)
26. Pinto-Bernal, M.J., et al.: Do different robot appearances change emotion recognition in children with ASD? Front. Neurorobot. **17** (2023)

27. Presidency of the Republic: Lei no. 12,764/2012 (lei berenice piana), available at: http://www.planalto.gov.br/ccivil_03/_ato2011-2014/2012/lei/l12764.htm
28. Presidency of the Republic: Lei no. 13,146, de 6 de julho de 2015, available at: http://www.planalto.gov.br/ccivil_03/_ato2015-2018/2015/lei/l13146.htm
29. Rogers, S.: Early start denver model. In: Comprehensive Models of Autism Spectrum Disorder Treatment: Points of Divergence and Convergence, pp. 45–62. Springer (2016)
30. Santos, L., et al.: Applications of robotics for autism spectrum disorder: a scoping review. Rev. J. Autism Develop. Disorders 1–22 (2023)
31. Santos, L., Geminiani, A., Schydlo, P., Olivieri, I., Santos-Victor, J., Pedrocchi, A.: Design of a robotic coach for motor, social and cognitive skills training toward applications with ASD children. IEEE Trans. Neural Syst. Rehabil. Eng. **29**, 1223–1232 (2021)
32. Scassellati, B.: How social robots will help us to diagnose, treat, and understand autism. Disabil. Rehabil. **29**(10), 779–792 (2007)
33. Silva, B., et al.: Attention analysis in robotic-assistive therapy for children with autism. IEEE Trans. Neural Syst. Rehabil. Eng. **32**, 2220–2229 (2024)
34. Silva, L.H.D.S.d.: Inclusion and development at school: an experience report on the autism project. Federal University of Tocantins (2023). Master's thesis
35. Silva, V., Soares, F., Esteves, J.S., Santos, C.P., Pereira, A.P.: Fostering emotion recognition in children with autism spectrum disorder. Multimodal Technol. Interact. **5**(10), 57 (2021)
36. Stiles, J.: The fundamentals of brain development: Integrating nature and nurture. Harvard University Press (2008)
37. Taheri, A., Meghdari, A., Alemi, M., Pouretemad, H.R.: Teaching music to children with autism: A social robotics challenge. Presented at the (2019)
38. Tamaral, C., Hernandez, L., Baltasar, C., Martin, J.S.: Design techniques for the optimal creation of a robot for interaction with children with autism spectrum disorder. Machines **13**(1), 67 (2025)
39. Tricco, A.C., et al.: Prisma extension for scoping reviews (prisma-scr): Checklist and explanation. Ann. Intern. Med. **169**(7), 467–473 (2018)
40. Yoshida, A., Kumazaki, H., Muramatsu, T., Yoshikawa, Y., Ishiguro, H., Mimura, M.: Intervention with a humanoid robot avatar for individuals with social anxiety disorders comorbid with autism spectrum disorders. Asian J. Psychiatr. **78**, 103315 (2022)

Optimizing Model Merging Configurations for Brazilian Portuguese Sentiment and Hate Speech Classification with TIES-Merging and SaDE

Viviane Galvão[(✉)] [iD] and Heder Bernardino[iD]

Universidade Federal de Juiz de Fora, Juiz de Fora, MG, Brazil
`viviane.galvao@estudante.ufjf.br`, `heder.bernardino@ufjf.br`

Abstract. The detection of emotions and opinions from textual data plays a critical role in diverse social applications, including political analysis, content moderation, online safety assurance, and the monitoring of emotional well-being in healthcare contexts. Large Language Models (LLMs) have demonstrated remarkable capabilities across diverse natural language processing (NLP) tasks, such as sentiment and hate speech detection. However, their effectiveness in specialized domains remains a challenge, often requiring adaptation techniques such as fine-tuning to optimize performance. For Brazilian Portuguese, sentiment and hate speech classification are tasks less explored compared to English, emphasizing the need for efficient adaptation strategies. Model merging methods have emerged as promising alternatives to obtain new language models without incurring the high computational costs or dataset requirements associated with fine-tuning techniques. This study investigates the integration of Self-adaptive Differential Evolution (SaDE) with the TIES-Merging method to optimize merging configurations of BERTimbau and its fine-tuned versions into a single model for Brazilian Portuguese sentiment and hate speech classification. Experimental results show that applying TIES-Merging, supported by evolutionary methods, produces models that outperform the existing fine-tuned model in the Brazilian Portuguese sentiment classification, while maintaining competitive performance in hate speech detection. In the comparison of evolutionary strategies, SaDE achieved results comparable to CMA-ES, a method commonly used in the literature, highlighting opportunities for further investigation into the tuning of the learning period parameter.

Keywords: LLM · Transformer · Differential Evolution · Merging Models · TIES-Merging · BERT · Sentiment Analysis

1 Introduction

Language models have transformed the way natural language processing (NLP) problems are addressed [38]. Since the publication of transformer architecture and attention mechanism [29], new language models with high text processing capabilities have been developed. While the transformer architecture enables parallel text processing with the attention mechanism, something not found in RNN [16] and LSTM [23] architectures, the memory required to store model parameters becomes a challenge.

As a result, training models or even fine-tuning their parameters becomes a challenge, as it requires not only storing the model parameters but also its optimizer states, gradients, and activation values for each parameter. Some studies have explored alternatives to make the training of these models more feasible. For example, the work in [6] proposes loading model parameters in 4-bit NormalFloat (NF4) format combined with the LoRA [9] method, allowing fine-tuning of large language models on a single GPU. Additionally, model and data parallelization techniques for GPUs have been proposed in [22] to facilitate processing under limited memory constraints.

As shown in [36], model merging methods have been explored as an alternative for obtaining new large language models without the same computational cost required for full training or fine-tuning, as well as the need for additional datasets. Model merging is the process of combining the parameters of multiple models into a single one that integrate expertise from different sources, allowing the resulting model to perform better across tasks or domains. Several merging methods have been proposed, including those designed for models with identical architectures and others capable of handling architectural differences. In this work, the focus are methods designed for identical architectures, such as TIES-Merging [35]. TIES-Merging is used to combine models with task-specific knowledge while mitigate interference caused by redundant parameter values across models.

Some model merging approaches assume access to a validation set [10,34,35], which enables the search for optimal merging coefficients. In this context, studies such as [1] and [15] employ evolutionary algorithms to optimize these coefficients, leading to an expanded search space and increasing the diversity of potential model combinations. Similarly, this work assumes access to a validation set but focuses on the application of model merging applied to Brazilian Portuguese.

In the context of Brazilian Portuguese, the use of language specific models have significantly advanced the development of high-quality language models, delivering better performance than the multilingual models alternatives for this language [3,17,26]. However, training and fine-tuning these models remain challenging due to limited access to hardware resources and the high cost associated with manual dataset labeling and preparation [11,17].

In the face of these challenges, this work investigates the potential of model merging methods in the context of Brazilian models. In particular, we propose the use of the TIES-Merging [35] method to combine BERTimbau [26] model and its fine tuned variants for sentiment and hate speech classification tasks. Moreover, to optimize the merging configuration for these tasks, it is used the evolutionary method SaDE [18], an adaptive version of Differential Evolution [27] that adjusts the mutation strategy and crossover rate during the optimization process.

The objectives are: (1) investigate if the abilities of specialized models can help to increase the performance on similar tasks; (2) integrate various abilities in a single multi-task model; (3) compare the performance of SaDE with CMA-ES [14] to examine the effectiveness and robustness of different optimization strategies in the model merging context.

2   BERT

Language models have become fundamental components in Natural Language Processing (NLP) field, enabling a wide range of solutions for tasks such as text classification, machine translation, sentiment analysis, question answering, information retrieval, and named entity recognition [38].

The development of transformer-based models [30] and the attention mechanism enabled the parallel processing, different from recurrent architectures [16, 23], and better handling of long sequences and contextual information. Some relevant transformers-based models are BERT [7], which introduced bidirectional training; GPT family models [2,19,20], which used causal language modeling; and T5 [21], which process all NLP tasks as a text-to-text problem.

BERT (Bidirectional Encoder Representations from Transformers) is a encoder based model proposed in [7] to provide text vector representations. BERT captures the context in a bidirectional way, using masked language approach in the pre-training phase, improving the text representations.

In the pre-training step, BERT is trained using self-supervised learning and using two tasks to guide the training: Masked Language Model (MLM) and Next Sentence Prediction (NSP). With MLM task, some random tokens in a sentence are masked and the model have to learn how to predict those masked tokens. The idea is to force BERT to predict missing tokens based on the context, allowing a deep bidirectional learning. In NSP task the model learns how to understand sentence relationships predicting whether two sentences are sequentially related.

To solve downstream tasks, a fine tuning step is executed, where the pre-trained parameters are modified using labeled data.

There are different variations of BERT, like RoBERTa [12] and DistilBERT [24]. RoBERTa (Robust Optimized BERT Pretraining Approach) is a BERT model version with improvements like (i) training on larger datasets using larger batch sizes and sequences, (ii) training with more epochs, (iii) and removing the NSP objective from pre-training. The DistilBERT model is a small version of BERT, with almost the same performance, developed using a knowledge distillation process where a smaller student model is trained to replicate the behavior of a larger teacher model, the original BERT model.

ModernBERT [31] is the latest version of BERT that incorporates several updates from previous work on LLM. The release of ModernBERT introduces a new Pareto-efficient model, improving accuracy in text retrieval and NLU (Natural Language Understanding) tasks without compromising inference speed.

Some Portuguese trained models based on BERT are BERTimbau [26] and BERTabaporu [4]. BERTimbau is the first BERT model trained from scratch for Brazilian Portuguese, designed with a Portuguese-specific tokenizer to improve tokenization quality and trained on the parameters of multilingual BERT (mBERT [7]) and BERT-Large as initialization for pretraining its base and large models versions, respectivelly. This model outperformed mBERT in processing Brazilian Portuguese across various NLP tasks.

In [4] is proposed BERTabaporu, a language model pre-trained on Twitter[1] Brazilian Portuguese dataset. Different from BERTimbau, a model for tasks involving more formal or general Portuguese, BERTabaporu is particularly effective for social media analysis, like stance detection, mental health analysis and political alignment prediction.

3   Model Merging Methods

Several works have presented methods for model merging, which explore the possibility of creating new models by combining the parameters of pre-trained neural networks [8,28]. The advantages are its low computational cost and the fact that it does not require access to raw or new training data [36].

While [8] proposes a classification of merging methods based on model architecture, such as same architecture with identical initialization, same architecture with different initialization, and different architectures, [36] classifies methods into pre-merging and during-merging approaches.

In the pre-merging class, the aim is to facilitate model merging by performing steps such as architecture transformation and weight alignment. These methods are designed for models with the same architecture but different initializations, or for models with different architectures. The during-merging class contains methods that directly merge the parameters of well-trained models and are most effective when the models share the same architecture and initialization.

This work focuses on studying merging methods for models with the same architecture and initialization. The simplest merging method is weight averaging [28,34]. The results in [34] show that averaging the weights of multiple model checkpoints can help with model selection on the held-out validation set when fine-tuning instead of selecting a single best model or conventional ensemble of model outputs, without additional inference cost.

While weight averaging is a simple and intuitive merging method, it may fail to preserve certain features of the models being combined, such as the spatial relationships between model parameters. The SLERP (Spherical Linear Interpolation) method, based on [32] and [25], aims to address this limitation by employing geometric and rotational interpolation, which preserves spatial characteristics of both original models.

In Task Arithmetic method [10], the concept of task vectors is introduced. These task vectors represent the differences between the parameters of a base

---

[1] X.com.

model and its fine-tuned versions and allows arithmetic operations over the tasks, such as addition, negation and analogies. Adding positive task vectors to the base model can improve performance in multiple tasks or a specific task. On the other hand, adding negative task vectors can help remove undesired biases learned during pre-training. Another potential application of task vectors is task analogies, where a new model can be obtained based on the analogy relationships between known models.

The studies in [35] and [37] investigates the impact of redundant parameters, based on the fact that in the fine tuning process some language models parameters are modified without necessarily impact the learning process.

The DARE (Drop And REscale) method, proposed in [37], involves dropping and rescaling delta parameters (task vectors) from fine tuned models before the merging application. By dropping some delta parameters and rescaling the remaining ones, DARE reduces redundancy of delta parameters and improves the merging results.

Proposed in [35], the TIES-Merging method addresses the issue of parameter interference when merging task vectors [10] from different fine-tuned models. Parameter interference can degrade final model performance due to redundant values and signal conflicts. The method consists in the following steps: (i) $(1-k)$ redundant task vectors are trimmed based on their magnitudes, k is the density hyper-parameter; (ii) the sign of the most significant task vector is elected; and (iii) only tasks vectors aligned with the elected sign are merged by a scale factor λ.

4   Evolutionary Model Merging

As seen in [13], evolutionary algorithms has been used in neural networks architecture search (ENAS). The main issues and challenges of ENAS methods remains on the quality of their solutions compared to baseline methods, like random search, and the trade-off between the computational cost of training and the accuracy of the evaluation.

In the field of merge methods, the study [1] proposed the use of evolutionary algorithms to identify optimal merging configurations of available open-source models. To combine models in the parameter space, the TIES-DARE merging method with CMA-ES is used for selecting the optimal TIES-DARE hyper-parameters. The approach also introduces the idea of merge in the data flow space, combining layers from different pre-trained or fine-tuned models to create new architectures. Unlike ENAS, this method has the advantage of not requiring model training to evaluate candidates, as the models are already trained.

Evolutionary methods can effectively explore merging configurations for language models, but they require frequent evaluation of candidate solutions. In this context, the fitness function is typically defined as the merged model performance on a validation set. However, running inference on large datasets with large language models can be computationally expensive. To address this, MERGE^3 [15] proposes evaluating each candidate on a small subset of the validation set and estimating their accuracy using Item Response Theory (IRT). By modeling each model latent abilities, this approach allows for an efficient approximation of full-dataset performance, significantly reducing evaluation costs during the evolutionary search.

5   Differential Evolution

Differential Evolution (DE) is a simple and efficient stochastic population-based algorithm designed to solve problems defined in continuous domain. The search space exploration is based on weighted differences between vectors. It was initially developed in [27] and has emerged as a very competitive evolutionary algorithm for continuous optimization [5].

The DE proposal is to evolve a population, where each individual is subject to mutation, crossover, and selection. The individual x_i in the population is a candidate solution, represented by a position in the search space, $x_i = [x_{i,1}, x_{i,2}, \ldots, x_{i,n}]$, where $i \in \{1, \ldots, N\}$, N is the population size, and n is the problem dimension.

The mutation process creates perturbations given by weighted differences between two individuals in the current population. A mutated individual v_i can be generated by:

$$v_i = x_{r_1} + F(x_{r_2} - x_{r_3}). \tag{1}$$

where v_i is the mutated individual, $r_1 \neq r_2 \neq r_3 \neq i$ are indexes of individuals randomly selected in $\{1, \ldots, N\}$, F is the weighting factor that controls the level of exploration, and $i \in \{1, \ldots, n\}$.

The crossover step is responsible to increase the diversity of the mutated population. The new individuals, the trial individuals, are created such that:

$$u_i = \begin{cases} v_i & \text{if } r_j \leq \text{CR} \\ x_i & \text{if } r_j > \text{CR} \end{cases} \tag{2}$$

where u_i is a trial individual, v_i is a mutated individual, x_i is an individual of the current population, r_j is a number drawn from a uniform distribution in $(0, 1)$, CR is a parameter defined in $[0, 1]$ which controls how similar the trial individual will be to mutated one, and $i \in \{1, \ldots, n\}$.

In the selection step, the new population will be constructed for the next generation preserving the best individuals the current ones and the trial individuals by a greedy criterion given by:

$$x_i^{t+1} = \begin{cases} u_i^t & \text{if } f(u_i^t) \leq f(x_i^t) \\ x_i^t & \text{otherwise} \end{cases} \tag{3}$$

5.1   SaDE

The Self-Adaptive Differential Evolution (SaDE) method was proposed in [18]. The advantage is that in this method the mutation strategy and the corresponding control parameters are chosen based on the learning obtained from previous generations.

The SaDE method considers a set of mutation strategies that are randomly selected according to their respective success and failure rates. The higher the success rate, the more likely the strategy is to be chosen. A strategy is considered successful when the mutated individual is better than the corresponding individual in the current population. For each mutation strategy, the weighting factor F is randomly obtained from the normal distribution $\mathcal{N}(0.5, 0.3)$, empirically defined in [18]. In Table 1 is shown the mutation variants used in this work.

The crossover rate (CR) parameter is randomly obtained from the normal distribution $\mathcal{N}(CRm, 0.1)$ for each strategy and individual. The parameter CRm is the median of the CR values in the memory associated with the winning mutation strategies from recent generations. Initially, the default value for CRm is 0.5 until the number of generations does not reach the learning period.

A new parameter, the learning period LP, is introduced. This parameter is important for defining how much information from previous generations will be used to calculate the mutation strategy probabilities and the CRm parameter.

During the selection step, in addition to the conventional selection of a new population, the success and failure rates are updated for each mutation strategy and the crossover control memory. The general SaDE structure is described in Algorithm 1.

6 Approach

In this section, we detail the approach employed to get a multitask BERTimbau to classify sentiment and hate speech with no training data or compute, using merging techniques and evolutionary method. Based on the procedure in [1], it is proposed to optimize the hyper-parameters of TIES-Merging in order to obtain the best combination of BERTimbau models (Table 2) using SaDE (Algorithm 1). We chose BERTimbau as our base model due to its efficiency, allowing it to be loaded and run effectively on an environment with limited resources. The adoption of TIES-Merging was driven by its favorable outcomes reported in previous work [1].

The optimization problem solved here can be described as

$$\min_{k,\lambda \in \mathbb{R}} \; - m(h(k_i, \lambda_i), D_{val})$$
$$s.a. \; 0 \leq k_i, \lambda_i \leq 1 \;\; \forall i = 1, \ldots, n \tag{4}$$

where k_i and λ_i represents the TIES-Merging hyperparameters density and scale, respectivelly, for each model to be combined; $m(\cdot, \cdot)$ is the evaluation metric of the models, with F1-Score being chosen; $h(k_i, \lambda_i)$ is the resulting model from the combination; D_{val} is the validation dataset used for model evaluation (Table 3); and n is the number of models to be combined.

In the evolutionary optimization process, the objective function was defined as the model evaluation metric to sentiment and hate speech detection tasks.

During model merging with Mergekit [8], classification layers were excluded, as the Bertimbau model lacks such layer. However, classification layers are essential for evaluating the merged model candidates on the target tasks. To simplify

---

Algorithm 1: Self-Adaptive Differential Evolution

Data: N: population size, LP: learning period

1 Initialize the individuals population $x_1, x_2, \ldots, x_N$;
2 Let $\hat{x}$ the best individual of the population;
3 Define the set of mutation strategies $\mathcal{M}$;
4 **while** *stop criteria false* **do**
5   Update the probabilities $\mathcal{P}$ for each strategy in $\mathcal{M}$;
6   Update CRm values for each strategy in $\mathcal{M}$;
7   Update CR values for each strategy in $\mathcal{M}$ and individual in the population;
8      $F \leftarrow \mathcal{N}(0.5, 0.3)$ for each strategy in $\mathcal{M}$;
9   **for** $i = 1, \ldots, N$ **do**
10   strategy = random_normal($\mathcal{M}, \mathcal{P}$);
11         $v_i \leftarrow$ Mutation(x_i, F, strategy);
12         $u_i \leftarrow$ Crossover(v_i, x_i, CR[strategy]);
13   **end for**
14   **for** $i = 1, \ldots, N$ **do**
15   **if** $f(u_i) < f(x_i)$ **then**
16             $x_i \leftarrow u_i$;
17   Update success_rate vector;
18   Update the CR_Memory;
19   **if** $f(x_i) < f(\hat{x})$ **then**
20                 $\hat{x} \leftarrow x_i$;
21   **end if**
22   **end if**
23   **else**
24   Update fail_rate vector;
25   **end if**
26   **end for**
27 **end while**
28 **return** $\hat{x}$;

---

the process and avoid potential biases introduced by additional training or fine-tuning, we opted to reuse the classification layers from pre-trained models rather than training new ones.

When a new merged candidate model is ready for evaluation, it is paired with external classification layers, each one corresponding to a specific task. For sentiment classification, the classification layer from the Model 1 (Table 2) is utilized. Similarly, for hate speech classification, the classification layer from the Model 3 (Table 2) is employed. As Models 2 and 3 address the same task, Model 3 was adopted here for this task due to its superior performance. According to the values presented on Hugging Face, Model 2 and 3 reached accuracies 0.781 and 0.907, respectively. This procedure is presented in Fig. 1.

F1-Score is used as the evaluation metric to assess the performance of the merged models on both tasks. The final evaluation score is obtained by summing all the F1-Score results from the sentiment analysis and hate speech classification tasks.

Table 1. Mutation variants used in the SaDE adopted here.

Variation	Mutation
DE/rand/1/bin	$v_i = x_{r_1} + F(x_{r_2} - x_{r_3})$
DE/rand/2/bin	$v_i = x_{r_1} + F(x_{r_2} - x_{r_3}) + F(x_{r_4} - x_{r_5})$
DE/current-to-best/2/bin	$v_i = x_i + F(x_{best} - x_i) + F(x_{r_1} - x_{r_2}) + F(x_{r_3} - x_{r_4})$
DE/current-to-rand/1	$v_i = x_i + F(x_{r_1} - x_i) + F(x_{r_2} - x_{r_3})$

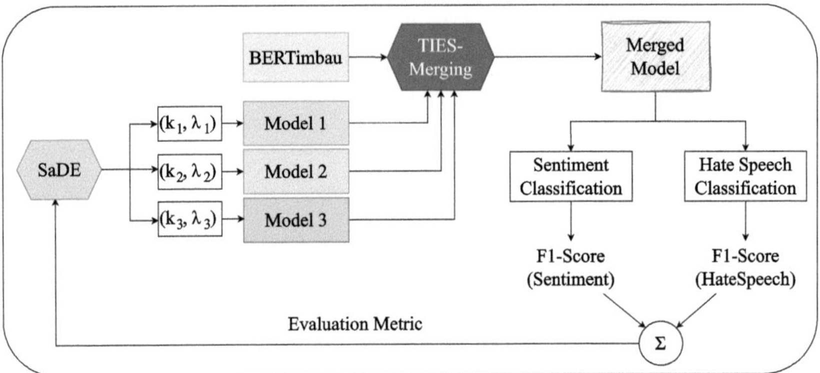

Fig. 1. A diagram illustrating the process of optimizing the model merging configurations using SaDE. The TIES-Merging hyperparameters densities (k_i) and scales (λ_i) are those from the evolutionary process provided by SaDE.

7   Experiments

To verify the potential of using the merging methods associated with Differential Evolution to create a multitask Portuguese BERTimbau model for sentiment and hate speech classification, computational experiments were carried out using the optimization problem defined in Sect. 6.

The Mergekit [8] framework was used with the following modifications: 1) merging pre-trained BERT model with its fine-tuned versions; 2) adapting the model evaluation function to support evolutionary methods, and 3) using SaDE into the framework to optimize the TIES-Merging merging configurations, as shown in Fig. 1.

For model merging, the version of TIES-Merging [35] method implemented by Mergekit was used, applied to the models listed in Table 2. During the optimization phase, evolutionary algorithms were used to determine the densities (k) and scales (λ) hyperparameters of TIES-Merging. In particular, we used the evolutionary method SaDE, implemented from scratch using the mutation variants presented in Table 1. To comparatively evaluate the results obtained by SaDE, experiments were performed with CMA-ES, which is available in the Mergekit framework.

Both evolutionary methods used a population size of 10 individuals and a maximum of 500 evaluation functions. Also, $\sigma_0 = \frac{1}{6}$ in CMA-ES and $LP = (2, 10)$ in SaDE. The number of design variables corresponds to the product of the number of models and the number of TIES-Merging coefficients, resulting in 6 design variables. We performed 20 independent runs for statistical analyzes and comparing the results. All the experiments were conducted in Google Colab environment, with a GPU NVIDIA T4 16GB.

Table 3 lists the datasets used to evaluate the merged models. The validation split was used to measure individual fitness during evolution, and the test split was used to check the final merged models performance. The validation and test splits were used to avoid data leak impact in the merge evaluation.

All datasets and models used here are available at Hugging Face[2]. Also, the source codes and supplementary resources supporting this study are publicly available[3].

Table 2. Models adopted here to merge.

Name	Model	Task of Classification
BERTimbau	neuralmind/bert-large-portuguese-cased	–
Model 1	danielribeiro/google-play-sentiment-analysis	Sentiment
Model 2	Nelci/bertimbau_hate_speech	Hate Speech
Model 3	SillyMachine/TuPyBertLargeBinaryClassifier	Hate Speech

Table 3. Datasets used in the computational experiments.

Dataset	Task	Split	Samples
maritaca-ai/sst2_pt	Sentiment Classification	Validation	872
ruanchaves/hatebr	Hate Speech Classification	Validation	655
maritaca-ai/imdb_pt	Sentiment Classification	Test	5000
Silly-Machine/TuPy-Dataset	Hate Speech Classification	Test	2000

8 Results

As described in Sect. 7, our experiments were designed to test the impact of merging models using Differential Evolution. In this section, we present the numerical results that emerged from these experiments.

Table 4 presents the models performance before the merge process, including F1-score and accuracy. These results will be as a benchmark for evaluating the improvements achieved of merging methods with SaDE.

---

[2] https://huggingface.co/.

[3] https://github.com/VivianeGalvao/mergekit.

Table 5 show the statistical results for merged models obtained with SaDE and CMA-ES in the sentiment classification tasks. For sentiment classification, the results were obtained by concatenating the Model 1 classification head to the merged models. Comparing these results with Model 1 performance (Table 4), it is possible to note that, in average, merging the models in Table 2 demonstrated a substantial improvement for sentiment classification task performance with both evolutionary methods and for validation and test datasets. For the evolutionary methods, one can see that the models achieved with CMA-ES have F1-Score and accuracy metrics slight better than SaDE.

The results of the merged models for the hate speech classification task are presented in Table 5. For both SaDE and CMA-ES, merging the models outlined in Table 2 led to an improvement in performance, in average, for both F1-Score and accuracy metrics on the validation dataset, compared to the results of Model 3 presented in Table 4. However, for the test dataset, neither the CMA-ES nor SaDE(LP=2, LP=10) merged models outperformed Model 3 in terms of F1-Score and accuracy. When comparing the two evolutionary methods, we observe that SaDE(LP=2) was able to produce merged models with superior performance on the validation dataset. On the other hand, for the test dataset, CMA-ES models achieved better overall performance.

The comparison between SaDE configurations with different learning periods (LP) values suggests that increasing the LP results in slight performance improvements, particularly in sentiment classification. This finding implies that allowing SaDE to accumulate information over more generations enables better adaptation of its control parameters, which helps in finding better solutions.

Moreover, our approach significantly improves multitask behavior by incorporating previously trained classification layers directly into the evolutionary evaluation process. This leads to more effective merged models across different tasks compared to simply concatenating these classification layers with a base model, such as Bertimbau (Table 4).

Although performance improvements for the hate speech classification task were not possible, the results obtained from the combined models remain highly competitive with those of the baseline model (Model 3). The improvements observed in the sentiment classification task demonstrate that, even with a limited amount of data, with (i) merging models approaches, (ii) high-quality models trained on similar tasks, and (iii) evolutionary methods to optimize the merging configuration, it was possible to achieve efficient transfer learning without additional training effort.

Table 6 presents the execution time required to find the best merged model using SaDE ($LP = 2$, $LP = 10$) and CMA-ES. In general, the execution times of both methods are comparable, with variations occurring on the order of minutes. The SaDE method demonstrated to be the slightly faster than compared to CMA-ES in all measured statistics.

Statistical tests with Wilcoxon signed-rank test [33] were conducted to compare the time distribution from both evolutionary methods. Comparing CMA-ES with SaDE ($LP = 10$) revealed a statistical significant difference (p-

value $= 0.0031$) between execution time distributions. In contrast, no significant difference (p-value $= 0.8408$) was observed between CMA-ES and SaDE (LP $= 2$). This finding indicates that increasing the learning period (LP) in SaDE helps reduce execution time by allowing the algorithm to accumulate more information for adjusting the control parameters, leading to more effective search guidance and faster convergence.

Table 4. Results obtained by the base models. The fine tuned models for classification task (Model 1 and Model 3), have better results than the BERTimbau model concatenated their classification head layers. Simply concatenating a classifier head from fine tuned models can lead to feature misalignment between the task-specific layers and BERTimbau model representations.

Model	Validation		Test	
	F1-Score	Accuracy	F1-Score	Accuracy
Model 1	87.01	84.31	78.34	81.83
Bertimbau + Model 1 (clf_head)	56.73	54.89	35.38	52.24
Model 3	92.13	97.86	90.77	98.15
Bertimbau + Model 3 (clf_head)	8.62	83.82	10.18	85.00

Table 5. Mean F1-Score and Accuracy ($\pm$ std) for Sentiment and Hate Speech classification tasks from 20 independent runs. The best results are highlighted in **boldface**. The underlined values are the best results when comparing only SaDE with different learning periods (LP$= 2$ and LP$=10$).

Task	Method	Validation		Test	
		F1-Score	Accuracy	F1-Score	Accuracy
Sentiment	CMA-ES	**95.84** $\pm$ 0.21	**93.44** $\pm$ 0.28	**91.70** $\pm$ 0.67	**90.41** $\pm$ 0.53
	SaDE (LP $= 2$)	95.31 $\pm$ 0.44	92.85 $\pm$ 0.58	90.33 $\pm$ 1.05	89.53 $\pm$ 0.63
	SaDE (LP $= 10$)	95.36 $\pm$ 0.35	92.84 $\pm$ 0.49	90.72 $\pm$ 0.92	89.77 $\pm$ 0.78
Hate Speech	CMA-ES	94.20 $\pm$ 0.45	98.39 $\pm$ 0.11	**89.24** $\pm$ 0.43	**97.83** $\pm$ 0.09
	SaDE (LP $= 2$)	**94.87** $\pm$ 0.46	**98.55** $\pm$ 0.12	88.72 $\pm$ 0.91	97.64 $\pm$ 0.23
	SaDE (LP $= 10$)	94.85 $\pm$ 0.38	98.54 $\pm$ 0.11	89.11 $\pm$ 0.64	97.73 $\pm$ 0.14

Table 6. Execution times (hours:minutes:seconds) required to find best merged model. Values obtained from 20 independent runs.

	CMA-ES	SaDE (LP $= 2$)	SaDE (LP $= 10$)
min	7:13:18.36	7:08:00.04	**6:42:51.13**
max	8:17:28.88	8:14:19.00	**8:09:02.49**
mean	7:44:34.98	7:41:57.80	**7:29:16.20**
std	0:20:19.80	**0:16:01.83**	0:17:21.08

9   Concluding Remarks and Future Works

This study investigates the application of TIES-Merging and adaptive version of Differential Evolution for merging Brazilian Portuguese language models. The objectives were to examine the role of specialized models in improving performance on related tasks and to explore how models with different capabilities can be integrated into a single model. Additionally, we compared the performance of SaDE and CMA-ES in identifying optimal TIES-Merging configurations for model merging.

Experimental results show that merging fine-tuned models, supported by evolutionary methods, can lead to performance improvements, particularly in sentiment analysis. Although the merged models did not outperform the baseline in hate speech classification, the final model remained competitive for both tasks.

Regarding the evolutionary approaches, CMA-ES achieved better results than SaDE. However, it is important to highlight that increasing the learning period of SaDE led to consistent improvements in the generated models and in the execution time. This points to promising opportunities for future work, specifically in exploring parameter tuning.

Furthermore, future work can investigate the proposal capabilities by evaluating the merged models across a more diverse set of tasks. Also, exploring the use of generative large language models as the base model is a promising opportunity for further research.

Acknowledgements. The authors thank the financial support provided by FAPEMIG (grants CEX APQ 03313/22 and 01832/22), CNPq (grants 316801/ 2021-6 and 313452/2025-3), CAPES, and UFJF.

References

1. Akiba, T., Shing, M., Tang, Y., Sun, Q., Ha, D.: Evolutionary optimization of model merging recipes. Nat. Mach. Intell. **7**(2), 195–204 (2025)
2. Brown, T., et al.: Language models are few-shot learners. In: Advances in Neural Information Processing Systems, vol. 33, pp. 1877–1901. Curran Associates, Inc. (2020)
3. Carmo, D., Piau, M., Campiotti, I., Nogueira, R., Lotufo, R.: Ptt5: pretraining and validating the t5 model on Brazilian Portuguese data. arXiv preprint arXiv:2008.09144 (2020)
4. Costa, P.B., Pavan, M.C., Santos, W.R., Silva, S.C., Paraboni, I.: Bertabaporu: assessing a genre-specific language model for Portuguese nlp. In: Proceedings of the 14th International Conference on Recent Advances in Natural Language Processing, pp. 217–223 (2023) (2023)
5. Das, S., Suganthan, P.N.: Differential evolution: a survey of the state-of-the-art. Trans. Evol. Comp **15**(1) (2011)
6. Dettmers, T., Pagnoni, A., Holtzman, A., Zettlemoyer, L.: Qlora: efficient finetuning of quantized llms. In: Oh, A., Naumann, T., Globerson, A., Saenko, K., Hardt, M., Levine, S. (eds.) Advances in Neural Information Processing Systems, vol. 36, pp. 10088–10115. Curran Associates, Inc. (2023)

7. Devlin, J., Chang, M.W., Lee, K., Toutanova, K.: BERT: In: Pre-training of Deep Bidirectional Transformers for Language Understanding, pp. 4171–4186. Association for Computational Linguistics (2019)

8. Goddard, C., et al.: Arcee's MergeKit: a toolkit for merging large language models, pp. 477–485. Association for Computational Linguistics (2024)

9. Hu, E.J., et al.: LoRA: low-rank adaptation of large language models (2022)

10. Ilharco, G., et al.: Editing models with task arithmetic (2023)

11. Larcher, C., Piau, M., Finardi, P., Gengo, P., Esposito, P., Caridá, V.: Cabrita: closing the gap for foreign languages (2023)

12. Liu, Y., et al.: Roberta: a robustly optimized bert pretraining approach (2019)

13. Liu, Y., Sun, Y., Xue, B., Zhang, M., Yen, G.G., Tan, K.C.: A survey on evolutionary neural architecture search. IEEE Trans. Neural Netw. Learn. Syst. $34(2)$, 550–570 (2023)

14. Lozano, J.A., Larrañaga, P., Inza, I.n., Bengoetxea, E.: Towards a New Evolutionary Computation: Advances on Estimation of Distribution Algorithms (Studies in Fuzziness and Soft Computing). Springer-Verlag, Cham (2006)

15. Mencattini, T., Minut, A.R., Crisostomi, D., Santilli, A., Rodolà, E.: Merge^3: efficient evolutionary merging on consumer-grade gpus (2025)

16. Mikolov, T., Karafiát, M., Burget, L., Cernocký, J., Khudanpur, S.: Recurrent neural network based language model. In: Interspeech, vol. 2, pp. 1045–1048. Makuhari (2010)

17. Pires, R., Abonizio, H., Almeida, T.S., Nogueira, R.: Sabiá: Portuguese Large Language Models, pp. 226–240. Springer, Cham (2023)

18. Qin, A.K., Huang, V.L., Suganthan, P.N.: Differential evolution algorithm with strategy adaptation for global numerical optimization. IEEE Trans. Evol. Comput. $13(2)$, 398–417 (2008)

19. Radford, A., Narasimhan, K., Salimans, T., Sutskever, I., et al.: Improving language understanding by generative pre-training. Technical report, OpenAI (2018)

20. Radford, A., Wu, J., Child, R., Luan, D., Amodei, D., Sutskever, I., et al.: Language models are unsupervised multitask learners. Technical Report 8, OpenAI (2019)

21. Raffel, C.: Exploring the limits of transfer learning with a unified text-to-text transformer. J. Mach. Learn. Res. $21(140)$, 1–67 (2020)

22. Rajbhandari, S., Rasley, J., Ruwase, O., He, Y.: Zero: memory optimizations toward training trillion parameter models. In: Proceedings of the International Conference for High Performance Computing, Networking, Storage and Analysis. SC '20. IEEE Press (2020)

23. Sak, H., Senior, A., Beaufays, F.: Long short-term memory based recurrent neural network architectures for large vocabulary speech recognition (2014)

24. Sanh, V., Debut, L., Chaumond, J., Wolf, T.: Distilbert, a distilled version of bert: smaller, faster, cheaper and lighter (2020)

25. Shoemake, K.: Animating rotation with quaternion curves. In: Proceedings of the 12th Annual Conference on Computer Graphics and Interactive Techniques, pp. 245–254 (1985)

26. Souza, F., Nogueira, R., Lotufo, R.: BERTimbau: Pretrained BERT Models for Brazilian Portuguese. In: Cerri, R., Prati, R.C. (eds.) BRACIS 2020. LNCS (LNAI), vol. 12319, pp. 403–417. Springer, Cham (2020). https://doi.org/10.1007/978-3-030-61377-8_28

27. Storn, R., Price, K.: Differential evolution - a simple and efficient adaptive scheme for global optimization over continuous spaces, vol. 3. ICSI Berkeley (1995)

28. Utans, J.: Weight averaging for neural networks and local resampling schemes. In: Proceedings of AAAI-96 Workshop on Integrating Multiple Learned Models, pp. 133–138. AAAI Press, Citeseer (1996)
29. Vaswani, A., et al.: Attention is all you need. In: Advances in Neural Information Processing Systems, vol. 30. Curran Associates, Inc. (2017)
30. Vaswani, A., et al.: Attention is all you need. In: Guyon, I., et al. (eds.) Advances in Neural Information Processing Systems, vol. 30. Curran Associates, Inc. (2017)
31. Warner, B., et al.: Smarter, better, faster, longer: a modern bidirectional encoder for fast, memory efficient, and long context finetuning and inference (2025)
32. White, T.: Sampling generative networks (2016)
33. Wilcoxon, F.: Individual Comparisons by Ranking Methods, pp. 196–202. Springer, New York (1992)
34. Wortsman, M., et al.: Model soups: averaging weights of multiple fine-tuned models improves accuracy without increasing inference time. In: Chaudhuri, K., Jegelka, S., Song, L., Szepesvari, C., Niu, G., Sabato, S. (eds.) Proceedings of the 39th International Conference on Machine Learning. Proceedings of Machine Learning Research, vol. 162, pp. 23965–23998. PMLR (2022)
35. Yadav, P., Tam, D., Choshen, L., Raffel, C., Bansal, M.: In: Ties-merging: resolving interference when merging models. In: Proceedings of the 37th International Conference on Neural Information Processing Systems. NIPS '23. Curran Associates Inc., Red Hook (2023)
36. Yang, E., et al.: Model merging in llms, mllms, and beyond: methods, theories, applications and opportunities (2024)
37. Yu, L., Yu, B., Yu, H., Huang, F., Li, Y.: Language models are super mario: absorbing abilities from homologous models as a free lunch. In: Proceedings of the 41st International Conference on Machine Learning. ICML'24. JMLR.org (2024)
38. Zhao, W.X., et al.: A survey of large language models (2025)

Perception of Guardians on the Use of Artificial Intelligence in Educational Geometry Games for Children

Leonardo Estevam[1]([✉]) [ID], Vitor Melo[1] [ID], João Carvalho[1] [ID],
Barbara da Silva[2] [ID], Walter Oliveira Júnior[2] [ID], Marcelle Mota[3] [ID],
Diego Lisboa[1] [ID], and Marcos Seruffo[1] [ID]

[1] Institute of Technology, Federal University of Pará, Belém, Brazil
leonardoestevam0605@gmail.com
[2] Inteceleri Technology for Education, Belém, Brazil
[3] Institute of Exact and Natural Sciences, Federal University of Pará, Belém, Brazil

Abstract. The study aims to evaluate caregivers' perceptions of the use of Artificial Intelligence (AI) in educational games for children, emphasizing the positive impact of this technology on the learning process. The research, conducted with 14 caregivers, utilized a comprehensive questionnaire to collect feedback on various aspects, such as the level of engagement fostered in children, the appropriateness and variety of the proposed activities, and the quality of AI-generated questions. The results revealed a positive response to the game, with a satisfaction rate of 93.4%, and indicated that most participants found the use of AI both engaging and enjoyable, highlighting the games' ability to capture children's attention in a meaningful way. Furthermore, the majority of caregivers rated the AI-generated questions as appropriate and diverse, considering the content well-suited to children's educational needs. This assessment demonstrates the effectiveness of AI in providing an interactive and personalized geometry learning experience, allowing each child to progress at their own pace in an engaging manner aligned with their comprehension levels. This adaptive learning approach, which adjusts content according to each child's progress, was widely recognized by caregivers as an important advancement for educational development, delivering a high-quality, engaging, and educational experience.

Keywords: Artificial Intelligence · Education · Geometry · Educational Games

1 Introduction

In recent years, the rapid evolution of digital technologies has been revolutionizing various sectors, especially education, which now benefits from increasingly sophisticated tools to promote learning and cognitive development among children and adolescents [15]. This transformation extends beyond mere access to

R. de Freitas and D. Furtado (Eds.): BRACIS 2025, LNAI 16181, pp. 321–334, 2026.
https://doi.org/10.1007/978-3-032-15990-8_22

information to encompass more interactive and adaptive teaching methods. The application of Artificial Intelligence (AI) in educational systems stands out as one of the most significant advancements, as it offers a dynamic and personalized way of teaching complex subjects such as mathematics and geometry in a playful and accessible environment that resonates with new generations [4].

AI integration allows educational games to transcend traditional teaching approaches, enabling learning experiences tailored to individual student needs. This personalization is achieved through algorithms that continuously adjust task difficulty levels based on each child's progress and ability. As a result, learning becomes not only more engaging but also more effective, promoting meaningful interaction with the content [5].

In the field of geometry education, AI-based technologies can make a particularly significant difference, as this area of mathematics involves spatial and visual concepts that benefit from interactive and adaptive approaches [3]. Educational games often utilize AI to automatically adjust question difficulty levels, providing content that evolves with the student's individual progress. This personalized approach is crucial for children's learning, as it prevents frustration from overly challenging questions and the lack of motivation generated by overly simple ones. Thus, children can experience continuous skill development, fostering self-confidence and curiosity for learning [22].

However, despite the transformative potential of these technological innovations, it is essential to understand how parents, who are primarily responsible for guiding and supervising technology use among children, perceive these educational innovations. Studies show that parents' perceptions of the effectiveness and safety of AI technologies in children's learning can directly influence the acceptance and use of these tools within the family context [13]. Caregivers often express concerns about the possible impacts of technology on their children's development and behavior. Therefore, understanding parents' perceived benefits regarding the use of AI in educational games is a vital aspect for the adoption and success of these platforms [7]. This perception not only shapes parents' attitudes but may also affect children's willingness to engage with the available educational tools.

In this study, we conducted research with caregivers of children who used the educational game GeoMeta [8], specifically focused on geometry education. The objective was to evaluate caregivers' perceptions of the impact of AI on the learning process. The research included a comprehensive questionnaire designed to assess not only the acceptance of AI use but also perceptions of its suitability and perceived effectiveness in geometry learning. By investigating these aspects, we aim to provide insights for developing educational games that are more efficient and meet both parents' expectations and children's needs, as well as to evaluate satisfaction with the quality of the generated questions [11]. The research results offer a comprehensive view of the perceptions and experiences related to the use of AI-based games in the educational context, highlighting not only the benefits but also the points of attention that should be considered when incorporating these technologies into early childhood education.

The article is structured into five main sections. In Sect. 2, we discuss related work, covering existing literature on educational games and the use of artificial intelligence in education. In Sect. 3, we present the research methodology, detailing the application of GeoMeta, AI customization, testing procedures, and ethical considerations related to the study. Section 4 discusses the results, focusing on caregivers' perceptions of the game application and its effectiveness in geometry learning. Finally, in Sect. 5, we provide a discussion of the results, exploring their implications for developing AI-based educational games and suggesting future directions for research and educational practice.

2   Theoretical Foundation

The theoretical framework of this study examines AI's role in early childhood education and caregiver perceptions, highlighting how these innovations transform pedagogy. Papert [17] shows AI-enabled games personalize learning by adapting to individual developmental needs. Norman [14] emphasizes that thoughtful UX design creates engaging environments where children develop problem solving skills safely.

Bloom's [2] research demonstrates how AI personalization in tools like GeoMeta prevents frustration by dynamically adjusting difficulty, maintaining optimal challenge levels. This adaptive approach increases motivation and self-confidence through responsive feedback systems.

Selwyn [19] and Plowman [18] establish caregivers as critical mediators of technology use, with adoption depending on perceived safety and developmental benefits. Long and Magerko [10] and Selwyn [20] further show that AI literacy among stakeholders increases trust and facilitates implementation through understanding both capabilities and ethical considerations.

Gardner and Davis [6] argue for balanced AI-human integration, where technology handles content adaptation while educators develop socioemotional skills like empathy and cooperation. This synergy creates inclusive learning environments that combine AI's personalization strengths with essential human guidance.

The framework thus identifies four key requirements for effective AI implementation: (1) child-centered UX design, (2) caregiver trust, (3) comprehensive AI literacy, and (4) balanced human-AI collaboration - all crucial for making educational AI tools like GeoMeta both pedagogically effective and developmentally appropriate.

3   Related Works

Recent studies have examined the integration of AI in education, particularly focusing on building critical thinking skills and AI literacy for students and educators. Research shows these efforts help understand how to implement AI effectively and ethically in learning environments.

The first study [9] demonstrates how informal AI learning helps youth make real-world connections, developing crucial critical thinking about technology. The second [1] reveals teacher training in AI leads to better classroom practices and student engagement. The third [21] proposes AI-driven collaborative models transforming higher education through interdisciplinary learning.

Practical applications appear in the fourth study [16], where simulation games teach AI concepts while addressing ethical implications. The fifth [12] shows how AI enhances educational games through adaptive challenges that maintain engagement.

This study uniquely examines caregivers' perspectives on educational AI - a previously underexplored area. While existing research focuses on skills development and teaching methods, our work directly investigates parental perceptions of AI's educational value and appropriateness. These insights prove vital since caregiver acceptance significantly impacts both children's adoption of learning technologies and institutional implementation decisions, ultimately promoting more ethical and effective AI use in education.

4   Methodology

The methodology employed in this study, illustrated in Fig. 1, encompassed five interrelated phases: initial GeoMeta configuration and AI integration for enhancing educational interactivity; customization of AI-generated content, including preliminary refinement tests; structured testing involving caregivers for real-time evaluation and feedback; administration of a detailed questionnaire to assess the effectiveness and appropriateness of AI-driven learning; and rigorous ethical considerations to maintain participant privacy and adherence to relevant research guidelines.

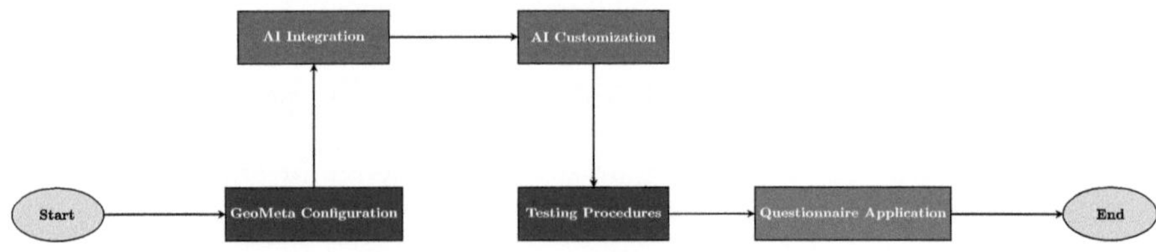

Fig. 1. Workflow of the Methodology.

4.1   GeoMeta Configuration

The GeoMeta educational application (Fig. 2) was designed and developed utilizing the Unity platform, renowned for creating interactive and immersive environments suitable for children's education. Unity's extensive capabilities facilitated the construction of engaging, three-dimensional interactive interfaces aimed at encouraging active exploration and learning. The platform supported high-quality graphical experiences, promoting visual and experiential learning, which significantly stimulated curiosity and involvement among children.

Fig. 2. Home screen of the GeoMeta application.

One critical innovation of GeoMeta was its integration with ChatGPT technology (Fig. 3), a sophisticated AI model based on transformer neural networks. This integration, enabled via OpenAI's API, allowed GeoMeta to dynamically generate tailored geometry questions and corresponding adaptive feedback in real-time. Such interaction ensured content remained relevant, appropriately challenging, and engaging for each individual learner, significantly personalizing and enhancing the educational experience.

Fig. 3. Home screen of the test version of the GeoMeta app integrated with ChatGPT.

4.2   Personalization of AI

The AI used in GeoMeta was developed to provide a learning experience exclusively aligned with the theme of geometry, applying a rigorous filter that prevents the creation of questions unrelated to this scope. This thematic precision is essential for ensuring that the game remains focused on relevant content, without distracting the user with off-context questions, thereby guaranteeing that progress is effective and targeted towards the development of geometric skills.

The game starts at the fifth-grade level, adapting to the player's performance based on specific criteria. When the child correctly answers three consecutive questions, the system automatically increases the difficulty level, advancing to the content of the next school year, as illustrated in Fig. 4. This encourages students to progressively challenge themselves, providing a sense of achievement and reinforcing learning. On the other hand, if the child makes two consecutive mistakes, the difficulty level decreases to the previous school year, ensuring that the content remains understandable and adjusted to the current knowledge level. This adjustment logic is particularly relevant for maintaining the child's motivation, avoiding both frustration with overly complex questions and disinterest with questions that are too easy.

The rationale behind this adjustment is to provide a balanced learning environment where children feel challenged but not overwhelmed. The alternation of difficulty levels allows GeoMeta to adapt to each student, promoting a personalized and continuous knowledge consolidation experience in geometry, as evidenced by research on the effectiveness of adaptive learning. The content covers both plane geometry—focusing on shapes such as squares, triangles, and circles—as well as spatial geometry, including three-dimensional shapes like cubes, pyramids, spheres, and cylinders.

Additionally, the personalization of the questions generated by the AI in GeoMeta aimed to provide a continuous and adaptive learning experience, which is essential for maintaining children's engagement and motivation. To facilitate understanding and increase student involvement, all questions were structured in multiple-choice format, presenting four alternatives, of which only one is correct. This structure allows students to practice their logical reasoning and decision-making skills, promoting an interactive and stimulating learning environment. The generation of questions is done indefinitely, allowing the game to adapt to each child's individual learning pace without content limitations, which is particularly important in educational contexts where each student may progress at their own speed.

Furthermore, the questions were designed to align with the geometry content outlined in the elementary school curriculum. This curricular compliance not only ensures that the learning is relevant and applicable but also enables children to connect what they learn in GeoMeta with what is taught in the classroom. This connection is vital for reinforcing knowledge and facilitating the transfer of skills from the gaming environment to the school setting, thereby enhancing the effectiveness of learning.

This personalization was crafted to allow parents to assess the appropriateness and relevance of the content generated by the AI, enabling closer monitoring of their children's educational progress. With the ability to track interactions and results obtained in GeoMeta, parents can gain clear insight into their children's performance and provide additional support when needed, fostering a collaborative and engaging approach to geometry education. This relationship among parents, children, and technology reinforces the importance of learning that not only adapts to individual needs but also integrates with traditional educational practices.

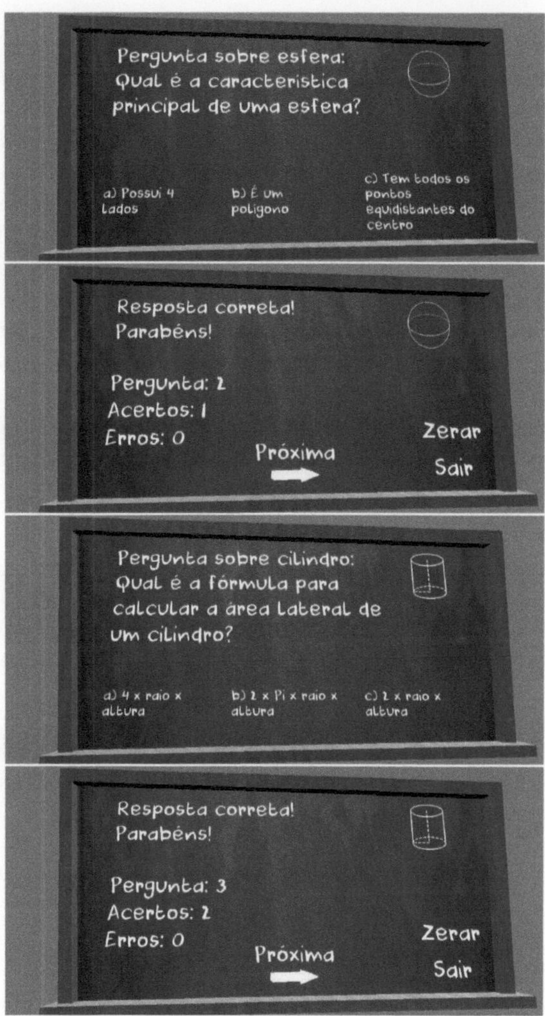

Fig. 4. GeoMeta game interface, showcasing the generation of geometry questions by AI, with dynamic difficulty adjustment based on user responses.

4.3   Testing Procedures

The tests with GeoMeta were conducted at a specific booth during a technology exhibition held at the Federal University of Pará. In this interactive and engaging environment, the application was presented to a diverse audience, capturing the attention of visitors who were curious about the game demonstration and the opportunity to observe their children's performance on the platform (Fig. 5). The atmosphere of the event was vibrant, featuring a mix of students, educators, and families, all interested in exploring technological innovations in the field of education.

Among the 14 guardians who participated in the experience, all were random individuals passing by the booth, creating a spontaneous and dynamic scenario for evaluating GeoMeta. This variety of participants brought different perspectives and interests, enriching the feedback obtained during the interactions. When invited to accompany their children while they interacted with the game, the guardians could not only observe their children's performance but also actively engage in the educational process provided by the platform.

Parents had the opportunity to see how their children tackled the challenges presented by GeoMeta, promoting enriching dialogue about the strategies employed. This interaction not only reinforced the importance of family support in learning but also highlighted GeoMeta's potential as an educational tool that can be used both at home and in school. By the end of the demonstration, many parents expressed enthusiasm and interest in how technology could complement traditional teaching, creating a conducive space for future discussions about integrating digital education into geometry learning.

Fig. 5. Children accompanied by their guardians using the GeoMeta application with the help of MiritiBoardVR VR glasses.

During this experience, caregivers were instructed to pay attention to three main aspects that were fundamental for evaluating the application. The first aspect was the quality of the questions generated by the AI, which involves the clarity, relevance, and complexity of the presented questions. A good set of questions is crucial to ensure that learning is meaningful and engaging, as research shows that the quality of educational content directly impacts student engagement and knowledge retention. The caregivers were also asked to focus on the appropriateness of the questions to the theme of geometry. This thematic alignment is vital to ensure that children receive instruction and practice skills that are pertinent to their school curriculum, which, in turn, facilitates the transfer of learning from the game environment to the classroom. By observing what their children were learning in school, caregivers could evaluate the effectiveness of GeoMeta in complementing formal education.

The third and final aspect observed by the caregivers was the perceived effectiveness of the child's learning. This includes observing how interaction with GeoMeta influenced the understanding of geometric concepts, whether children felt motivated and engaged during the game, and whether the platform contributed to meaningful learning. The direct involvement of caregivers was essential for collecting immediate and direct feedback on their perception of the quality and effectiveness of the content generated by the AI. This feedback is crucial for continuously improving the application, adapting it to user needs, and maximizing its educational impact.

Additionally, the participation of caregivers in observing and evaluating GeoMeta provided a rich context for discussions about the integration of technology in education. This interaction not only encouraged a collaborative environment between parents and children but also highlighted the importance of technology being accessible and effective in promoting learning. The information collected through the tests can serve as a foundation for future improvements to the application, always aiming to strengthen education in geometry and develop critical skills in children.

4.4 Questionnaire

The questionnaire administered to caregivers aimed to evaluate the interaction between AI and children's learning processes. The analyzed aspects included the clarity and relevance of the questions generated by the AI, which are essential for students to understand and apply geometric concepts. The appropriateness of the questions in relation to the appropriate difficulty level for the children's age group was also assessed, ensuring that they were challenged without feeling overwhelmed. Additionally, caregivers were asked about the relevance of the content concerning the school curriculum, aiming to understand if GeoMeta complemented classroom learning and whether the knowledge acquired was applied in contexts outside the virtual environment.

The information collected from the questionnaire is fundamental for analyzing the impact of AI on learning and guiding future improvements in GeoMeta. Caregivers' feedback not only contributes to the educational effectiveness of the AI but also ensures that their needs are met during the development process. Thus, the questionnaire provides a comprehensive view of how to effectively integrate educational technologies, reinforcing the utility of AI as a learning tool. The questionnaire addressed the following aspects:

- **(P1) Engagement and Interest:** Do you find it fun or interesting for your child to play a game that uses AI to generate questions and answers?
- **(P2) Appropriateness and Variety:** Did the questions generated by the AI seem appropriate and varied for your child's knowledge level?
- **(P3) Quality of Questions:** How would you rate the overall quality of the questions and answers generated by the AI in the game?
- **(P4) Personalization Based on Performance:** Did you feel that the AI adequately personalizes the questions based on your child's performance?
- **(P5) Improvement in Geometry Knowledge:** Do you believe that the game, by using AI, helps to improve your child's knowledge of geometry?

4.5   Ethical Considerations

In accordance with the ethics committee guidelines, this study did not require formal approval as established by CNS Resolution No. 446/11 and Resolution 370, since it did not involve direct interventions with children and focused solely on observing interactions with freely accessible educational content. Furthermore, the involvement of caregivers was limited to passive observation, with no collection of sensitive data, thereby exempting the process from strict ethical restrictions. The research adhered to principles of ethics and transparency, and all caregivers were informed in advance about the study's objective and provided their consent to participate, ensuring that the experience was conducted in an ethical and safe manner for all involved.

5   Results

The analysis of questionnaire responses from caregivers revealed a highly positive perception of the GeoMeta application, emphasizing its effectiveness in using AI for teaching geometry. The caregivers recognized the educational value of GeoMeta, highlighting satisfaction with its interactive and immersive format, which successfully engaged children.

Responses were evaluated using a 5-point Likert scale (Fig. 6), capturing both quantitative scores and qualitative insights into the application's integration into children's learning routines. Statistical measures, including mean, standard deviation, and satisfaction index, facilitated a comprehensive understanding of caregiver feedback, emphasizing critical factors such as question clarity, content relevance, and appropriateness.

The mean (M) for each question was calculated, providing a clear representation of caregivers' general perceptions. The **standard deviation** (σ), indicating the variability of responses, was calculated as follows by (1):

$$\sigma = \sqrt{\frac{\sum_{i=1}^{n}(x_i - M)^2}{n}} \tag{1}$$

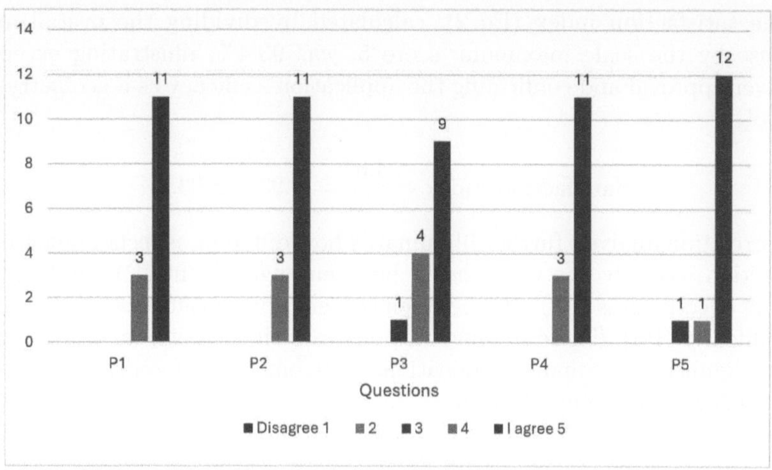

Fig. 6. Graph showing the caregivers evaluations of the GeoMeta application using AI, employing a 5-point Likert scale.

Table 1. Descriptive Statistics Table

Question	Mean (M)	Standard Deviation (σ)
P1	4.79	0.42
P2	4.79	0.42
P3	4.57	0.52
P4	4.79	0.52
P5	4.71	0.52

Results from these calculations are presented in Table 1.

In evaluating engagement and interest (P1), 78.6% rated the application at the highest score, number 5 of the Likert scale, and 21.4% rated it at 4, resulting in a mean of 4.79 ($\sigma = 0.42$), indicating strong acceptance of the AI-driven format. Similarly, for question appropriateness and variety (P2), caregivers showed comparable satisfaction (mean of 4.79, $\sigma = 0.42$), underscoring AI's effectiveness in generating diverse and suitable content.

Regarding the quality of questions (P3), responses varied slightly more, with 64.3% rating 5, 28.6% rating 4, and 7.1% rating 3. The mean score was 4.57 ($\sigma = 0.52$), reflecting overall high satisfaction despite minor suggestions for improvement. Customization of difficulty (P4) again showed high approval, with a mean of 4.79 ($\sigma = 0.52$), highlighting AI's adaptive capacity.

The effectiveness in improving geometry knowledge (P5) achieved a mean score of 4.71 ($\sigma = 0.52$), with 85.7% assigning the highest rating. These outcomes underscore GeoMeta's significant educational impact.

The satisfaction index (Eq. 2), calculated by dividing the overall average response by the scale maximum, score 5, was 93.4%, illustrating exceptional caregiver approval and confirming the application's efficacy as a geometry learning tool.

$$\text{Satisfaction Index} \approx \frac{4.67}{5} = 0.934 \text{ or } 93.4\% \tag{2}$$

Correlation analysis further illuminated how different aspects influenced user satisfaction, notably the relationship between engagement (P1) and perceived learning effectiveness (P5), and between content appropriateness (P2) and adaptive difficulty (P4). These findings demonstrate that emotional and interactive design significantly enhances educational outcomes, reinforcing GeoMeta as a robust, effective learning platform.

6   Conclusion

The conclusion of this study focuses on caregivers' perceptions regarding the use of AI in educational geometry games for children. The results obtained demonstrate a high level of approval among caregivers, indicating that many view AI as an effective tool for making learning more dynamic and tailored to the individual needs of children. This technology is seen as capable of generating questions that stimulate the interest and engagement of young players, creating a more immersive educational experience. The interactivity provided by AI allows children to explore geometric concepts in a playful manner, contributing to a better understanding and retention of knowledge. As such, the integration of AI not only enhances the educational experience but also encourages children to develop a positive attitude towards learning.

However, it is essential to consider that the analyzed sample was relatively small, which may limit the ability to make broader generalizations about the effectiveness of AI in the educational context. Future research will be important to include a larger number of participants, as well as the implementation of new AI features such as interactive avatars and geometric shape recognition mechanisms. These enhancements could expand learning opportunities, making the experience even richer and more personalized. A diversity of approaches in the use of AI may provide valuable insights into how different tools impact learning in geometry, potentially leading to innovative pedagogical strategies that can be adapted to various educational settings.

Moreover, the use of AI should be carefully balanced with human interactions, which are fundamental for the holistic development of children. While AI can personalize and optimize learning experiences, interactions with educators and caregivers are crucial for fostering social and emotional skills. Children benefit not only from academic knowledge but also from the ability to relate to and communicate with others, which is essential for their overall development. Therefore, promoting an educational environment that harmonizes technology with human contact will be vital to maximizing the benefits of AI in educational geometry games. This integrated approach can contribute to more effective and meaningful learning experiences, preparing students not only for academic challenges but also for the complexities of everyday life, including problem-solving and critical thinking.

Finally, it is important to emphasize that the integration of AI in education is not a one-size-fits-all solution, but rather part of a broader educational ecosystem. Continuous development and research in this area are essential to better understand how technology can be utilized responsibly and beneficially. This understanding ensures that education not only capitalizes on technological advancements but also preserves the human aspect of teaching and learning. As we move forward, it will be critical to engage stakeholders, including educators, parents, and policymakers, in discussions about the ethical implications and best practices surrounding AI in education. This collaborative approach will help create a sustainable educational framework that leverages technology while maintaining a focus on the needs and well-being of students.

References

1. Addo, S.A., Sentance, S.: Teachers' motivation for teaching AI in k-12 settings. In: Proceedings of the 2023 Conference on Human Centered Artificial Intelligence: Education and Practice (HCAIep '23), p. 43, New York. Association for Computing Machinery (2023)
2. Bloom, B.S.: The 2 sigma problem: the search for methods of group instruction as effective as one-to-one tutoring. Educ. Res. **13**(6), 4–16 (1984)
3. Calaça de Sousa, C.: Inteligência Artificial No Ensino De Geometria Em Nível Fundamental Da Educação Básica: contribuições e perspectivas (2023)
4. de Souza, F.W.M., da Cruz Foncesa, N., Dias, V.S., Borges, R.L., Coutinho, D.J.G.: O ensino e aprendizado matemÁtico com inteligncia artificial: Uma anÁlise de algumas ferramentas e tecnologias disponÍveis. Revista Ibero-Americana de Humanidades, Ciências e Educação **10**(7), 1908–1923 (2024)
5. Fachini, J. D., Willemann, T. E., dos Reis Bezerra, W.: O desenvolvimento de jogos utilizando inteligncia artificial e linguagem de programaÇÃo nas aulas de licenciatura em matemÁtica. In: Anais da Feira do Conhecimento Tecnológico e Científico, number **24** (2024)
6. Davis, K., Gardner, H.: The App Generation: How Today's Youth Navigate Identity, Intimacy, and Imagination in a Digital World. Yale University Press (2013)
7. Huang, P., Chen, Y., Lin, Y., Li, J.: The intersection of artificial intelligence and education: Exploring the opportunities and challenges. In: Proceedings of the 2nd International Conference on Educational Knowledge and Informatization (EKI '24), pp. 415–419, New York. Association for Computing Machinery (2024)
8. Oliveira Júnior, W., Estevam, L., Silva, B., Silva, J., Reis, M., Seruffo, M.: Geometa: realidade virtual e aumentada no ensino de geometria. In: Anais do II Workshop sobre Interação e Pesquisa de Usuários no Desenvolvimento de Jogos,, pp. 43–53. , Porto Alegre. SBC (2023)
9. Lee, S., Choi, D., Lee, M., Choi, J., Lee, S.: Fostering youth's critical thinking competency about AI through exhibition. In: Proceedings of the 2023 CHI Conference on Human Factors in Computing Systems (CHI '23), Article 451, pp. 1–22, New York. Association for Computing Machinery (2023)

10. Long, D., Magerko, B.: What is AI literacy? competencies and design considerations. In: Proceedings of the 2020 CHI Conference on Human Factors in Computing Systems, pp. 1–16 (2020)
11. Lu, X., Fan, S., Houghton, J., Wang, L., Wang, X.: Readingquizmaker: um sistema colaborativo humano-pnl que dá suporte aos instrutores para criar perguntas de teste de leitura de alta qualidade. In: Anais da Conferência CHI de 2023 sobre Fatores Humanos em Sistemas de Computação (CHI '23), pp. Artigo 454, 1–18, Nova York. Association for Computing Machinery (2023)
12. Lyu, A.: Research on online game design based on artificial intelligence algorithm. In: Proceedings of the 6th International Conference on Information Technologies and Electrical Engineering (ICITEE '23), vol. '23, pp. 501–504. Association for Computing Machinery, New York (2024)
13. Marassi, L.: Assessing user perceptions of bias in generative AI models: Promoting social awareness for trustworthy AI. In: Proceedings of the 2023 Conference on Human Centered Artificial Intelligence: Education and Practice (HCAIep '23), p. 46. New York. Association for Computing Machinery (2023)
14. Norman, D.: The Design of Everyday Things: Revised and Expanded Edition. Basic Books (2013)
15. Nunes, A.P., et al.: O uso de telas e tecnologias pela população infanto-juvenil: revisão bibliográfica sobre o impacto no desenvolvimento global de crianças e adolescentes. Brazilian J. Heal. Rev. **6**(5), 19926–19939 (2023)
16. Simone Opel, Michael Schlichtig, and Carsten Schulte. Developing teaching materials on artificial intelligence by using a simulation game (work in progress). In: Proceedings of the 14th Workshop in Primary and Secondary Computing Education (WiPSCE '19) Article 11, pp. 1–2, New York. Association for Computing Machinery (2019)
17. Papert, S.: Mindstorms: Children, Computers, and Powerful Ideas. Basic Books (1980)
18. Plowman, L., McPake, J., Stephen, C.: The technologisation of childhood? young children and technology in the home. Children Soc. **24**(1), 63–74 (2010)
19. Selwyn, N.: Distrusting Educational Technology: Critical Questions for Changing Times. Routledge (2013)
20. Selwyn, N.: Education and Technology: Key Issues and Debates. Bloomsbury Publishing (2021)
21. Wei, W., Xie, H., Li, S., Chen, Z.: Explore the innovation of "artificial intelligence + education" in the education domain. In: 2021 4th International Conference on Information Systems and Computer Aided Education (ICISCAE 2021), pp. 2309–2312, New York. Association for Computing Machinery (2021)
22. Bella Yang, K., et al.: Pair-up: prototyping human-AI co-orchestration of dynamic transitions between individual and collaborative learning in the classroom. In: Proceedings of the 2023 CHI Conference on Human Factors in Computing Systems (CHI '23), pp. 453, 1–17, New York. Association for Computing Machinery (2023)

Predicting and Interpreting Clinical Deterioration in the Intensive Care Unit Using Machine Learning and Explainable AI

Vanderleicio Carvalho Leite Junior, Matheus Giovanni Pires$^{(\boxtimes)}$, and Fabiana Cristina Bertoni

State University of Feira de Santana, Feira de Santana 44036-900, BA, Brazil
vanderleiciojr397@gmail.com, {mgpires,fcbertoni}@uefs.br

Abstract. Intensive Care Units in hospitals have been the focus of significant research efforts, as patients require continuous monitoring of their physiological parameters due to their elevated risk of rapid clinical deterioration. In this study, we evaluated eighteen predictive models for clinical deterioration in ICU patients. Fifteen of these models were composed by combining three machine learning algorithms – LightGBM, Random Forest and XGBoost – with five data imputation techniques: linear interpolation, forward filling, carry forward, indicator imputation, and zero imputation. The use of data imputation techniques aims to address the challenge of missing clinical information. The remaining three were formed using each machine learning algorithm, with the inclusion of statistical metrics for each feature in the dataset. For all models, hyperparameter tuning was performed using the grid search method, and model efficiency was assessed using the G-mean metric. The results demonstrated that models based on the Random Forest algorithm achieved the best performance. Finally, we applied the SHAP technique to identify the most influential variables for predicting clinical deterioration in the best-performing models.

Keywords: Pacient Deterioration · Intensive Care Unit · Machine Learning · Explainable AI

1 Introduction

Intensive Care Units (ICU) patients require more attention and monitoring than those in other departments to detect potential deterioration or life-threatening changes, given their critical condition [1]. However, acute and intensive care have been primarily reactive, and interventions are typically initiated only after clinical deterioration. This is in part because the data generated during medical care in ICU are vast, complex, and unstructured, which complicate interpretation by physicians. Such data cover all aspects of a patient journey into intensive care and typically include demographic information, repeated physiological measurements, clinical observations, laboratory test results, and therapeutic interventions.

Performing predictive analysis can enable proactive actions to mitigate potential complications or deteriorations, such as forecasting sepsis, respiratory distress, cardiac events, and especially mortality risk. Predicting mortality risk contributes to effective ICU management, which is essential for optimizing patient outcomes and ensuring the sustainability of healthcare systems [3]. Models for evaluating mortality risk have frequently been used to support resource allocation and treatment decisions, including the globally recognized Acute Physiology and Chronic Health Evaluation II (APACHE-II) score [9].

However, several limitations are associated with these score-based models. Firstly, their performance tends to decline relatively quickly over time, leading to a calibration drift. This loss of calibration is often due to evolving patient populations and medical practices, which typically results in an overestimation of mortality. In addition to calibration issues, other studies have indicated that limited consideration of diverse patient cohorts has also negatively impacted model performance [2].

The limitations of existing scoring systems have led to a growing interest among researchers in exploring Machine Learning (ML) algorithms for mortality prediction [2]. ML approaches offer the advantage of being relatively easy to update and continuously recalibrate, with algorithms that can be configured for ongoing training using new data collected in real-time clinical environments [2]. These methods can also make predictions more quickly and at a larger scale than humans, and are increasingly regarded as indispensable tools in modern healthcare systems [3].

In this context, this study aims to explore the use of machine learning to develop a prediction model for mortality risk in ICU, based on patient data and clinical measurements. These algorithms offer the potential to improve outcome prediction and hence, enhance both patient care and ICU resource management. More specifically, we assessed and compared the performance of three ML algorithms–namely, LightGBM (LGBM), Random Forest, and XGBoost–using the real-world dataset Medical Information Mart for Intensive Care (MIMIC) [7]. These ML approaches are known for their strong predictive capabilities [8] [3] [10].

While ML algorithms have demonstrated superior performance compared to traditional methods, they are not without limitations. A notable challenge is the presence of missing clinical information within datasets. Incomplete data can introduce bias and reduce sample sizes, thereby compromising the robustness and accuracy of ML algorithms. To mitigate this issue, we applied five data imputation techniques–linear interpolation, forward filling, carry forward, indicator imputation, and zero imputation–to estimate and replace missing values, thereby ensuring a complete and reliable dataset for model development, training, and subsequent analysis.

Furthermore, the data must be structured into time-series vectors, where each row corresponds to a specific day of a patient ICU stay and aggregates all features recorded within that timeframe. Two methods were used to compose these vectors, both based on a 24-h observation window.

Another limitation is the lack of interpretability of these algorithms. Therefore, an Explainable AI (XAI) technique was applied to interpret the output of ML models. Understanding the features that contribute towards the prediction is crucial for supporting clinical decision-making [12].

This paper is organized as follows: Sect. 2 introduces prior research on ML in predict clinical deterioration in ICU. Section 3 presents the methodology used in this work. Section 4 presents the experiments and results followed by conclusions in Sect. 5.

2 Literature Review

Machine learning applications in the ICU can be categorized into prognostic modeling, treatment recommendation systems, disease phenotyping, resource allocation, and early warning systems for the timely detection of clinical deterioration–most notably, predicting mortality risk. In recent years, the use of ML-based models for such purpose has been extensively investigated. This section highlight representative studies that illustrate these applications.

The paper proposed by [2], developed a hybrid neural network model that combines convolutional layers (CNN) with bidirectional long short-term memory (BiLSTM), to predict mortality from statistics describing the variation of heart rate, blood pressure, respiratory rate, blood oxygen levels, and temperature. They concluded that the use of a hybrid CNN-BiLSTM network is highly effective in determining mortality risk for the 3, 7, and 14 day windows from vital signs.

The work presented in [12], conducted a systematic literature review to evaluate the effectiveness of applying ML in the ICU using the MIMIC dataset. A quantitative descriptive analysis was performed on 61 qualified articles that applied ML techniques in ICU settings. The authors assembled the qualified articles to provide insights into the areas of application, clinical variables used, and treatment outcomes that can pave the way for further adoption of this promising technology and possible use in routine clinical decision. In their review, studies have employed both ML and Deep Learning (DL) methods to predict mortality. Among traditional ML techniques, Random Forest, Decision Tree, and Logistic Regression were the most commonly used algorithms. Recent studies have also applied DL methods for mortality prediction with promising accuracy. However, they point out that ML models are generally more interpretable compared to DL models, which involve many levels of features and hidden layers to predict outcomes.

The investigation described in [1], evaluated whether the following measurements: blood pressure, oxygen saturation, temperature and heart rate can predict deterioration in ICU patients. Additionally, they aimed to identify which of these measurements contributes most significantly to the prediction. Lastly, they sought to determine the most accurate classifier for real-world data applications, evaluating models such as logistic regression, support vector machines, k-nearest neighbors (KNN), eXtreme Gradient Boosting (XGBoost), and Naive Bayes. A comprehensive comparison of these techniques was performed, focusing on accuracy, precision, recall, and F-measure. The results showed that the XGBoost model achieved the highest accuracy in predicting patient deterioration or survival.

In [3], the authors evaluated the performance gap between interpretable and black-box models in two healthcare prediction tasks: mortality and length of stay prediction in ICU settings. They focused specifically on the family of Generalized Additive Models (GAMs) as powerful interpretable ML models. The models were evaluated based on (i) predictive performance, (ii) the impact of compact feature sets on predictive accuracy, and (iii) interpretability and consistency with medical knowledge. The findings suggest that interpretable models can achieve performance close to that of state-of-the-art black-box models such as Random Forest (RF), XGBoost, Decision Tree (DT), and Logistic Regression (LR).

Finally, the study conducted in [13], presented the development of a real-time prediction model using digital and automatically generated clinical variables for the early detection of patients at risk of deterioration. Five different models were trained, tested, and compared: an artificial neural network (ANN), a random forest (RF), a support vector machine (SVM), a linear discriminant analysis (LDA), and a logistic regression (LR). The conclusions indicated that the ANN, using automatically recorded vital signs, was the most effective in predicting deterioration, based on its sensitivity. In terms of specificity, the Random Forest outperformed the other models.

Taking into account the recent research reported in the literature, some analyses are necessary. Studies that utilize ANN must address the high dimensionality of physiological and vital signs time series datasets, which demands an expensive feature selection process– a critical factor in the success of a neural network. Studies that use deep learning (DL) face the challenge of interpreting the results obtained, due to the complexity of the model. ML models such as XGBoost outperform traditional algorithms like KNN and SVM, as observed in [1]. Although interpretable ML models, such as GAMs, show promise, they still fall short in terms of accuracy and efficiency when compared to state-of-the-art black-box models.

In this context, and considering the limitations identified in previous studies from the literature, this work assessed three promising black-box machine learning models for mortality risk prediction in the ICU, based on patient data and clinical measurements. Additionally, we employed XAI techniques to interpret the predictions generated by the ML models, thereby addressing their lack of interpretability.

3   Methodology

This section outlines all procedures applied in the present study, including dataset preprocessing, data imputation techniques, classifiers hyperparameter tuning, performance metrics and model explanation. Preprocessing involved data formatting to ensure consistency and compatibility across all variables. Missing values were handled using appropriate imputation methods tailored to the type and distribution of the missing data. Hyperparameter tuning was performed to optimize the performance of the machine learning algorithms, using grid search and cross-validation strategies. Performance metrics were applied to assess model efficiency, and Explainable Artificial Intelligence was used to interpret the model outcomes.

3.1   Dataset Preprocessing

The data used in this study were obtained from the Medical Information Mart for Intensive Care (MIMIC-IV) clinical dataset [7], which contains detailed clinical information from patients admitted to the Beth Israel Deaconess Medical Center (BIDMC). For the purposes of this study, data were specifically selected from ICU patients, including patient data, vital signs and laboratory test results. Table 1 lists the names of the selected clinical information.

Table 1. Patient data, vital signs and laboratory test results.

Event Name	Type
Gender	Categorical
Age	Numeric
Daily Weight	Numeric
Respiratory Rate	Numeric
O2 saturation pulseoxymetry	Numeric
Temperature Celsius	Numeric
Arterial Blood Pressure systolic	Numeric
Arterial Blood Pressure diastolic	Numeric
Heart Rate	Numeric
Level of Consciousness	Categorical
PAR-Respiration	Categorical
Glucose (whole blood)	Numeric
Sodium (whole blood)	Numeric
Creatinine (whole blood)	Numeric
Potassium (whole blood)	Numeric

In the MIMIC-IV dataset, each medical record is stored as a separate row, containing the patient identifier, timestamp, event code, and corresponding value. To facilitate analysis, this raw data was restructured into time-series vectors, with each row representing a single day of the ICU stay of the patient and including all features observed on that day. The target variable indicates whether the patient survived or died.

Two distinct methods were used to generate these time vectors. The first method, proposed by [4], creates a daily vector by including the last three recorded values for each feature within a 24-hour window. The second method, proposed by [2], also generates one vector per 24-hour period, but computes and includes seven statistical metrics for each feature: first value, last value, mean, median, minimum, maximum, and standard deviation.

Missing data is a common issue in the MIMIC-IV dataset. Addressing this problem is crucial, as simply ignoring or discarding records with missing values can introduce bias and negatively affect both analysis and model performance. Several strategies exist to handle missing data, including imputation techniques. Based on the study in [11], five imputation techniques were considered in this work: linear interpolation, forward filling, carry-forward, indicator imputation, and zero imputation. These methods were selected due to their suitability for time-series clinical data, where temporal continuity and feature sparsity are common.

Another challenge with the MIMIC dataset is data imbalance. To deal with class imbalance, a frequent issue in medical datasets where adverse outcomes (e.g., mortality) are relatively rare, the Random Undersampling technique was applied to the training set. This method reduces the number of majority class instances to match the minority class, thus balancing the class distribution. Statistically, this helps prevent the model from learning a trivial decision boundary biased toward the majority class, which could artificially inflate accuracy while degrading performance on the minority class. By ensuring class balance during training, the models are encouraged to learn discriminative features for both classes.

3.2 Classifiers Hyperparameter Tuning

To predict clinical deterioration in the ICU, we evaluated the performance of three ML algorithms: LightGBM (LGBM), Random Forest, and XGBoost, using the MIMIC-IV dataset. The hyperparameters of these algorithms, showed in Table 2, were optimized using a grid search approach, intending to identify the best parameter combinations for each model. The Geometric Mean (G-Mean) was employed as the primary performance metric to evaluate and compare model effectiveness, as it balances sensitivity and specificity, making it suitable for imbalanced classification problems. A ten-fold cross-validation strategy was applied, in which models were trained on a balanced dataset but validated on an imbalanced one to simulate real-world clinical conditions.

Following the grid search procedure, the ten best hyperparameter combinations were selected to train and test the models across each fold. The resulting performance metrics were used to determine the most effective configuration.

Table 2. Hyperparameter Tuning.

Model	Parameters	Values
Random Forest Classifier	n_estimators	100, 200, 300, 600
	max_depth	None, 2, 4, 6, 8, 10, 12, 14
	min_samples_split	2, 4, 6, 8
	min_samples_leaf	1, 3, 5, 7
XGBoost	gamma	0, 1, 2, 3
	eta	0.1, 0.3, 0.6
	max_depth	2, 4, 6, 8, 10, None
	grow_policy	depthwise, lossguide
	sampling_method	uniform, gradient_based
LightGBM	num_leaves	7, 10, 15, 30, 31, 40, 50
	max_depth	-1, 2, 3
	learning_rate	0.012, 0.025, 0.05, 0.1, 0.2
	n_estimators	50, 100, 200, 300

3.3 Model Performance Analysis

Subsequently, each model was evaluated using its optimal hyperparameter configuration on the original imbalanced dataset in order to preserve the real-world outcome distribution. Three performance metrics were assessed: Sensitivity, Specificity, and G-Mean, using a ten-fold cross-validation approach. Sensitivity and specificity correspond to the True Positive Rate (TPR) and True Negative Rate (TNR), respectively. G-Mean is calculated as the square root of the product of sensitivity and specificity. It provides a balanced assessment of model performance by accounting for both the ability to correctly classify positive and negative cases, making it particularly useful in scenarios where one class significantly outnumbers the other.

To statistically evaluate whether the differences among model performances were significant, the Friedman test with Nemenyi post hoc was conducted, which is appropriate for comparing multiple algorithms over multiple datasets [5]. The corresponding results are presented in Sect. 4.

3.4 Model Explanation

As stated in Sect. 1, one of the limitations of ML algorithms is their lack of interpretability. Their black-box nature is problematic because patients, physicians, and even designers, do not understand why or how a prediction is produced by AI technologies [6]. Therefore, we employed SHapley Additive exPlanations (SHAP), an Explainable AI (XAI) technique, to interpret the output of ML models by quantifying the contribution of each feature to a given prediction. Interpreting the predictive contribution of individual features plays a key role in aiding clinical decisions.

4   Experimental Results

This section presents the experimental setup, evaluation metrics, and results obtained to assess the performance of the ML models. The experiments were conducted using Python 3.12.3. As described in Sect. 3, three ML algorithms – LightGBM, Random Forest, and XGBoost – were combined with five data imputation techniques: linear interpolation, forward filling, carry-forward, indicator imputation, and zero imputation, resulting in fifteen models. Each of these fifteen models was evaluated using the method proposed by [4] for creating time-series vectors, which includes the last three recorded values for each feature within a 24-h window.

The first fifteen models were named by combining the name of the data imputation technique with the machine learning algorithm, resulting in names like 'zrRF', which stands for Random Forest + zero imputation. For LightGBM, the abbreviation 'LGBM' was used, and for XGBoost, 'XGB' was used. As for the data imputation techniques, 'zr' refers to zero imputation, 'ff' to forward filling, 'cf' to carry-forward, 'id' to indicator imputation, and 'it' to linear interpolation.

An additional three models were analyzed – without applying data imputation techniques – using the same three ML algorithms, but employing the method proposed by [2] to construct the time-series vectors. This approach generates one vector per 24-hour period and adds seven statistical metrics for each feature: first value, last value, mean, median, minimum, maximum, and standard deviation. These models were named by combining the abbreviation 'sta' (from statistical) with the ML algorithm, resulting in staLGBM, staRF, and staXGB.

As already mentioned, the hyperparameters of each of the eighteen models were then tuned using a grid search approach, aiming to identify the optimal parameter combinations for each case. The combinations demonstrating the highest performance and the lowest computational cost were selected to compose the models.

To evaluate the effectiveness of the eighteen models in predicting mortality risk in ICU patients, tests were conducted on the original imbalanced dataset to reflect real-world prevalence. Three performance metrics were assessed: G-Mean, Sensitivity (Sens.), and Specificity (Spe.), using a ten-fold cross-validation approach. Table 3 summarizes the average (avg) and standard deviation (sd) of the metrics obtained from ten executions. The ranking of the models is based on their G-Mean average.

As observed, the top three models are based on the Random Forest algorithm, followed by one utilizing LightGBM and another using XGBoost. The models staRF, zrRF, idRF, staLGBM, and staXGB achieved the best performance, with G-mean values of 0.9553, 0.9497, 0.9461, 0.9409, and 0.9330, respectively. All these five models also exhibited strong predictive capability for both classes, as evidenced by their high sensitivity and specificity values. Among the three ML models, the statistical approach was particularly effective in generating the time-series vectors.

Table 3. Model results.

Rank	Model	G-Mean(avg)	G-Mean(sd)	Sens.(avg)	Sens.(sd)	Spe.(avg)	Spe.(sd)
1	staRF	0.9553	0.0011	1.0000	0.0000	0.9127	0.0021
2	zrRF	0.9497	0.0012	1.0000	0.0000	0.9019	0.0023
3	idRF	0.9461	0.0020	0.9984	0.0017	0.8965	0.0033
4	staLGBM	0.9409	0.0038	0.9792	0.0075	0.9041	0.0020
5	staXGB	0.9330	0.0038	0.9643	0.0073	0.9027	0.0018
6	itXGB	0.9088	0.0067	0.9344	0.0136	0.8838	0.0012
7	cfRF	0.8990	0.0062	0.8928	0.0127	0.9052	0.0023
8	ffRF	0.8952	0.0066	0.8847	0.0132	0.9059	0.0026
9	itLGBM	0.8926	0.0103	0.9050	0.0210	0.8803	0.0014
10	idXGB	0.8861	0.0089	0.8834	0.0163	0.8889	0.0044
11	zrLGBM	0.8772	0.0070	0.8558	0.0142	0.8991	0.0018
12	zrXGB	0.8736	0.0066	0.8449	0.0131	0.9033	0.0017
13	cfLGBM	0.8607	0.0093	0.8345	0.0193	0.8877	0.0027
14	cfXGB	0.8595	0.0094	0.8259	0.0185	0.8945	0.0023
15	ffXGB	0.8594	0.0128	0.8259	0.0251	0.8943	0.0022
16	idLGBM	0.8591	0.0104	0.8129	0.0207	0.9080	0.0030
17	itRF	0.8563	0.0102	0.7970	0.0203	0.9199	0.0017
18	ffLGBM	0.8508	0.0122	0.8090	0.0236	0.8948	0.0023

In order to determine whether there are statistically significant differences among the G-Mean outcomes of the all models, statistical analyses were conducted using the Friedman test with Nemenyi post hoc, with level of significance $= 0.05$. The *p-values* results are shown in Table 4.

Table 4. Statistical results.

		1	2	3	4	5	6	7	8	9	10	11	12	13	14	15	16	17
		zrRF	idRF	staLGBM	staXGB	itXGB	cfRF	ffRF	itLGBM	idXGB	zrLGBM	zrXGB	cfLGBM	cfXGB	ffXGB	idLGBM	itRF	ffLGBM
1	staRF	0.9000	0.9000	0.9000	0.9000	0.3983	0.1923	0.1113	0.7914	0.0119	0.0010	0.0010	0.0010	0.0010	0.0010	0.0010	0.0010	0.0010
2	zrRF		0.9000	0.9000	0.9000	0.7092	0.4897	0.3367	0.9000	0.0597	0.0062	0.0010	0.0010	0.0010	0.0010	0.0031	0.0010	0.0010
3	idRF			0.9000	0.9000	0.9000	0.7366	0.5995	0.9000	0.1739	0.0257	0.0052	0.0010	0.0010	0.0010	0.0140	0.0010	0.0010
4	staLGBM				0.9000	0.9000	0.9000	0.8462	0.9000	0.3983	0.0875	0.0222	0.0010	0.0010	0.0010	0.0521	0.0010	0.0010
5	staXGB					0.9000	0.9000	0.9000	0.9000	0.7092	0.2832	0.0984	0.0044	0.0022	0.0044	0.1923	0.0010	0.0010
6	itXGB						0.9000	0.9000	0.9000	0.9000	0.9000	0.6818	0.1391	0.0875	0.1391	0.8462	0.0222	0.0052
7	cfRF							0.9000	0.9000	0.9000	0.9000	0.9000	0.3092	0.2131	0.3092	0.9000	0.0682	0.0191
8	ffRF								0.9000	0.9000	0.9000	0.9000	0.4604	0.3367	0.4604	0.9000	0.1250	0.0397
9	itLGBM									0.9000	0.5721	0.2832	0.0222	0.0119	0.0222	0.4604	0.0022	0.0010
10	idXGB										0.9000	0.9000	0.9000	0.7914	0.9000	0.9000	0.5173	0.2582
11	zrLGBM											0.9000	0.9000	0.9000	0.9000	0.9000	0.9000	0.6818
12	zrXGB												0.9000	0.9000	0.9000	0.9000	0.9000	0.9000
13	cfLGBM													0.9000	0.9000	0.9000	0.9000	0.9000
14	cfXGB														0.9000	0.9000	0.9000	0.9000
15	ffXGB															0.9000	0.9000	0.9000
16	idLGBM																0.9000	0.7914
17	itRF																	0.9000

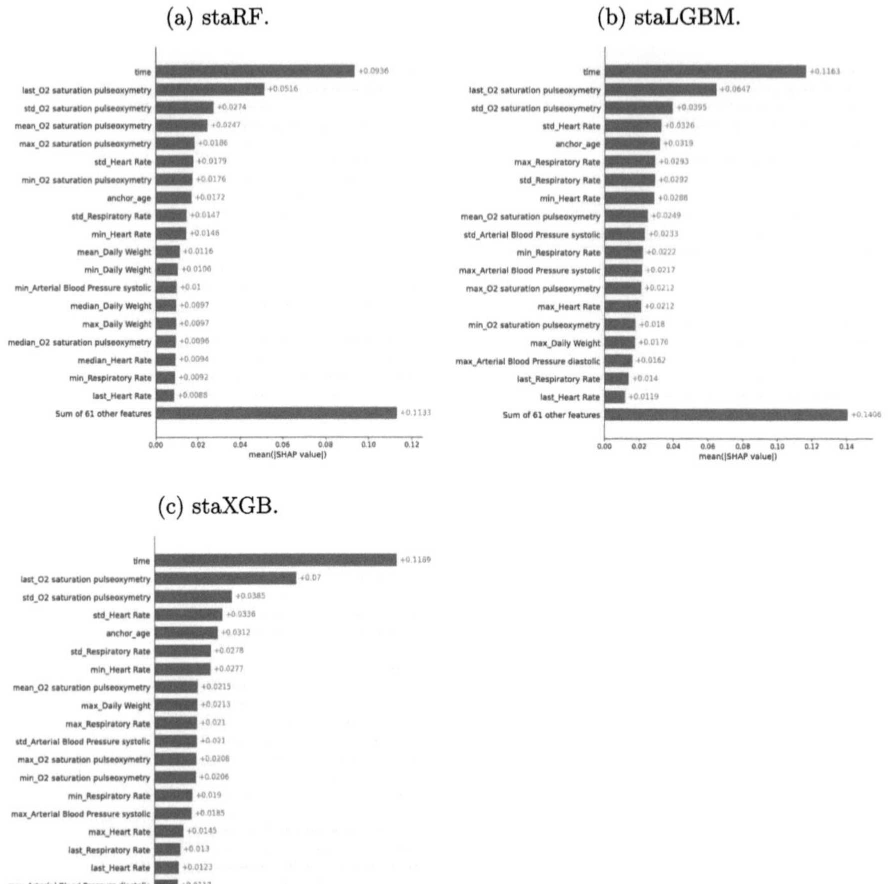

Fig. 1. SHAP analysis.

Based on Table 4, when considering the metric G-Mean and analyzing each row of the table, it can be observed that there is no statistically significant difference between staRF (the top-ranked model) and all other models listed in columns 1 to 8. The same holds true for zrRF model in columns 2 to 9, and idRF model with respect to the models in columns 3 to 9. The staLGBM model showed no statistically significant difference when compared to the models in columns 4 to 10, as well as column 15. Finally, the staXGB model did not exhibit a statistically significant difference compared to the models in columns 5 to 11 and column 15. In summary, considering the top five models in the ranking, we observe that there is no statistically significant difference among them, despite the differences in their G-Mean values. Thus, it is inferred that the three machine learning algorithms – LightGBM, Random Forest, and XGBoost – can be effectively applied to estimate the risk of mortality in ICU patients.

Finally, the SHAP technique was employed to explain the outputs of the ML models. It quantifies the contribution of each feature to a given prediction and helps to understand how features influence model outcomes. Considering that the three ML algorithms analyzed in this study are among the top five models with the highest G-Mean, and that there is no statistically significant difference among them, we applied the SHAP technique to the staRF, staLGBM, and staXGB models. Figure 1 displays the most important features in descending order for each model.

Figure 1(a) presents the SHAP values for the staRF model. Length of stay (time) is identified as the most important feature, followed by statistical measures related to the O2 saturation (pulse oximetry) variable, which were incorporated through the statistical approach used to construct the time-series vectors. Figures 1(b) and 1(c) show the SHAP values for the staLGBM and staXGB models, respectively. These values also indicate that length of stay has a stronger impact on the prediction. Other relevant features include statistical measures associated with O2 saturation (pulse oximetry), heart rate, and respiratory rate, as well as the anchor age variable. Based on the results obtained from the three models under analysis, it can be inferred that the features length of stay, O2 saturation (pulse oximetry), heart rate, and anchor age exhibit a greater influence on the predictive outcomes.

5   Conclusion

In this paper, we presented a study evaluating eighteen predictive models for assessing mortality risk in ICU patients. Of these, fifteen were constructed by combining three machine learning algorithms with five data imputation techniques. The remaining three models were developed using each machine learning algorithm individually, incorporating statistical metrics derived from the dataset features. Hyperparameter tuning was conducted to optimize model performance, employing grid search in conjunction with a ten-fold cross-validation strategy.

The algorithms were evaluated using G-Mean, Sensitivity, and Specificity metrics, employing a ten-fold cross-validation approach. The results indicated that the top three models were based on the Random Forest algorithm, followed by one using LightGBM and another using XGBoost. Notably, all five models demonstrated strong predictive performance for both classes, as reflected by their high Sensitivity and Specificity scores. An important observation is that among top five models, three models used only ML algoritms, employing the method proposed by [2] to construct the time-series vectors. Another important consideration is that there is no statistically significant difference among the top five models identified.

Given that the three machine learning algorithms analyzed in this study are represented among the top five models with the highest G-Mean scores– and that no statistically significant differences were observed among them–the

SHAP technique was applied to the staRF, staLGBM, and staXGB models. The findings showed that the features length of stay, O2 saturation (pulse oximetry), heart rate, and anchor age exert a greater influence on the predictive outcomes.

In future work, we intend to compare our results with score-based models, given that these models are widely used by physicians. Additionally, we plan to advance the current XAI-based analysis by employing explainability techniques as a feature selection strategy, conducting further analyses using only the most relevant features contributing to mortality risk prediction.

Acknowledgments. The authors would like to thank the CAPES Postgraduate Support Program (PROAP) and the State University of Feira de Santana for the financial support.

References

1. Aldhoayan, M.D., Aljubran, Y.: Prediction of icu patients' deterioration using machine learning techniques. Cureus **15** (2023). https://doi.org/10.7759/cureus.38659
2. Baker, S., Xiang, W., Atkinson, I.: Continuous and automatic mortality risk prediction using vital signs in the intensive care unit: a hybrid neural network approach. Sci. Rep. **10** (2020). https://doi.org/10.1038/s41598-020-78184-7
3. Bohlen, L., Rosenberger, J., Zschech, P.M.K.: Leveraging interpretable machine learning in intensive care. Ann. Oper. Res. (2024). https://doi.org/10.1007/s10479-024-06226-8
4. Cheng, F.Y., et al.: Using machine learning to predict ICU transfer in hospitalized covid-19 patients. J. Clin. Med. **9**(6), 1668 (2020)
5. Demšar, J.: Statistical comparisons of classifiers over multiple data sets. J. Mach. Learn. Res. **7**, 1–30 (2006)
6. Hanhui, X., Kyle, M.J.S.: Medical artificial intelligence and the black box problem: a view based on the ethical principle of "do no harm". Intell. Med. **4**(1), 52–57 (2024). https://doi.org/10.1016/j.imed.2023.08.001
7. Johnson, A.E., et al.: Mimic-iv, a freely accessible electronic health record dataset. Sci. Data **10**(1), 1 (2023). https://doi.org/10.1038/s41597-022-01899-x
8. Ke, G., et al.: Lightgbm: a highly efficient gradient boosting decision tree. In: Proceedings of the 31st International Conference on Neural Information Processing Systems, NIPS'17, pp. 3149–3157. Curran Associates Inc., Red Hook (2017)
9. Knaus, W., Draper, E., Wagner, D., Zimmerman, J.: Apache ii: a severity of disease classification system. Care Med. 818–829 (1985)
10. Lim, L., et al.: Multicenter validation of a machine learning model to predict intensive care unit readmission within 48 hours after discharge. eClinicalMedicine **81**, 103112 (2025). https://doi.org/10.1016/j.eclinm.2025.103112
11. Solís-García, J., Vega-Márquez, B., Nepomuceno, J.A., Riquelme-Santos, J.C., Nepomuceno-Chamorro, I.A.: Comparing artificial intelligence strategies for early sepsis detection in the ICU: an experimental study. Appl. Intell. **53**(24), 30691–30705 (2023)

12. Syed, M., et al.: Application of machine learning in intensive care unit (icu) settings using mimic dataset: systematic review. Informatics **8**(1) (2021). https://doi.org/10.3390/informatics8010016
13. Thiele, D., et al.: Machine learning models for the early real-time prediction of deterioration in intensive care units–a novel approach to the early identification of high-risk patients. J. Clin. Med. **14**(2) (2025). https://doi.org/10.3390/jcm14020350

Predicting College Student Mental Health Levels: A Machine Learning Approach Using Sociodemographic and Quality of Life Data

Lucas J. L. Braz[1]([envelope]), Lucas S. Fonseca[1], and C. Alexandre R. Fernandes[2]

[1] Universidade Federal do Ceará (UFC), Fortaleza, Brazil
`{lucas.jlb19,lucas.santosfonseca}@alu.ufc.br`
[2] Universidade Federal do Ceará (UFC), Sobral, Brazil
`alexandrefernandes@ufc.br`

Abstract. Worldwide, mental health (MH) issues among students, including anxiety and depression, are rising. Predictive models are crucial for early intervention. This study proposes a novel MH prediction model for college students using data mining (DM) and machine learning (ML) techniques. The model integrates sociodemographic data and Quality of Life (QoL) assessments, employing various classification and regression methods, alongside feature selection. Using a database of 880 students and data from the Mental Health Inventory (MHI), WHOQOL-Bref, and a sociodemographic questionnaire, the model achieved a high accuracy of 82.62%, with an R^2 of 0.7139. Furthermore, the study identifies key factors influencing MH prediction. This data-driven approach provides a valuable tool for identifying students needing support, potentially improving intervention strategies and campus well-being programs.

Keywords: Mental health · Quality of life · Machine learning · Prediction model · Data mining

1 Introduction

The number of scientific studies in the field of Mental Health (MH) has considerably increased in recent years. MH is now recognized as a major factor impacting various aspects of individuals' lives [32]. World Health Organization (WHO) defines MH as a state of well-being enabling individuals to cope with life's stresses, utilize their abilities, and contribute to their communities [3]. According to the WHO, MH is influenced by individual, social, and structural factors throughout life.

Indeed, psychological and biological factors such as emotional skills and substance use, along with social, economic, and geopolitical circumstances, all contribute to a person's vulnerability or resilience to MH challenges. One such key factor is Quality of Life (QoL), a multifaceted concept encompassing physical,

R. de Freitas and D. Furtado (Eds.): BRACIS 2025, LNAI 16181, pp. 348–362, 2026.
https://doi.org/10.1007/978-3-032-15990-8_24

psychological, social, and environmental dimensions relevant to overall well-being [2].

While MH challenges affect the broader population, the college student demographic faces a particularly acute and growing crisis. Recent evidence consistently points to alarmingly high prevalence rates of anxiety, depression, and significant stress among university students globally [22]. These conditions are far from benign academic stressors; they profoundly impact students' lives, significantly impairing academic performance, interfering with daily functioning, hindering the development of crucial social connections, and tragically increasing the risk of dropout and suicide [13,14]. The urgency for effective early identification and intervention strategies within higher education settings cannot be overstated.

Understanding and predicting MH outcomes in this population is complicated by the intricate interplay of numerous factors. Beyond academic pressures, students navigate financial stress, significant life transitions, and complex social dynamics, all of which are further modulated by individual sociodemographic backgrounds [11]. Crucially, the various domains of QoL, including perceived physical health, psychological state, social relationship quality, and environmental satisfaction, are strongly intertwined with mental health status [12]. Lower QoL across these domains often correlates with greater mental distress, suggesting that QoL indicators may hold significant predictive value [29]. Yet, their comprehensive integration into predictive models remains an area needing further exploration.

Accordingly, Data Mining (DM) and Machine Learning (ML) techniques are increasingly popular tools across multiple fields due to their usefulness in dealing with high-dimensional datasets to identify important patterns and address diverse problems, including those in medicine, health, biology, and psychology [18,19]. These computational systems utilize datasets to improve clinical decision-making through the use of pattern recognition as predictive systems for pre-diagnosis, which is particularly relevant given the complexities outlined above.

This study proposes a predictive model for MH levels among college students employing the Knowledge Discovery in Databases (KDD) methodology. The proposed model incorporates ML techniques with sociodemographic data and QoL indicators to predict MH levels and analyze the influencing factors. These findings could contribute to a more informed approach to policy recommendations in healthcare settings.

The predictive model uses the KDD process [15] for effective database management and efficient use of ML algorithms. Through extensive testing of multiple classification and regression models, this study aimed to identify those which performed optimally. To enhance predictive performance and address feature complexity, the feature selection methods Sequential Forward Floating Selection (SFFS) and Sequential Backward Floating Selection (SBFS) were applied. The dataset consists of data from three questionnaires [29]: Mental Health Inventory (MHI), World Health Organization Quality of Life (WHOQOL-Bref), and a sociodemographic questionnaire. The WHOQOL-Bref was designed to measure the multidimensional QoL [17], while the sociodemographic survey covers basic participant details, serving as independent variables and input into the system. Data collection occurred through in-person interviews with 880 college student participants.

The MHI, established as a metric of MH from the United States Department of Health, Education, and Welfare [33], identifies the output of this dataset (as a dependent variable), functioning as the predicted output for these models. For regression analyses, the raw MHI score is used and, for classification analyses, the MHI underwent a stratification with three levels: low, medium, and high. The results demonstrate the good ability of the proposed models, achieving an accuracy of 82.62% and an R^2 value of 0.7139.

This paper proceeds with the following structure: Sect. 2 contextualizes our contribution by outlining relevant prior studies. Section 3 lays the groundwork, offering background on the fundamental concepts of MH and QoL. The proposed methodology is described in Sect. 4, which covers the dataset characteristics and the predictive models. Section 5 is dedicated to presenting and comparing the empirical results regarding model performance, followed by an analysis of the dataset's most salient features. The paper concludes in Sect. 6 with a summary of findings, potential applications, and avenues for future work.

2   Related Works

This section reviews relevant research applying ML techniques to MH and related areas. Several studies highlighted the application of diverse ML algorithms for MH level prediction in varied populations, such as high school and college students, and working professionals [30]. These studies analyze factors like engagement, perseverance, optimism, and happiness as potential predictors. For instance, [30] achieved 90% accuracy in predicting MH levels using a range of classifiers.

The impact of psychoactive substances on MH has also been investigated through the use of ML. Research analyzing the correlation between psychoactive drug use, depression, and Common Mental Disorders (CMD) found age, income, frequency of drug use, and dependence were significant predictors [9]. Using ML, an accuracy rate of approximately 82% was achieved for both CMD and depression prediction.

Other studies have investigated the potential of ML in MH prediction among working populations, using Decision Trees (DT), Random Forest (RF), and Naive Bayes (NB) in online surveys using the Open Sourcing Mental Illness dataset (OSMI) [21]. A DT model yielded the highest accuracy (82%), while also revealing relevant factors like work problems, family history, and gender.

Predictive modeling has been explored to evaluate poor physical and mental Health-Related Quality of Life (HRQoL) among individuals with rheumatoid arthritis. Two Logistic Regression (LR) models in [4] were developed that achieved an accuracy of 83.7% for mental HRQoL and 75.4% for physical HRQoL, indicating predictors including pain, family income (below \$300), comorbidities, and depression.

ML models have also been employed in the early identification and intervention of MH disorders. A study applying LR, K-Nearest Neighbors (KNN), DT, and RF algorithms achieved an accuracy of 86% for early MH disorder detection, based on inputs of age, gender, lifestyle, and MH history [5].

The present work expands on the aforementioned existing ML approaches by using multiple regression and classification ML techniques, as well as feature selection methods, to model scores in college students in Brazil. Specifically, in addition to considering socioeconomic data, this work evaluates the impact of QoL indices on MH, which have not been considered by similar works, offering insights that refine models and strengthen MH predictive systems in comparison to the above-mentioned works.

3   Background

Understanding the fundamental concepts of MH and QoL provides the necessary foundation for the methodology and results presented herein. The following subsections elaborate on these key terms.

3.1   Mental Health

The WHO defines MH as a state of well-being where individuals realize their potential, cope with life's stresses, work productively, and contribute to their communities [1]. Despite its pervasive influence, misconceptions and barriers to services surround MH. Many people remain unaware of their conditions, delaying treatment until symptoms worsen [5]. The prevalence of MH disorders is significant: one in three women and one in five men experience major depressive episodes [31], highlighting a broader range of MH challenges alongside major depression and the risk of suicide, with the WHO noting that in 2023 over 700,000 suicides occurred worldwide [24].

MH encompasses a broad spectrum beyond common conceptions of anxiety and depression, which highlights a wider range of dysfunctions and psychopathological states, requiring rigorous assessments for proper diagnosis [33]. In 1971, after 15 years of research, the U.S. Department of Health, Education and Welfare developed the MHI, a crucial tool for MH assessment that measures various dimensions including psychological distress, psychological well-being, anxiety, depression, emotional ties, general positive affection, and emotional/behavioral control. This assessment has greatly informed the tracking of mental illnesses, in order to identify populations most affected, so that those at risk may be addressed earlier and more proactively [33]. The MHI's 38 items cover several domains relevant to the MH spectrum, allowing for a clearer distinction of cases by quantifying them [33].

3.2 Quality of Life

Although the term QoL emerged around 1930, a complete and standardized definition didn't gain general acceptance until the 1990s [10,28]. Now widely recognized as both subjective and multifaceted [28], the WHO emphasizes that QoL includes emotional and physical well-being along with personal abilities, which together generate overall satisfaction levels [16]. QoL encompasses physical, psychological, social, and environmental dimensions [2].

The WHO's World Health Organization Qualiy of Life (WHOQOL) group developed comprehensive scales for QoL measurement, including the full WHOQOL and the shorter 26-item WHOQOL-Bref, which addresses four key domains: physical, psychological, social relationships, and environment. This reduced instrument retains strong predictive potential for both happiness and overall well-being [25]. While acknowledging the contribution of multiple parameters to QoL, studies point out the significant influence of the psychological dimension to QoL and overall MH [12,26].

4 Methodology

The development of our predictive models involved defining the data foundation, described below, and implementing a systematic KDD process for analysis and evaluation.

4.1 Mental Health Database

The dataset used in this study was constructed by the authors of [29] and comprises data from three questionnaires: the MHI, WHOQOL-Bref, and a sociodemographic survey. The sociodemographic survey collects data such as gender, age, education level, socioeconomic status, living arrangements, frequency of family visits, and relevant clinical information, including leisure hours, health conditions, participation in social activities, and psychoactive substance use. The WHOQOL-Bref questionnaire, consisting of 24 items, measures different facets of QoL in four domains (physical, psychological, social relationships, and environment).

The MHI, serving as the dependent variable, assesses levels of MH. This data is used as the output. For regression analysis, the raw MHI index was used. However, for classification analyses, the MHI index undergoes quantization into three distinct levels (low, medium, high), using the following classification rule:

$$\hat{y}_i = \begin{cases} \text{low}, & y_i \leq \mu - \sigma \\ \text{medium}, & \mu - \sigma < y_i < \mu + \sigma \\ \text{high}, & y_i \geq \mu + \sigma \end{cases} \qquad (1)$$

where y_i is the raw MHI score of the ith sample, $\hat{y}_i$ is the stratified MHI score, μ is the mean and σ standard deviation of the MHI scores.

Data collection involved in-person interviews with 880 participants, all college students across 19 different undergraduate programs at Vale do Acaraú University, Brazil. Data was collected anonymously and voluntarily between April and June 2019. A basic statistical analysis was conducted previously using the dataset in [29], without using ML and associated techniques.

The distribution of samples across these three stratified classes reveals an imbalance, with the 'Medium' mental health level being the majority class. Specifically, out of 880 participants, 574 (65.83%) were classified as 'Medium', while 149 (17.09%) were 'Low' and 149 (17.09%) were 'High'. This class distribution was considered during model evaluation.

4.2   Predictive Model

The proposed predictive model adheres to the five steps of the KDD approach: (1) data selection, (2) preprocessing, (3) transformation, (4) data mining, and (5) interpretation [15]. The complete KDD process used in the present work involved these sequential steps. Step 1 (data selection) involved removing duplicated entries, entries with missing values, and those with irrelevant or redundant features. After this step, 872 samples remained for analysis

In Step 2 (*preprocessing*), categorical variables were converted into numerical form using one-hot encoding for binary variables. Complex categorical variables (e.g., place of birth) were simplified, retaining only the most relevant information. In Step 3 (*transformation*), the feature selection techniques SFFS and SBFS are applied to improve performance by minimizing dimensionality. SFFS iteratively adds features which contribute maximally while SBFS progressively eliminates least significant features to achieve optimal performance [20,27].

Step 4 (*data mining*) encompassed the application of ten classification models (NB, RF, eXtreme Gradient Boosting (XGBoost), Support Vector Machine (SVM), DT, Adaptive Boost (ADABoost), EXtra-Trees Classifier (EXT), LR, Multilayer Perceptron (MLP), and KNN) and seven regression models (Multiple Linear Regression (MLR), Support Vector Regression (SVR), XGBoost, MLP, RF, DT, and KNN). Hyperparameter tuning employed a random search technique to optimize performance, considering computational costs and outcomes [7]. A five-fold cross-validation was employed to further ensure robustness.

The final step (Step 5, *interpretation*) involves analyzing the results and interpreting them within the larger context (detailed in the following section). Evaluation metrics encompassed accuracy, precision, recall, F1-score, and the confusion matrix for classification; R-squared, mean squared error (MSE), and mean absolute error (MAE) were used to evaluate the regression models.

5   Results and Discussion

This section presents and discusses simulation results evaluating the performance of the developed prediction models. First, classification results are presented, followed by regression results. In both cases, the objective is to predict the level of MHI using sociodemographic and WHOQOL-Bref responses.

Table 1. Selected Hyperparameters Using Only Sociodemographic Data

Classifier	Parameters
RF	N $^{\underline{o}}$ of Estimators = 42, Max N $^{\underline{o}}$ of Features = 24, Max Depth = 9, Criterion = Entropy.
EXT	N $^{\underline{o}}$ of Estimators = 15, Max N $^{\underline{o}}$ of Features = 23, Max Depth = 8, Criterion = Entropy.
LR	Solver = 'saga', Penalty = 'l1', Max Iterations = 1864, L1 Ratio = 0.3333, Regularization Strength (C) = 0.4291.
XGBoost	Subsample = 0.4, Number of Estimators = 51, Max Depth = 1, Learning Rate = 0.1112, Gamma = 0.4444, Colsample by Tree = 0.5.
KNN	Weights = 'uniform', Distance Metric = Minkowski (p=1), Number of Neighbors = 15, Leaf Size = 32, Algorithm = Ball Tree.
ADA	Number of Estimators = 143, Learning Rate = 0.0699.
SVM	Kernel = RBF, Gamma = 1, Degree = 3, Regularization Strength (C) = 10.
MLP	Momentum = 0.3667, Max Iterations = 968, Initial Learning Rate = 0.1112, Hidden Layer Sizes = (466, 466).
NVB	Variance Smoothing = 1.1864
DT	Splitter = 'best', Minimum Samples Split = 0.8958, Minimum Samples Leaf = 0.4226, Max Depth = 6, Criterion = Entropy.

5.1   Classification of MHI using Sociodemographic Data

This subsection presents results for classifying the MHI level using only sociodemographic data, i.e. without using the QoL information. Table 1 lists the hyperparameters selected by the random search for each tested classifier. Table 2 shows the accuracy achieved by each classification technique after hyperparameter tuning. The results robustly indicate that, when using only sociodemographic data, the classifiers achieved relatively low accuracy in predicting the MHI class. The minimal variation in performance observed across the ten different algorithms in this stage further suggests that sociodemographic data alone possess limited predictive power for college student mental health levels within this context.

Table 3 presents the accuracy of the best-performing classifier from Table 2 (RF) after applying SBFS and SFFS feature selection techniques. Table 3 also shows the number of features selected by each method. A small improvement in accuracy is observed after feature selection, accompanied by a substantial reduction in the number of features.

Specifically, the number of features decreased significantly from the original 54 features to 15 (SFFS) and 6 (SBFS). The SFFS method resulted in a larger feature set (15) and slightly higher accuracy (69.43%) compared to SBFS (6 features, 68.29%). This aligns with the general behaviour of SFFS, which often selects more features than SBFS in its search for optimal model accuracy.

Table 2. Accuracy Using Only Sociodemographic Data

Classifier	Accuracy (%)
RF	68.04
EXT	67.68
LR	67.50
XGBoost	67.14
KNN	67.14
ADA	67.14
SVM	66.96
MLP	66.78
NVB	66.61
DT	66.60

Table 3. Accuracy Using Sociodemographic Data with Feature Selection (RF Classifier)

Method	Accuracy (%)	N º of Features
SBFS	68.29	6
SFFS	**69.43**	15

5.2 Classification of MHI using Sociodemographic and WHOQOL-Bref Data

This subsection evaluates the impact of including the WHOQOL-Bref data input features, alongside the sociodemographic data, to perform MHI classification. Table 4 lists the hyperparameters of the classifiers obtained through grid search, and Table 5 shows the accuracies obtained by the classification models after tuning. The EXT classifier achieved the highest accuracy (80.08%), followed by RF (79.36%), XGBoost (78.99%), and ADA (78.46%). Comparing the results of Table 5 with those using only sociodemographic data (Table 2), a significant improvement in accuracy is achieved when the WHOQOL-Bref data is included. Specifically, the top accuracy increased from 68.04% to 80.08%.

Table 6 displays the accuracy and the number of selected features for the best-performing classifier (EXT) after applying SBFS and SFFS to the combined dataset of features. This table shows that feature selection further improved the EXT accuracy. SBFS achieved 82.62% (an increase of approximately 2.5% points over the 80.08% baseline) using 18 features, while SFFS achieved 81.64% (an increase of approximately 1.6% points) using 36 features. Again, a significant reduction in the feature count was achieved compared to using the full feature set. Comparing the number of selected features here (Table 6) with the previous case using only sociodemographic data (Table 3), more features were selected when WHOQOL-Bref data was included (18 and 36 vs. 6 and 15). This suggests

Table 4. Selected Hyperparameters Using Sociodemographic and WHOQOL-Bref Data

Classifier	Parameters
EXT	Number of Estimators = 39, Max Features = 49, Max Depth = 10, Criterion = Entropy.
RF	Number of Estimators = 51, Max Features = 29, Max Depth = 39, Criterion = Gini.
XGBoost	Subsample = 0.7, Number of Estimators = 2, Max Depth = 16, Learning Rate = 0.1112, Gamma = 0.2222, Colsample by Tree = 0.8888.
ADA	Number of Estimators = 112, Learning Rate = 0.6211.
DT	Splitter = 'best', Minimum Samples Split = 0.1663, Minimum Samples Leaf = 0.0874, Max Depth = 27, Criterion = Gini.
NVB	Variance Smoothing = 0.1695.
SVM	Kernel = RBF, Gamma = 1e-05, Degree = 2, Regularization Strength (C) = 1000.
KNN	Weights = 'uniform', Distance Metric = Minkowski (p=1), Number of Neighbors = 9, Leaf Size = 42, Algorithm = Brute Force.
LR	Solver = 'saga', Penalty = 'l1', Max Iterations = 1728, L1 Ratio = 1.0, Regularization Strength (C) = 0.1437.
MLP	Momentum = 0.8111, Max Iterations = 589, Initial Learning Rate = 0.0001, Hidden Layer Sizes = (541).,

that WHOQOL-Bref variables provide substantial predictive information for the MHI.

Table 7 details the recall, precision, and F1-score per class for the best overall model (EXT with SBFS). The weighted averages for these metrics across all classes provide a comprehensive overview of the model's classification performance, yielding a recall of approximately 0.8233, precision of 0.8265, and F1-score of 0.8212

The "Medium" class exhibits the highest recall, precision, and F1-score, indicating the model is most effective at identifying individuals with a medium MHI level. The observed lower performance in predicting the 'High' MH class, characterized by its lower recall, precision, and F1-score, is noteworthy. This disparity is consistent with the class imbalance present in the dataset, where the 'High' (and 'Low') MH categories represent minority classes compared to the 'Medium' class. While overall accuracy provides a general measure of performance, the detailed per-class metrics presented in Table 7 are crucial for understanding the model's nuanced predictive capabilities, particularly in the presence of imbalanced datasets.

Table 5. Accuracy Using Sociodemographic and WHOQOL-Bref Data

Classifier	Accuracy (%)
EXT	80.08
RF	79.36
XGBoost	78.99
ADA	78.46
DT	77.74
NVB	77.39
SVM	76.66
KNN	76.30
LR	74.87
MLP	72.71

Table 6. Accuracy Using Sociodemographic and WHOQOL-Bref Data With Feature Selection (EXT Classifier)

Method	Accuracy (%)	N º of Features
SBFS	**82.62**	18
SFFS	81.64	36

5.3 Regression of MHI using Sociodemographic and WHOQOL-Bref Data

This section presents the results obtained by the regression models when predicting the raw MHI score using both sociodemographic and WHOQOL-Bref data. The objective here is to complement the classification analysis by evaluating the ability of ML techniques to predict the continuous MHI score.

Table 8 reports the coefficient of determination (R^2), Mean Squared Error (MSE) and Mean Absolute Error (MAE) for various regression models. The MLR model achieved the best performance, with an R^2 of 0.7139, MSE of 0.0320, and MAE of 0.1383. The MLP, SVR, and XGBoost models followed closely. The performance of these top four regressors ($R^2 > 0.70$) suggests a reasonably good fit to the data, further highlighting the predictive value of the combined sociodemographic and WHOQOL-Bref features for the continuous MHI score.

To investigate potential improvements of dimensionality reduction, feature selection (SBFS and SFFS) was applied to the best-performing regressor (MLR). Table 9 presents the resulting R^2 values and the number of selected features. Feature selection did not improve the R^2 score for the MLR model. However, similarly to the classification task, both SBFS and SFFS substantially reduced the number of features (to 22 and 25, respectively) with only a minimal decrease in R^2 compared to the model using the full feature set.

Table 7. Recall, Precision and F1-Score of the EXT with SBFS Model

Class	Recall	Precision	F1-Score
Low	0.8381	0.7395	0.7857
Medium	0.8367	0.9150	0.8741
High	0.7556	0.5714	0.6507

Table 8. R^2, MSE and MAE of Various Regression Techniques

Regressor	R^2	MSE	MAE
MLR	0.7139	0.0320	0.1383
MLP	0.7131	0.0321	0.1385
SVR	0.7091	0.0326	0.1402
XGBoost	0.7035	0.0332	0.1436
RF	0.6502	0.0392	0.1558
KNN	0.6279	0.0418	0.1632
DT	0.5621	0.0489	0.1742

5.4   Importance of Features

This subsection analyzes the most influential factors for predicting the MHI. Feature importance was evaluated using information gain (based on entropy) derived from the classification task with the combined dataset. Table 10 lists the ten features with the highest information gain values. The features "Psychological Domain", "Physical Domain", and "Environmental Domain" in this table represent aggregated scores from the WHOQOL-Bref questionnaire. As described previously, these domain scores are calculated by averaging the scores of their constituent items and scaling them to a 0–100 range.

All ten features listed in Table 10 come from the WHOQOL-Bref questionnaire. This strongly corroborates the earlier finding that WHOQOL-Bref data significantly improves MHI prediction accuracy. The high ranking of the WHOQOL-Bref domain scores indicates they encapsulate substantial predictive information, logically so, as they aggregate responses from multiple related questions. Notably, the "Psychological Domain" and "Physical Domain" exhibit the highest information gain values, with the "Environmental Domain" also ranking highly (sixth).

The strong predictive power of these domains aligns with findings by [29], who reported correlations between higher WHOQOL-Bref domain scores and lower prevalence of issues like depression and anxiety (components related to MHI), ultimately indicating better MH.

Furthermore, the individual question "How often do you have negative feelings such as blue mood, despair, anxiety, depression?" ranked third in information gain. This highlights the direct importance of self-reported negative affect

Table 9. R^2 Using Combined Data With Feature Selection (MLR Regressor)

Method	R^2	N º of Features
SBFS	**0.7128**	22
SFFS	0.7035	25

Table 10. Top Ten Features by Information Gain for MHI Classification

Information Gain	Feature Description
0.496	Psychological Domain
0.338	Physical Domain
0.317	How often do you have negative feelings such as...
0.309	How satisfied are you with yourself?
0.267	How safe do you feel in your daily life?
0.240	Environment Domain
0.230	To what extent do you feel your life to be meaningful?
0.200	How satisfied are you with your health?
0.196	Do you have enough energy for everyday life?
0.191	How much do you enjoy life?

in predicting the overall MHI level. This finding is consistent with literature indicating a strong association between the frequency of such negative feelings and lower self-reported MH [23].

The question regarding perceived safety ("How safe do you feel in your daily life?") also demonstrated a high importance (fifth highest information gain). This aligns with research showing that perceived lack of safety and fear of crime can negatively impact MH through increased stress and reduced trust [8], and is specifically associated with depression, anxiety, and psychological distress [6].

Similarly, the question "To what extent do you feel your life is meaningful?" ranked highly (seventh). This is consistent with findings that perceived meaning in life is a strong predictor of psychological well-being [34].

6   Conclusion and Future Work

This paper presented the development and evaluation of ML models, following the KDD process, to predict the MH level of college students. Data from sociodemographic and WHOQOL-Bref questionnaires served as input features, while the MHI score was the target variable. Several ML techniques and feature selection methods were evaluated for both classification (predicting MH levels: low, medium, high) and regression (predicting the raw MHI score) tasks to identify approaches yielding optimal predictive performance.

The results demonstrated strong predictive performance for the classification task. Ensemble tree-based models, specifically EXT, RF, XGBoost, and

ADA, achieved accuracies ranging from 78% to 80%. Applying feature selection (SBFS) to the best-performing classifier (EXT) further increased accuracy to 82.62%. A key finding was that incorporating WHOQOL-Bref data substantially improved prediction accuracy compared to using sociodemographic data alone, which demonstrated limited predictive capabilities in isolation. This highlights the critical importance of QoL indicators for a more comprehensive and accurate estimation of mental health status.

Furthermore, an analysis of feature importance using information gain revealed the predominant contribution of WHOQOL-Bref features to MHI prediction. Questions related to subjective psychological and physical well-being, particularly the aggregated "Psychological Domain" and "Physical Domain" scores, emerged as the most influential predictors. This finding underscores the close relationship between perceived quality of life and mental health status within this student population.

Collectively, these results suggest that ML models integrating sociodemographic and QoL data offer a promising approach for estimating the MH status of college students. Such predictive tools have the potential to serve as valuable aids for healthcare professionals, facilitating the early identification of students requiring support and informing targeted interventions or public health strategies within educational institutions.

Future work should focus on enhancing the robustness and generalizability of these findings. Expanding the dataset to include more samples and participants from diverse institutional settings (e.g., multiple universities, public and private) would be beneficial. This could strengthen the statistical power and allow for exploration of how MH predictors might vary across different student populations. Additionally, refining the sociodemographic questionnaire by incorporating variables identified as relevant in related literature could potentially uncover further predictive insights. Further exploration of advanced ML techniques, such as deep learning architectures or alternative feature engineering approaches, could also be pursued to potentially improve prediction accuracy. The ultimate aim is to refine these models into practical, validated tools that can effectively support student well-being initiatives.

Acknowledgments. This work is partially supported by the FUNCAP/Brazil agency (grant N. BP5-0197-00183.01.06/23 and grant N. BP5-0197-00183.01.02/23).

References

1. Mental health. https://www.who.int/news-room/fact-sheets/detail/mental-health-strengthening-our-response
2. The World Health Organization quality of life assessment (WHOQOL): Position paper from the World Health Organization. Soc. Sci. Med. **41**(10), 1403–1409 (1995). https://doi.org/10.1016/0277-9536(95)00112-K
3. The world health report. 2001: Mental health: new understanding, new hope, p. iSSN: 1020-3311. (2001)

4. Alishiri, G.H., Bayat, N., Fathi Ashtiani, A., Tavallaii, S.A., Assari, S., Moharamzad, Y.: Logistic regression models for predicting physical and mental health-related quality of life in rheumatoid arthritis patients. Mod. Rheumatol. **18**(6), 601–608 (2008)

5. Bajaj, M., Rawat, P., Diksha, V., S., Sharma, V., Gopal, L.: In: Prediction of Mental Health Treatment Adherence using Machine Learning Algorithms, pp. 716–720. IEEE, Ghaziabad, India (2023). https://doi.org/10.1109/CICTN57981.2023.10141520

6. Baranyi, G., Di Marco, M.H., Russ, T.C., Dibben, C., Pearce, J.: The impact of neighbourhood crime on mental health: A systematic review and meta-analysis. Soc. Sci. Med. **282**, 114106 (2021). https://doi.org/10.1016/j.socscimed.2021.114106

7. Bergstra, J., Bengio, Y.: Random search for hyper-parameter optimization. The. J. Mach. Learn. Res. **13**(null), 281–305 (2012)

8. Bhugra, D., Ventriglio, A., Castaldelli-Maia, J., McCay, L.: Urban Mental Health. Oxford University Press (Jun 2019)

9. Ximenes de Brito, R., Rolim Fernandes, C.A., Martins Moreira, R.M., Oliveira, E.N.: Prediction model for common mental disorder and depression in users of psychoactive drugs. IEEE Lat. Am. Trans. **21**(3), 399–407 (Mar 2023https://doi.org/10.1109/tla.2023.10068843, number: 3

10. Campbell, A.: Subjective measures of well-being. Am. Psychol. **31**(2), 117–124 (1976). https://doi.org/10.1037/0003-066X.31.2.117

11. De Groot, K., Wieman, S.M., Van Strien, J.W., Lindemann, O.: To each their own: sociodemographic disparities in student mental health. Frontiers in Education **9**, 1391067 (Sept 2024). https://doi.org/10.3389/feduc.2024.1391067

12. Dos Santos De Brito, L., et al.: Impact of students assistance policies on quality of life and mental health. Front. Psychol. **14**, 1266366 (Nov 2023). https://doi.org/10.3389/fpsyg.2023.1266366

13. Duffy, A., et al.: Predictors of mental health and academic outcomes in first-year university students: Identifying prevention and early-intervention targets. BJPsych Open **6**(3), e46 (2020). https://doi.org/10.1192/bjo.2020.24

14. Eisenberg, D., Downs, M.F., Golberstein, E., Zivin, K.: Stigma and help seeking for mental health among college students. Med. Care Res. Rev. **66**(5), 522–541 (2009). https://doi.org/10.1177/1077558709335173

15. Fayyad, U., Piatetsky-Shapiro, G., Smyth, P.: From data mining to knowledge discovery in databases. AI Mag. **17**(3), 37–37 (1996). https://doi.org/10.1609/aimag.v17i3.1230, number: 3

16. Felce, D., Perry, J.: Quality of life: Its definition and measurement. Res. Dev. Disabil. **16**(1), 51–74 (1995). https://doi.org/10.1016/0891-4222(94)00028-8

17. T.W., Group: Development of the World Health Organization WHOQOL-BREF Quality of Life Assessment. Psychol. Med. **28**(3), 551–558 (1998). https://doi.org/10.1017/S0033291798006667, publisher: Cambridge University Press

18. Harlow, L.L., Oswald, F.L.: Big data in psychology: introduction to special issue. Psychol. Methods **21**(4), 447–457 (Dec 2016). https://doi.org/10.1037/met0000120

19. Koh, H., Tan, G.: Data mining applications in healthcare. Journal of healthcare information management : JHIM **19**, 64–72 (02 2005)

20. Kudo, M., Sklansky, J.: Comparison of algorithms that select features for pattern classifiers. Pattern Recogn. **33**(1), 25–41 (2000). https://doi.org/10.1016/S0031-3203(99)00041-2

21. Laijawala, V., Aachaliya, A., Jatta, H., Pinjarkar, V.: Mental health prediction using data miningâĂŕ: a systematic review. SSRN Electron. J. (2020). https://doi.org/10.2139/ssrn.3561661
22. Lipson, S.K., et al.: Trends in college student mental health and help-seeking by race/ethnicity: Findings from the national healthy minds study, 2013–2021. J. Affect. Disord. **306**, 138–147 (Jun 2022). https://doi.org/10.1016/j.jad.2022.03.038
23. Lombardo, P., Jones, W., Wang, L., Shen, X., Goldner, E.M.: The fundamental association between mental health and life satisfaction: Results from successive waves of a Canadian national survey. BMC Public Health **18**(1), 342 (2018). https://doi.org/10.1186/s12889-018-5235-x
24. Marrapu, H.K., Maram, B., Reddi, P.: New analytic framework of public mental health prediction using data science. In: 2022 International Conference on Smart Technologies and Systems for Next Generation Computing (ICSTSN), pp. 1–6. IEEE, Villupuram, India (Mar 2022). 10.1109/ICSTSN53084.2022.9761324
25. Medvedev, O.N., Landhuis, C.E.: Exploring constructs of well-being, happiness and quality of life. PeerJ **6**, e4903 (2018). https://doi.org/10.7717/peerj.4903, publisher: PeerJ Inc
26. Nouri, F., Feizi, A., Roohafza, H., Sadeghi, M., Sarrafzadegan, N.: How different domains of quality of life are associated with latent dimensions of mental health measured by GHQ-12. Health Qual. Life Outcomes **19**(1), 255 (2021). https://doi.org/10.1186/s12955-021-01892-9
27. Pudil, P., Novovičová, J., Kittler, J.: Floating search methods in feature selection. Pattern Recogn. Lett. **15**(11), 1119–1125 (1994). https://doi.org/10.1016/0167-8655(94)90127-9
28. Seidl, E.M.F., Zannon, C.M.L.D.C.: Qualidade de vida e saúde: aspectos conceituais e metodológicos. Cad. Saúde Pública **20**(2), 580–588 (Apr 2004). https://doi.org/10.1590/S0102-311X2004000200027
29. da Silva Oliveira, L.: Qualidade de Vida e Saúde Mental de Estudantes Universitários. Mestrado acadêmico em saúde da família, Universidade Federal do Ceará-UFC, Faculdade de Medicina-. , Campus Sobral, Sobral, Ceará, Brasil (2020)
30. Srividya, M., Mohanavalli, S., Bhalaji, N.: Behavioral modeling for mental health using machine learning algorithms. J. Med. Syst. **42**(5), 88 (2018). https://doi.org/10.1007/s10916-018-0934-5
31. Tam, J., Mezuk, B., Zivin, K., Meza, R.: U.S.: Simulation of lifetime major depressive episode prevalence and recall error. Am. J. Prev. Med. **59**(2), e39–e47 (2020). https://doi.org/10.1016/j.amepre.2020.03.021
32. Van Lente, E., et al.: Measuring population mental health and social well-being. Int. J. Public Health **57**(2), 421–430 (2012). https://doi.org/10.1007/s00038-011-0317-x
33. Veit, C.T., Ware, J.E.: Mental health inventory. Psychol. Assessment (1983). https://doi.org/10.1037/t02354-000
34. Zika, S., Chamberlain, K.: On the relation between meaning in life and psychological well-being. Br. J. Psychol. **83**(1), 133–145 (1992). https://doi.org/10.1111/j.2044-8295.1992.tb02429.x

Pseudo-labeling for Multi-label Legal Text Classification

Lucas Freitas[1], Thais Rodrigues[2(✉)], Guilherme Rodrigues[2],
Pamella Edokawa[3], and Ariane Farias[4]

[1] AI and Data Office, Brazilian Supreme Federal Court (STF), Brasília, Brazil
[2] Department of Statistics, University of Brasilia, Brasília, Brazil
`thaisrodrigues@unb.br`
[3] Strategic Management Office, Brazilian Supreme Federal Court (STF), Brasília,
Brazil
[4] Department of Data Processing and Innovation, Regional Electoral Court of
Roraima (TRE-RR), Boa Vista, Brazil

Abstract. Data augmentation is a widely used strategy to improve classification performance, yet it is only applied to labeled training data. In many real-world scenarios, however, vast amounts of unlabeled data remain underutilized. Pseudo-labeling offers a semi-supervised approach to incorporate this unlabeled data into model training. In this paper, we propose a simple yet effective pseudo-labeling method that combines clustering and label propagation to enhance performance in multi-label text classification tasks. Our approach addresses common challenges such as biases arising from decision boundaries and class imbalance. As a case study, we apply this method to the classification of legal cases in accordance with the United Nations 2030 Agenda for Sustainable Development Goals. In this context, the proposed augmentation strategy led to notable improvements in both accuracy and sensitivity metrics when compared to models trained solely on the original labeled dataset. This approach provides a valuable means to expand the existing knowledge base without the need for labor-intensive manual classification efforts.

Keywords: 2030 UN Agenda · Natural Language Processing ·
Semi-Supervised Classification · Unbalanced data

1 Introduction

Courts around the world are adopting open data policies to promote greater transparency and increase access to justice. Notable examples include the European Union's CURIA and EUR-Lex portals, the United Kingdom's BAILII, India's National Judicial Data Grid (NJDG), and the Brazilian Federal Supreme Court's open data platform. These platforms provide public access to case law, judicial statistics, and court performance indicators. As a result, quantitative methods are being employed in legal research worldwide. Among the techniques most used in the legal context, approaches based on data science and machine

R. de Freitas and D. Furtado (Eds.): BRACIS 2025, LNAI 16181, pp. 363–377, 2026.
https://doi.org/10.1007/978-3-032-15990-8_25

learning stand out [24]. These methods utilize learning strategies to train algorithms in repetitive tasks, such as clustering and classification of legal texts.

When labeled data is scarce, supervised learning frameworks cannot be applied effectively, highlighting the need for additional labeling efforts and data augmentation strategies [11]. Data augmentation encompasses a range of techniques designed to increase the diversity of training examples in machine learning workflows, without the need to explicitly acquire new data through collection [9] or artificial simulations (synthetic data). Among the most widely used approaches is Easy Data Augmentation (EDA) [28], which expands labeled text using simple operations, such as synonym replacement and random insertion. While effective, these techniques rely solely on labeled data and fail to leverage the large volumes of unlabeled data that are often readily available, limiting their capacity to further improve model performance.

Semi-supervised text classification approaches have emerged as effective strategies for incorporating unlabeled data into model training. Among these, pseudo-labeling approaches focus on training models using a combination of labeled data and unlabeled data that have been automatically annotated with pseudo-labels [30]. Here we propose a pseudo-labeling method for multi-label legal text annotation. Multi-label classification assumes that each instance may be associated with multiple class labels rather than just one. The proposed method integrates clustering of both unlabeled and expert-labeled data, followed by a label propagation step designed to mitigate biases introduced by decision boundaries. To address class imbalance, traditional data augmentation strategies are applied prior to clustering, enhancing the robustness of the pseudo-labeling process.

As a case study, we apply this method to the classification of legal cases according to the United Nations 2030 Agenda for Sustainable Development Goals (SDG)[1]. In Brazil, the Supreme Federal Court (STF) has been making efforts to incorporate the 2030 Agenda into its activities since 2020, particularly through the manual classification of legal processes. In 2021, the STF further advanced this initiative by implementing a machine learning tool, RAFA 2030 [1], to assist in the automated classification of selected legal cases according to the relevant SDGs. However, the expert-labeled database is limited and there is a large number of unlabeled cases. In this context, we showed that the proposed pseudo-label strategy led to notable improvements in both accuracy and sensitivity metrics when compared to models trained solely on the original labeled dataset.

This article is organized as follows: the next section reviews related work on machine learning and legal text classification; Sect. 3 presents the proposed pseudo-labeling method for SDG classification; Sect. 4 covers experiments and results; and the final section provides discussions and conclusions.

---

[1] https://sdgs.un.org/goals.

2   Related Work

Recent advancements in large language models (LLMs) have led to the development of compelling solutions for semi-supervised text classification based on generative models. GAN-BERT [5], for instance, considers training BERT with unlabeled data in a generative adversarial setting. GenCo [31] introduces a generation-driven contrastive self-training strategy designed for zero-shot text classification. GPT-3 [3], a large autoregressive language model, demonstrates strong few-shot learning capabilities. However, LLMs often require extensive domain-specific fine-tuning and substantial computational resources [4,31].

Pseudo-labeling introduces a simpler yet efficient approach within the semi-supervised learning paradigm. In the context of single-label classification, several notable methods have been proposed. [30] proposes a prototype-guided pseudo-labeling method that formulates class prototypes for label assignment. Whereas, Unsupervised Data Augmentation (UDA) [29] and JoinMatch [32] combines various semi-supervised learning strategies with the idea of consistency learning.

In multi-label classification, recent studies have focused on capturing correlations from labels and instances through more sophisticated models, such as graph-based approaches and ensemble learning [6,17]. An alternative strategy involves transforming the multi-label dataset into a multi-class by treating each unique combination of labels as a distinct class [2]; however, this increase in the number of classes can be inefficient. Another straightforward solution is to decompose the multi-label learning problem into independent binary learning problems, one for each class label, as considered in this work and also implemented in methods like Random k-Labelsets (RAkEL) and its variants [26].

Lastly, given the limited resources available for the Portuguese language, optimizing classifier performance in this context remains particularly challenging. Many applications still depend on databases that have been painstakingly curated by legal experts [10]. To address this, [20] explores the use of UDA strategies to enhance the classification of brief legal reports written in Portuguese. In contrast, the present work introduces a novel pseudo multi-labeling approach tailored for the classification of Portuguese legal cases, and designed to handle imbalanced data and long-form legal texts.

3   Methodology

Here we propose a new approach for improving the performance of text classification models given a database containing labeled and unlabeled documents. The data and methodological framework are described in detail next.

3.1   Data

The current study uses two datasets: one with labels corresponding to the SDGs of the 2030 Agenda, and another without such labels. The labeled dataset was compiled by the court's own staff and consists of approximately 2,000 texts, including judgments and initial petitions from cases handled by the STF. Judgments are records of collective court rulings, whereas initial petitions are the original requests submitted to initiate legal cases. The allocation of SDG labels in the labeled dataset is outlined in Table 1.

Table 1. Label distribution for manually labeled processes.

SDG	Labels 0	Labels 1
SDG 3	1635	370
SDG 4	1877	128
SDG 8	1559	446
SDG 9	1937	68
SDG 10	1635	370
SDG 11	1914	91
SDG 15	1909	96
SDG 16	763	1242
SDG 17	1787	218

Label 1 indicates that the case examined is related to the specific SDG, while label 0 indicates that the case has been reviewed and does not have any association with the SDG. Considering that each case can carry multiple labels, the sum of each row in Table 1 represents the total count of cases in the labeled dataset. The limited occurrences of label 1 and the label imbalance justify the data augmentation strategy proposed in this article. SDGs with fewer positive instances were excluded from the analysis.

The unlabeled dataset comprises more than 40,000 STF judgments between 2015 and 2018. These are cases that have not been evaluated in terms of the SDGs, as such labels use started in 2020 and are not mandatory for initiating judicial proceedings. These texts will be employed here to enrich the initially labeled dataset, introducing new contexts/words and addressing the original data imbalance. All documents can be accessed through the court official website[2], provided that they are not subject to judicial confidentiality and their disclosure does not violate the Brazilian General Data Protection Law (LGPD).

3.2 Workflow

Considering that there are scarce labeled instances, we demonstrate how initially unlabeled entities can automatically receive pseudo labels, without the need for manual classifications. For that, we propose a semi-supervised learning routine with a clustering step followed by a label propagation strategy to augment the database prior to classification. This strategy was similarly considered for solving a digit detection problem in images [11].

---

[2] https://portal.stf.jus.br/internacional/default.asp?idioma=en_us.

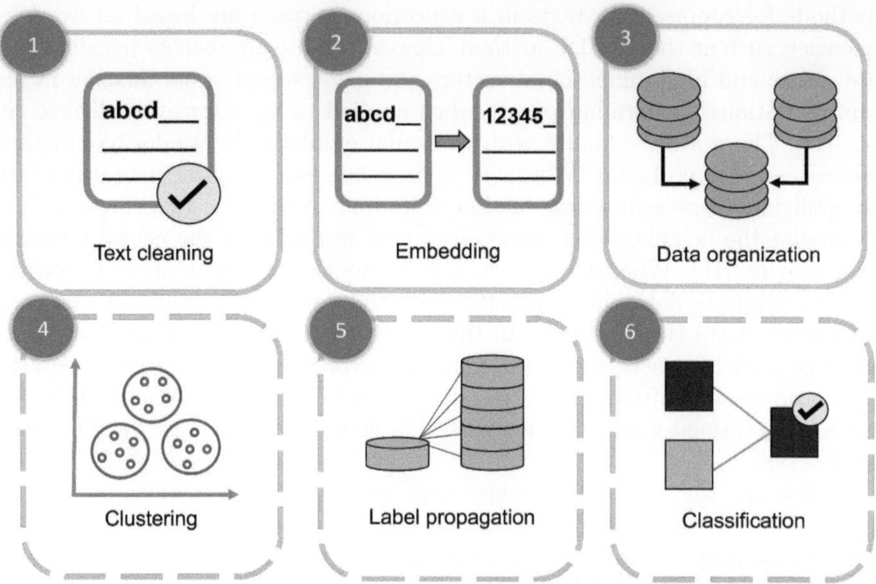

Fig. 1. Basic flowchart. Text cleaning, embedding and data organization are performed for all SDGs in batch (solid line steps), while clustering, label propagation and classification are performed individually for each of the SDGs (dashed line steps)

A high-level overview of the proposed workflow is illustrated in Fig. 1. Text cleaning, embedding, data organization and classification are traditional blocks for preprocessing and classifying text data. Here we propose the additional clustering and label propagation steps to generate pseudo-labels and improve final classification. The clustering mechanism is employed on the full dataset (labeled and unlabeled) to create clusters of processes with similar textual content. Disregarding the cluster boundaries, processes initially lacking labels are assigned artificial labels based on the presence or absence of labeled processes in their proximity (label propagation), increasing the number of positive examples for specific labels. The main steps presented in Fig. 1 are detailed next.

3.3   Preprocessing Steps

The preprocessing steps include text cleaning, embedding, and data organization. These procedures are applied to both labeled and unlabeled data, as well as across all classes (SDGs), and are depicted as solid-line steps in Fig. 1. Specifically, for this application, text cleaning involved removing non-informative elements such as numbers, stop words, and punctuation, along with a part-of-speech (pos-tag) strategy, retaining only words classified as nouns, verbs, or adjectives.

Embedding involves transforming text into numerical vectors, which are entities that can be easily interpreted and processed by computers. The simplest methods for representing texts in a collection (corpus) are based on word frequencies, such as the TF-IDF method. However, these approaches usually generate sparse and high-dimensional vectors and neglect contextual nuances in text representations, performing poorly when applied to an extensively diverse corpus [14]. The word2vec family, with particular emphasis on the doc2vec method, addresses these problems. Word2vec approaches use two-layer neural networks to artificially represent words hidden according to their neighboring words, or to predict the neighborhood based on central words using the neural network's own weights [19]. Whereas, doc2vec [16] trains the textual representation vector, via weight updates, in conjunction with the word representation vectors that collectively form the text itself. In this study, the texts were vectorized using a doc2vec model trained from scratch on approximately 150,000 legal documents from appeals submitted to the Brazilian Federal Supreme Court (STF). The model was trained with a window size of 5, 80 epochs, and a vector dimensionality of 300.

Following the embedding step, data organization encompasses splitting labeled data in training, validation and test datasets. For an imbalanced data set, we also propose an upsampling operation to reinforce the label signals with few entries and mitigate biases. The upsampling strategy used here considered replacing 10% of words with contextual synonyms using BERT transformers [23].

3.4   Clustering and Label Propagation

The clustering and label propagation steps are designed to assign high-confidence pseudo-labels to a subset of previously unclassified texts. In the case of the study, processes began to be labeled with SDG tags from the 2030 Agenda only in 2020, even though there are many usable texts (cases) predating the 2030 Agenda itself. The goal of assigning labels to new texts is to reinforce signals, especially for less common labels, and enhance the performance of classification algorithms.

As shown previously in Table 1, the number of labeled instances for training an artificial neural network for classification is limited. However, given the abundance of unlabeled data, it is important to consider this extra information rather than relying solely on traditional data augmentation techniques. In this study, the proposed approach involves merging the original labeled texts with an unlabeled dataset, followed by the use of a clustering algorithm to assign pseudo labels within well-established groups. A portion of the labeled dataset (60%) is dedicated to training or adjustment of the clustering stage using k-means, along with the entire unlabeled dataset. 20% of the labeled data set is reserved for validating the clustering parameters, and the remaining 20% is used to test the clustering algorithm. Due to the limited amount of data, the clustering, label propagation, and classification steps are better performed separately for each SDG (indicated by the dashed-line steps in Fig. 1), so the multi-label learning problem is decomposed into a set of independent binary classification tasks. Figure 2 illustrates the clustering strategy.

The diagram showcases both originally labeled (crosses) and unlabeled texts (triangles). Here both data sets are grouped using the k-means clustering algo-

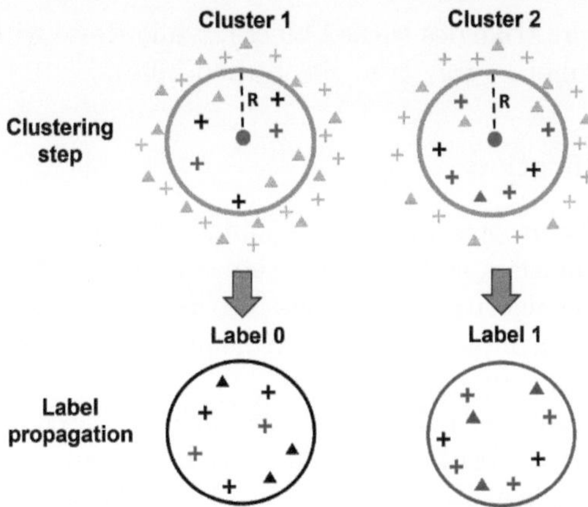

Fig. 2. Clustering strategy to pseudo labeling. To illustrate, data was divided into 2 clusters and unlabeled legal processes (gray triangle) in the radius R were selected. Crosses illustrate originally labeled text (black cross denotes label 0 and blue cross denotes label 1). Label propagation is performed according to the proportion of labeled processes in each selected region. Pseudo label 0 was assigned to the first cluster (black triangles) and pseudo label 1 was assigned to the second cluster (blue triangles). (Color figure online)

rithm based on their text embeddings. Initially, we select K initial centroids, with K being a user-specified parameter representing the desired number of clusters. Each point is assigned to the nearest centroid, forming clusters. Then the centroid of each cluster is updated based on the points within it. This assignment and update process continues until no point changes clusters or until the centroids stabilize. For simplicity, the figure presents only two groups, although the number of clusters can be adjusted as a model hyperparameter.

For the label propagation step, we propose to assign pseudo labels only to processes within the vicinity of the cluster center. By avoiding the cluster edges, greater similarity among processes in the group is achieved and we can mitigate decision boundary bias. Within this proximity (gray circle with radius R), we have processes associated with the specified SDG (blue crosses denoting label 1), processes not associated with the SDG (black crosses denoting label 0), and processes that have not been evaluated yet (gray triangles).

Figure 2 also shows the assignment of labels (colors) to certain unlabeled processes. Unclassified processes (triangles) located within the radius of the circle are assigned pseudo labels on the basis of the proportion of original labels in their vicinity. The threshold proportion also serves as a model parameter and is optimized individually for each class. In Fig. 2, for explanatory purposes, we considered the criterion of at least 50% positive labels (processes related to the specific SDG) within the vicinity to assign label 1 to nearby unclassified processes. This means that unlabeled processes within the vicinity of cluster 1 received label 0 (gray triangles turned black), while those within the vicinity of cluster 2 received label 1 (gray triangles turned blue).

3.5 Text Classification

Since the goal of the proposed pseudo labeling strategy is to enhance classification model performance, augmented datasets containing pseudo labels are used to train classification algorithms. The idea is to assess whether an increased number of positive label examples impacts textual classification models, particularly for labels with limited original records.

There are numerous methods for text classification based on machine learning and deep learning [7]. Algorithms such as Naive Bayes, Support Vector Machines (SVM), Extreme Gradient Boosting (XGBoost), CatBoost and deep neural networks are popular choices for text labeling [25].

In particular, LSTM neural networks are widely used in natural language processing due to their ability to better manage long-term dependencies. In essence, they can effectively capture relationships among distant segments within a given text. The memory mechanism of these networks combines three different types of gates - namely, input gates, output gates, and forget gates - to determine what information to remember and what to forget in each layer of the network. In this paper, LSTM networks were chosen for the classification stage, as they are already employed in the classification of legal texts within the context of the 2030 Agenda's Sustainable Development Goals in the Brazilian judicial system. Classification was conducted individually for each SDG, which improved efficiency given the limited amount of available data. It is important to note that each document may be associated with multiple SDG labels.

This study employed simple methods to establish a baseline and present the strategy in a clear way. Nevertheless, within the proposed workflow, new methods for preprocessing, embedding, clustering, and classification can be considered given the application at hand.

4 Experiments and Results

The series of experiments carried out here encompasses studies on the optimal parameters for clustering, a task associated with pseudo-labeling method. Additionally, these experiments evaluate whether the augmented datasets generated by the proposed method lead to improved performance in the classification task.

4.1 Clustering

The parameters required for the clustering step are the number of clusters, centroid distance radius, and the threshold proportion for label propagation. While some ranges of values were established for each parameter based on the dataset at hand, practical applications may require broader intervals at the start of calibration, before refining the search space. Here, the models were fitted considering the parameter variations within the designated grid. Furthermore, the selection of the best model took into account optimizing accuracy and sensitivity metrics, given that an upsampling procedure had previously been applied to balance the distribution of SDG-related entries.

In semi-supervised learning considering non-hierarchical clustering algorithms, the choice of the number of clusters plays a pivotal role in shaping the distribution of original labels within the generated groups. A limited number of clusters could lead to a dense concentration of original labels in each group, potentially causing overly generalized or less precise label propagation. Conversely, employing a larger number of clusters may result in fewer original labels per group, potentially leading to the generation of inaccurate pseudo labels. In this study, we fine-tuned the k-means algorithm across different settings, specifically exploring 5, 10, 25, 50, and 100 clusters to determine the optimal configuration.

The centroid distance radius determines how far from the cluster edges candidate processes for receiving pseudo labels are positioned. Larger radii indicate that more processes will receive pseudo labels during the propagation step, while the opposite occurs with smaller radii. The idea behind avoiding the cluster edges is to exclude texts that may have relevant associations with more than one cluster, implying higher uncertainty in their classification. The selected radii were 5%, 10%, 25%, and 100%. A 5% distance implies that only the closest 5% of processes to the centroid were retained, whereas a 100% radius means that all processes within the cluster were retained for the label propagation step.

The classification threshold proportion plays an important role during the label propagation step. It defines the decision-making rule associated with label propagation. When examining processes within the cluster radius, the proportion of occurrences of label 1 among the originally labeled processes is evaluated. If this proportion is high, surpassing the classification threshold proportion, then label 1 is extended to all unlabeled processes within the same radius. If the ratio of labeled processes with label 1 falls below the threshold, then pseudo label 0 is assigned to the unlabeled processes within the radius. The thresholds under evaluation here were 50%, 60%, and 70%. The rule tied to the threshold 50% is straightforward: if more than 50% of processes within the radius carry label 1 (indicating the presence of SDGs), the same label is applied to processes initially unlabeled within the radius. The same rule applies to the thresholds of 60% and 70%, which are designed to mitigate false positive labels.

For parameter selection, a validation set consisting of 20% of the labeled dataset was used. This means that these processes labels were masked during the clustering step, and the labels assigned during modeling were compared to the original masked labels. In the experiment, all possible combinations of cluster number, centroid distance radius, and propagation threshold proportion were evaluated. After parameter selection, 20% of the remaining labeled dataset was used for the testing phase. This approach seeks to assess the performance of clustering on a distinct dataset after identifying the optimal parameters for each label. The proposed clustering strategy for label propagation has the advantage of controlling the classification efficiency, preventing incorrect label propagation in poor clusters. Table 2 presents the optimal parameter configuration and evaluation metrics for each SDG on test data.

Table 2. Parameter choices and evaluation metrics on test data.

SDG	Clusters	Distance (%)	Threshold (%)	Accuracy	Sensitivity
SDG 3	25	10	60	0.77	0.77
SDG 4	25	10	60	0.75	0.73
SDG 8	25	10	70	0.75	0.72
SDG 9	25	10	70	0.73	0.78
SDG 10	25	10	70	0.81	0.76
SDG 11	25	10	70	0.72	0.73
SDG 15	25	10	70	0.74	0.71
SDG 16	25	25	60	0.79	0.80
SDG 17	50	25	60	0.65	0.66

As shown in Table 2, for most SDGs, the optimal model parameters for clustering and label propagation were 25 clusters, a 10% centroid distance radius, and classification thresholds of 60% and 70%. It is also interesting that SDGs with a broader scope often exhibit poorer performance, as exemplified by SDG 17 - Partnerships for the Goals.

Due to variations in the centroid distance radius, approximately 5%, 10%, 25%, or 100% of the validation and test cases were considered when computing the evaluation metrics for each respective radius scenario. As a result, higher variability in these metrics is expected for smaller radii. Nevertheless, a substantial number of validation and test cases were retained even in the 5% scenario, and model performance remained consistent across both sets (results omitted).

Following the upsampling procedures and the application of the proposed pseudo-labeling strategy, the resulting label distribution is shown in Table 3. As observed, all SDGs experienced a substantial increase in the number of positive instances (label 1). For example, SDGs 9 and 11 exceed 500 positive examples, compared to fewer than 100 in the original dataset (Table 1). This augmentation holds particular significance as it effectively doubles the overall datasets sizes.

4.2   Classification

LSTM networks was trained on both the original and augmented datasets using the PyTorch framework [22]. The syntax of the PyTorch library is distinctive, and its embedding mechanism for adjusting LSTM networks is based on one-hot encoding (Bag of Words) and weights initialized arbitrarily.

During the forward pass, LSTM layers of the networks receive the outputs from the embedding stage and undergo consecutive dimension reductions. These

Table 3. Label distribution after pseudo-labeling process

SDG	Labels 0	Labels 1	Total
SDG 3	3590	590	4180
SDG 4	3908	509	4417
SDG 8	3453	654	4107
SDG 9	3964	548	4512
SDG 10	3604	642	4246
SDG 11	3953	535	4488
SDG 15	3934	529	4463
SDG 16	3957	6438	10395
SDG 17	3692	663	4355

reductions take into account weights for distant term distances, dropout layers, and activation layers. After completing the network's execution, the model returns probabilities of belonging to the classes of the proposed problem. In the context of this study, class 0 indicates that the text has no association with the evaluated SDG and class 1 otherwise. By default, a threshold of 0.5 is considered, where probabilities exceeding 0.5 indicate label 1.

The networks were trained for 100 epochs using the Adam optimizer with a learning rate of 0.001 and Binary Cross-Entropy (BCELoss) loss function. Additionally, two dropout layers were integrated into the architecture, with dropout probabilities of 0.8 and 0.6. The computational cost of training LSTM networks is higher for augmented datasets. Consequently, instances of Google Colab Pro+ were used. On average, computational times were approximately 59 min, benefiting from hardware acceleration through TPUs V2 and 52 GB of RAM. In the case of the original dataset, this time was under 10 min per SDG.

Network performance was evaluated using a bootstrap strategy [13] with 10,000 iterations. In this process, 80% of the dataset was resampled with replacement for training purposes, while the remaining data not used in the training samples was considered for testing. Table 4 presents the average accuracy and sensitivity metrics for both the original and augmented datasets.

From Table 4, we note that all SDGs exhibited greater accuracy when using augmented data, with a noteworthy mention of SDG 15 - Life on Land, which shows a 17% increase in this measure. The average accuracies and sensitivities exceed 80% for all SDGs, except for SDG 17. The sensitivity metric is of particular importance, as one of the objectives of this study is to amplify the volume of texts associated with SDGs that inherently have limited examples.

T-tests used to compare the bootstrap samples show a significant improvement, at 5% significance level, in both the mean accuracy and sensitivity measures for the augmented datasets compared to the original datasets in almost all SDGs. An exception is noted for SDGs 4, where average sensitivities slightly decreased in the augmented data set. In summary, the proposed pseudo-labeling

Table 4. Average LSTM networks performance on the original and augmented datasets.

SDG	Original Dataset		Augmented Dataset	
	Accuracy	Sensitivity	Accuracy	Sensitivity
SDG 3	0.83	0.80	0.89	0.82
SDG 4	0.79	0.83	0.84	0.81
SDG 8	0.86	0.81	0.87	0.83
SDG 9	0.81	0.79	0.89	0.87
SDG 10	0.83	0.79	0.85	0.79
SDG 11	0.78	0.75	0.82	0.81
SDG 15	0.72	0.72	0.83	0.83
SDG 16	0.87	0.82	0.91	0.85
SDG 17	0.73	0.75	0.74	0.76

strategy has proven effective, leading to a substantial improvement in the classification neural network's performance for nearly all SDGs.

Notably, the pseudo labels were not generated to formally expand the originally labeled dataset or replace human assessments. Pseudo labels were applied to originally unlabeled texts for the purpose of investigating improvements in the neural networks - the current classification algorithm in use within the tribunal itself. The classification through clustering does not label all cases within the unlabeled dataset, but rather focuses on cases closer to the centroids of clusters. Therefore, it is not intended to replace more sophisticated classification methods but rather to serve as a complementary tool to enhance overall performance.

5   Conclusion and Discussion

The present work proposes a pseudo labeling method for multi-label text classification problems, with immediate application in legal contexts. The main idea is to enhance text classification pipelines using a semi-supervised pseudo labeling approach based on clustering and label propagation strategies. This approach is less computationally demanding than competing methods and has the potential to replace rapid annotation strategies based on tools like Doccano and Brat (Browser-Based Rapid Annotation Tool). These tools involve human analysis, which can lead to work overlap for employees who work in sectors related to case filing and classification, such as in the Brazilian judiciary sector.

The proposed pipeline was applied to the classification of legal texts according to the SDGs of the 2030 Agenda. The observed performance difference between original and augmented dataset underscores the effectiveness of the proposed method in generating diverse, high-quality pseudo-labeled data. In particular, some SDGs have increased from fewer than 100 positive examples to around 500 labels, considering both original and pseudo labels. This is highly valuable for class balancing and the fine-tuning of machine learning models. Furthermore, improvements in SDG classification performance were observed, with metrics such as accuracy and sensitivity increasing from 72% to 83% on test data for SDG 15, for example.

The methodology presented here is advantageous in scenarios where the absence of labels is accompanied by a substantial amount of unlabeled data of a similar nature. This aligns well with the context of SDG labels in the Brazilian Supreme Federal Court, as these labels were introduced in 2020, and a substantial volume of texts exists prior to this time point.

In this work, simple clustering (k-means) and classification (LSTM networks) models were used to establish the foundational baseline for the proposed flowchart presented in Fig. 1. A simple approach was also chosen to propagate pseudo labels, which was based on the proportion of original labels within the established neighborhood. However, other models can be considered at each step of the pipeline. For instance, in future works, ModernBERT models [27] trained on legal contexts in the Brazilian Portuguese [4] and LLMs [21] could be used to enhance the text abstraction capability in the embedding stage. Adjustments can also be made to other clustering models, such as those from the DBSCAN [8], WEclustering [18], and BERTopic [12] families. Label propagation can be aided by graphical models [15] and by handling legal metadata by legal experts. Finally, numerous classification models can be fine-tuned, and the vast range of methods includes simple approaches based on textual similarity using cosine similarity, ensemble models, and various modern neural network architectures.

Disclosure of Interests. There are no conflicts of interest to disclose.

References

1. Documentação - RAFA 2030. https://agenda2030rafa.github.io/rafa_documentacao/. Accessed 24 June 2025
2. Ahmed, M.S., Khan, L., Oza, N.C.: Pseudo-label generation for multi-label text classification (2011)
3. Brown, T., et al.: Language models are few-shot learners. In: Larochelle, H., Ranzato, M., Hadsell, R., Balcan, M., Lin, H. (eds.) Advances in Neural Information Processing Systems, vol. 33, pp. 1877–1901. Curran Associates, Inc. (2020)
4. Chalkidis, I., Fergadiotis, M., Malakasiotis, P., Aletras, N., Androutsopoulos, I.: LEGAL-BERT: the muppets straight out of law school. In: Findings of the Association for Computational Linguistics: EMNLP 2020, pp. 2898–2904. Association for Computational Linguistics, Online (2020). https://doi.org/10.18653/v1/2020.findings-emnlp.261
5. Croce, D., Castellucci, G., Basili, R.: GAN-BERT: generative adversarial learning for robust text classification with a bunch of labeled examples. In: Jurafsky, D., Chai, J., Schluter, N., Tetreault, J. (eds.) Proceedings of the 58th Annual Meeting of the Association for Computational Linguistics, pp. 2114–2119. Association for Computational Linguistics, Online (2020). https://doi.org/10.18653/v1/2020.acl-main.191, https://aclanthology.org/2020.acl-main.191/

6. Du, G., Zhang, J., Zhang, N., Wu, H., Wu, P., Li, S.: Semi-supervised imbalanced multi-label classification with label propagation. Pattern Recogn. **150**(C) (2024). https://doi.org/10.1016/j.patcog.2024.110358
7. Eisenstein, J.: Introduction to Natural Language Processing. MIT Press, Cambridge (2019)
8. Ester, M., Kriegel, H.P., Sander, J., Xu, X., et al.: A density-based algorithm for discovering clusters in large spatial databases with noise. In: KDD, vol. 96, pp. 226–231 (1996)
9. Feng, S.Y., et al.: A survey of data augmentation approaches for NLP. In: Zong, C., Xia, F., Li, W., Navigli, R. (eds.) Findings of the Association for Computational Linguistics: ACL-IJCNLP 2021, pp. 968–988. Association for Computational Linguistics, Online (2021). https://doi.org/10.18653/v1/2021.findings-acl.84, https://aclanthology.org/2021.findings-acl.84/
10. Francia, O., Nunez-del Prado, M., Alatrista-Salas, H.: Survey of text mining techniques applied to judicial decisions prediction. Appl. Sci. **12**, 10200 (2022). https://doi.org/10.3390/app122010200
11. Géron, A.: Hands-on Machine Learning with Scikit-Learn, Keras, and TensorFlow. O'Reilly Media Inc., Sebastopol (2022)
12. Grootendorst, M.: Bertopic: neural topic modeling with a class-based TF-IDF procedure. arXiv preprint arXiv:2203.05794 (2022)
13. James, G., Witten, D., Hastie, T., Tibshirani, R.: An Introduction to Statistical Learning: with Applications in R. Springer Texts in Statistics. Springer, New York, New York (2014)
14. Jurafsky, D., Martin, J.H.: Speech and Language Processing: An Introduction to Natural Language Processing, Computational Linguistics, and Speech Recognition with Language Models, 3rd edn (2025). https://web.stanford.edu/~jurafsky/slp3/, online manuscript released January 12, 2025
15. Koller, D., Friedman, N.: Probabilistic Graphical Models: Principles and Techniques. Adaptive Computation and Machine Learning. MIT Press, Cambridge, Massachusetts, USA (2009)
16. Le, Q., Mikolov, T.: Distributed representations of sentences and documents. In: International Conference on Machine Learning, pp. 1188–1196. PMLR (2014)
17. Liu, R., Lu, Y., Shi, L., Tan, S.: Research on multi-label semi-supervised learning algorithm based on dual selection criteria. IEEE Access **12**, 31357–31365 (2024). https://doi.org/10.1109/ACCESS.2024.3369919
18. Mehta, V., Bawa, S., Singh, J.: Weclustering: word embeddings based text clustering technique for large datasets. Complex Intell. Syst. **7**(6), 3211–3224 (2021). https://doi.org/10.1007/s40747-021-00512-9
19. Mikolov, T., Chen, K., Corrado, G., Dean, J.: Efficient estimation of word representations in vector space. arXiv preprint arXiv:1301.3781 (2013)
20. Noguti, M., Vellasques, E., Soares de Oliveira, L.: A small claims court for the NLP: judging legal text classification strategies with small datasets, pp. 1840–1845 (2023). https://doi.org/10.1109/SMC53992.2023.10394189
21. OpenAI: GPT-4 technical report (2023)
22. Paszke, A., et al.: PyTorch: An Imperative Style, High-Performance Deep Learning Library, pp. 8024–8035. Curran Associates, Inc, Canada (2019). http://papers.neurips.cc/paper/9015-pytorch-an-imperative-style-high-performance-deep-learning-library.pdf
23. Souza, F., Nogueira, R., Lotufo, R.: BERTimbau: pretrained BERT models for Brazilian Portuguese. In: Cerri, R., Prati, R.C. (eds.) BRACIS 2020. LNCS

(LNAI), vol. 12319, pp. 403–417. Springer, Cham (2020). https://doi.org/10.1007/978-3-030-61377-8_28

24. Surden, H.: Machine learning and law. Washington Law Rev. **89**, 87 (2014). https://scholar.law.colorado.edu/faculty-articles/81

25. Taha, K., Yoo, P.D., Yeun, C., Homouz, D., Taha, A.: A comprehensive survey of text classification techniques and their research applications: observational and experimental insights. Comput. Sci. Rev. **54**, 100664 (2024)

26. Wang, R., Kwong, S., Wang, X., Jia, Y.: Active k-labelsets ensemble for multi-label classification. Pattern Recogn. **109**(C), 107583 (2021). https://doi.org/10.1016/j.patcog.2020.107583

27. Warner, B., et al.: Smarter, better, faster, longer: a modern bidirectional encoder for fast, memory efficient, and long context finetuning and inference (2024). https://arxiv.org/abs/2412.13663

28. Wei, J., Zou, K.: EDA: easy data augmentation techniques for boosting performance on text classification tasks. In: Inui, K., Jiang, J., Ng, V., Wan, X. (eds.) Proceedings of the 2019 Conference on Empirical Methods in Natural Language Processing and the 9th International Joint Conference on Natural Language Processing (EMNLP-IJCNLP), pp. 6382–6388. Association for Computational Linguistics, Hong Kong, China (2019). https://doi.org/10.18653/v1/D19-1670, https://aclanthology.org/D19-1670/

29. Xie, Q., Dai, Z., Hovy, E., Luong, M.T., Le, Q.V.: Unsupervised data augmentation for consistency training. In: Proceedings of the 34th International Conference on Neural Information Processing Systems. NIPS '20. Curran Associates Inc., Red Hook, NY, USA (2020)

30. Yang, W., Zhang, R., Chen, J., Wang, L., Kim, J.: Prototype-guided pseudo labeling for semi-supervised text classification. In: Rogers, A., Boyd-Graber, J., Okazaki, N. (eds.) Proceedings of the 61st Annual Meeting of the Association for Computational Linguistics (Volume 1: Long Papers), pp. 16369–16382. Association for Computational Linguistics, Toronto, Canada (2023). https://doi.org/10.18653/v1/2023.acl-long.904

31. Zhang, R., Wang, Y.S., Yang, Y.: Generation-driven contrastive self-training for zero-shot text classification with instruction-following LLM. In: Graham, Y., Purver, M. (eds.) Proceedings of the 18th Conference of the European Chapter of the Association for Computational Linguistics (Volume 1: Long Papers), pp. 659–673. Association for Computational Linguistics, St. Julian's, Malta (2024). https://aclanthology.org/2024.eacl-long.39/

32. Zou, H., Caragea, C.: JointMatch: a unified approach for diverse and collaborative pseudo-labeling to semi-supervised text classification. In: Bouamor, H., Pino, J., Bali, K. (eds.) Proceedings of the 2023 Conference on Empirical Methods in Natural Language Processing, pp. 7290–7301. Association for Computational Linguistics, Singapore (2023). https://doi.org/10.18653/v1/2023.emnlp-main.451

Swin Transformer for Classification of Whole-Body PET Cancer Images

Celso Luiz Silva Soares Filho[1(✉)] , Anselmo Cardoso de Paiva[1] ,
Darlan Bruno Pontes Quintanilha[1] , Ramsey D. Badawi[2] ,
Vivek Swarnakar[3] , Cláudio de Souza Baptista[4] ,
and Mateus Queiroz Cunha[4]

[1] Núcleo de Computação Aplicada, Universidade Federal do Maranhão (UFMA),
Caixa Postal, 65085-580 São Luís, MA, Brazil
{celso,paiva,dquintanilha}@nca.ufma.br
[2] Department of Radiology, University of California Davis Health, Sacramento, CA,
USA
rdbadawi@health.ucdavis.edu
[3] Department of Radiology, University of California Davis, Davis, CA, USA
vswarnakar@health.ucdavis.edu
[4] Universidade Federal de Campina Grande (UFCG), R. Aprígio Veloso, 882 -
Universitário, Campina Grande - PB 58429-900, Brazil
baptista@computacao.ufcg.edu.br, mateusqueiroz@copin.ufcg.edu.br

Abstract. Cancer remains a critical global health challenge, with the
World Health Organization (WHO) projecting 35 million new cases by
2050, necessitating advanced diagnostic tools such as whole-body FDG-
PET imaging, which detects metabolic activity in pathologies. While 3D
PET scans are powerful, their computational demands become excessive when dealing with deep learning, motivating the use of efficient 2D
representations, moreover, this representation would assist radiologists in
analyzing exams, since there are too few specialized professionals to interpret all the scans. This work proposes a Swin Transformer-based method
to classify 2D Maximum Intensity Projection (MIP) images from FDG-
PET scans into binary categories (cancerous vs. healthy), addressing
challenges of multi-cancer detection (melanoma, lymphoma, lung cancer) and variability in image coverage. The approach achieved results of
$82.08\% \pm 4.3\%$ accuracy, $82.43\% \pm 2.9\%$ F1-Score, $84.31\% \pm 4.4\%$ recall,
and $81.35\% \pm 7.1\%$ precision. These results demonstrate the viability of
the proposed approach, which combines the computational efficiency of
2D representations with the discriminative capability of the Swin Transformer architecture for medical image analysis.

Keywords: FDG PET · Whole Body PET Scan · Classification ·
Swin Transformer

1 Introduction

Cancer diagnosis, monitoring, and treatment are critically important, as the
disease is often silent and aggressive. According to the World Health Organi-

© The Author(s), under exclusive license to Springer Nature Switzerland AG 2026
R. de Freitas and D. Furtado (Eds.): BRACIS 2025, LNAI 16181, pp. 378–392, 2026.
https://doi.org/10.1007/978-3-032-15990-8_26

zation (WHO), an estimated 35 million new cancer cases will occur by 2050–a 77% increase compared to 2022 projections [1]. Whole-Body Positron Emission Tomography (PET) serves as a key tool for diagnosing and monitoring the disease by scanning the entire body for pathologies.

A crucial factor in PET imaging is the radiopharmaceutical used. The most common, 18F-FDG (Fluorodeoxyglucose F-18), is a glucose analog that carries the radioactive isotope Fluorine-18 to areas of high metabolic activity, such as the brain, heart, kidneys, and cancerous regions [5]. As the isotope decays, it emits positrons that annihilate with electrons, producing gamma-ray photon pairs traveling in opposite directions. The PET scanner detects these photons to generate a 3D image of the patient's body [5]. While whole-body PET can detect pathologies globally, the scan typically covers only the base of the skull to the upper thighs (mid-femoral region) [5].

Automated classification of PET images using deep learning models (e.g., CNNs or Transformers) can benefit both clinicians and the general population [4]. These models enable earlier cancer detection, improving treatment efficacy [2], while their ability to identify subtle patterns reduces diagnostic errors and enhances patient safety [17]. Thus, they complement specialist workflows by enabling faster and more precise image analysis.

Advances in computer vision and deep learning have expanded their use in medical applications [15]. However, processing 3D PET images is computationally expensive to train deep learning models, making 2D representations a viable alternative due to their lower resource demands [8]. Notably, Transformer-based networks have demonstrated superior performance compared to Convolutional Neural Networks (CNNs) [22].

The proposed solution uses image processing techniques and Swin Transform [16] to create a 2D representation of PET scans. Furthermore, a method is developed to classify these images into two categories: positive, when some type of cancer is present (such as melanoma, lymphoma, and lung cancer), and negative, corresponding to images of healthy patients. Next, Sect. 2 highlights the related work, Sect. 3 describes the proposed method, and Sect. 4 presents the results, experiments, comparisons, and discussions of the proposed method.

2   Related Works

This section presents related work, covering both the neural network model used and studies performing classification and detection on whole-body FDG PET images. Furthermore, many studies that used the same dataset as this work employed classification as a preliminary step to lesion segmentation.

Li et al. (2021) proposed the Swin Transformer architecture, an improvement over the Vision Transformer. The model splits input images into smaller patches, computing attention both within individual patches and globally (across patches). Additionally, the Shifted Window mechanism was introduced to establish connections between different image regions. These features enable the model to capture fine-grained details, proving particularly useful in contexts where the region of interest may be located anywhere in the image and can be extremely small.

In Heiliger et al. (2022), the primary research objective was to perform 3D segmentation on images from the AutoPET Challenge II dataset, which comprises the same FDG PET scans used in the present study. As a preliminary step to pathology segmentation, classification was performed using an ensemble of ResNet-18 and ResNet-50 applied to 2D MIP projections of FDG PET scans along the coronal and sagittal axes. Additionally, experiments were conducted by excluding the brain region, as it could be interpreted as a false positive. The classification aimed to minimize false negatives, achieving average results of 74.4% accuracy, 2.4% false negatives, and 49.6% false positives after five-fold cross-validation.

Pang et al. (2024) developed and validated a universal lesion detection algorithm for PET/CT and PET/MRI, integrating 2D/3D F-Res models with a network to synthesize MR-derived CT (sCT). The study analyzed 1,014 PET/CT scans (AutoPET Challenge 2022) and 41 MR/CT datasets, with validation on 38 patients. For PET/CT scans, the algorithm achieved 78% accuracy, 84% precision, 98% recall, and 89% Dice score, demonstrating superior performance when processing 3D volumes.

Häggström et al. (2024) proposed LARS (Lymphoma Artificial Reader System), a ResNet34-based deep learning model to classify lymphoma scans into Deauville scores 1–3 (no hypermetabolic disease) or 4–5 (with disease). Trained on 16,583 PET-CTs from 5,072 patients at the Memorial Sloan Kettering Cancer Center (80% training, 20% internal test) and externally validated with 1,000 scans from the Medical University of Vienna, LARS achieved high precision. The LARS-avg variant (accuracy-optimized) reached 94.9% AUC, 89.0% accuracy, 86.8% sensitivity, and 91.3% specificity, while LARS-max (sensitivity-optimized) attained 94.9% AUC, 86.8% accuracy, 90.9% sensitivity, and 82.6% specificity. In external validation, LARS-avg maintained superior performance (95.3% AUC, 90.7% accuracy, 87.4% sensitivity, and 94.9% specificity).

Therefore, it can be noted that the best results, as observed in [10, 12, 18], involve a problem that was solved using a 3D approach or are specific to a particular type of cancer, since there is a scarcity of research addressing the classification of these images in datasets with multiple pathologies, even in binary classification scenarios. In most studies, one class corresponds to a single type of cancer, while the other comprises scans of healthy patients.

Another important factor is that the cited works that use a 2D MIP approach normalize the scans considering each scan individually, leading to significant differences in each new representation obtained. In the proposed method, the images are normalized taking into account the maximum SUV level value in the areas with lesions, without losing information from the regions of interest. Finally, the use of the Swin Transformer becomes viable, since its windowing mechanism, together with sliding windows, can capture fine-grained features of the regions of interest. Thus, the present work stands out for its methodology, which analyzes the SUV levels of the exams to build 2D MIP representations and performs binary classification using Swin Transformer Base, where the anomalous class includes three types of cancer (lung cancer, lymphoma and melanoma).

3   Materials and Method

In this section, the image database used and the proposed method for solving the PET image classification problem (Fig. 1) are presented. The method consists of two steps: The first involves preprocessing the 3D scan volumes into 2D representations, along with image resizing. Then, image classification is performed using the Swin Transformer network. Each step is detailed below.

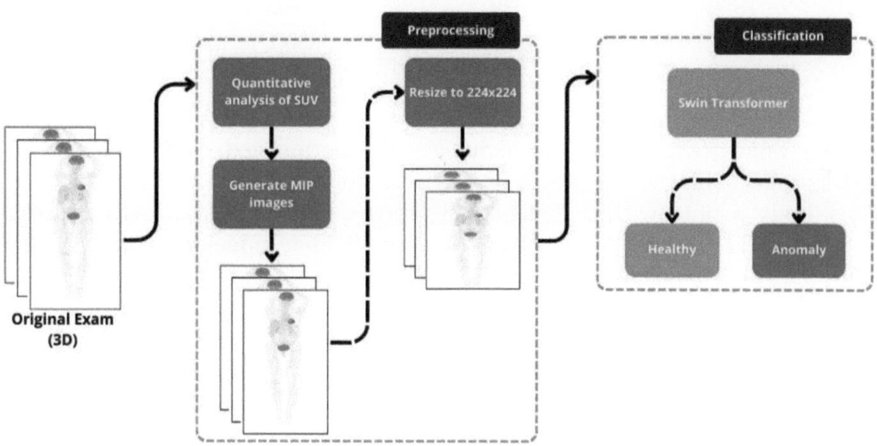

Fig. 1. Proposed Method

3.1   Dataset

In this work, experiments were conducted using FDG PET scans from the Autopet Challenger III dataset [7,14]. The dataset is divided into two subsets: the first includes computed tomography (CT) and PET scans with the radiotracer FDG, comprising 501 patients diagnosed with malignant melanoma, lymphoma, and lung cancer, along with 513 negative control patients. All images were acquired using a Biograph mCT PET/CT scanner (Siemens Healthcare GmbH, Erlangen, Germany) [7]. The second subset consists of pre- and post-therapeutic PSMA PET/CT scans from male patients with prostate carcinoma, containing 537 pathology-positive images and 60 pathology-negative images [14]. However, only the images from the first subset were used, being the FDG PET exams, with the intention of classifying only this type of exam. Table 1 shows the demographic distribution of the patients of the FDG PET exams.

Table 1. Patient Information

Diagnosis	Gender	Number of Studies	Age [Mean ± SD]
Melanoma	Female	77	65.0 ± 12.8
	Male	111	65.7 ± 13.7
Lymphoma	Female	69	45.1 ± 19.7
	Male	76	47.3 ± 17.9
Lung Cancer	Female	65	64.2 ± 8.7
	Male	103	67.0 ± 9.0
Negative	Female	233	59.1 ± 14.7
	Male	280	58.7 ± 15.1
Total	Female	444	58.5 ± 16.1
	Male	570	60.1 ± 15.9

The values of the FDG PET images are normalized in SUV (Standardized Uptake Value) levels, which is a method for measuring metabolic activity. Thus, body regions with higher pixel activation correspond to areas of greater metabolic activity, such as the brain, urinary bladder, kidneys, heart, inflammations, infections, and cancerous regions [5]. Finally, all data were annotated by a radiologist with 10 years of experience in hybrid imaging and machine learning research [7]. Figure 2 shows an example of the slice with the highest activation in the expert's annotation of a patient diagnosed with lymphoma, in the coronal and sagittal views, followed by the expert's annotation and their overlap.

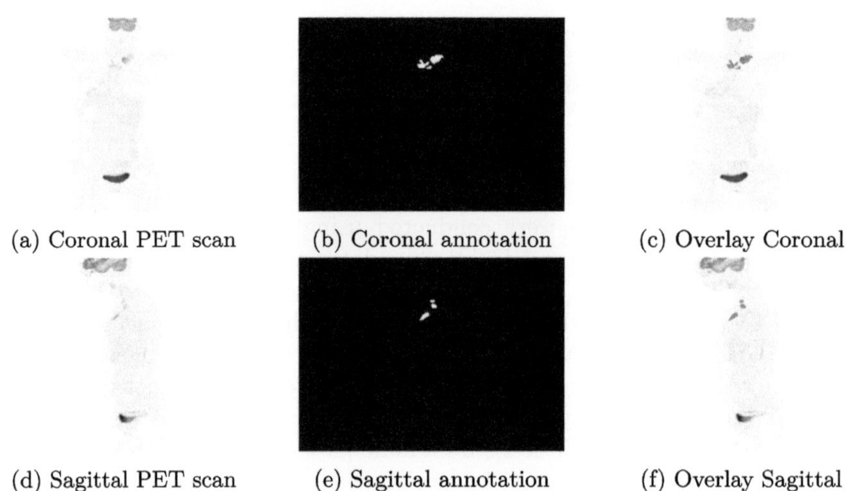

(a) Coronal PET scan   (b) Coronal annotation   (c) Overlay Coronal

(d) Sagittal PET scan   (e) Sagittal annotation   (f) Overlay Sagittal

Fig. 2. Visualization of the slices with the highest activation in the expert's annotation on the Coronal and Sagittal axis of the same patient

3.2   Preprocessing

During the preprocessing stage, several phases are crucial, ranging from handling the data related to SUV levels in the scans to resizing their 2D representations. The first step consists of a general quantitative analysis of SUV values across all scans, focusing both on the classes present in the dataset and specifically on pathological areas. The main objective is to define a range of SUV levels to subsequently perform image quantization [9].

After analyzing the maximum and minimum SUV levels in the lesion areas, a 2D Maximum Intensity Projection (MIP) representation of the images is generated [20]. This is done by initially defining a study plane for the exam – the coronal plane – since this view allows a clear view of the patient's entire body. Furthermore, comparative preliminary tests were conducted between the coronal and sagittal planes using a subset of previously annotated scans, and the results indicated that the coronal plane showed superior performance in terms of accuracy and sensitivity in identifying cancer-suspected areas. Then, for each projection line perpendicular to the selected plane, the algorithm identifies and selects the voxel with the highest SUV value, discarding lower intensity information. Thus, the resulting MIP image highlights the regions with the highest metabolic uptake, facilitating the identification of potentially pathological areas.

Finally, with the generated images, a resizing process via interpolation to 224×224 pixels is performed [9]. This is essential for input into the Swin Transformer, as it allows the use of the network's pre-trained weights.

3.3   Classification

For the classification stage, several architectures were tested, namely EfficientNet B0, DenseNet 121, ResNet 50 and ViT [6,11,13,21], since they are widely used architectures and validated by several works, however the Swin Transformer network was chosen because it has the best performance. It is used with images already resized to 224×224 pixels during the pre-processing stage [16]. The use of the Swin-Base Transformer with pre-trained weights is motivated by its ability to improve results in cases with few training images available, in addition to having already been compared with other architectures, demonstrating to be superior. [16,19].

The Swin Transformer is based on the Transformer originally designed for NLP (Natural Language Processing) tasks, which uses attention mechanisms [22]. Furthermore, it represents an improvement over the Vision Transformer (ViT) [6], with its key innovation being the introduction of shifted windows. This approach divides the image into local regions and computes self-attention only within these windows, reducing computational costs and enabling efficient processing of high-resolution images compared to ViT [16].

Figure 3 shows the Swin Transformer architecture on the left and the Swin Transformer blocks on the right. The workflow begins by splitting the image into non-overlapping patches, which are then converted into linear embeddings. The data is processed through four sequential stages, where each phase progressively reduces the spatial resolution, allowing the model to capture features at different scales, from local details to global patterns [16].

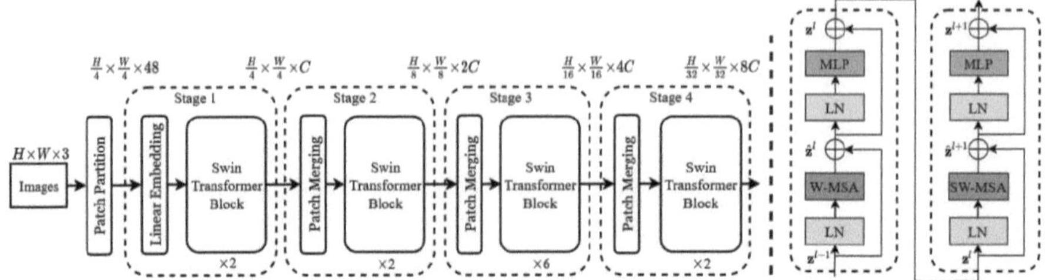

Fig. 3. Swin Architecture [16]

Regarding the Swin Transformer blocks, it is noted that there are two distinct types of attention mechanisms. The first block (W-MSA) applies multi-head self-attention within fixed windows, reducing computational complexity since calculations are limited to local regions. The second block (SW-MSA) introduces a Shifted Window, allowing the model to establish connections between different areas of the image.

4 Results and Discussion

In this section, the experiment settings and an evaluation of the results achieved in all stages of the developed method are presented.

4.1 SUV Level Analysis

FDG PET scans are normalized in SUV levels, a metric that measures metabolic activity. Therefore, to generate 2D images that best represent the original scans, qualitative experiments were conducted on SUV levels. When analyzing all SUV values found in the 3D volume, most values were close to 0, with an average of 0.09 ± 0.57, and minimum and maximum values of 0.00 and 2415.16, respectively. Such low values are due to the fact that the volume is being evaluated as a whole, not just the region of the patient's body.

Thus, an analysis was performed based on the classes present in the dataset, considering the mean SUV levels per patient. It was observed that the per-patient mean values remain very low, with the following averages: Melanoma: 0.09 ± 0.03, Lung cancer: 0.10 ± 0.02, Lymphoma: 0.10 ± 0.02, Negative (healthy) class: 0.09 ± 0.02. Given these findings, the SUV levels in cancerous regions become more relevant for defining a value range that can be used for image quantization. Figure 4 shows a histogram of SUV level distribution specifically in pathological areas.

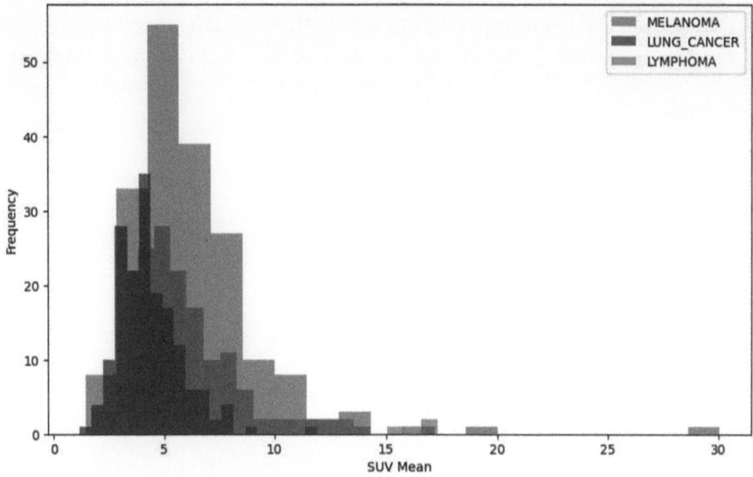

Fig. 4. Histogram of mean SUV levels by type of abnormality

For this case, the intersection between the expert's annotated volumes and the scans was calculated, obtaining the values as shown in Table 2. Based on this, the range between SUV levels 1 and 31 was selected for image quantization, as this interval ensures no risk of losing pathological values. All values less than 1 or greater than 31 were discarded, redistributing the values in this range between 0 and 255.

Table 2. SUV Levels in Cancer Areas

Diagnosis	SUV [Mean ± SD]	Maximum SUV	Minimum SUV
Melanoma	6.25 ± 3.19	30.03	1.44
Lung Cancer	4.37 ± 1.48	11.91	1.17
Lymphoma	6.35 ± 2.67	17.30	2.31

4.2   MIP Image Generation

The 2D representations of FDG PET scans are generated using Maximum Intensity Projection (MIP), considering only the predefined SUV level range (between 1 and 31). First, an axis is selected for image generation–in this work, the coronal axis was chosen, as it provides a clear view of the patient's entire body in the scan. Next, the highest-intensity voxel values along this axis are projected as pixels in the new image, which is then subjected to quantization.

After generating the new scan representations, the images are resized to 224 × 224 pixels via bicubic interpolation. This step is necessary to ensure compatibility with the pre-trained weights of the Swin Transformer. Figure 5 illustrates an example of the MIP-generated representations, with cancerous regions segmented based on expert annotations, as well as the final resized images.

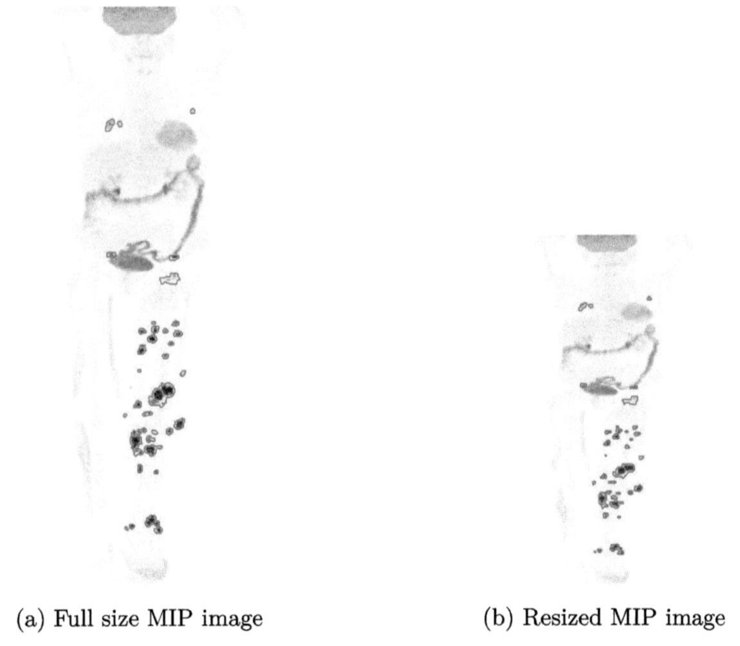

(a) Full size MIP image   (b) Resized MIP image

Fig. 5. Example of original size and resized MIP representation

4.3 Experiment Settings

The experiments were conducted using the Python programming language with the PyTorch framework, running on a machine equipped with 16 GB of RAM, an Intel Core i7-7700 processor, and an NVIDIA GeForce GTX 1080 Ti GPU with 11 GB of dedicated VRAM.

The image dataset was divided into training, validation, and test sets, with images being randomly distributed while maintaining class balance. To prevent data leakage, all scans from the same patient were kept within the same subset. The final distribution was as follows: training set: 80% of the data, validation set: 10% of the training set, test set: 20% of the total data. The Table 3 shows the number of images and their class distribution across each subset. This approach ensures proper data segregation and maintains representative class proportions in all subsets.

The hyperparameters for the Swin Transformer were defined through a grid search [3] aiming to achieve the best F1 Score, with training conducted over 300 epochs and an early stopping criterion of 30 epochs. The tested hyperparameters

Table 3. Data Distribution by Class

	Lung Cancer	Melanoma	Lymphoma	Healthy	Total
Training	120	138	103	376	**737**
Validation	14	17	12	34	**77**
Test	34	33	30	103	**200**

can be seen in Table 4, with the best results obtained using a learning rate of 5e−5, batch size of 24, AdamW optimizer, and Binary Cross Entropy loss function.

Table 4. Hyperparameters Tested in Grid Search

Learning Rate	Batch Size	Optimizers	Loss Function
1e−4	**24**	Adam	**BCE**
1e−5	28	**AdamW**	Focal
5e−4	32	SGD	-
5e−5	-	-	-

Furthermore, to validate the method, Cross Validation was performed using 5 Folds while maintaining the same distribution proportions and rules previously established for the training, test, and validation split. Table 5 shows the class distribution across each fold. Finally, the method's performance was evaluated using Accuracy, F1 Score, Recall, and Precision metrics.

Table 5. Dataset distribution for Cross Validation

	Lung Cancer	Melanoma	Lymphoma	Healthy	Total
Fold 1	32	44	25	103	**204**
Fold 2	31	39	32	100	**202**
Fold 3	33	28	39	104	**204**
Fold 4	43	45	24	93	**205**
Fold 5	29	32	25	113	**199**

4.4 Performance Metrics Assessment

After the training, validation, and test split was performed, several experiments were conducted to determine which model would be used. Among them were

EfficientNet B0, DenseNet 121, ResNet 50, Visual Transformer (ViT), and Swin Base, all with the same hyperparameters: trained for 300 epochs with early stopping set at 30, learning rate of 1e-4, batch size of 32, AdamW optimizer, and Focal Loss function. Table 6 shows the results for each one, with the decision made to proceed with experiments using Swin Base as it achieved the best F1 Score and Recall, resulting in a balance between False Positives (FP) and False Negatives (FN).

In the medical field, this balance is crucial because classifications with FN can lead to lack of or delayed treatment of the disease, while FP can cause unnecessary interventions. Thus, the high Recall ensures greater sensitivity in detecting critical cases, while the F1-Score maintains adequate precision, making the model more reliable for clinical applications.

Table 6. Comparative Performance of Architectures in PET Image Classification

	Accuracy	F1 Score	Recall	Precision
EfficientNet B0	73.50%	74.88%	81.44%	69.30%
DenseNet 121	**77.50%**	76.92%	77.32%	76.53%
ResNet 50	76.00%	73.63%	69.07%	**78.82%**
ViT	68.50%	68.66%	71.13%	66.35%
Swin Transformer	76.50%	**77.51%**	**83.51%**	72.32%

After defining the model and its new hyperparameters, superior results were achieved on the test set. Furthermore, to validate the method, Cross-Validation was performed, generating the results shown in Table 7.

Table 7. 5-Fold Cross-Validation Result with Swin Transformer

	Accuracy	F1 Score	Recall	Precision
Fold 1	74.02%	77.06%	68.46%	88.12%
Fold 2	85.15%	85.15%	84.31%	86.00%
Fold 3	82.84%	83.09%	86.00%	80.37%
Fold 4	81.95%	82.13%	75.89%	89.47%
Fold 5	86.43%	84.75%	87.21%	82.42%
Mean ± SD	82.08% ± 4.3%	82.43% ± 2.9%	84.31% ± 4.4%	81.35% ± 7.1%

Based on the F1 Score metrics, Fold 2 showed the best performance with 85.15%, with a mere 0.4% difference from Fold 5. However, Fold 5 achieved the highest Recall among all folds at 87.21%, representing a 2.9% improvement over Fold 2. Given the minimal difference in F1 Scores and the significant advantage in Recall, Fold 5 was selected as having the best overall performance, and its results were used for subsequent case studies.

Table 8 presents the performance metrics of Swin Base in comparison with related works, which performed classification and detection on the same dataset. Compared to Heiliger et al. (2022), the results of this research have a higher accuracy, in addition to using an ensemble with the ResNet18 and ResNet50 architectures, in MIP representations in the coronal and sagittal slices, in addition to a technique called "de-brain", which removes the brain from the images.

Compared to Pang et al. (2025), the results were inferior, which is attributed to their use of a combination of 3D scans and 2D slice representations in their method. Nevertheless, the proposed approach is simpler, has lower computational costs, and does not rely on multiple imaging modalities. Furthermore, the images from the CT scans were used together with the PET scans, providing a better representation of the morphology of the human body in the scan. This approach allows the architecture to understand with greater precision the shape and location of regions of interest and areas of lesions.

Table 8. Performance Comparison of Swin Transformer with Related Works

	Accuracy	F1 Score	Recall	Precision
Heiliger et al. (2022)	74.3%	-	-	-
Pang et al. (2025)	78%	89%	98%	84%
Proposed Method	82.08% ± 4.3	82.43% ± 2.9	84.31% ± 4.4	81.35% ± 7.1

4.5 Case Studies

For the case studies, one example classified as FP (False Positive) and another as FN (False Negative) were selected as representative samples. Figure 6 displays these cases, with expert annotations marked in red for the FN instance.

In the FP case, a high-intensity spot is observed in the patient's arm (left side of the brain image), showing some difficulty of the method in dealing with False Positive characteristics overall, since there is very high intensity in the region - something very common in cancerous areas. For the FN cases, the opposite occurred, with worse performance where pathologies are very small and have very low intensity, making these cases particularly difficult to identify since these characteristics closely resemble other body areas that have natural activation.

In illustration D, it is possible to see an example of FN where the abnormality can only be seen in the sagittal axis section. Even though the anomaly is not in the brain, when seen in the coronal axis, it appears in the same region, making it difficult to visualize and having a very similar insufficiency, hindering the model's ability to classify the image correctly.

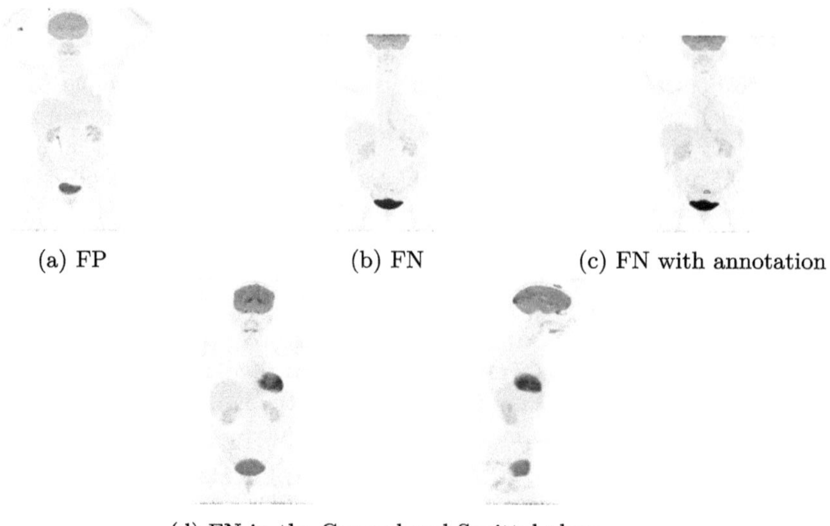

(a) FP   (b) FN   (c) FN with annotation

(d) FN in the Coronal and Sagittal plane

Fig. 6. Examples of FP and FN cases with expert annotations (Color figure online)

4.6   Discussion

After running the experiments, it was possible to arrive at a method capable of making a classification using only the images in the coronal axis with the Swin Transformer Base. It was also possible to obtain a better result than that of Heiliger et al. (2022), who made a classification using an ensemble of architectures and two different types of view of the same exam (coronal and sagittal).

Furthermore, it was observed that in certain cases it is very difficult to classify the images due to features that resemble regions of interest in FP cases, as well as regions with low activation, small and similar to areas that normally have high metabolic activity but are not cancerous. Furthermore, another challenge encountered was that the dataset contains four different classes – three types of cancer and cases of healthy patients.

Even though the experiments aimed only to perform binary classification (distinguishing between anomaly and healthy images), the diversity of cancer classes complicates the task, since cancer can appear anywhere in the body–especially in melanoma cases. Furthermore, the whole-body FDG PET images vary in coverage: some scans include only the upper brain to mid-thigh, while others capture the entire patient. These differences directly affect how pathologies appear after image resizing, often reducing their visibility significantly. Regarding resizing, even in cases where the original images had the maximum height (661 pixels), the anomalies did not disappear when downscaled to 224×224 pixels.

5   Conclusion

Given the above, it can be concluded that the methodology proposed in this work was effective in classifying FDG PET images from the AutoPET Challenge III dataset, maintaining considerable metric values of 82.08% ± 4.3% accuracy, 82.43% ± 2.9% F1 Score, 84.31% ± 4.4% Recall, and 81.35% ± 7.1% precision. Additionally, the approach using 2D MIP representations of the original scan volumes also proved consistent, generating images where cancerous regions remain highlighted, while eliminating regions with low metabolic activity that are not relevant for classification.

As future work, the use of 2D images from the Sagittal axis is being considered, with the intention of combining two different views of the same scan. This could be done by concatenating the output of the feature extractor and using a final classifier. The use of images in another plane is also justified by the fact that in some exams the cancer in the Coronal axis is considerably small, but presents greater activation in the Sagittal axis (Fig. 6d), which may be beneficial for cases in which the activation of the region of interest is small in one of the two planes.

Acknowledgements. This work was carried out with the support of the Coordination for the Improvement of Higher Education Personnel - Brazil (CAPES) - Financing Code 001, Maranhão Research Support Foundation (FAPEMA), National Council for Scientific and Technological Development (CNPq) and Brazilian Company of Hospital Services (Ebserh) Brazil (Proc. 409593/2021-4).

References

1. Global cancer burden growing, amidst mounting need for services. https://www.who.int/news/item/01-02-2024-global-cancer-burden-growing--amidst-mounting-need-for-services. Accessed 02 Apr 2025
2. Ardila, D., et al.: End-to-end lung cancer screening with three-dimensional deep learning on low-dose chest computed tomography. Nat. Med. **25**(6), 954–961 (2019)
3. Bergstra, J., Bengio, Y.: Random search for hyper-parameter optimization. J. Mach. Learn. Res. **13**(1), 281–305 (2012)
4. Bi, W.L., et al.: Artificial intelligence in cancer imaging: clinical challenges and applications. CA: Cancer J. Clinicians **69**(2), 127–157 (2019)
5. Bushberg, J., Seibert, J., Leidholdt, E., Boone, J.: The Essential Physics of Medical Imaging, 3rd edn. Lippincott Williams & Wilkins, Philadelphia, PA (2012)
6. Dosovitskiy, A., et al.: An image is worth 16x16 words: transformers for image recognition at scale. arXiv preprint arXiv:2010.11929 (2020)
7. Gatidis, S., Kuestner, T.: A whole-body FDG-PET/CT dataset with manually annotated tumor lesions (FDG-PET-CT-lesions) (2022). https://doi.org/10.7937/gkr0-xv29
8. Gil, J., Choi, H., Paeng, J.C., Cheon, G.J., Kang, K.W.: Deep learning-based feature extraction from whole-body PET/CT employing maximum intensity projection images: preliminary results of lung cancer data. Nucl. Med. Mol. Imaging **57**(5), 216–222 (2023)

9. Gonzalez, R., Woods, R.: Processamento de imagens digitais. Edgard Blucher (2000). https://books.google.com.br/books?id=d3MnAgAACAAJ
10. Häggström, I., et al.: Deep learning for [18f] fluorodeoxyglucose-pet-ct classification in patients with lymphoma: a dual-centre retrospective analysis. Lancet Digit. Health **6**(2), e114–e125 (2024)
11. He, K., Zhang, X., Ren, S., Sun, J.: Deep residual learning for image recognition (2016)
12. Heiliger, L., et al.: Autopet challenge: combining nn-unet with swin unetr augmented by maximum intensity projection classifier. arXiv preprint arXiv:2209.01112 (2022)
13. Huang, G., Liu, Z., Van Der Maaten, L., Weinberger, K.Q.: Densely connected convolutional networks (2017)
14. Jeblick, K., et al.: A whole-body PSMA-PET/CT dataset with manually annotated tumor lesions (PSMA-PET-CT-lesions) (version 1) (2024). https://doi.org/10.7937/r7ep-3x37
15. Litjens, G., et al.: A survey on deep learning in medical image analysis. Med. Image Anal. **42**, 60–88 (2017)
16. Liu, Z., et al.: Swin transformer: hierarchical vision transformer using shifted windows (2021)
17. McKinney, S.M., et al.: International evaluation of an AI system for breast cancer screening. Nature **577**(7788), 89–94 (2020)
18. Pang, L., et al.: Comparison of the accuracy of a deep learning method for lesion detection in PET/CT and PET/MRI images. Mol. Imag. Biol. **26**(5), 802–811 (2024)
19. Rana, N., et al.: Improved swin transformer-based thorax disease classification with optimal feature selection using chest x-ray. PLoS ONE **20**(6), e0327099 (2025)
20. Rana, N., Singh, H., Vatsa, R., Watts, A., Mittal, B.R.: Correction of positron emission tomography maximum intensity projection image artifact using retro reconstruction method. Indian J. Nuclear Med. **35**(3), 235–237 (2020)
21. Tan, M., Le, Q.: Efficientnet: rethinking model scaling for convolutional neural networks. In: International Conference on Machine Learning, pp. 6105–6114. PMLR (2019)
22. Vaswani, A., et al.: Attention is all you need. In: Advances in Neural Information Processing Systems, vol. 30 (2017)

Synthetic Data for Mental Health: A Comparative Analysis of LLMs, BERT, and Copy-Based Augmentation

Matheus Yasuo Ribeiro Utino[1(✉)], Elton H. Matsushima[2], Aline Paes[3], and Paulo Mann[4]

[1] Institute of Mathematics and Computer Science, University of São Paulo, São Paulo, Brazil
`matheusutino@usp.br`
[2] Department of Psychology, Fluminense Federal University, Niterói, Brazil
`eh.matsushima@gmail.com`
[3] Institute of Computing, Fluminense Federal University, Niterói, Brazil
`alinepaes@ic.uff.br`
[4] Institute of Computing, Federal University of Rio de Janeiro, Rio de Janeiro, Brazil
`paulomannjr@gmail.com`

Abstract. Depression screening through social media has emerged as a promising research avenue; however, the scarcity of annotated data remains a significant barrier to effective model training. In this work, we evaluate several textual data augmentation strategies for screening users with depression through Brazilian-Portuguese Instagram posts. We explore three techniques of increasing complexity: simple post duplication, contextual word substitution using BERT-based models, and synthetic posts generation via Large Language Models (LLMs), both with and without the modulation of psychometric data from the Beck's Depression Inventory (BDI-II) to create new instances. Experiments were conducted under both Single-Instance Learning (SIL) and Multiple-Instance Learning (MIL) frameworks, using multilingual sentence embeddings and an XGBoost classifier. Results reveal statistically significant differences among augmentation strategies, with LLM-based generation without BDI-II modulation achieving the highest performance. Contextual substitution proved to be a competitive and computationally efficient alternative. In contrast, psychometric modulation reduced model effectiveness, suggesting that artificially aligning emotional tone may compromise data quality. These findings underscore the importance of semantically coherent augmentation for sensitive applications in mental health. Code and supplementary material: https://github.com/Matheusutino/depression-data-augmentation.

Keywords: Depression · MDD · Data augmentation · Large Language Models · Social Media

R. de Freitas and D. Furtado (Eds.): BRACIS 2025, LNAI 16181, pp. 393–408, 2026.
https://doi.org/10.1007/978-3-032-15990-8_27

1   Introduction

Mental health disorders, particularly Major Depressive Disorder (MDD), pose a growing global challenge, with prevalence rates steadily increasing worldwide [9]. Depression significantly impacts individuals' professional and social functioning due to symptoms such as anhedonia, disturbances in sleep and concentration, and broader cognitive impairments [9]. These debilitating effects contribute significantly to global disability and impose considerable economic burdens, with costs estimated to surpass hundreds of billions of dollars annually [13,14].

In response to this crisis, researchers have developed automated methods that leverage social media data to screen for depression and identify individuals who may be suffering but remain undiagnosed [6,11,16,17]—however, these approaches face critical data limitations. While collecting raw social media content is relatively straightforward, obtaining reliable annotations presents significant challenges: annotating data without clinical knowledge of users is problematic, and recruiting volunteers for assessing depressive symptoms through standardized psychometric tests—such as Beck's Depression Inventory [3]—yields limited data points. This annotation scarcity becomes particularly acute for limited-resource countries. To address these constraints, data augmentation emerges as a promising alternative, though it requires careful implementation in sensitive domains like mental health.

Previous research has investigated various data augmentation techniques to address annotation scarcity in mental health applications. Several studies have employed approaches such as Easy Data Augmentation (EDA), conditional BERT, and Back-Translation (BT) [2,10]. More advanced strategies have involved augmenting data using intent-aware prompts for LLMs [19], text summarization [18], and paraphrasing [8]. Although summarization techniques effectively augment extensive text content, such as Reddit posts, their suitability decreases for shorter-text platforms such as Instagram and X (formerly Twitter). Moreover, to the best of our knowledge, previous studies have neither integrated psychometric data into LLM-based augmentation approaches nor evaluated these methods' effectiveness at the user level regarding a subset of their posts. Instead, most of the previous research has augmented single posts, neglecting the context in which they were posted.

In this study, we address these gaps by systematically investigating three augmentation strategies of increasing complexity: (1) simple instance duplication as a baseline, (2) contextual word substitution using BERT-based models to ensure greater semantic and distributional similarity to original data, and (3) synthetic post generation with LLMs both with psychometric guidance (LLM - BDI) and without (LLM - No BDI), offering varied capabilities including paraphrasing and latent feature extraction. We benchmark each approach under two learning paradigms: Single-Instance Learning (SIL), which treats individual posts as independent labeled examples, and Multiple-Instance Learning (MIL), which aggregates all posts per user into a single training instance. Our comparative analysis quantifies how each augmentation strategy affects classification accuracy, robustness, and computational efficiency. Our main contributions are:

- The MIL approach consistently outperforms SIL, based on F1-scores, across all data augmentation methods, demonstrating that user-level information improves performance when augmenting data.
- Among LLMs, Dolphin 3 outperformed larger ones, showing that compact models can generate high-quality synthetic data at lower computational cost.
- The experiments reveal that, for both the LLM and Contextual (BERT) methods, the best performance is achieved with an augmentation factor of $n = 1$. This suggests that adding more synthetic data may introduce noise, ultimately hindering model performance.

2 Related Work

In automated mental health screening, psychometric questionnaires—standardized instruments designed to assess psychological symptoms and traits through structured self-reports—are often employed to generate high-quality labels for machine learning. When applied to social media data, this strategy involves recruiting participants to complete clinically validated inventories, such as the Beck's Depression Inventory (BDI-II) [3]. The BDI-II is a 21-item questionnaire in which each item is scored from 0 (no symptom) to 3 (severe symptom), yielding a total score between 0 and 63. Established cut-offs categorize respondents into minimal (0–13), mild (14–19), moderate (20–28), and severe (29–63) levels of depressive symptomatology. Subsequently, studies link participants' responses to BDI-II to their online activity history [4,16,17]. Although this method yields high-quality, trustworthy annotations, it is resource-intensive and generally limited to small samples. As a less costly alternative, researchers have also relied on self-reported disclosures found directly within social media profiles or posts, where individuals voluntarily share information about their mental health status, such as mentioning a diagnosis of depression [5,11]. While this approach enables the construction of larger datasets at lower cost, it carries the risk of introducing label noise and biases, as such disclosures may be incomplete, informal, or context-dependent.

As a result, researchers have explored a variety of text-based augmentation strategies to mitigate data scarcity in mental health applications. Rule-based methods such as Easy Data Augmentation (EDA) apply operations like synonym replacement, random insertion, token swapping, and deletion to diversify training texts [2,10]. Back-Translation (BT) approaches translate posts into an intermediate language and then back again, producing paraphrases that retain original meaning while introducing lexical variation [2,15]. For longer documents—particularly Reddit posts—abstractive summarization has generated concise new examples and helped rebalance class distributions [18]. More recently, studies have leveraged LLMs with intent-aware prompting, creating "same-intent" and "opposite-intent" variants, to enhance stress-detection performance beyond traditional augmenters [19]. A graph-based framework for structuring clinical interview data has also been proposed, where the authors used LLM-generated content with explicit principles [8]. One study integrated BDI-II scores into prompt design, generating N synthetic Reddit posts per inventory item, but observed no performance gains when augmenting lengthy text Reddit posts [4]; unlike their item-level approach, we feed the model the user's complete BDI-II response—all 21 items. In contrast, our study systematically compares three augmentation strategies, where the LLM-based synthesis is evaluated with and without psychometric (BDI-II) modulation.

3   Methodology

3.1   Original Dataset

The primary dataset for our experiments comes from a Brazilian-Portuguese Instagram corpus of university students [16]. In that study, 221 participants provided informed consent, granted access to their Instagram histories, and completed the BDI-II questionnaire. To create binary user-level labels, participants whose BDI-II scores fell into the minimal or mild ranges were annotated as nondepressed, whereas those in the moderate or severe ranges were labeled depressed, a safe threshold provided by the Beck's Depression Inventory [3]. We use the same training, validation, and test splits as the original study [16]. This study was conducted with approval from the Institutional Review Board (IRB), as reported by the authors.

3.2   Data Augmentation

This paper devises three textual data augmentation strategies to enhance the performance of depression screening classifiers. They are simple instance duplication, contextual word substitution using a BERT-based approach, and synthetic instance generation with LLMs. Each approach introduces synthetic instances with varying sophistication and computational cost levels, enabling a comparative analysis between simpler and more advanced data generation methods.

Simple duplication (Copy) involves directly replicating instances from the original dataset without any textual modifications. Although elementary, this approach serves as a baseline to isolate the effects of increased data volume without introducing new semantic or syntactic information. Despite its simplicity, it can help mitigate class imbalance bias and reinforce patterns already present in the original data. This method was adopted as the baseline for these reasons, given its low computational cost and ease of implementation.

Contextual substitution aims to introduce lexical variation while maintaining the semantic coherence of messages. This technique selects words within each sentence and replaces them based on the global context, using semantic representations learned by language models. The goal is to generate alternative versions of the texts that preserve the original meaning while introducing subtle lexical differences [21]. This controlled modification increases dataset diversity and encourages the model to learn more generalizable representations. For this purpose, we apply this strategy using two Transformer-based language models: BERTimbau, a large-scale BERT model trained specifically on Brazilian-Portuguese corpora, and BERT Base Multilingual Cased, to evaluate the benefits of cross-lingual semantic knowledge. For each sentence, we randomly mask and replace 20% of its tokens.

The third approach is based on generating new textual instances using LLMs. Unlike the previous techniques, which operate locally on text, this strategy adopts a global perspective by considering a user's entire set of posts in an attempt to infer patterns of style, thematic focus, and emotional tone. The model can generate new content from these extracted latent features that simulates the original discursive behavior while maintaining stylistic and semantic coherence with the input data [23]. In one variant, named LLM - No BDI, texts are generated solely based on the user's textual history. In another variant, named LLM - BDI, psychometric information, namely, the user responses and score from the BDI-II questionnaire, is incorporated to adjust the emotional tone of the generated posts, aligning it with the user's reported affective state. Prompt templates and implementation details for both variants are available in our GitHub repository. This approach, by enabling complete and contextualized paraphrases, significantly enhances the linguistic diversity of the dataset, contributing to more robust semantic representations during training. The LLMs employed in this study were Dolphin 3–8B, Mistral Small 3.1–24B, and Gemini 2.0 Flash. These models were selected with varying model sizes to ensure diversity in performance and capabilities, covering a range from smaller models to more powerful, large-scale architectures. Moreover, we select models that could be run locally to avoid sending user data to API-based models.

All augmentation procedures are executed at the user level: for each original user u, we generate a synthetic user u' whose timeline consists of new posts. In the Copy strategy, u' replicates u's posts verbatim, with no changes. In the Contextual Substitution strategy, u' preserves the same post count but introduces lexical variation by selectively replacing words via contextual embeddings. In the LLM-based strategy, we construct a prompt containing (1) u's original posts, (2) the user's BDI-II responses, and (3) instructions to generate a new set of posts u'. Prompt design and examples are available in our GitHub repository. In this process, a data augmentation factor $n \in \{1, 2, 3, 4, 5\}$ was employed, such that for each original user, n synthetic counterparts were generated. Consequently, the total number of synthetic users corresponds to n times the size of the original dataset. This design allows for a systematic assessment of how varying synthetic data volumes influence model performance. Finally, two types of augmented datasets were evaluated: augmented, containing exclusively synthetic instances, and combined, which merges original and synthetic data. This distinction allows us to measure both the standalone value of synthetic data and its added benefit when mixed with original samples.

3.3 Classification

This study investigates two supervised user-level classification strategies: SIL and MIL. In the SIL approach, each textual instance (e.g., a user's post) is treated independently during training. The model is trained to classify individual posts, and the final user-level prediction is obtained by aggregating the instance-level outputs, using majority voting. This method assumes that each post independently carries sufficient information to infer the user's label, which may be limiting in scenarios where the relevant information may be fragmented across multiple posts or extracted from how posts were organized through time or subsets of posts. In contrast, the MIL approach treats the complete set of a user's posts as a single unit, represented as a bag of instances associated with one label. Embeddings are generated for each instance and aggregated using a mean pooling operation to produce a single vector representation per user, which is then used for classification. This strategy is particularly suited for situations where only a subset of instances is informative, enabling the model to capture latent and distributed patterns.

We employed three distinct pre-trained embedding models to obtain dense semantic representations. First, we incorporated paraphrase-multilingual-mpnet-base-v2 (paraphrase), a widely adopted model known for its strong performance in capturing semantic similarity across languages, which produces 768-dimensional embeddings. Second, we leveraged multilingual-e5-base (e5), an encoder trained with retrieval-style instructions that has shown promising results in various multilingual information retrieval and ranking benchmarks, also generating 768-dimensional embeddings. Lastly, we utilized granite-embedding-107m-multilingual (granite), a compact yet effective model, which outputs 384-dimensional vectors. Combining these models allowed us to compare different architectures and training objectives and evaluate their ability to produce meaningful and comparable dense representations across diverse languages and tasks.

User-level embeddings were constructed differently depending on the learning strategy. In the SIL approach, embeddings were generated individually for each textual instance (e.g., each post), and user-level predictions were later obtained by aggregating the instance-level outputs through majority voting. In the MIL approach, embeddings corresponding to all posts of a user were first generated and then aggregated into a single vector by applying a mean pooling operation. This resulted in one dense and standardized representation per user, which was subsequently used for training the classifier.

For classification, we employed the XGBoost algorithm, which has demonstrated strong performance across a wide range of supervised learning tasks. XGBoost builds an ensemble of decision trees sequentially, where each new tree is trained to correct the residual errors of the previous ensemble. It incorporates regularization techniques to prevent overfitting and supports parallel processing, making it particularly robust in real-world settings [7]. In this study, XGBoost was trained to predict post-level embeddings for SIL, and the user-level embeddings for MIL. The model was configured with a binary logistic objective function and optimized using the logarithmic loss as the evaluation metric. The number of boosting iterations was set to 1000, and an early stopping mechanism was employed, halting the training process if the validation performance did not improve after 50 consecutive rounds.

We employed Bayesian optimization for hyperparameter tuning, which constructs a probabilistic surrogate model to approximate the objective function. It iteratively selects the most promising hyperparameter configurations based on a balance between exploration and exploitation [20]. We performed 20 iterations of the optimization process. The range of hyperparameters is detailed in the supplementary material on GitHub.

We relied on the original training (60%), validation (20%), and test (20%) stratified sets [16]. These splits ensure that each user's entire post history is contained within a single partition, preventing any overlap between sets. Only the training set was subjected to data augmentation, while the validation and test sets remained unaltered to ensure fair and unbiased evaluation. The training set was used to fit the model parameters, the validation set guided model selection and hyperparameter tuning, and the test set was reserved for the final performance evaluation to assess generalization capability.

4   Results

In general, as shown in Fig. 1, the combined version consistently outperforms the augmented one, regardless of the embedding used. This indicates that the original data still plays a crucial role in the model's performance. It also suggests that, despite their refinement, synthetic samples have not yet reached a sufficient quality level to replace the richness and authenticity of real data fully.

Moreover, the LLM - BDI method shows greater instability under the SIL framework than MIL (also observed in Fig. 2 by std error bars). This discrepancy can be attributed to the way each approach processes input data. In SIL, where each post is evaluated in isolation, the BDI-II-driven emotional modulation can clash with users' own voice—since the sober, technical tone of the questionnaire starkly contrasts the laid-back, informal style of social media posts—often yielding outputs that are unnaturally negative or overly positive. These deviations might compromise the coherence of individual samples, making it possibly more challenging for the model to classify them correctly. In contrast, MIL benefits from analyzing multiple posts from the same user simultaneously, enabling it to capture more robust semantic patterns and to smooth out the effects of emotionally modulated outliers. Consequently, MIL proves to be more resilient to the distortions introduced by the LLM - BDI strategy, which explains its greater stability and more consistent performance in this context.

In Fig. 3, it is observed that the BERT models showed similar performance; however, on average, the multilingual version achieved a slight advantage over the version specialized in Portuguese. Regarding the LLM-based models, the configuration without the BDI-II outperformed in most scenarios, suggesting that, in the absence of explicit symptom information, these models are more effective at capturing implicit patterns in the texts. When considering the presence of BDI-II, it is noteworthy that only Dolphin 3 maintained relative stability, while the Mistral and Gemini models experienced significant performance drops compared to their counterparts without BDI.

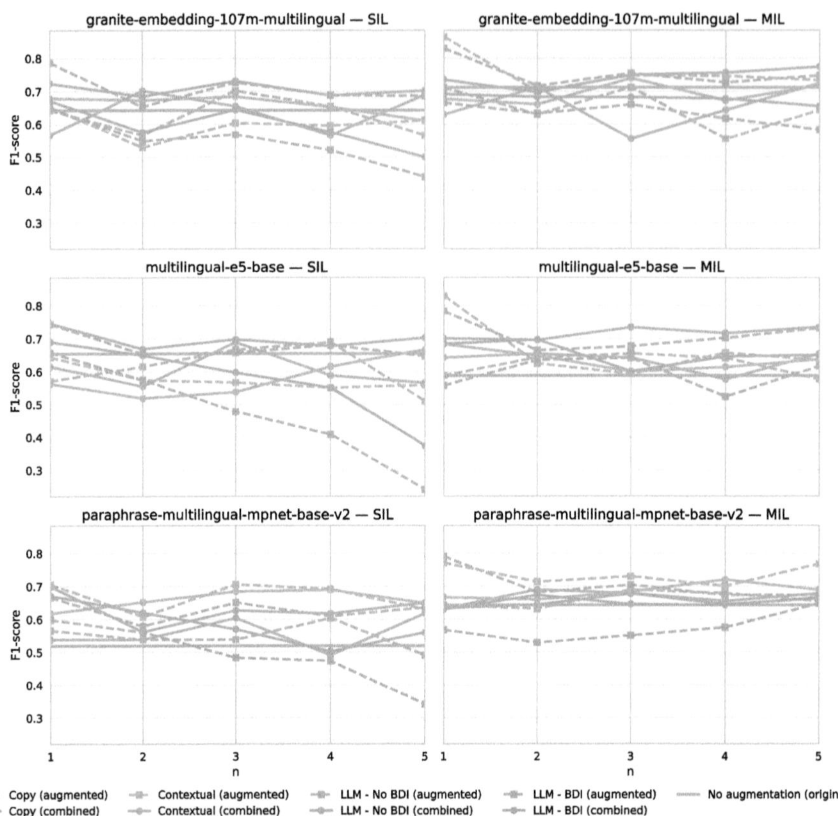

Fig. 1. F1 results for SIL and MIL, across three embedding representations and different data augmentation scenarios: using only synthetic data (augmented) and combining original with synthetic data (combined). The results are shown as a function of the augmentation factor n, ranging from 1 to 5, highlighting the impact of the amount of synthetic data on model performance.

Figure 2 displays the mean F1-scores for the different augmentation techniques and classifier types. The results indicate that the MIL approach consistently outperforms the SIL approach, irrespective of the data augmentation method employed. As anticipated, the comparison between SIL and MIL highlights an intrinsic advantage of the MIL framework, given the nature of the task. Since posts authored by the same user are inherently correlated, analyzing them in isolation—as in the SIL framework—may overlook important contextual cues. Therefore, treating the collection of posts as a unified instance, as done in MIL, is more appropriate for depression screening. Depression is a mental condition diagnosed when a patient presents a specific temporal pattern of symptoms onset and persistence of at least two weeks to be considered a MDD episode [1].

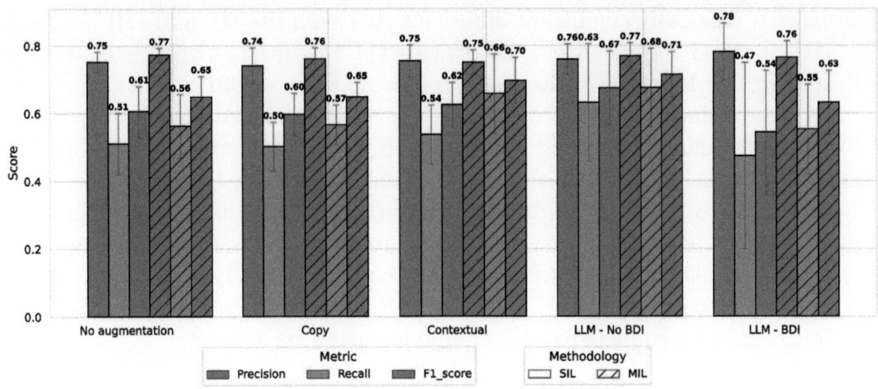

Fig. 2. Mean precision, recall and F1-scores for each combination of augmentation type and classifier type averaged over all embeddings, models and n, with error bars indicating standard deviation.

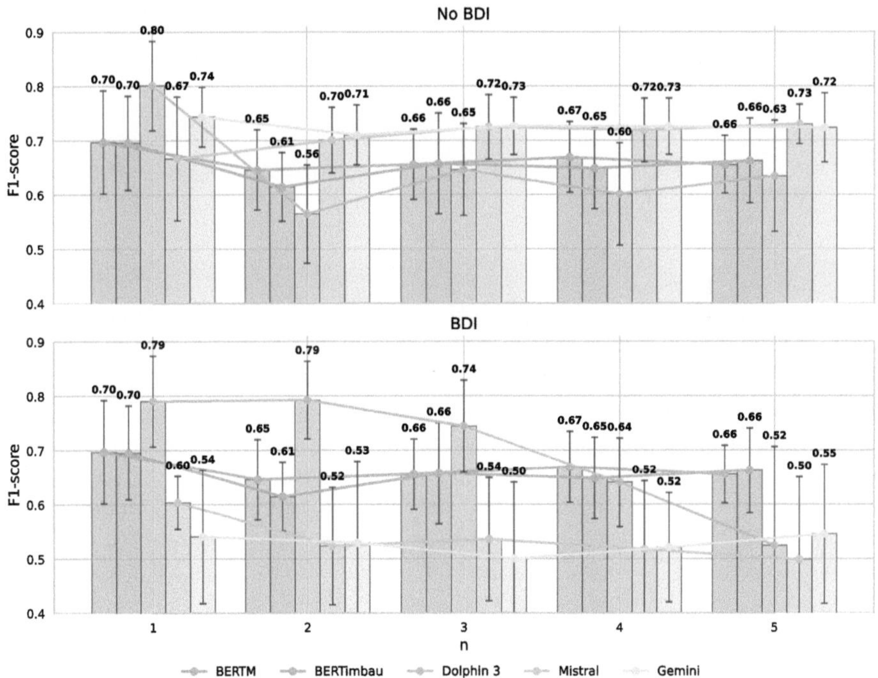

Fig. 3. Mean F1-score across the models, varying the number of augmented samples n, averaged over all embeddings, type augmentation, and classification types. Error bars indicate the standard deviation.

The non-parametric Kruskal-Wallis H-test was applied to assess whether there were statistically significant differences between the SIL and MIL methods. The MIL method significantly outperforms the SIL method in this context, as indicated by the Kruskal-Wallis test, $H(1) = 36.04$, $p < .001$.

The results indicate that, on mean, the LLM - No BDI method achieved the best performance, standing out for its effectiveness compared to other data augmentation techniques. This superior performance can be attributed to the LLM's ability to generate high-quality synthetic data that complements the original dataset, enhancing the model's robustness. The contextual augmentation method ranked second. Although less computationally demanding, it still yielded satisfactory results, demonstrating the effectiveness of approaches that replace words with context-aware synonyms within posts.

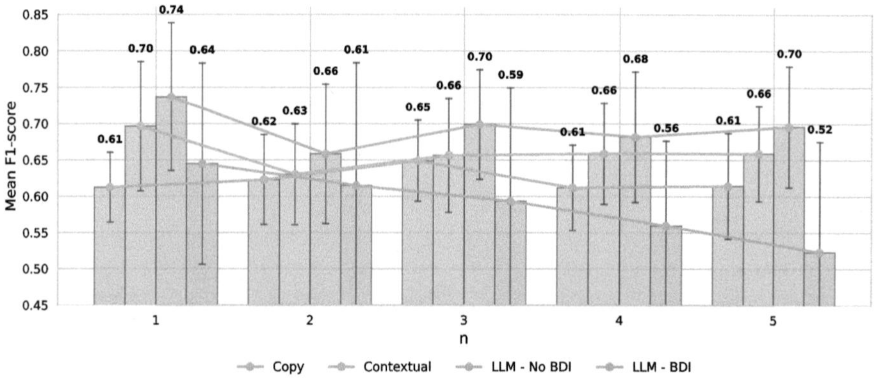

Fig. 4. Mean F1-score across data augmentation methods, varying the number of augmented samples n, averaged over all embeddings, type augmentation, classification types, and models. Error bars indicate the standard deviation.

In contrast, the copy-based augmentation method performed slightly worse than without augmentation. This suggests that simply duplicating existing instances in the dataset added little value to the model, resulting in suboptimal performance and increased computational cost. The lack of diversity introduced by this method may have constrained its potential to improve the model.

The LLM - BDI method yielded the poorest performance, marked by a substantial decrease in F1-score. This decline is likely due to the noise introduced by incorporating synthetic data generated based on BDI-II questionnaire. By generating synthetic instances that stray from the true data distribution—amplified by BDI-II's sober, technical tone—, this approach can introduce samples misaligned with the usual social media style, ultimately undermining model performance. This is illustrated in Table 1, where the original text conveys an emotional and uplifting tone centered on resilience. A similar tone is preserved in the "no BDI" version, as it closely follows the structure and sentiment of the original post. In contrast, the version with BDI-II exhibits a markedly more negative tone. This shift can be attributed to the user's high BDI-II score of 36, which is indicative of depressive symptoms. According to the self-reported questionnaire, the user expressed feeling sad all the time and perceiving many past experiences as failures, both of which likely influenced the generation of content with a more pessimistic perspective. This issue may also stem from the common tendency of individuals to mask their true emotions on social media [12,22], meaning that the posts themselves may not consistently reflect the psychological states assessed by the BDI-II. Therefore, while the BDI-II questionnaire may accurately capture emotional states, the synthetic data generated from the posts and BDI-II together might not always align with those states, potentially introducing inconsistencies that impair the model's performance.

Table 1. Illustrative example of data augmentation using prompts without and with BDI. Original Text: *As our anthem says: "He's got true grit." Strength to the survivors and to the families who have lost their loved ones.* All examples have been paraphrased to prevent author identification.

No BDI	BDI
This is a time to cherish life and acknowledge the victories achieved. May faith continue to guide those facing hardships and seeking hope.	Today, even the small moments feel hollow. Just another day going by...

As shown in Fig. 4, the LLM - No BDI method consistently achieved the highest average performance across all values of n, indicating greater robustness compared to the other data augmentation techniques. It is also noteworthy that, for most methods, the highest mean F1-scores were observed at $n = 1$. This pattern suggests that excessive use of augmented samples may introduce noise into the dataset, ultimately hindering model performance. The only exception was the Copy method, which reached its best performance at $n = 3$, indicating a higher dataset expansion tolerance in this case.

The Kruskal-Wallis H-test was applied to assess whether statistically significant differences exist among the data augmentation methods (Copy, Contextual, LLM - No BDI, and LLM - BDI). The results revealed a statistically significant difference among the groups, $H(3) = 80.15$, $p < .001$, leading to the rejection of the null hypothesis and indicating that at least one method performs significantly differently from the others. Dunn's post hoc test with Holm-Sidak correction was applied to examine these differences further, and the results are presented in Table 2.

The results demonstrate that the LLM - No BDI method exhibits statistically significant differences in performance when compared to all other methods. The p-values for all comparisons were below the 0.05 threshold, indicating that the observed performance differences are statistically reliable. This finding suggests

Table 2. Dunn's post hoc test (Holm-Sidak) among augmentation methods.

Comparison	P-value	Comparison	P-value
Copy vs Contextual	0.017	Contextual vs LLM-BDI	0.000
Copy vs LLM-No BDI	0.000	LLM-No BDI vs LLM-BDI	0.000
Copy vs LLM-BDI	0.627	Contextual vs LLM-No BDI	0.002

that the inclusion of BDI-II information significantly modified the dataset, which, in turn, negatively impacted the model's performance for screening depression in augmented datasets.

In contrast, the LLM - BDI method does not differ significantly from the Copy method, indicating that the inclusion of BDI-II does not lead to a meaningful improvement over simpler augmentation strategies. This lack of statistical distinction suggests that incorporating BDI-II may introduce noise or constrain the generative process in a way that limits potential performance gains. Additionally, the Contextual method shows statistically significant differences when compared to Copy and LLM - BDI, but not when compared to LLM - No BDI. This suggests that the performance of the Contextual method is more aligned with that of LLM - No BDI, reinforcing its potential as a competitive alternative. These findings highlight that, although LLM - No BDI demonstrates superior performance, it entails a higher computational cost. Therefore, approaches such as Contextual, which are simpler and computationally less demanding, emerge as viable alternatives, offering a favorable trade-off between performance and resource efficiency.

Table 3 presents the highest F1-score achieved by each data augmentation technique evaluated. Among them, the Contextual method stands out for achieving the best overall performance, highlighting its effectiveness in generating synthetic data that enhances classification tasks. Within the LLM-based approaches, the Dolphin 3 model delivered the best results. This finding is particularly noteworthy as it shows that smaller and more computationally efficient models, such as Dolphin 3, can still produce high-quality synthetic data, rivaling more complex alternatives. It reinforces the feasibility of using compact LLMs in resource-constrained scenarios without significantly compromising performance. An additional noteworthy observation is that, whereas the Contextual and LLM-based methods attain strong performance with low values of n and solely with the augmented dataset, the Copy method demonstrates improved results as n increases.

Despite the promising result previously observed, Fig. 5 shows that, according to the Interquartile Range (IQR) method, the highest F1-score obtained by the Contextual method is identified as an outlier. This suggests that the exceptional performance may not reflect the typical behavior of the method, raising questions about its consistency. In contrast, the LLM - No BDI approach exhibits a higher median performance compared to the other methods, indicating a stronger central tendency. Although it presents a few lower-end outliers, the overall distribution is more concentrated, suggesting greater robustness and

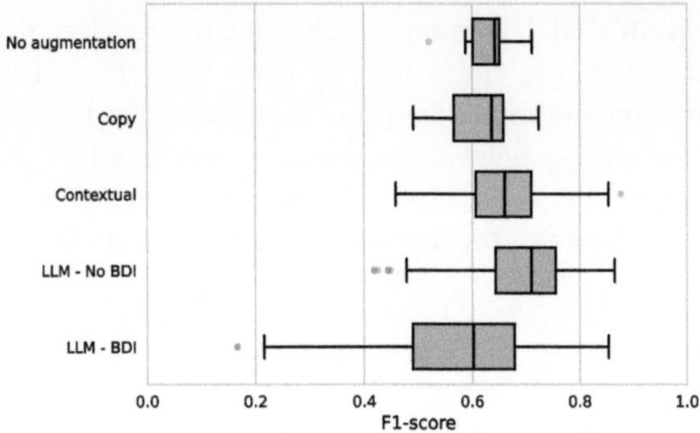

Fig. 5. F1-score boxplot by augmentation method over all embeddings, type augmentation, classification types, models and n.

Table 3. Best F1-score achieved by method across all configurations for MIL. The hyperparameters used in these experiments are available in the repository.

Method	Model	Embedding	Dataset Fold	n	F1-score
Contextual	BERTimbau	Granite	Augmented	1	0.877
LLM - No BDI	Dolphin 3	Paraphrase	Augmented	1	0.865
LLM - BDI	Dolphin 3	Paraphrase	Augmented	2	0.853
Copy	-	Granite	Combined	5	0.724
No augmentation	-	Granite	-	-	0.712

reliability in its typical results. The Copy remains stable, but consistently below those of No augmentation, Contextual and LLM - No BDI, reinforcing the limited impact of simpler augmentation strategies. The LLM - BDI method displays the greatest variability among all approaches, as evidenced by its wide interquartile range spanning nearly the full range of observed values. This high dispersion reflects lower consistency and, consequently, reduced reliability, which may limit the practical utility of this method in scenarios requiring stable and predictable performance.

The analysis of similarity metrics between embeddings, using OpenAI's text-embedding-3-large model, both original and augmented—including Paired Cosine Similarity (PSC), Centroid Cosine Similarity (CCS), and Hausdorff Distance (HD)—reveals consistent differences between the conditions with and without the BDI-II intervention. Overall, LLM models with BDI-II-based prompts exhibited lower similarity (e.g., Dolphin 3: PSC = 0.305, CCS = 0.652, HD = 1.226) and greater distance between embeddings, indicating an increase in the diversity of the generated representations. This trend was less pronounced in the BERT-based models. For instance, BERTM showed intermediate values (PSC = 0.316, CCS = 0.813, HD = 1.152), and BERTimbau had similar behavior (PSC = 0.331, CCS = 0.832, HD = 1.144), suggesting moderate diversity – higher than the LLMs with BDI-II but lower than those without it. Among all evaluated models, Dolphin's BDI-II version achieved the highest diversity across all metrics used, outperforming the others in both average and maximum values. These results not only highlight Dolphin 3's sensitivity to changes induced by BDI-II prompts but also suggest its superior semantic adaptability. The full set of numerical results—and a detailed description of how the similarity metrics were computed—can be found in the supplementary materials on our GitHub.

5   Conclusion

This study examined the impact of various data augmentation strategies on detecting depressive symptoms in Instagram posts. Strategies ranged from simple instance duplication to content generation with LLMs. Results showed that context-aware LLM generation, without psychometric data, outperformed other methods. Conversely, using psychometric questionnaires in generation negatively impacted performance, suggesting that emotional tone alignment may harm semantic coherence. BERT-based contextual word substitution was an effective and resource-efficient alternative. Additionally, the MIL approach significantly outperformed SIL, supporting the aggregation of user posts to capture depressive patterns. These findings highlight the importance of preserving semantic integrity in data augmentation for sensitive tasks.

Given the inherently multimodal nature of platforms like Instagram, future work could benefit from incorporating visual data, such as shared images or story content, alongside textual inputs. Integrating image features–potentially extracted via vision-language models–may enrich user representations and offer complementary cues about emotional states that are not explicitly verbalized. In addition, while the current augmentation strategies focused on generating synthetic posts based on the full set of a user's history, alternative granularity levels merit exploration. Future research could investigate post-level augmentation, where each message is individually modified or paraphrased to introduce diversity. This finer-grained approach may allow for more controlled perturbations and could prove especially useful in contexts where user histories are limited or fragmented.

The third author acknowledges the grants from CNPq (National Council for Scientific and Technological Development) and FAPERJ - *Fundação Carlos Chagas Filho de Amparo à Pesquisa do Estado do Rio de Janeiro*, processes SEI-260003/002930/2024, SEI-260003/000614/2023.

References

1. American Psychiatric Association: Diagnostic and Statistical Manual of Mental Disorders, 5th edn, text revision (DSM-5-TR®). American Psychiatric Association Publishing, Arlington, TX (2022)
2. Ansari, G., Garg, M., Saxena, C.: Data augmentation for mental health classification on social media. In: Proceedings of the 18th ICON, pp. 152–161. NLPAI (2021)

3. Beck, A.T., Steer, R.A., Brown, G.: Beck depression inventory–ii. Psychological assessment (1996)
4. Bucur, A.M.: Utilizing ChatGPT generated data to retrieve depression symptoms from social media. arXiv preprint arXiv:2307.02313 (2023)
5. Bucur, A.M., Cosma, A., Rosso, P., Dinu, L.P.: It's just a matter of time: detecting depression with time-enriched multimodal transformers. In: Kamps, J., et al. (eds.) ECIR 2023. LNCS, vol. 13980, pp. 200–215. Springer, Cham (2023). https://doi.org/10.1007/978-3-031-28244-7_13
6. Bucur, A.M., Moldovan, A.C., Parvatikar, K., Zampieri, M., KhudaBukhsh, A.R., Dinu, L.P.: On the state of NLP approaches to modeling depression in social media: a post-COVID-19 outlook. IEEE J. Biomed. Health Inform. (2025)
7. Chen, T., Guestrin, C.: XGBoost: a scalable tree boosting system (2016)
8. Chen, Z., Deng, J., Zhou, J., Wu, J., Qian, T., Huang, M.: Depression detection in clinical interviews with LLM-empowered structural element graph. In: Proceedings of the 2024 NAACL, pp. 8181–8194. ACL (2024)
9. Cui, L., et al.: Major depressive disorder: hypothesis, mechanism, prevention and treatment. Sig. Transduct. Target. Ther. **9**(1), 30 (2024)
10. Ding, X., Lybarger, K., Tauscher, J., Cohen, T.: Improving classification of infrequent cognitive distortions: domain-specific model vs. data augmentation. In: Proceedings of the 2022 NAACL Student Research Workshop, pp. 68–75. ACL (2022)
11. Filho, S.L., Silva, M., Oliveira, J.: Identificação de sintomas de depressão por dados de mídias sociais: Aplicando design science research para desenvolver um modelo de classificação. In: SBSI, pp. 1–15. SBC, Porto Alegre, RS, Brasil (2024)
12. Fox, J., Vendemia, M.A.: Selective self-presentation and social comparison through photographs on social networking sites. Cyberpsychol. Behav. Soc. Netw. **19**(10), 593–600 (2016)
13. Greenberg, P.E., et al.: The economic burden of adults with major depressive disorder in the united states (2010 and 2018). Pharmacoeconomics **39**(6), 653–665 (2021)
14. Health, T.L.G.: Mental health matters. Lancet. Glob. Health **8**(11) (2020)
15. Liyanage, C., Garg, M., Mago, V., Sohn, S.: Augmenting Reddit posts to determine wellness dimensions impacting mental health. In: Demner-fushman, D., Ananiadou, S., Cohen, K. (eds.) The 22nd BioNLP, pp. 306–312. ACL (2023)
16. Mann, P., Matsushima, E.H., Paes, A.: Detecting depression from social media data as a multiple-instance learning task. In: 10th ACII, pp. 1–8 (2022)
17. Mann, P., Paes, A., Matsushima, E.H.: See and read: detecting depression symptoms in higher education students using multimodal social media data. In: Proceedings of the AAAI ICWSM, vol. 14, pp. 440–451 (2020)
18. Nilsson, F., Kovács, G.: Filipn@ lt-edi-acl2022-detecting signs of depression from social media: examining the use of summarization methods as data augmentation for text classification (2022)
19. Saleem, M., Kim, J.: Intent aware data augmentation by leveraging generative AI for stress detection in social media texts. PeerJ Comput. Sci. **10**, e2156 (2024)
20. Watanabe, S.: Tree-structured parzen estimator: understanding its algorithm components and their roles for better empirical performance. arXiv preprint arXiv:2304.11127 (2023)
21. Wu, X., Lv, S., Zang, L., Han, J., Hu, S.: Conditional BERT contextual augmentation. In: Rodrigues, J.M.F., et al. (eds.) ICCS 2019. LNCS, vol. 11539, pp. 84–95. Springer, Cham (2019). https://doi.org/10.1007/978-3-030-22747-0_7
22. Zheng, A., Duff, B.R., Vargas, P., Yao, M.Z.: Self-presentation on social media: When self-enhancement confronts self-verification. JIA **20**(3), 289–302 (2020)

23. Zhou, Y., Guo, C., Wang, X., Chang, Y., Wu, Y.: A survey on data augmentation in large model era. arXiv preprint arXiv:2401.15422 (2024)

Author Index